# applied business research:
## QUALITATIVE AND QUANTITATIVE METHODS

# applied business research:
## QUALITATIVE AND QUANTITATIVE METHODS

**ROBERT Y. CAVANA**
Victoria University of Wellington

**BRIAN L. DELAHAYE**
Queensland University of Technology

**UMA SEKARAN**
Professor Emerita
Southern Illinois University at Carbondale

**WILEY**
John Wiley & Sons Australia, Ltd

First published 2001 by
John Wiley & Sons Australia, Ltd
42 McDougall Street, Milton, Qld 4064

Typeset in 10.5/12 pt Berkeley

US edition © 2000 by John Wiley & Sons, Inc.

Australian edition © John Wiley & Sons Australia, Ltd 2001

The moral rights of the authors have been asserted.

Authorised adaptation of *Research Methods for Business*,
3rd edition (ISBN 0 471 33166-X), published by
John Wiley & Sons, Inc., New York

National Library of Australia
Cataloguing-in-Publication data

Cavana, R. Y.
　Applied business research: qualitative and quantitative
　methods.

　Bibliography.
　Includes index.
　ISBN 978 0 471 34126 0.

　1. Business — Research — Methodology. I. Sekaran, Uma.
　II. Delahaye, Brian L. 1946–. III. Title.

650.072

**Reproduction and communication for educational purposes**
The Australian *Copyright Act 1968* allows a maximum of one chapter or 10% of the pages of this work, whichever is the greater, to be reproduced and/or communicated by any educational institution for its educational purposes provided that the educational institution (or the body that administers it) has given a remuneration notice to Copyright Agency Limited (CAL).

**Reproduction and communication for other purposes**
Except as permitted under the Act (for example, a fair dealing for the purposes of study, research, criticism or review), no part of this book may be reproduced, stored in a retrieval system, communicated or transmitted in any form or by any means without prior written permission. All inquiries should be made to the publisher.

Cover and internal images: © 2001 Digital Vision.

Illustrated by the John Wiley art department

Printed in Singapore by
Markono Print Media Pte Ltd.

10 9 8 7 6

All URLs were checked and current at the time of publication. However, owing to the dynamic nature of the Internet, some sites may since have changed, moved or disappeared.

# DEDICATION

For Bob: To my wife, *Carolyn*, for her support and encouragement

For Brian: To my best friend and loving wife, *Yvonne*

For Uma: In memory of beloved *P. S. Mani*

# BRIEF CONTENTS

Preface   xiii
About the authors   xv
Acknowledgements   xvi

Part I — A scientific approach to business research   1

   CHAPTER 1   *Introduction to business research*   3

   CHAPTER 2   *Scientific investigations and the research process*   27

Part II — Initial stages and design of a research project   45

   CHAPTER 3   *Preliminary information gathering and problem definition*   47

   CHAPTER 4   *Framework development and research objectives*   76

   CHAPTER 5   *Research design and planning*   105

Part III — Qualitative business research   131

   CHAPTER 6   *Qualitative data gathering*   133

   CHAPTER 7   *Qualitative data analysis and interpretation*   168

Part IV — Quantitative business research   183

   CHAPTER 8   *Measurement of variables*   185

   CHAPTER 9   *Scaling, reliability and validity*   202

   CHAPTER 10   *Questionnaire design*   224

   CHAPTER 11   *Sampling design*   250

   CHAPTER 12   *Experimental designs*   284

   CHAPTER 13   *Quantitative data analysis and interpretation*   313

Part V — Research reporting and managerial decision making   347

   CHAPTER 14   *Research reporting*   349

   CHAPTER 15   *Managerial decision making and evaluating research*   385

References   393
Appendix I   401
Appendix II   447
Glossary   453
Index   465

# CONTENTS

Preface xiii

About the authors xv

Acknowledgements xvi

## Part 1 — A scientific approach to business research 1

**CHAPTER 1  Introduction to business research 3**
What is research? 4
   Why managers should know about research 4
Business research 5
   Definition of research 5
   Research and the manager 6
The context of business research 8
Philosophical bases of business research 8
   Positivist research 8
   Interpretivist research 9
   Critical research 10
   An approach for business 11
Business research methods: Quantitative and qualitative 12
Types of business research: Applied and basic 12
   Applied research 13
   Basic or fundamental research 13
Managers and research 15
The manager and the consultant or researcher 16
   How to locate and select a researcher 17
   The manager–researcher relationship 17
   Values 18
Internal versus external consultants or researchers 18
   Advantages of internal consultants or researchers 18
   Disadvantages of internal researchers 19
External consultants or researchers 19
   Advantages of external consultants 19
   Disadvantages of external consultants 20
Knowledge about research and managerial effectiveness 20
Ethics and business research 21
   Societal accountability 22
   The sponsor or client of the research 23
   The research subjects 23
   Conflict among the accountabilities 24
Summary 25
**Discussion points 26**

**CHAPTER 2  Scientific investigation and the research process 27**
The hallmarks of scientific research 28
   Purposiveness 29
   Rigour 29
   Testability 29
   Replicability 30
   Accuracy 30
   Objectivity 30
   Generalisability 31
   Parsimony 31
Limitations to scientific research in management 32
Some basic definitions 32
   Observations 32
   Concepts 33
   Constructs 34
Approaches to research 34
   Quantitative research 34
   Qualitative research 34
   Deduction 35
   Induction 36
The research process 37
   Catalyst for research 37
   Preliminary information gathering and literature survey 39
   Problem definition 39
   Framework development 39
   Research objectives 39
   Research design 40
   Data collection 40
   Data analysis 40
   Interpretation of findings 41
   Report preparation and presentation 41
   Management action 41
   Review of the research process 43
Summary 44
**Discussion points 44**

**Part II — Initial stages and design of a research project  45**

### CHAPTER 3  *Preliminary information gathering and problem definition*  47

The practical application of the research process  48
Catalyst for business research  49
Preliminary information gathering  50
    Nature of the information to be collected  50
    Sources of information  54
The literature survey  56
    Reasons for the literature survey  57
    Conducting the literature survey  58
    Writing up the literature survey  59
    Examples of two literature surveys  60
Problem definition  61
    Examples of well-defined problems  63
Managerial implications  63
Ethical issues  64
Summary  64
**Discussion points  64**
**Practice projects  65**
**Appendix  66**
Section 1: Some useful databases for business research  66
    Newspaper indexes of current events  68
    Other databases  68
    On the World Wide Web  69
Section 2: Search engines  71
Section 3: The bibliography and reference list  71
    Specimen format for citing different types of references  72
Section 4: Referencing and quotation in the business article or report  73

### CHAPTER 4  *Framework development and research objectives*  76

The need for a framework  77
Concepts and variables  78
Concepts and the conceptual framework  79
    The components of the conceptual framework  82
Variables and the theoretical framework  82
    Types of variables  82
Developing the theoretical framework  91
    The components of the theoretical framework  91
Research objectives  95
    Research questions  96
    Hypothesis development  98
Summary  103
**Discussion points  103**
**Practice project  104**

### CHAPTER 5  *Research design and planning*  105

The research design  106
The purpose of the study  107
    Exploratory study  108
    Descriptive study  109
    Hypothesis testing  111
    Case studies  112
    Review of the purpose of the study  112
Type of investigation  113
Purpose of the study and the research method  114
Researcher interference  115
Study setting: contrived and non-contrived  117
Units of analysis: Individuals, dyads, groups, organisations or cultures  119
Time horizon: Cross-sectional versus longitudinal studies  121
    Cross-sectional studies  121
    Longitudinal studies  122
    Review of elements of research design  123
The research proposal  123
Managerial implications  127
Summary  128
**Discussion points  128**

## Part III — Qualitative business research  131

### CHAPTER 6  Qualitative data gathering  133
The assumptions of qualitative research  134
Accuracy and replicability  135
Sampling  137
Qualitative research methods  137
Interviewing  138
- The pattern of an interview  138
- Listening  142
- Questioning  142
- Paraphrasing  143
- Probing  144
- Summarising  146
- Non-verbal behaviour  147
- Structured and unstructured interviews  148
- The three levels of interviewing  150
- Types of interviews  150

The focus group  153
- Structured and unstructured focus groups  154
- Logistics  154
- Group composition  154
- Conducting the focus group  155
- Summary of focus groups  159

Observational studies  159
- Types of observer roles  160
- Structured versus unstructured observational studies  160
- Advantages and disadvantages of observational studies  161
- Bias in observational studies  161
- Summary of observational studies  162

Other special data sources  162
- Projective methods  162
- Secondary data  163
- Panels  164

Ethics in data collection  165
- Ethics and the researcher  165
- Ethical behaviours of respondents  166

Summary  166
**Discussion points  166**

### CHAPTER 7  Qualitative data analysis and interpretation  168
The overlap of data gathering and analysis  169
The purpose of qualitative analysis  170
Structured and unstructured methods  170
Content analysis  171
- Conducting content analysis  171
- A rich, messy and complex process  175

Using a computer package  176
- The NVivo program  176
- The NVivo program and content analysis  178

Summary  181
**Discussion points  182**

## Part IV — Quantitative business research  183

### CHAPTER 8  Measurement of variables  185
How variables are measured  187
Operational definition: Dimensions and elements  188
- What an operational definition is not  192
- A measure of student learning  194
- Review of operational definition  194

Measurement scales  194
- Nominal scale  195
- Ordinal scale  196
- Interval scale  196
- Ratio scale  198
- Review of scales  200

Summary  201
**Discussion points  201**

### CHAPTER 9  Scaling, reliability and validity  202
Rating scales  203
- Dichotomous scale  203
- Category scale  203
- Likert scale  205
- Semantic differential scale  205
- Numerical scale  205

Itemised rating scale   206
  Fixed or constant sum rating scale   206
  Stapel scale   207
  Graphic rating scale   207
  Consensus scale   208
  Other scales   208
Ranking scales   208
  Paired comparison   208
  Forced choice   208
  Comparative scale   209
Goodness of measures   209
  Item analysis   210
Reliability   210
  Stability of measures   210
  Internal consistency of measures   211
Validity   212
  Face validity   212
  Content validity   213
  Criterion-related validity   213
  Construct validity   213
Summary   215
**Discussion points   215**
**Appendix   216**
Examples of some measures   216
  Measures from management research   216
  Measures from marketing research   220

## CHAPTER 10   Questionnaire design   224

Why are questionnaires important?   225
Guidelines for questionnaire design   227
Principles of wording   228
  Content and purpose of the question   228
  Language and wording of the questionnaire   229
  Type and form of questions   229
  Biases in questions   230
  Sequencing of questions   232
  Classification data or personal information   232
Principles of measurement   234
General appearance of the questionnaire   234
  Introduction to respondents   234
  Instructions and organising questions   235
  Demographic data   235
  Sensitive personal data   236
  Open-ended question at end   237
  Concluding the questionnaire   237
Pre-testing questionnaires   238
  Face validity   238
  Content validity   238
  Pilot study   238
Gathering the data   239
  Personally administered questionnaires   239
  Mail questionnaires   240
  Electronic questionnaires   240
Cross-cultural research   241
  Special issues in instrumentation   241
  Issues in data collection   242
Multimethods of data collection   242
  Comparison of data collection methods   243
  Managerial perspective   246
Summary   246
**Discussion points   247**
**Appendix   249**
Management's best MBAs   249

## CHAPTER 11   Sampling design   250

Population, element, sampling frame, sample and subject   252
Sampling   253
  Reasons for sampling   254
  Representativeness of samples   255
Probability and non-probability sampling   257
Probability sampling   257
  Simple random sampling   257
  Complex probability sampling   257
  Review of probability sampling designs   262
Non-probability sampling   262
  Convenience sampling   262
  Purposive sampling   263
  Review of non-probability sampling designs   265
Examples of sampling designs   265
  Review of sampling plan decisions   271
Sampling in cross-cultural research   272

Issues of precision and confidence in determining sample size    272
    Precision    273
    Confidence    273
Sample data, precision and confidence in estimation    274
Trade-off between precision and confidence    275
Determining the sample size    276
Importance of sampling design and sample size    279
Efficiency in sampling    279
    Review of sample size decisions    280
Summary    280
**Discussion points**    281

**CHAPTER 12    *Experimental designs*    284**
Introduction to experimental designs    285
Laboratory experiments    287
    Controlling the extraneous variables    287
    Manipulating the independent variable    288
    Selecting and assigning subjects    289
    Internal validity    291
    External reliability    291
Field experiments    292
Validation issues    292
    Validation comparison: Lab and field experiments    292
    Trade-off between internal and external validity    293
    Factors affecting internal validity    293
    Scenario case: Identifying threats to internal validity    297
    Internal validity in case studies    298
    Factors affecting external validity    298
    Review of factors affecting internal and external validity    299
Types of experimental designs    299
    Quasi-experimental designs    299
    True experimental designs    300
    Solomon four-group design    301
    Double-blind studies    303
    Ex post facto designs    303
Simulation    303
Ethical issues in experimental research    305
Managerial implications    306
Summary    307
**Discussion points**    308
**Appendix**    309
Further experimental designs    309
    The completely randomised design    309
    Randomised block design    310
    Latin square design    310
    Factorial design    311

**CHAPTER 13    *Quantitative data analysis and interpretation*    313**
Getting data ready for analysis    315
    Editing data    315
    Handling blank responses    316
    Coding    316
    Categorising    318
    Entering data    318
Data analysis    319
Getting a feel for the data    319
Testing goodness of data    320
    Reliability    320
    Validity    321
Hypothesis testing    322
Case: Research done in Wollongong Enterprises    322
    Some preliminary steps    324
    Checking the reliability of measures: Cronbach's alpha    324
    Obtaining descriptive statistics    325
    Inferential statistics: Pearson correlation    327
    Hypothesis testing    328
    Overall interpretation and recommendations    333
Use of expert systems    334
Summary    334
**Discussion points**    335
**Appendix**    337
Data analysis using Excel    337
    Analysis of the accounting chair data set using Excel    337
    Analysis using Excel    337

## Part V — Research reporting and managerial decision making 347

### CHAPTER 14 Research reporting 349

The written report 351
- The written report and its purpose 351
- The written report and its audience 353
- Characteristics of a well-written report 354
- Contents of the research report 355

Integral parts of the report 356
- The title page of the research report 356
- Table of contents 356
- Authorisation letter 356
- The executive summary or synopsis 357
- The introductory section 358
- The body of the report 358
- The final part of the report 358
- Acknowledgements 358
- References 358
- Appendices 360

Oral presentation 360
- Deciding on the content 360
- Visual aids 361
- The presenter 361
- The presentation 361
- Handling questions 362

Summary 362
**Discussion points** 362
**Appendix** 363

Report 1: Example of a report involving a descriptive study 363
Report 2: Example of a report where an idea has to be 'sold' 367
Report 3: Example of a report offering alternative solutions and explaining the pros and cons of each alternative 369
Report 4: Example of an abridged basic research report 371
Report 5: Example of an abridged applied business research report 375
- Executive summary 376
- 1. Introduction 376
- 2. Methodology 378
- 3. Results 380
- 4. Qualitative analysis of comments 381
- 5. Conclusions 384
- Acknowledgements 384

### CHAPTER 15 Managerial decision making and evaluating research 385

Scientific research and managerial decision making 386
- Purposive research 388
- Decision-making processes and different types of research 388

Evaluating business research 389
- Conceptual/overview questions 390
- Framework questions 390
- Method questions 391
- Results or conclusions questions 391
- Reader's abstract 392

A final comment 392
**Discussion points** 392

**References** 393

**Glossary of statistical symbols** 400

**Appendix I: A refresher on some statistical terms and tests** 401

Introduction 402
Descriptive statistics 405
- Frequencies 405
- Measurement of central tendencies 408
- Measures of dispersion 409

Inferential statistics 414
- Statistical hypothesis testing 414
- Correlations 418
- Relationship between two nominal variables: chi-square test 422
- Significant mean differences between two groups: the $t$-test 425
- Significant mean differences among multiple groups: ANOVA 430
- Regression analysis 432
- Factor analysis 439

Other tests and analyses 441
Managerial relevance 443
Summary 443
**Discussion points** 444

**Appendix II: Statistical tables** 447

**Glossary** 453

**Index** 465

# PREFACE

In many ways this book is the story of the coming together of three strangers. Uma's highly successful *Research Methods for Business: A Skill-building Approach*, published in the United States, is now in its third edition. It is a book with many strengths. However, market research undertaken by Judith Fox in Australia and by Bob in New Zealand revealed a need for wider coverage of a number of business research topics. These include: the main research philosophies and paradigms; preparing research proposals; evaluating business research articles and reports; a deeper examination of the quantitative research applications and methods; a more integrated and practical coverage of qualitative research; Australian and New Zealand examples of business research; and a fuller coverage of ethics in business research. We have attempted to address these requirements in this book.

Bob, from New Zealand, with his wide experience in business economics and the decision sciences, had used Uma's text for teaching business research methods at Victoria University of Wellington for more than 10 years. He had a number of ideas for adapting the quantitative research aspects of the text to suit New Zealand and Australian needs. Brian, from Australia, had a long background in teaching interviewing, focus groups and other qualitative research methods. He had just completed another text, which covered some of the qualitative research concepts. Our publisher, Judith Fox, invited Brian to join the team. For both of us, this team experience proved to be a robust learning journey as we continually reviewed our assumptions of business research and how it might best be taught, challenging while at the same time respecting each other's ideas.

Our initial hurdle, of course, was to add to the value of Uma's text without complicating or diluting her wonderful ideas. From the outset we were determined to keep the 'skill-building approach' we saw as the foundation of the parent text, and we believe we have achieved this goal. The text is written so the reader will be equipped to carry out business research. Wherever possible we have endeavoured to convert discussion of the theoretical aspects of business research into practical steps and advice. We hope this will allow readers to navigate their way through the complexities that often surround solid, applied business research. We have tried to make this book accessible to both practising managers, and undergraduate and graduate students of business and management.

We would like to thank all the people who have assisted us with this book, including our families, students and colleagues who have shared their ideas with us. We would like to acknowledge a few individuals in particular. First, Judith Fox, a former publisher with John Wiley & Sons: this book would never have been completed without her vision and perseverance! We would also like to thank our developmental editor, Catherine Spedding, for the difficult task of keeping the project on target, and our project editor, Jem Bates, for his patience and superb editorial assistance in the final stages. We are very grateful to Janet Keilar, the Faculty of Commerce and Administration Librarian at Victoria University of Wellington, for her assistance with the information sources for New Zealand, and the library staff at the Kelvin Grove Campus of the Queensland University of Technology for their advice, assistance and information sources in Australia. Our thanks also go to the unnamed reviewers of earlier drafts of the text. Some of the information in chapters 6, 7 and 10 were based on work from B. L. Delahaye's *Human Resource Development: Principles and Practice* (2000, John Wiley & Sons Australia). Also, a very special acknowledgement to Professor Lyn Richards and Ted Barrington of Research Services, QSR International Pty Ltd, for their thoughtful advice on the content of chapter 7 and the provision of screenshots for the figures in that chapter.

Finally, we wish our readers well in their learning journey and hope that our enjoyment of business research will be reproduced, to some extent, in the process.

Happy researching!

Bob Cavana and Brian Delahaye
*May 2001*

# ABOUT THE AUTHORS

Dr Robert Y. Cavana is currently a senior lecturer in decision sciences with the School of Business and Public Management at Victoria University of Wellington, where he has taught business research methods for 10 years and has supervised about 80 business research projects. He holds an MCom in economics from the University of Auckland and a PhD in management science from the University of Bradford, UK. His research and consultancy interests cover the theoretical and applied aspects of decision sciences, business research, strategic/policy modelling and business economics. He has published in a wide range of international and New Zealand journals, and recently co-authored the book *Systems Thinking and Modelling: Understanding Change and Complexity*. Between 1988 and 1990 he was the President of the Operational Research Society of New Zealand. He has previously worked in a number of public and private sector organisations in New Zealand, where he has been involved in economic, strategic and business research projects spanning most sectors of the economy. Before joining Victoria University in 1989 he was Corporate Economist with the New Zealand Railways Corporation.

Brian L. Delahaye is Associate Professor, Adult and Workplace Education, in the School of Professional Studies at Queensland University of Technology. Before taking up this position in 1990 he was a senior training officer, staff development officer and administration manager with Telecom Australia, and a lecturer and senior lecturer in human resource management in the School of Management at Queensland University of Technology. Brian's research, including his doctoral thesis, has concentrated on self-directed learning, developing the human resource developer and the management of knowledge capital. He has published more than 30 articles in national and international refereed journals and is co-author of the successful text *How to Be an Effective Trainer* (Wiley New York), now in its third edition, and author of *Human Resource Development: Principles and Practice* (Wiley Australia). He has taught research methodology at the postgraduate level and was nominated as 'Supervisor of the Year' in 1996 by the Postgraduate Students Association at QUT. He consults widely with commercial, non-profit and government organisations on the management of change, managing knowledge, management development and human resource development.

Uma Sekaran is Professor Emerita of Management, Southern Illinois University, at Carbondale (SIUC), Illinois. She obtained her MBA degree from the University of Connecticut at Storrs, and her PhD from the University of California, Los Angeles. She has authored or co-authored seven books, 12 book chapters and more than 45 refereed journal articles. She has presented more than 70 papers in national, international and regional conferences, and is the recipient of meritorious research awards from both the Academy of Management and SIUC. She has also received the Best Teacher Award from the university. Professor Sekaran has won recognition for significant research contributions to cross-cultural research by US and international professional organisations. She was Chair of the Department of Management and Director of University Women's Professional Advancement at SIUC before her retirement.

# ACKNOWLEDGEMENTS

The authors and publisher wish to thank the following people and institutions for permission to reproduce material covered by copyright.

## Figures

Page 22 (figure 1.1): from *Social Research Methods: Qualitative and Quantitative Approaches*, 3rd edition, by W. Lawrence Neuman, © 1997, Allyn & Bacon. Reprinted with permission; page 139 (figure 6.2): from *Human Resource Development: Principles and Practice* by Brian L. Delahaye, © 2000, John Wiley & Sons Australia; pages 177-81 (figures 7.2-7.8): screenshots of the NVivo qualitative analysis software reproduced by permission of QSR International Pty Ltd, www.qsrinternational.com. NVivo, NUD*IST Vivo, NUD*IST are registered trade marks of QSR International Pty Ltd; page 204 (figure 9.1): from *Business Research Methods*, 6th edition, by William G. Zikmund, © 2000, The Dryden Press. Reproduced by permission of the publisher; page 227 (figure 10.3): from *A Guide to Good Survey Design*, 1995, Statistics NZ; page 304 (figure 12.4): from *Computer Simulation in Management Science*, 3rd edition, by M. Pidd, 1992, John Wiley & Sons, Chichester, UK. Reproduced with permission; pages 404-33 (figures A1, A2, A11, A12, A19(a) and (b)): SPSS screenshots and data output reproduced with permission of SPSS Inc.; page 418 (figure A10): from *Marketing Research*, 5th edition, by D. A. Aaker, V. Kumar and G. S. Day, © 1995, John Wiley & Sons, New York; pages 448-52 (graphs accompanying statistical tables): from *Business Statistics: A Decision-making Approach* by D. F. Groebner and P. W. Shannon, © 2001. Reproduced by permission of Pearson Education Inc., Upper Saddle River, New Jersey 07458.

## Text

Page 13 ('Xerox tries to clear a paper jam of debts'): Adam Jones, *The Times*, 6 December 2000, © Times Newspaper Limited, London; pages 80-81: adapted case study reproduced by permission of Dr Jennifer Pierce; page 216 ('Job involvement' table): page 218: scale excerpted from *A Theory of Leadership Effectiveness* by Fred E. Fiedler, © 1967, McGraw-Hill, New York. Reproduced by permission of the author; page 219 ('V. Management Priorities'): from *Decision Sciences* 29 (4), 1998. Reproduced by permission of the publisher, The Decision Sciences Institute; page 221: reproduced with permission from the *Journal of Marketing*, published by the American Marketing Association, J. F. Gaski and M. J. Etzel, volume 50, 71-81; page 222 ('II. SERVQUAL-P Battery'): from B. Mittal and W. M. Lassar 1996, 'The role of personalization in service encounters', *Journal of Retailing* 72, 95-109. Reproduced with permission; page 223 ('IV. Brand image'): reproduced with permission from the *Journal of Marketing Research*, published by the American Marketing Association, M. S. Roth, XXXII, May, 173; pages 238-9: excerpted and adapted from *Human Resource Development: Principles and Practice* by Brian L. Delahaye, © 2000, John Wiley & Sons Australia; page 248 (Exercise 10.4): *from Human Resource Development: Principles and Practice* by Brian L. Delahaye, © 2000, John Wiley & Sons Australia; page 249: survey reproduced from *Management Magazine*, © *Management Magazine*/Profile Publishing, Auckland; page 448 (appendix II, table I): from *Business Statistics: A Decision-making Approach* by D. F. Groebner and P. W. Shannon, © 2001. Reproduced by permission of Pearson Education Inc., Upper Saddle River, New Jersey 07458.

Every effort has been made to trace the ownership of copyright material. Information that will enable the publisher to rectify any error or omission in subsequent editions would be welcomed. In such cases please contact the Permissions Section of John Wiley & Sons Australia, Ltd, who will arrange for payment of the usual fee.

# part I

# A SCIENTIFIC APPROACH TO BUSINESS RESEARCH

1 Introduction to business research
2 Scientific investigation and the research process

# chapter 1

# INTRODUCTION TO BUSINESS RESEARCH

## OUTLINE

WHAT IS RESEARCH?

BUSINESS RESEARCH

THE CONTEXT OF BUSINESS RESEARCH

PHILOSOPHICAL BASES OF BUSINESS RESEARCH

BUSINESS RESEARCH METHODS: QUANTITATIVE AND QUALITATIVE

TYPES OF BUSINESS RESEARCH: APPLIED AND BASIC

MANAGERS AND RESEARCH

THE MANAGER AND THE CONSULTANT OR RESEARCHER

INTERNAL VERSUS EXTERNAL CONSULTANTS OR RESEARCHERS

EXTERNAL CONSULTANTS OR RESEARCHERS

KNOWLEDGE ABOUT RESEARCH AND MANAGERIAL EFFECTIVENESS

ETHICS AND BUSINESS RESEARCH

SUMMARY

DISCUSSION POINTS

REFERENCES

## CHAPTER OBJECTIVES

After reading this chapter, you should be able to:
- describe what research is and state how it is defined
- distinguish between applied and basic research, giving examples, and discussing why they would fall into one or other of the two categories
- distinguish between positivist, interpretivist and critical research
- explain why managers should know about research
- discuss what managers should and should not do in order to interact most effectively with researchers
- identify and fully discuss specific situations in which a manager would be better off using an internal research team, and when an external research team would be more advisable, giving reasons for the decisions
- discuss what research means to you and describe how you, as a manager, might apply the knowledge gained about research
- describe the role of ethics in business research.

As a manager, you will be making decisions each day at work. What would help you to make the right decisions? Will it be your experience on the job, your sixth sense or hunch, or will you just trust to good luck? Certainly, all these will play a part after you have thoroughly investigated or researched the problem situation and generated some alternative solutions to choose from. Whether or not managers realise it, they are constantly engaged in research as they try to find solutions to the day-to-day problems, big and small, which confront them at work. Some of the issues are solved with relative ease, as when a machine on the shop floor stops working and the foreman, applying past experience, hastens to do the necessary repair and gets it to run smoothly again. A few problems may present moderate difficulty, requiring time and effort for the manager to investigate and find a solution — as, for example, when many employees absent themselves from work frequently. Yet other problems can be quite complex and the manager may proceed to seek the help of an 'expert researcher' to study the issue and offer solutions, as in the case of a company consistently incurring losses, a situation perplexing to everyone.

## WHAT IS RESEARCH?

Just close your eyes for a moment and utter the word 'research' to yourself. What images does this word conjure up for you? Do you visualise a lab with scientists at work with bunsen burners and test tubes, or an Einstein-like character writing dissertations on some complex subject, or someone collecting data to study the impact of a newly introduced day-care system on the morale of employees? Most certainly, all these images do represent different aspects of research. **Research**, a somewhat intimidating term for some, is simply the process of thoroughly studying and analysing the situational factors surrounding a problem in order to seek out solutions to it. Managers in organisations constantly engage themselves in studying and analysing issues and hence are involved in some form of research activity as they make decisions at the workplace. As is well known, sometimes managers make good decisions and the problem is solved; sometimes they make poor decisions and the problem persists; and on occasion they make such colossal blunders that the organisation gets stuck in the mire. The difference between making good decisions and committing blunders lies in how managers go about the decision-making process. In other words, good decision making fetches a 'yes' answer to the following questions: Do managers identify where exactly the problem lies? Do they correctly recognise the relevant factors in the situation needing investigation? Do they know what types of information are to be gathered and how? Do they know how to make use of the information so collected and draw appropriate conclusions to make the right decisions? And finally, do they know how to implement the results of this process to solve the problem? This is the essence of research, and to be a successful manager it is important that you know how to go about making the right decisions by being knowledgeable about the various steps involved in solving problematic issues. This is what this book is all about.

### WHY MANAGERS SHOULD KNOW ABOUT RESEARCH

Modern technology has made research an exciting and relatively smooth process. Today a personal computer and a modem place us within easy reach of knowledge of what is happening in the global markets and how the world economy is impacting on business. By grasping the fundamentals of the research process and keeping abreast of modern computer technology, which has provided computers with enormous capability to store and retrieve information, you as a manager can face the competitive global market, with its multitude of complex and confusing factors, with greater confidence.

Knowledge of research not only helps us to look at the available information in sophisticated and creative ways in the fast-paced global environment in which businesses exist, but also helps in other ways. For example, you can interact more effectively with research consultants who work for you, you can discriminate between good and bad studies published in professional journals and, if you wish, you yourself can undertake research to solve problems. Moreover, knowledge in the business area is exploding: there is an overwhelming maze of information available through the **Internet**, which has to be sifted for reliability. Identifying the critical issues, gathering relevant information, analysing the data in ways that would help decision making, and implementing the right course of action are all facilitated by understanding business research. After all, decision making is concerned with the process of choosing from among alternative solutions to resolve a problem, and research helps to generate viable alternatives for effective decision making.

## BUSINESS RESEARCH

Business research can be described as a systematic and organised effort to investigate a specific problem or opportunity encountered in the work setting that needs a solution. Managers also need to recognise that most problems are opportunities in disguise. For example, a customer complaint can be an opportunity to increase market share. Business research, then, comprises a series of steps designed and executed with the goal of finding answers to the issues that are of importance to the manager in the work environment. This means that the first step in research is to know where the problem or opportunity areas exist in the organisation, and to identify as clearly and specifically as possible the problems and opportunities that need to be studied and resolved. Once the problem or opportunity that needs attention is clearly defined, then steps can be taken to gather information, analyse the data, determine the factors that are associated with the problem or opportunity, and take the necessary actions to solve the problem or secure the opportunity.

This entire process by which we attempt to resolve issues is called research. Thus, research involves a series of well-thought-out and carefully executed activities that will enable the manager to know how organisational problems can be resolved, or at least considerably minimised. Research thus encompasses the processes of inquiry, investigation, examination and experimentation. These processes have to be carried out systematically, diligently, critically, objectively and logically. The expected end results are the discovery that will help the manager to deal with the problem or opportunity.

The difference between the manager who uses common sense alone to analyse and make a decision in a given situation and the investigator who uses a scientific method is that the latter makes a systematic inquiry into the matter and proceeds to describe, explain or predict phenomena based on data carefully collected for the purpose.

## DEFINITION OF RESEARCH

We can now define business research as an *organised, systematic, data-based, critical, objective, scientific inquiry or investigation into a specific problem or issue* with the purpose of finding solutions to it or clarifying it. In essence, research provides the needed information that guides managers to make *informed* decisions to deal successfully with organisational issues. The information provided could be the result of a careful analysis of data gathered first-hand or of data that are already available (in the company, industry, archives etc.). Data can be quantitative (as generally gathered through structured questions) or qualitative (as generated from the broad answers to specific questions in interviews, from responses to open-ended questions in a questionnaire, through observation, or from already available information gathered from various sources).

## RESEARCH AND THE MANAGER

A common aspect of all organisations is that each day managers encounter problems big and small, which they have to solve by making the right decisions. In business, research is usually primarily conducted to resolve problematic issues in, or interrelated among, the areas of accounting, finance, management and marketing. In accounting, budget control systems, practices and procedures are frequently examined. Inventory costing methods, accelerated depreciation, time-series behaviour of quarterly earnings, transfer pricing, cash recovery rates and taxation methods are some of the other areas researched. In finance, the operations of financial institutions, optimum financial ratios, mergers and acquisitions, leveraged buyouts, intercorporate financing, yields on mortgages, the behaviour of the stock exchange and the like become the focus for investigation. *Management research* could encompass the study of employee attitudes and behaviours, human resources managment, the impact of changing demographics on management practices, production operations management, strategy formulation, **information systems** and so on. *Marketing research* could address issues pertaining to product image, advertising, sales promotion, distribution, packaging, pricing, after-sales service, consumer preferences, new product development and other marketing aspects.

Below we have listed some commonly researched topical areas in business.

---

**Examples of commonly researched areas in business**

- employee behaviours such as performance, absenteeism and turnover
- employee attitudes such as job satisfaction, loyalty and organisational commitment
- supervisory performance, managerial leadership style and performance appraisal systems
- employee selection, recruitment, training and retention
- validation of performance appraisal systems
- human resource management choices and organisational strategy
- evaluations of assessment centres
- the dynamics of rating and rating errors in the judgement of human performance
- strategy formulation and implementation
- just-in-time systems, continuous-improvement strategies and production efficiencies
- updating policies and procedures in keeping with the latest government regulations and organisational changes
- organisational outcomes such as increased sales, market share, profits, growth and effectiveness

- distribution channels, advertising effectiveness and effective test marketing strategies
- brand loyalty, product life cycle and product innovation
- consumer complaints
- location analysis
- impression management, logos and image building
- market feasibility studies and market testing
- product positioning, product modification and new product development
- cost of capital, valuation of firms, dividend policies and investment decisions
- portfolio management, pricing models and future options
- financial institutions and their operations
- risk assessment, exchange rate fluctuations and foreign investment
- tax implications of reorganisation of firms or acquisition of companies
- collection of accounts receivable
- accelerating depreciation
- developing effective cost accounting procedures
- auditing practices
- qualified pension plans and cafeteria type of benefits for employees
- deferred compensation plans
- installing effective management information systems
- use of **expert systems** in daily decision making
- models of executive information systems
- mathematical models for assessing organisational effectiveness
- advanced manufacturing technologies and information systems
- designing career paths for spouses in dual-career families
- creative management of a diverse work force
- cultural differences and the dynamics of managing a multinational firm
- alternative work patterns: job sharing, flexitime, flexiplace and part-time work
- creating and managing corporate culture and socialisation processes
- downsizing
- participative management and performance effectiveness
- differences in leadership positions, salaries and leadership styles
- instrument development for assessing 'true' gender differences
- pollution emission and consequences
- installation, adaptation and updating of computer networks and software suitable for creating effective information systems for organisations
- installing an effective Data Warehouse and Data Mining system for the organisation
- keeping ahead of the competition in the new millennium.

Not only are the issues within any sub-area related to many factors within that particular system, but they must also be investigated in the context of the external environment facing the business. For example, economic, political, demographic, technological, competitive and other relevant global factors could impinge on some of the dynamics related to the firm. These factors have to be scrutinised as well to assess their possible impact on the problem researched.

# THE CONTEXT OF BUSINESS RESEARCH

All professional areas — anthropology, medicine, sociology and engineering, to name a few — seek out new knowledge and answers to critical issues through research. As we have discussed, business must also search for new knowledge and base decisions on a systematic process of data collection and data analysis.

However, business operates within a specific environment, so we first need to understand the context within which business is carried out. To understand business research, we need to examine the research philosophies that underpin it, the methodical options used and the basic types of business research that can be undertaken.

# PHILOSOPHICAL BASES OF BUSINESS RESEARCH

Research is a complex process, laden with values and, at times, complicated by a variety of expectations. Given this complexity, perhaps it is not surprising that researchers base their endeavours on differing beliefs about how research should be conducted and what the results of research should accomplish. These differing beliefs can be broadly categorised under three schools of thought, or paradigms — namely, positivist, interpretivist and critical research.

The term 'paradigm' has come to be widely used among business and social researchers in recent years owing to the work of Thomas Kuhn (1962). In the context of business research:

> A *paradigm* reflects a basic set of philosophical beliefs about the nature of the world. It provides guidelines and principles concerning the way research is conducted within the paradigm. The methods and techniques used in the research should be in sympathy with these guidelines and principles (Ticehurst & Veal 1999:25).

The three main paradigms in business research will now be discussed.

## POSITIVIST RESEARCH

Positivist research is rooted in the natural sciences, which have a longer history than the social sciences. Broadly, the natural sciences research elements of the natural world while the social sciences examine the world of people. Accordingly, a number of the assumptions used in the natural sciences are inherent in the positivist approach to social science.

Positivist research uses precise, objective measures and is usually associated with quantitative data. Positivist researchers use a linear strategy of formulating a hypothesis (a statement of the relationships between the observed phenomena) then attempt to disprove these assumed relationships by concentrating on the *null hypothesis* — that is, the researcher tries to disprove the research **hypothesis**. Data gathering follows rigorous steps and the quantitative data are analysed using statistical methods. The hallmark of good positivist research is replicability — that is, another researcher should be able to conduct the same research in the same way and come up with comparable results.

Positivist research uses deductive reasoning — beginning with a theoretical position and moving towards concrete empirical evidence — to identify a set of universal laws that can be used to predict general systems of human activity. Accordingly, positivist research is based on the assumption that there is a set of universal laws out there waiting to be discovered.

The positivist researcher is expected to remain aloof and separate from the research subjects to ensure total objectivity during data gathering and analysis.

**EXAMPLE 1.1** The manager of the student union complex at Victoria University wants feedback on the performance of the contractors servicing the student café. She is interested in the reasons why students use the café, their frequency and time of use, and their opinions about the range and quality of the food, drinks and service provided in the café.

This would be structured as a fairly straightforward positivist research project.

Criticisms of positivist research include that:
- it is superficial, in that it attempts to reduce all aspects of human endeavour to numbers
- it fails to deal with the meaning systems of people, including the way they think and feel
- the independence of the researcher is a myth, and the use of statistical procedures in particular is an attempt to hide the fact that all researchers have subjective responses and involvement with their research
- statistical **samples** often do not represent specific social groups, and do not allow either illuminating generalisation or understanding of individual cases.

## INTERPRETIVIST RESEARCH

Whereas positivist research assumes that all people share the same meaning systems, interpretivist research believes that it is more likely that people experience physical and social reality in different ways. These meaning systems, or patterns of conventions, are created out of social interactions between people. The interpretivist researcher assumes that the world is largely what people perceive it to be. Reality, therefore, is socially constructed. The interpretivist researcher is interested in understanding the lived experience of human beings. The researcher identifies what is meaningful to each individual being investigated and becomes fully involved with these individual subjects. This involvement allows the researcher to uncover the socially constructed meaning as it is understood by an individual or a group of individuals.

**EXAMPLE 1.2** A manager institutes an annual review process that examines the output of each staff member during the year and in this way establishes the expected output of each staff member for the following year. For the manager, this annual review process appears to be a sound communication system that rewards staff for their achievements and provides motivational energy to increase production in the following year. However, the staff see the review as a heavy-handed control mechanism which forces them to promise the achievement of targets for the following year when they do not know the conditions under which they will be expected to work.

For the manager and the staff, the annual review process has two different socially constructed meanings.

Rather than producing general, predictive laws about human behaviour, interpretivist research presents a rich and complex description of how people think, react and feel under certain contextually specific situations. This description allows others to understand the world of the subjects being investigated.

Criticisms of interpretivist research include that:
- it is too subjective
- it focuses on local, micro-level or short-term events
- it does not seek to initiate change.

# CRITICAL RESEARCH

The basic aim of critical research is to empower people to create a better world for themselves. The approach achieves this aim by uncovering, and going beyond, surface illusions. Research should concentrate on uncovering myths and revealing hidden meanings. These meanings are hidden because reality has multiple layers, with underlying meaning systems behind the observable, surface reality. Critical research assumes that, once people see these surface illusions for what they are, the less powerful will be motivated to make changes to their lives. The critical researcher should present the research findings in such a way that they become a catalyst that leads to transformation.

**EXAMPLE 1.3**

When examining the relationship between a teacher and students, interpretivist research may present a rich and colourful description of the interactions between the parties. Critical research will look, for example, for power issues in the relationship. Why is the teacher allowed to roam about the room while the students sit captured and passive behind desks? Why does access to the chalkboard give the teacher power? Should there be unequal power between the teacher and the numerically superior students? How can this power relationship be changed?

Critical research, then, assumes that people have a great deal of unrealised potential and have the ability to adapt and transform themselves. Criticisms of critical research include that:

- in common with positivist research, it assumes that laws of social order are out there waiting to be discovered
- it may force change on people before they are ready
- it focuses on destroying current reality without providing processes for building a new reality.

**Table 1.1** Comparison of the three major paradigms underpinning business research

|  | Positivist | Interpretivist | Critical |
| --- | --- | --- | --- |
| **Assumptions** | Objective world which science can measure and 'mirror' with privileged knowledge | Intersubjective world which science can represent with concepts; social construction of reality | Material world of structured contradictions and/or exploitation which can be objectively known only by removing tacit ideological biases |
| **Aim** | To discover universal laws that can be used to predict human activity | To uncover the socially constructed meaning of reality as understood by an individual or group | To uncover surface illusions so that people will be empowered to change their world |

|  | **Positivist** | **Interpretivist** | **Critical** |
|---|---|---|---|
| **Stance of researcher** | Stands aloof and apart from research subjects so that decisions can be made objectively | Becomes fully involved with research subjects to achieve a full understanding of subjects' world | Involved with research subjects so that surface illusions can be identified, but urges subjects to change their world |
| **Values** | Value free; their influence is denied | Values included and made explicit | Values included and made explicit |
| **Types of reasoning** | Deductive | Inductive | Deductive and inductive |
| **Research plan** | Rigorous, linear and rigid, based on research hypothesis | Flexible, and follows the information provided by the research subject | The imperative for change guides the actions of the researcher |
| **Research methods and type(s) of analysis** | Experiments; questionnaires; secondary data analysis; quantitatively coded; documents statisticial analysis | Ethnography; participant observation; interviews; focus groups; conversational analysis; case studies | Field research, historical analysis, dialectical analysis |
| **Goodness or quality of criteria** | Conventional benchmarks of 'rigour'; internal and external validity; reliability and objectivity | Trustworthiness and authenticity | Historical situatedness; erosion of ignorance and misapprehensions; action stimulus |

**Sources:** Lincoln and Guba (2000); Gephart (1999).

## AN APPROACH FOR BUSINESS

Some researchers claim specific allegiance to one or another of the research paradigms or approaches, and so claim to be positivist, interpretivist or critical researchers. This preference is, most probably, based on the individual researcher's personality, past experiences and training. However, it is as well to recognise that the topic of research and the **research objectives** may indicate the advantages of a particular approach. For example, if the organisation is looking for a strategic change towards a more independent staff decision-making process, then a critical research perspective may enhance the change process considerably.

What can be said is that each approach brings with it a unique perspective, and that the distinctive assumptions of each have their own strengths. Some researchers, therefore, take a more eclectic view and use aspects of each approach to suit their needs. So, for example, recognising the benefits of encouraging replicability, interpretivist researchers often describe the research design followed in the project in considerable detail in the hope that other researchers may be able to replicate the investigation for comparative purposes.

Each researcher, then, must make an informed decision on which approach, or combination of approaches, to follow.

## BUSINESS RESEARCH METHODS: QUANTITATIVE AND QUALITATIVE

Generally, research can be divided into two broad methods — quantitative and qualitative. Quantitative methods rely on the ability of the researcher to measure the phenomena under investigation and the use of statistics to analyse the raw data. Quantitative methods in business research include **questionnaires**, field and laboratory experiments and also use statistical data gathered by organisations such as the Australian Bureau of Statistics and Statistics New Zealand.

Qualitative research methods include **interviews**, **focus groups** and **observations**, and are aimed at understanding the rich, complex and idiosyncratic nature of human phenomena. These qualitative approaches rely on the researcher being a 'human-as-an-instrument' both to gather and to analyse the information.

A more detailed discussion on quantitative and qualitative research is included in chapter 2.

## TYPES OF BUSINESS RESEARCH: APPLIED AND BASIC

Research can be undertaken for two different purposes. One is to solve a current problem faced by the manager in the work setting that demands a timely solution. For example, a particular product may not be selling well and the manager may want to find the reasons for this in order to take corrective action. Such research is called *applied research*. The other is to generate a body of knowledge by trying to comprehend how certain problems that occur in organisations can be solved. This is called *basic research*. It is quite possible that some organisations may later apply the knowledge gained by the findings of such basic research to solve their own problems. For instance, a university professor may be interested in investigating the factors that contribute to employee absenteeism as a matter of mere academic interest. After gathering information on this topic from several institutions and analysing the data collected, the professor may identify specific factors such as inflexible work hours, inadequate training of employees and low morale as primarily influencing absenteeism. Later, a manager who encounters employee absenteeism in his or her organisation may be able to use this information to determine if these factors are relevant to that particular work setting.

Thus, research done with the intention of applying the results to solving specific problems currently being experienced in the business is called **applied research**. Research done chiefly to enhance the understanding of certain problems that commonly occur in organisational settings and seek methods of solving them is called **basic** or **fundamental research**. It is also known as **pure research**. The findings of such research contribute to the building of knowledge in the various functional areas of business. Such knowledge is applied in organisational settings for problem solving.

## APPLIED RESEARCH

Consider the following situation cited in *The Australian*.

> ### Xerox tries to clear a paper jam of debts
>
> Xerox, the company that invented the office photocopier, is on the verge of bankruptcy.
>
> The American firm is desperately trying to raise billions of dollars amid fears it could run out of money. Xerox, which has debts of US$17 billion ($A31.5 billion), must raise as much as US$4 billion from selling parts of its empire.
>
> But in a monumental 'paper jam', the only documents Xerox seems to be capable of churning out these days are gloomy warnings for its investors.
>
> Xerox traces its history back to 1906, when it was called the Haloid Corporation. After World War II it commercialised a process that transferred electrostatic images to paper and a business giant was born.
>
> But mismanagement and competition from rival manufacturers such as Canon have seen its stock decline.
>
> Xerox shares have gone into freefall and doors have been slamming in the company's face all over Wall Street.
>
> The company's stock market value has collapsed from nearly US$20 billion earlier this year to US$2.8 billion on Tuesday.
>
> A Xerox spokeswoman refused to entertain suggestions that the company might be forced to seek protection from bankruptcy.
>
> The cash crisis is so serious at Xerox that it might have to give up its research laboratory at Palo Alto in California, where many features that are commonplace in personal computers were invented. Xerox has said that it would seek joint venture partners to keep the research centre afloat.
>
> **Source:** *The Australian*, 7 December 2000, p. 25.

It is obvious that Xerox has a multitude of problems, including mismanagement and competition from competitors. These problems are reflected in the collapse of its share market value, which lost nearly US$17 billion in 2000 alone. A business researcher could design a scientific study to examine the issues that have led to this situation and also examine possible solutions. Once the options are identified, Xerox could then look for opportunities to change its strategic direction, rather than — as they are doing now — merely churning out gloomy warnings.

## BASIC OR FUNDAMENTAL RESEARCH

The following example is an instance of basic research, where knowledge was generated to understand a phenomenon of interest to the researcher. Most research and development departments in industry, as well as many academics in universities, do basic or fundamental research, so that more knowledge is generated in particular areas of interest to industries, organisations and researchers. Though the primary objective of engaging in basic research is to gain additional knowledge of certain phenomena and problems that occur in organisations and industries with a view to finding solutions, the knowledge generated from such research is often applied later for solving specific business problems.

> From her days as a clerical employee in a bank, Sandra had observed that her colleagues, although extremely knowledgeable about the nuances and intricacies of banking, were doing very little to improve the efficiency and effectiveness of the bank in the area of customer relations and service. They took on the minimum workload, availed themselves of long tea and lunch breaks, and showed no interest in their dealings with customers or management. That they were highly knowledgeable about banking policies and practices was clearly evident from their discussions about these subjects as they processed applications from customers. Sandra herself was very hardworking and enjoyed dealing with customers. She always used to think what a huge waste it was for talented employees to fool around rather than contribute to the GNP. When she left the bank and wrote her dissertation for her PhD, her topic of investigation was 'Job Involvement', or the ego investment of people in their jobs. The conclusion of her investigation was that the single most important contributory factor to job involvement is the fit or match between personality characteristics and the characteristics of the job people engaged in. For example, challenging jobs allowed employees with high capabilities to get job-involved, and people-oriented employees got job-involved with service activities. Sandra then understood why the highly intelligent bank employees could not get job-involved or find job satisfaction in the routine jobs that required almost no use of their abilities.
>
> Subsequently, when Sandra joined the internal research team of a Fortune 500 company, she applied this knowledge to solve problems of motivation, job satisfaction and job involvement in the organisation.

As we have stated, the primary purpose of conducting basic research is to generate knowledge and understanding of the phenomena of interest and to build theories based on the research results. Such theories subsequently form the foundation of further studies of many aspects of the phenomena. This process of building on existing knowledge is the genesis for theory building, particularly in the management area.

Several examples of basic research can be provided. For instance, researching the causes and consequences of global warming will offer many solutions to minimise the phenomenon, and will lead to further research on it, and suggest how global warming can be totally averted. While the primary purpose of global warming research might be to understand the nuances of the phenomenon, its findings will ultimately be applied usefully to the agricultural industry and the building industry, among others.

Many large companies engage in basic research. For instance, General Electric generates knowledge regarding the different applications of electrical energy (their motto is 'We bring good things to life'). Computer companies are constantly engaged in generating knowledge on how to increase the usefulness of microcomputers in industry, for the special benefit of managers and technicians in all organisations. This, ultimately, results in increased sales of computers for the companies.

University academics engage in basic research in an effort to understand and generate more knowledge about various aspects of businesses. Common areas of investigation include how to:
- improve the effectiveness of information systems
- integrate technology into the overall strategic objectives of an organisation
- assess the impact of logos
- increase the productivity of employees in service industries

- monitor sexual harassment incidents at the workplace
- increase the effectiveness of small businesses
- evaluate alternative inventory valuation methods
- change the institutional structure of the money and capital markets.

The findings from such research later become useful for application in business situations.

As illustrated, the main distinction between applied and basic business research is that the former is specifically aimed at solving a currently experienced problem, whereas the latter has the broader objective of generating knowledge and understanding of phenomena and problems that occur in various organisational settings. Despite this distinction, both types of research follow the same steps of systematic inquiry to arrive at solutions to problems. As current or prospective practising managers in organisations, you would be directly or indirectly engaged in applied research. You would also stay abreast of new basic knowledge generated by keeping up with the published research in the business journals related to your sphere of work, some of which could be applicable to your own business organisation.

In sum, both applied and basic business research are scientific in nature; the main difference is that the former is undertaken specifically to solve a current business problem whereas the latter is primarily resorted to because of the importance of the subject to the researcher. A deeper understanding of the phenomenon would be useful for its own sake as well as for later application. Both basic and applied research have to be undertaken in a scientific manner (discussed in the next chapter) so that the findings or results generated by the research can be relied upon to solve the problem investigated. However, some applied research could have a shorter time frame than some basic research. Overall, this book has a leaning towards applied research as it is conducted in various business organisations and industries.

## MANAGERS AND RESEARCH

Managers familiar with research have an advantage over those who are not. As a manager, although you yourself may not be doing any major research, you will have to understand, predict and control events that are dysfunctional to the organisation. For example, a newly developed product may not be 'taking off', or a financial investment may not be 'paying off' as anticipated. Such disturbing phenomena have to be *understood* and explained. Unless this is done, it will not be possible to *predict* the future of that product or the prospects of that investment, or how future catastrophic outcomes can be *controlled*. A grasp of research methods will enable managers to understand, predict and control their environment.

Since you may be bringing in researchers to solve problems instead of doing the research yourself, you may wonder why you should bother to study research. The reasons become clear when one considers the consequences of *not* knowing about research. With the ever-increasing complexity of modern businesses, and the uncertainty of the environment they face, the management of organisational systems has come to involve constant troubleshooting in the workplace. It would be helpful if managers could sense, identify and deal with potential problems. Knowledge of research and problem-solving processes helps managers to identify problem situations *before* they get out of control. While minor problems can be fixed by the manager, major problems would warrant the hiring of outside researchers or consultants. The manager who is knowledgeable about research can interact effectively with consultants. Knowledge of the research processes, design and interpretation of data also helps managers to become discriminating recipients of the research findings presented, and to determine whether or not the recommended solutions are appropriate for implementation.

Another reason why today's professional managers need to know about research methods is that they will become more discriminating when sifting through information in business journals. Some journal articles are more scientific and objective than others. Even among the scientific articles, some are more appropriate for application or adaptation to particular organisations and situations than others. This is a function of the **sampling** design, the types of organisations studied and other factors reported in the journal articles. Unless the manager is able to assess how scientific a study is, and grasp what the published empirical research actually conveys, she or he is likely to err in incorporating some of the suggestions such publications offer. Such an understanding also helps managers to handle their own problems at considerable cost savings by reading the results of 'good' published research (discussed in the next chapter) which has addressed similar issues.

There are several other reasons why professional managers should be knowledgeable about research and research methods in business. First, such knowledge sharpens managers' sensitivity to the myriad variables operating in a situation and reminds them of the multicausality and multifinality of phenomena, thus avoiding inappropriate, simplistic notions of one variable 'causing' another. Second, when managers understand the research reports on their organisations handed to them by professionals, they will be in a position to take intelligent, educated, calculated risks with known probabilities attached to the success or failure of their decisions. Research then becomes a useful decision-making tool rather than a mass of incomprehensible statistical information. Third, when managers become knowledgeable about **scientific investigations**, vested interests inside or outside the organisation will not prevail. For instance, an internal research group within the organisation will be unable to distort information or manipulate the findings to their advantage, if managers are aware of the **biases** that could creep into research and know how data are analysed and interpreted. As an example, an internal research team might state that a particular unit to which it is partial (for whatever reason) has shown increased profits and hence should be allocated more resources to buy sophisticated equipment to further enhance its effectiveness. However, the increased profit could have been a one-time windfall phenomenon due to external environmental factors such as market conditions, bearing no relation whatever to the unit's operating efficiency. Thus, awareness of the different ways in which data can be camouflaged will help the manager to relate to, and share pertinent information with, the researcher or consultant hired for problem solving.

In sum, being knowledgeable about research and research methods helps professional managers to:
- identify and effectively solve minor problems in the work setting
- know how to discriminate good from bad research
- appreciate and be aware of the multiple influences and multiple effects of factors impinging on a situation
- take calculated risks in decision making, knowing the probabilities attached to the different possible outcomes
- prevent possible vested interests from exercising their influence in a situation
- relate to hired researchers and consultants more effectively
- combine experience with scientific knowledge while making decisions.

# THE MANAGER AND THE CONSULTANT OR RESEARCHER

As a manager, you will often need to engage a consultant to study some of the more complex, time-consuming problems you might encounter, as in the case of Xerox noted earlier. It is thus important to know how to locate and select a researcher, how to interact effectively with the consultant (the terms *researcher* and *consultant* are used interchangeably), what the manager–researcher relationship should be, and the advantages and disadvantages of **internal** versus **external consultants**. It has to be emphasised that the genuine motive of the manager in hiring consultants should be for problem solving and not for promoting self-interest or advancing one's pet projects and ideas.

## HOW TO LOCATE AND SELECT A RESEARCHER

Many business consulting firms are listed in telephone directories and can be used for consulting on various types of projects. If a broad indication is given about what areas or issues need to be researched, the consulting firm will provide lists of individuals who have expertise in those particular areas. The credentials of these individuals are also usually presented by the consulting firm, or they can be requested. Other organisations that have used their services can also be contacted to ascertain the merits and effectiveness of the individuals and the reputation of the firm.

Many universities also have academics who take on business consulting work. Some of them have vast experience working with different types of organisation. These consultants can also be contracted and hired, if they are available and agree to do the study. In all cases, however, it is advisable to check their credentials and those of their institutions before hiring.

## THE MANAGER–RESEARCHER RELATIONSHIP

During the course of their careers, it often becomes necessary for managers to deal with consultants. Many academics have their students do research projects for the class, and some organisations allow access to these students, asking only that a copy of the research project be made available to them. Some academics interested in publishing the results of basic research also approach organisations and are afforded the facilities to conduct research. If the research has been done scientifically, then the study results will be beneficial to the manager, who will have obtained useful information without paying for it. By being able to point out the relevant variables of concern to the researchers engaging in basic research, and by helping them with useful insights, the manager stands to benefit a great deal. When the manager is knowledgeable about research, then the interactions between the manager and the researcher become more meaningful, purposeful and beneficial to both the organisation and the researcher.

Quite frequently, organisations hire outside research agencies to identify and solve problems for them. In such a case, the manager must not only interact effectively with the research team, but also explicitly delineate the roles of researchers and management. The manager has to inform the researchers what types of information could be provided to them and, more important, which of their records would *not* be made available to them. Such records might include personnel files or those containing trade secrets. Making these facts explicit at the outset can avoid a lot of frustration for both parties. Managers who are knowledgeable about research can more easily foresee what information the researchers might require, and if certain documents containing such information cannot be made available to the investigators, they can inform the research team at the start. It is vexing for the researchers to discover at a later stage that the company will not give them access to certain information. If they know the constraints from the beginning, the researchers may be able to identify alternative ways of tackling the problems and to design the research in such a way as to provide the answers needed.

## VALUES

Beyond specifying the roles and constraints, the manager should also make sure that the value systems of management and the consultants are compatible. For example, the research team might strongly believe and recommend that reducing the work force and streamlining the work system is the ideal way to cut down operating costs. Management's consistent philosophy, however, might be *not* to fire employees who are experienced, loyal and senior. Thus, there might be a clash of ideologies between management and the research team. Research knowledge will help managers to identify and explicitly state, ahead of time, the values the organisation holds dear, so that there are no surprises down the road. Clarification of the issue offers the research team the opportunity either to accept the assignment, knowing alternative ways of dealing with the problem, or to regret its inability to undertake the project. In either case, both the organisation and the research team would be better off for having discussed their value orientations and avoided potential frustration on both sides.

Exchange of information in a straightforward and forthright manner also helps to increase the rapport and trust levels between the parties, which in turn motivates the two sides to interact effectively. Under these conditions, the researchers feel free to approach the management to seek assistance in making the research more purposeful. For instance, the research team is likely to request that management inform the employees of the ensuing research and its broad purpose to allay any fears that might be entertained.

To summarise, the manager should make sure while hiring researchers or consultants that:
- the roles and expectations of both parties are made explicit
- relevant philosophies and value systems of the organisation are clearly stated, and constraints, if any, communicated
- a good rapport is established with the researcher, and between the researchers and the employees in the organisation, so that the latter cooperate fully with the researchers.

## INTERNAL VERSUS EXTERNAL CONSULTANTS OR RESEARCHERS

Some organisations have their own consulting or research department, which may be called the Management Services Department, the Corporate Planning Department, R & D (research and development department) or some other name. This department serves as the internal consultant to subunits of the organisation that face certain problems and seek help. Such a unit within the organisation is useful in several ways, and enlisting its help may be advantageous under some circumstances, but not under others. The manager often has to decide whether to use internal or external researchers. To reach such a decision, the manager should be aware of the strengths and weaknesses of both, and weigh the advantages and disadvantages of using either, based on the needs of the situation. Some of the advantages and disadvantages of internal and external teams are now discussed.

### ADVANTAGES OF INTERNAL CONSULTANTS OR RESEARCHERS

There are at least four advantages in engaging an internal team to undertake the research project.
1. An internal team would stand a better chance of being accepted by the employees in the subunit where research needs to be done.
2. They would require much less time to understand the structure, the philosophy and climate, and the functioning and work systems of the organisation.

3. They would be available for implementing their recommendations after the research findings are accepted. This is very important, because any 'bugs' in the implementation of the recommendations could be removed with their help. They would also be available for evaluating the effectiveness of the changes, and for considering further changes when necessary.
4. The internal team might cost considerably less than an external team for the department enlisting help in problem solving, because they will need less time to understand the system owing to their continuous involvement with various units of the organisation. For problems of low complexity, the internal team would be suitable.

## DISADVANTAGES OF INTERNAL RESEARCHERS

There are also certain disadvantages to engaging internal research teams for the purposes of problem solving. The four most critical ones are described below.
1. In view of their status as insiders, the internal team may fall into a stereotypical way of looking at the organisation and its problems. This would inhibit any fresh ideas and perspectives that might be needed to correct the problem, which would be a definite handicap where weighty issues and complex problems are to be investigated.
2. There is scope for certain powerful coalitions in the organisation to influence the internal team to conceal, distort or misrepresent certain facts. In other words, certain vested interests could dominate, especially in securing a sizeable portion of the available scant resources.
3. Even the most highly qualified internal research teams may not be perceived as 'experts' by the staff and management, and hence their recommendations may not be highly regarded and given the attention they deserve.
4. Certain organisational biases of the internal research team may in some instances make the findings less objective and hence less scientific.

## EXTERNAL CONSULTANTS OR RESEARCHERS

The disadvantages of the internal research teams turn out to be the advantages of the external teams, and the former's advantages work out to be the disadvantages of the latter. The specific advantages and disadvantages of the external teams will now be outlined.

## ADVANTAGES OF EXTERNAL CONSULTANTS

The advantages of the external team are described below.
1. The external team can draw on a wealth of experience from having worked with different types of organisation that have had the same or similar types of problem. This wide range of experience enables them to think both divergently and convergently rather than rushing to an instant solution on the basis of the apparent facts of the situation. They are able to consider several alternative ways of looking at the problem because of their extensive problem-solving experiences in various other situations. Having viewed the situation from several possible angles and perspectives (divergently), they can critically assess each of these, discard the less viable options and alternatives, and focus on specific feasible solutions (think convergently).
2. The external teams, especially those from established research and consulting firms, may have more knowledge of current sophisticated problem-solving models through their periodic training programs, to which the teams within the organisation may not have access. Because knowledge obsolescence is a real threat in the consulting area, external research institutions ensure that their members are kept current on the latest innovations through periodic organised training programs.

The extent to which internal team members are kept abreast of the latest problem-solving techniques may vary considerably from one organisation to another.

## DISADVANTAGES OF EXTERNAL CONSULTANTS

The major disadvantages in hiring an external research team are now described.
1. The cost of hiring an external research team is usually high and is the main deterrent, unless the problems are critical.
2. In addition to the considerable time required for the external team to gain an understanding of the organisation to be researched, they may not be readily accepted or welcomed by employees. Departments and individuals likely to be affected by the research study may perceive the study team as a threat and resist them. Therefore, enlisting their cooperation in the study is a little more difficult and time-consuming for the external researchers, compared with the internal teams.
3. The external team also charges extra for their assistance in the implementation and evaluation phases.

Keeping in mind these advantages and disadvantages of the internal and external research teams, the manager who needs research services has to weigh up the pros and cons of engaging each before making a decision. If the problem is a complex one, if there are likely to be vested interests, or if the very existence of the organisation is at stake because of one or more serious problems, it would be advisable to engage external researchers despite the increased costs involved. However, if the problems are fairly straightforward, if time is of the essence in solving moderately complex problems, or if there is a system-wide need to establish procedures and policies of a fairly routine nature, the internal team would probably be the better option.

Knowledge of research methods and an appreciation of the comparative advantages and disadvantages of the external and internal teams help managers to determine which would be the appropriate choice to investigate and suggest solutions for the problem.

## KNOWLEDGE ABOUT RESEARCH AND MANAGERIAL EFFECTIVENESS

As already mentioned, managers are responsible for making the critical decisions in the organisation. This is greatly facilitated by research knowledge. Such knowledge heightens managers' sensitivity to the innumerable internal and external factors operating in their environment. It also helps to facilitate effective interactions with consultants and comprehension of the nuances of the research process.

Sophisticated technology involving **simulation** and model building, for instance, is now available and may lend itself to profitable application in certain business areas. The recommendations of the external consultant who is proficient in this technology, and who urges its application in a particular situation, may make no sense to the manager and can create misgivings. Even a superficial knowledge of these techniques helps the manager to relate to the researcher in a mature and confident manner, so that dealing with 'experts' does not cause uneasiness. As the manager, *you* will be the one who makes the final decision on the implementation of the recommendations made by the research team. Remaining objective, focusing on problem solutions, fully understanding the recommendations made, and why and how they are arrived at, make for good managerial decision making. While company traditions are to be respected, there may be occasions where today's rapidly changing, turbulent environment demands the substitution or adaptation of some, based on research findings. Once again, knowledge of research greatly enhances the decision-making skills of the manager.

# ETHICS AND BUSINESS RESEARCH

**Ethics** in business research refers to the application of a code of conduct or expected societal norm of behaviour while conducting research. Ethical conduct applies to the organisation and notably the members that sponsor the research, those who undertake the research and the respondents who provide them with the necessary data. Ethical behaviour begins with the person instituting the research, who should do so in good faith, pay attention to what the results indicate and, surrendering the ego, pursue organisational interests rather than self-interest. Ethical conduct should also be reflected in the behaviour of the researchers who conduct the investigation, the participants who provide the data, the analysts who provide the results, and the entire research team that presents the interpretation of the results and suggests alternative solutions.

The relationship between the researcher and the person providing information to the researcher — often called the **subject** — is unique. First, the relationship is contrived for the benefit of the researcher and for other parties who may be interested in the research. Second, the researcher uses a variety of skills to encourage the subject to disclose information which the subject might not normally disclose. This situation of open communication poses risks for the subject and places the researcher in a position of power, in that the researcher could use the disclosed information against the subject. On the other hand, the researcher has a commitment to investigate a particular phenomenon which is causing concern to others or may result in distinct advantages to others or even the long-term benefit of the subject. For example, a research project investigating the problems faced by dual-career couples might result in the organisation agreeing to more flexible working arrangements for dual-career couples.

The need to be fair to a variety of stakeholders confronts all researchers (see figure 1.1). Two somewhat opposing views have been proposed which reflect this dilemma (see, for example, Bibby 1997 and Jackson 1995). The **consequentialist view** focuses on what is good or bad by concentrating on the consequences of the actions. The most extreme position of the consequentialist view is the belief (sometimes termed utilitarianism) that a researcher should act to produce the greatest good for the greatest number. However, the **deontological view** asserts that the end cannot justify the means. This view proposes absolute moral strictures which can never be violated. Underlying it is the belief in the significance of every person, and that individuals and minorities should be defended against the interests of majorities. As is often the case, there is significant value in both views and the researcher makes a choice based on personal preference. However, in practice, the issue of ethics in research is even more complicated than the consequentialist and deontological views suggest.

Ehrich (2000) contends that three competing accountabilities face people, such as researchers, who are in positions of control or power over others. *Professional accountability* is concerned with upholding the standards of one's profession. Some authors (for example Davis & Cosenza 1993 and Neuman 1997) expand this accountability to include the overall component of **societal accountability**. **Corporate accountability** means being accountable to the sponsor or client of the research project. In many cases, this accountability is to the organisation (or, more specifically, the managers in the organisation) that has commissioned the research. **Moral accountability** focuses on the relationship between the researcher and the subject. The researcher, therefore, has responsibilities to three major stakeholders —

society, the sponsor or client of the research and the subjects (people) who are the focus of the research.

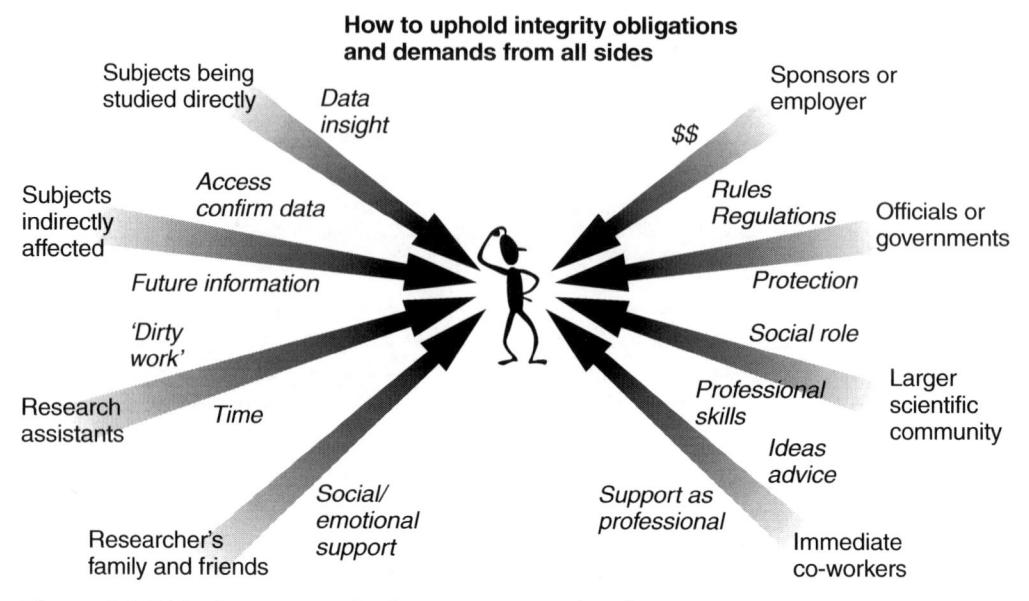

**Figure 1.1** Ethical pressures the business researcher faces

**Source:** Adapted from Neuman (1997:459).

# SOCIETAL ACCOUNTABILITY

All researchers carry the responsibilities that accrue to being a member of the human community. A good community member attempts to enhance the community and avoid instigating any actions that may have deleterious effects on society. Researchers also have a duty to uphold the moral standards of the research profession. These moral standards focus particularly on their responsibilities to the sponsors of, and participants in, the research projects. Finally, many researchers — for example engineers, medical practitioners, human resource managers, marketers, accountants or economists — belong to professional disciplines, and these professional bodies advocate strict ethical practices, often referred to as 'professional codes of conduct'. The researcher should adhere to these professional requirements since they are invariably based on many decades of experience. It could also be noted that many of these ethical practices share common ground with the ethical stance required of all researchers.

At the very minimum, researchers must not transgress in the following areas.

- **Plagiarism** is the act of using another writer's work and either not citing the source or presenting it as the researcher's own work. All work borrowed from another author must be acknowledged through a referencing system.
- **Fraud** comes in many guises, from using research grant monies for personal purchases to falsifying data. Researchers must be able to account for all assets allocated to the research, and must be absolutely transparent in identifying and describing the data-gathering and analytic processes used.
- **Deception** includes presenting untrue information, or omitting information, in an attempt to persuade an individual to become involved in a research project or to provide data for a research project. Deception can also include presenting untrue

information or omitting information in the final report in an attempt to persuade the readers of a particular argument. Researchers among both the consequentialists and those holding deontological views argue against the use of deception. For a deeper discussion on this issue, see Lawson (1997).

In Australia, social research is governed by the National Health and Medical Research Council, who have published the National Statement on Ethical Conduct in Research Involving Humans. In New Zealand, such research is not governed by any specific organisation.

## THE SPONSOR OR CLIENT OF THE RESEARCH

When a researcher undertakes a research project, the client may be the researcher's present employer or a paying customer. In either event, the researcher has a number of responsibilities to that client or sponsor. These responsibilities are outlined below.

- Often the sponsor or client does not have specialised knowledge of research and is therefore in a vulnerable position. The researcher must produce *high quality research*. This means that the research is conducted in a professional manner, that the research design is the most effective and cost-efficient possible, and that the final report is an honest and a true reflection of the issue being investigated.
- The sponsor or client has a right to expect that all matters pertaining to the research project will remain *confidential*. Often the very nature of the research project is of commercial importance to the sponsor. The sponsor depends on the researcher to ensure that any commercially sensitive information does not come to the attention of any other parties, either deliberately or accidentally. In addition, during the course of the research project, the researcher may encounter other sensitive information that has nothing to do with the research project. The sponsor has a right to expect that such information is also treated confidentially.

## THE RESEARCH SUBJECTS

The most vulnerable party in the research project is undoubtedly the research subject — the person who provides the information. It is not surprising, then, that the research profession has invested a lot of thought and energy into the ethical relationship between the researcher and the subject. The main responsibilities of the researcher are outlined below.

- The subject must be protected from *physical, psychological and legal harm*. Most people accept that a research subject should not suffer any physical harm during the research project. Indeed, in most cases, protection from physical harm is easy to achieve with a little forethought, as physical injury is clearly observable. Psychological harm is more insidious. It may not be easy to detect. Of particular concern is psychological harm caused by stress or loss of self-esteem, since these may not be obvious to the researcher. Finally, the researcher must protect the subject from the possibility of being sued or arrested for any breach of state or federal laws. Most researchers do not have a detailed knowledge of the country's laws, so protection from legal harm may be problematic. In such cases, the researcher should seek legal advice.
- Most research institutions, such as universities, recognise the potential for harm to research subjects and have established ethics committees to oversee research. Researchers are required to clear all research with these ethics committees before proceeding, and this requirement is a significant safeguard to researchers. Such a review brings to bear an unbiased clarity, as well as specific knowledge, on the research design, which can identify potential physical or psychological harm as well as potential legal problems.

- Research subjects have a right to absolute *confidentiality*. Researchers must do all in their power to preserve the anonymity of the research subjects. No third party should be able to link the information provided by the subject to that subject. For example, if a subordinate has criticised a supervisor, no one reading the final report should be able to identify the person who made the comments. Further, personal identifying information (for example names and addresses) must not be passed on to another party.
- Research subjects must be protected from coercion and undue pressure. The most basic ethical principle of business research is that of *informed consent*. Participation in a research project must be voluntary, and potential research subjects must be given sufficient information so that they can make an informed choice whether or not to participate. Research subjects should be advised of:
  - the nature and purpose of the study
  - how long their involvement will last (for example the duration of the interview)
  - their right to withdraw from the research project at any time
  - why they were selected
  - a clear description of any possible risks or discomfort
  - who is sponsoring the research
  - a guarantee of confidentiality
  - what will happen to the data once they are analysed.

## CONFLICT AMONG THE ACCOUNTABILITIES

When considered individually, few people would disagree with the three areas of accountability — social and professional, corporate and moral. However, researchers cannot afford to consider each accountability as a single entity. Rather, they operate within an environment in which the three operate concurrently. Accordingly, researchers will sometimes find themselves facing a conflict between the demands of at least two areas of accountability.

Situations that may produce a conflict of accountabilities include those outlined below.
- The sponsor indicates, directly or indirectly, that the researcher should arrive at a particular finding, or places limits on the conduct of the research, such that the researcher would have to act unprofessionally. This introduces a conflict of corporate accountability and societal accountability.
- The researcher, during the course of the project, finds that an individual is acting illegally. This presents a conflict between societal accountability and moral accountability.
- The government, by limiting research grants to a particular topic, reduces the opportunity for researchers to investigate problems faced by a disadvantaged group. This exposes a conflict between corporate accountability and societal accountability.
- During an interview, a research subject discloses information that his supervisor is committing fraud against the sponsoring organisation. This presents a conflict between moral accountability and corporate accountability.

During their career, researchers may come across a variety of such conflicts between accountabilities. Researchers need to think deeply about such possible conflicts and identify personal principles on which they would make a decision. For example, some researchers place moral accountability above all. As a new researcher, you are encouraged to consider how you would react to such scenarios as those described above. Table 1.2 provides a checklist for researchers to review their research from an ethical standpoint.

**Table 1.2** Checklist for ethical research*

| Yes or No | Ethical question |
|---|---|
| | Will any person experience pain (other than mild discomfort), sickness or psychological stress? |
| | Will any blood, body fluid or tissue samples be taken? |
| | Does the research involve the use of drugs or any other form of treatment? |
| | Does the research involve the collection or disclosure of personal information? |
| | Will any individual or definable group be identified by the published data? |
| | Will the research involve subjects who are unable to provide informed consent? |
| | Does the research require the active involvement of minors? |
| | Does the research involve subjects who are in a dependent relationship with the researcher or the sponsor? |
| | Will subjects be offered payments or other inducements to encourage their participation? |
| | Does the research involve questions about sensitive aspects of subjects' behaviour (e.g. criminal record, use of drugs, sexual behaviour, religious beliefs)? |
| | Does the research involve the participation of Aboriginal or Torres Strait Islander groups or other identifiable cultural/minority groups? |
| | Does the project involve the deception of participants? |

*Adapted from the research ethic requirements at the Queensland University of Technology and the Victoria University of Wellington.

Answering yes to any of the above questions does not necessarily mean that the research project should not continue. However, the researcher may wish to have the research design checked by a competent authority before proceeding.

Thus, ethical behaviour pervades each step of the research process — data collection, data analysis, reporting and the dissemination of information anywhere, including on the Internet. How the subjects are treated and how confidential information is safeguarded are guided by business ethics. We will highlight these ethical considerations as they relate to different aspects of research in the relevant chapters of the book.

## SUMMARY

In this chapter we have discussed research, defined business research and examined the role of the manager in research. At times the manager may conduct the research project and at other times the manager may oversee the research being conducted by a consultant. The manager should be able to build a good relationship with the consultant researcher and be aware of the advantages and disadvantages of external and internal consultants. The manager must also recognise the context of sound business research, including the three fundamental philosophies or paradigms that contribute to business research — the posititivist, interpretivist and critical views. The manager should be able to use both qualitative and quantitative research, and recognise the two types of business research — applied and basic. Finally, the ethical responsibilities of business researchers have been outlined.

## DISCUSSION POINTS

1 Define *research* and explain the difference between applied and basic research.

2 Why is it important for managers to know about research?

3 Explain why handling the manager–researcher relationship effectively is important.

4 Describe a situation in which it would be more beneficial to engage an external research team rather than an internal one.

5 'Because basic research is not applied immediately to a problem, it is less valuable and useful than applied resesarch.' Comment on this statement.

6 'If managers learned how to conduct good research by taking a course such as this book offers, there would be no need to hire anyone to solve problems in organisations.' What is your response to this statement?

7 Describe a situation in which research will help you as a manager to make a good decision.

8 Given the following situation, discuss with reasons (a) whether it falls into the category of applied or basic research, (b) who will conduct the research, and (c) whether a positivist, interpretivist or critical research approach would be better.

> **To acquire or not to acquire: that is the question**
> Companies are very interested in acquiring other firms even when the latter operate in totally unrelated realms of business. For example, Gencore Industries, manufacturing asphalt plants for road construction, acquired Ingersoll-Rand in 1996, and later acquired yet another company engaged in the business of food processing. Such acquisitions are claimed to 'work miracles'. However, given the volatility of the share market and the slowing down of business, many companies wonder whether such acquisitions are becoming too risky. At the same time, they also wonder if they are missing out on a great business opportunity if they fail to engage in this activity. Some research is needed here!

9 Discuss the ethical responsibilities of a business researcher.

10 Who are the major stakeholders in a business research project, and what are their main interests and concerns?

# chapter 2

# SCIENTIFIC INVESTIGATION AND THE RESEARCH PROCESS

## OUTLINE
THE HALLMARKS OF SCIENTIFIC RESEARCH
LIMITATIONS TO SCIENTIFIC RESEARCH IN MANAGEMENT
SOME BASIC DEFINITIONS
APPROACHES TO RESEARCH
THE RESEARCH PROCESS
SUMMARY
DISCUSSION POINTS

## CHAPTER OBJECTIVES
After reading this chapter, you should be able to:
- explain what is meant by scientific investigation, giving examples of both scientific and nonscientific investigation
- explain the eight hallmarks of science
- briefly explain why research in the organisational behaviour and management areas cannot be completely scientific
- compare and contrast quantitative and qualitative research
- discuss the 11 steps of the research process, using an example of your own.

The heading of this chapter uses the word 'scientific'. A common misconception is that scientific means measurable and quantifiable. This is incorrect. Rather, scientific research refers to the need for an honest, truthful, accurate and complete investigation. In this book, we refer to various types of research — qualitative, quantitative, exploratory, descriptive and experimental. Whatever the type of research undertaken, the processes used must be scientific — that is, they must be honest, truthful, accurate and complete.

Managerial decisions based on the results of scientific research are effective. In chapter 1 we defined research as an organised, systematic, data-based, critical, objective, scientific inquiry into a specific problem or issue that needs a solution. Decisions based on the results of scientific investigations tend to be more effective than those that are not. Scientific research is focused on the goal of problem solving and pursues a step-by-step, logical, organised and rigorous method to identify problems, gather data, analyse them and draw valid conclusions from them. Thus, scientific research is not based on hunches, experience and intuition (though these may play a part in final decision making), but is purposive and rigorous. Because of the rigorous way in which it is carried out, scientific research enables all those who are interested in researching and learning about the same or similar issues to undertake research and come up with comparable findings. Scientific research also helps researchers to state their findings with accuracy and confidence. This helps other organisations to apply those solutions when they encounter similar problems. Furthermore, scientific investigation tends to be more objective than subjective, and helps managers to highlight the most critical factors in the workplace that need specific attention so as to avoid, minimise or solve problems. Scientific investigation and managerial decision making are integral aspects of effective problem solving.

The term *scientific research* applies to both basic and applied research. Applied research may or may not be generalisable to other organisations, depending on the extent to which differences exist in such factors as size, nature of work, characteristics of the employees and structure of the organisation. Nevertheless, applied research also has to be an organised and systematic process by which problems are carefully identified, data scientifically gathered and analysed, and conclusions drawn in an objective manner for effective problem solving.

Do organisations always follow this rigorous step-by-step process? No. Sometimes the problem may be so simple that it does not call for elaborate research, and past experience may offer the necessary solution. At other times, exigencies of time (where quick decisions are required), unwillingness to expend the resources needed for good research, lack of knowledge and other factors may prompt businesses to try to solve problems based on hunches. However, the probability of making wrong decisions in such cases is high. Even such business gurus as Lee Iacocca confess to making big mistakes owing to errors of judgement. *Business Week, Fortune,* the *Wall Street Journal,* the *Australian Business Review,* the *New Zealand Business Times* and other business periodicals and newspapers feature articles from time to time about organisations that face difficulties because of bad decisions made on the basis of hunches and/or insufficient information. Many implemented plans fail because not enough research is done in formulating them.

## THE HALLMARKS OF SCIENTIFIC RESEARCH

There are eight hallmarks or main distinguishing characteristics of scientific research. They are:
- **purposiveness**
- **rigour**

- testability
- replicability
- accuracy
- objectivity
- generalisability
- parsimony.

Each of these characteristics can be explained in the context of a concrete example. Let us consider the case of a manager who is interested in investigating how employees' commitment to the organisation can be increased. We will examine how the eight hallmarks of science apply to this investigation so that it may be considered scientific.

## PURPOSIVENESS

The manager has started with a definite aim or purpose for the research. The focus is on increasing the commitment of employees to the organisation, which will be helpful in many ways. An increase in employee commitment would mean lower staff turnover, less absenteeism and probably increased performance levels, all of which would benefit the organisation. The research thus has a purposive focus.

## RIGOUR

A good theoretical base and a sound methodological design would add rigour to a purposive study. **Rigour** connotes carefulness, scrupulousness and the degree of exactitude in research investigations. In the case of our example, let us say the manager of an organisation asks 10 to 12 employees in the organisation to indicate what would increase their level of commitment to it. If, on the basis of their responses alone, the manager reaches several conclusions on how employee commitment can be increased, the whole approach to the investigation would be unscientific. It would lack rigour because, to mention just a few reasons, (1) the conclusions would be incorrectly drawn since they would be based on the thoughts of a few employees whose opinions may not represent those of the entire work force; (2) the manner of framing and addressing the questions could have introduced bias or incorrectness in the responses; and (3) there might be many other important influences on organisational commitment that this small sample of respondents did not or could not verbalise during the interviews, and the researcher would have failed to include them.

For the reasons given above, conclusions drawn from an investigation that lacks a good theoretical foundation, as evidenced by reason 3, and methodological sophistication, as evident from 1 and 2 above, would be unscientific. Rigorous research involves a good theoretical or conceptual base and a carefully thought-out methodology. These factors enable the researcher to collect the right kinds of information, using an appropriate research methodology and an appropriate sample with the minimum degree of bias, and to facilitate appropriate analysis of the data gathered. The following chapters address these theoretical and methodological issues. Rigour in research design also makes possible the achievement of the other six hallmarks of science, which will now be discussed.

## TESTABILITY

If, after talking to a random selection of employees of the organisation and after studying the previous research done in the area of organisational commitment, the manager or researcher develops certain hypotheses on how employee commitment can be enhanced, then these can be tested. For instance, the researcher might hypothesise that those employees who perceive greater opportunities for participation in decision making would have a higher level of commitment. This is a hypothesis that can be tested when the data are collected. A correlation analysis would indicate whether or not the hypothesis is substantiated. The use of several other tests, such as the chi-square test and the *t*-test, is discussed in appendix I, A Refresher on Statistical Terms and Tests, at the end of this book, and in chapter 13.

Scientific research thus lends itself to testing logically developed research objectives to see whether or not the data support the educated conjectures, research questions or hypotheses developed after a careful study of the problem situation. **Testability** thus becomes another hallmark of scientific research.

# REPLICABILITY

Let us suppose that the manager or researcher concludes, based on the results of the study, that participation in decision making is one of the most important factors influencing the commitment of employees to the organisation. We will place more faith and credence in these findings and conclusion if similar findings emerge on the basis of data collected by other organisations employing the same methods. To put it differently, the results of the tests of research objectives should be supported again and again when the same type of research is repeated in other, similar circumstances. To the extent that this does happen (that is, the results are *replicated* or repeated), we will have confidence in our research being scientific. In other words, our research objectives would not have been supported merely by chance but would reflect the true state of affairs in the **population**. **Replicability** is thus another hallmark of scientific research.

# ACCURACY

In management research we seldom have the luxury of being able to draw 'definitive' conclusions based on the results of data analysis. This is because we are unable to study the universe of items, events or populations we are interested in, and have to base our findings on a sample that we draw from the universe. The sample in question may not reflect the exact characteristics of the phenomenon we try to study (these difficulties are discussed in greater detail in a later chapter). Measurement errors and other problems are also bound to introduce an element of bias or inaccuracy into our findings. However, we would like to design the research in a manner that ensures that our findings are as close to reality (that is, the true state of affairs in the universe) as possible, so we can put faith or confidence in our findings.

Accuracy refers to how close the findings, based on a sample, are to 'reality'. In other words, accuracy reflects the degree of exactitude of the results based on the sample. For example, if I estimated the number of production days lost during the year through absenteeism at between 30 and 40, while the actual number of days lost happens to be 35, the accuracy of my estimate compares more favourably than if I had indicated that the loss of production days was somewhere between 20 and 50. You may recall the term *confidence interval* in statistics; this is what is referred to here as accuracy.

# OBJECTIVITY

The conclusions drawn through the interpretation of the results of data analysis should be objective; that is, they should be based on the facts derived from the findings from actual data, and not based on our own subjective or emotional values. For instance, if we had a research question that asked whether greater participation in decision making would increase organisational commitment, and this hypothesis was not supported by the results of our interviews, it would make no sense for the researcher to continue to argue that increased opportunities for employee participation would still help! Such an argument would be based not on factual, data-based research findings, but on the subjective opinion of the researcher. If this was the researcher's conviction all along, then there would have been no need to do the research in the first place!

Much damage can be sustained by organisations that implement non-data-based or misleading conclusions drawn from research. For example, if the research question relating to organisational commitment in our previous example was not supported, considerable time and effort would be wasted in finding ways to create opportunities for employee participation in decision making. We would discover only later that employees still keep quitting or taking time off and do not develop any sense of commitment to the organisation. Similarly, if research shows that increased pay is not going to increase the job satisfaction of employees, then implementing a revised increased pay system will only drag down the company financially without attaining the desired objective. Such a futile exercise, then, is based on non-scientific interpretation and implementation of the research results.

The more objective the interpretation of the data, the more scientific the research investigation becomes. Though managers or researchers might start with some initial subjective values and beliefs, their interpretation of the data should be stripped of personal values and bias. If managers attempt to do their own research, they should be particularly sensitive to this aspect. **Objectivity** is thus another hallmark of scientific investigation.

## GENERALISABILITY

**Generalisability** refers to the applicability of the research findings in one organisational setting to other settings. Obviously, the wider the applicability of the solutions generated by research, the more useful the research is to the users. For instance, if a researcher's findings that participation in decision making enhances organisational commitment are found to be true in a variety of manufacturing, industrial and service organisations, and not merely in the particular organisation studied by the researcher, then the generalisability of the findings to other organisational settings is demonstrated. The more generalisable the research, the greater its usefulness and value. However, not many research findings can be generalised to all other settings, situations or organisations.

For wider generalisability, the research sampling design has to be logically developed, and a number of other meticulous details in the data-collection methods need to be followed. However, a more elaborate sampling design, which would doubtless increase the generalisability of the results, would also increase research costs. Most applied research is confined to research within the particular area in which the problem arises, and the results, at best, are generalisable only to other identical situations and settings. Although such limited applicability does not necessarily decrease its scientific value (if the research is properly conducted), its generalisability is restricted.

## PARSIMONY

Simplicity in explaining the phenomena or problems that occur, and in generating solutions for the problems, is always preferred to complex research frameworks that consider an unmanageable number of factors. For example, identifying three specific variables in the workplace which, when changed, raise the organisational commitment of employees by 45 per cent would be more valuable to the manager than identifying 10 different variables that increase organisational commitment by 48 per cent. Such an unmanageable number of variables might well be totally beyond the manager's control to change. Therefore, the achievement of a meaningful and parsimonious, rather than an elaborate and cumbersome, model for problem solution becomes a critical issue in research.

Economy in research models is achieved when we can build into our research framework a lesser number of variables that would explain the variance far more efficiently than a complex set of variables that would contribute only marginally to the result. **Parsimony** can be introduced with a good understanding of the problem and the important factors that influence it. A good conceptual theoretical model can be realised through unstructured and structured interviews with the concerned people, and a thorough **literature review** of the previous research work in the particular problem area.

In sum, scientific research encompasses the eight criteria introduced above. These are discussed in more detail later in the book. At this point, we might ask why a scientific approach is necessary for investigations, when systematic research involving simply collecting and analysing data would produce results that can be applied to solve the problem. The reason for following a scientific method is that the results will be less prone to errors and we will have more confidence in the findings because of the greater rigour we apply to the design details. This also increases the replicability and generalisability of the findings.

## LIMITATIONS TO SCIENTIFIC RESEARCH IN MANAGEMENT

In the management and behavioural areas, it is not always possible to conduct investigations that are 100 per cent scientific; unlike in the physical sciences, the results obtained will not be exact and error-free. This is primarily because of difficulties we are likely to encounter in the measurement and collection of data in the subjective areas of feelings, emotions, attitudes and perceptions. These problems occur whenever we attempt to investigate human behaviour. We might also encounter difficulties in obtaining a representative sample, which would restrict the generalisability of the findings. Thus, it is not always possible to meet all the hallmarks of science completely. Comparability, consistency and wide generalisability are often difficult to obtain in research. Still, to the extent that we can design our research to ensure purposiveness, rigour, and the maximum possible testability, replicability, generalisability, objectivity, parsimony and accuracy, we will have endeavoured to engage in scientific investigation. Several other possible limitations in research studies are discussed in subsequent chapters.

## SOME BASIC DEFINITIONS

In research textbooks, you will come across words such as 'facts', 'constructs', 'concepts' and 'variables'. We need to differentiate between these words as they have different meanings in research.

### OBSERVATIONS

**Observations** are perceptions of reality and can be expressed in the form of 'facts' or 'opinions'. A *fact* is an observation that represents a universal truth. A fact can often be supported by measurable evidence. For example, you are a certain height and this height can be measured. However, it is as well to recognise that such objective measures may not be as exact as initially presumed. Suppose you were measured and were found to be 1729 mm. Is this exact? Perhaps with a more accurate measuring device you may be found to be 1729.12 mm. Or an even more precise instrument may find you to be 1729.12923 mm. So the precision of measurement may become an issue in providing evidence of a 'fact'. In addition, height may not be the consistent idea that we originally throught. As your hair grows, your height increases. So, you may find that, in a few weeks' time, your height is actually 1729.12925 mm. Or you may have been standing on your feet all day, so, at the end of the day, your height may be only 1729.1291 mm, as your joints have become compressed during the day. So the 'truth' of a fact is not necessarily as immutable as first thought. However, for all such pedantic assertions, a fact is usually defined as a phenomenon that has consensual support. We would usually take a measured height of 1729 mm as a fact. For certain research objectives the finer differences in the measurement might be important, but for most research purposes a height measurement to the nearest millimetre would be an acceptable fact.

An *opinion* is a person's belief about a phenomenon. A research project may use a series of interviews to ascertain people's opinions on a product for marketing purposes. These opinions are then recorded as verbal statements, which are the observations of the particular phenomenon under investigation. A researcher may attempt to measure such an opinion — for example using a five-point **scale** in a questionnaire — but such a 'measure' is simply an artifice to enable the researcher to observe the phenomenon.

It is important for a researcher to differentiate fact from opinion. Using the example of the questionnaire, the response on the five-point scale remains an opinion even though it has been given a numerical value.

# CONCEPTS

Concepts have long been held to be the basic building blocks of scientific investigation (see, for example, Hempel 1952; Reynolds 1971). A concept is an idea expressed as a symbol or in words (Neuman 1997). They are used to communicate the essence of an observation. In the physical sciences, symbols are often used to communicate an idea. The formula $E = MC^2$ represents a relatively abstract idea that is generalised from a series of facts or opinions. In the social sciences, a relatively abstract idea may be communicated by a word or phrase. The word 'weight' communicates a relatively abstract idea about a physical phenomenon. The phrase 'self-directed learning' communicates a relatively abstract idea about a way of learning and can be contrasted with another relatively abstract idea termed 'teacher-directed learning'. So concepts are general representations of ideas to be studied and become the building blocks of a research project (Ticehurst & Veal 1999).

A concept that can be *operationalised* is called a **variable**. A researcher operationalises a concept so that it can be observed and measured. At its most limited form of operationalisation, a variable can take on at least two values (for example, gender can be either male or female). In its most unlimited form of operationalisation, a variable can assume wide variety of values (for example height). So, while concepts are the basic building blocks of scientific research, a special form of concept is a variable. Both concepts and variables are used in business research. The reporting of concepts is usually referred to as soft data.

# CONSTRUCTS

A **construct** is an abstract representation of a phenomenon and is invented for special theoretical purposes. Constructs, unlike concepts, cannot be directly linked to observations and have to be inferred. This inference can then be measured indirectly — for example using a specially compiled questionnaire.

# APPROACHES TO RESEARCH

Given the creative nature of human beings, it is not surprising that a variety of research methods have been suggested. The various methods can be clustered under two broad themes — quantitative and qualitative. The main differences are discussed below and summarised in table 2.1. Unfortunately, as Neuman (1997:14) points out, there is often ill will between the followers of the respective styles of research, as some researchers find it difficult to understand or appreciate the alternative styles and the set of assumptions that underpin them.

Typically, quantitative research methods are used within the positivist research paradigm, and qualitative methods are used within the intepretivist paradigm.

## QUANTITATIVE RESEARCH

Quantitative research is based broadly on the ideals of positivism which arose some two hundred years ago with the ideas of Auguste Compte (1798–1857). These ideas espouse precise quantitative data and value rigorous, exact measures. The hallmarks of 'good' research are seen as objective observation, precise measurements, statistical analysis and verifiable truths. Hypotheses are tested by carefully analysing the data, usually using statistics. The aim of positivist research is to identify universal laws of human behaviour so that we can control and predict events. There is an overriding perception that 'reality' is out there waiting to be discovered and an assumption that universal laws of nature operate according to deductive, logical reasoning. The ideal quantitative research design is to identify the research hypothesis (the expected solution to the problem or challenge) and then to attempt to prove that this research hypothesis is not correct — that is, to prove the **null hypothesis**.

## QUALITATIVE RESEARCH

Qualitative researchers believe that humans are complex, somewhat unpredictable beings and that individual differences and idiosyncratic needs override any notion of universal laws of human behaviour. The role of research is seen to be the deep understanding of human behaviour. True meaning can be discovered only by detailed study and contemplation of rich and multifarious evidence of human thoughts and behaviour. The aim of qualitative research is to discover how humans construct meanings in their contextual setting. 'Reality' is seen as constructed by individuals, and the exigencies of life are what people perceive them to be. Qualitative research reveals people's values, interpretative schemes, mind maps, belief systems and rules of living so that the respondents' reality can be understood. Rather than concerning itself primarily with representative samples, qualitative research emphasises careful and detailed descriptions of social practices in an attempt to understand how participants experience and explain their own world (Jackson 1995).

With such opposing belief systems, it is not surprising that the two schools of thought have been at loggerheads. However, taking an exclusive stance that argues that one approach is better than the other ignores the reality that there are many paths to the goal of fundamental knowledge. As we will see, both methods of research have rich potential to uncover relevant and salient information that can be critical to business decision making. Indeed, a combination of both qualitative and quantitative research designs often generates a synergistic energy which provides unique and important insights. This power is created by the fundamental difference between the two approaches — that quantitative research is based on deductive reasoning while qualitative research involves inductive reasoning.

**Table 2.1** Differences between quantitative and qualitative research

| Quantitative research | Qualitative research |
|---|---|
| • Reality is objective and singular, and apart from the researcher | • Reality is subjective and multiple, as seen by paticipants in a study |
| • Researcher is independent of that being researched | • Researcher interacts with that being researched |
| • Research is assumed to be value-free and unbiased | • Research is value-laden and biased, with values generally made explicit |
| • Theory is largely causal and deductive | • Theory can be causal or non-causal, and is often inductive |
| • Hypotheses that the researcher begins with are tested | • Meaning is captured and discovered once the researcher becomes immersed in the data |
| • Concepts are in the form of distinct variables | • Concepts are in the form of themes, motifs, generalisations, taxonomies |
| • Measures are systematically created before data collection and are standardised | • Measures are created in an ad hoc manner and are often specific to the individual setting or researcher |
| • Data are in the form of numbers from precise measurement | • Data are in the form of words from documents, observations and transcripts |
| • There are generally many cases or subjects | • There are generally few cases or subjects. |
| • Procedures are standard, and replication is assumed | • Research procedures are particular, and replication is rare |
| • Analysis proceeds by using statistics, tables or charts, and discussing how what they show relates to hypotheses | • Analysis proceeds by extracting themes or generalisations from evidence and organising data to present a coherent, consistent picture. |

**Sources:** Cresswell (1994:5); Neuman (1997:14, 329).

# DEDUCTION

**Deduction** is the process by which the researcher begins with a theoretical proposition and then moves towards concrete empirical evidence (as illustrated in figure 2.1(a)). For example, we may theorise that all high performers are highly efficient in their jobs. We would gather data on the two concepts (for example a psychological questionnaire measuring efficiency in specific tasks, and a measure of performance based on the number of items produced) and then conduct a correlational analysis. Quantitative research, therefore, is

> an organised method for combining deductive logic with precise empirical observations of individual behaviour in order to discover and confirm a set of probabilistic causal laws that can be used to predict general patterns of human activity (Neuman 1997:63).

# INDUCTION

**Induction**, on the other hand, is a process by which we observe certain phenomena and arrive at certain conclusions (see figure 2.1(b)). The researcher begins with detailed observations of the world and moves towards more theoretical generalisations and ideas. In other words, in induction, we establish a general proposition logically based on observed facts. For instance, we may observe in a work setting that some people are very efficient at their work. After further observations, reviewing work output records and discussions with supervisors, we may identify evidence that those who are efficient are also high performers. Qualitative research, therefore, is seen as:

> the systematic analysis of socially meaningful action through the direct detailed observation of people in natural settings in order to arrive at understandings and interpretations of how people create and maintain their social worlds (Neuman 1997:68).

**(a) Deductive reasoning**

Develop theory → Formulate hypotheses → Collect and analyse data → Accept/reject hypotheses

**(b) Inductive reasoning**

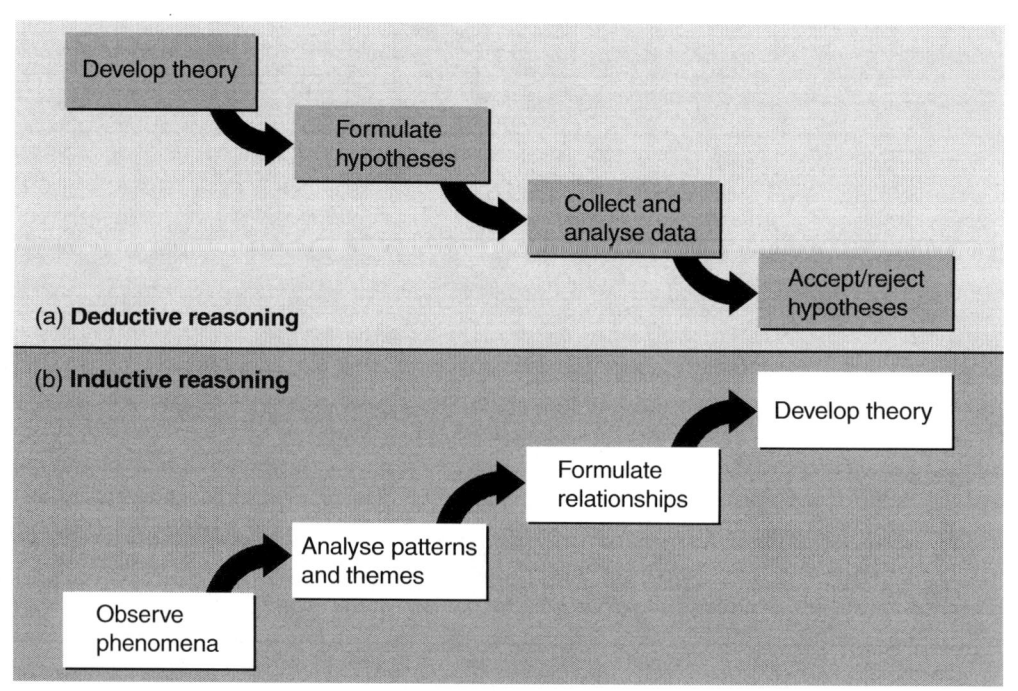

Observe phenomena → Analyse patterns and themes → Formulate relationships → Develop theory

**Figure 2.1** Deductive and inductive reasoning in business research

In business research, the advantages of both qualitative and quantitative research are harnessed to provide accurate and comprehensive information on which to base decisions. If you examine the two examples provided under the explanations of deduction and induction, you can see that the conclusions of a qualitative research investigation may be further confirmed using a more quantitative approach. Conversely, a quantitative research project may uncover some unexplained phenomenon which needs further clarification using a qualitative approach.

> **EXAMPLE 2.1** An investigation into the research question 'What are the critical issues faced by dual-career couples in the workplace?' may commence with a series of interviews (qualitative research) to identify the range of issues. From the analysis of this qualitative data, the researcher can then design a questionnaire (quantitative research) to confirm which issues are considered critical.

> **EXAMPLE 2.2** An investigation into the research question 'Do young people share adult learning characteristics?' may commence with a quantitative design using a number of questionnaires to measure the existence in young people of various adult learning characteristics and then move on to a series of focus groups (qualitative research) that will allow the young learners to explain the findings from the quantitative data.

Methods of research, then, can be broadly classified as qualitative or quantitative. Qualitative research methods include interviews, observations and focus groups. The data collected are based on words — hence the name qualitative. Qualitative research tends to use inductive reasoning. Quantitative research, on the other hand, collects numbers, and the methods used include questionnaires and laboratory experimentation, and tend to be based on deductive reasoning. Generally, positivist research concentrates on quantitative research while interpretivist and critical research are usually based on qualitative methods.

When examining data collection and data analysis, this text has been divided into qualitative research (chapters 6 and 7) and quantitative research (chapters 8 to 13).

## THE RESEARCH PROCESS

Whether using a qualitative or a quantitative approach, business research follows the same general process, which involves 11 steps. These are:
- catalyst for research
- preliminary information gathering and literature survey
- problem definition
- framework development
- research objectives
- research design
- data collection
- data analysis
- interpretation of findings
- report preparation and presentation
- management action

These 11 phases are illustrated in figure 2.2.

### CATALYST FOR RESEARCH

The first stage of research occurs when someone senses that certain changes are happening, or that some new behaviours, attitudes or feelings are surfacing in one's environment (that is, the workplace). If it is believed that the sensed changes or new events may have potentially important consequences, then one needs to verify the existence of the changes or events.

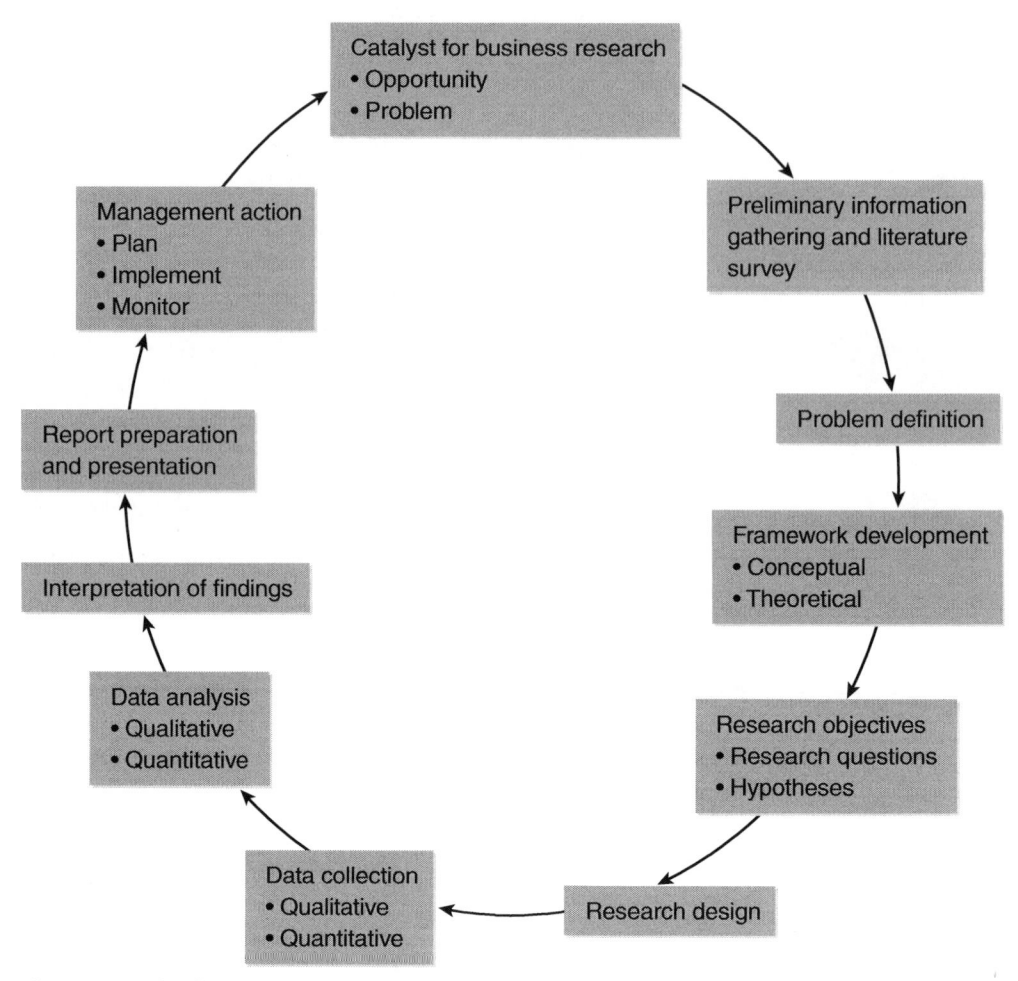

**Figure 2.2** The business research process

How does one observe phenomena and changes in the environment? The information systems of the organisation will often provide a signal. In addition, of course, the people-oriented manager is always sensitive to and aware of what is happening in and around the workplace. Changes in attitudes, behaviours, communication patterns and styles, and a score of other verbal and non-verbal cues, can be readily picked up by managers who are sensitive to the various nuances. Whether we are dealing with finance, accounting, management, marketing or administrative matters, and whatever the sophistication of the machines, ultimately it is people who achieve the goals and make things happen. Whether it is the installation of an effective management information system or a new manufacturing technology, distribution channel, strategic plan, cost accounting system, investment plan or training scheme, it is only through the efforts of the employees that the goals are attained. The vast majority respond positively or negatively to various factors in the work environment, and knowingly or unwittingly transmit cues, which the manager can easily pick up. The manager may not understand exactly what is happening but can certainly sense that things are not what they should be.

Similarly, a drop in sales, frequent production interruptions, incorrect accounting results, low-yielding investments or employees' lack of interest in their work could easily come to the manager's attention, though why they occur might remain a mystery.

## PRELIMINARY INFORMATION GATHERING AND LITERATURE SURVEY

Preliminary information gathering involves the search for information in depth concerning the observed phenomenon. This could be done by observation or talking informally to several people in the work setting or to clients or other relevant sources, thereby gathering information on what is happening and why. Through these unstructured interviews, one gets an idea or 'feel' for what is happening in the situation. Once the researcher gains a greater awareness of what is happening, he or she can then focus on the problem and the associated factors through further structured, formal interviews with the relevant groups. It must be emphasised that the preliminary information gathering must be cost effective. The investigator is looking for quick information at the least cost.

Additionally, by doing library research, or obtaining information through other sources, the investigator is able to identify how such issues have been tackled in other situations. This information gives additional insights into factors that may be operating in the particular situation — over and above those that have not surfaced in previous interviews.

## PROBLEM DEFINITION

Thus, a mass of information will have been collected through the interviews, observation and a library search. At this stage, the manager or researcher can usually convert the original catalyst of a problem or opportunity into a tentative research problem definition. The next step is to make sense of the factors that have been identified in the information-gathering stage by piecing them together in a meaningful fashion.

## FRAMEWORK DEVELOPMENT

Framework development, the next step, is an attempt to integrate all the information in a logical manner, so that the reason for the research problem can be conceptualised and tested. Framework development is often guided by experience and intuition. In this step, the critical concepts and/or variables are examined for their contribution to or influence in explaining why the research problem occurs and how it can be solved. The network of associations identified among the concepts or variables would then be woven together with a justification as to why they might influence the problem.

If the findings from the preliminary information gathering and literature survey are mainly concepts, then a **conceptual framework** is developed. If the findings consist almost entirely of variables, then a **theoretical framework** is developed. The process of developing conceptual and theoretical frameworks is discussed in greater depth in chapter 4.

One might wonder, at this juncture, why a concept or theory has to be formulated each time a problem or opportunity is investigated, and why one cannot act on the information contained in the previously published research findings, as the literature is surveyed. There are two reasons for this. First, different studies may have identified different variables, some of which may not be relevant to the situation at hand. Also, in the previous studies, some of the research objectives may have been substantiated while others may not, presenting a perplexing situation. Hence, problem solving in every complex situation is facilitated by formulating and testing theories and concepts relevant to that particular situation.

## RESEARCH OBJECTIVES

Once the problem or opportunity has been placed within an appropriate conceptual or theoretical context, the research objectives can be formulated.

In qualitative research, a research objective is usually framed in the form of a *research question*, which identifies the probable direction of the research project and at the same time limits the boundaries of the research project. An example of a research question is, *What are the concerns of the staff over the introduction of the new production system?* With this research question, the researcher would concentrate on (a) the concerns of (b) the staff over (c) the new production system. The investigation would not examine the concerns of staff over the management style in the organisation.

In quantitative research, the research objective is conventionally interpreted as a *hypothesis*. From the theorised network of associations among the variables, certain testable hypotheses or educated conjectures can be generated. For instance, the researcher may hypothesise that if a sufficient number of items are stocked on the shelves, customer dissatisfaction will be considerably reduced. The hypothesis would be written as a definite statement indicating the relationship of one variable to another. For example: *When the amount of stock on the shelves increases, customer satisfaction will be increased.*

## RESEARCH DESIGN

Once the research objective is defined, the design of the research can be planned. The initial question, of course, is to decide whether a qualitative or quantitative approach will be used. This is partly answered by the formulation of the research objective — a research question tends to use a qualitative design, and a hypothesis a quantitative design.

However, other issues need to be decided. First, the researcher will need to decide whether the investigation will be exploratory, descriptive or hypothesis testing in nature. This issue is discussed further in chapter 5. Second, within these approaches, various methods might be followed. If a qualitative design is used, will the researcher use interviews, focus groups, observations or panels? Or will a combination of these be used? Third, the respondents have to be identified and selected. Who will be interviewed? Who will receive the questionnaires? How will the participants be identified? Will the whole population be investigated or will a sample suffice? Fourth, various concepts or variables may have to be operationalised. Look at the examples provided above. Who do we mean by staff? Only those using the new production system, or will management be involved as well? What is meant by 'stock on the shelves increases'? Is this a 10 per cent increase, a 40 per cent increase or a 200 per cent increase?

Research design addresses these basic questions as well as ensuring that the research is conducted within the accepted parameters of the particular research method used.

## DATA COLLECTION

After the development of the research questions and/or hypotheses, data need to be collected. Data can be collected by using either qualitative (e.g. focus groups) or quantitative (e.g. questionnaires) methods. So, for example, when investigating the concerns of the staff over the introduction of the new production system, the researcher may conduct several focus groups involving staff members, but when investigating whether customer satisfaction increases when the amount of stock increases, the researcher may use a questionnaire to measure customer satisfaction.

## DATA ANALYSIS

In the data analysis step, the data gathered are analysed appropriately to see if the research questions or hypotheses have been supported. Analyses of both quantitative and qualitative data can be carried out to determine whether certain research objectives are substantiated. For instance, to see if stock levels influence customer satisfaction, one might want to do a correlational analysis and determine the relationship between the two factors. Similarly, other hypotheses could be tested through appropriate statistical analysis. Qualitative data refer to information gathered in a narrative form, for example, through interviews and observations. For example, to test the theory that budgetary constraints adversely affect managers' responses to their work, several interviews might be conducted with managers after budget restrictions are imposed. The responses from the managers who verbalise their reactions in different ways might then be organised to determine the different categories under which they fall and the extent to which the same kinds of response are articulated by the managers.

## INTERPRETATION OF FINDINGS

The next step is the process of arriving at conclusions by interpreting the meaning of the data analysis results. For instance, if it is found from the data analysis that increasing the stock was positively correlated to (increased) customer satisfaction (by, say, 0.5), then one can deduce that if customer satisfaction is to be increased, the shelves have to be better stocked. Another inference from this data analysis is that stocking of shelves accounts for (or explains) 25 per cent of the variance in customer satisfaction ($0.5^2$). Based on these deductions, the researcher would make recommendations on how the 'customer dissatisfaction' problem could be solved.

## REPORT PREPARATION AND PRESENTATION

Once the data have been interpreted, the *research report* has to be written (see chapter 14). This report describes the purpose of the study, provides background information, lists the research objectives and the research questions and/or hypotheses, explains and justifies the research design, including the data analysis protocols, and presents and justifies the findings and recommendations. Of course, while planning and writing the report, the researcher is always comparing the conclusions and recommendations with the original catalyst for the research. This comparative process ensures that the original opportunity is achieved or the original problem is solved. This stage may also involve an oral presentation of the research results to the client or sponsor of the research.

## MANAGEMENT ACTION

We have seen how the original catalyst for research is often perceived by the manager or at least brought to the attention of the manager. The last step, management action, is also the responsibility of the manager rather than of the researcher. This final phase ensures that the action recommended in the report is indeed carried out (providing, of course, that the manager accepts the recommendations!). The manager will draft a plan, organise the required resources, implement the action and establish monitoring processes to ensure that the action achieves the original purpose of the research project.

Let us now briefly review two examples in an organisational setting and the course of action taken through the 11 steps.

### EXAMPLE 2.3 THE CIO DILEMMA

**Catalyst for research**

The Chief Information Officer (CIO) of a firm observes that the newly installed management information system (MIS) is not being used by middle managers as much as was originally expected. The managers often approach the CIO or go to some other 'computer expert' for help, or worse still, make decisions without facts. 'There is surely a problem here', the CIO observes.

### Information gathering through informal interviews
Talking to some of the middle-level managers, the CIO finds that many of them have very little idea of what MIS is all about, what kinds of information it could provide, and how to access and utilise the information.

### Obtaining more information through a literature survey
The CIO immediately uses the Internet to explore additional information on the lack of use of MIS in organisations. The search indicates that many middle-level managers — especially the old-timers — are not familiar with operating personal computers and experience 'computer anxiety'. Lack of knowledge about what MIS offers is found to be another main reason why some managers do not use MIS.

### Problem definition
Managers appear to be unfamiliar with personal computer processes and are unaware of what MIS offers.

### Framework development
Based on all this information, the CIO develops a conceptual framework incorporating all the relevant factors contributing to the lack of access of the MIS by managers in the organisation.

### Research objective
From such a theory, the CIO generates various research questions for investigation, one of them being to what extent will knowledge of the usefulness of MIS help managers to put MIS to greater use?

### Research design
The CIO then designs a structured inteview based on the various factors theorised to influence the use of MIS by managers, such as the extent of knowledge of what MIS is, what kinds of information MIS provides, how to access the information, the level of comfort felt by managers in using computers in general and, finally, how often managers have accessed the MIS in the preceding three months.

### Data collection
The CIO conducts the interviews.

### Data analysis
The CIO then analyses the data obtained through the interviews to determine what factors prevent the managers from using the system.

### Interpretation of data
Based on the results, the manager concludes that managers do not use MIS owing to certain factors.

### Report preparation
The manager writes a report, which includes recommendations for future action.

### Management action
These conclusions help the CIO to take necessary action to rectify the situation, which might include, among other things, seminars for training managers in the use of computers, and on MIS and its usefulness.

---

## EXAMPLE 2.4 — THE UNINTENDED CONSEQUENCES OF BUDGET CUTS

### Catalyst for research
The Finance Director senses that the budgetary process is not working as well as it should. Managers seem to be overcautious; they tend to pad their budgets excessively, and generally seem to be acting defensively. The Finance Director observes various phenomena and senses that there is a problem.

### Information gathering through informal interviews
The Finance Director chats with a few of the managers and their staff. He finds that there is much anxiety among the managers that the budgets for all departments are likely to be slashed. There is also a perception that the new information system that is planned for installation will deprive the managers of much of their original power and control. A general notion that the managers who have bigger budgets will be evaluated more favourably also seems to prevail.

### Obtaining more information through a literature survey
Amused by these findings, the Finance Director reads materials on the subject and finds that many factors, including those identified through the interviews, are instrumental in thwarting the idea of effective budgeting.

### Problem definition
Effective budgeting appears to be hindered by incorrect perceptions of managers.

### Framework development
Piecing together the information obtained from the interviews and the literature, the Finance Director develops a theory of possible factors that may be influencing ineffective budgeting practices; that is, a theoretical framework of the factors that could account for the padding of budgets is developed.

### Research objective
From the theory, the Finance Director conjectures the relationships among the factors; one of the hypotheses is that fear of budget cuts influences excessive padding of the budget.

### Research design
In this phase, the Finance Director designs a questionnaire based on various concepts such as the extent of anxiety regarding perceived budget cuts and concern regarding the installation of the proposed information systems.

### Data collection
The Finance Director collects data anonymously from the other managers using the questionnaire.

### Data analysis
The Finance Director then has the data analysed using a statistical package to see if there are indeed significant correlations between each of the different factors and if there is slack in the budget (that is, the hypotheses are tested).

### Interpretation of data
If significant correlations are in fact found, the Finance Director would deduce (or conclude) that misperceptions about budget cuts and the proposed information system did influence the managers to pad their budgets.

### Management action
After writing a research report, the Finance Director may then clarify the real situation to the managers, allay their fears and educate them on how they would all benefit by proposing realistic budgets. The Finance Director would also institute a checking procedure to detect any further misperceptions.

## REVIEW OF THE RESEARCH PROCESS
In summary, the research process involves the 11 steps of catalyst for business research, preliminary information gathering and literature search, problem definition, framework development, research objectives, research design, data collection, data analysis, interpretation of findings, report preparation and presentation, and management action. Later chapters in this book will examine each of these steps in the research process in more detail.

# SUMMARY

In this chapter we obtained a general understanding of what constitutes scientific investigation in the business environment. We discussed the hallmarks of scientific research and examined the basic definitions of observations, concepts, variables and constructs. The two approaches to research, qualitative and quantitative, were compared and contrasted, and we concluded that ideal business research should use both of these approaches to advantage. Finally, the 11 steps of the business research process were explained.

## DISCUSSION POINTS

1. Describe the hallmarks of scientific research.

2. What are the steps in the research process? Explain them, using an example not in the book.

3. Compare and contrast qualitative and quantitative research.

4. What is the difference between a concept and a variable?

5. One hears the word *research* mentioned by various groups, including research organisations, university professors, doctoral students, graduate assistants working for faculty, graduate and undergraduate students doing their assignments, research departments in industries, newspaper reporters, journalists, lawyers, doctors, and other professionals and non-professionals. In the light of what you have learned in this chapter, which among these groups do you think may be doing 'scientific' investigations in the areas of basic or applied research? Why?

6. Explain the processes of deduction and induction, giving an example of each.

7. If research in the management area cannot be 100 per cent scientific, why bother to do it at all?

8. Critique the following research carried out in a service industry: to what extent does it meet the hallmarks of scientific investigation discussed in this chapter?

> **The Friendly Telephone Company**
>
> Customer complaints were mounting, and letters of complaint regarding the problems they experienced with the residential telephones lines were constantly pouring in at the Friendly Telephone Company. The company wanted to pinpoint the specific problems and take corrective action.
>
> Researchers were called in, and they spoke to a number of customers, keeping notes on the nature of the specific problems they faced. Since the problem had to be attended to very quickly, they developed a theoretical base, collected relevant detailed information from a sample of 100 customers, and analysed the data. The results are expected to be fairly accurate, with at least an 85 per cent chance of success in problem solving. The researchers will make recommendations to the company based on the results of data analysis.

# part II

# INITIAL STAGES AND DESIGN OF A RESEARCH PROJECT

3 Preliminary information gathering and problem definition

4 Framework development and research objectives

5 Research design and planning

# chapter 3

# PRELIMINARY INFORMATION GATHERING AND PROBLEM DEFINITION

## OUTLINE

THE PRACTICAL APPLICATION OF THE RESEARCH PROCESS
CATALYST FOR BUSINESS RESEARCH
PRELIMINARY INFORMATION GATHERING
THE LITERATURE SURVEY
PROBLEM DEFINITION
MANAGERIAL IMPLICATIONS
ETHICAL ISSUES
SUMMARY
DISCUSSION POINTS
PRACTICE PROJECTS
APPENDIX
 SECTION 1: SOME USEFUL DATABASES FOR BUSINESS RESEARCH
 SECTION 2: SEARCH ENGINES
 SECTION 3: THE BIBLIOGRAPHY AND REFERENCE LIST
 SECTION 4: REFERENCING AND QUOTATION IN THE BUSINESS ARTICLE
  OR REPORT

## CHAPTER OBJECTIVES

After reading this chapter, you should be able to:
- identify problem areas that are likely to be studied in organisations
- discuss how problem areas can be identified in work settings
- state research problems clearly and precisely
- develop relevant and comprehensive bibliographies for any business research topic
- write a literature review on any given topic, documenting the references in the prescribed manner
- apply all you have learned to a group project that might be assigned to you.

# THE PRACTICAL APPLICATION OF THE RESEARCH PROCESS

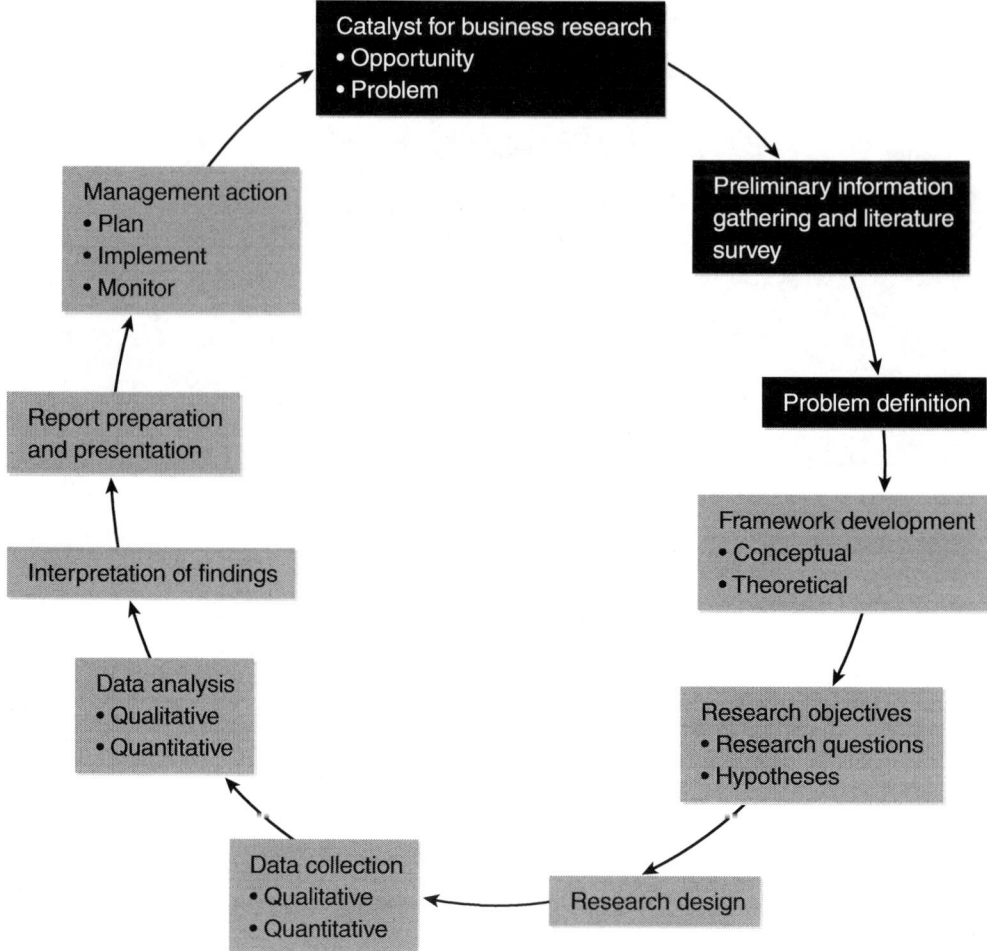

**Figure 3.1** The business research process: preliminary information collection and problem definition

In chapter 2 we discussed and illustrated through figure 2.2 the research process used for scientific inquiry in business, and this is returned to in figure 3.1. However, despite the fact that the research model is depicted and discussed in this book as if it were a step-by-step, *linear* process, it is not actually so in practice. For example, although the initial observations and interviews in the preliminary information gathering may be conducted before the framework is formulated, one may have to go back and conduct more interviews and/or seek additional information from the literature for a clearer understanding in order to refine the concepts. The research site, the sample, measurement of the variables and other design issues may also have to be considered simultaneously as one identifies the problem, formulates the conceptual or theoretical framework, and generates the research questions or hypotheses. So, while the communicative process of reading this book demands a linear logic, keep in mind the constant interactions between the various stages of the research model.

This chapter will discuss the first three stages of the research process — the catalyst for research, preliminary information gathering, and literature review and problem definition.

# CATALYST FOR BUSINESS RESEARCH

The initial situation — whether an opportunity for the organisation or a problem that may present some current or future threat — eventually comes to the attention of someone in the organisation who has the authority to decide that some investment of energy and money should be incurred. Thus, the initial situation becomes the catalyst for an official research investigation.

The specific issues that need to be researched within this situation may not be identified at this stage. Such issues might pertain to:
- problems currently existing in an organisational setting that need to be solved
- areas in the organisation that a manager believes need to be improved
- a conceptual or theoretical issue that needs to be tightened up for the basic researcher to understand certain phenomena
- some research questions that a basic researcher wants to answer *empirically*.

Examples of each type can be provided by taking the issue of sexual harassment, which is a problem that arises in some organisations.

As an example of a *currently existing* issue, a situation might present itself in which a manager receives written complaints from women in some departments who claim they are not being treated fairly by their bosses. From the generalised nature of these complaints, the manager might become aware of a gender-related problem situation, but might be unable to pinpoint exactly what it is; that is, the matter calls for further investigation before the exact problem can be identified and attempts made to resolve it. On the other hand, if the company has already formulated policies on discrimination and sexual harassment, and legitimate complaints of discrimination continue to come in, then it is obvious that the policies are ambiguous and need improvement in how they have been framed, how they are understood or how they are enforced. This is an example of a situation *requiring improvement*.

It may be that there is a *conceptual issue that needs to be tightened*. Say the basic researcher studies sexual harassment so as to define that concept in precise terms. Currently, sexual harassment might be broadly defined as *any unwelcome sexual advances, requests for sexual favours, or other verbal or physical conduct of a sexual nature*. In practice, however, certain non-verbal or nonphysical attention, such as ogling, might also be unpalatable to some women and could be termed 'harassment'. Thus, the researcher might want to come up with a precise statement of what sexual harassment is and expand the definition of the term. Here is a clear case for a better understanding and definition of the concept itself. The issue of perceived or actual sexual harassment and its impact on individuals (e.g. psychological stress) and organisations (e.g. poor performance) is explored by gathering data and testing the relationships. This is a situation in which specific answers to a research question are sought *empirically*.

Examples of catalysts for research areas that a manager could observe at the workplace are outlined below.
- Training programs are perhaps not as effective as anticipated.
- The sales volume of a product is not picking up.
- Minority groups in organisations are not progressing in their careers.
- The daily balancing of accounting ledgers is becoming a continuing concern.

- The newly installed information system is not being used by the managers for whom it was primarily designed.
- The introduction of flexible work hours has created more problems than it has solved in many companies.
- The anticipated results of a recent merger have not been forthcoming.
- Inventory control is not effective.
- The installation of an MIS keeps getting stalled.
- The management of complex, multidepartmental team projects is getting out of hand in the R & D department of a firm.

The **broad problem area** would be narrowed down to specific issues for investigation after some preliminary data are gathered by the researcher. This may be achieved through interviews, observations and a literature research.

## PRELIMINARY INFORMATION GATHERING

Preliminary information gathering allows the researcher to gain a wider perspective on the possible problem or business opportunity. It is important to recognise that at this stage the information gathering is indeed preliminary. Any information-gathering exercise is costly in terms of resources such as time and money. At this early stage, the investigator is gathering information to answer two fundamental questions.

1. Is the problem or opportunity worth ongoing investigation?
2. How can the problem or opportunity be clearly and efficiently described?

In gathering this information, the researcher will use such research methods as interviewing, focus groups and statistical analysis of existing quantitative data. However, at this stage, a full investigation is not undertaken. The preliminary investigation is a quick run through readily available information to provide a fundamental direction for the later research investigation.

Information is gathered from four main sources — organisational records, the knowledge of the staff, the Internet and a library search. Before examining these sources in detail, we will examine the nature of the information the preliminary investigation is targeting.

## NATURE OF THE INFORMATION TO BE COLLECTED

The information to be gathered during this preliminary phase can be classified as specific to the problem or challenge yet broad in nature.

### Specific information

Although the problem or opportunity has been initially identified, the researcher usually needs to clarify the situation; that is, the researcher needs to be able to describe what the issue is and what it is not. This is achieved through asking questions such as those below.

- When was the issue first noticed?
- How do we know that the issue exists? Are any indicators available? Are these indicators quantitative or qualitative? If quantitative, are the measures hiding more complex issues? If qualitative, are the opinions or feelings widespread and/or do they have significant impact?
- Who is affected by the issue?
- What is the perceived impact of the issue? Is the impact best described in qualitative or quantitative terms or a combination of both?
- What are the perceived causes?
- What is the time frame of both the causes and the impact?

## Broader issues and context

The researcher cannot afford to concentrate solely on the specific problem or opportunity. Indeed, possible causes and impacts demand that the researcher take a wider view. In addition, the researcher needs to place the specific issue within the context of the organisation and the external environment in which the organisation operates. This broader information is also essential to the researcher in the next phase of the research process — developing a conceptual or theoretical framework. The nature of this broader information can be classified under three headings. These are:

- background information of the organisation — that is, the **contextual factors**
- managerial philosophy, company policies and other structural aspects
- perceptions, attitudes and behavioural responses of organisational members and client systems (as applicable).

Certain types of information, such as background details of the company, can be obtained from available published records, the website of the company, its archives and other sources. Other types of written information, such as company policies, procedures and rules, can be obtained from the organisation's records and documents. Data gathered through such existing sources are called **secondary data** — that is, data that already exist and do not have to be collected by the researcher. Some secondary sources of data are statistical bulletins, government publications, information published or unpublished and available either within or outside the organisation, data available from previous research, case studies and library records, on-line data, websites and the Internet. In contrast, certain other types of information, such as the perceptions and attitudes of employees, are best obtained by talking to them, by observing events, people and objects, or by administering questionnaires to individuals. Such data, gathered for research from the actual site of occurrence of events, are called **primary data**.

We will now see how the three broad types of information mentioned earlier can be gathered.

### Background information of the organisation

It is important for the researcher or research team — especially if an outside agency conducts the research — to be well acquainted with the background of the company or organisation studied before even conducting the first interview with its officials. Such background information may include contextual factors, which may be obtained from various published sources such as trade publications, business guides and services, records available within the organisation and the **World Wide Web**. These sources will provide essential information such as:

- the origin and history of the company — when it came into being, the business it is in, its rate of growth, ownership and control, and so on
- its size in terms of employees, assets or both
- the company charter (its purpose and ideology)
- its location — regional, national or other
- corporate resources — human and other
- interdependent relationships with other institutions and the external environment
- its financial position during the previous five to 10 years, and other relevant financial data.

Information gathered on these aspects will be useful in talking knowledgeably with others in the company during the interviews and raising the appropriate issues related to the problem. For example, problems with cash flow (which can be gleaned from the balance sheets) may be related to the poor quality of raw materials purchased, resulting in a high rate of return of goods sold by the company. This issue can be tactfully investigated during the course of discussions with the appropriate staff members if this basic information is known in advance. Or an industry analysis might reveal that some of the problems encountered, such as competition from foreign producers, consumer resistance to spending money and the like, are not unique to this company but are faced industry-wide. In such a case, more questions can focus on strategies (such as sales and advertising efforts) developed by the company to promote sales in the face of foreign competition.

### Information on structural factors and management philosophy

Information on company policies, structure, workflow, management philosophy and the like can be obtained by asking management direct questions. When questions are directed at several managers individually, some of the responses may be conflicting and contradictory. Frequent instances of such contradictions may in themselves indicate problems such as poor communication or misperceptions of the organisation's philosophy, goals, values and so forth. These issues can be pursued by the researcher in subsequent interviews to get an idea of the extent to which differences in perceptions exist in the organisation.

Such information gathering is particularly useful when newly installed systems, processes and procedures fail to produce the desired results. The failure of many new technologies, well-meant benefit policies, strategic plans, or marketing or production practices is often due to misunderstandings and misperceptions of the goals and motives of top administration rather than any inherent faults in the mechanisms themselves. Once the misperceptions are resolved, the problem may well disappear. Hence, it is useful right at the start to gauge the extent to which perceptual and communications problems exist.

Questions about managerial and company philosophy offer an excellent idea of the priorities and values of the company regarding issues such as:
- whether product quality is really deemed important by the company, or if only lip-service is paid to the concept
- whether the company has short-term or long-term goals
- whether controls are so tight that creativity is stifled, or so loose that nothing gets done, and whether they are conducive to good performance
- whether the company always wants to play it safe or is prepared to take calculated risks
- whether it is people-oriented or solely profit-oriented.

Frequently, aspects of structure also influence the problem and need to be explored. Structural factors include:
- roles and positions in the organisation, and the number of employees at each job level
- the extent of specialisation
- communication channels
- control systems
- coordination and span of control
- reward systems
- workflow systems and the like.

The respondents' perceptions of the **structural variables** may not match the formal written structural policies and procedures of the organisation. Where this is the case, these become relevant leads to follow during unstructured and structured interviews with various levels of employees in the organisation.

## Perceptions, attitudes and behavioural responses

Employee perceptions of the work and work environment, and their attitudinal and behavioural responses, can be tapped by talking to the employees, observing them and seeking their responses through questionnaires. A general idea of people's perceptions of their work, the organisational climate and other aspects of interest to the researcher can be obtained through both unstructured and structured interviews. By establishing a good rapport with the individuals and following the right questioning techniques (discussed in detail in chapter 6), the researcher will be able to obtain useful information. An understanding of the attitudinal and behavioural reactions of organisational members is often very helpful in arriving at a precise problem definition.

**Attitudinal factors** comprise people's beliefs about and reactions to:
- the nature of the work
- workflow interdependencies
- their superiors in the organisation
- participation in decision making
- client systems
- their co-workers
- rewards provided by the organisation, such as pay rises and fringe benefits
- opportunities for advancement in the organisation
- the organisation's attitudes towards employees' family responsibilities
- the company's involvement with community, civic and other social groups
- the company's tolerance of employees' taking time off from the job.

**Behavioural factors** include actual work habits such as industriousness and performance on the job, and the extent of absenteeism.

The respondents may be encouraged at the interviewing stage to talk about their jobs, other work- and non-work-related factors, and their attitudes, values, perceptions and behaviours, some of which might influence outcomes in the workplace. Talking to people at various levels in the organisation will give the interviewer a good idea of the dynamics that operate in the system. Detailed discussions on how the unstructured and structured interviews are to be conducted are in chapter 6.

## Is it worth the effort?

At this stage, questions may arise as to whether seeking all this information on management philosophy, structure, perceptions and attitudes is *always* necessary, how the materials will be utilised in the research project and how much time should be expended in collecting such particulars. The answer to these questions is that there is no substitute for good judgement. Depending on the situation, the type of problem investigated and the nature of initial responses received, certain aspects may have to be explored in greater depth than others. For example, if the problem as identified by the manager is related to individuals' attitudes and behaviours, then the value system, the corporate culture and employee perceptions may have to be examined more deeply than the structural aspects. On the other hand, if reorganisation of the work layout is the subject for the study, then the workflow interdependencies and coordination aspects will need more attention. The main idea in gathering information on values, structures and processes, instead of merely dealing with the manifest symptoms, is that these often reveal the root of the *real problem*. These distinctions are elaborated later in this chapter. For now, as an illustration, many companies are introducing employee store ownership plans (ESOP). Not all employees are necessarily enthusiastic about this. Rather than taking immediate steps towards making the package more attractive through cosmetic changes, talking to individuals might reveal that the employees perceive ESOP merely as a tool to deter takeovers and save taxes, and as providing no true opportunities for employee involvement and participation. The understanding so gained helps the manager to attack the *real issues* (in this case, employees' concerns and fears), rather than work on the surface symptoms (making cosmetic changes to the package to make it more attractive).

As another example, a manager might think that refining a just-in-time (JIT) system will help reduce inventory and production costs, whereas the real problem could involve the type of machinery used in the production process. It is for reasons such as these that talking with people at different levels helps the researcher to understand their concerns. Spending two or three days interviewing individuals at different levels in the system should generally suffice to get a grasp of the establishment and understand the culture of the organisation.

To summarise, the nature of the information that the researcher gathers at this preliminary stage is both specific and broad. This combination leads the researcher to a clearer understanding of the problem or opportunity as well as its overall importance.

## SOURCES OF INFORMATION

There are four main sources of information used by the researcher. These are:
- organisational records
- the knowledge of the staff
- the Internet
- the library search.

## Organisational records

The organisational records provide the researcher with factual information that is organisation specific and can range from written documentation, such as the minutes of meetings and organisational policies, to strategic plans and financial statements. Organisational records have another advantage — they are enduring and therefore provide a historical account of the organisation. Often this provides the researcher with an insight into the development of a problem or challenge. The researcher should also recognise that organisational records consist of secondary data.

Most organisations today have data warehouses and management information systems. **Data warehouses** serve as central repositories of relevant information pertaining to the company's finance, manufacturing, sales, staff and administrative processes. The data warehouse is usually built from data collected from the different departments of the enterprise. **Data mining** is the term used for the process of extracting and integrating data for the purpose of analysis and decision making. Various on-line analytic processing (OLAP) tools are used to support this analytical decision-making process. For example, a hotel that had retained four of its eighteen floors of rooms for non-smoking patrons found, after analysing its data warehouse, that requests for non-smoking rooms accounted for over 75 per cent of room booking requests. While this becomes a very simple calculation once data are available for analysis in a warehouse, such a trend is not easily identified without such a resource. A **management information system (MIS)** provides a regular and systematic analysis of data in a warehouse. An MIS usually consists of three subsystems. The operating subsystem provides data used daily in business operations, such as data on production and inventory control. The reporting subsystem generates management reports of various types, such as costs of production and return on investment figures, and even reports on a competitor's strategy or financial standing, which is independent of the operating subsystem. The decision-making subsystem provides information that helps the manager to decide among many competing alternative courses of action in any given situation. This subsystem often provides mathematical models and simulations created using different assumptions.

## Knowledge of the staff

The staff within an organisation possess a unique, complex and abundant array of information. Extracting relevant information from this rich source presents the researcher with at least two distinctive challenges. First, the researcher must identify which staff have information relevant to the investigation. Unlike organisational records, there is rarely an index or list of contents that will provide a guide. Second, eliciting the relevant knowledge from an individual requires professional skills and abilities. These skills and abilities are discussed in detail in chapter 6, where the processes of interviewing and conducting focus groups are examined. Usually, at this preliminary stage questionnaires are not used as there is insufficient understanding of the variables involved (see chapter 4).

The **intranet** consists of the network of computers and computer programs within the company. Through an Internet link, the researcher is connected to the various databases within the organisation, such as the human resource information system (HRIS), and also the individual members of the organisation via the **e-mail** system. It greatly facilitates data gathering from within the organisation. For example, surveys can be conducted through the intranet to assess employee morale or the popularity of benefit packages. The intranet can be put to many creative uses. Cronin (1998) noted that Ford's intranet success is such that the car maker's in-house website could save the company billions and fulfil the dream of building cars on demand. Cronin explains how the car maker's product development system documents thousands of steps that go into manufacturing, assembling and testing vehicles. By opening its intranet to selected suppliers, Ford encouraged research and created a variety of opportunities — not only from within its own organisation but among suppliers as well.

So for the researcher, the staff of an organisation represent a very valuable source of information. Further, this information is primary data and is thus unique to the research issue. However, the effort required to unlock this information varies in direct relation to the value of the information. In the preliminary information-gathering stage, this presents a dilemma, since the information is valuable but the effort required to extract it is likely to be costly. At this stage, the researcher must make a decision on whether the data gathered is sufficient to draw preliminary conclusions. If not, then further interactions with staff — interviews and focus groups — will be necessary.

## Response patterns and outside information gathering

The information gathered from organisational records and the staff represents *information from within* the organisation. The next step for the researcher is to quickly analyse this internal information and determine if there are patterns in the responses. For instance, it might be determined from the qualitative data that some problems are frequently mentioned by employees at several levels of the organisation. Certain factors, such as insufficient lighting, untrained personnel or inadequate tools, may be brought out forcefully in the interviews by several workers. When the analysis reveals that such issues have been raised frequently, it gives the researcher some good ideas about how to proceed in the next step — surveying information from outside the organisation.

By accessing *information from outside* the organisation, the researcher can determine how others, in other work settings, have perceived such factors and defined the problem before arriving at solutions. Of course, this information is classified as secondary data. The two main sources of information from outside the organisation are the Internet and libraries.

## The Internet

The Internet is a vast web of networks of computers linking people and information that interconnects us globally to a wealth of data and information. The Internet has opened up tremendous possibilities for research and expanding the realms of business opportunities. However, its immense capacity and complexity presents time-consuming challenges to the researcher who must navigate the labyrinth of options and pitfalls. Indeed, the Internet has been described as the world's most badly organised library.

To help navigate the Internet, researchers use **search engines** such as 'GOeureka' and 'HotBot'. Search engines are software programs designed to help users search World Wide Web and other Internet sources by entering keywords that describe the topic. The search engine will then search for these keywords in files and databases linked to the Internet. A list of common search engines is included in the appendix at the end of this chapter. On the Internet, files, documents, databases and other information sources are usually referred to as **websites**. Commonly, large organisations will have their own website which describes their operations and provides a means for public access and promotion. A list of websites useful to researchers in Australia and New Zealand is included in the appendix at the end of this chapter. An *information source* may be a journal article or other written material on the topic. It is possible also to obtain files with text, graphics, sound and video through the electronic mail exchange.

## Libraries

Most people are conversant with libraries with their collections of books, journals and other reference material. Researchers need to be very familiar with the means of accessing this rich resource so they can extract information easily and efficiently. Most libraries have a computer system that allows the researcher to examine the collections of materials under author, title or topic headings, and that also indicates the location of the item in the library. For a wider subject search, the researcher needs to examine the various indexes available such as ABI/INFORM or the Business Periodicals Index (BPI). Many of these indexes are listed in the appendix at the end of this chapter.

## THE LITERATURE SURVEY

Because the literature survey is one way of summarising secondary data and is an important step in the process of defining the research problem, we will now discuss it in some detail as one of the preliminary data-gathering tools.

It is important to keep in mind that secondary data can be extracted from various sources, including books and periodicals, government publications and information sources, the media, census records, stock market reports, and mechanised and electronic information of all kinds, from bar codes and scanner data to the Internet. Secondary data can be culled from the historical records of the organisation itself, from information available on the company intranet, and from external sources such as those already mentioned.

A literature survey or review is the documentation of a comprehensive review of the published and unpublished work from secondary sources in the areas of specific interest to the researcher. The library is a rich source of secondary data, and researchers used to spend weeks, sometimes months, going through books, journals, newspapers, magazines, conference proceedings, doctoral dissertations, master's theses, government publications, and financial, marketing and other reports, to obtain information on their research topic. With computerised databases now readily available and accessible, a literature search is much faster and easier, and can be done without entering the library building.

The researcher could start the literature survey even as the information from inside the organisation is being gathered. Reviewing the literature on the topic area at this time helps the researcher to focus the interviews and observations more meaningfully on certain aspects found to be important in the published studies, even if these did not surface during the preliminary information gathering.

## REASONS FOR THE LITERATURE SURVEY

The purpose of the literature review is to ensure that no important variable is ignored that has in the past been found to have had an impact on the problem. For example, it is possible that some of the critical variables are never brought out in the interviews, either because the employees cannot articulate them or because they are unaware of their impact, or because the variables seem so obvious to the interviewees that they are not specifically stated. If there are variables that are not identified during the interviews, but influence the problem critically, then research done without considering them would be an exercise in futility. In such a case, the true reason for the problem would remain unidentified even at the end of the research. To avoid such mistakes, the researcher needs to delve into all the important research work relating to the particular problem area. The following example will help to highlight the importance of the literature survey.

In establishing employee selection procedures, a company may be doing all the right things, such as administering the appropriate tests to assess the applicants' analytical skills, judgement, leadership, motivation, oral and written communication skills and the like. Yet it may be consistently losing excellent MBAs, hired as managers, within a year, despite their being highly paid. The reasons for the turnover of MBAs may not be identified while conducting interviews with the candidates. However, a review of the literature might indicate that when employees have unmet job expectations (that is, their original expectations of their role and responsibilities do not match their actual experiences), they will be inclined to leave the organisation. Talking further to company officials, it may be found that *realistic job previews* are never offered to the candidates at the time of the interview. This might explain why the candidates experience frustration on the job and eventually leave. This important factor, significantly influencing the turnover of managerial employees, might not have come to light but for the literature survey. If this variable is not included in the research investigation, the problem may never be solved!

Sometimes an investigator may expend considerable time and effort to 'discover' something that has already been thoroughly researched. A literature review would prevent such wastage of resources on reinventing the wheel. However, because every situation is unique, further research needs to take into consideration the relevant variables applicable to each unique situation. Finally, a good literature survey could in itself be the basis for qualitative research — for instance in tracing the origins and progress of technology and predicting where it is headed in the future.

A survey of the literature not only helps the researcher to include all the relevant variables in the research project, but also facilitates the creative integration of the information gathered from inside the organisation with what is found in previous studies. In other words, it gives a good basic framework to proceed further with the investigation. A good literature survey thus provides the foundation for developing a comprehensive conceptual or theoretical framework from which research objectives can be developed for testing. The development of the conceptual or theoretical framework and research objectives therefore is discussed in the next chapter.

A good literature survey has the following advantages.

- Important variables that are likely to influence the problem situation are not left out of the study.
- A clearer idea emerges as to what variables would be most important to consider (parsimony), why they would be considered important and how they should be investigated to solve the problem. Thus, the literature survey helps to develop the conceptual or theoretical framework and research objectives for testing.
- Testability and replicability of the findings of the current research are enhanced.
- The research problem statement can be made with precision and clarity.
- One does not run the risk of 'reinventing the wheel' — that is, wasting effort on trying to 'discover' something that is already known.
- The research problem investigated is perceived by the scientific community as relevant and significant.

## CONDUCTING THE LITERATURE SURVEY

Based on the specific issues of concern to the manager and the factors identified during the interview process, a literature review needs to be carried out on these variables. The first step in this process is to identify the various published and unpublished materials that are available on the topics of interest, and gain access to these. The second step is to gather the relevant information either by going through the necessary materials in a library or by accessing the sources on line. The third step is to write up the literature review. These steps are now discussed.

### Identifying the relevant sources

Previously, one had to manually pore through the bibliographical indexes that are compiled periodically, listing the journals, books and other sources in which published work in the area of interest can be found. However, with modern technology, locating sources where the topics of interest have been published has become easy. Almost every library now has computer on-line systems to help locate and print out the published information on selected topics.

Global business information, published articles in newspapers and periodicals, and conference proceedings, among other sources, are all now available on databases. Computerised databases include bibliographies, abstracts and full texts of articles on many business topics. Statistical and financial databases are also easily accessible. Computer hardware and software enable the storage, updating and display of information on global activities. Economic indicators and other data for various countries can be tracked easily. Statistical abstracts, and other publications, now available on CD-ROM and on the Internet, bring to the researcher all the necessary information at the press of the relevant computer keys.

Three types of database are useful in reviewing the literature, as indicated below.

1. *Bibliographic databases* display only bibliographic citations — that is, the name of the author, the title of the article (or book), source of publication, year, volume

and page numbers. These have the same information as found in bibliographic index books in libraries, which are periodically updated, and include articles published in periodicals, newspapers, books and so on.
2. *Abstract databases*, in addition, provide an abstract or summary of the articles.
3. *Full-text databases* provide the full text of the article.

Databases are also available for obtaining statistics — marketing, financial and so on — and directories are organised by subject, title, geographic location, trade opportunities, foreign traders, industrial plants and other categories. Some of these on-line databases are listed in section 1 of the appendix at the end of this chapter.

On-line searches provide a number of advantages. Besides saving enormous amounts of time, they are comprehensive in their listing and review of references, and the researcher can focus on materials most central to the research effort. In addition, accessing them is relatively inexpensive.

Some of the important research databases available on line and on the World Wide Web are provided in the appendix to this chapter. If a source of information is not known, the search strategies on the Internet will help to find it. Databases include listings of journal articles, books in print, census data, dissertation abstracts, conference papers and newspaper abstracts that are useful for business research.

## Extracting the relevant information

Accessing the on-line system and getting a printout of all the published works in the area of interest from a bibliographical index (some useful indexes are provided in section 1 of the appendix to this chapter) will provide a comprehensive **bibliography** on the subject, which will form the basis for the next step. Whereas the printout could sometimes include as many as 100 or more listings, a glance at the titles of the articles or books will indicate which of these may be pertinent and which are likely to be peripheral to the contemplated study. Abstracts of articles that seem to be relevant can then be obtained through the on-line system. This will give an idea of the articles that need to be examined, the full text of which can then be printed out. While reading these articles, detailed information on the problem that was researched, the design details of the study (such as the **sample size** and data-collection methods) and the ultimate findings may be systematically noted in a convenient format. This facilitates the writing up of the literature review with minimum disruption and maximum efficiency. While reading the articles, certain other factors may be found that are closely related to the problem at hand. For instance, while reading articles on the effectiveness of information systems, the researcher may discover that the size of the company has also been found to be an important factor. The researcher may then want to know more about how the size of organisations is categorised and measured by others, and hence may want to read materials on organisation size. All the articles considered relevant to the current study can then be listed as references using the appropriate referencing format, which is discussed in section 3 of the appendix to this chapter.

## WRITING UP THE LITERATURE SURVEY

The documentation of the relevant studies, citing the author and the year of the study, is called the literature review or literature survey. The literature survey is a clear and logical presentation of the relevant research work carried out thus far in the area of investigation. As stated earlier, the purpose of the literature survey is to identify and highlight the important variables, and to document the significant findings from earlier research that will serve as the foundation on which the conceptual or theoretical framework for the current investigation can be based and the hypotheses developed. Such documentation is important in order to convince the reader that the researcher is knowledgeable about the problem area and has done the preliminary groundwork necessary to conduct the research, and also that the conceptual or theoretical framework will be built on the solid foundation of existing knowledge.

A point to note is that the literature survey should bring together all relevant information in a cogent and logical manner instead of presenting all the studies in chronological order with fragments of uncoordinated information. A good literature survey also leads logically to a good problem statement.

There are several accepted methods of citing references and using quotations. The *Publications Manual of the American Psychological Association* (the *APA Manual*) (1994) offers detailed information regarding citations, quotations, references and so on, and presents one of the accepted styles of referencing in the management area. Other formats include the Harvard system, detailed in the *Chicago Manual of Style* (1993), and the AGPS *Style Manual* (1994). Details of the referencing and quotation style outlined in the *APA Manual* are given in section 3 of the appendix at the end of this chapter along with a short description of the Harvard system.

## EXAMPLES OF TWO LITERATURE SURVEYS

Let us take a *section* of two literature reviews and examine how the activity has helped to introduce the subject of study, identify the research question, and build on previous research to offer a basis for moving on to the next steps of theoretical framework and hypotheses development.

### EXAMPLE 3.1 — RISK-TAKING BEHAVIOURS AND ORGANISATIONAL OUTCOMES

Managers handle risks and face uncertainties in different ways. Some of these styles are functional and others adversely affect corporate performance. Living in times of dramatic organisational change (mergers, for instance), and with company performance varying vastly in this turbulent environment, it is important to investigate the relationship between risk-taking behaviours of managers and organisational outcomes.

A vast body of knowledge exists regarding risk-taking behaviours in decision making. Some studies have shown that the context which surrounds the decision maker exerts an influence on the extent of risk the individual is prepared to take (Shapira 1995; Starbuck & Milken 1988). Other studies, such as those by Sankar (1997) and Velcher (1998), indicate that the position of the risk taker, and whether the decision is taken by an individual or is the result of group effort, account significantly for the variance in risk-taking behaviours and, ultimately, for the performance of the organisation. Schwartz (1994) argues that research carried out using subjects participating in activities in a laboratory setting shows different results compared with those found in research done in organisational settings. Additionally, MacCrimmon and Wehrung (1984, 1986, 1990) suggest that the differences in the measurement tools used in research studies account for the differences in the findings of managerial risk attitudes.

You will note that the preceding example first introduces the subject of risk-taking behaviours and corporate performance, and why it is an important topic to be studied. Through the literature survey, it identifies the problem to be studied as one of investigating the factors that account for risk-taking behaviours. This example also indicates the important factors to be considered in the research — factors that would enable the researcher to formulate a theory based on which research objectives can be formulated and tested.

> **EXAMPLE 3.2**
>
> **ORGANISATIONAL EFFECTIVENESS**
>
> Organisational theorists have defined organisational effectiveness (OE) in various ways. OE has been described in terms of objectives (Georgopolous & Tannenbaum 1957), goals (Etzioni 1960), efficiency (Katz & Kahn 1966), resource acquisition (Yuchtman & Seashore 1967), employee satisfaction (Cummings 1977), interdependence (Pfeffer 1977) and organisational vitality (Colt 1995). As Coulter (1996) remarks, there is little consensus on how to conceptualise, measure or explain OE. This should not come as a surprise since OE models are essentially a value-based classification of the construct (the values being those of the researchers), so the number of potential models that can be generated by researchers is virtually limitless. Researchers are now moving away from a single model and are adopting contingency approaches to conceptualising OE (Cameron 1996; Wernerfelt 1998; Yetley 1997). However, they are still limiting themselves to examining the impact of the dominant constituencies served and the organisation's life cycle instead of taking a broader, more dynamic approach (Dahl 1998:25).

From the survey of the literature above, several insights can be gained. First, the literature review introduces the subject of study (organisational effectiveness). Second, it highlights the problem (that we do not have a good conceptual framework for understanding what OE is). Third, it summarises the work done thus far on the topic in a manner that convinces the reader that the researcher has indeed surveyed the work done in the area of OE and wants to contribute to an understanding of the concept, moving beyond the earlier contingency approaches in a more creative way. The scholar has carefully paved the way for the next step, which is to develop a more viable and robust model of organisational effectiveness. This model will be logically developed, integrating several streams of research undertaken in other areas (for example cross-cultural management and sociology), which will be woven further into the literature review. Once the scholar has explicated the framework as to what constitutes OE and the factors that influence OE, the next step is to develop testable research questions or hypotheses to see if the new model is indeed viable.

The literature survey thus provides a foundation on which to develop a conceptual or theoretical framework for looking at the problem in a more useful and creative way. This, in turn, helps to develop testable research questions or hypotheses that would substantiate or disprove our theory.

Examples of a good literature survey can be found at the beginning of any article in the *Academy of Management Journal* and most other academic or practitioner-oriented journals. Specimens of a literature survey can also be found later in this book.

One important benefit derived from a well-written literature survey is that the researcher is able to delineate a logical and well-defined, tentative problem for research investigation. This delineation or definition of the tentative problem, which is the next step in the research process, is now discussed.

## PROBLEM DEFINITION

After information has been gathered from within and outside the organisation, the researcher is in a position to narrow down the situation highlighted by the catalyst for research from its original broad base and define more clearly the issues of concern. It is critical that the focus for further research be unambiguously identified and defined. No amount of good research can find solutions to the situation if the critical issue to be studied is not clearly pinpointed.

To this point, we have referred to the situation being investigated as a 'problem or opportunity'. From the organisational perspective, the manager will want to solve the problem or achieve the opportunity. However, for the researcher, at this stage of the investigation, the situation becomes a 'research problem'.

A research problem does not necessarily imply that something is seriously wrong with a current situation which needs to be rectified immediately. It could simply indicate an interest in an issue and a sense that finding the right answers might help to improve an existing situation. Thus, it is useful to define a research problem as *any situation where a gap exists between the actual and the desired ideal states*. Basic researchers usually define their research problems for investigation from this perspective. For instance, we would ideally like to see zero defects, low inventory of unsold goods, high share quotations on the stock market and so on. These 'problems' could then very well become the foci of research. Thus, research problem definitions could encompass both existing problems in a current setting and the quest for ideal states in organisations. We might find some managers defining their problem as a severe decline in productivity, or the company fast losing its market share, where the goal is to rectify the situation with a heightened sense of urgency. Other managers might define the 'problem' as a situation in which there is considerable interest in attracting highly qualified engineers to the firm, or enhancing the quality of life for their employees.

For simplicity, we will now refer to 'research problems' as 'problems'. Whatever the problem, one should know exactly what the issue is for which one seeks answers. It is very important that *symptoms* of problems are not defined as the real problem. For instance, a manager might have tried to increase productivity by increasing the piece rate, but have met with little success. Here the real problem may be the low morale and motivation of employees, who feel they are not being recognised as valuable contributors to the system and get no praise for the good work they do. The low productivity may merely be a *symptom* of a deep-rooted morale and motivation problem. Under these conditions, a higher piece rate will not improve productivity. Finding the 'right' answers to the 'wrong' problem definition will not help. Hence, it should be recognised that correct problem identification is critical for finding solutions to vexing issues.

Frequently, managers describe the problem in terms of symptoms during the interviews. Rather than accepting it as such, the researcher needs to identify the problem more accurately after talking to the employees and reviewing the literature, as discussed earlier. One way of determining that the problem, rather than the symptom, is being addressed is to ask the question (after gathering sufficient information through observations, MIS, interviews and literature search), 'Is this factor I have identified an *antecedent*, the real problem or the *consequence*?' These terms can be discussed in the context of the earlier example of low productivity. The real issue or problem here is low morale and motivation. The consequence of the problem is low productivity. Note that the consequence (or effect) of low motivation can also manifext itself in absenteeism, sabotage or any number of other adverse effects for the firm. The antecedent of the problem (that is, the contributing factor) in the given situation seems to be nonrecognition of the employees' contributions. Until such time as the employees are recognised for their work, their motivation and morale will not improve, and neither will their productivity. Without addressing the central issue, if more money is spent, or better equipment installed to increase productivity, the desired results will not ensue because the right problem has not been addressed.

**Problem definition**, or **problem statement**, as it is also often called, involves a *succinct statement of the question or issue that is to be investigated with the goal of*

*finding an answer or solution*. As mentioned earlier, problem definitions could pertain to:
- existing business problems to which a manager is looking for a solution
- situations that may not pose any current problems but that the manager feels can stand improvement
- areas in which some conceptual clarity is needed for better theory building
- situations in which a researcher is trying to answer a research question empirically because of interest in the topic.

The first two fall within the realm of applied research; the last two are basic research. However, at this stage the problem is tentatively defined to provide some direction to the following stages. As the research process progresses, the problem will be either confirmed or refined.

## EXAMPLES OF WELL-DEFINED PROBLEMS

1. To what extent do the structure of the organisation and type of information systems installed account for the variance in the perceived effectiveness of managerial decision making?
2. To what extent has the new advertising campaign been successful in creating the high-quality, customer-centred corporate image that it was intended to produce?
3. How has the new packaging affected the sales of the product?
4. Has the new advertising message resulted in better recall?
5. How do price and quality rate in consumers' evaluation of products?
6. Is the effect of participative budgeting on performance moderated by control systems?
7. Does better automation lead to greater asset investment per dollar of output?
8. Does expansion of international operations result in an enhancement of the firm's image and value?
9. What are the effects of downsizing on the long-range growth patterns of companies?
10. Can cultural differences account for the differences in the nature of hierarchical relationships between superiors and subordinates in India, Japan, Singapore, New Zealand and Australia?
11. What are the components of 'quality of life'?
12. What specific factors should be considered in creating a data warehouse for a manufacturing company?
13. What network system is best suited to Speights Breweries?

## MANAGERIAL IMPLICATIONS

Managers sometimes look at the symptoms in problematic situations and treat them as if they are the real problems, becoming frustrated when their remedies do not work. Understanding the *antecedents–problem–consequences* sequence, and gathering the relevant information to get a true grasp of the problem, go a long way towards pinpointing it.

Managers' input helps researchers to define the broad problem area and confirm their own theories about the situational factors affecting the central problem. Managers who realise that correct problem definition is critical to ultimate problem solution do not begrudge the time spent in working closely with researchers, particularly at this stage. Awareness of information sources and ability to access the requisite information at will through the Internet are great assets to the manager. Using this facility, the manager can learn how similar businesses throughout the world deal with similar situations, and gain a better understanding of the issues at hand.

## ETHICAL ISSUES

Once a problem is recognised and an investigation is decided on, it is important to inform all employees, particularly those who will be contacted for preliminary data gathering. Although it is not necessary to acquaint them with the actual reasons for the study (since this might bias responses), knowing that the research is intended to help them in their work environment will encourage their cooperation. The element of unpleasant surprise will thus be eliminated for the employees. It is also necessary to assure them that their responses will be kept confidential by the researcher/s and that individual responses will not be divulged to anyone in the organisation. These two steps will make the employees comfortable with the research project and ensure their cooperation. Attempts to obtain information through deceptive means should be avoided at all costs, because this approach engenders distrust and anxiety within the system. In essence, employers have the right to gather information relating to work, and employees have the right to privacy and confidentiality, but respondent cooperation assures good information.

## SUMMARY

In this chapter we have examined the first three steps of the research process — awareness of the research issue, preliminary information gathering and literature searches, and the research problem definition. As the organisation becomes aware of a problem or opportunity, a decision is made on whether the problem or opportunity is worth further investigation. If the decision is in the affirmative, then the preliminary data gathering commences. This initial investigation gathers information on the organisation (such as structural factors, managerial philosophy, perceptions and attitudes), examines the organisational information systems, and then may expand the information gathering by accessing knowledge bases on the Internet and using a literature search. From this preliminary data gathering, a research problem definition is identified. This problem definition is then used for the next step in the research process — the framework development.

## DISCUSSION POINTS

1 How would you describe the research process?

2 Explain the preliminary data-collection methods.

3 Why is it important to gather information on the background of the organisation?

4 Should a researcher *always* obtain information on the structural aspects and job characteristics from those interviewed? Give reasons for your answer with examples.

5 How would you go about doing a literature survey in the area of business ethics?

6 What is the purpose of a literature survey?

7 Why is appropriate citation important? What are the consequences of not giving credit to the source from which materials are extracted?

8 'The problem definition stage is perhaps more critical in the research process than the problem solution stage.' Discuss this statement.

9 Why should one get hung up on problem definition if one already knows the broad problem area to be studied?

10 Access the on-line system in your library and (a) generate a list of the references that relate to the performance of Telstra or Telecom NZ, and (b) obtain the abstracts of these studies.

11 Access the on-line system and obtain a list of references that deal with product image.

12 Offer a clearly focused problem statement in the broad area of corporate culture.

13 After studying and extracting information from all the relevant work carried out previously, how does the researcher know which particular references, articles and information should be given prominence in the literature survey?

14 Given the following situation, (a) identify the broad problem area; (b) define the problem; and (c) explain how you would proceed further.

---

**Problem at Pioneer**

Pioneer's minivans and pickups take a big share of the truck market in India, while its cars lag behind those of its competitors — Maruti, Premier Automobiles and Hindustan Motors. Quality problems include such things as water leaks and faulty headlights.

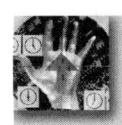

---

## PRACTICE PROJECTS

1 Do the project assigned below, following the step-by-step process delineated.
   (a) Compile a bibliography on any one of the following topics, or any other topic of interest to you, from a business perspective: (i) child care; (ii) product development; (iii) open-market operations; (iv) information systems; (v) manufacturing technology; (vi) assessment centres; (vii) transfer pricing.
   (b) From this bibliography, select 15 references that include books, periodicals and newspaper items.
   (c) Based on these 15 articles, write a literature review using different forms of citation as described in the appendix.
   (d) Formulate a problem statement.

2 Visit the following websites and complete the exercises below.
   (a) IBM          http://www.ibm.com
       FORD         http://www.ford.com
       What similarities and differences do you notice?
   (b) Intel        http://www.intel.com
       Microsoft    http://www.microsoft.com
       Apple        http://www.apple.com
       Write a paragraph on each of these companies.

# APPENDIX

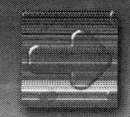

## SECTION 1: SOME USEFUL DATABASES FOR BUSINESS RESEARCH

Databases contain raw data stored on disks or CD-ROMs. Computerised databases deal with statistical data, financial data, text and so on. Computer network links allow access to these databases, which are updated on a regular basis. Most university libraries have computerised databases pertaining to business information which can be readily accessed.

On-line servers such as America Online, CompuServe, BigPond, Ozemail and Microsoft Network provide, among other things, facilities for electronic mail, discussion forums, real-time chat, business and advertising opportunities, share quotes, on-line newspapers and access to many databases. Some databases useful for business research are listed below.

**ABI/INFORM Global** and **ABI/INFORM** provide the capability to search most major business, management, trade and industry, and scholarly journals from 1971 onwards. The information search can be made by keying in the name of the author, periodical title, article or company name. Full texts from the journals and business periodicals are also available on CD-ROMs and electronic services.

**ABIX** contains more than one million citations to business, financial and economic news items on companies and industries covered in the Australian financial press.

**ABS Time Series Service** contains time series data from many Australian Bureau of Statistics publications and the Reserve Bank of Australia Bulletin Statistics.

**AIM Management and Training Database** (AIMMAT) contains citations relating to management and training since 1991.

**Anbar Management Intelligence Library** includes a comprehensive coverage of 450 journals in management.

**Asian Business** provides 75 Asian business periodical titles in full text.

**Australian Accounting and Taxation Database** (AATD) contains more than 12 000 citations to articles appearing in Australian journals, conference papers and academic publications covering accounting and taxation.

**Australian Business Research (ABR) Stock Data** provides information about Australian publicly listed companies.

**Australian Industrial Relations Database** (IREL) contains 11 250 citations, with abstracts, to industrial relations news and information.

**Australian Public Affairs Information Services** (APAIS) indexes current journals and newspapers in Australia and overseas for material on Australia's political, economic, legal, social and cultural affairs.

**Australian Tourism Index** contains bibliographical details of Australian material in the areas of tourism and travel.

**Australian Vocational Education Database** (VOCED) contains internationally relevant information on vocational and adult education and training, acquired from various Australian and New Zealand clearing houses.

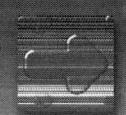

**Bibliographical Index** is an index that lists, by subject, sources of bibliographies.

**Business Books in Print** indexes by author, title and business subject the books in print in the areas of finance, business and economics.

**Business Investment Service** analyses production in basic industries and presents stock market trends and indexes, as well as earnings of stocks in selected industries.

**Business Periodicals Index** (BPI) provides an index of more than 3000 business and management periodicals.

**CDATA96** allows the analysis of the 1996 Census data using Mapinfo mapping software.

**CLIB96** contains information from the Australian Census of Population and Housing.

**Dun and Bradstreet Credit Service** collects, analyses and distributes credit information on manufacturers, wholesalers and retailers. It includes information on the enterprise and offers a detailed statement of the methods of operation, financial statement analysis, management progress and payment record.

**ECONLit** provides bibliographical citations, with selected abstracts, to the literature on economics since 1961.

**Education Resources Information** (ERIC) is the main bibliographical and abstract database on educational literature, including adult learning, human resource development and training.

**Index New Zealand** is an index of general New Zealand publications, covering areas such as business, health, education and general social issues — available via Te Puna.

**INFOS** is Statistics New Zealand's database (mainly New Zealand trade related).

**INFOTRAC** has a CD-ROM with expanded academic, business and investment periodicals index covering more than 1000 periodicals in social sciences and business, updated monthly.

**Human Resources Abstract** is a quarterly abstracting service that covers human, social, HR planning and organisational behaviour.

**New Zealand Business Who's Who** is a general directory of businesses in New Zealand.

**New Zealand Company Register** has general information on New Zealand–listed companies.

**NewzIndex** is an index of 55 New Zealand business and trade-related publications (magazines, newspapers and trade journals) which cover the economy, government, social policy, health, education, companies and international trade.

**Newztext-INL** is a searchable archive of the full text of most INL newspapers, from 1995.

**Newztext-Mags** is a searchable archive of the full text of several New Zealand magazines and weekly newspapers.

**Psychological Abstracts** summarises the literature in psychology, covering several hundred journals, reports, monographs and other scientific documents.

**Public Affairs Information Service** (PAIS) indexes books, periodicals, business articles and government documents in business.

**Supermap** contains New Zealand census data on CD-ROM, which can be mapped according to selected variables.

**Te Puna** is a database of the National Library of New Zealand which includes records of both international and New Zealand publications.

**Topicator** is a classified guide to articles in advertising, communications and marketing periodicals.

**Work Related Abstracts** contains abstracts of articles, dissertations and books relating to labour, personnel and organisational behaviour.

## NEWSPAPER INDEXES OF CURRENT EVENTS

**Electric Library** covers 235 international newspapers and nearly 100 newspapers and magazines from Australia and New Zealand.

**New York Times Index**, published every two weeks, summarises and classifies news alphabetically by subject, persons and organisations.

**Wall Street Journal Index**, published monthly, gives a complete report on current business. Grouped under 'Corporate News' and 'General News', the subject index of all articles that appeared in the *Journal* is also given.

## OTHER DATABASES

The following databases can also be accessed through the Internet:
- Business and Industry Database*
- Guide to Dissertation Abstracts
- Guide to Newspaper Abstracts
- Conference Papers
- Conference Proceedings
- Operations Research/Management Science
- Periodicals Abstracts
- Personnel Management Abstract
- Social Science Citation Index
- Conference Board Cumulative Index (covers publications in business, finance, personnel, marketing and international operations)

\* Includes information on whether the company is private or public, description of business, company organisation and management, product lines and brand names, financial information, share prices and dividends, foreign operations, marketing and advertising, sales, R & D, and articles available on the company in newspapers and periodicals.

*Note:* A cumulated annotated index to articles on accounting and in business periodicals arranged by subject and by author is also available. The Lexis-Nexis Universe provides specific company and industry information including company reports, share information, industry trends and the like.

# ON THE WORLD WIDE WEB

Some of the many websites useful for business research which can be accessed through a **browser** such as Netscape Navigator or Internet Explorer are provided below.

**Academy of Management** aom@academy.pace.edu

**Access New Zealand** http://www.accessnz.co.nz
General Internet searching on New Zealand topics.

**American Society of Training and Development** http://www.astd.org

**AT&T Business Network** http://www.bnet.att.com
Good business resources and the latest business news and information.

**Australian Bureau of Statistics** http://www.abs.gov.au/websitedbs
Statistics on key national indicators (such as consumer price index, unemployment and building approvals), the census of population and housing and more than 160 tables, providing a broad statistical picture of Australia's economic and social environment.

**Australian Department of Finance and Administration**
http://www.dofa.gov.au/index.html
Full-text publications relating to Australian public sector finance and accounting, federal government operations, and public sector reform and management.

**Australian Financial Review** http://www.afr.com.au
A three-week archive of articles from the website of the *Australian Financial Review* and a three-month archive of Fairfax Publications.

**Australian Human Resources Institute** http://www.ahri.com.au
Information on curent events, courses, journals and directories concerning the human resource industry.

**Australian Journal of Management** http://www.agsm.unsw.edu.au/~eajm
Research in the fields of applied economics, finance, industrial relations, psychology and political science as applied to management.

**Australian National Audit Office** http://www.anoa.gov.au
Guides, speeches, reports and some full-text publications on Australian public sector performance, management, financial management, reforms and initiatives.

**Australian Securities and Investments Commission** http://www.asic.gov.au
Information for companies, small business, investors and consumers, and financial service providers, and procedures for the Companies and Securities Advisory Commission.

**Australian Stock Exchange** http://www.asx.com.au
Share prices, guides for investors, broker referral system, companies listed and market news.

**Australian Tourist Commission** http://www.atc.net.au/index.htm
Australian tourism statistics, market intelligence reports, current news and marketing opportunities.

**Dow Jones Business Directory** http://www.Businessdirectory.dowjones.com

**Harvard Business School Publishing** http://www.hbsp.harvard.edu

**Human Resource Management on the Internet** http://www.members.gnn.com/hrm-basics/hrinet.htm

**Human Rights and Equal Opportunity Commission** http://www.hreoc.gov.au
The Commission's functions, powers and legislation, and information on freedom of information legislation

**Index of Business Topics** http://www1.usa1.com/~ibnet/iccindex.html
A vast range of subjects for companies engaged in international trade.

**International Labour Organization** http://www.ilo.org

**International Monetary Fund** http://www.imf.org

**National Occupational Health and Safety Commission** http://www.worksafe.gov.au
News items, information about the organisation and a number of searchable databases, such as full-text NOHSC publications, research grants, designated hazardous substances, and Australia and New Zealand bibliographic OHS resources.

**New Zealand Government Online** http://www.govt.nz
Overview of New Zealand Government, access to government services information, central and local government agency contacts.

**New Zealand Institute of Economic Research** http://www.nzier.org.nz
Economic data and commentary.

**New Zealand Stock Exchange** http://www.nzse.co.nz
Information on the New Zealand Stock Exchange, with links to other exchanges.

**New Zealand Trade Development Board** http://www.tradenz.govt.nz
Information for marketers and exporters, including country profiles.

**Organisation for Economic Co-operation and Development** http://www.oecd.org

**OSIRIIS** http://indrel.agps.gov.au
Full text of Australian federal awards, agreements, decisions, variations and decision summaries of the Australian Industrial Relations Commission.

**Reserve Bank of Australia** http://www.rba.gov.au
Policy material, financial statistics and banking information on Australia.

**Reserve Bank of New Zealand** http://www.rbnz.govt.nz
Policy material, financial statistics and banking information on New Zealand.

**SearchNZ** http://www.sesarchnz.co.nz
General Internet searching on New Zealand topics

**Statistics New Zealand** http://www.stats.govt.nz
An introduction to the range of print and electronic sources available from Statistics New Zealand — includes the *New Zealand Official Yearbook*.

**Te Puna Web Directory** http://tepuna.natlib.govt.nz/web_directory
Selected New Zealand and Pacific websites, with good access by broad subject area.

For more information on useful websites for business researchers, refer to T. Denison and J. M. Stewart (eds) 1998, *Electronic Sources of Information for Business in Australia and New Zealand*, 3rd edition, University of Otago Press, Dunedin.

## SECTION 2: SEARCH ENGINES

Search engines help you navigate the World Wide Web to locate information. There is a variety of search engines, using different software and accessing different sites. No single search engine covers the entire Web and no two search engines cover all the same websites. You usually need to use several search engines to gain a comprehensive sampling of the material available. Some of the more common general search engines are listed below.

| | |
|---|---|
| AltaVista | One of the biggest search engines. Provides basic and advanced facilities and offers a directory, translation, image finder and shopping services. |
| Beaucoup | Provides hundreds of search services grouped into categories such as topic area subjects. |
| GOeureka | Using AltaVista technology, emphasises Australian websites in the directory services. |
| HotBot | Uses a number of advanced search features with a menu system for easier searching. |
| Northern Light | Uses selected 5000+ quality information sources to overcome the difficulties of information overload. |
| Yahoo | Provides a wide range of search and browse options. |

## SECTION 3: THE BIBLIOGRAPHY AND REFERENCE LIST

A distinction has to be made between a bibliography and references. A *bibliography* is the listing of the work that is relevant to the main topic of research interest arranged in alphabetical order according to the last names of the authors. A *reference list* is a subset of the bibliography which includes details of all the citations used in the literature survey and elsewhere in the paper, again arranged in alphabetical order by the last names of the authors. These citations credit the author and enable the reader to find the works cited. All the citations mentioned in the research report will find a place in the References section at the end of the report.

There are two main styles of referencing — footnoting and author–date. The author–date style predominates in business research. At least two modes of author–date referencing are followed in business research. These are based on the formats provided in the *APA Manual* (1994) and the *Chicago Manual of Style* (1993). *Chicago* follows the traditional Harvard conventions for referencing. Each manual specifies, with examples, how books, journals, newspapers, dissertations and other materials are to be referenced in manuscripts. Since the APA format is followed for referencing by many journals in the management area, we will highlight this system in the examples given below. (The Harvard and APA systems are relatively similar. You will note that this book adopts a variant of the Harvard system that differs only slightly from the style outlined in the following pages.) In section 4, we will discuss how these references will be cited in the literature review section.

# SPECIMEN FORMAT FOR CITING DIFFERENT TYPES OF REFERENCES

## Specimen format for referencing

*Book by a single author*
Leshin, C. B. (1997). *Management on the World Wide Web.* Englewood Cliffs, NJ: Prentice Hall.

*Book by more than one author*
Cornett, M., Wiley, B. J., & Sankar, S. (1998). *The pleasures of nurturing.* London: McMunster Publishing.

*More than one book by the same author in the same year*
Roy, A. (1998a). *Chaos Theory.* New York: McMillan Publishing Enterprises.
Roy, A. (1998b). *Classic Chaos.* San Francisco, CA: Jossey Bamar.

*Edited book*
Pennathur, A., Leong, F. T., & Schuster, K. (Eds) (1998). *Style and substance of thinking.* New York: Publishers Paradise.

*Chapter in an edited book*
Riley, T., & Brecht, M. L. (1998). The success of the mentoring process. In R. Williams (Ed.), *Mentoring and career success* (pp. 120–60). New York: Wilson Press.

*Book review*
Nichols, P. (1998). A new look at Home Services [Review of the book *Providing Home Services to the Elderly* by Girch, S.]. *Family Review Bulletin,* 45, 12–13.

*Journal article*
Jeanquart, S., & Peluchette, J. (1997). Diversity in the workforce and management models. *Journal of Social Work Studies,* 43 (3), 72–85.

*Conference proceedings publication*
Yeshwant, M. (1998). Revised thinking on Indian Philosophy and Religion. In S. Pennathur (Ed.). *Proceedings of the Ninth International Conference on Religion* (pp. 100–107). Madras, India.

*Doctoral dissertation*
Kiren, R. S. (1997). Medical advances and quality of life. Unpublished doctoral dissertation, Omaha State University, USA.

*Paper presentation at conference*
Bajaj, L. S. (1996). Practical tips for efficient work management. Paper presented at the annual meeting of entrepreneurs, San Jose, CA.

*Unpublished manuscript*
Pringle, P. S. (1991). Training and development in the '90s. Unpublished manuscript, Southern Illinois University, Diamondale, IL.

*Newspaper article*
The new GM pact (1998, July 28). *Concord Tribune,* p.1.

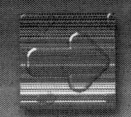

## Referencing electronic sources

### Individual work from the Internet

Author/editor. (year). *Title of document* (edition), [type of medium]. Available: URL [access date].

James, L. N. (1999). *Management for the new millennium — challenges and fables.* [Web document]. Available: http://www.public.access/management/bd-online/part5 [2000, 20 May].

### Journal article from the Internet

Author. (year). Title of article. *Journal Title* [type of medium], *volume* (issue), paging or indicator of length. Available: URL [access date].

Singh, P. L. R. (2001). Developing knowledge capital. *Journal of Organizational Assets* (Web document], *8* (21), 9 pages. Available: http://www.orgassets.edu/knowledge/fremt/821 [2001, 3 February].

### Journal article from commercial supplier

Author. (year). Title of article. *Journal Title* [type of medium], *volume* (issue), paging or indicator of length. Available: Supplier/Database name (database identifier or number, if available)/Item or accession number [access date].

Wysocki, Y. (2000). Economic shifts in rural New Zealand. *Rural management* [CD-ROM], *3* (2), 21–23. Available: NI Retrieval Service/R1999/Monograph21 [January 2001].

## Referencing non-print media

### Film

Maas, J. B. (Producer), & Gluck, D. H. (Director). (1979). *Deeper into hypnosis* (film). Englewood Cliffs, NJ: Prentice Hall.

### Cassette recording

Clark, K. B. (Speaker). (1976). *Problems of freedom and behavior modification* (Cassette Recording No. 7612). Washington, DC: American Psychological Association.

# SECTION 4: REFERENCING AND QUOTATION IN THE BUSINESS ARTICLE OR REPORT

Cite all references in the body of the paper using the author–year method of citation; that is, the surname of the author(s) and the year of publication are given at the appropriate places. Examples of this are as follows:

a. Todd (1998) has shown ...
b. In recent studies of dual-career families (Hunt, 1999; Osborn, 1998) it has been shown ...
c. In 1997, Kyle compared dual-career and dual-career families and found that ...

As can be seen from the above, if the name of the author appears as part of the narrative, as in the case of (a), the year of publication alone needs to be cited in parentheses. In case (b), both the author and the year are cited in parentheses, separated by a comma. If the year and the author are a part of the textual discussion, as in (c) above, the use of parentheses is not warranted.

Note also the following:

1. Within the same paragraph, you need not include the year after the first citation so long as the study cannot be confused with other studies cited in the article. For example:

    Gutek (1985) published her findings in the book titled *Sex and the Workplace*. Gutek indicated ...

2. When a work is authored by *two* individuals, always cite both names every time the reference occurs in the text.

3. When a work has *more than two* authors but fewer than six authors, cite all authors the first time the reference occurs, and subsequently include only the surname of the first author followed by 'et al.', as in the example below.

    Sekaran, Martin, Trafton, and Osborn (1980) found ... (first citation)

    Sekaran et al. (1980) found ... (subsequent citations)

4. When a work is authored by *six or more* individuals, cite only the surname of the first author followed by 'et al.' and the year for the first and subsequent citations. Join the names in a multiple-author citation in running text by the word 'and'. In parenthetical material, in tables and in the reference list, join the names by an ampersand (&). Examples are given below.

    As Tucker and Snell (1989) pointed out ...

    As has been pointed out (Tucker & Snell, 1989), ...

5. When a work has no author, cite in text the first two or three words of the reference list entry. Use quotation marks around the title of the article. For example, while referring to the newspaper article cited earlier, the text might read as follows:

    While examining unions ('With GM pact', 1990) ...

6. When a work's author is designated as 'Anonymous', cite in text the word 'Anonymous' followed by a comma and the date: (Anonymous, 1979). In the reference list, an anonymous work is alphabetised by the word 'Anonymous'.

7. When the same author has several works published in the same year, cite them in the order they occur in the reference list, with the in-press citations coming last. For example:

    Research on the mental health of dual-career family members (Sekaran, 1985a, 1985b, 1985c, 1999, in-press) indicates ...

8. When more than one author must be cited in the text, these should be in alphabetical order by the first author's surname, and the citations should be separated by semicolons, as in the illustration below.

    In the job design literature (Aldag & Brief, 1976; Alderfer, 1972; Beatty, 1982; Jeanquart, 1998), ...

**Personal communcation** through letters, memos, telephone conversations and the like should be cited in the text only and not included in the reference list since these are not retrievable data. In the text, provide the initials as well as the surname of the communicator together with the date, as in the following example.

> L. Peters (personal communication, June 15, 1998) feels ...

In this section we have seen different modes of citation. We will next see how to include quotations from others in the text.

## Quotations in the text

Quotations should be given exactly as they appear in the source. The original wording, punctuation, spelling and italics must be preserved, even if they are erroneous. The citation of the source of a direct quotation should always include the page number(s) as well as the reference.

Use quotation marks for quotations in the text. Use double within the single quotation marks to identify material that was enclosed in quotation marks in the original source. If you want to emphasise certain words in a quotation, underline them for italic treatment and immediately after the underlined words, inset within brackets the words *italics added*. Use three ellipsis points (...) to indicate that you have omitted material from the original source.

If the quotation is of more than 40 words, set it in a free-standing style starting on a new line and indenting the left margin an additional five spaces. Type the entire quotation double spaced on the new margin, indenting the first line of succeeding paragraphs five spaces from the new margin. For example:

> In discussing the importance of knowledge capital in organisations, Delahaye (2000) states:
>
> > Knowledge has now become an equally critical resource. Unfortunately, though, there is no simple exchange equation between money and time, on the one hand, and knowledge, on the other. Knowledge has to be created, learned and maintained ...
> >
> > Knowledge is a complex resource that needs careful management. Knowledge may be held in organisational systems, such as computer systems and manuals of procedures, but it also resides within the minds of individual staff members (p. 374).

If you intend publishing an article in which you have quoted extensively from a copyrighted work, it is important that you seek written permission from the owner of the copyright. Make sure that you also footnote the permission obtained with respect to the quoted material. Failure to do so may result in unpleasant consequences, including legal action taken through copyright protection laws.

# chapter 4

# FRAMEWORK DEVELOPMENT AND RESEARCH OBJECTIVES

## OUTLINE

THE NEED FOR A FRAMEWORK
CONCEPTS AND VARIABLES
CONCEPTS AND THE CONCEPTUAL FRAMEWORK
VARIABLES AND THE THEORETICAL FRAMEWORK
DEVELOPING THE THEORETICAL FRAMEWORK
RESEARCH OBJECTIVES
SUMMARY
DISCUSSION POINTS
PRACTICE PROJECT

## CHAPTER OBJECTIVES

After completing this chapter, you should be able to:
- differentiate between concepts and variables
- trace and establish the links among variables and evolve a theoretical framework
- develop a research question
- develop a set of hypotheses to be tested and state them in the null and the alternate
- apply what you have learned to a research project.

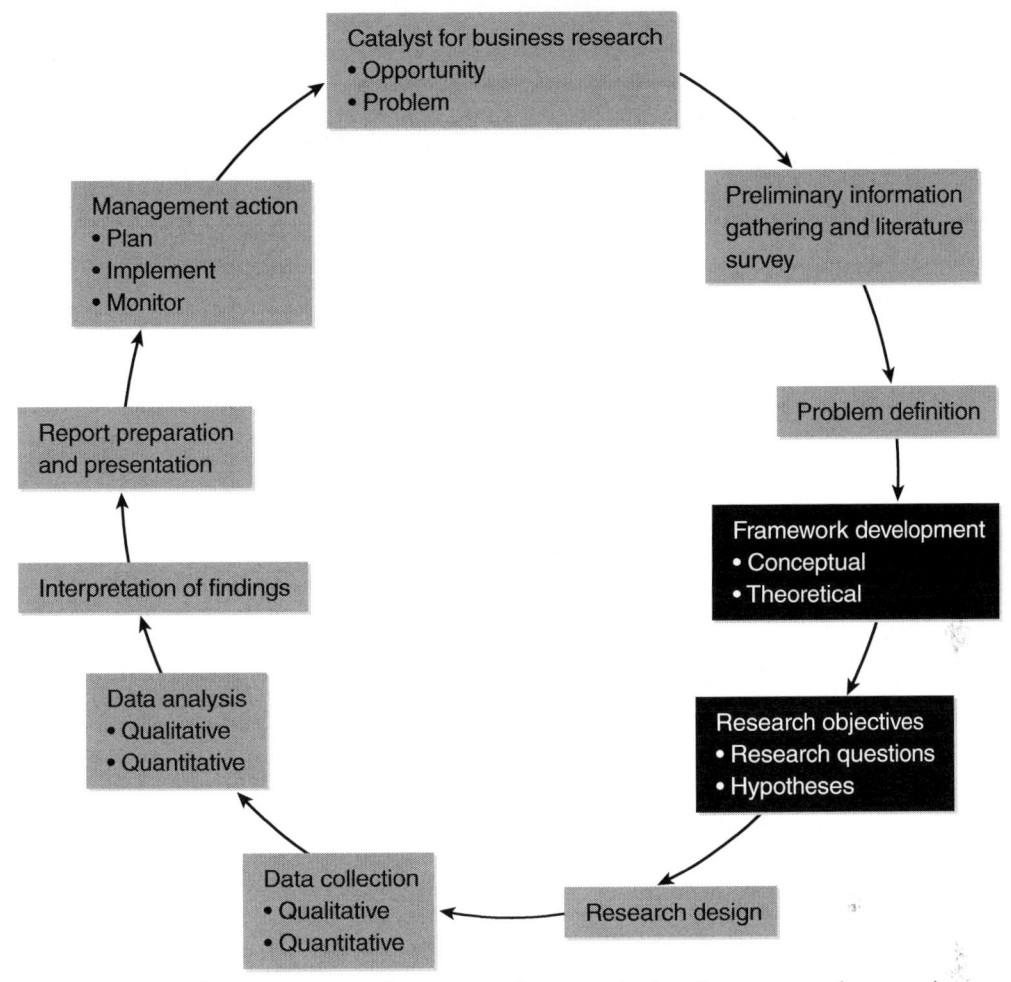

**Figure 4.1** The business research process: framework development and research objectives

The focus in the previous chapter was on learning how to narrow down and clearly define the research problem. We can now examine steps 4 and 5 in the research process model — the shaded portions in figure 4.1. Step 4 relates to developing a conceptual or theoretical framework, and step 5 is concerned with deriving research objectives. In this chapter we will discuss both topics in some depth.

As you work through this chapter, you will be instructed to work out certain exercises. Tackling these exercises at the time you are asked to, before reading further, will help you to become adept at developing frameworks in a logical manner without becoming confused.

## THE NEED FOR A FRAMEWORK

After conducting the preliminary information gathering, completing a literature survey and defining the research problem, you are ready to develop a framework. A framework offers a model of how to make logical sense of the relationships among the several factors that have been identified as important to the problem. These relationships flow logically from the documentation of previous research in the problem area. Integrating your logical beliefs with published research, taking into consideration the boundaries and constraints governing the situation, is pivotal to developing a scientific basis for investigating the research problem. In sum, the framework discusses the interrelationships among the concepts and/or variables that are deemed to be integral to the dynamics of the situation being investigated. Developing such a framework helps us to formulate research questions and, perhaps, postulate or hypothesise and test certain relationships so as to improve our understanding of the dynamics of the situation.

From the framework, then, research objectives can be developed to examine whether the relationships formulated are valid or not. The suggested relationships can thereafter be tested through appropriate analyses. Being able to test and replicate the findings will also further convince you of the rigour of your research. Thus, the framework is the basis on which the entire research rests. Even if testable hypotheses are not necessarily generated (as in some applied research projects), developing a good framework is central to examining the problem under investigation.

The conceptual/theoretical framework is a logically developed, described and elaborated network of associations among concepts or variables deemed relevant to the problem situation, which have been identified through preliminary information gathering and the literature search. Experience and intuition also guide you in developing the framework.

It becomes evident, at this stage, that to find solutions to the research problem being investigated, one should first identify the problem or opportunity and then identify the concepts and/or variables that contribute to it. The importance of the preliminary information gathering and the literature review now becomes clear. After identifying the appropriate concepts and/or variables, the next step is to elaborate the network of associations, if possible. This definition, description and elaboration of the concepts and variables provides the justification for the research objective and the resultant research questions and/or hypotheses.

To summarise, the preliminary information gathering and literature search provide a solid foundation for developing the conceptual/theoretical framework; that is, this preliminary work identifies the concepts and/or variables that may be important. This, in addition to other logical connections that may be conceptualised by the researcher, forms the basis for the framework. The framework, therefore, defines the concepts, explains the theory underlying these concepts, elaborates the relationships among them if possible, and may even describe the nature and the direction of the relationships. It should also be noted that, just as this preliminary work sets the stage for the conceptual/theoretical framework, the framework, in turn, provides the logical base for developing the research objectives.

## CONCEPTS AND VARIABLES

As discussed in chapter 2, a concept is an idea expressed as a symbol or in words while a variable can be observed and measured. Have a look at the following examples.

### EXAMPLE 4.1 ORGANISATIONAL CULTURE

The organisational culture of a firm or business is a multifaceted concept, and providing a clear description can be quite difficult. When referring to organisational culture, some people may refer to a 'feeling' when entering the organisation; others may allude to the stories told about the organisation or to the rituals followed within the organisation; yet other people may mention the organisational hierarchy. All these factors have some bearing on the concept 'organisational culture'.

> **EXAMPLE 4.2 MOTIVATION**
>
> The levels of motivation to learn among members in a work team may take on varying values ranging from 'very low' to 'very high'. An individual's motivation to learn in different work teams may also take on differing values. But how one *measures* the level of motivation is an entirely different matter. The factor called motivation has to be removed from its level of abstraction and operationalised in such a way that it becomes measurable.

> **EXAMPLE 4.3 EXAM SCORE**
>
> A student's score in exams one, two and three for a particular subject may be different (take on varying values). Equally, the scores of different students for the same exam may differ. In both cases the exam score takes on different values and hence is a variable.

> **EXAMPLE 4.4 ABSENTEEISM**
>
> Today three class members may be absent; tomorrow five students may not show up in class; the day after, there may be no one absent. The value of the absenteeism variable can thus theoretically range from 'none' to 'all'.

In example 4.1 you can see that organisational culture is obscure and difficult to measure; it could be described as a *concept*. However, in example 4.4, absenteeism can be clearly identified and is easy to measure; thus, absenteeism can be described as a *variable*. Similarly, exam score in example 4.3 could be classed as a variable. Motivation, in example 4.2, is more debatable. In many ways, motivation is a concept. However, motivation may be 'operationalised' so that it can be measured in some form (for example, by using a questionnaire such as the Myers Brigg Type Indicator). However, this operationalisation is a researcher's artefact that allows measurement, and many experts would suggest that such operationalisation does not represent the true and rich meaning of the concept 'motivation'. Operationalisation is discussed further in chapter 8.

This basic consideration — whether a concept can be 'converted' to a variable — has a significant bearing on the presentation of the framework. If the researcher decides to remain at the concept level, then a conceptual framework is developed. This is an important consideration because, as we shall see later in the chapter, a conceptual framework allows the researcher to convert the research objective into a research question. On the other hand, if the researcher operationalises the concepts to variables, then a theoretical framework can be formulated. A theoretical framework usually allows a more precise hypothesising of the relationships between the variables, and often even of the strength and direction of the relationships. Further, a theoretical framework allows the researcher to convert the research objective to either a research question or a research hypothesis, and this can allow the use of statistical procedures in the data analysis.

First, let us look at concepts and conceptual frameworks.

# CONCEPTS AND THE CONCEPTUAL FRAMEWORK

When the preliminary investigation reveals concepts that are difficult to operationalise, the researcher will concentrate on defining these issues as clearly as possible in a conceptual framework. These concepts will be described in terms of the descriptions

provided, for example, by the interviewees and also from the writings discovered during the literature search. In presenting the conceptual framework under such conditions, the researcher will be careful to acknowledge that:
- the description of each concept may not be complete
- there may be other concepts that have not yet been discovered.

As the preliminary investigation has identified the concepts, the emphasis of the subsequent research project is often based on a qualitative design, such as interviews, observations and/or focus groups. These qualitative approaches allow the researcher to investigate, and subsequently identify and describe, the concepts in a more distinct form.

**EXAMPLE 4.5**

The Human Resource (HR) manager of a Federal Government department in Queensland had just completed an exit interview. The interviewee, a lawyer, had recently submitted her resignation after working in the department for five years. Her husband also worked in the department, as an information technology programmer. Some of the information that the interviewee provided worried the HR manager. She had indicated that her primary reason for leaving the department was the problems caused by her and her husband both trying to develop their separate careers in the same organisation. The concern had come to a head recently when their two-year-old daughter became ill. Both she and her husband were involved in projects that demanded their attendance at the office — indeed, both had been required to work overtime to meet the deadlines. They had managed to overcome the problem with the help of friends who looked after their daughter, but both parents felt guilty and this was putting a strain on their marriage. The interviewee and her husband had discussed the problem for some considerable time and decided that one of them had to leave the department and find an organisation that was more friendly to family life. The interviewee was not entirely happy about this decision as she felt that her husband's professional career had taken precedence over her own.

After the interview, the HR manager started to wonder how many other married couples worked for the department. On reviewing the staff records, the HR manager was surprised to learn that the figure was nearly 15 per cent of the total staff in the state. Further, this figure represented only those who had volunteered this information for the staff records. The HR manager realised that there were probably many others who either had declined to provide the information or lived in some other type of permanent relationship. The worrying aspect was that these dual-worker couples could be facing similar problems, with subsequent pressures on their work life that could result in a high turnover of these people. Given that the records indicated that a large number of these dual-worker couples were in the professional ranks, and these professionals were often hard to recruit, the issue raised significant potential problems for the department.

The HR manager decided to conduct six interviews with one member of six dual-worker couple partnerships. The results were quite worrying although a little confusing. All of the interviewees reported conflicts between their work commitments and their home lives. However, these conflicts seemed to be more severe for some couples than for others. When reviewing the data from the interviews, the HR manager realised that those who felt the pressures most acutely were those couples who were both members of the professional ranks. The couples who were not members of the professional ranks seemed to be able to avail themselves of leave and more flexible work arrangements. The professional couples seemed to have a very strong need to fulfil their professional obligations, and also seemed to be more concerned about their future careers. The professional couples also spoke of problems of confidentiality of information — one partner having information on something in the organisation that should not be shared with his or her partner.

The HR manager conducted a literature review and found that the problems faced by couples working in the same organisation had been the basis for some initial research.

Writers such as Sekaran (1986) noted that, when organisations dealt only with males from traditional families, they did not have to worry about the family aspects of their employees' lives, but that, in the last decade, the changing composition and values of the work force have made it imperative for organisations to change their structures, policies and processes. Several other issues came to light. Stolz-Loike (1992) and Parker, Peltier and Wolleat (1981) differentiated between dual-career couples — where both partners are highly committed to their careers and view work as essential to their psychological sense of self — and dual-earner couples, where both spouses are working but are not necessarily committed to a long-term developmental progression of occupational pursuits. The literature revealed a range of issues that affect dual-career couples. Bruce and Reed (1991) suggested that HRM policies and practices could be categorised under two headings — recruitment and retention; and ability to balance work and family roles. The HR manager found that the issues raised by various authors could be listed under those two headings.

**Recruitment and retention**
- Relocation poses a unique dilemma for dual-career couples. They are faced with the stark reality that, while a promotion and subsequent change of geographical location may be of benefit to one partner's career, the relocation may have negative consequences for the other's.
- Anti-nepotism policies — originally designed to prevent relatives gaining unfair employment advantages — are a potential barrier to married couples working in the same organisation. While few organisations prevent married couples from working in the same organisation, there is some research evidence of anti-nepotism operating at unofficial levels — for example, no married partners working in the same department or section within the organisation.
- A conflict of interest arises when information from one person can benefit another at the expense of a third party. While exposure to conflicts of interest is not the sole preserve of dual-career couples, their position in the professional ranks of an organisation and their close personal relationship make them particularly vulnerable. Information from one partner could provide the other partner with an advantage over the employer — for example, by providing opportunities for promotion.

**Balancing work and family lives**
- Historically, organisations have viewed child care as a 'women's issue' — an outdated concept in today's society. However, the literature noted child care as one of the most significant issues confronting dual-career couples. Friedman (1986) identifies four ways that organisations can become involved in child care — by providing direct services; by providing informational services (for example locating already existing sources of child care); by providing financial assistance (for example by negotiating discounts at local child-care centres); and by offering alternative work arrangements, such as flexitime and job share arrangements.
- Family leave benefits — such as paternity leave, time off to care for a sick child and personal days to attend to other family business — are a direct means for organisations to provide relief to dual-career couples.
- The rigidity or work schedules and excessive work hours are a common source of stress for dual-career couples. A number of studies indicated that time flexibility is the employees' first choice to improve their ability to balance their work and family responsibilities. Telecommuting — working at home but being in touch with the workplace by various telecommunication technologies — was also seen as a worthy contributor to flexible work practices.

In analysing these initial data, the HR manager first decided to concentrate on dual-career couples, rather than dual-earner couples, and then outlined the following conceptual framework for a research project.

This case study is based on a PhD thesis by Dr J. Pierce (1998).

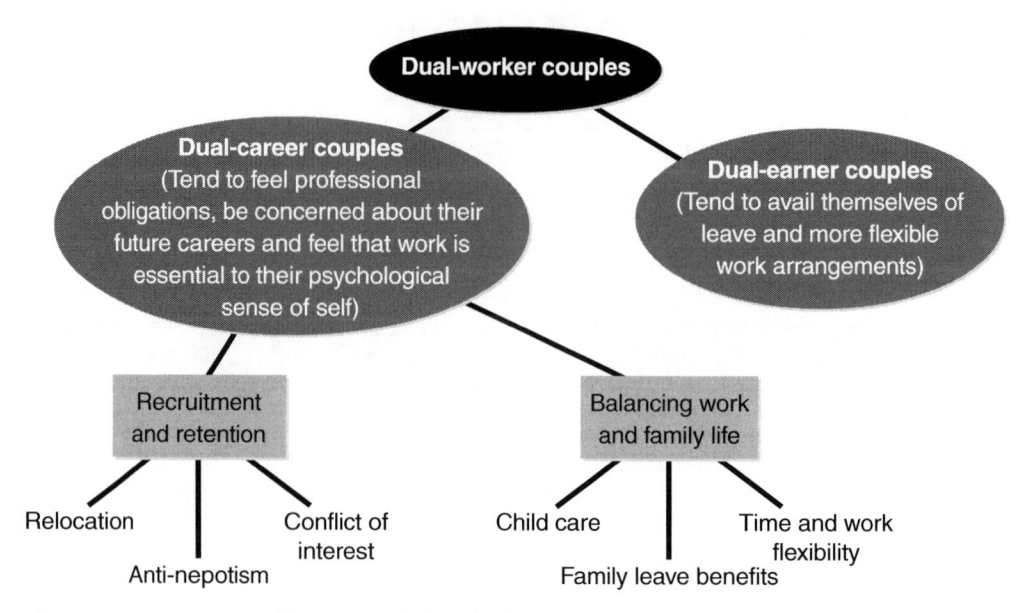

**Figure 4.2** Conceptual framework for dual-career couples

# THE COMPONENTS OF THE CONCEPTUAL FRAMEWORK

Several comments can be made about the conceptual framework outline presented in figure 4.2. First, the outline itself will become a structure for a more detailed initial report to be written by the HR manager. Also, note that there has been a *clear descriptive differentiation* between dual-career couples and dual-earner couples. This differentiation will become important later in the project when selecting subjects to be part of the investigation. In addition, the HR manager has decided to *limit the topic* to the dual-career couple, most probably because professionals are much harder to recruit. Finally, recognise that only concepts have been identified. There is no indication of the relationship between the concepts other than a hierarchy (for example, relocation is a subset of recruitment and retention, which, in turn, is a subset of dual-career couples). In fact, because they can be classed as concepts, the aim of the research project will be to describe and explain these concepts more clearly, to identify any other concepts that have not surfaced so far in the initial data-gathering stage and to identify possible relationships between the concepts.

# VARIABLES AND THE THEORETICAL FRAMEWORK

When the preliminary investigation reveals mainly variables, the researcher will concentrate on trying to confirm these variables and to identify possible relationships among the variables. Because the researcher has been able to identify more detail about the variables in the initial information gathering, the researcher can build a more robust model. As a first stage in outlining a theoretical framework, the researcher categorises the variables.

## TYPES OF VARIABLES

Four main types of variables are discussed in this chapter. These are:
- the dependent variable (also known as the **criterion variable**)
- the independent variable (also known as the **predictor variable**)
- the **moderating variable**
- the **intervening variable**.

Variables can be discrete (e.g. male/female) or continuous (e.g. the age of an individual). Extraneous variables that confound cause and effect relationships are discussed in chapter 12. In this chapter, we will concern ourselves primarily with the four types of variables listed above.

## Dependent variable

The **dependent variable** is the variable of primary interest to the researcher. The researcher's goal is to understand and describe the dependent variable, or to explain its variability or predict it. In other words, it is the main variable that lends itself as a viable factor for investigation. Through analysis of the dependent variable (that is, finding what variables influence it), it is possible to find solutions to the problem. For this purpose, the researcher will be interested in quantifying and measuring the dependent variable, as well as the other variables that influence this variable.

> **EXAMPLE 4.6** A manager is concerned that the sales of a new product introduced after test marketing is not as high as he had expected. The dependent variable here is sales. Because the sales of the product can vary — can be low, medium or high — it is a variable; since sales is the main factor of interest to the manager, it is the dependent variable.

> **EXAMPLE 4.7** A basic researcher is interested in investigating the debt-to-equity ratio of manufacturing companies in Tasmania. Here the dependent variable is the ratio of debt to equity.

> **EXAMPLE 4.8** A Human Resource director is concerned that the employees are not loyal to the organisation and, in fact, switch their loyalties to other institutions. The dependent variable in this case is *organisational loyalty*.

Here again, variance is found in the levels of organisational loyalty among employees. The HR director might want to know what accounts for the variance in the loyalty of organisational members, so that he can control the variance. If he finds that higher pay levels would ensure their loyalty and their retention, he can then offer employees pay rises that would help control the variability in organisational loyalty, and keep them in the organisation.

It is possible to have more than one dependent variable in a study. For example, there is always a tension between quality and volume of output, between low-cost production and customer satisfaction, and so on. In such cases, the manager is interested in knowing what factors influence all the dependent variables of interest and how some of the factors might differ in regard to different dependent variables. These investigations may call for multivariate statistical analyses.

Now respond to exercises 4.1 and 4.2.

**Exercise 4.1** An applied researcher wants to increase the commitment of organisational members in a particular bank.
*What would be the dependent variable in this case?*

**Exercise 4.2** A marketing manager wonders why the recent advertising strategy does not work.
*What would be the dependent variable here?*

## Independent variable

An **independent variable** is one that influences the dependent variable in either a positive or a negative way; that is, when the independent variable is present, the dependent variable is also present, and with each unit of increase in the independent variable, there is an increase or decrease in the dependent variable also. In other words, the variance in the dependent variable is accounted for by the independent variable. To establish causal relationships, the independent variable is manipulated, as described in chapter 12.

---

**EXAMPLE 4.9**

Research studies indicate that successful new product development has an influence on the share market price of the company. Here the development of a successful new product influences the share market price and explains the variance in it; that is, the more successful the new product turns out to be, the higher will be the share market price of that firm. Therefore, the *success of the new product* is the independent variable, and *share market price* is the dependent variable. The degree of perceived success of the new product will explain the variance in the share market price of the company. This relationship and the labelling of the variables are illustrated in figure 4.3.

New product success (Independent variable) → Share market price (Dependent variable)

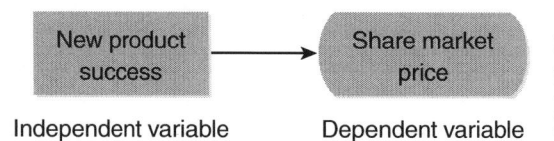

**Figure 4.3** The relationship between the independent variable (new product success) and the dependent variable (share market price)

---

**EXAMPLE 4.10**

Cross-cultural research indicates that managerial values govern the power distance between superiors and subordinates. Here, power distance (that is, egalitarian interactions between the boss and the employee versus the high-power superior in limited interaction with the low-power subordinate) is the subject of interest and hence the *dependent variable*. Managerial values, which explain the variance in power distance, are the *independent variable*. This relationship is illustrated in figure 4.4.

Managerial values (Independent variable) → Power distance (Dependent variable)

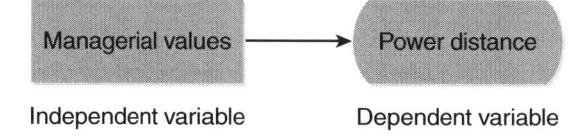

**Figure 4.4** The relationship between the independent variable (managerial values) and the dependent variable (power distance)

---

Now do exercises 4.3 and 4.4.
*List the variables in these exercises individually, and label them as dependent or independent, explaining why they are so labelled. Illustrate the relationships diagrammatically.*

Exercise 4.3   A manager believes that good supervision and training would increase the production level of the workers.

Exercise 4.4   A consultant is of the opinion that much benefit would accrue from buying and selling at the appropriate times in a financial environment in which the shares are volatile.

## Moderating variable

A moderating variable is one that has a strong *contingent* effect on the independent variable–dependent variable relationship. That is, the presence of a third variable (the moderating variable) modifies the original relationship between the independent and the dependent variables in that the relationship holds true for some categories of the sample but not for other categories. This will become clear through the following examples.

**EXAMPLE 4.11**

Number of books → Reading abilities

Independent variable     Dependent variable

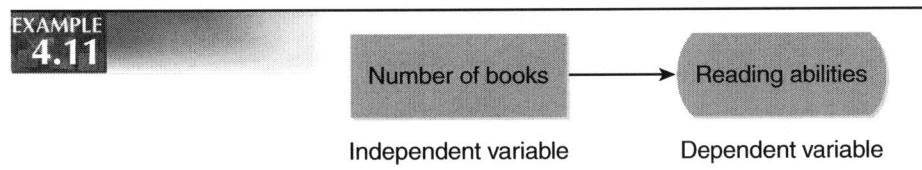

**Figure 4.5A** The relationship between the independent variable (number of books) and the dependent variable (reading abilities)

A relationship has been found between the number of books that five- and six-year-old children have access to at home and their reading abilities. That is, if five- and six-year-olds are provided with a lot of children's books, their reading skills and abilities improve because they have greater opportunities to read more books — an activity in which they are assisted by their parents — and hence read better. As a corollary, if children are raised in homes where there are no books, they are deprived of the opportunities to cultivate the reading habit, and hence their reading skills and abilities will be deficient. Thus, there is a relationship between the independent variable, number of books, and the dependent variable, reading abilities, which is illustrated in figure 4.5A.

Although this relationship can be said to hold true generally for all children, it is nevertheless contingent on the extent of literacy of the parents who enable preschool children to learn to read at home. With totally illiterate parents (one category of parents' literacy), no amount of books in the home will help the child to develop reading skills and abilities, but the presence of totally literate parents (another category of parents' literacy) helps children develop good reading abilities. Thus, *parents' literacy* moderates the relationship between the number of books and reading abilities. To put it differently, the relationship between the number of children's books at home and the reading abilities of five- and six-year-old children is contingent on the literacy of the parents. This influence of parents' literacy on the relationship between the independent and dependent variables is illustrated in figure 4.5B.

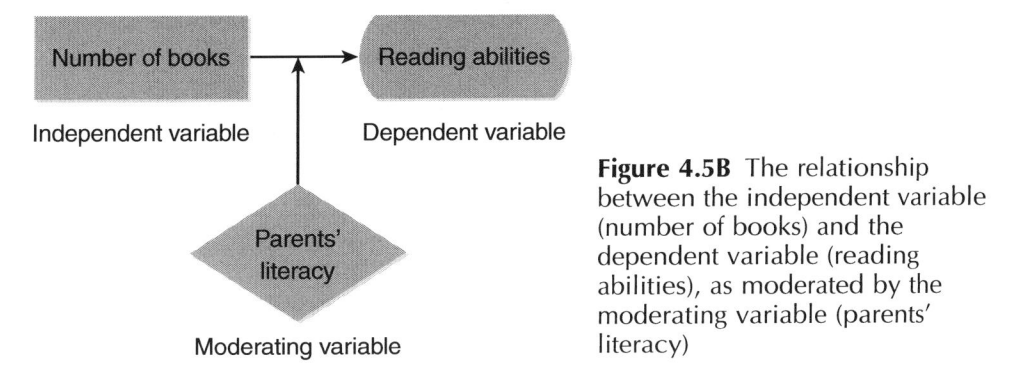

Number of books → Reading abilities
↑
Parents' literacy

Independent variable     Dependent variable

Moderating variable

**Figure 4.5B** The relationship between the independent variable (number of books) and the dependent variable (reading abilities), as moderated by the moderating variable (parents' literacy)

As in the preceding case, whenever the relationship between the independent variable and the dependent variable becomes contingent or dependent on another variable, we say that the third variable has a moderating effect on the independent variable–dependent variable relationship. The variable that moderates the relationship is known as the moderating variable.

**EXAMPLE 4.12**

Let us take another example of a moderating variable related to the organisational setting. A prevalent theory is that the diverse work force (comprising people of different ethnic origins and nationalities) contributes more to organisational effectiveness because each group brings its own special expertise and skills to the workplace. This synergy can be captured, however, only if managers know how to harness the special talents of the diverse work group; otherwise they will remain untapped.

In the preceding scenario, organisational effectiveness is the **dependent variable**, which is positively influenced by work force diversity — the independent variable. However, to harness the potential, managers must know how to encourage and coordinate the talents of the various groups to make things work. If not, the synergy will not be captured. In other words, the effective utilisation of different talents, perspectives and eclectic problem-solving capabilities to enhance organisational effectiveness is contingent upon the skill of the managers (categorised as either high or low) in acting as catalysts. This managerial expertise then becomes the moderating variable. These relationships are depicted in figure 4.6.

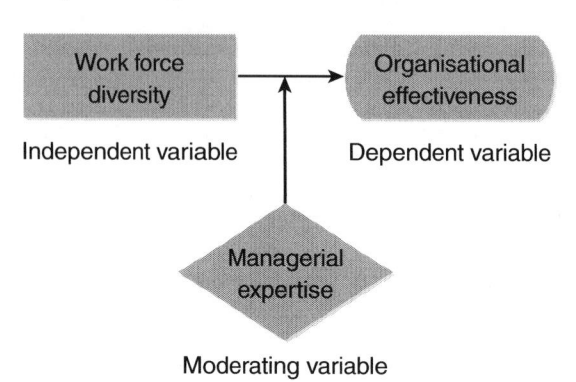

**Figure 4.6** The relationship among three variables: work force diversity, organisational effectiveness and managerial expertise

## The distinction between an independent variable and a moderating variable

At times, deciding when a variable should be treated as an independent variable and when it is a moderating variable can be confusing. Consider the two situations that follow.

### Situation 1

A research study indicates that the better the quality of the training programs in an organisation and the greater the growth needs of the employees (that is, when the need to develop and grow on the job is strong), the greater their willingness to learn new ways of doing things.

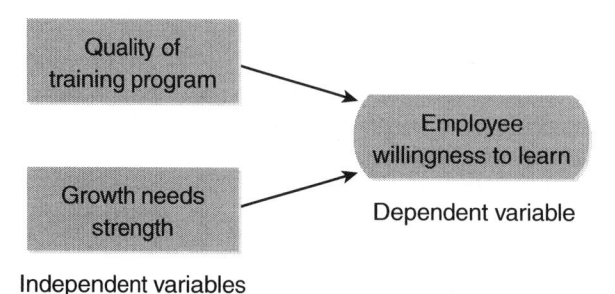

**Figure 4.7** 'Growth needs strength' is considered an independent variable.

APPLIED BUSINESS RESEARCH: QUALITATIVE AND QUANTITATIVE METHODS

*Situation 2*
Another research study indicates that the willingness of employees to learn new ways of doing things is not influenced by the quality of the training programs offered by the organisation for *all* people. Only those who have high growth needs seem to be willing to learn to do new things through specialised training.

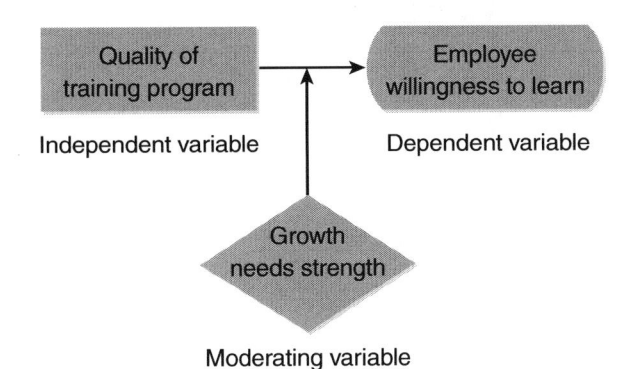

**Figure 4.8** 'Growth needs strength' is considered a moderating variable.

In the preceding two situations, we have the same three variables. In the first case, the training programs and the strength of growth needs are the independent variables that influence employees' willingness to learn — the dependent variable. In the second case, however, the quality of the training program is the independent variable, and although the dependent variable remains the same, growth needs strength becomes a moderating variable. In other words, only those who have high growth needs show a greater willingness to learn to do new things when the quality of the training program is improved. Thus, the relationship between the independent and dependent variables has now become contingent on the existence of a moderator.

Figure 4.8 makes it clear that even though the variables used may be the same, the decision whether to label them dependent, independent or moderating depends on how they affect one another. The differences between the effects of the independent and the moderating variables are visually depicted in figures 4.9A and 4.9B.

Note the steep incline of the top line and the relative flatness of the bottom line in figure 4.9B.

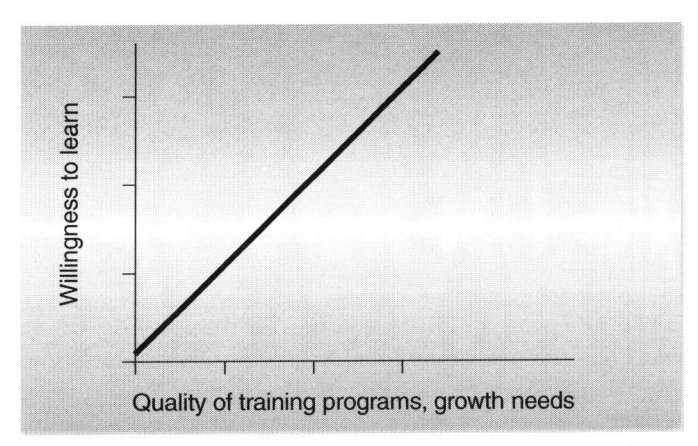

**Figure 4.9A** The influence of independent variables on the dependent variable when no moderating variable operates in the situation

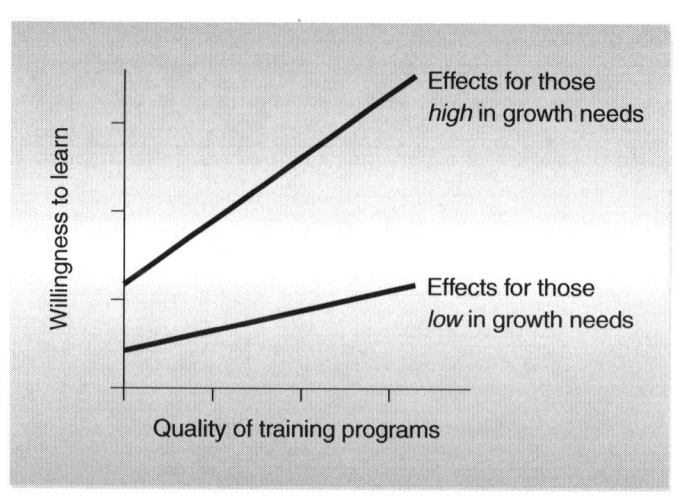

**Figure 4.9B** The influence of independent variables on the dependent variable when a moderating variable is operating in the situation

> Now do exercises 4.5 and 4.6.
> *List and label the variables in these exercises and explain and illustrate in a diagram the relationships among the variables.*
>
> **Exercise 4.5** A manager finds that off-the-job classroom training has a great impact on the productivity of the employees in her department. However, she also observes that employees over 50 years of age do not seem to derive much benefit and do not improve with such training.
>
> **Exercise 4.6** A visitor to a factory observes that the workers in the packing department have to interact with one another to get their jobs done. The more they interact, the more they seem to tend to stay after hours and go to the local pub together for a drink. However, the women packers, even though they interact with the others as much as the men do, do not stay late or visit the pub after work hours.

## Intervening variable

An **intervening variable** is one that surfaces between the time the independent variables operate to influence the dependent variable and its impact on the dependent variable. An intervening variable is both a product of the independent variable and a cause of the dependent variable. There is thus a time dimension to the intervening variable. The intervening variable surfaces as a function of the independent variable(s) operating in any situation, and helps to conceptualise and explain the influence of the independent variable(s) on the dependent variable. Unlike the moderator variable, all categories of the intervening variable affects *all* categories of the dependent variable. The following example illustrates this point.

**EXAMPLE 4.13**

In example 4.12 where the independent variable *work force diversity* influenced the dependent variable *organisational effectiveness*, an intervening variable that surfaces as a function of the diversity in the work force is *creative synergy*. This creative synergy results from a multi-ethnic, multiracial and multinational (that is, diverse) work force interacting and bringing together their multifaceted expertise in problem solving. This helps us to understand how organisational effectiveness can result from having diversity in the work force. Note that creative synergy, the intervening variable, surfaces at time $t_2$, as a function of work force diversity, which was in place at time $t_1$, to bring about organisational effectiveness in time $t_3$. The intervening variable of creative synergy helps us to conceptualise and understand how work force diversity brings about organisational effectiveness. The dynamics of these relationships are illustrated in figure 4.10A.

Time: $t_1$ ⟶ $t_2$ ⟶ $t_3$

| Work force diversity | → | Creative synergy | → | Organisational effectiveness |

Independent variable — Intervening variable — Dependent variable

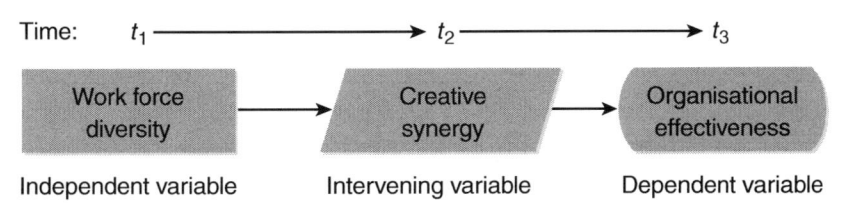

**Figure 4.10A** The relationship among the independent, intervening and dependent variables

**EXAMPLE 4.14**

It would be interesting to see how the inclusion of the moderating variable *managerial expertise* in the previous example would change the model or affect the relationships. The new set of relationships that would emerge in the presence of the *moderator* are depicted in figure 4.10B. As can be seen, managerial expertise moderates the relationship between work force diversity and creative synergy. In other words, creative synergy will not emerge from the multifaceted problem-solving skills of the diverse work force unless the manager is capable of harnessing that synergy by creatively coordinating the different skills. If the manager lacks the expertise to perform this role, then no matter how many different problem-solving skills the diverse work force has, synergy will not occur. Instead of functioning effectively, the organisation might remain static.

Time: $t_1$  $t_2$  $t_3$

Work force diversity → Creative synergy → Organisational effectiveness

Independent variable — Intervening variable — Dependent variable

Managerial expertise

Moderating variable

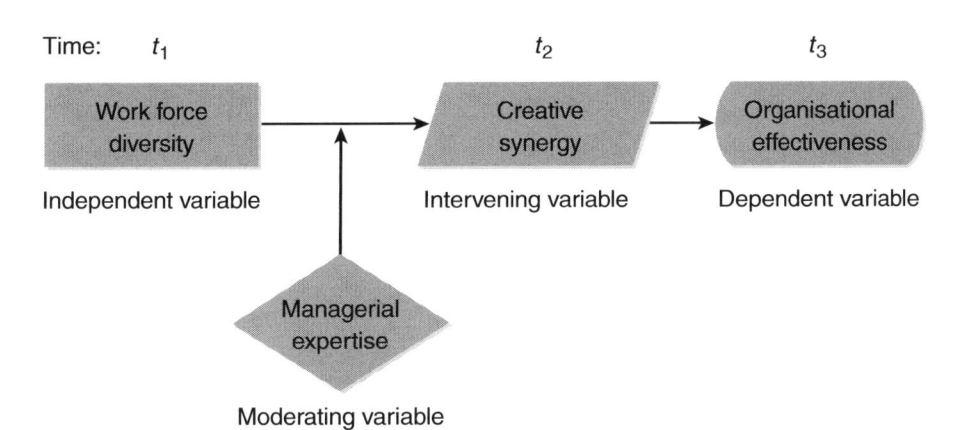

**Figure 4.10B** The relationship among the independent, intervening, moderating and dependent variables

It is now easy to see differences among an independent variable, an intervening variable and a moderating variable. The independent variable helps to *explain* the variance in the dependent variable; the intervening variable surfaces at time $t_2$, as a function of the independent variable, which also helps us to conceptualise the relationship between the independent and dependent variables; and the moderating variable has a *contingent effect* on the relationship between two variables. To put it differently, while the independent variable explains the variance in the dependent variable, the intervening variable does not add to the variance already explained by the independent variable, whereas the moderating variable has an interactive effect with the independent variable in explaining the variance. That is, unless the moderating variable is present, the theorised relationship between the other two variables considered will not hold.

Whether a variable is an independent variable, a dependent variable, an intervening variable or a moderating variable should be determined by a careful reading of the dynamics operating in any given situation. For instance, a variable such as motivation to work could be a dependent variable, an independent variable, an intervening variable or a moderating variable, depending on the theoretical model being advanced.

Now do exercises 4.7, 4.8 and 4.9.

**Exercise 4.7** Make up three different situations in which motivation to work would be, respectively, an independent variable, an intervening variable and a moderating variable.

**Exercise 4.8** List and label the variables in the following situation, explain the relationships among the variables and illustrate these in a diagram.

> Failure to follow accounting principles causes immense confusion, which in turn creates a number of problems for the organisation. Those with vast experience in bookkeeping, however, are able to avert the problems by taking timely corrective action.

**Exercise 4.9** List and label the variables in the following situation. Explain the relationships among the variables and illustrate them in a diagram. What might be the problem statement or problem definition for the situation?

> The manager of Haines Company observes that the morale of employees in his company is low. He thinks that if the working conditions, the pay scales and the holiday benefits of the employees are improved, morale will improve. He doubts, though, that increasing the pay scales is going to raise the morale of all employees. His guess is that those with good side incomes will just not be 'turned on' by higher pay. However, those without side incomes will be happy with increased pay and their morale will improve.

# DEVELOPING THE THEORETICAL FRAMEWORK

Having examined the different kinds of variable that could operate in a situation and how the relationships among these can be established, it is now possible to see how we can develop the theoretical framework for our research.

The theoretical framework is the foundation on which the entire research project is based. It is a logically developed, described and elaborated network of associations among the variables that are deemed relevant to the problem situation and have been identified through such processes as interviews, observations and a literature survey. Experience and intuition also guide in developing the theoretical framework.

It is apparent at this stage that to find solutions to the research problem, one should first identify the problem and then identify the variables that contribute to it. The importance of conducting purposeful interviews and doing a thorough literature review now becomes clear. After identifying the appropriate variables, the next step is to elaborate the network of associations among the variables, so that relevant hypotheses can be developed and subsequently tested. Based on the results of hypotheses testing (which would indicate whether or not the hypotheses have been supported), the extent to which the problem can be solved becomes evident. The theoretical framework is thus an important step in the research process.

In the relationship between the literature survey and the theoretical framework, the literature survey provides a solid foundation for developing the theoretical framework; that is, the literature survey identifies the variables that might be important, as determined by previous research findings. This, in addition to other logical connections that can be conceptualised, forms the basis for the theoretical model. The theoretical framework elaborates the relationships among the variables, explains the theory underlying these relations, and describes the nature and direction of the relationships. Just as the literature survey sets the stage for the theoretical framework, a good theoretical framework, in turn, provides the logical base for developing testable hypotheses.

## THE COMPONENTS OF THE THEORETICAL FRAMEWORK

A good theoretical framework identifies and labels the important variables in the situation that are relevant to the problem defined. It logically describes the interconnections among these variables, if possible. The relationships among the independent variables, the dependent variables and, if applicable, the moderating and intervening variables are elaborated. Should there be any moderating variables, it is important to explain how and what specific relationships they would moderate. An explanation of why they operate as moderators should also be presented. If there are any intervening variables, a discussion on how or why they are treated as intervening variables would be necessary. Any interrelationships among the independent variables themselves, or among the dependent variables themselves (if there are two or more dependent variables), if any, should also be clearly spelled out and adequately explained.

The elaboration of the variables in the theoretical framework thus addresses the issues of why or how we expect certain relationships to exist, and the nature and direction of the relationships among the variables of interest. A schematic diagram of the conceptual model described in the theoretical framework will also help the reader to visualise the theorised relationships.

It may be noted that we have used the terms *theoretical framework* and *model* interchangeably. There are differences of opinion as to what a model actually represents. Some describe models as simulations, whereas others view a model as a representation of relationships between and among variables. We use the term here in the latter sense, as a conceptual scheme connecting variables.

There are five basic features that should be incorporated in any theoretical framework.
1. The variables considered relevant to the study should be clearly identified and labelled in the discussions.
2. The discussions should state how two or more variables are related to one another. This should be done for the important relationships that are theorised to exist among the variables.
3. If the nature and direction of the relationships can be theorised on the basis of the findings from previous research, then there should be an indication in the discussions as to whether the relationships would be positive or negative.
4. There should be a clear explanation of why we would expect these relationships to exist. The arguments could be drawn from the previous research findings.
5. A schematic diagram of the theoretical framework should be given so that the reader can see and easily comprehend the theorised relationships.

Let us illustrate how these five features are incorporated in the following example of Delta Airlines. Note that, in this example, the preliminary information gathering and the literature search provided detailed information on the variables. Thus, the five features can be incorporated.

### EXAMPLE 4.15 — DELTA AIRLINES

With airline deregulation, price wars among the various airlines cut costs in different ways. According to reports, Delta Airlines faced charges of air-safety violations after several near midair collisions and one accident that resulted in 137 deaths in 1987. The four important factors that seem to have influenced these accidents are poor communication among the cockpit crew members themselves, poor coordination between ground staff and cockpit crew, minimal training given to the cockpit crew and a management philosophy that encouraged a decentralised structure. It would be helpful to know if these factors did indeed contribute to the safety violations, and if so, to what extent.

## Theoretical framework for example 4.15

The dependent variable is *safety violation*, which is the variable of primary interest, the variance in which is to be explained by the four independent variables of communication among crew members, communication between ground control and the cockpit crew, training received by the cokpit crew, and decentralisation.

The less the communication among the crew members themselves, the greater the probability of air-safety violations, because very little information is shared among the members. For example, when there are threats to safety, the navigator and the pilot will not communicate with each other in a timely manner. Each member will be doing his or her work and lose sight of the big picture. When ground crew do not give the right information at the right time, mishaps are bound to occur, with aborted flights and collisions. Coordination between ground and cockpit crew is at the very heart of air safety. Thus, the less the coordination between ground control and cockpit crew, the greater the possibility of air-safety violations taking place. Both of the preceding factors are exacerbated by the management philosophy of Delta Airlines, which emphasises decentralisation. This philosophy might have worked before the deregulation of the airlines, when the number of flights was manageable; however, with increased numbers of planes in the air and especially with all airlines operating many more flights after deregulation, centralised coordination and control assume great importance. Thus, the greater the degree of decentralisation, the greater the scope for lower levels of communication both among in-flight staff and between ground staff and cockpit crew, and the greater the scope for air-safety violations. Also, when the cockpit crew are not well trained, they may not have adequate knowledge of safety standards or may be unable to handle emergency situations and avoid collisions. Poor training, therefore, also adds to the probability of increased safety violations. These relationships are illustrated in figure 4.11.

Independent variables → Dependent variable

- Communication among cockpit members
- Communication between ground control and cockpit
- Decentralisation
- Training of cockpit crew

→ Air-safety violations

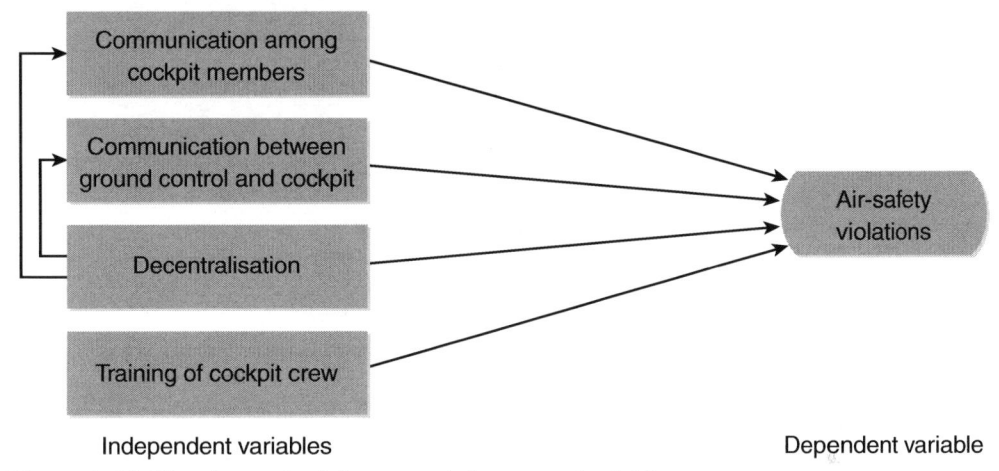

**Figure 4.11** The theoretical framework in example 4.15

Note how the five basic features of the theoretical framework have been incorporated in the example.

The theoretical framework identified and labelled the dependent and independent variables. The relationships among the variables were discussed, establishing that the four independent variables are related to the dependent variable, and that the independent variable, decentralisation, is related to the other two independent variables — namely, communication among the cockpit crew members and between ground control and the cockpit crew. The nature and direction of the relationship of decentralisation to the two independent variables were clearly stated.

For example, it was indicated that the lower the training level of the cockpit crew, the greater the chances of air-safety violations. Thus, as training levels are lowered, the hazard is increased, or conversely, the higher the training levels, the less likely the air-safety violations, indicating a negative relationship between the two variables. Such a negative relationship exists between each of the independent variables (except decentralisation) and the dependent variable. There is also a negative relationship between decentralisation and communication among cockpit members (the more the decentralisation, the less the communication) and between decentralisation and coordination (the more the decentralisation, the less the coordination).

Why these relationships can be expected was explained through several logical statements — for example describing why decentralisation, which worked before deregulation, would not work now. More specifically, it was argued that:
- less communication among cockpit crew would fail to alert the pilot about impending hazards
- poor coordination between ground control and cockpit crew would be detrimental because such coordination is the very essence of safety
- encouragement of decentralisation would only reinforce poorer communication and coordination efforts
- inadequate training of cockpit crew would fail to build survival skills.

The relationships among the variables were schematically illustrated in figure 4.11.

It would now be interesting to see if we can interject an intervening variable into the model. For example, we can say that lack of adequate training makes the pilots *nervous and diffident*, and that this in turn explains why they are not able to handle midair situations confidently. Nervousness and diffidence are related to lack of training and help to explain why inadequate training would result in air-safety hazards. This scenario is depicted in figure 4.12.

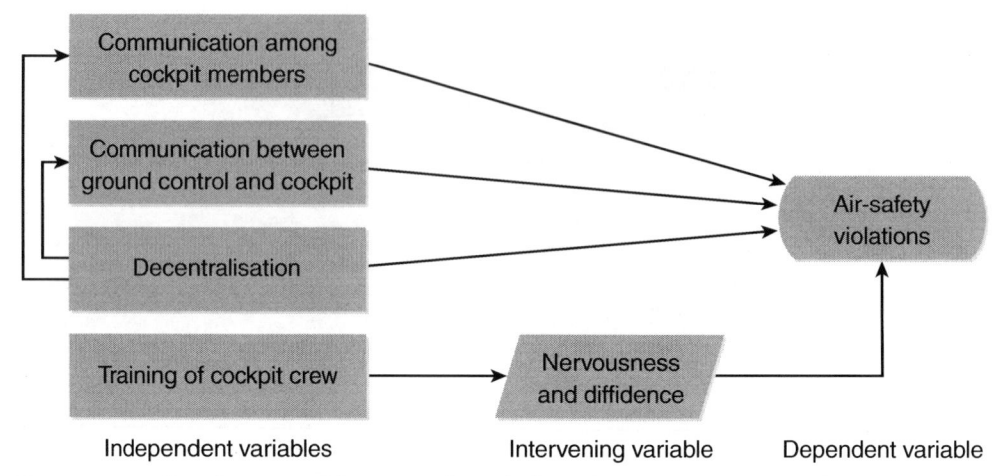

**Figure 4.12** The theoretical framework including the intervening variable

We can also change the model substantially by using (poor) training as a moderating variable, as shown in figure 4.13. Here we are theorising that poor communication, poor coordination and decentralisation are likely to result in air-safety violations only in cases in which the pilot in charge has had inadequate training. In other words, those who have had adequate training in handling hazardous situations through simulated training sessions and so forth would not be handicapped by poor communication and coordination, and in cases where the aircraft is in the charge of well-trained pilots, poor communication and coordination will not result in hazards to safety.

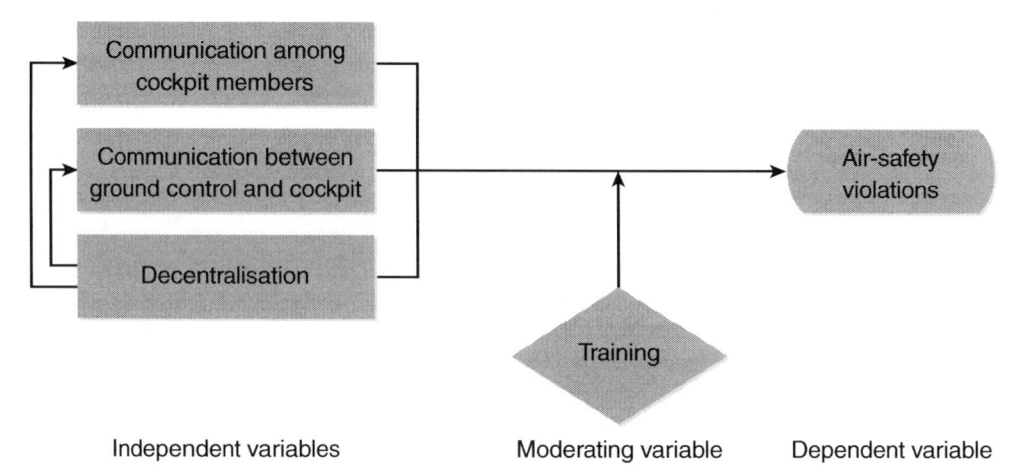

**Figure 4.13** The theoretical framework including a moderating variable

These examples illustrate that the same variable could be an independent, an intervening or a moderating variable, depending on how we conceptualise our theoretical model.

Now do exercises 4.10 and 4.11.

**Exercise 4.10** *Develop a theoretical framework for the following situation after stating what the problem definition of the researcher would be in this case.*

A family counsellor, engaged in counselling married couples who are both professionals, is caught in a dilemma. He realises that the focus of the counselling sessions should be on both family satisfaction and job satisfaction; however, he is not sure how job and family satisfactions can be integrated in the dual-career family. Husbands, the traditional breadwinners, seem to derive more job satisfaction as they get more involved in their jobs and also spend more discretionary time on job-related activities. This, however, does not seem to be true in the case of their wives, who perform the dual role of career person and homemaker. However, both husbands and wives seem to enjoy high levels of family satisfaction when they spend more time together at home and help each other in planning family-oriented activities.

**Exercise 4.11** *Define the problem and develop the theoretical framework for the following situation.*

The probability of cancer victims successfully recovering under treatment was studied by a medical researcher in a hospital. She found three variables to be important for recovery. These were:
- early and correct diagnosis by the doctor
- the nurse's careful follow-up of the doctor's instructions
- peace and quiet.

In a quiet atmosphere, the patient rested well and recovered sooner. Patients who were admitted in advanced stages of cancer did not respond to treatment even though the doctor's diagnosis was performed immediately on arrival, the nurses did their best, and there was plenty of peace and quiet.

This definition, description and elaboration of the variables provides the justification of the research objectives and the resultant research questions and/or hypothesis.

# RESEARCH OBJECTIVES

A conceptual/theoretical framework allows the researcher to explore the concepts in the research project to the fullest extent possible. As indicated earlier, in the preliminary investigation the concepts may differ on the extent to which they can be clearly defined and, therefore, easily measured. If the concepts cannot be clearly defined, then the research effort is more likely to be based on a qualitative research strategy.

# RESEARCH QUESTIONS

Qualitative research strategies include interviews, focus groups and **observational studies**. These strategies are ideally suited to investigating the research topic more deeply. If the answers to the originally identified organisational problem or challenge did not surface in the preliminary information gathering and literature search, the researcher has no recourse but to search for answers from knowledgeable people. These knowledgeable people may be academic experts or people who are affected by the phenomenon under investigation. The assumption is that these people may throw further light on the conundrum by providing insights, examples and information that will allow the researcher to define the variables more clearly and also identify the relationships between the variables.

In qualitative research, the research objectives are formulated as **research questions**. A research question identifies the issues that will be investigated by describing the concepts that will be the focus of the research.

**EXAMPLE 4.16** What are the factors that contribute to the organisational culture in Delta Airlines?

**EXAMPLE 4.17** What issues are of most concern to dual-career couples in retail organisations?

As you can see, research questions allow the researcher to clarify particular concepts that the preliminary information gathering and literature search have indicated would be of specific interest in the research project. Thus, the research objectives limit the researcher to those particular variables.

While research questions are frequently investigated using qualitative research methods, the researcher may at times use a quantitative approach. However, using quantitative methods will necessitate the researcher being able to operationalise the concept in some manner. So in example 4.16 the researchers may use a questionnaire that has been designed to measure organisational culture. The researcher would, however, need to acknowledge that some of the complexities and richness of the concept 'organisational culture' may be lost with this operationalisation.

The following is an example of a literature search that leads to a conceptual framework, which, in turn, leads to appropriate research questions.

**EXAMPLE 4.18 LITERATURE REVIEW, CONCEPTUAL FRAMEWORK AND RESEARCH QUESTIONS FOR QUALITATIVE RESEARCH**

### Introduction
Despite the dramatic increase in the number of managerial women during the current decade, the number of women in top management positions continues to be very small and static, suggesting that women currently experience a glass ceiling effect (Morrison, White & Vura 1998; VanVelsor 1996). Given the projected demographics of the workplace, which forecast that for every six or seven women entering the work force in the future, there will be only about three males joining the labour market, it becomes important to examine the organisational factors that would facilitate the *early* advancement of women to top executive positions. This study is an effort to identify the factors that currently impede women's advancement to the top in organisations.

### A brief literature survey
It is often declared that since women have only relatively recently embarked on careers and entered the managerial ranks, it will take more time for them to rise to top executive

positions. However, many women in higher middle management positions feel that there are at least two major stumbling blocks to their advancement: gender-role stereotypes and inadequate access to critical information (Crosby 1985; Daniel 1990; Welch 1997).

Gender stereotypes, or sex-role stereotypes as they are also known, are societal beliefs that men are better suited to taking on leadership roles and positions of authority and power, whereas women are more suited to taking on nurturing and helping roles (Eagly 1989; Kahn & Crosby 1985; Smith 1997). These beliefs influence the positions assigned to organisational members. Whereas capable men are given line positions and developed to take on higher responsibilities and executive roles in the course of time, many capable women are assigned to staff positions and dead-end jobs. With little exposure to management of budgets and few opportunities for significant decision making, women are seldom groomed for top-level positions.

Women are also excluded from the 'old boys' network'. Information exchange, development of career strategies, clues regarding access to resources and other important information vital to upward mobility are thus lost to women (*The Chronicle* 1998). While many other factors impinge on women's upward mobility, these two factors, sex-role stereotypes and exclusion from critical information, are particularly detrimental to women's advancement to senior positions.

**Conceptual framework**

The literature search confirms that two factors — sex-role stereotyping and access to critical information — can have adverse effects on women's employment in organisations, including career advancement.

Sex-role stereotypes adversely affect women's career prospects. Since women are perceived as ineffective leaders but good nurturers, they are not assigned line positions in their early career but offered staff responsibilities. It is only in line positions that managers make significant decisions, control budgets and interact with top-level executives who have an impact on their careers. These opportunities to learn, grow and develop on the job, and gain visibility in the system, help managers to advance to top-level positions. However, because women in staff positions do not gain these experiences or have the visibility to be identified as key people in the organisation with the potential to be successful top managers, their advancement to top-level positions is rare and they are usually overlooked.

Limited access to critical information — through not participating in the networks in which men informally interact with one another, including on the golf course and in pubs and so on — also bars women from gaining access to key information and resources vital for their advancement. For example, many significant organisational changes and events are discussed informally among men outside the work setting. Women are generally unaware of the most recent developments since they are not part of the informal group that interacts and exchanges information away from the workplace. This is definitely a handicap. For example, knowledge of an impending vacancy for an executive position enables one to strategise in order to secure that position. One can become a key contender by procuring critical information relevant to the position so as to present the appropriate credentials to the right people at the right time, and thus pave the way for success. Thus, access to critical information is important for the progress of all employees, including women. When women do not have the critical information that is shared in informal networks, their chances of advancement to top positions are severely restricted.

Gender-role stereotypes also hinder access to information. If women are not considered to be decision makers and leaders, but are perceived merely as support personnel, they are not apprised of critical information, because this is not seen as relevant for them. When both stereotyping and exclusion from critical information are in operation, women have little chance of reaching the top.

Therefore, gender-role stereotypes and lack of access to critical information can adversely affect women in organisations. There is certainly evidence in the literature that gender-role stereotyping affects women's career prospects. What is the extent of this? Do male managers have better access to critical information and what effect does this have on women in the workplace? How else does gender stereotyping and lack of critical information hinder women?

**Research questions**
1. What are the effects of gender stereotyping in organisations?
2. To what extent do male managers have more access to critical information than female managers at the same rank?
3. To what extent does lack of access to critical information hinder women's employment in the workplace?

---

This discussion on research questions highlights the initial relationship between qualitative and quantitative research. The variables have to be clearly defined before quantitative research can be undertaken and this clear definition is provided by qualitative research. Of course, quantitative research may discover variables that are not clearly understood and the researcher would then return to qualitative research to investigate these variables further — and so the research cycle continues. Once the variables have been clearly defined, the researcher can move towards a quantitative research strategy. Because of this clearer definition, the researcher can be more specific about the research objective. These more specific statements are termed hypotheses.

# HYPOTHESIS DEVELOPMENT

If we have clearly identified the important variables in a situation and established the relationships among them through logical reasoning in the theoretical framework, we are in a position to test whether the relationships that have been theorised do, in fact, hold true. By testing these relationships scientifically through appropriate statistical analyses, we are able to obtain reliable information on what kinds of relationship exist among the variables operating in the problem situation. The results of these tests offer us some clues as to what could be changed in the situation to solve the problem. Formulating such testable statements is called hypothesis development.

## Definition of hypothesis

A hypothesis can be defined as a logically conjectured relationship between two or more variables expressed in the form of a testable statement. Relationships are conjectured on the basis of the network of associations established in the theoretical framework formulated for the research study. By testing the hypothesis and confirming the conjectured relationships, it is expected that solutions can be found to correct the problem encountered.

---

**EXAMPLE 4.19**

Several testable statements or hypotheses can be drawn from the theoretical framework formulated in example 4.15. One of them could be as follows:

*If the pilots are given adequate training to handle midair crowded situations, air-safety violations will be reduced.*

This is a testable statement. By measuring the extent of training given to the various pilots and the number of safety violations committed by them over a period of time, we can statistically examine the relationship between these two variables to see if there is a significant negative correlation between the two. If we do find a significant negative correlation, then the hypothesis is substantiated. That is, giving more training to pilots in handling crowded air space will reduce safety violations. If a significant negative correlation is not found, then the hypothesis would not have been substantiated. By convention in the social sciences, to call a relationship 'statistically significant', it should be possible to find the observed relationship *by chance* only five times out of 100. To put it differently, we should be confident that 95 times out of 100 the observed relationship will hold true.

Note that in the above example, the researcher has a clear definition of the variables and some indications of the relationship between the variables — that is, 'training' is the independent variable and 'air-safety violations' is the dependent variable.

## Statement of hypotheses: propositions or if–then statements

As already stated, a hypothesis is a testable statement of the relationship between variables. A hypothesis can also test whether there are differences between two groups (or among several groups) with respect to any variable or variables. To examine whether or not the conjectured relationships or differences exist, these hypotheses can be put either as propositions or in the form of if–then statements. The two formats can be seen in the following two examples.

**EXAMPLE 4.20** *Employees who are more healthy will take sick leave less frequently.*

**EXAMPLE 4.21** *If employees are more healthy, **then** they will take sick leave less frequently.*

## Directional and non-directional hypotheses

If, in stating the relationship between two variables or comparing two groups, terms such as *positive*, *negative*, *more than* or *less than* are used, then these hypotheses are directional, because the direction of the relationship between the variables (positive/negative) is indicated, as in example 4.22, or the nature of the difference between two groups on a variable (more than/less than) is postulated, as in example 4.23.

**EXAMPLE 4.22** *The greater the stress experienced in the job, the lower the job satisfaction of employees.*

**EXAMPLE 4.23** *Women are more motivated than men.*

On the other hand, **non-directional hypotheses** postulate a relationship or difference, but offer no indication of the direction of these relationships or differences. In other words, although it may be conjectured that there would be a significant relationship between two variables, we may not be able to say whether the relationship would be positive or negative, as in example 4.24. Similarly, even if we can conjecture that there will be differences between two groups on a particular variable, we will not be able to say which group will be more and which less on that variable, as in example 4.25.

**EXAMPLE 4.24** *There is a relationship between age and job satisfaction.*

**EXAMPLE 4.25** *There is a difference between the work ethic values of Australian and New Zealand employees.*

Note that in examples 4.24 and 4.25, while the variables are clearly defined, the relationship between them is less clear. In fact, this non-directional hypothesis is the closest type of hypothesis to a research question. Non-directional hypotheses are formulated either because the relationships or differences have never been previously explored and hence there is no basis for indicating the direction, or because there have been conflicting findings in previous research studies on the variables. In some studies a positive relationship may have been found, while in others a negative relationship may have been traced. Hence, the current researcher may be able to hypothesise only that there would be a significant relationship, but the direction may not be clear. In such cases, the hypothesis could be stated non-directionally. Note that in example 4.24 there is no clue as to whether age and job satisfaction are positively or negatively correlated, and in example 4.25 we do not know whether the work ethic values are stronger in Australians or in New Zealanders. However, in example 4.24 it would have been possible to state that age and job satisfaction are positively correlated, since previous research has indicated such a relationship. Whenever the direction of the relationship is known, it is better to develop **directional hypotheses**, for reasons that will become clear in our discussions in a later chapter.

## Null and alternate hypotheses

The null hypothesis is a proposition that states a definitive, exact relationship between two variables. That is, it states that the population correlation between two variables is equal to zero or that the difference in the means of two groups in the population is equal to zero (or some *definite* number). In general, the null statement is expressed as no (*significant*) relationship between two variables or no (*significant*) difference between two groups, as we will see in the various examples in this chapter. The **alternate hypothesis**, which is the opposite of the null, is a statement expressing a relationship between two variables or indicating differences between groups.

To explain it further, in setting up the null hypothesis, we are stating that there is no difference between what we might find in the population characteristics (that is, the total group we are interested in knowing something about) and the sample we are studying (that is, a limited number representative of the total population or group we have chosen to study). Since we do not know the true state of affairs in the population, all we can do is draw inferences based on what we find in our sample. What we imply through the null hypothesis is that any differences found between two sample groups or any relationship found between two variables based on our sample is simply due to random sampling fluctuations and not due to any 'true' differences between the two population groups (say, men and women), or relationships between two variables (say, sales and profits). The null hypothesis is thus formulated so that it can be tested for possible rejection. If we reject the null hypothesis, then all permissible alternative hypotheses relating to the particular relationship tested could be supported. It is the theory that allows us to have faith in the alternative hypothesis that is generated in the particular research investigation. This is one more reason why the theoretical framework should be grounded in sound, defensible logic to start with. Otherwise, other researchers are likely to refute and postulate other defensible explanations through different alternative hypotheses.

The *null* hypothesis in respect of group differences stated in our example 4.23 would be

$$H_0: \mu_M = \mu_W$$

or

$$H_0: \mu_M - \mu_W = 0$$

where $H_0$ represents the term null hypothesis
$\mu_M$ is the mean motivational level of the men
$\mu_W$ is the mean motivational level of the women.

The *alternate* for the preceding example would statistically be set as follows:

$$H_A: \mu_M < \mu_W$$

which is the same as

$$H_A: \mu_W > \mu_M$$

where $H_A$ represents the term alternate hypothesis and $\mu_M$ and $\mu_W$ are the mean motivation levels of men and women, respectively.

For the non-directional hypothesis of mean group differences in work ethic values in example 4.25, the null hypothesis would be

$$H_0: \mu_{OZ} = \mu_{NZ}$$

or

$$H_0: \mu_{OZ} - \mu_{NZ} = 0$$

where $H_0$, represents the null hypothesis
$\mu_{OZ}$ is the mean work ethic value of Australians
$\mu_{NZ}$ is the mean work ethic value of New Zealanders.

The alternate hypothesis for the preceding example would statistically be set as

$$H_A: \mu_{OZ} \neq \mu_{NZ}$$

where $H_A$ represents the term alternate hypothesis and $\mu_{OZ}$ and $\mu_{NZ}$ are the mean work ethic values of Australians and New Zealanders respectively.

The null hypothesis for the relationship between the two variables in example 4.22 would be:

$H_0$: There is no relationship between stress experienced on the job and the job satisfaction of employees.

This would be statistically expressed by

$$H_0: \rho = 0$$

where $\rho$ represents the correlation between stress and job satisfaction, which in this case is equal to 0 (that is, no correlation).

The alternate hypotheses for the above null, which has been expressed directionally in example 4.22, can be statistically expressed as:

$$H_A: \rho < 0 \text{ (The correlation is negative.)}$$

For example, 4.24, which has been stated non-directionally, while the null hypothesis would be statistically expressed as:

$$H_0: \rho = 0$$

The alternate hypothesis would be expressed as:

$$H_A: \rho \neq 0$$

Having thus formulated the null and alternate hypotheses, the appropriate statistical tests (e.g. $t$-tests, $F$ tests) can then be applied, which would indicate whether or not support has been found for the alternate — that is, that there is a significant difference between groups or that there is a significant relationship between variables as hypothesised.

The steps to be followed in hypothesis testing are listed below.
1. State the null and the alternate hypotheses.
2. Choose the appropriate statistical test depending on whether the data collected are parametric or non-parametric (discussed in a later chapter).

3. Determine the level of significance desired ($p = 0.05$, or more, or less).
4. See if the output results from computer analysis indicate that the significance level is met. If, as in the case of Pearson correlation analysis in Excel software, the significance level is not indicated in the printout, look up the critical values that define the regions of acceptance in the appropriate table (($t, F, X^{c2}$) — see tables at the end of the book). This critical value demarcates the region of rejection from the region of acceptance of the null hypothesis.
5. When the resultant value is larger than the critical value, the null hypothesis is rejected and the alternate accepted. If the calculated value is less than the critical value, the null is accepted and the alternate rejected.

Now do exercises 4.12, 4.13 and 4.14.

**Exercise 4.12**  For the theoretical framework developed for the Haines Company in exercise 4.9, develop five different null hypotheses and the alternate hypothesis for each null.

**Exercise 4.13**  A production manager is concerned about the low output levels of his employees. The articles he has read on job performance frequently mention four variables as important to job performance: skill required for the job, rewards, motivation and satisfaction. Several of the articles also indicate that only if the rewards are valent (attractive) to the recipients will motivation, satisfaction and job performance increase.

Given this situation:
1. Define the problem.
2. Evolve a theoretical framework.
3. Develop at least six hypotheses.

**Exercise 4.14**  Retention of minority women in the workplace is becoming more and more difficult. Not finding an influential mentor in the system who is willing to help them, lacking the informal network with influential colleagues, a lack of role models and a dearth of high visibility projects result in dissatisfaction at work, and the minority women ultimately decide to leave the organisation. Of course, not all minority women quit. Only those who have the wherewithal (for example the resources and the self-confidence) to start their own business leave the organisation.

*For the preceding situation, define the problem, develop a theoretical framework and formulate six hypotheses.*

Before concluding the discussion on hypotheses, it must be reiterated that hypotheses generation and testing can be done through both deduction and induction. In deduction, first the theoretical model is developed, then testable hypotheses are formulated and data collected, and finally the hypotheses are tested. In the inductive process, new hypotheses are formulated based on what is known from the data already collected, which are then tested.

New hypotheses not originally thought of, or previously untested, might be developed after data are collected. Creative insights might compel researchers to test a new hypothesis from existing data, which, if substantiated, would add new knowledge and help theory building. Through the growth in our understanding of the dynamics operating in different situations using the deductive and the inductive processes, we add to the total body of knowledge in the area.

## SUMMARY

In this chapter we discussed the importance of a conceptual/theoretical framework. In a conceptual framework, concepts are identified in the preliminary information gathering. The conceptual framework will concentrate on identifying those concepts and variables that need further investigation and will describe the research questions that the researcher will attempt to answer. These research questions will often be investigated using qualitative research methods, although sometimes more quantitative approaches are used. If a concept can be operationalised, then it is called a variable. Variables can be divided further into dependent, independent, moderating and intervening types. By using these distinctions between variables, a theoretical framework can be constructed. The theoretical framework then forms the basis for the development of hypotheses, which in turn will foreshadow the types of testing that will be conducted. Hypotheses are usually investigated using quantitative research.

## DISCUSSION POINTS

1 'Because a literature survey is a time-consuming exercise, a good, in-depth interview should suffice to develop a theoretical framework.' Discuss this statement.

2 Discuss the differences between a conceptual framework and a theoretical framework.

3 There is an advantage in stating the hypothesis both in the null and in the alternate; it adds clarity to our thinking about what we are testing. Explain.

4 Why is quantitative research used for variables?

5 'It is advantageous to develop a directional hypothesis whenever we are sure of the predicted direction.' How would you justify this statement?

6 For the following case:
   (a) identify the main problem
   (b) develop a theoretical framework
   (c) develop at least four hypotheses.

### Problems at Southern Cross Hospitality

John Campbell, the CEO of Southern Cross Hospitality, was wondering how to differentiate among the three types of facilities offered under the Southern Cross Hospitality flagship so as to attract the right type of clients to each of the facilities. The Southern Cross Deluxe was meant for business travellers, the Southern Cross Express was meant for those looking for the least expensive accommodation, and the Southern Cross Royal was meant to provide high quality services for big spenders. Campbell felt that revenues could be quadrupled if clients only understood the distinctions among the three types of facilities offered.

Keen on developing a viable strategy to eliminate the brand confusion and make clear the distinctions, John Campbell conducted a customer survey of those who had used each type of facility and found the following. Consumers were blissfully unaware of the differences among the three types of facilities. Many complained about how old the buildings were and how poorly the facilities were maintained. The quality of services was also rated as poor. Furthermore, when a rumour spread that one of Campbell's ideas was a name change to differentiate the facilities, franchise owners became angry and the mixed messages they gave to customers had not helped clients to understand the differences.

Campbell thought that he first needed to understand how the different classifications would be important to the several classes of clients, and then he could develop a marketing strategy that would enhance revenues. Simultaneously, he recognised that unless the franchise owners cooperated with him fully in all his plans, mere facelifting and improvement of customer service would not bring in the added revenues he hoped for.

## PRACTICE PROJECT

For your project topic from the previous chapter, do the following:

1. Go through the computer-generated bibliography again.
2. Define a problem statement that, in your opinion, would be most useful for researchers to investigate.
3. Write up a literature review that would seem to offer the greatest potential for developing a good theoretical framework, using about 20 references.
4. Identify the important variables based on this literature review.
5. Develop the theoretical framework incorporating its five basic features as discussed in the chapter.
6. Generate a set of testable hypotheses based on the theoretical framework, stating them both in the null and in the alternate.

# chapter 5

# RESEARCH DESIGN AND PLANNING

## OUTLINE

THE RESEARCH DESIGN
THE PURPOSE OF THE STUDY
TYPE OF INVESTIGATION
PURPOSE OF THE STUDY AND THE RESEARCH METHOD
RESEARCHER INTERFERENCE
STUDY SETTING: CONTRIVED AND NON-CONTRIVED
UNITS OF ANALYSIS: INDIVIDUALS, DYADS, GROUPS, ORGANISATIONS OR CULTURES
TIME HORIZON: CROSS-SECTIONAL VERSUS LONGITUDINAL STUDIES
THE RESEARCH PROPOSAL
MANAGERIAL IMPLICATIONS
SUMMARY
DISCUSSION POINTS

## CHAPTER OBJECTIVES

After completing this chapter, you should be able to:
- understand the different aspects relevant to designing a research study
- identify the scope of any given study and the purposes for which the results will be used
- decide for any given situation the type of investigation needed, the study setting, the extent of researcher interference, the unit of analysis and the time horizon of the study
- identify whether a clarification, a causal or a correlational study would be more appropriate in a given situation
- list and describe the main components of a research proposal.

# THE RESEARCH DESIGN

The research design, which involves a series of rational decision-making choices, is represented in the shaded box in figure 5.1. The various issues involved in the research design, which will be discussed in this chapter, are shown in detail in figure 5.2. As may be seen, issues relating to decisions regarding the purpose for the study (exploratory, descriptive, hypothesis testing or **case study**), where the study will be conducted (that is, the study setting), the extent to which the researcher manipulates and controls the study (the extent of researcher intereference), the temporal aspects of the study (the time horizon) and the level at which the data will be analysed (the **unit of analysis**) are integral to research design. These factors are discussed in this chapter. In addition, decisions have to be made as to the type of sample to be used (sampling design), how the data will be collected (data collection methods), how variables will be measured (measurement), and how the concepts and variables will be analysed (data analysis). These issues are discussed in subsequent chapters.

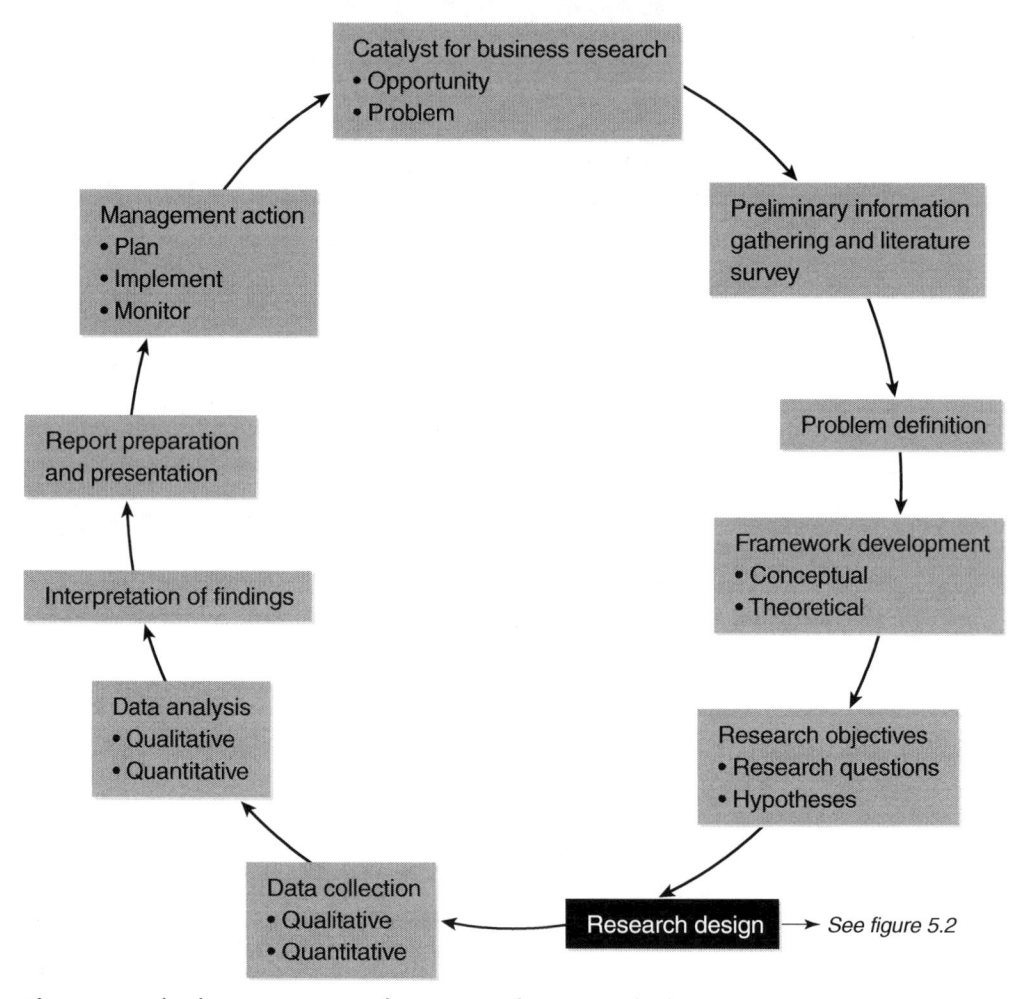

**Figure 5.1** The business research process: the research design

As shown in figure 5.2, each component of the research design offers several critical choice points. The extent of scientific rigour in a research study depends on how clearly the variables can be defined and on how carefully the manager or researcher has chosen the appropriate design alternatives, taking into consideration the specific purpose of the study. For instance, if a critical financial decision to invest millions of dollars in a project is to be based on the results of a research investigation, then careful attention to details is necessary to ensure that the study is carried out with precision and confidence. This implies, as we will see later in the book, that close attention is paid to sampling, measurement, data collection and similar factors. Contrast this with the research goal of generating a profile of managers in an organisation to publish a newsletter, which will not call for elaborate research design decisions.

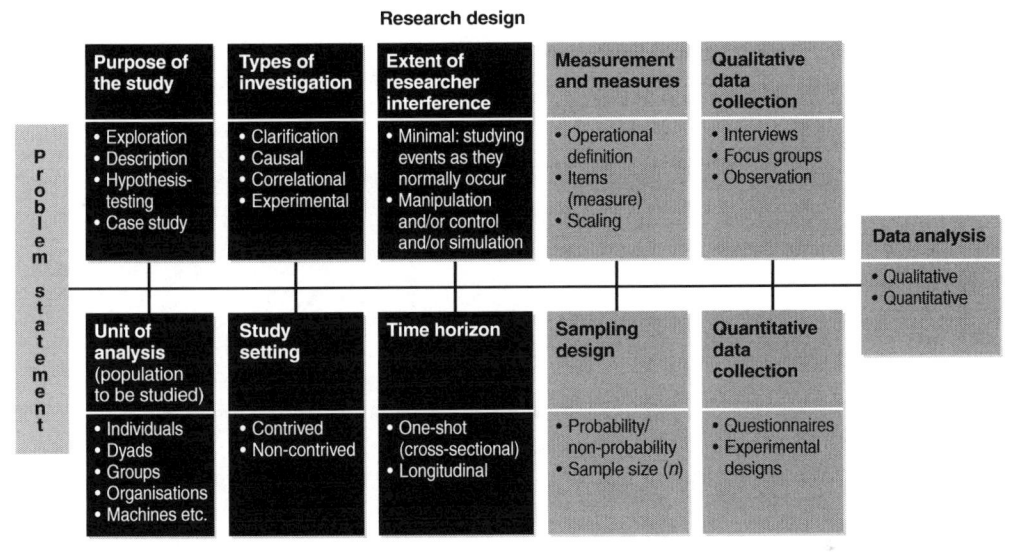

**Figure 5.2** The research design: details of the study

It is important to note that the more sophisticated and rigorous the research design, the greater the time, costs and other resources expended on the study. It is therefore relevant to ask the question at every decision point whether the benefits that result from a more sophisticated design to ensure accuracy, confidence, generalisability and so on are commensurate with the investment of greater resources.

In this chapter we will examine the six basic aspects of research design. Specifically, we will discuss the purpose of the study, the types of investigation, the extent of **researcher interference**, the study setting, the unit of analysis and the time horizon of the study (the shaded parts in figure 5.2). The other aspects of measurement, data-collection methods, sampling design and data analysis will be discussed in subsequent chapters.

# THE PURPOSE OF THE STUDY

Studies can be either exploratory or descriptive in nature, or they can be conducted to test hypotheses. The case study, which is an examination of studies done in other similar organisational situations, is also a method of solving problems, or of understanding phenomena of interest and generating additional knowledge in that area. The nature of the study — whether it is exploratory, descriptive or hypothesis testing — depends on the stage to which knowledge about the research topic has advanced.

The design decisions commence with qualitative assumptions and move to be more quantitative as we proceed from the exploratory stage, at which we attempt to explore new areas of organisational research, to the descriptive stage, at which we try to describe certain characteristics of the phenomenon on which interest centres, to the hypothesis-testing stage, where we examine whether or not the conjectured relationships have been substantiated and an answer to the hypothesis has been obtained. We will now look at each of these stages in some detail.

## EXPLORATORY STUDY

An **exploratory study** is undertaken when little is known about the situation at hand, or when no information is available on how similar problems or research issues have been resolved in the past. In such cases, extensive preliminary work needs to be done to gain familiarity with the phenomena in the situation, and understand what is occurring, before we develop a model and set up a rigorous design for comprehensive investigation.

In essence, exploratory studies are undertaken to better comprehend the nature of the problem that has been the subject of very few studies. Extensive interviews with many people might have to be undertaken to get a handle on the situation and to understand the phenomena. After obtaining a better understanding, more rigorous research can proceed.

Some **qualitative studies** (as opposed to quantitative data gathered, for example, through questionnaires), where data are collected through observation, interviews or focus groups, are exploratory in nature. Conceptual and theoretical frameworks are developed and research objectives formulated for subsequent investigation. For example, Henry Mintzberg interviewed managers to explore the nature of managerial work. Based on the analysis of his interview data, he formulated theories of managerial roles and the nature and types of managerial activities. These theories are now being tested in different settings through both interviews and questionnaire surveys. Case studies, too, are qualitative in nature and are useful in applying solutions to current problems based on past problem-solving experiences. They are also useful in understanding certain phenomena and generating further theories for empirical tesing.

Exploratory studies are important for obtaining a good grasp of the phenomena of interest and for advancing knowledge through good theory building and hypothesis testing. Example 5.1 illustrates a situation in which exploratory research would be necessary.

---

**EXAMPLE 5.1** The manager of a multinational corporation is curious to know if the work ethic values of employees working in its subsidiary in Papua New Guinea are different from those of Australians. Since there is considerable controversy about what work ethic values mean to people in other cultures, the manager's curiosity can only be addressed by an exploratory study, interviewing employees in organisations in Papua New Guinea. Religion, political, economic and social conditions, upbringing and cultural values all play a big part in how people in different parts of the world view work. Because very little is known about work ethic values in Papua New Guinea (or even if it is a viable concept for study in that country), an exploratory study will have to be undertaken.

---

Many topics of interest and concern to managers in the management and organisational behaviour areas have been studied, and information is available in the library on these subject areas. Although few exploratory studies are currently undertaken in the management area, from time to time researchers do explore new grounds with the changing dynamics that occur at the workplace. Not long ago, for instance, exploratory research on the topics of women in management and dual-career families was conducted. Because of subsequent studies, research on these topics has now progressed beyond the exploratory to the hypothesis-testing stage.

The same is true of research on *quality of life*. At one time, exploratory studies were undertaken to understand what the concept *quality of work life* means. After extensive interviews with various groups of people, the concept was considered to encompass such factors as enriched jobs, a healthy work environment, stress-free work relationships, job satisfaction, work role involvement and other work-related factors. Current thinking is that the concept quality of work life is too narrow to be useful for research and that the concept quality of life is more helpful, because work and non-work cannot be viewed as two discretely compartmentalised aspects of an individual's life. Current research now takes both the work and non-work factors (family, community and so on) into consideration when examining quality of life. This advance of knowledge would not have been possible without the initial exploratory studies.

Currently, exploratory studies about organisationally relevant differences in ethnic and country origins are being undertaken so that sound theories about managing a diverse work group can be evolved for the future. Such exploratory studies are necessary since we do not now know if there are differences in communication styles, interpretation schemas, superior–subordinate relationship expectations and the like among the groups. If conflict and stress in the system are to be reduced and productivity is to be maintained and increased in the future, such understanding is essential. The demographics of the workplace are constantly changing, and learning to value differences and adopting new styles of management are important to organisational success.

Exploratory studies can be done by interviewing individuals and through focus groups. For instance, if a company manufacturing cosmetics wants to learn what arouses emotive appeal for the product and induces people to buy cosmetics, several focus groups can be convened to discuss the related issues. This exploratory study will offer the needed preliminary information for a later full-fledged study on the matter. With advances in technology, the Internet and **video-conferencing** facilities offer the advantage of contacting focus groups on line at minimal cost. An analysis of their views would be very useful for a further in-depth study.

It is important to note that carrying out a study for the first time in a particular organisation does not make the research exploratory in nature; only when knowledge is scant and a deeper understanding is required does the study become exploratory — hence the emphasis on qualitative research in exploratory studies.

# DESCRIPTIVE STUDY

A **descriptive study** is undertaken in order to ascertain and be able to describe the characteristics of the variables of interest in a situation. For instance, a study of a class in terms of the percentage of members who are in their senior and junior years, gender composition, age groupings, number of semesters until graduation, and number of business courses taken, can only be considered descriptive in nature. Quite frequently, descriptive studies are undertaken in organisations in order to learn about and describe the characteristics of a group of employees — for example the age, educational level, job status and length of service of indigenous persons,

Caucasians or Asians working in the system. Descriptive studies are also undertaken to gain an understanding of the characteristics of organisations that follow certain common practices. For example, one might want to know and be able to describe the characteristics of the organisations that implement flexible manufacturing systems (FMS) or that have a certain debt-to-equity ratio.

The goal of a descriptive study, therefore, is to offer a profile or to describe relevant aspects of the phenomenon of interest to the researcher from an individual, organisational, industry-oriented or other perspective. In many cases, such information may be vital before even considering certain corrective steps such as changing the organisation's practices. If a study of the firms in the industry indicates that most of them resort to *just-in-time* systems to cut inventory costs, maybe organisation Z should also seriously consider the feasibility of this practice. Or if a descriptive study indicates the need to introduce flexible work hours for parents of children under three years of age, this may have to be seriously considered, and a further, more focused study initiated to decide on the matter.

Descriptive studies that present data in a meaningful form thus help us to:
- understand the characteristics of a group in a given situation
- think systematically about aspects in a given situation
- offer ideas for further research
- make certain simple decisions (such as how many and what types of individual should be transferred from one department to another).

Below are examples of situations warranting a descriptive study.

**EXAMPLE 5.2**

A bank manager wants a profile of the individuals who have loan payments outstanding for six months or more. It should include details such as their average age, earnings, type of occupation and employment status (full-time or part-time). This information might help him to ask for further information or make an immediate decision on the types of individuals to whom he would not extend loans in the future.

**EXAMPLE 5.3**

A CEO is interested in having a description of organisations in her industry that follow the LIFO system. In this case, the report may include the age of the organisations, their locations, their production levels, assets, sales, inventory levels, suppliers and profits. Such information might help to compare the performance levels of specific types of companies later.

**EXAMPLE 5.4**

A marketing manager wants to develop a pricing, sales, distribution and advertising strategy for her product. With this in mind, she asks for information regarding the competitors with respect to the following factors:
- the percentage that have prices higher and lower than the industry norm; a profile of the terms of sale; and the percentage of companies whose prices are controlled regionally as opposed to those controlled from a central headquarters
- the percentage of competitors hiring in-house staff to handle sales and of those that use independent agents
- the percentage of sales groups organised by product line, by accounts and by region
- the types of distribution channels used and the percentage of customers using each
- the percentage of competitors spending more advertising/promotion dollars than the firm and of those spending less; a categorisation of their target audience, and the types of media most frequently used.

Descriptive studies thus become essential in many situations. Whereas qualitative data obtained by interviewing individuals may help an understanding of phenomena at the exploratory stages of a study, a combination of qualitative data and quantitative data in terms of frequencies, or mean and standard deviations, becomes necessary for descriptive studies. A report on a descriptive study of the reaction of organisational members to a proposal to introduce an on-site child-care facility, for instance, might look something like this:

> Whereas 30 per cent of the employees were in favour of the idea, at least 40 per cent felt that an on-site child-care facility was unnecessary. Twenty per cent indicated that it would benefit only those with preschool children and hence would be unfair to the others who had no use for the facility. The remaining 10 per cent suggested the introduction of a cafeteria style of benefits, so that employees could opt for what they preferred.
>
> More women than men were favourably inclined towards the proposal (almost 2:1). Parents with two or more preschool children overwhelmingly desired this; employees who had no such children were opposed to the idea.
>
> Employees over 50 years of age and those below 25 did not seem to favour this scheme. However, women between 25 and 45 (a total of 45 women) seemed to desire it the most.
>
> The mean on the preference scale indicated for the child-care facility by all employees is rather low (1.5 on a five-point scale), but the dispersion is rather high, the standard deviation being 1.98. This indicates that there were some who registered a strong liking for the proposed project, while some were totally against it.
>
> The average preference indicated by women between the ages of 30 and 45 with children is the highest (4.75 on a five-point scale), with very little dispersion (the standard deviation for this group of 42 women was .38). This is the group that desires the on-site facility the most.

Introductory descriptive narratives in some research reports, as you might have noticed, are drawn from government statistical publications such as the Australian Bureau of Statistics and Statistics New Zealand census, from which data are culled for presentation as and when appropriate.

## HYPOTHESIS TESTING

Studies that engage in **hypothesis testing** usually explain the nature of certain relationships, or establish the differences among groups or the independence of two or more factors in a situation. Examples of such studies are given below. Hypothesis testing is undertaken to explain the variance in the dependent variable or to predict organisational outcomes.

**EXAMPLE 5.5**

A marketing manager would like to know if the sales of the company will increase if he doubles the advertising dollars. Here, the manager wants to know the nature of the relationship between advertising and sales that can be established by testing the hypothesis: *If advertising is increased, then sales will also go up.*

**EXAMPLE 5.6**

A university lecturer may be interested in predicting the factors that would significantly account for the variance in students' perceptions of what contributes to a good lecture. After conducting a literature search and some interviews, the lecturer may theorise that four variables — careful preparation on the part of the lecturer, student motivation, appropriate use of visual aids and realistic examples of using theory in the real world — will significantly account for the variance in the students' perception of a good lecture. The researcher is interested in understanding and accounting for the variance in the dependent variable (a good lecture) through hypothesis testing.

**EXAMPLE 5.7** The testing of a hypothesis such as *More men than women are whistle-blowers* establishes the difference between two groups — men and women — in regard to their whistle-blowing behaviours.

**EXAMPLE 5.8** The independence between two variables that are qualitative in nature can also be established through hypothesis testing. Consider the hypothesis *Working the night shift (as opposed to the day shift) is related to whether or not one is married.* A chi-square test of independence will determine the truth of this hypothesis.

As may be seen, in hypothesis testing, the researcher goes beyond merely describing the variables in a situation to determining the relationships among factors of interest.

## CASE STUDIES

When using the case study approach, the researcher systematically gathers in-depth information on a single entity — an individual, a group, an organisation or a community — using a variety of data gathering methods. Case studies can involve contextual analyses of similar situations in other organisations, in which the nature of the problem and the problem definition happen to be the same as the one experienced in the current situation. As in all research investigations, research objectives can be developed in case studies as well.

The case study, as a problem-solving technique, is seldom undertaken in organisations because case studies dealing with problems similar to the one experienced by a particular organisation of a particular size and in a particular type of setting are difficult to find. Moreover, authentic case studies are difficult to find because many companies prefer to guard them as proprietary data. However, by carefully going through documented case studies, the manager is in a position to obtain several clues as to what could be happening in the current situation and how the problem might be solved. Picking the right cases for study, and understanding and correctly translating the dynamics to one's own situation are critical for successful problem solving. It should be noted, though, that application of case study analysis to certain organisational issues is relatively easy. For instance, a study of what contributes to the successful installation of a good MIS system in organisations similar to the one that is planning to install it, and applying that knowledge, would be very beneficial.

## REVIEW OF THE PURPOSE OF THE STUDY

It is not difficult to see that in exploratory studies, the researcher is basically interested in exploring the situational factors so as to understand the characteristics of the phenomena of interest. Also, pilot studies on a small scale, interviewing individuals or gathering information from a limited number of occurrences, are not uncommon in exploratory research.

Descriptive studies are undertaken when the characteristics or phenomena to be tapped in a situation are known to exist, and one wants to be able to describe them more clearly by offering a profile of the factors. Hypothesis testing offers an enhanced understanding of the relationships that exist among variables. Hypothesis testing can also establish cause and effect relationships, as we will see in the next chapter. Case studies are generally qualitative in nature and are sometimes used as a tool in managerial decision making.

Methodological rigour increases as we move from an exploratory study to a hypothesis-testing study, and with this the costs of research also increase. As we will see in later chapters, increases in sample size, multiple methods of data collection and the development of sophisticated measuring instruments add to research costs. Further, as we move from an exploratory study to a hypothesis-testing study, we tend to move from a qualitative to a quantitative design. These designs are based on different assumptions of research methodology and these differences will be explored in later chapters.

## TYPE OF INVESTIGATION

When deciding the type of investigation path to follow, the researcher can consider four approaches — clarification, correlational, causal and experimental.

In a clarification investigation the researcher is trying to gain a clearer understanding of the concepts involved in the research problem. Exploratory and descriptive studies often follow this path. Qualitative methods are often used as this allows the researcher to explore issues in a flexible manner. However, quantitative methods can also be useful as these approaches can sometimes provide a definitive answer.

Once a clear understanding of the concepts is achieved, the researcher's interest usually turns to the relationship between the concepts or variables. When considering the relationships between concepts or variables, the researcher must differentiate between a correlational and a causal relationship. A correlational relationship indicates that at least two concepts or variables move simultaneously. A causal relationship indicates that one concept or variable causes a movement in another concept or variable.

A manager should determine whether a causal or a correlational study is needed to find an answer to the issue at hand. The former type of study is done when it is necessary to establish a definitive cause and effect relationship. However, if the manager simply wants to identify the important factors 'associated with' the problem, then a correlational study is called for. In the former case, the researcher is keen on delineating one or more factors that are undoubtedly *causing* the problem. In other words, the intention of the researcher conducting a causal study is to be able to state that variable *X* causes variable *Y*. So, when variable *X* is removed or altered in some way, problem *Y* is solved. Quite often in organisations, however, it is not just one or more variables that cause a problem. Because at most times there are multiple factors that influence one another and the problem, the researcher might be asked to identify the crucial factors that are *associated* with the problem, rather than establish a cause and effect relationship.

When the researcher wants to delineate the *cause* of one or more problems, then the study is called a **causal study**. When the researcher is interested in delineating the important variables that are *associated* with the problem, it is called a **correlational study**. Attempts are sometimes made to establish cause and effect relationships through certain types of correlational or regression analysis, such as cross-lagged correlations and path analysis (Billings & Wroten 1978; Namboodiri, Carter & Blalock 1975). Whether a study is causal or correlational thus depends on the type of research questions asked and how the problem is defined. The following example will illustrate the difference.

**EXAMPLE 5.9**

A *causal* study question: Does smoking *cause* cancer?
A *correlational* study question: Are smoking and cancer related?
or
Are smoking, drinking and chewing tobacco *associated* with cancer? If so, which of these contributes most to the variance in the dependent variable?

The answer to the first question will help to establish whether people who do not smoke will not develop cancer. The answer to the second question will determine if smoking and cancer are correlated. The third situation recognises that there are perhaps several other factors that influence cancer apart from the three identified, but do these three help to explain a significant amount of the variance in cancer? If they do, then which among the three variables examined is the one that has the greatest association with it, which is the next and which the third? The answer to the correlational study would help determine the extent of cancer risk that people expose themselves to by smoking, drinking and chewing tobacco. The intention here is not to establish a causal connection between one factor and another, but merely to see if some relationship does exist among the variables investigated.

The distinction between causal and correlational studies can be further clarified by the following two examples.

**EXAMPLE 5.10**
The uncertainty over the coming federal elections was instrumental (i.e. causal) in the slowdown in the number of building applications received by local councils in capital cities.

**EXAMPLE 5.11**
The introduction of the Goods and Services Tax, increases in interest rates and uncertainty over the coming election considerably slowed down building applications in capital cities.

Note that example 5.10 indicates a causal relationship between the elections and building applications, whereas example 5.11 indicates that several factors, including the uncertainty over the coming elections *influenced* (not caused) the building applications to slow down. This is a correlational study, the goal of which was not aimed at establishing a cause and effect relationship.

## PURPOSE OF THE STUDY AND THE RESEARCH METHOD

Once conclusions on the purpose of the study and type of investigation have been reached, the researcher can then make a decision on the research method to be used. These research methods — interviews, focus groups, observation, questionnaires, experimental projects — are described in detail in the following chapters.

Selecting an appropriate research method is, of course, at the heart of the research design. An inappropriate research method will not achieve the research objective defined in the theoretical framework. So the researcher must carefully consider the research method options available. While it is difficult to establish hard and fast rules to be followed by the researcher, figure 5.3 provides a basic structure for deciding on an appropriate research method.

Figure 5.3 suggests that, where the conceptual framework indicates there is little information or knowledge of the variables affecting the problem or challenge being investigated, the researcher is more likely to be involved in exploratory research. Accordingly, the research objectives are likely to be framed as research questions and the research methods that are more likely to be appropriate are observation, unstructured interviews and unstructured focus groups. At the other end of the continuum, where the theoretical framework shows an extensive understanding of the variables, the research objective is more likely to be framed as a research hypothesis or even a null hypothesis. Accordingly, the researcher is more likely to be interested in the relationship between the variables and would use hypothesis-testing methods such as field and laboratory experiments and structured questionnaires. At the middle of the continuum, where the theoretical framework demonstrates a reasonable knowledge of the variables, the researcher is more likely to be interested in more detailed information about the variables (for example differentiating between the independent and dependent variables and the intervening and moderating variables) and indicators of possible relationships between the variables. Accordingly, the researcher would be more likely to use structured interviews, focus groups and questionnaires.

Little information or knowledge of situation (or research topic) — Extensive information or knowledge of situation (or research topic)

**Exploratory**
- Observation
- Unstructured interview
- Unstructured focus group

**Descriptive**
- Structured interview
- Structured focus group
- Questionnaire

**Hypothesis testing**
- Structured questionnaire
- Field experiment
- Laboratory experiment

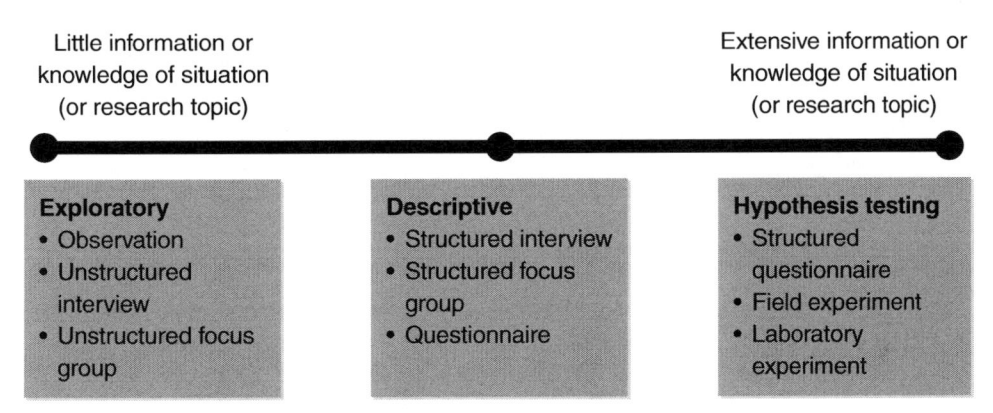

**Figure 5.3** The appropriate research method

# RESEARCHER INTERFERENCE

The extent to which the researcher interferes with the normal flow of work in the workplace has a direct bearing on any research decision. Exploratory and descriptive studies are conducted in the natural environment of the organisation, the researcher usually interfering minimally with the normal flow of work. For example, if a researcher wants to study the factors influencing training effectiveness (a descriptive study), the individual simply has to develop a theoretical framework, collect the relevant data and analyse them to come up with the findings. Although there is some disruption to the normal flow of work as the researcher interviews employees and administers questionnaires in the workplace, the researcher's interference in the system is minimal compared with that in causal studies.

In studies conducted to establish cause and effect relationships, the researcher tries to *manipulate* certain variables so as to study the effects of such **manipulation** on the dependent variable of interest. In other words, the researcher deliberately changes certain variables in the setting and interferes with the events as they normally occur in the organisation. As an example, a researcher might want to study the influence of lighting on worker performance, and hence manipulates the intensity of lighting in the work situation to varying degrees. Here, there is considerable researcher interference with the natural and normal setting. In other cases the researcher might even want to create an altogether new artificial setting where the cause and effect relationships can be studied by manipulating certain variables and tightly controlling others, as in a laboratory. Thus, there could be varying degrees of interference by the researcher in the manipulation and control of variables in the research study, either in the natural setting or in an artificial lab setting.

Here are three examples of research with varying degrees of interference — minimal, moderate and excessive.

**EXAMPLE 5.12**

A hospital administrator wants to examine the relationship between the perceived emotional support in the system and the stresses experienced by the nursing staff. In other words, she wants to do a correlational study.

Here, the administrator/researcher will collect data from the nurses (perhaps through a questionnaire) on how much emotional support they get in the hospital and to what extent they experience stress. (We will learn in a later chapter how to measure these variables.) By correlating the two variables, the answer that is being sought could be found.

In this case, beyond administering a questionnaire to the nurses, the researcher has not interfered with the normal activities in the hospital. In other words, researcher interference has been *minimal*.

**EXAMPLE 5.13**

The same researcher is now no longer content with finding the correlation but wants to establish a firm causal connection. That is, the researcher wants to demonstrate that having emotional support does indeed *cause* the nurses to experience less stress. If this can be established, then the stress experienced by nurses can definitely be reduced by offering them emotional support.

To test the cause and effect relationship, the researcher will measure the stress currently experienced by the nurses in three wards in the hospital, and then deliberately manipulate the extent of emotional support given to the three groups of nurses in the three wards for perhaps a week, and measure the amount of stress at the end of that period. For one group, the researcher will ensure that a number of lab technicians and doctors help and comfort the nurses when they face stressful events — such as when they care for patients suffering severe pain and distress in the ward. Under similar conditions, for a second group of nurses in another ward, the researcher might arrange for only a moderate amount of emotional support, and that given only by the lab technicians. The third ward might operate without any emotional support.

If the experimenter's theory is correct, then the difference in the stress levels before and after the one-week period should be greatest for the nurses in the first ward, moderate for those in the second ward, nil for the nurses in the third ward.

We find that not only does the researcher collect data from nurses on their experienced stress at two different points in time, but has also 'played with' or manipulated the normal course of events by deliberately changing the amount of emotional support received by the nurses in two wards, while leaving things in the third ward unchanged. Here, the researcher has interfered *more than minimally*.

**EXAMPLE 5.14**

The preceding researcher, after conducting the previous experiment, feels that the results may or may not be valid because other external factors might have influenced the stress levels experienced by the nurses. For example, during that particular experimental week, the nurses in one or more wards may not have experienced high stress levels because there were no serious illnesses or deaths in the ward. Hence, the emotional support received might be unrelated to the levels of stress experienced.

The researcher might want to make sure that extraneous factors that might affect the cause and effect relationship are controlled, so she might take three groups of medical students, put them in different rooms and confront them with the same stressful task. For example, she might ask them to describe in the minutest detail the procedures in performing surgery on a patient who has not responded to chemotherapy, and keep bombarding them with more and more questions even as they respond. Although all are exposed to the same intensive questioning, one group might get help from a doctor who voluntarily offers clarifications and help when students stumble. In the second group, a doctor might be available, but might offer clarifications and help only if the group seeks it. In the third group, there is no doctor present and no help is available.

In this case, not only is the support manipulated, but even the setting in which this experiment is conducted is artificial, inasmuch as the researcher has removed the subjects from their normal environment and put them in a totally different setting. The researcher has intervened *maximally* with the normal setting, the participants and their duties.

In chapter 12 we will see why such changes are necessary to establish cause and effect relationships beyond doubt. The extent of researcher interference will depend on whether the study is exploratory, descriptive, correlational or causal and also the importance of establishing causal relationships beyond any doubt.

Most organisational problems seldom require a causal study. In any case, researcher interference through a change in the setting in which the causal study is conducted is rare, except in some market research areas.

## STUDY SETTING: CONTRIVED AND NON-CONTRIVED

As we have just seen, business research can be carried out in the natural environment where work proceeds normally (i.e. in **non-contrived settings**) or in artificial, **contrived settings**. Exploratory and descriptive studies are invariably conducted in non-contrived settings, whereas rigorous causal studies are undertaken in contrived lab settings.

Exploratory, descriptive and some correlational studies undertaken in organisations are called **field studies**. Studies conducted to establish correlational or cause and effect relationships using the same natural environment in which employees normally function are called **field experiments**. Here, as we have seen earlier, the researcher does interfere with the natural occurrence of events inasmuch as the independent variable is manipulated. For example, a manager wanting to know the effects of pay on performance would raise the salary of employees in one unit, decrease the pay of employees in another unit, and leave the pay of the employees in a third unit untouched. Here there is a tampering with or manipulation of the pay system to establish a cause and effect relationship between pay and performance, but the study is still conducted in the natural setting and hence is called a field experiment.

Experiments to establish cause and effect relationships beyond the least doubt require the creation of an artificial, contrived environment in which all the extraneous factors are strictly controlled. Similar subjects are chosen carefully to respond to certain manipulated stimuli. These studies are referred to as **lab experiments**. Let us give another example to understand the differences among a field study (a non-contrived setting with minimal researcher interference), a field experiment (a non-contrived setting but with researcher interference to a moderate extent) and a lab experiment (a contrived setting with excessive researcher interference).

### EXAMPLE 5.15 FIELD STUDY

A bank manager wants to identify the bank deposit decision patterns of clients. She identifies clients who use different types of accounts — savings, interest-bearing deposits and the bank's new 'golden passbook' account. The bank manager then interviews 10 clients who use each of these accounts to discover the reasons for selecting that type of account.

This is a field study in which the bank manager has merely identified the clients using the accounts and interviewed them. Research here is done in a non-contrived setting with no interference with the normal work routine.

## EXAMPLE 5.16 — FIELD EXPERIMENT

The bank manager now wants to determine the cause and effect relationship between interest rates and the inclinations of clients to save and deposit money in the bank. She selects four branches within a 60-kilometre radius for the experiment. For one week only, she advertises the annual rate for new certificates of deposit received during that week in the following manner: the interest rate would be 9 per cent in one branch, 8 per cent in another and 10 per cent in the third. In the fourth branch, the interest rate remains unchanged at 5 per cent. Within the week, she would be able to determine the effects, if any, of interest rates on deposit mobilisation.

The preceding would be a field experiment since nothing but the interest rate is *manipulated*, with all activities occurring in the normal and natural work environment. All four branches chosen should be more or less compatible in size, number of depositors, deposit patterns and the like, so that the interest–savings relationships are not influenced by a third factor. But other factors might affect the findings. For example, one area may have more retirees, who may not have additional disposable income that they could deposit, despite the attraction of a good interest rate! The banker may have been unaware of this fact when setting up the experiment.

## EXAMPLE 5.17 — LAB EXPERIMENT

The banker in example 5.16 may now want to establish beyond a doubt the causal connection between interest rates and savings. Because of this she wants to create an artificial environment and trace the true cause and effect relationship. She recruits 40 students who are all business majors in their final year of study and are approximately the same age. She splits them into four groups and gives each of them chips that count for $1000 which they may utilise for spending, or saving for the future, or both. The bank manager manipulates the interest rates by offering a 6 per cent interest rate on savings for group 1, 8 per cent for group 2, 9 per cent for group 3, and by keeping the interest at the low rate of 1 per cent for group 4.

Here, the manager has created an artificial laboratory environment and has manipulated the interest rates for savings. She has also chosen subjects with similar backgrounds and exposure to money matters (business students). If the banker finds that the students who are offered more interest are inclined to save more — there being significant differences in the desire to save among those who were offered very low interest by way of incentive and those who were offered progressively more — then she would be able to establish a cause and effect relationship between interest rates and the disposition to save.

In this laboratory experiment with the contrived setting, the researcher interference has been maximal, inasmuch as the setting is different, the independent variable has been manipulated, and most external **nuisance** factors such as age and experience have been controlled.

**Experimental designs** are discussed more fully in chapter 12. However, the preceding examples have shown that it is important to decide the various design details before conducting the research study, because one decision criterion might have an impact on others. For example, if one wants to conduct an exploratory, descriptive or some types of correlational hypothesis-testing study, then the necessity for the researcher to interfere with the normal course of events in the organisation will be minimal. However, if causal connections are to be established, then experimental designs need to be set up either within the organisation where the events normally occur (the field experiment) or in an artificially created setting (the lab experiment).

We have thus far made a distinction among:
1. *field studies*, in which various factors are examined in the natural setting in which daily activities go on as normal with minimal researcher interference
2. *field experiments*, in which correlational or cause and effect relationships are studied with some amount of researcher interference, but still in the natural setting where work continues in the normal fashion
3. *lab experiments*, in which the researcher explores cause and effect relationship exercising a high degree of control in an artificially created setting.

In chapter 12 we will see the advantages and disadvantages of using contrived and non-contrived settings for establishing cause and effect relationships. Depending on the degree to which establishing the cause and effect relationship *unequivocally* is important to a research project, a contrived or a non-contrived setting would be relevant for causal studies. Thus, the choice of the setting becomes an important issue in research design. As stated earlier, an artificial setting is rarely called for in business research.

## UNITS OF ANALYSIS: INDIVIDUALS, DYADS, GROUPS, ORGANISATIONS OR CULTURES

The unit of analysis refers to the level of aggregation of the data collected during the subsequent data analysis stage. If, for instance, the problem statement focuses on how to raise the motivational levels of employees in general, then we are interested in individual employees in the organisation and would like to find out what we can do to raise their motivation. Here, obviously, the unit of analysis is the *individual*. We will be looking at the data gathered from each individual and treating each employee's response as an individual data source. If the researcher is interested in studying two-person interactions, then several two-person groups, also known as dyads, will become the unit of analysis. Analysis of husband–wife interactions in families and supervisor–subordinate relationships in the workplace are good examples of the *dyad* as a unit of analysis. If the problem statement is related to group effectiveness, however, then obviously the unit of analysis would be at the group level. In other words, even though we may gather relevant data from all individuals comprising, say, six groups, we would aggregate the individual data into *group* data so as to see the differences among the six groups. If we compare different departments in the organisation, then the data analysis will be done at the departmental level — that is, the individuals in the department will be treated as one unit — and comparisons made treating the department as the unit of analysis.

Our research objective determines the unit of analysis. For example, if we wish to study group decision-making patterns, we would probably be examining such aspects as group size, group structure, cohesiveness and the like in trying to explain the variance in group decision making. Here, our main interest is not in studying individual decision making but in group decision making, and we will be studying the dynamics that operate in several different groups and the factors that influence group decision making. In such a case, the unit of analysis will be groups.

As our research objective addresses issues that move away from the individual to dyads, and to groups, organisations, and even nations, the unit of analysis similarly shifts from individuals to dyads, groups, organisations and nations. The characteristic of these 'levels of analysis' is that the lower levels are subsumed within the higher levels. Thus, if we study buying behaviours, we can collect data from, say, 60 individuals, and analyse the data. If we want to study group dynamics, we may need to study, say, six or more groups, and then analyse the data gathered by examining the patterns in each of the groups. If we want to study cultural differences among nations, we will have to collect data from different countries and study the underlying patterns of culture in each country. Some critical issues in cross-cultural research are discussed in later chapters.

Individuals do not have the same characteristics as groups (e.g. structure or cohesiveness), and groups do not have the same characteristics as individuals (e.g. IQs or stamina). There are variations in the perceptions, attitudes and behaviours of people in different cultures. Hence, the nature of the information gathered, as well the level at which data are aggregated for analysis, are integral to decisions made in the choice of the unit of analysis.

It is necessary to decide on the unit of analysis even as we formulate the research question, since the data collection methods, sample size and even the variables included in the framework may sometimes be determined or guided by the level at which data are aggregated for analysis.

Let us examine some research scenarios that would call for different units of analysis.

### EXAMPLE 5.18 — INDIVIDUALS AS THE UNIT OF ANALYSIS

The Chief Financial Officer of a manufacturing company wants to know how many of the staff would be interested in attending a three-day seminar on making appropriate investment decisions. For this purpose, data will have to be collected from each individual staff member and the unit of analysis is the individual.

### EXAMPLE 5.19 — DYADS AS THE UNIT OF ANALYSIS

Having read about the benefits of mentoring, an HR manager wants first to identify the number of employees in three departments of the organisation who are in mentoring relationships, and then to find out what the jointly perceived benefits (i.e. by both the mentor and the one mentored) of such a relationship are.

Here, once the mentor and mentored pairs are identified, their joint perceptions can be obtained by treating each pair as one unit. Hence, if the manager wants data from a sample of 10 pairs, he will have to deal with 20 individuals, a pair at a time. The information obtained from each pair will be a data point for subsequent analysis. Thus, the unit of analysis here is the dyad.

### EXAMPLE 5.20 — GROUPS AS THE UNIT OF ANALYSIS

A manager wants to see the patterns of usage of the newly installed Information System (IS) by the production, sales and operations personnel. Three groups of personnel are involved and information on the number of times the IS is used by each member in each of the three groups, and other relevant issues, will be collected and analysed. The final results will indicate the mean usage of the system per day or month for each group. Here the unit of analysis is the group.

### EXAMPLE 5.21 — DIVISIONS AS THE UNIT OF ANALYSIS

Procter and Gamble wants to find out which of its various divisions (soap, paper, oil etc.) have made profits of more than 12 per cent during the current year. Here the profits of each of the divisions will be examined and the information aggregated across the various geographical units of the division. Hence, the unit of analysis will be the division, at which level the data will be aggregated.

> **EXAMPLE 5.22**
>
> **INDUSTRY AS THE UNIT OF ANALYSIS**
>
> An employment survey specialist wants to know the proportion of the work force employed by the health care, utilities, transportation and manufacturing industries. In this case, the researcher has to aggregate the data relating to each of the subunits of each of the industries and report the proportions of the work force employed at the industry level. The health care industry, for instance, includes hospitals, nursing homes, mobile units, small and large clinics, and other health care providing facilities. The data from these subunits will have to be aggregated to see how many employees are employed by the health care industry. Similarly, for each of the other industries, data will have to be aggregated at each subunit level of the industry.

> **EXAMPLE 5.23**
>
> **COUNTRIES AS THE UNIT OF ANALYSIS**
>
> The Chief Financial Officer (CFO) of a multinational corporation wants to know the profits made during the last five years by each of the subsidiaries in Australia, Fiji, New Zealand and Singapore. It is possible that there are many regional offices of these subsidiaries in each of these countries. The profits of the various regional centres for each country have to be aggregated and the profits for each country for the past five years have to be provided for the CFO. In other words, the data will now have to be aggregated at the country level.

As can be easily seen, the data collection and sampling processes become more cumbersome at higher levels of units of analysis (industry, country) than at the lower levels (individuals and dyads).

It is obvious that the unit of analysis has to be clearly identified, as dictated by the research objective. Sampling plan decisions will also be governed by the unit of analysis. For example, if we compare two cultures, say those of India and Australia — where our unit of analysis is the country — our sample size will be only two, despite the fact that we will have to gather data from several hundred individuals from a variety of organisations in the different regions of each country, incurring huge costs. However, if our unit of analysis is individuals (as when studying the buying patterns of customers in the South Island of New Zealand), we can perhaps collect data from a representative sample of 100 individuals in that region and conduct our study at a low cost!

It is now easier to see why the unit of analysis should be given serious consideration even as the research objective is being formulated and the research design planned.

# TIME HORIZON: CROSS-SECTIONAL VERSUS LONGITUDINAL STUDIES

## CROSS-SECTIONAL STUDIES

A study can be carried out in which data are gathered just once, perhaps over a period of days, weeks or months, in order to meet a research objective. Such studies are called **one-shot** or **cross-sectional** studies.

> **EXAMPLE 5.24**
>
> Data were collected from sharebrokers between April and June of last year to study their concerns in a turbulent share market. Data with respect to this particular research had never been collected from these sharebrokers, nor will they be collected again from them for this research.

> **EXAMPLE 5.25**
> A drug company wishing to invest in research for a new obesity (reduction) pill conducted a survey among obese people to see how many of them would be interested in trying the new pill. This is a one-shot or cross-sectional study to assess the likely demand for the new product.

The purpose of both of the studies in the two foregoing examples was to collect data pertinent to finding the solution to a research objective. Data collection at one point in time was sufficient. Both were cross-sectional designs.

## LONGITUDINAL STUDIES

In some cases, however, the researcher might want to study people or phenomena at more than one point in time in order to meet the research objective. For instance, the researcher might want to study employees' behaviour before and after a change in the top management to learn the effects of the change. Here, because data are gathered at two different points in time, the study is not cross-sectional or of the one-shot kind, but is carried longitudinally across a period of time. Such studies, as when data on the dependent variable are gathered at two or more points in time to answer the research question, are called longitudinal studies.

> **EXAMPLE 5.26**
> A government railway department experienced a shutdown for 15 days during a railway workers' walkout, and their clients shifted their business to other carriers such as private delivery services and the post office. After the termination of the strike, the railway department tried to woo their customers back through several strategies and collected data month after month to see what progress they were making in this regard.
> Here, data were collected every month to assess whether the railway department had regained the business volume. Because data were collected at various points in time to answer the same research question (have we regained lost ground?), the study is a longitudinal one.

> **EXAMPLE 5.27**
> A marketing manager is interested in tracing the pattern of sales of a particular product in four different regions of the country on a quarterly basis for the next two years. Since data are collected several times to answer the same issue (tracing the pattern of sales), the study falls into the longitudinal category.

Longitudinal studies take more time and effort and cost more than cross-sectional studies. However, well-planned longitudinal studies could, among other things, help to identify cause and effect relationships. For example, one could study the sales volume of a product before and after an advertisement, and provided other environmental changes have not impacted on the results, one could attribute any increase in the sales volume to the advertisement. If there is no increase in sales, one could conclude that either the advertisement is ineffective or it will take longer to take effect.

Experimental designs invariably are longitudinal studies because data are collected both before and after a manipulation. Field studies could also be longitudinal. For example, a study of the comparison data pertaining to the reactions of managers in a company towards working women now and in 10 years' time will be a longitudinal field study. Most field studies conducted, however, are cross-sectional in nature because of the time, effort and costs involved in collecting data over several time periods. Longitudinal, studies will, of course, be necessary if a manager wants to keep track of certain factors (e.g. sales or debt–equity ratio) over a period of time to assess improvements, or to detect possible causal connections (sales promotions and actual sales data; frequency of drug testing and reduction in drug usage etc.). Though more expensive, longitudinal studies can offer some good insights.

## REVIEW OF ELEMENTS OF RESEARCH DESIGN

This concludes our discussion on the basic design issues regarding the purpose and type of the study, the extent of researcher interference, the study setting, the unit of analysis and the time horizon. The researcher would determine the appropriate decisions to be made in the study design based on the problem definition, the research objectives, the extent of rigour desired and cost considerations. Sometimes, because of the time and costs involved, a researcher might be constrained to settle for less than the 'ideal' research design. For instance, the researcher might have to conduct a cross-sectional instead of a **longitudinal study**, do a field study rather than an experimental design, choose a smaller rather than a larger sample size and so on, thus sub-optimising the research design decisions and settling for a lower level of scientific rigour because of resource constraints. This trade-off between rigour and resources will be a deliberate and conscious decision made by the manager or researcher based on the scope and reasons for the study, and will have to be explicitly stated in any written **research proposal**. Such compromises may also be the reasons why business studies are not entirely scientific, as discussed in chapter 2.

A rigorous research design, which might involve higher costs, is essential if the results of the study are critical for making important decisions affecting the organisation's survival and/or the wellbeing of the vast majority of the publics of the system. It is best to think about the research design decision issues even as the conceptual or theoretical framework is being developed. The researcher has to be very clear about each aspect discussed in this chapter before embarking on data collection.

> Now respond to exercises 5.1–5.3 at the end of the chapter.

## THE RESEARCH PROPOSAL

The design stage of the research process is a watershed phase. The challenge, problem or issue has been investigated sufficiently to indicate that a need exists and the research approach has been planned. At this time a series of decisions have to be made, usually by someone in authority. Among these decisions are (a) should the investigation continue? and (b) who should conduct the investigation? These two critical decisions have to be based on accurate and reliable information. This information is supplied by the research proposal. The research proposal, then, becomes a very important part of the research process.

The research proposal is simply a plan for conducting the research. It serves several purposes. First, it allows the researcher to document the logic supporting the various decisions made during the previous stages. This documentation process can help the researcher clarify a number of issues in his or her mind. Second, the proposal must justify the investment in the research. Third, the proposal is often used to persuade other people to support the research project, perhaps to give their approval, or even to invest resources such as time or money. Fourth, the proposal should provide a budget and time frame for completion.

Authors who have identified the basic components of a research proposal include Davies, Smith and Underhill (1989); Delahaye (2000); Neuman (1997); and Ticehurst and Veal (1999).

1. *Title*
   The title of the proposal should come directly from the research objective, and should indicate the scope and content of the project.

> **EXAMPLE 5.28** The effect of organisational culture on training programs

Notice, in the above example, how the content is defined — organisational culture and training programs — and also how the words constrain the scope of the study. The study will not examine national cultures and will focus only on how organisational culture affects training programs, not on other issues such as dual-career couples or absenteeism. This definition of content and scope, of course, reflects the influence of the research objective.

2. *Introduction*
   The introduction should give the reasons for undertaking the research project; outline how the challenge, problem or issue first came to the attention of the organisation, and who first authorised the initial investigation; and define the challenge, problem or issue to be investigated. This background information orientates the reader to the context within which the research project will operate. The way the challenge, problem or issue is presented can influence the direction of the research project, as demonstrated in the following two examples.

> **EXAMPLE 5.29** The management of the Fly Fishing Components company must determine how to reduce absenteeism in order to achieve high-quality products and production targets.

> **EXAMPLE 5.30** The Fly Fishing Components company is a major manufacturing company in the Hutt Valley region. Management faces high absenteeism in the Associated Components Department, which is leading to high material wastage and delays in meeting production targets.

Example 5.29 is overly concerned with 'ends' — it dictates the end result expected and this unnecessarily narrows the research project. Example 5.30, however, describes the situation as it exists at the moment and allows the researcher to investigate fully a number of options. Thus, example 5.30 allows an open perspective, does not imply a negative situation, does not imply that a return to the previous state is necessarily the best option.

3. *Research objective*
   The research objective achieves at least two outcomes. First, it identifies the purpose of the research project. Second, whereas the problem definition used in the introduction may be relatively broad, the research objective identifies explicitly the domains to be investigated. A possible research objective for example 5.30 is shown in example 5.31.

**EXAMPLE 5.31**

To minimise the impact of absenteeism on work allocation and production targets in the Associated Components Department by:
a. identifying the actual levels, timing and length of absences in the Associated Components Department
b. comparing the absence figures from the Associated Components Department with those from other departments in the company and with the industry standard
c. determining the causes of the absences in the Associated Components Department
d. identifying the quantitative and qualitative consequences of absenteeism on work allocation and production targets
e. identifying ways of minimising absenteeism
f. identifying other ways of minimising the impact of absenteeism on work allocation and production targets.

Several aspects of this research objective should be noted. First, if the investigation was confined to 'a', 'b' and 'c', the research project would explore only absenteeism. The link with absenteeism and work allocation/production targets would not be studied. Second, someone in authority may decide that the cost of the investigation is too high. By limiting the research objective — for example deleting 'f' — the research costs could be decreased. However, the person in authority would also need to recognise that the investigation is then that much less valuable. Third, both qualitative and quantitative research methods are indicated. So 'a' and 'b' are certainly quantitative research, 'e' is qualitative research and 'd' is both qualitative and quantitative.

4. *Justification*

   The research project has to be justified. The need for the research has to be 'sold' to the key stakeholders. The reasons for the research should have been identified in the preliminary information gathering stage. The justification may come via the data gathering from the organisational records, from the preliminary interviews or focus groups or from the literature search — or, more commonly, from a combination of all these sources.

5. *Research design*

   The research methods to be used have to be described and justified. In this component of the research proposal, the six basic aspects of research design discussed in this chapter — the kind of design (exploratory, descriptive, hypothesis testing), type of investigation (clarification, correlational, causal), researcher interference, study setting, unit of analysis and time horizon — are examined.

   Importantly, the research objectives have to be converted to research questions or research hypotheses. So, from example 5.31, 'd. Identifying the quantitative and qualitative consequences of absenteeism on work allocation and production targets', may be converted into:

**EXAMPLE 5.32**

(i) a hypothesis: *Increased absenteeism has a negative effect on work allocation and production targets.*

(ii) a research question: *What other consequences does increased absenteeism have on work allocation and production targets?*

In addition, the research methods — interviews, focus groups, observations, questionnaires, organisational records — have to be discussed in detail. These details are discussed further in later chapters. For example, if a questionnaire is to be used, its validity, reliability and relevance to the study have to be documented. The type and number of respondents for the study have to be defined, as does the sampling process and other actions to be taken to ensure quality.

Finally, the expected methods of data analysis need to be explained. If a quantitative approach is to be followed, the statistical processes to be used (for example descriptive or inferential statistics) should be nominated as well as the statistical package that will be utilised (for example SPSS or Excel). If a qualitative design is needed, the data analytic technique (for example, constant comparative analysis) should be identified, brief but relevant descriptions of the people to be used in the analysis should be documented, as should whether any computerised packages (such as **NVivo**) are to be used. Needless to say, these data analysis techniques should be appropriate to the relevant research questions and hypotheses to be tested.

6. *Research schedule*
   The research schedule includes a timetable of the duration and expected completion dates of the critical steps in the research project. This is usually presented in the form of a table.

**EXAMPLE 5.33 — RESEARCH SCHEDULE**

| Activity | Working days | Completion date |
|---|---|---|
| Literature search | 12 | 15 July |
| Write proposal | 3 | 20 July |
| Gain approval | 5 | 25 July |
| Design interview protocol | 5 | 30 July |
| Conduct pilot study | 2 | 2 August |
| Analyse results of pilot study | 1 | 3 August |
| Conduct interviews | 15 | 23 August |
| Arrange transcripts of interviews | 20 | 18 September |
| Analyse interview data | 20 | 13 October |
| Relate findings to conceptual framework | 3 | 18 October |
| Write draft report | 6 | 26 October |
| Review and edit report | 2 | 28 October |
| Allowance for overruns | 5 | 4 November |
| Forward report | 2 | 6 November |

7. *Approvals*

    The need for any specific approvals — to enter certain locations, from government departments, ethical clearances — should be documented. The ethical implications of the research should be clearly identified. For example, are there potential conflicts of interest, or areas of ethical sensitivity that may occur during or after the research?

8. *Resources*

    It is common to include a listing of other resources needed. These resources may range from certain computer analysis packages to the skills and experience of the researchers to office accommodation.

9. *Budget*

    The budget should include all the financial costs that can be attributed to the research project. These costs should include allowances for major items such as wages for research assistants and accommodation and travel expenses and minor costs such as photocopying, stationery and postage.

10. *Report preparation and distribution*

    The form of the final report and its distribution should be documented. This can become an important issue at the end of the project, and agreement now can save a lot of arguments at a later stage. Issues relating to copyright should also be clarified at this point. This can save arguments later on whether the researchers or the research sponsors hold the copyright on the final report and what use can be made of the final report — for example converting the report into a paper or article for a professional or research journal.

## MANAGERIAL IMPLICATIONS

Knowledge about research design issues helps the manager to understand what the researcher is attempting to do. The manager also understands why the reports sometimes indicate data analytic results based on small sample sizes, when a lot of time has been spent in collecting data from several score individuals, as in the case of studies involving groups.

One of the important decisions a manager must make before starting a study pertains to how rigorous the study ought to be. Knowing that more rigorous research designs consume more resources, the manager is in a position to weigh the gravity of the problem and decide what kind of a design would yield acceptable results in an efficient manner. For example, the manager might decide that knowledge of which variables are associated with employee performance is good enough to enhance performance results, and there is no need to ferret out the cause. Such a decision would not only result in economy in resources, but also cause the least disruption to the smooth flow of work for employees and preclude the need for collecting data longitudinally. Knowledge of interconnections among various aspects of the research design helps managers to select the most effective study, after weighing the nature and magnitude of the problem encountered, and the type of solution desired.

One of the main advantages in fully understanding the difference between causal and correlational studies is that managers do not fall into the trap of making implicit causal assumptions when two variables are associated only with each other. They realise that A could cause B, or B could cause A, or both A and B could co-vary because of some third variable.

## SUMMARY

In this chapter we examined the basic research design issues and the choice points available to the manager or researcher. We discussed the situations in which exploratory, descriptive, hypothesis-testing and case studies are called for. We examined clarification, causal and correlational studies, and the implications of either for determining the study setting, the extent of researcher interference and the time horizon of the study. We noted that the unit of analysis refers to the level at which data are aggregated for analysis, and that the time horizon of studies could be one-shot or longitudinal. Finally, we examined the circumstances in which each design decision would be appropriate and the components of a research proposal.

## DISCUSSION POINTS

1. What are the basic research design issues? Describe them in some detail.
2. Why are the basic design issues important to consider before conducting the study and even as early as at the time of formulating the research objective?
3. Is a field study totally out of the question if one is trying to establish cause and effect relationships?
4. 'An exploratory study is just as useful as a predictive study.' Discuss this statement.
5. Why is the unit of analysis an integral part of the research design?
6. Discuss the interrelationships among non-contrived setting, purpose of study, type of investigation, researcher interference and time horizon of study.
7. List and briefly describe the components of a research proposal.
8. Discuss the importance of preparing a good research proposal.
9. Below are two scenarios. Indicate how the business researcher should proceed in each case; that is, determine the following, giving reasons:
   (a) the purpose of the study
   (b) the type of investigation
   (c) the extent of researcher interference
   (d) the study setting
   (e) the time horizon for the study
   (f) the unit of analysis.

*Scenario A*

Joyce Lynn, the owner of a small business (a women's dress boutique), has invited a consultant to tell her how her business is different from similar small businesses within a 60-kilometre radius with respect to usage of computer technology, sales volume, profit margin and staff training.

*Scenario B*

Paul Hodge, the owner of several restaurants in Victoria, is concerned about the wide differences in their profit margins. He would like to try some incentive plans for increasing the efficiency levels of those restaurants that lag behind. But before he does this, he would like to make sure that the idea would work. He asks a business researcher to help him on this issue.

| | |
|---|---|
| Exercise 5.1 | A foreman believes that the low efficiency of the machine tool operators is directly linked to the high level of fumes emitted in the workshop. He would like to prove this to his supervisor through a research study.<br>1 Would this be a causal or a correlational study? Why?<br>2 Is this an exploratory, descriptive or hypothesis-testing (analytical or predictive) study? Why?<br>3 What kind of a study would this be — a field study, lab experiment or field experiment? Why?<br>4 What would be the unit of analysis? Why?<br>5 Would this be a cross-sectional or a longitudinal study? Why? |
| Exercise 5.2 | Many people were concerned about banks increasing their charges while enjoying record profits. If the government had wished to probe into the details, would this investigation have called for:<br>1 a descriptive, exploratory or hypothesis-testing study?<br>2 a hypothesis-testing study? If so, would this be correlational or causal? Why?<br>3 a field study, lab experiment or field experiment? Why?<br>4 a cross-sectional or longitudinal study? Why? |
| Exercise 5.3 | Below is the story of BFI. The newly appointed Chief Executive of BFI wishes to conduct a study to effect improvements and asks you to work out the research design details. After reading the short case that follows, discuss fully the design decisions that you, as a researcher, will make to investigate the situation, giving reasons for your choices. |

### The Sad Saga of BFI

Brown Ferris Industries (BFI), a waste management company, grew rapidly by snapping up local dump sites, collection routes and recycling businesses across the country during the 1980s and early 1990s. But, while BFI was paying a lot of money for acquiring collection routes, it had not linked these routes to the company-owned landfills, and this cost BFI dearly. As a consequence, it had to pay outsiders a lot of money to dispose of its rubbish.

However, BFI's recycling business was booming, since the profits in recycling were high. But in the mid-1990s profits from recycling dropped drastically, and BFI finished the fiscal year ended in June 2000 with a heavy loss.

# part III

# QUALITATIVE BUSINESS RESEARCH

6 Qualitative data gathering

7 Qualitative data analysis and interpretation

# chapter 6

# QUALITATIVE DATA GATHERING

## OUTLINE
THE ASSUMPTIONS OF QUALITATIVE RESEARCH
ACCURACY AND REPLICABILITY
SAMPLING
QUALITATIVE RESEARCH METHODS
INTERVIEWING
THE FOCUS GROUP
OBSERVATIONAL STUDIES
OTHER SPECIAL DATA SOURCES
ETHICS IN DATA COLLECTION
SUMMARY
DISCUSSION POINTS
EXERCISES

## CHAPTER OBJECTIVES
After completing this chapter, you should be able to:
- discuss the assumptions of qualitative research
- describe how qualitative researchers respond to the demands of accuracy and replicability
- explain the process of planning and conducting a research interview
- discuss the face-to-face interview, the telephone interview and the computer-assisted interview
- explain the process of planning and conducting a focus group
- describe non-participant and participant observational studies
- identify other special data sources
- describe the ethical issues involved in qualitative research.

While quantitative research has had a longer history, there has been growing recognition of another major stream of investigation — qualitative research. Qualitative research sees the world as complex and interconnected and therefore a rich and fertile opportunity for understanding the nature of humanity. As a research process, it attempts to come to terms with the meaning, not the frequency, of naturally occurring phenomena in the social world (Van Maanen 1983). As discussed in chapter 2, the strengths of qualitative research become apparent when there is little known about the concepts under investigation or about the relationship between those concepts. The focus of qualitative research, therefore, is on identifying these hitherto unknown concepts.

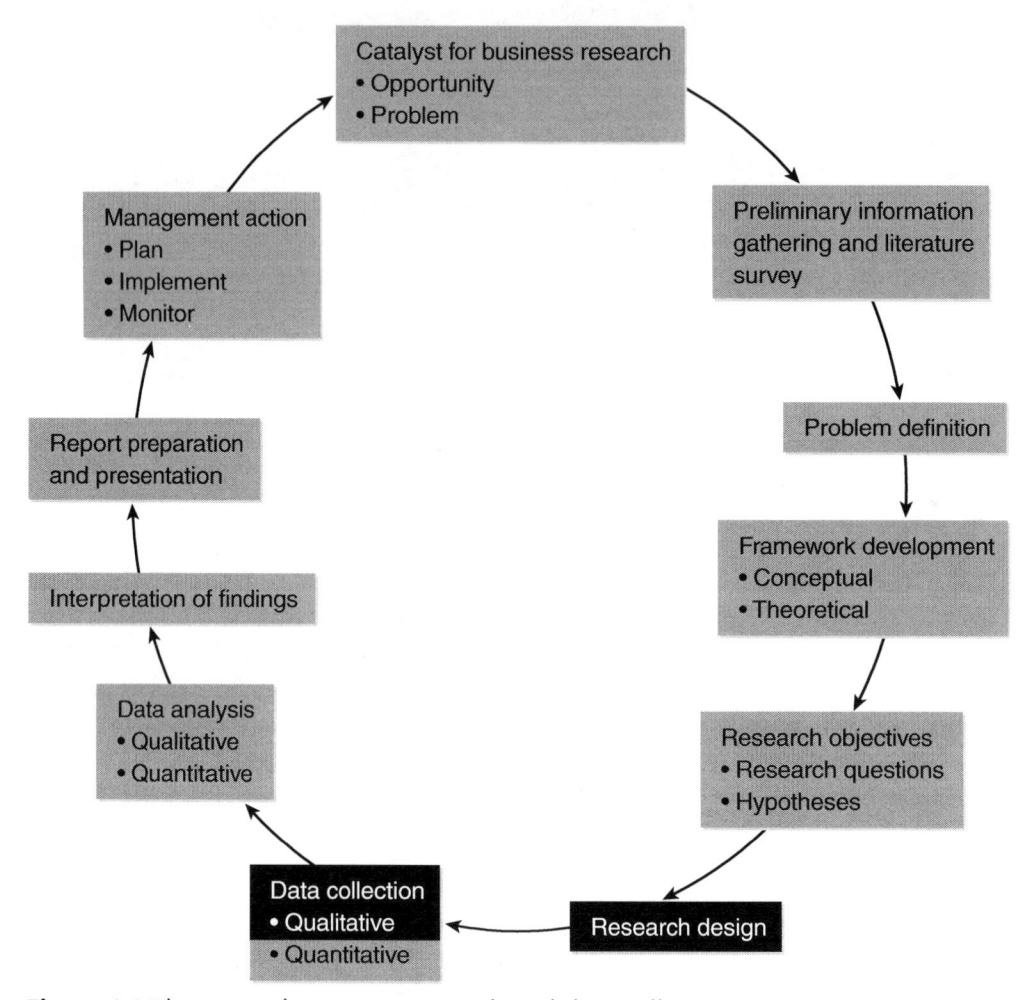

**Figure 6.1** The research process: research and data collection

## THE ASSUMPTIONS OF QUALITATIVE RESEARCH

Maykut and Morehouse (1994) identify several important parameters on which qualitative research differs from the traditional positivist assumptions.
1. Qualitative research places emphasis on *understanding* through closely examining people's words, actions and records rather than assigning mathematical symbols to these words, actions and records.

2. Rather than an objective stance, qualitative research takes a **perspectival view**. Qualitative research believes that meaning is co-constituted — reality is socially and subjectively construed rather than objectively determined (Ticehurst & Veal 1999). Therefore, qualitative research is interested in the subjective perception of the respondent — that is, in examining the perspective of the respondent's beliefs and interpretation of the phenomena being researched.
3. The goal of qualitative research is to *discover the patterns* that emerge after close observation, careful documentation and thoughtful analysis. Until these patterns are identified, the quantitative proof of the causal nature of the variables cannot be investigated.
4. Qualitative research assumes the posture of **indwelling** by being at one with the person under investigation and by understanding the respondent's point of view from an empathic rather than a sympathetic position. Indwelling also involves reflection — that is, pausing to think and process what has gone before.
5. Qualitative research looks to the **human-as-an-instrument** for the collection and analysis of data. Only a human can be responsive, adaptable and holistic so as to explore the atypical or idiosyncratic responses that surface during an interaction with a respondent. As a human-as-an-instrument, the researcher intervenes through speech and actions to understand the 'web of meaning' the respondent attributes to the phenomena under investigation.
6. Polanyi (1997) has differentiated between tacit knowledge and explicit knowledge. Tacit knowledge is defined by the saying 'We know more than we can tell' (136), while explicit knowledge is that knowledge an individual can readily articulate. While quantitative research can access explicit knowledge, the qualitative researcher, by her or his unique combination of position and human ability, is the best instrument to surface the *hidden tacit knowledge* of the respondent.

As Ticehurst and Veal (1999:95) point out, qualitative research tends to concentrate on collecting a great deal of 'rich' information from relatively few people, and recognises a more fluid and recursive relationship among the various elements of the research. Accordingly, the research question or hypothesis evolves as the research progresses, data collection and analysis often take place concurrently, and writing can be an evolutionary, ongoing process.

## ACCURACY AND REPLICABILITY

Qualitative research is open to criticism for being subjective and biased. Its advantage, however, is the ability to amass rich and highly useful data. Qualitative researchers, therefore, respond to the demands of accuracy and replicability in a number of ways. Writers such as Burns (1994:270–3) and Neuman (1997:332–5) list a number of options.

### Trustworthiness

To a qualitative researcher integrity is everything. A qualitative researcher always endeavours to observe, report and interpret the complex field experience as accurately and faithfully as possible.

### Verification

A basic tenet of qualitative research is not to accept anything at face value. Qualitative researchers try to ensure that their research accurately reflects the evidence, and they have checks on their evidence and interpretations.

As an aid to **verification**, **triangulation** is a common theme in qualitative research. Cohen and Manion (1989) suggest three types. Researcher–subject corroboration involves cross-checking the meaning of data between the researcher and the respondents. This cross-checking may occur during data gathering or after interpretations of the raw data have been made, for confirmation of accurate reporting. Second, confirmation from other sources about specific issues or events identified is always paramount. Third, two or more methods of data collection should be used and the resultant interpretations should be compared. A fourth triangulation option is called *researcher convergence* (Huberman & Miles 1998) — using another researcher to analyse the same raw data and then comparing the two analyses.

## Acknowledging subjectivity and bias

Qualitative researchers assume that it is impossible to eliminate the effect of the researcher's bias and subjectivity and suggest that quantitative researchers sometimes hide behind supposed 'objective' techniques. A qualitative researcher takes advantage of personal insights, feelings and values but uses two techniques to limit the contamination. First, the researcher overtly takes measures to guard against inappropriate personal influences by being aware of his or her frames of reference, which may contaminate any analysis of the topic under investigation. Second, it is common for a brief description of the researcher to be incorporated in the final report. This brief description includes any relevant personal history of the researcher that may affect the interpretations — either in providing a unique insight, or in causing subjectivity and bias in the interpretation. Frequently, personal research assumptions and biases are also shared with the reader.

## Process and sequence

The passage of time is an integral part of qualitative research. The sequence of events (what happened first, second, third and so on) provides confirmational evidence for the qualitative researcher.

## Interpretation

Interpreting the complex behaviours, messages, forces and conditions of an event is the central theme of qualitative research. As a safeguard to accuracy, the qualitative researcher uses two techniques. The first is to report 'in the voice of the source' by using the actual words of the respondent — either in the phrasing of a sentence or verbatim as an example of an opinion or fact. As Burns (1994:12) comments, the task of the qualitative methodologist is to capture what people say and do as a product of how they interpret the complexity of their world, to understand events from the viewpoints of the participants. The second technique is to report the logic of interpretation used to come to a particular conclusion.

## Referential adequacy

The comments and descriptions in the report should be of sufficient detail and richness that the reader has no difficulty in imagining the context, situations and themes discussed (Eisner 1991). Thus, citations of the raw data collected in qualitative research should be frequent enough to give the reader confidence that the raw data has been reported accurately and that the themes extracted are valid.

## Paint the path

It is impossible to exactly replicate a qualitative study — there are too many complex variables involved. For example, just having a different researcher introduces an immediate variant to qualitative research, since the researcher is such a central part of qualitative research.

However, to help the reader of the report understand the source and theme of the interpretations, the qualitative researcher provides a detailed description of the research process in the final report. Huberman and Miles (1998) call this *transparency* and suggest that description should be provided of, for example, sampling decisions, data collection operations, database summary (size, how produced), software used (if any), an overview of the analytic strategies used and the key data displays supporting the main conclusions. To this list could be added timing and timeliness of observations, spatial arrangements of interviews, relationships with subjects, categories developed for analysis and protocols of analysis.

## Summary

When involved in qualitative research, the researcher should ensure that triangulation is built into the research design. At the very least, two methods of data gathering should be used, and preferably more. Frequently, this means the use of either interviews or focus groups and survey questionnaires, but the researcher need not be limited to this qualitative/quantitative combination. During the report-writing stage, adequate references and support for interpretations are prime requirements. Describing the data gathering and analysis choices — painting the path — needs to be sufficiently detailed.

## SAMPLING

As discussed in chapter 5, selecting the unit of analysis for research purposes is an important task. In qualitative research, the units of analysis are either individuals, dyads or groups. Care must be taken that the respondents provide information that is representative of the target population. However, the non-probability methods — for example, purposive, convergence and snowball sampling — have the distinct advantage of quickly accessing participants who are most likely to provide rich information (see chapter 11). For this reason, non-probability methods of sampling are more commonly used in qualitative research (Minichiello et al. 1990:199).

Selecting a representative sample of respondents so that no systematic bias occurs in the data gathered is an important task. At the same time, the investigator should not suffer from 'paralysis by analysis'. As Kruger (1994:82) comments, the investigator should recognise that sometimes compromises are needed between the cost of finding the perfect participants and the likely increased quality of the data gathered. As a specific warning, Kruger advises caution with participants who have expressed concern about the topic, who are clones of the supervisor, who can best be spared by the supervisor because they are the least productive, or who are picked from memory by the supervisor or other 'expert'. The cautious investigator always reviews the sampling options for the most efficient selection process and potentially worthwhile participants.

## QUALITATIVE RESEARCH METHODS

Social science provides a number of qualitative research methods ranging from phenomenography to ethnography to structured interviews. In business research, the most common research methods used are interviewing, focus groups and observation, and these will now be discussed in turn.

# INTERVIEWING

One wit has suggested that everyone claims to be a good driver, a good lover and a good interviewer. The last claim, at least, is not true! Successful interviewing is the result of the complex interaction of high-level skills, empathy and understanding of others, and an inexhaustible curiosity. Interviews may be conducted face to face, over the telephone or via a video link. While there are some minor variations, the same general principles apply, whatever the medium.

The interview provides a unique opportunity to uncover rich and complex information from an individual. The face-to-face interactive process can, under the guidance of an experienced interviewer, encourage the interviewee to share intrinsic opinions and to dredge previously unthought-of memories from the unconscious mind. This rich and rare material invariably includes tacit knowledge from the interviewee.

The key to uncovering this rich information is a well-designed and professionally conducted interview. Socialisation and natural resistance mean that people tend not to disclose information, particularly to a stranger. Further, we often 'grade' the information we are willing to disclose. There is a difference between responding to such questions as *How did you travel to work this morning?* and *What tasks did you carry out at work yesterday?* and questions such as *Have you ever been convicted of taking prohibited drugs?* and *Would you describe your feelings when you experience your worst nightmare?* Whether interviewees would respond to any of these questions and how much they would disclose depends a lot on the context of the interview. However, certain interview skills will increase the likelihood that the interviewee will provide the desired information. A well-designed interview is based on six factors. These are:

- the pattern of the interview
- listening
- questioning
- paraphrasing
- probing
- non-verbal behaviour.

## THE PATTERN OF AN INTERVIEW

A well-patterned interview has a number of benefits. The basic aim of the interview is achieved in less time by removing communication barriers and encouraging the flow of information. The interviewee feels at ease and tends to provide more complete answers. Finally, a well-patterned interview looks professional. Figure 6.2 is an overview of the **pattern of an interview**; this model provides a general guideline for an interviewer involved in a one-on-one interaction.

The first challenge for an interviewer is to bring the interviewee into the **rapport zone**; this is the area of minimum stress where the interviewee will disclose all information. We all retain natural barriers so that we do not disclose personal information inappropriately. The first task of the skilled interviewer is to encourage the interviewee to lower these barriers so that information will flow more easily. This easy flow of information occurs in the rapport zone. The interview proper cannot start until the interviewee enters this zone, and the interviewer will need to invest some time and energy in encouraging the interviewee to lower his or her natural barriers.

The interview pattern consists of four stages — the entrance investment time, activity no. 2, intimacy and the exit investment time.

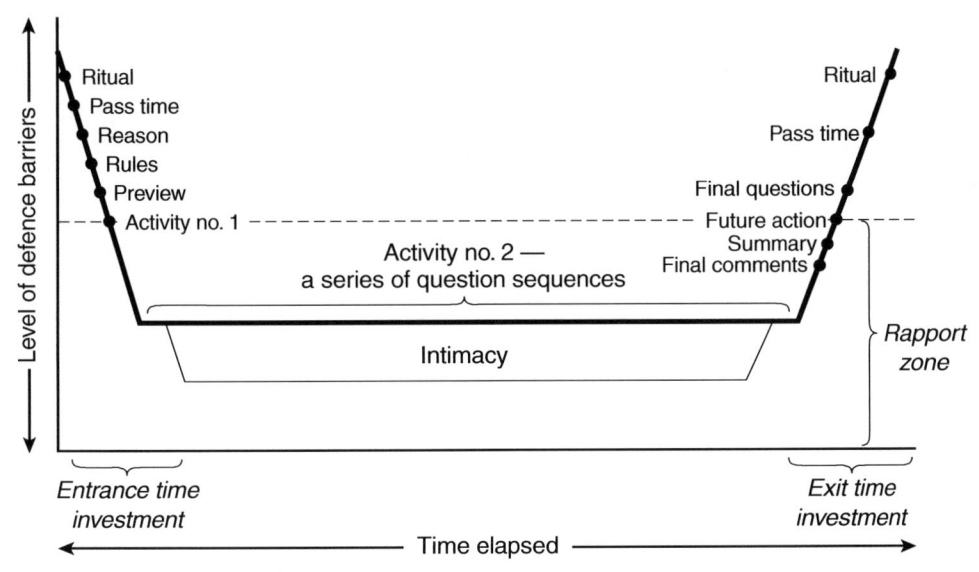

**Figure 6.2** The pattern of an interview

**Source:** Delahaye (2000:166).

## Stage 1: entrance time investment

This is the time invested at the start of the interview to ensure the interviewee enters the rapport zone. The rapport zone is where the interviewee will disclose information honestly and openly. It has six steps — the *ritual*, the *pass time*, the *reason*, the *rules*, the *preview* and *activity no. 1*. The first two — the ritual and the pass time — may seem superficial. Far from being a waste of time, however, these exchanges provide information, as well as a time space, for the interviewee to become accustomed to the interviewer and the interview situation. Any attempt to 'shortcut' the proceedings will often result in barriers being re-formed as a means of protection against insecurity.

- **Rituals** are the simple, stereotyped greetings that we use every day and can be regarded as common good manners — for example, 'Good morning'. A frequent addition to the ritual is an introduction — for example, 'My name is Yvonne'.
- A **pass time** carries on from the ritual and extends the time space available to the interviewee to adjust to the interview situation. Common pass times include observations or questions about the weather ('It's a windy day today, isn't it?') or health ('How are you today?'). The point of the pass time is that it does not expect a literal reply — in fact, such a reply to a pass time is often considered quite odd. However, a pass time should be reasonably relevant to the situation. A comment on the immediate environment may be more acceptable than the health pass time — for example, 'It's quite cool in here, isn't it?' or, if the interviewee is unfamiliar with the interview location, a comment such as 'Ah, good, you found the room, then' would suffice.
- By this time the interviewee's mind should be coming off any events that occurred prior to the interview, his or her curiosity piqued about the *reason* for the interviewer's presence. Needless to say, this curiosity should be immediately satisfied by sharing with the interviewee the objectives of the business research project. However, a decision needs to be made about the degree of specificity to be shared about the objectives of the business research project. If the interview is to be unstructured, then the interviewer may prefer to give a more general description, as anything specific may bias the direction of the interview.

- An interview is a somewhat artificial situation: two strangers come together to share information in an open relationship that would normally take some time to establish. Therefore, there is a need to establish *basic ground rules* early. One frequent concern of interviewees is the confidentiality of the information and how the information will be used. Assurances need to be given at this stage. Permission on the type of recording — whether note taking or audio recording — needs to be obtained from the interviewee.
- Very briefly, *preview* the interview by telling the interviewee how it will proceed. This may simply be: 'I have six questions to ask and expect that this will take about 45 minutes'. More detail can be given, depending on the context, but be careful not to talk for too long. The sign of a good interview is a very high proportion of interviewee participation.
- The ritual, the pass time and the reason would have occupied a time space of about 60 seconds and the rules and the preview perhaps another 30 seconds. While the interviewee may now be willing to disclose some information, it would be naive to assume that no filtering would take place. It is now time for *activity no. 1*.

The role of activity no. 1 is to bring the interviewee fully into the rapport zone. Once people start on a perceived relevant activity, information flows increasingly easily as the natural barriers are forgotten and trust increases. However, activity no. 1 needs to be designed to meet two conflicting goals. On the one hand, it has to be related to the objective of the research project, as any hint of artificiality will raise the interviewee's natural barriers, not lower them. On the other hand, it has to be recognised that the interviewee is not yet in the rapport zone, so at least the initial information of activity no. 1 will be filtered by the interviewee. In addition, the activity needs to be based on a question that the interviewee can answer easily and is willing to answer — lack of early success on the part of the interviewee is likely to increase the barriers to free information flow, so activity no. 1 needs to be carefully planned.

As indicated in figure 6.2, activity no. 1 sits on the boundary between stage 1 (entrance investment time) and the rapport zone. This positioning indicates that activity no. 1 helps the interviewee enter the rapport zone and, at the same time, can also provide useful information. However, this information will need checking at a later time, through triangulation, since there is a possibility that stress or lack of trust may have filtered the data.

The entrance investment time is needed to help reduce the interviewee's natural barriers to sharing information. As a final comment, the entrance investment time has two conflicting roles. It needs to be detailed and take sufficient time to allow the interviewee to lower his or her natural barriers, but it should not take so much time that the interviewee becomes exasperated.

## Stage 2: activity no. 2

As the interviewee enters the rapport zone (which is indicated by his or her non-verbal behaviour), the interview proper can start. In activity no. 2 the interviewer uses the skills of questioning, paraphrasing and probing. These skills will be discussed later in the chapter.

Research projects investigating explicit knowledge will remain at this activity no. 2 stage. As discussed later in the chapter, interviews that stay at the activity no. 2 level are usually more structured and rely for the most part on questions that are pre-planned and content based.

## Stage 3: intimacy

Research projects researching deeper knowledge that is not explicit will usually encounter complexity, uncertainty and emotions. This type of interview will need to progress deeper into the rapport zone. Such a step involves genuine caring and authenticity, and requires expert interviewing skills and sensitivity. Interviews at the intimacy level are usually less structured and rely heavily on the researcher's interview skills.

It should be noted that interviews moving this deep into the rapport zone will need to go through the steps of ritual, pass time, activity no. 1 and activity no. 2 before the interviewee will risk full disclosure of emotions and inner feelings.

## Stage 4: exit time investment

Just as an investment of time was required to lower the defences of the interviewee at the beginning of the interview, so further time investment is needed to allow the interviewee to rebuild his or her natural defences. It is quite unethical for an interviewer not to provide this time space, since no interviewee should be pushed defenceless into the cold outside world again. There are six steps that make up this exit time investment.

- When the interviewer believes all the necessary information has been gathered a comment such as 'Well, that is all the questions I have. Do you have any final comments?' is needed. This achieves three aims. First, the interviewee can add any further information that he or she considers important. This often leaves the interviewee with a feeling of satisfaction that he or she has completed a good job. Second, it sometimes uncovers unexpected information, which the interviewer may or may not choose to follow up. Third, the word 'final' gives the interviewee a cue that the interview is coming to a close.
- Some interviewers prefer to give a summary at this point, highlighting the main issues discussed. Again, this may encourage the interviewee to add some finer points and, by explicitly demonstrating all the issues covered, emphasises that the interview was worthwhile. On the other hand, particularly if the interviewee is concerned about the amount of time the interview has taken, this step may take up too much valuable time and therefore may be omitted.
- The interviewee may be curious and/or concerned about what will happen to the information that he or she has supplied. It is good practice to advise the interviewee of the *future actions* that you will take. This is also a good time to re-emphasise the confidentiality of these actions.
- To check if there are any other issues or concerns held by the interviewee, a comment such as 'Do you have any *final questions*?' gives the interviewee the opportunity to satisfy any curiosity and also indicates that the interview is just about finished.
- A pass time gives the interviewee the chance to prepare to leave. Some interviewers like to use the same pass time as was used at the beginning of the interview, but such a perfectly rounded ending is most probably not needed. This pass time can also be accompanied by non-verbal behaviours, such as standing up and moving towards the door of the interview room.
- In a similar fashion to the entry ritual, a verbal leave-taking is common good manners — a 'Good-bye and thank you for your time' is usually all that is necessary.

Each of these steps in the exit time investment signals to the interviewee that the interview is coming to a close and allows the interviewee to rebuild his or her defences in an orderly and dignified fashion.

# LISTENING

Listening is the most important skill of an interviewer. Seidman (1991:56) suggests that there are two levels of listening. First, the interviewer listens to what the interviewee is saying — the content of the reply as constructed by the words used. The interviewer must concentrate on the substance to make sure that the message is understood and to assess whether the answer is on the right track and is as detailed and complete as expected. Second, the interviewer listens for the 'unstated message' — what is not being said, or what is said but is being contradicted by non-verbal messages. Does the interviewee continually avoid answering questions on a specific topic? Does his tone of voice match the verbalised message? Is he saying 'Yes, it's okay' while looking despondent or even shaking his head?

As Fowler and Mangione (1990) comment, in an interview the participants have different roles, and it is the interviewee who provides the answers. The answers are the raw data for the investigation so the interviewer must listen very carefully. This means that the interviewer must be comfortable with silence, allowing the interviewee to think rather than rushing in and contaminating the outcome.

# QUESTIONING

While the pattern of the interview defines the overall strategy of the interview, questioning is the real heart of the process. Well-designed questions allow the interviewer to control the direction of the interview and investigate areas of relevance and interest, to say nothing of ensuring that the objectives of the research project are achieved. There are two types of questions — open questions and closed questions.

## Open questions

There are two aspects to the **open question** (Delahaye & Smith 1998). Open or open-ended questions allow the interviewee a wide choice of possible answers. While the interviewee may have only one opinion or remember only one point, as far as the interviewer is concerned the *possible opinions* or points are many. Second, the open question should be arranged in what is called the *stem-plus-query design*. So an open question may look like this: *I am interested in the concerns you may have about the new financial system. Would you tell me about some of these concerns, please?* Compare this to the style of questioning that is often used in ordinary conversations: *What are your concerns about the new financial system?*

Compared to the ordinary style, the stem-plus-query structure of open questions first gives the interviewee the subject to be investigated. This allows the interviewee to start focusing his or her attention on the topic. It also 'softens' the question; the ordinary style can become inquisitorial when used in a succession of questions. Also, as we will see later in this chapter, the stem-plus-query design fits in well with the skill of probing.

## Closed questions

**Closed questions** are used for identifying explicit facts or for confirmation — for example, *How many times have customers complained?* or *So, in your opinion, blue would be a better colour for the background?* Because of the very short interviewee response required, the stem-plus-query structure is usually inappropriate for the closed question.

## In combination

During the interview, the first question is usually referred to as the *primary question*. All other questions are called *secondary questions*. The types of questions used as primary and secondary questions lead to different questioning sequences that have different uses.

A question sequence that starts with an open question and, in turn, has a secondary question as a less open question, then a relatively closed question and finally a closed question is called a **funnel sequence**. The funnel sequence is most common in qualitative research. The *inverted funnel sequence* starts with a closed question and the questions then become broader until the sequence finishes with an open question. An interviewer uses the inverted funnel sequence when the interviewee is reluctant to be interviewed or there is some uncertainty that the interviewee has any knowledge of the topic area. Theoretically, the inverted funnel sequence allows the interviewer to cease the interview early so that time is not wasted. However, as discussed later, there are more sophisticated ways of gathering data in these difficult situations that have a higher probability of success. The *tunnel sequence* is made up of either a series of closed questions or a series of open questions. A series of closed questions becomes an interrogation; this type of tunnel sequence is rarely used in business research (although it is a favourite with the police!). A tunnel sequence of open questions requires high levels of interviewing skills, as the interviewee can easily become bored or frustrated with the inability to cover any particular area in depth.

## PARAPHRASING

From the point of view of the interviewer, questions are the key to the interview as they provide the cues to which the interviewee responds. However, from the interviewee's point of view, the answers are the most important component — and who can argue? The answers provide the material that will become the raw data of the research project.

So, let us look at the interview from the interviewee's perspective. The interviewee hears each question and provides a detailed answer. The interviewer then asks another (possibly unrelated) question. The interviewee is left wondering. Has the interviewer heard the detailed answer? More important, has the interviewer understood the meaning of the reply? These unspoken queries will divert the interviewee's attention and, worse, de-motivate the interviewee so that less detail is given to the next question — not the ideal interviewing environment.

Of course, what the interviewee needs is confirmation that the interviewer has heard and does understand. This confirmation is achieved by **paraphrasing**. With paraphrasing, the interviewer repeats back to the interviewee, in a concise form, the essential message of the interviewee's reply. If there has been a misunderstanding, the interviewee can then correct the interviewer's perception. As well as reassuring the interviewee that the message has been understood, paraphrasing has three additional benefits. First, as the interviewer is paraphrasing, the interviewee is often reminded of additional information and will provide this when the interviewer finishes paraphrasing. Second, paraphrasing establishes a sympathetic atmosphere within the interview that increases the trust between the participants. Third, paraphrasing allows the interviewee time to think, giving the interview a slightly slower but more methodical, measured and professional quality.

A special type of paraphrasing is called *reflection of feeling*. Whereas ordinary paraphrasing concentrates on the content of the message, reflection of feeling acknowledges the emotions of the interviewee. Reflection of feeling often becomes more important during the intimacy stage of the interview. Being able to reflect feelings is a much more complex skill than ordinary paraphrasing as it demands of the interviewer the ability to empathise with the interviewee's emotions. In turn, empathising with another's feelings needs an ability to be in touch with one's own feelings.

In most western societies, feelings and emotions come second to the more factual aspects of the interview, so developing the skill to reflect feelings often requires considerable effort. (See Cormier & Cormier (1991:95–100) for an excellent discussion on reflection of feeling.)

# PROBING

**Probing** combines the funnel sequence of questions with paraphrasing and allows the interviewer to delve into the memories of the interviewee. The steps in probing are as follows:

1. The interviewer asks the primary, usually open question, using the stem-plus-query structure.
2. The interviewee responds.
3. The interviewer notes the salient points of the interviewee's answer to the first primary question.
4. The interviewer paraphrases the salient points back to the interviewee.
5. Selecting one of the salient points, the interviewer asks the first secondary question, using the salient point as the stem of the question.
6. The process continues on that first salient point, with each response paraphrased and with the questions becoming more closed (i.e. a funnel sequence), until the interviewer is satisfied that the point has been fully explored.
7. The interviewer then briefly summarises the main issues that have come out of the first salient point. This overall summary uses a special type of paraphrasing that briefly brings together what has been covered to this stage.
8. The interviewer then moves on to the second salient point, using it as the stem for the next secondary question, and continues to explore this second salient point using the funnel sequence so that the questions become more closed and more factual information is uncovered. The main issues of this second salient point are summarised.
9. The interviewer then progresses to the third salient point of the first primary question or goes on to the next primary question. Thus, the interview becomes a series of funnel sequences.

Several points should be made about the probing process. Paraphrasing in the early stages of each funnel sequence is essential, but as the interview progresses down each funnel, paraphrasing may become too annoying for the interviewee. Therefore, as the questions become more closed, paraphrasing usually becomes redundant. Second, the interviewer decides which salient points of the interviewee's response to explore. Some points may be fully explained as part of the response to the primary question; other points may not be worth following up. Only those points which contribute to the objectives of the research project are worth the interviewer's time investment in the interview. Third, the interviewer can decide how far down the funnel the questions should commence. For an interviewee who has limited knowledge of the topic, it may be easier to start with a less open question — that is, to start lower down the funnel. With interviewees who have a better knowledge of the topic, the interviewer can afford to start with a broader, more open question — that is, higher up the funnel. Finally, the interviewer decides how far down the funnel the interview should progress. Remember, closed questions are used to confirm an issue or to gather a specific fact. If confirmation or a specific fact is not needed, then the interviewer finishes that funnel sequence (usually with a summary) before the closed questions and then goes on to the next area to be explored.

## EXAMPLE 6.1   PROBING

-ER: As you know, there are a number of problems with the Human Resource Information System we use in the company. What type of problems have you come across when using the system?

-EE: Well, trying to access information is always a problem. You know, you need to find out various bits and pieces. I guess it is to do with the system not linking the various parts. When someone takes leave without pay, then the system does deduct the right amount from their pay but it does not deduct the day from their leave records. You would think that the system would do the lot, wouldn't you? And another thing, when someone goes to a training course, the system does note their training record, but nothing is transferred to their department's Skills Matrix. We have to enter that information in by hand a second time.

-ER: So the main problem with the current Human Resource Information System is that the various parts are not linked. There are two specific problems — let's concentrate on the first. Tell me more about the problems between the pay record and the leave record.

-EE: Well, when someone goes on leave-without-pay they fill out a form. This leave form goes to the leave clerk, who enters the information into the computer under the Individual Leave Record. But then the leave clerk has to complete another form which he sends to the pay office. The computer system should automatically deduct the amount from both the leave record and the person's salary.

-ER: So the leave clerk has to do two actions — enter the leave into the computer and also complete another form. This other form that the leave clerk completes, what is it called?

-EE: Oh, that's the Salary Deduction Form. It has to be signed by the manager as well.

-ER: Okay, the leave clerk enters the information and also completes the Salary Deduction Form when someone has leave-without-pay. You also spoke about the problem when someone goes on a training course. Would you tell me more about that?

-EE: When someone gets trained we have to update their personal record on the HRIS. But the personnel records of each department are separate. It's the same problem really. We then have to open another field in the HRIS and enter the same information. It's a waste of time. And, of course, sometimes it is not done so it makes problems when we have to look up the information — and it can cause quite a bit of confusion.

-ER: So, it is the same general problem — you have to do two actions when a single entry should be all that is needed. I would just like to go back to the Salary Deduction Form. You said that the manager had to sign it. If the computer did both jobs — note the leave record and also deduct the salary — how would the manager approve the salary deduction?

[... and so the interview would continue.]

**Some points to note:**
1. The interviewer started with an open question in the stem-plus-query format.
2. The interviewee has provided information. The reply is fairly typical in that the first few sentences are not very clear. The interviewee is trying to make some sense of his or her thoughts and often, in the initial stages, they are not too logical. However, as the answer progresses, the meaning becomes more articulate.
3. The interviewer paraphrased the information back to the interviewer.
4. The interviewer chose to follow the first point about the leave and salary record.
5. The interviewer used a closed question to identify a fact — the name of the Salary Deduction Form.
6. The interviewer summarised the main information from this first point then followed up on the second point with another open question in the stem-plus-query format.
7. This information was again paraphrased. There was no need for a summary on the second as the paraphrasing did this role.

8. The interviewer then investigated a new point disclosed by the interviewee from the earlier closed question. The interviewer could have followed up this point when it was raised but this would have interfered with the flow of the interview. Instead, the interviewer chose to make it a third major point, as the interviewer considers it to be a very important issue.

## SUMMARISING

**Summarising** provides a break in the relentless search for information — a break for both the interviewer and the interviewee. Zima (1991:47) defines a summary as a restatement of the major ideas, facts, themes and/or feelings that the interviewee has expressed. He suggests that summaries are like internal summaries in a good speech. From our knowledge of adult learning, a summary can be seen as a good example of at least two principles of learning. First, the recency element refreshes the interviewee's memory. Second, the feedback provided is of two types — informational and motivational. The advantages of recency and feedback alone point up the importance of the skill of summarising.

Interviewers should summarise at the end of each questioning sequence (for example at the bottom of the funnel). This allows the interviewer to highlight the important points covered and to refresh the memories of each party regarding the salient points. The interviewee also has the opportunity to correct any misinterpretations that have occurred.

---

**EXAMPLE 6.2 — SUMMARISING**

Here is an example of inadequate summarising.
-ER: Yes, well, that was very interesting. You have made some very good points. They should be very useful for my enquiry. Thank you very much. Now I have some more questions.

Here is an example of good summarising.
-ER: Good, thank you. Looking at my notes here, you have made four very good points about helping customers at the library. First, on the return of books. The customers have no record of the return of their books and, if there is a later enquiry, the customers cannot prove that they have returned their books. Second, the returned books are not put back on the shelves quickly enough. You have found that, even though the library records indicate that books are available, they are not on the shelves, and sometimes you have found them on the return trolleys. Third, when lining up to check out books, you have noticed that some staff seem to be confused by the 'hold system' and have to ask their supervisor what to do. However, as a fourth point, you do like the friendly and helpful atmosphere in the library. You always feel that you can go to staff members and ask questions.

Okay, is there anything you would like to add to those points? No? Right, I would like to go on to the next point, which is about the computer services.
[... and so the interview would continue.]

**Some points to note:**
1. In the inadequate summary, the interviewer has given motivational feedback and has indicated that the interview will move on to further questions, but little else has been achieved.
2. In the good example, the interviewer has provided positive motivational feedback and then gone on to list and paraphrase the four points the interviewee made. The interviewer has also referred to the notes, indicating that the notes are not a secret record but can be shared.

3. In the good example, the interviewer has given the interviewee an opportunity to add more information.
4. In the good example, the interviewer has previewed the next area of questioning.

## NON-VERBAL BEHAVIOUR

The interviewer needs to be aware of non-verbal behaviour on two fronts. First, the non-verbal behaviour exhibited by the interviewer can have a dynamic effect on the interview. Second, reading the interviewee's non-verbal behaviour can provide useful insights into the progress of the interview and useful cues on when to press for more information or when to proceed more carefully on a particular topic.

Egan (1994:91–2) has provided a robust model that can be used successfully either for appropriate interviewer behaviour or for interpreting the interviewee's orientation. This model is called the SOLER System. Its main constituents are outlined below.

- Square on. The interviewer needs to stand or sit so that he or she is fully facing the interviewee. This gives the message that the interviewer is paying full attention to the interviewee's responses.
- Open posture. The interviewer should not be hunched down or 'closed off' from the interviewee (for example by having arms or legs crossed so that they form a barrier) but should sit up straight in an open posture. This indicates that the interviewer is willing to accept all the information from the interviewee and is usually interpreted as being non-defensive.
- Lean forward. Leaning slightly forward indicates involvement and interest. This posture says, 'I'm with you, I want to understand your message'. However, it should be noted that leaning too far forward suggests aggressiveness and should be avoided.
- Eyes. In our society, the eyes play an important part in communication. There are two issues to consider here. First, the distance from the eyes of the interviewer to the eyes of the interviewee should be at least a metre. This distance varies from culture to culture but a metre seems to be a comfortable distance for most western people. Any less and the interviewee may become unconsciously defensive, with a resultant suppression of information. Much more and the interviewee may feel that the interviewer is uninterested. Second, the amount of eye contact is important, although this also varies between cultures. However, in most cultures there is an accepted level of contact, with too little being just as inhibiting as too much.
- Relax. A relaxed interview atmosphere is usually more conducive to easy information flow. If the interviewer models relaxed non-verbal behaviour — slow, smooth rather than jerky movements, a calm facial expression and slower speech patterns — then the interviewee is more likely to follow this example.

The SOLER System provides a useful 'checklist' at the start of the interview. If the interviewer consciously concentrates on these non-verbal behaviours at the beginning, they tend to become automatic as the interview progresses and the interviewer becomes more interested in the topic of the interview itself.

The SOLER System also provides a very useful guide to assessing the involvement of the interviewee. The more defensive the interviewee, the more the interviewee's behaviour will appear to be anti-SOLER, with a tendency to stand or sit side on, to show a smaller profile by hunching down, to avoid eye contact and to seem anything but relaxed. Such anti-SOLER behaviour is a sure sign that the interviewee is not in the rapport zone. This usually means that the interviewee has not reacted positively to the ritual and the pass time, so the interviewer will need to spend more time on activity no. 1.

Another option is for the interviewer first to mimic, very subtly, the anti-SOLER non-verbal behaviour of the interviewee and then to gradually move to the SOLER posture. Frequently, if the changes in non-verbal behaviour are carefully gauged, the interviewee will gradually emulate the SOLER posture of the interviewer and, at the same time, become more open psychologically to allowing information to flow.

## STRUCTURED AND UNSTRUCTURED INTERVIEWS

Interviews can be categorised as highly structured or highly unstructured, these two points being the poles of a continuum. In other words there are infinite degrees of being structured or unstructured.

In an **unstructured interview** the interviewer does not enter into the interview setting with a planned sequence of questions for the respondent. The objective of the unstructured interview is to cause some preliminary issues to surface so that the researcher can decide what variables need further, in-depth investigation. In the unstructured interview, the interviewer starts with a broad, open primary question and then relies entirely on the interview skill of probing — questioning, paraphrasing and summarising — to manage the process and direction of the interview. An unstructured interview has the advantage of being unbiased by any pre-ordained ideas of the interviewer and, theoretically, more truly reflects the world of the interviewee. The disadvantage of the unstructured interview is that it can be very time-consuming and can wander away from the objectives of the research project. This means that no two interviews are the same and the breadth of the investigation can become very wide.

A **structured interview** is conducted when it is known at the outset what information is needed. The interviewer has a list of predetermined, standardised questions which are carefully ordered and worded in a detailed interview schedule, and each research subject is asked exactly the same questions, in exactly the same order (Minichiello et al. 1990:90). Each question is pre-planned and explores a specific topic — that is, the content of the questions is used to manage the direction of the interview. Structured interviews are used in situations where the differences in the interviewees' responses can be compared and interpreted as indicating real differences in what is being measured. The structured interview ensures that each interviewee answers the same questions and that opinion is canvassed for specific areas of enquiry only. However, the interview direction is heavily biased by the predetermined questions, and there is usually limited opportunity for the interviewee to provide further information. In structured interviews, the questions are posed either personally or over the telephone or through the medium of a personal computer.

The decision to use a structured or unstructured interview revolves around two factors. The first and main factor is whether a reasonable amount of information on the issues is already known. If so, then specific primary questions can be formulated for each of the issues. If only limited information is available on the issues, then the interviewer will have no recourse but to use a more unstructured format and rely on interviewing skills to manage the process to ensure that the objectives of the research project are accomplished. The second factor is the interview skills of the interviewer. The unstructured interview demands that the interviewer be highly experienced. On the other hand, the strict scheduling of the structured interview can often be used successfully by an unskilled interviewer.

Another option, of course, is to conduct a *semi-structured interview*. There are two basic strategies for this. The first is to commence the interaction as an unstructured interview — present the primary, overall question and then concentrate on managing the process by using interview skills to elicit information. When the information elicited appears to be drying up, the interviewer switches to planned questions based on defined, pre-identified topics — that is, questions based on content. So, for example, the investigator may start the interview with a very open question such as:

> The records indicate that customer complaints for the whole company have increased in the last three months by 32 per cent. In your experience, what do you see as some of the possible reasons for these complaints?

When the interviewer has used all her interview skills to explore the respondent's ideas, she may then choose to switch to some prepared questions on topics such as:
- the customer delivery systems
- the location of the complaints office
- the training of staff to handle difficult customers.

These are questions based on content. Where did the investigator find the content for these questions? Most probably from the preliminary information gathering stage. For example, before conducting the interviews, the investigator may have examined organisational records and gained some insights into possible causes of the customer complaints.

Another strategy for semi-structured interviews is to use a pre-planned, logical approach to manage the interview process. Writers such as Tregoe (1983), Zima (1991) and Egan (1994) have provided insights that could be combined into a five-step model to manage the process of a semi-structured interview.

- **Exploring the current situation:** The interviewer probes for a description of the current situation by identifying, clarifying and exploring the problem situations and unused opportunities. The interviewer will tend to concentrate on:
  - what is actually happening and the identity of the issue
  - where it is happening, or the location
  - when the event occurred
  - the extent of the event — how often; how serious or important.
- **Possible causes/options:** For example, the research project assumes that the people at the workfront have a wealth of knowledge and the interview should provide an opportunity for this knowledge to come to the fore. If the research project is examining a problem, then this step will concentrate on causes; if exploring an opportunity, the options will be the emphasis. Some techniques for assisting the process include:
  - listing the historical sequence of events to highlight the link that was most at risk or had the greatest impact on creating the problem, or the link that is easiest to repair
  - brainstorming — that is, asking people to come up with a list of ideas, no matter how far-fetched, without assessing them
  - asking people to compare and contrast how it used to be with how it is now; this product with that one; utopia with reality
  - concentrating on what has changed.
- **Identifying untrue causes/adverse consequences:** The investigator finds out if the suggested cause would eliminate the problem or if the suggested option would have other effects in another system.
- **Preferred scenario:** The investigator has people describe the preferred future scenario — defining activities that would occur, goals that would be achieved and people who would be affected. This is a good time to gather ideal examples, either

in descriptive form or as actual artefacts. These ideal solutions can often be used in formulating learning objectives or as part of the learning experience.
- **Planning the future:** The investigator gathers suggestions on how the proposed scenario should be planned, identifying the resources that will be needed, the timing of key events, the people who should be involved and any dangers that should be avoided.

## THE THREE LEVELS OF INTERVIEWING

The interview is a dynamic vehicle for exploring the rich and complex body of information possessed by an individual. The interview, as an interaction, is itself a very complex activity. The interviewer must operate on three levels. These are:
- the *content level*, at which the interviewer listens to and records the information the interviewee provides
- the *process level*, at which the interviewer uses the skills of questioning, paraphrasing, probing and attending to control the direction of the interview and encourage the interviewee to provide information
- the *executive level*. As Seidman (1991:57) points out, the interviewer must be conscious of time during the interview and be aware of how much has been used and how much there is to go. An interviewer must be sensitive to the interviewee's energy levels and continually make judgements on how to move the interview forward.

## TYPES OF INTERVIEWS

Particularly in business research, interviews are of three types — **face-to-face interviews**, **telephone interviews** and computer-assisted interviews.

### Face-to-face and telephone interviews

Interviews can be conducted either face to face or over the telephone. They can also be computer-assisted. Although most unstructured interviews in business research are conducted face to face, structured interviews can be either face to face or through the medium of the telephone, depending on the level of complexity of the issues involved, the likely duration of the interview, the convenience of both parties, and the geographical area covered by the survey. Telephone interviews are best suited when quick information from a large number of respondents spread over a wide geographic area is to be obtained, and the likely duration of each interview is, say, 10 minutes or less. Many market surveys, for instance, are conducted through structured telephone interviews. In addition, **Computer-assisted telephone interviews** (CATI) are also possible and easy to manage.

Face-to-face interviews and telephone interviews each have their advantages and disadvantages. These will now be briefly discussed.

### Face-to-face interviews

**Advantages**

The main advantage of face-to-face or direct interviews is that the researcher can adapt the questions as necessary, clarify doubts and ensure that the responses are properly understood by repeating or rephrasing the questions. The researcher can also pick up non-verbal cues from the respondent. Any discomfort, stress or problems that the respondent experiences can be detected through frowns, nervous tapping and other body language unconsciously exhibited by the respondent. These would obviously be impossible to detect in a telephone interview.

### Disadavantages

The main disadvantages of face-to-face interviews are the geographical limitations they may impose on the interviews and the vast resources needed if such interviews need to be carried out nationally or internationally. The costs of training interviewers to minimise interviewer biases (for example differences in questioning methods and interpretation of responses) are also high. Another drawback is that respondents might feel uncertain of the anonymity of their responses when they interact face to face with the interviewer.

## Telephone interviews

### Advantages

The main advantage of telephone interviewing, from the researcher's point of view, is that a number of different people can be reached (across the country or even internationally) in a relatively short period of time. Respondents often prefer the relative anonymity of a telephone interview. Some people feel less uncomfortable disclosing personal information over the phone than face to face.

### Disadvantages

A major disadvantage of telephone interviewing is that the respondent can unilaterally terminate the interview without warning or explanation by hanging up the phone. Caller ID may further aggravate the situation. This is understandable given the numerous telemarketing calls people are bombarded with on a daily basis. To minimise this type of a non-response problem, it would be advisable to contact the interviewee ahead of time to request participation in the interview, giving an approximate idea of how long the interview would last, and setting up a mutually convenient time. Interviewees usually appreciate this courtesy and are more likely to cooperate. It is also a good policy not to prolong the interview beyond the time originally stated. As mentioned earlier, another disadvantage of the telephone interview is that the researcher will not be able to see the respondent to read the non-verbal signs of impatience.

Interviewing is a useful data collection method, especially during the exploratory and descriptive stages of research. Where a large number of interviews are conducted with a number of different interviewers, it is important to train the interviewers with care in order to minimise interviewer bias manifested in voice inflections, particular wording and differences in interpretation, for instance. Good training decreases interviewer biases.

## Computer-assisted interviewing

With computer-assisted interviews (CAI), thanks to modern technology, questions are flashed onto the computer screen and interviewers can enter the respondent's answers directly into the computer. The accuracy of data collection is considerably enhanced since the software can be programmed to flag the 'off-base' or 'out-of-range' responses. CAI software also prevents interviewers from asking the wrong questions or asking them in the wrong sequence, since the questions are automatically flashed to the respondent in an ordered sequence. To some extent, this eliminates interviewer-induced biases.

## CATI and CAPI

There are two types of computer-assisted interview programs: CATI (computer-assisted telephone interviewing) and CAPI (computer-assisted personal interviewing).

CATI, used in research organisations, is useful inasmuch as responses to surveys can be obtained from people all over the world, since the PC is networked into the telephone system. The PC monitor prompts the questions with the help of software and the respondent provides the answers. The computer selects the telephone number, dials and places the responses in a file. The data are analysed later. Computerised, voice-activated telephone interviews are also possible for short surveys. Data can also be gathered during field surveys through hand-held computers which record and analyse responses.

CAPI involves big investments in hardware and software. CAPI has an advantage in that it can be self-administered; that is, respondents can run the program themselves on their own computers and enter their own responses, thereby reducing errors in recording. However, not everyone is comfortable using a personal computer.

The *voice recording system* assists CATI programs by recording interviewee's responses. Courtesy and ethics, as well as legal requirements, require that the respondent's permission to record be obtained before the *voice capture system* (VCS) is activated. The VCS allows the computer to capture the respondent's answers, which are recorded in a digital mode and stored in a data file. They can be played back later — for example to listen to customers by region, industry or any combination of factors.

In sum, the advantages of computer-assisted interviews are simply quick and more accurate information gathering, plus faster and easier analysis of data. The field costs are low and automatic tabulation of results is possible. Indeed, they are more efficient in terms of costs and time, once the initial heavy investment in equipment and software is made. However, to be really cost-effective, the surveys should be large and done frequently enough to warrant the heavy front-end investment and programming costs.

## Computer-aided survey services

Several research organisations offer their services to companies that engage in occasional data gathering. For instance, the National Computer Network provides computer survey services for conducting marketing studies. Some of the advantages of using these services are listed below.

- The researcher can start analysing the data even as the field survey is progressing, since results can be transmitted to clients through their modem in raw or tabulated form.
- Data can be automatically 'cleaned up' and any errors fixed even as they are being collected.
- Biases due to ordering questions in a particular way (known as the ordering effects) can be eliminated, since meaningful random start patterns can be incorporated into the questioning process.
- Skip patterns (for example, *if the answer to this question is NO, skip to question #19*) can be programmed into the process.
- Questions can be customised to incorporate the respondents' terminology of concepts into subsequent questions.

Computer surveys can be conducted either by mailing the disks to respondents or through on-line surveys, with the respondents' personal computers being hooked up to computer networks. Survey System, provided by Creative Research Systems, and Compaq Co.'s Interview System are two of several computer survey systems that are currently available on the market.

## Advantages of computer packages

Field notes taken by interviewers as they collect data have generally to be transcribed, hand-coded and hand-tabulated — all of which are tedious and time-consuming. Computers vastly facilitate the interviewer's job with regard to these activities. Automatic indexing of the data can be achieved with special programs. The two modes in operation are *indexing*, so that specific responses are coded in a particular way, and *retrieval* of data with a fast search speed — going through 10 000 pages in less than five seconds. A text-oriented database management retrieval program allows the user to go through the text, inserting marks that link related units of text. The associated links formed are analytical categories specified by the researcher. Once the links are created, the program allows the user to activate them by opening multiple windows on the screen.

We can see that computers have a large impact on data collection. With greater technological advances and falling hardware and software costs, computer-assisted interviews will become a primary method of data collection in the future.

## Review of interviewing

Interviews are one method of obtaining data; they can be either unstructured or structured, and can be conducted face to face, over the telephone or through the medium of a PC. Unstructured interviews are usually conducted to obtain definite ideas about what is and is not important and relevant to particular problem situations. Structured interviews give more in-depth information about specific variables of interest. To minimise bias in responses, the interviewer must establish rapport with the respondents and ask **unbiased questions**. The face-to-face interview and that conducted over the telephone have their advantages and disadvantages; both are useful under different circumstances. Computer-assisted interviewing, which entails a heavy initial investment, can greatly facilitate interviewing and the analysis of qualitative, spontaneous responses. We can expect computer interactive interviews to become an increasingly important mode of data collection in the future.

The interview is ideally suited for extracting information from an individual. Where qualitative information from two or more people is required, the focus group is used.

## THE FOCUS GROUP

The focus group method is a research technique that collects information through group interaction on a topic determined by the researcher; the researcher's interest provides the focus while the information come from the group interaction (Morgan 1997:6).

As a data gathering device for a research project, the focus group has a number of similarities with the interview. First, the facilitator of a focus group must operate at three levels — the content, the process and the executive. As with the interview, the management of the process is the most complex of these levels. Second, the conduct of the focus group is based on the same six factors:

1. The overall pattern is based on an entry time investment, with the steps of ritual, pass time, reason, rules, preview and activity no. 1, activity no. 2, intimacy (if needed) and exit time investment, with final comments, summary, future, final questions, pass time and ritual.
2. The ability to listen is still paramount.
3. Questioning by the facilitator still guides and controls the interaction.

4. The participants still need to hear paraphrasing to be reassured that their message has been received and understood.
5. The facilitator probes to uncover all the information required.
6. Non-verbal behaviour of the facilitator is used to encourage responses, and the facilitator observes the non-verbal behaviour of the participants to check for levels of involvement and understanding.

However, the differences between the interview and the focus group highlight the role that the facilitator will need to play in managing the process of a focus group. Morgan (1997:10–11) points out that the focus group method provides direct and immediate evidence about similarities and differences in participants' opinions and experiences, as opposed to reaching such conclusions from post hoc analysis of separate statements from each interviewee. He goes on to acknowledge that the individual interviews have the distinct advantage with regard to the amount of control the interviewer has and the greater amount of time that each informant has to provide information. However, it is interesting to note that an investigation by Fern (1982) showed that focus groups did not produce significantly more or better quality information than an equivalent number of individual interviews.

In conducting a focus group, a facilitator has to be aware of a number of specific issues — among them, whether the focus group should be structured or unstructured, the logistics, group composition and the processes of conducting the focus group.

## STRUCTURED AND UNSTRUCTURED FOCUS GROUPS

As with the interview, a decision needs to be made on whether the focus group should be structured or unstructured. A structured focus group is governed by predetermined content questions, while the unstructured approach uses an initial open primary question and then relies on the skills of the facilitator to manage the process. A semi-structured focus group starts off being unstructured, then the facilitator brings in the predetermined, content-based questions.

## LOGISTICS

A focus group brings together a number of people at a common time in a relatively large space that is comfortable, quiet and free from interruptions. Associated equipment such as chairs, tables, audio or video taping facilities, visual aids and writing material is also usually needed. While the steps in planning a focus group are the same as those discussed for the interview, planning the logistics, so that a focus group runs smoothly, can take considerable time.

Accessing financial resources is also usually more involved. Morgan (1997:32) points out that major cost factors include salaries to facilitators, travel to research sites, rental of research workshop rooms, payments to participants, and producing and transcribing tapes.

## GROUP COMPOSITION

The investigator must give careful thought to the membership of the groups. One of the assumed benefits of focus groups is that the individuals in the group can 'piggy-back' and 'leapfrog' off one another's ideas, thus generating a richer accumulation of data. Unfortunately, this interaction can also contaminate the outcome, if not carefully managed, with stronger participants taking over the group.

Another problem that can occur with inappropriate group composition results from having a group with too diverse a background. The diversity of interests can result in too many, and even inappropriate, issues being raised, with the result that the time investment increases significantly. Accordingly, several factors need to be considered when assembling a group.

## Homogeneity

The degree of homogeneity or sameness in the group will depend on the objectives of the research project. If in-depth discussion is needed on a particular issue, then the group will need to be homogeneous in a number of ways. For example, if the perceptions of upper management on a particular situation are to be compared with those of operating staff, then there may be a need for at least two focus groups — one consisting of upper managers and another of operating staff. On the other hand, if the objective is to gather information from a wide variety of staff, then a mixture of participants may produce richer and more relevant data. Kruger (1994:77) suggests that the focus group is characterised by homogeneity but with sufficient variation among participants to allow for contrasting opinion.

## Representation

Quite often the entire target population cannot be canvassed, so a sample of representatives are brought together in the focus group. It is important to ensure that these representatives are likely to mirror the opinions of the target population. Previous comments on sampling should be considered here.

## Strangers versus acquaintances

Whether it is preferable to select individuals who do or do not know one another is debatable. Morgan (1997) suggests that the rule of thumb favours strangers, although he acknowledges that this is not a necessity. Indeed, avoiding acquaintanceships within organisations is virtually impossible.

## Size of group

There are conflicting issues to consider when deciding the optimum size of a group. The smaller the group, the more time each participant has to contribute views. However, the smaller the group, the less chance there is of representation of the target population and the greater the chance that one strong individual can hijack the agenda. Morgan (1997) considers that small groups can be easily disrupted by friendship pairs, 'experts' or uncooperative participants — therefore, small groups are likely to work best when the participants are interested in the topic and respectful of one another. Large groups, on the other hand, simply because of the tyranny of numbers, require considerable skill to manage the group processes. In addition, as groups increase in size, they tend to become more complex and formally structured (Forsyth 1990).

Kruger (1994) suggests as a rule of thumb a range of six to nine members, although one should not feel confined by this upper and lower limit.

## CONDUCTING THE FOCUS GROUP

Figure 6.2 provides a good outline for the conduct of a focus group and allows the facilitator to work though the stages of entry investment time, activity stage and exit investment stage. Focus groups rarely descend to the intimacy level as the public context usually inhibits such disclosures. Fontana and Frey (1998) believe that the skills required by a group facilitator are not significantly different from those needed by an interviewer of individuals. The facilitator will use the same process skills — questioning, probing and encouraging non-verbal behaviour.

Fontana and Frey (1998) report that a facilitator of focus groups has three specific goals: first, the facilitator must keep one person or a small coalition of persons from dominating the group; second, he or she must encourage reluctant respondents to participate; and third, he or she must obtain responses from the entire group to ensure the fullest possible coverage. To achieve these goals there are five specific considerations that need attention while conducting focus groups.

## Facilitator team

Kruger (1994) recommends considering using a facilitator team — perhaps comprising a facilitator and an assistant facilitator. The facilitator can concentrate on directing the discussion and recording the group's views on a whiteboard, while the assistant can take more comprehensive notes.

## Recording

Consider if technology is needed to assist with data gathering. Using audio or video recording devices can preserve a range of detail and be a significant memory aid during the analytic stage. However, recognise that such recording can cause participants to suppress information.

## Use of visual aids

When talking to a group, it is difficult to be sure that you have the attention of everyone. It is also more difficult to recognise feedback from so many people. Using visual aids (i.e. multiple sense learning) can help overcome these problems, particularly on the following three occasions.

- During the introduction, the *objectives* of the research project can be shown on the overhead projector.
- Each *new question* can also be displayed on the overhead projector. If the question is presented only orally, misinterpretations can occur. In addition, the question can remain on the overhead projector for some time, allowing the participants to refer to it and helping to keep the discussion on track.
- The *ideas* offered by the group should be recorded on a whiteboard or similar device. This has at least three advantages. The offeree is rewarded by seeing her or his idea accepted visually. This reward is doubled if the facilitator paraphrases at the same time. Second, other participants can use an idea displayed on the whiteboard to generate new ideas. Third, the list can be easily used to summarise at strategic points during the focus group interaction.

## Thinking time

Borrowing from the Nominal Group Technique, it is often advisable to allow group members to think about and write down ideas individually on a piece of paper when each question or cue is presented. This gives everyone a chance to collect their thoughts and tends to mitigate the overbearing predilections of the opinionated individual who likes to take over the focus group agenda. If someone has written down an idea, he or she usually shares it with limited encouragement, thus assuring contribution from all members.

## Group dynamics

A variety of forces operate within a group, and these forces are known collectively as group dynamics. Early work by such researchers as Benne and Sheats (1948) and Bales (1950) suggested two important functions carried out by groups — task and maintenance — and that within these functions a variety of roles are performed by the group members. The *task roles* encompass all behaviours that help the group achieve its goal or objective. In a focus group this task activity is the answering of questions. They contribute to the good working relationships of the group by encouraging a collaborative attitude. A number of more recent authors (for example Dunphy with Dick 1981; Forsyth 1990; Napier & Gershenfeld 1993) have expanded on this early work on group roles. Roles within each of the functions that are important to focus groups are described in tables 6.1 and 6.2.

**Table 6.1** Task roles in focus groups

| Initiator | Provides new ideas or solutions concerning the problem at hand or suggests different ways to approach the problem; is often deferred to by the group |
|---|---|
| Information giver | Being a topic expert, provides facts and data; acts in an advisory capacity to the group |
| Information seeker | Calls for background, factual information from other members |
| Elaborator | Gives additional information in the form of examples or rephrases others' contributions |
| Opinion giver | Provides opinions, values and feelings |
| Opinion seeker | Seeks more qualitative data, such as attitudes, values and feelings |
| Coordinator | Points out the relevance of each idea and its relationship to the focus group objective |
| Evaluator | Appraises the quality of the group's offerings, logic and results; questions the validity or relevance of the facts raised by the group; seeks clarification of vague ideas or issues |
| Representative | Acts as a spokesperson for others outside the group and speaks for the group as a whole. |

The facilitator must be able to differentiate between task and maintenance functions and recognise the roles of each. Schein (1969) recommends that group facilitators should stay at the process level and not stray into the content. Following this recommendation, the facilitator of focus groups should not become involved in any of the task roles. Rather, the facilitator should recognise and encourage the contributions of each role within the task function. So, if the group is not making any progress, the facilitator may ask the person who has been filling the initiator role for a contribution. However, it is important to recognise that any group member may fill any of the roles at various points — for example, as the discussion moves from topic to topic, different members may fill the information-giver role.

**Table 6.2** Maintenance roles in focus groups

| Encourager | Rewards others through agreement, warmth and praise; asks for additional examples or inquires if others have a similar opinion |
|---|---|
| Harmoniser | Mediates conflict among group members or between different points of view |
| Gatekeeper | Ensures equal participation from members; establishes procedures and ground rules that encourage smooth communications |
| Orienter | Refocuses discussion on topic when necessary |
| Energiser | Stimulates the group to continue working when discussion flags |
| Expresser | Expresses the emotions the group is feeling and sometimes 'triggers' emotional responses from other members |
| Confronter | Tends to take the 'hard-nosed' approach and exposes interpersonal conflicts; is impatient with delays and confusion |
| Tension reliever | Introduces humour when group tension is high; encourages a relaxed atmosphere |
| Recorder | Provides a record of the information provided by the participants. This record is of two types — a visual record to help the group in processing the data and a permanent record for later analysis. |

If the facilitator attends to the maintenance roles, then he or she will fulfil Schein's recommendation to concentrate on managing the process. However, group members will also often perform maintenance roles. The facilitator therefore needs to decide when to use one of the roles and when to allow or encourage one of the participants to fill the role. Typically, the facilitator tends to use the roles of recorder, encourager, gatekeeper, orienter and energiser. While the facilitator does enter the other roles, it is sometimes better to allow one of the group members to take on the responsibility. For example, tension reliever is a role sometimes best occupied by a participant, particularly if the tension reliever is also the expresser. Of course, the facilitator may find the need to become the tension reliever, but must be careful that this contribution is not viewed as flippant or as demonstrating a lack of concentration on the goal of the focus group.

Benne and Sheats (1948) and Bales (1950) also suggested that some *individual idiosyncratic behaviours* can compromise the achievement of the group goals. The facilitator needs to be on the lookout for these behaviours and plan ways of overcoming them. Napier and Gershenfeld (1993:257) suggest being aware of five of these behavioural types. The *aggressor* questions the very use and existence of the focus group using thinly veiled sarcasm, and makes personal attacks on the facilitator and individual group members. The *blocker* criticises every suggestion and idea. The *self-confessor* uses the audience to express personal problems, seeking sympathy and atonement. The *recognition-seeker* boasts of personal conquests and past successes. The *dominator* likes to be 'top dog' and uses strategies such as interrupting, flattery and asserting superior status. The thing to remember about these dysfunctional behaviours is that they represent personal agendas that run contrary to the needs and goals of the group. The behaviours are games that satisfy the needs of the aberrant individual. The facilitator can draw on a number of strategies to cope with these situations.

- Allow the group the chance to retain control. Often the confronter is good at this role.
- Use non-verbal behaviour to discourage the individual — for example, go against the SOLER method: do not look them in the eyes and stand sideways to them.
- Do not paraphrase their aberrant offerings but reward them for positive contributions.
- Remind the group of the question by pointing to the overhead projector and restating the question.
- Summarise the progress so far and go back to the question.
- As a last resort, confess that you cannot see how the aberrant contribution helps the focus group achieve its goals. Be careful of this option as it can have negative repercussions.

Three of these considerations in particular — use of visual aids, thinking time and group dynamics — and the associated skills separate the focus group from the interview. They are also what makes the facilitation of focus groups both exciting and challenging.

## SUMMARY OF FOCUS GROUPS

Focus groups collect data from groups of respondents and have a number of similarities with interviews, including the use of an overall pattern to structure the focus group and the importance of the skills of listening, questioning, probing and summarising. When planning a focus group, the facilitator has to pay special attention to the logistics of bringing the group together and the group composition. When conducting the focus group, the facilitator should consider the use of visual aids, the recording process and particularly the role of group dynamics.

## OBSERVATIONAL STUDIES

Whereas interviews and questionnaires elicit responses from the subjects, it is possible to gather data without asking questions of respondents. People can be observed in their natural work environment or in the lab setting, and their activities and behaviours or other points of interest recorded.

Apart from the activities performed by the individuals under study, their movements, work habits, the statements made and meetings conducted by them, their facial expressions of joy, anger and other emotions, and body language can be observed. Other environmental factors, such as workplace layout, workflow patterns, how close the seating arrangement is, can also be noted. Children can be assessed as to their interests and attention span with various stimuli, such as their involvement with different toys. Such observation would help toy manufacturers, child educators, day-care administrators and others responsible for children's development to design and model ideas based on children's interests, which are more easily observed than traced in any other manner.

The researcher can play one of two roles while gathering field observational data — that of **nonparticipant-observer** or participant-observer.

# TYPES OF OBSERVER ROLES

## Nonparticipant-observer

The researcher can collect the needed data in the role of a researcher without trying to become an integral part of the organisational system. For example, the researcher might sit in the corner of an office and observe and record how the manager spends her time. Observation of all the activities of managers over a period of several days will allow the researcher to make some generalisations on how managers typically spend their time. By merely observing the activities, recording them in a systematic way and tabulating them, the researcher comes up with some findings. For this purpose, observers must be physically present in the workplace for extended periods of time, which makes observational studies time-consuming.

## Participant-observer

The researcher can also play the role of the **participant-observer**. Here, the researcher enters the organisation or the research setting, becoming a part of the work team. For instance, if a researcher wants to study group dynamics in work organisations, then she may enter the organisation in the role of an employee and observe the dynamics in groups while being a part of the work organisation and work groups. Much anthropological research is conducted in this manner, with researchers becoming a part of the alien culture they are interested in studying in depth.

# STRUCTURED VERSUS UNSTRUCTURED OBSERVATIONAL STUDIES

## Structured observational studies

As we have seen, observational studies can be of either the nonparticipant-observer or the participant-observer type. Both of these, again, can be either structured or unstructured. Where the observer has a predetermined set of categories of activities or phenomena to be studied, it is a **structured observational study**. Formats for recording the observations can be specifically designed and tailored to each study to suit the goal of the research.

Usually, such matters that pertain to the feature of interest, like the duration and frequency of the event, and also certain activities that precede and follow the feature of interest, are recorded. Environmental conditions, and any changes in setting, are also noted if they are considered relevant. Task-relevant behaviours of the actors, their perceived emotions, verbal and non-verbal communication and so on are recorded. Observations that are recorded in worksheets or field notes are systematically analysed, with minimal personal inferences made by the investigator. Categories can then be developed for further analysis, as described in chapter 7.

## Unstructured observational studies

At the beginning of a study it is possible that the observer has no definite ideas of the particular aspects that need focus. Observing events as they happen may be part of the plan, as in many qualitative studies. In such cases, the observer will record almost everything that is observed. Such a study will be an **unstructured observational study**.

Unstructured observational studies are claimed to be the hallmark of qualitative research. The investigator might entertain a set of tentative research objectives that serve as a guide as to who, when, where and how the individual will observe. Once the information needed is observed and recorded over a period of time, patterns can be traced, and inductive discovery can then pave the way for subsequent theory building and hypothesis testing.

# ADVANTAGES AND DISADVANTAGES OF OBSERVATIONAL STUDIES

The specific advantages and disadvantages to gathering data through observation are listed below.

## Advantages of observational studies

The following are among the advantages of observational studies.
1. The information obtained through observation of events as they normally occur are generally more reliable and free from respondent bias.
2. In observational studies, it is easier to note the effects of environmental influences on specific outcomes. For example, the weather (hot, cold, rainy), the day of the week (midweek as opposed to Monday or Friday), and other factors that might have a bearing on, say, the sales of a product, traffic patterns or absenteeism can be noted and meaningful patterns might emerge from these types of data.
3. It is easier to observe certain groups of individuals (for example very young children and extremely busy executives) from whom it may be otherwise difficult to obtain information.

The preceding three advantages are perhaps unique to observational studies.

## Disadvantages of observational studies

The following drawbacks of observational studies should also be noted.
1. It is necessary for the observer to be *physically* present (unless a camera or another mechanical system can capture the events of interest), often for prolonged periods of time.
2. This method of collecting data is not only slow, but also tedious and expensive.
3. Because of the long periods for which subjects are observed, observer fatigue can easily set in, which may bias the recorded data.
4. Although moods, feelings and attitudes can be guessed by observing facial expressions and other non-verbal behaviours, the cognitive thought processes of individuals cannot be captured.
5. Observers have to be trained in what and how to observe, and ways to avoid observer bias.

# BIAS IN OBSERVATIONAL STUDIES

Information observed from the researcher's point of view is likely to be prone to observer bias. There could be recording errors, memory lapses and errors in interpreting activities, behaviours, events and non-verbal cues. Moreover, where several observers are involved, interobserver reliability has to be established before the data can be accepted. Observation of events day in and day out, over extended periods of time, can fatigue or bore the observers and introduce biases in the recording of the observations. To minimise observer bias, observers are usually trained in how to observe and what to record. Good observational studies also establish interobserver reliability. This can also be established during the training of the observers, when videotaped stimuli can be used to determine interobserver reliability. A simple formula can be used for the purpose — dividing the number of agreements among the trainees by the number of agreements and disagreements, thus establishing the **reliability** coefficient.

Respondent bias can also pose a threat to the validity of the results of observational studies, because those who are observed may behave differently during the period the study is conducted, especially if the observations are carried out for a short period of time. However, in studies of longer duration, as the study progresses the employees become more relaxed and tend to behave normally. For these reasons, researchers undertaking observational studies discount the data recorded in the initial few days if they seem to be different from what is observed later.

## SUMMARY OF OBSERVATIONAL STUDIES

Observational studies have a formulated research purpose and are systematically planned. Such studies can be structured or unstructured, with the investigator being a participant or a nonparticipant in the study setting. All phenomena of interest are systematically recorded, and quality control can be exercised by eliminating biases. Observational studies can provide rich data and insights into the nature of the phenomena observed. Such studies have contributed greatly to our understanding of interpersonal and group dynamics. Interestingly, observational data can be quantified.

## OTHER SPECIAL DATA SOURCES

There are situations where machines can provide data by recording the events of interest as they occur, without a researcher being physically present. Nielsen ratings are an oft-cited example in this regard. Other examples include collection of details of products sold by types or brands tracked through optical scanners and bar codes at the checkout counter, and tracking systems by keeping a record of how many individuals utilise a facility or visit a website. Film and electronic recording devices such as video cameras can also be used to record data. Such mechanically observed data are error-free.

## PROJECTIVE METHODS

Certain ideas and thoughts that cannot easily be verbalised or that remain at unconscious levels in the respondents' minds can usually be brought to the surface through **motivational research**. This is typically done by trained professionals who apply different probing techniques in order to uncover deep-rooted ideas and thoughts in the respondents. Familiar techniques for eliciting such data are word associations, sentence completion, thematic apperception tests (TAT) and inkblot tests.

**Word-association** techniques, such as asking the respondent to quickly associate a word — say, *work* — with the first thing that comes to mind, are often used to uncover true attitudes and feelings. The reply indicates what work means to the individual. Similarly, *sentence completion* requires the respondent to quickly complete a sentence, such as 'Work is ...'. One respondent might say, 'Work is a lot of fun', whereas another might say, 'Work is drudgery'. These responses provide insights into individuals' feelings and attitudes towards work.

**Thematic apperception tests (TAT)** ask the respondent to develop a story around a picture that is shown. Several need patterns and personality characteristics in employees can be traced through these tests. **Inkblot tests**, another form of motivational research, use coloured inkblots that are interpreted by the respondents, who explain what they see in the various patterns and colours.

Although these types of **projective tests** are useful for tapping attitudes and feelings that are difficult to obtain otherwise, they cannot be engaged in by researchers who are not trained to conduct motivational research.

Consumer preferences, buying attitudes and behaviours, product development and other marketing research strategies make substantial use of in-depth probing. TAT and inkblot tests are on their way out in marketing research since advertisers and others are now utilising the sentence completion tests and word-association tests more frequently. Sketch drawings, collages from magazine pictures, filling in the balloon captions of cartoon characters and other strategies are also being followed to see how individuals associate different products, brands and advertisements in their minds. Agencies frequently ask subjects to sketch 'typical' users of various brands and narrate stories about them. The messages conveyed through the unsophisticated drawings are said to be very powerful, helping development of different marketing strategies.

The idea behind motivational research is that 'emotionality' ('I identify with it' feeling) rather than 'rationality' ('it is good for me' thought) — which is what keeps a product or practice alive — is captured. Emotionality is a powerful motivator of actions and knowledge of what motivates individuals to act is very useful. The failure of attempts to trade in the 'New Coke' for 'Classic Coke' is an oft-cited example of the emotional aspect. Emotionality is clearly at the non-rational, subconscious level, lending itself to capture by projective techniques alone.

# SECONDARY DATA

Secondary data are indispensable for much business research. As discussed in chapter 3, secondary data refer to information gathered by someone other than the researcher conducting the current study. Such data can be internal or external to the organisation and can be accessed through the computer or by going through recorded or published information.

There are several sources of external data, including books and periodicals, government publications of economic indicators, census data, statistical abstracts and databases (as discussed in chapter 3), the media, annual reports of companies and so on. Much internal data could be proprietary and not accessible to all.

Secondary data can be used for such things as forecasting sales by constructing models based on past sales figures and through extrapolation. Financial databases are also available for research. The Compustat Database contains information on thousands of companies organised by industry, and information on global companies is also available through Compustat.

The advantage of secondary data is the savings in time and costs of acquiring information that are generated. However, secondary data as the sole source of information have the drawbacks of becoming obsolete and not meeting the specific needs of the particular situation or setting.

## Other secondary sources of information

We discussed secondary sources of data in some detail earlier. Case studies and other archival records can provide a lot of information for research and problem solving. Such data are mostly qualitative in nature. Included in the secondary sources are the schedules maintained for or by key personnel, the desk calendar of executives and the speeches delivered by them.

*Trace measures* or **unobtrusive measures** as they are also called, come from a source that does not involve people. One example is the wear and tear on journals in a university library, which offers a good indication of their popularity, their use or both. The number of different brands of soft drink cans found in garbage bins can also provide a measure of their consumption levels. Signatures on cheques exposed to ultraviolet rays can indicate the extent of forgery and frauds; actuarial records are good sources for collecting data on births, marriages and deaths in a community; and company records disclose a lot of personal information about employees, the level of company efficiency and other data. These unobtrusive sources of data and their use are also important in research.

## PANELS

Panels are another source of information for research purposes. Whereas focus groups meet for a one-time group session, panels (of members) meet more than once. In cases where the effects of certain interventions or changes are to be studied over a period of time, **panel studies** are very useful. Several individuals are randomly chosen to serve as panel members for a research study. For instance, if the effects of a proposed advertisement for a certain brand of coffee are to be assessed quickly, the panel members can be exposed to the advertisement and their intentions of purchasing that brand assessed. This can be taken as indicating the response that could be expected of consumers if they were exposed to the advertisement. A few months later, the product manager might consider changing the flavour of the same product and might explore its effects on this panel. Thus, a continuing set of 'experts' serve as the sample base or sounding board for assessing the effects of change. These members are called a panel, and research that uses this panel is called a panel study.

The Nielsen Television Index is based on the television viewing patterns of a panel. The index is designed to provide estimates of the size and nature of the audience for individual television programs. The data are gathered through Audimeter instruments attached to the television sets in approximately 1200 cooperating households. The Audimeters are connected to a central computer, which records when the set is turned on, and what channel is tuned. From these data, Nielsen develops estimates of the number and percentage of all TV households viewing a given TV show. Other panels used in marketing research include the National Purchase Diary Panel, the National Family Opinion Panel and the Consumer Mail Panel.

### Static and dynamic panels

Panels can be either *static* (that is, the same members serve on the panel over extended periods of time) or *dynamic* (the panel members change from time to time as various phases of the study are in progress). The main advantage of the static panel is that it offers a sensitive measurement of the changes that take place between two points in time — a much better option than using two different groups at two different times. The disadvantage, however, is that the panel members could become so sensitive to the changes as a result of continuous interviews that their opinions might no longer be representative of those held by others in the population. Members could also drop out of the panel from time to time for various reasons, thus raising issues of bias due to mortality. The advantages and disadvantages of the **dynamic panel** are the reverse of the ones discussed for the static panel.

## ETHICS IN DATA COLLECTION

Several ethical issues should be addressed while collecting data. As previously noted, these pertain to those who sponsor the research, those who collect the data and those who offer it. The *sponsors* should ask for the study to be undertaken in the interests of the organisation, and not for any self-serving reason. They should respect the confidentiality of the data obtained by the researcher, and not ask for the individual or group responses to be disclosed to them or ask to see the questionnaires. Once the report is submitted, they should be open-minded in accepting the results and recommendations presented by the researchers.

## ETHICS AND THE RESEARCHER

1. Treating the information given by the respondent as strictly confidential and guarding his or her privacy is one of the primary responsibilities of the researcher. If the confidentiality of the survey has been communicated to the organisational executives before the survey starts, then, should a general manager or another top executive desire to take a look at the completed questionnaires, the prior understanding can be brought to their attention. Also, reports on data for a subgroup of, say, fewer than 10 individuals, should be dealt with tactfully to preserve confidentiality. The data can be combined with other information or treated in another unidentifiable manner. It is difficult to sanitise reports to protect sources and still preserve the richness of detail of the study. An acceptable alternative has to be found, since preserving confidentiality is the fundamental goal.
2. Researchers should not misrepresent the nature of the study to subjects, especially in laboratory experiments. The purpose of the research must be explained to them.
3. Personal or seemingly intrusive information should not be solicited, and if it is absolutely necessary for the project, it should be tapped from the respondent with high sensitivity, with specific reasons given.
4. Whatever the nature of the data collection method, the self-esteem and self-respect of the subjects should never be violated.
5. No one should be forced to respond to the survey, and if someone turns down the opportunity to participate, the individual's desire should be respected. Informed consent of the subjects should be the goal of the researcher. This holds true even when data are collected through mechanical means, like recording interviews, videotaping and the like.
6. Nonparticipant observers should be as unintrusive as possible. In qualitative studies, personal values can easily bias the data. It is necessary for the researcher to make explicit his or her assumptions, expectations and biases, so that informed decisions regarding the quality of the data can be made by the manager.
7. In laboratory studies, the subjects should be debriefed with full disclosure of the reason for the experiment after they have participated in the study.

8. Subjects should never be exposed to situations in which they could be subject to physical or mental harm. The researcher should take personal responsibility for their safety.
9. There should be absolutely no misrepresentation or distortion in reporting the data collected during the study.

# ETHICAL BEHAVIOURS OF RESPONDENTS

1. The subject, once having exercised the choice to participate in a study, should cooperate fully in the tasks ahead, such as responding to a survey or taking part in an experiment.
2. The respondent also has an obligation to be truthful and honest in the responses. Misrepresentation, or giving information knowing it to be untrue, should be avoided.

## SUMMARY

In this chapter we examined the assumptions of qualitative research, including the emphasis on understanding and taking the perspectival view, the goal of discovering patterns and accepting the role of indwelling. The need for accuracy and replicability is recognised by qualitative researchers by using triangulation, acknowledging subjectivity and bias, and ensuring referential adequacy. Three main methods of qualitative research were discussed — the interview, focus groups and observational studies. In addition, other data gathering methods were introduced, including projective methods, secondary data and panels. Finally, the importance of ethical behaviour in qualitative research was emphasised.

## DISCUSSION POINTS

1 List and discuss at least five ways that a qualitative researcher ensures accuracy and replicability.

2 What is bias and how can it be reduced during interviews?

3 Describe, and explain the benefits of, a well-patterned interview.

4 What are projective techniques and how can they be profitably used?

5 Using examples, describe how you would use probing in an interview.

6 What is the difference between an unstructured and a structured focus group?

7 Discuss four factors that should be considered about the group composition of a focus group.

8 Describe how the task and maintenance roles can be used to help the facilitation of a focus group.

9 How have technological advances helped data gathering?

10 How would you use the data from an observational study to reach scientific conclusions?

11 'The fewer biases in measurement and in data collection procedures, the more scientific the research.' Comment on this statement.

| | |
|---|---|
| Exercise 6.1 | A production manager wants to assess the reactions of the blue-collar workers in her department (including supervisors) to the introduction of computer-integrated manufacturing (CIM) systems. She is particularly interested in knowing how they would perceive the effects of CIM on:<br>a. their future jobs<br>b. additional training they would have to receive<br>c. future job advancement.<br>Plan a focus group for the production manager and describe how you would conduct the focus group. |
| Exercise 6.2 | Seek permission from a lecturer at your university to sit in on two sessions of his or her class, and conduct an unstructured, nonparticipant observational study. Give your conclusions on the data, and include in a short report your observation sheets and tabulations. |
| Exercise 6.3 | Conduct first an unstructured, and later a structured, interview with any lecturer at your university who is unknown to you. The research objective is to identify her or his values and strategy in teaching courses. Write up the results, and include the formats you used for both stages of the research. |

# chapter 7

# QUALITATIVE DATA ANALYSIS AND INTERPRETATION

## OUTLINE
THE OVERLAP OF DATA GATHERING AND ANALYSIS
THE PURPOSE OF QUALITATIVE ANALYSIS
STRUCTURED AND UNSTRUCTURED METHODS
CONTENT ANALYSIS
USING A COMPUTER PACKAGE
SUMMARY
DISCUSSION POINTS

## CHAPTER OBJECTIVES
After completing this chapter, you should be able to:
- describe the overlap between data gathering and data analysis in qualitative research
- explain the difference between the analysis of qualitative data gathered by structured methods and that gathered by unstructured methods
- list and describe the 15 steps of content analysis
- discuss how the analysis of qualitative data is a rich, messy and complex process
- describe how a computer package can assist the researcher in analysing qualitative data.

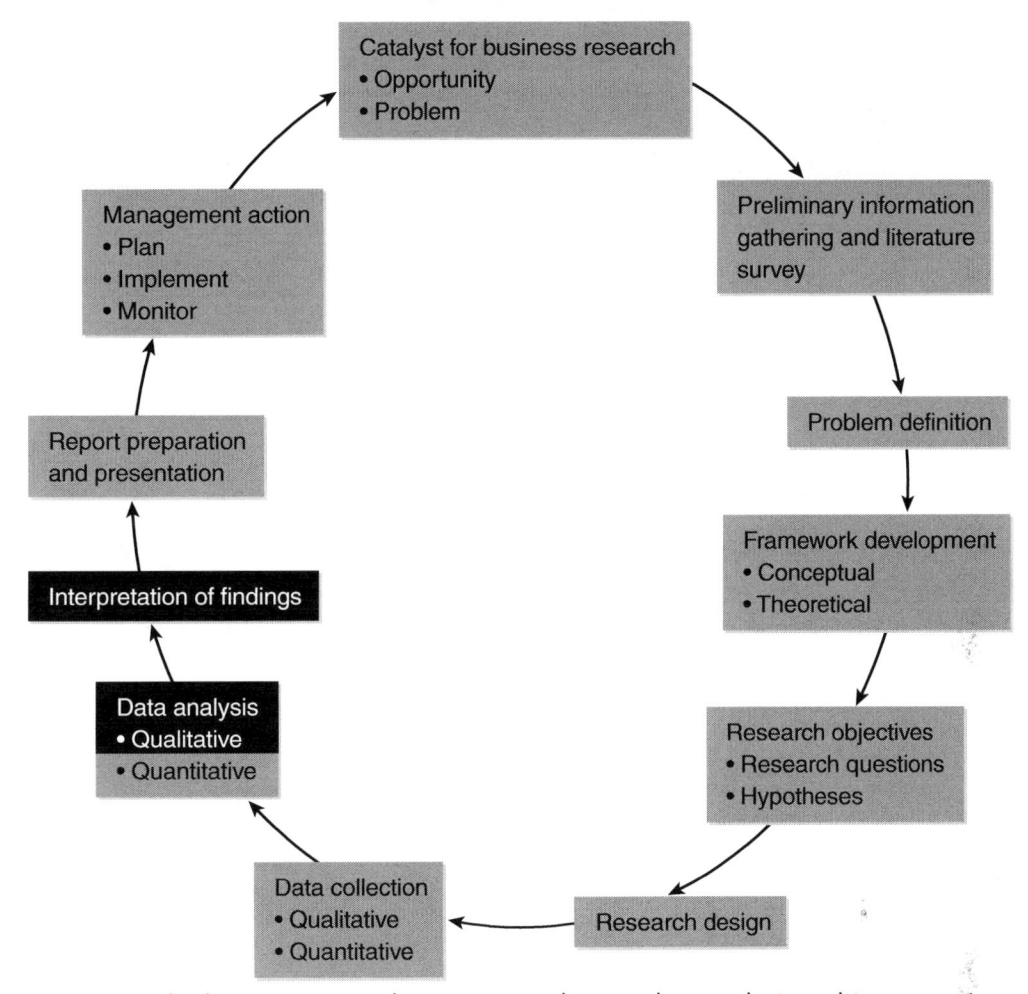

**Figure 7.1** The business research process: qualitative data analysis and interpretation

Researchers share a common motivational drive — the need to discover the secrets about the phenomena they are investigating. In the analytic phase, the researcher explores the raw data collected in an attempt to identify the underlying themes, insights and relationships within the phenomena being researched. While the process of qualitative data analysis can follow many paths, it is basically a non-mathematical procedure that analyses the meaning of people's words and behaviours.

# THE OVERLAP OF DATA GATHERING AND ANALYSIS

When we come to data analysis, there is another significant difference between quantitative and qualitative research. In quantitative research, data are collected in one time period and those data are then analysed in a later time period. However, as discussed in the previous chapter, qualitative research looks to the human-as-an-instrument for the collection and analysis of data. In reality, this means that there is no natural split between the data gathering and the analysis of the data. As the researcher is gathering data, he or she is also analysing those data.

This overlap can be both a strength and a weakness of qualitative research. It can be a weakness when the simultaneous analysis contaminates the direction of the data gathering by diverting the research away from the research objectives. The overlap is a significant strength when the researcher uses the results of the simultaneous analysis to probe further and uncover additional material. The experienced qualitative researcher, therefore, always uses the research objective as a pole star. The research objective can then be used as a comparative standard when deciding whether to further probe a particular response from a research subject. Some researchers go one step further and keep a diary to record thoughts on the data being gathered and to record the reasons for making certain decisions during data gathering or for following specific points.

As Maykut and Morehouse (1994) comment, the qualitative researcher's perspective is a paradoxical one. It is to be acutely tuned in to the experiences and meaning systems of others and, at the same time, to be aware of how one's own biases and preconceptions may be influencing what one is trying to understand.

## THE PURPOSE OF QUALITATIVE ANALYSIS

The overall purpose of analysing qualitative data is to understand the phenomenon being studied. Usually, qualitative researchers wish to go beyond the journalistic approach of only reporting what occurred. They need to interpret what has occurred, and achieve this by identifying the themes and subthemes in the raw data which will provide an understanding of the phenomenon — the issue, opportunity or problem — being investigated.

Themes can be identified in two ways — by using pre-planned questions or by **content analysis**.

## STRUCTURED AND UNSTRUCTURED METHODS

In chapter 6 we discussed the difference between structured and unstructured data gathering methods, especially as applied to interviewing and focus groups.

In structured and semi-structured interviews and focus groups, pre-planned questions are used to explore certain specific topics. These cue questions, then, automatically provide themes for investigation and subsequent analysis of the data gathered. For example, if a question used was: 'Staff expect their supervisors to take on several roles. What do you think some of these roles are?', then the researcher would have gathered a list and description of a variety of roles based on the expectations of the respondents. Therefore, using the pre-planned questions as the analytic 'blueprint' places an *a priori* structure on the outcome of the analysis. If the pre-planned questions have been carefully devised and are cues accurately representing the concept or issue being investigated, then any resultant contamination will be minimal.

However, the responses within each of the pre-planned questions will still have a large degree of variety. The task of the analyst is to uncover the various subthemes that are present within each of the responses to each of the questions.

With the unstructured interview or focus group, the analyst does not have the luxury of a predetermined structure. The themes and subthemes have to be prospected from the morass of raw data collected. The process of uncovering these themes and subthemes is called content analysis.

# CONTENT ANALYSIS

Content analysis is the process of identifying, coding and categorising the primary patterns in the data (Patton 1990). This type of analysis allows the themes to emerge from the raw data, and this describes the main focus of the qualitative analyst. However, simply identifying themes is not sufficient. The analyst must also ensure that each theme has a separate identity from the other themes. It should be noted that the term 'content analysis' can also refer to the statistical analysis of key word or phrase occurences (see, for example, Krippendorff 1980). However, in this chapter we are using Patton's more general definition.

Much of our knowledge on analysing qualitative data has come from *grounded theory*. This chapter will use only certain aspects of grounded theory to provide an introduction to analysing qualitative data. For a more in-depth review of grounded theory, see Glaser and Strauss (1967) and Strauss and Corbin (1990).

Glaser and Strauss (1967) coined the term *constant comparative method* to describe this process of separating themes. When using constant comparative analysis, the researcher reads the raw data and identifies an important point (or theme, as it is called in qualitative research). The researcher continues reading until an apparent second theme is identified. The researcher compares this second theme with the first theme identified to ensure that the two are different, then continues reading until an apparent third theme is identified. This third theme is compared with the first and second themes. So the process of constant comparative analysis continues — each newly identified theme compared with previously identified themes to ensure that the new theme does indeed add more understanding about the phenomenon under investigation.

Content analysis can be conducted by the researcher using a manual decision support system or by using a computer program such as QSR NUD*IST Vivo (NVivo). (QSR International are developers of the NUD*IST software, now in two packages — NVivo and N5. Details on the programs are on the website www.qsrinternational.com.) When using a manual decision support system, the researcher highlights each theme as it occurs in the raw data being perused. Each highlighted theme is given a *theme code* and the theme code name is written in a *data index*, so that a record of the list of themes is kept. At appropriate times, the highlighted segments are collated into separate files, so that each theme has a collection of quotes from each respondent. Computer programs allow the researcher to achieve this outcome without the need to physically undertake the activities, saving time and also allowing the researcher to concentrate on the art of analysis.

## CONDUCTING CONTENT ANALYSIS

There are 15 steps in conducting a content analysis using the constant comparative method. Recognise, however, that these steps are not necessarily followed in a strict linear order, as interaction and overlapping does occur. The following description is discussed in terms of the manual decision support system. The use of the computer program NVivo will be discussed later in the chapter.
1. Prepare and organise your raw data. All field notes should be easily readable (having them typed from the written form is a good idea) and audio tapes should be transcribed.
2. Source code all raw data. Each interview, focus group or document should have a **source code** that is:
    - unique, so that any future reference can be traced easily to each piece of raw data
    - logical, so that it is easily remembered
    - efficient, as the code will be used a number of times in the content analysis.

A source code is usually a short line of alphanumeric symbols.
- It is common for the first code segment to refer to the type of data (for example 'I' for interview or 'FG' for focus group).
- The second segment should describe the respondent (for example 'JF' for the name of the respondent Judith Fox or 'E1' for the first engineer interviewed or 'A3' for the third administrator).
- The third segment refers to the number of the interaction, if there was more than one interaction for the respondent (for example 'E1a' for the first interaction with engineer 1 and 'E1b' for the second interaction).
- The last segment is a page number if the raw data cover more that one page (for example '3' or 'p3' for the third page of a transcription of an interview).

So 'IA3b4' would be the source code for the fourth page of the transcript and the second interaction in an interview with administrator 3. Most researchers settle on a personal source coding system for themselves. Just make sure that yours is unique, logical and efficient.

3. Photocopy all the written or typed raw data. Some researchers make several copies, as the subsequent constant comparative analysis using a manual system tends to destroy each copy as the copy is marked, written on or even cut up with scissors.
4. Store the originals of all raw data in a safe place. Some researchers even store a copy of the raw data in another safe place. In qualitative research the field notes, transcripts of interviews and focus groups and other documents are the only evidence that the researcher has of hundreds of hours of data gathering time. The researcher has to be extremely security conscious of this valuable and expensive evidence and has to be able to return to the originals.
5. Read through your notes, transcripts and other evidence. While this step takes only one sentence to describe, it is the major and most time-consuming part of the analysis. Reading cannot be completed quickly and high levels of concentration are essential.
6. As you read through the notes and other evidence, themes will emerge for you. As Maykut and Morehouse (1994) comment, the process of content analysis is one of culling meaning from the words and behaviours of the participants in the study, framed by the researcher's focus of inquiry. Code these themes as they surface.

    A **theme coding system** is a means of reorganising the data according to conceptual themes recognised by the researcher (Minichiello et al. 1990:293). Theme coding can be achieved in a number of ways, such as putting an abbreviation representing the theme next to the sentence or paragraph which contains the theme; using a number, in place of an abbreviation; or using highlighter pens of different colours to accent different themes. For example, the researcher may note 'PSDL' for 'preference for self-directed learning' against some passage in an interview transcript and 'LM' for 'low motivation' against another passage.

    This coding process is the central activity of content analysis. As Patton (1990:381) comments, coming up with topics or themes is similar to constructing an index for a book or labels for a filing system; look at what is there and give it a name or a label.
7. When you find what you think is a second theme, compare it with the first theme. When you find a third theme, compare it with the first and second themes, and so on. This is the process called **constant comparative analysis**.

**EXAMPLE 7.1**

IR { Well, originally, I was not too keen on this contract learning stuff. There just did not seem to be anything to grasp onto. All wishy-washy, you know. Then I started thinking. Really, I guess it had been going around in my head for some time. Being able to learn what I wanted to learn and making it so much more practical, more use to me. I would be able to show employers what I had been able to do. As the semester went on, I got really excited about the various ways of identifying customer needs and I could really see how this was going to help me next year when I got a job. } PSDL

Some of the other students whinged a fair bit. Kept going on about how much work they had to do. Why did they have to do so many assignments! I tried to tell them that they were learning and producing evidence of their learning at the same time. And they didn't have to go to every lecture. Most of us seemed to like it though. } OPP

It was good being able to make your own decisions, a bit scary too, of course. } PSDL

Note: IR = Initial reaction; PSDL = Preference for self-directed learning; OPP = Other people's preferences.

8. Maintain a list of the abbreviations and a brief description of the themes on a separate sheet of paper. Keep adding to this list as you discover new themes. This provides a **data index** and is the first stage of **classification**.

9. At reasonable intervals during this process (say, every couple of hours or so), or at the end of the process, transfer the indicated passages to a file — one file for each theme. These days this is usually achieved by using a computer and word processing package. Another option is the 'cut and paste' technique — simply cut the coded segments from your notes or transcripts and paste them onto other sheets of paper under the appropriate categories. As this destroys the documents, the cut and paste process needs to be undertaken using copies.

   As each passage is transferred, note the source code of the passage so that each passage in a theme can be traced back to the original raw data.

   This transferring process classifies the data into specific *categories* and provides fuller descriptions and examples of the themes. Usually, one category consists of one theme. Guba (1978) suggests two criteria for judging a theme or category. These are:
   - *internal homogeneity* — the extent to which the data in the theme 'dovetail' or hold together in a meaningful way
   - *external heterogeneity* — the extent to which differences between themes are bold and clear.

   Do not be concerned if a sentence or paragraph contributes to more than one theme. Just incorporate the sentence or paragraph in all the themes to which it contributes. However, re-examine these themes to see if this commonality indicates a relationship.

10. Steps 5 to 9 describe what Strauss and Corbin (1990) call **open coding**. Neuman (1997) describes open coding as the first pass through the raw data when the researcher locates themes and assigns initial codes or labels in a first attempt to condense the mass of data categories. The first pass allows the researcher to open up the text, create new concepts and explore them immediately.

11. The second reading of the raw data is for **axial coding** (Neuman 1997). This name most probably comes from the researcher's role of working around the central axis of the theme, 'worrying away' at the data until the theme becomes clear. While additional or new ideas may emerge during this pass, the researcher's primary task is to review, examine and develop the initial themes assigned during the open coding step. During this second pass, the researcher investigates causes and consequences, conditions and interactions, strategies and processes and looks for categories or concepts that cluster together.

    Read through each of the theme files and look for subthemes within each. Again, reread it several times to check for relationships between the subthemes or even with another theme. Do not be surprised if one theme splits into two or more new themes or if two themes combine to make one. Your judgement is the critical element here, since it is you who are trying to make sense of the wealth of raw data.

12. After reviewing each category, identify rules for inclusion (Lincoln & Guba 1985). Rules for inclusion identify the properties or characteristics of the various passages from the raw data in the category and serve as a basis for including or not including subsequent data. Rules for inclusion are, of course, based on internal homogeneity and external heterogeneity.

---

**EXAMPLE 7.2**

Category and code: Low motivation (LM)
Rule for inclusion: Any personal statement or non-verbal indication from the respondent that signifies he or she did not like self-directed learning. Will not include statements about other people's preferences (see category OPP — 'Other people's preferences')

---

Some researchers construct rules for inclusion during the open coding stage (steps 5–9), as it gives them an early focus. Other researchers wait until the axial coding stage (step 11), as they believe an earlier construction of rules of inclusion creates an initial bias that may be hard to break.

13. **Selective coding** (Neuman 1997) occurs during the third reading of the raw data. The researcher first looks selectively for evidence that illustrates or justifies themes and then makes comparisons and identifies contrasts between subthemes and between themes.

    During this third stage, Morgan (1997) suggests that for focus group data it is important to include the number of participants who mentioned a particular code and whether each group's discussion contained a particular code. In other words, numerical scores can indicate the strength of opinion on a particular theme — although this should not be confused with importance, which is largely a judgement of the analyst. Neuman (1997) suggests that negative evidence should also be identified, in that the non-appearance of something can reveal a great deal and provide valuable insights — for example when an event does not occur, or the target population is not aware of certain issues.

14. Mapping allows the researcher to investigate relationships across categories. To this stage the researcher has concentrated internally on the categories to ensure that each has a sense of homogeneity and purity. However, most research projects are also interested in the connection between categories in order to draw a fuller picture of the phenomenon being studied. A number of researchers use very large pieces of paper pinned to a wall or even whiteboards to explore the possible relationships.

Review the material in chapter 4 on dependent, independent, moderating and intervening variables before taking this step. The researcher should also be cautioned to note the difference between a causal relationship and a correlational relationship.
15. The researcher writes the report. Surprisingly, this step is also an important last step in the analytic process. The researcher is forced to convert tacit knowledge to explicit information, and logic deficiencies often come to the surface during this period. Once again, this can be an iterative process, with the researcher often visiting the theme files and also the raw data to check, question or support various arguments to be enunciated in the report.

In summary, then, the researcher uses content analysis and the constant comparative method to explore the raw data. During this process, themes and subthemes are identified and are then converted into categories. Each category consists of a full description and examples from the raw data of the theme and subthemes. Each category is given a name and a theme code to represent that label. These category names and codes are also listed in a data index. Further, a rule for inclusion is formulated for each category. Finally, a map representing the relationships between the categories is constructed.

## A RICH, MESSY AND COMPLEX PROCESS

Four important comments should be made about the analysis of qualitative data.
1. Analysis of qualitative data is a messy process. Even the description of the 15 steps of content analysis discussed above is a simplified representation of reality.

    First, as discussed earlier in the chapter, analysis tends to start during the data gathering phase. It is difficult for the analyst not to see trends and categories as the data unfold. Some authors argue that the analyst should ignore the urge to start analysing at the data gathering stage. This is unrealistic. The best strategy is to acknowledge that this early analysing is natural and to record any ideas on trends or categories. However, recognise that these early ideas are tentative, use them as possible sources for probing questions but do not fall into the error of assuming that reality has been found. Maintain a healthy scepticism. Second, the analyst will work back and forth between the themes and subthemes, and even between the themes and the raw data, again and again, until a level of satisfaction is felt that the reconstituted data are a true and accurate reflection of the phenomena being studied.
2. Further, Minichiello et al. (1990:290) suggest that there can be at least two levels of data — the manifest content and the latent content. The **manifest content** is the data physically present and accountable in the evidence (for example the words in a quote from an interviewee). The **latent content** is the symbolism underlying the physically present data — reading between the lines, if you like. The analyst may choose to interpret the manifest content or the latent content, or even both. However, Minichiello et al. emphasise that, when reading between the lines, it is essential to continually ask whether our reading is consistent with the informant's perspective.
3. The decisions are yours. Do not be overwhelmed by this. Look for the evidence that supports your choices of themes and go with them. Most people severely underestimate their ability to identify trends or themes in data — yet the human brain is superbly designed for just this purpose.
4. Gathering data, analysing the data and writing the report are not mutually exclusive activities. As Morgan (1997) comments, decisions about how to collect the

data will depend on decisions about how to analyse and report the data. So, when planning a research project, the investigator needs to project forward and consider the implications of data analysis and the make-up of the final report as well as planning the data gathering techniques.

It is a fact of life that the best instrument to analyse qualitative data is the human brain. This is the only instrument that possesses the required breadth of perception, complex appreciation and ability to reduce data. There is a danger of contamination. However, the principles of qualitative research are the means of mitigating this danger. Always striving for the ideals of accuracy and replicability and following the conventions of content analysis are the hallmarks of good qualitative research.

## USING A COMPUTER PACKAGE

We have already discussed the overlap between data gathering and analysis in qualitative research and how this is different from quantitative research. We now come to another difference. In quantitative research, the analytic procedures are quite transparent as they are based on mathematical functions. However, the complex, critical and in-depth analysis demanded by qualitative data can be achieved only by the human brain. No computer system can supplant the ability of the human brain to perceive trends in data that are so vivid, multifaceted and intricate. Therefore, it is important to recognise that any computer program can only support the decision-making processes of the researcher/analyst in qualitative data analysis.

Several computer packages designed to support qualitative data analysis have been around for a number of years. One of the most popular is a package called NUD*IST — for non-numerical unstructured data * indexing, searching and theorising. This package has recently been updated and improved significantly: there are now two packages, one called NUD*IST Vivo — or NVivo for short — and the other called N5. NVivo is a full generation ahead of any other package for the analysis of qualitative data and is the first package to fully support the 15 steps of content analysis discussed earlier in this chapter.

## THE NVIVO PROGRAM

The NVivo program recognises that qualitative research is varied, and that different qualitative methodologies have very different goals (Richards 1999). The program assumes that the researcher has a project and that this project is supported by a variety of databases — from written field notes to files in a computer-based word processing package to scanned documents to video and audio tapes. The program also recognises that these records are likely to change and grow richer as the analyst evaluates, makes decisions and produces further insights.

The program allows the researcher to manage this diversity of data, to record decisions and to create new records. There are three systems in NVivo for managing the data (Richards 1999). These are:

- the *documents* system, which accepts plain or rich text records. These documents can be imported from a word processor or can be created inside NVivo and can be browsed and analysed at any time.
- the *nodes* system, which is the container for themes or categories and coding. These nodes can be kept without any organisation (called free nodes) or organised into an hierarchy (called tree nodes). These nodes can be browsed and explored at any time. Further, the researcher can move between the documents system and the nodes system quite easily.

- the *attributes* system, which allows the researcher to assign values to the nodes and documents — for example, a gender node identifying male or female, or the document files being assigned a location (where the data were collected) and the date collected. This is very useful when searching the raw data.

When opening NVivo, the 'Launch Pad' menu appears, which allows the researcher to commence a new project or to open an existing project. If a new project is to be commenced, the 'New Project Wizard' submenu allows the researcher to choose a typical project set-up (which assumes just one user) or a custom project option, which provides the allocation of different team members and passwords. Under the custom project option, the person creating the project is called the 'administrator', whose role becomes one of housekeeping. This allows the person creating the project to separate the responsibilities of administration and researching.

Once the project has been initiated, the researcher turns to the 'Project Pad', the key menu for managing the research. It is the heart of NVivo and is very user-friendly. The project pad has two tabs — the documents tab and the nodes tab.

- Using the documents tab in the project pad, the researcher can import and create documents and then browse, explore, edit and code the documents. The documents can also be given attributes to describe or identify each document. When the researcher is analysing the documents, each coding decision automatically creates a theme or category. In NVivo terms, each one of these themes or categories is called a 'node'.
- The researcher can then turn to the node tab in the project pad to further examine and analyse the data held within each node (or category). In addition, attributes can be assigned to describe or identify each node. The 'Node Explorer' called from the Node tab provides the researcher with a variety of options for viewing and managing the nodes. In this way, various links and relationships between the nodes can be explored.
- The search button allows the researcher to ask questions of the information stored, to identify and make sense of patterns.
- Finally, the modelling option on the project pad gives researchers the ability to draw diagrams to represent their ideas visually.

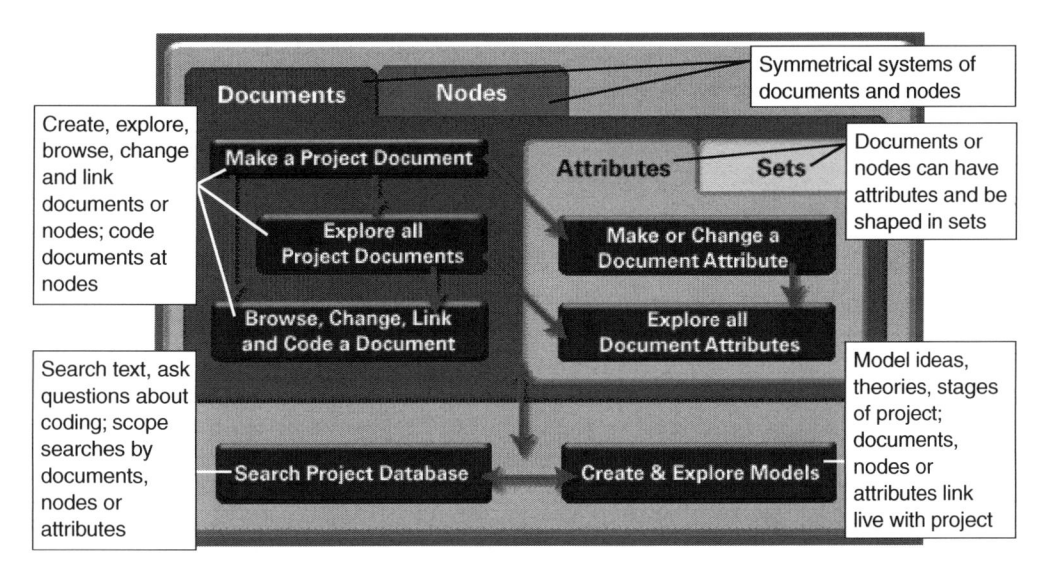

**Figure 7.2** The Project Pad in NVivo

# THE NVIVO PROGRAM AND CONTENT ANALYSIS

The NVivo package is a dynamic decision support tool for the qualitative researcher. The package fits in very well with the 15 steps of qualitative data analysis.

1. *Prepare and organise your data.* Rich text and plain text files can be imported into NVivo or can be represented by a 'Proxy Document' if you do not wish to, or cannot, import directly (for example a book or a video tape), or a document can be created within NVivo.
2. *Source code all raw data.* All documents and nodes can be assigned attributes.
3. *Make backup copies of all the written data.* This step is not needed for NVivo, just for security purposes.
4. *Store the originals of all raw data in a safe place.* This is an important practice for the safety of any qualitative research.
5. *Read through the documents* managed by NVivo using the *explore* and *browse* options. The explore option allows the researcher to see the list of all documents held by NVivo for that project and also to select a particular document for analysis (see figure 7.3).

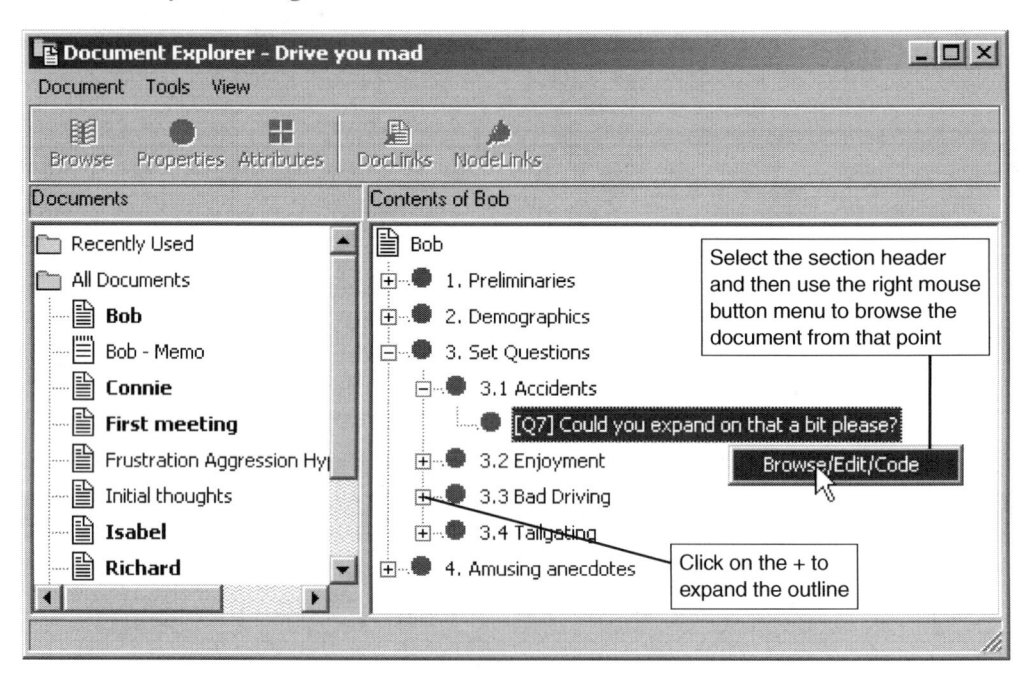

**Figure 7.3** Document Explorer in NVivo

The browse option allows the researcher to read a particular document and to conduct a constant comparative analysis (see figure 7.4).

6. *Identify themes and code.* NVivo allows the researcher to highlight passages in the document in different colours. When satisfied that a particular passage represents a specific theme, the researcher uses an icon at the bottom of the display to create a category (or node, in NVivo terms). The researcher will then be asked to give each new category a name. This name can be nominated by the researcher or can be drawn from the passage in the document (for example a word used by the respondent). Technically, when a category is named using a word drawn directly from the document, the naming is called '**in vivo**' — this is where NVivo acquires its name (see figure 7.5).

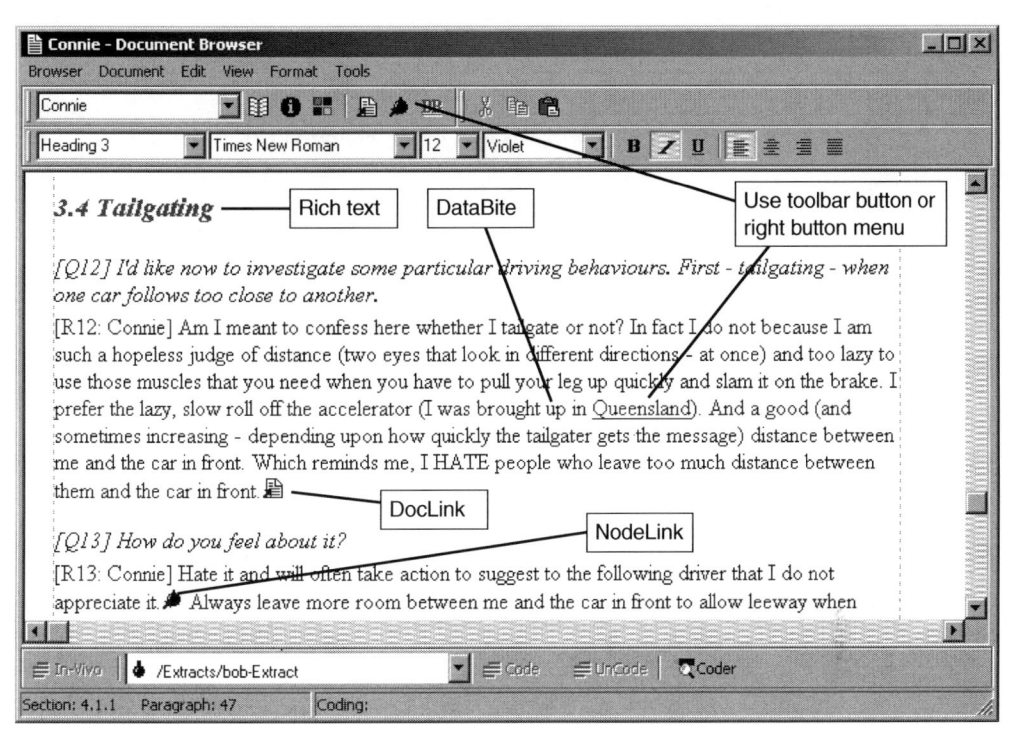

**Figure 7.4** Document Browser in NVivo

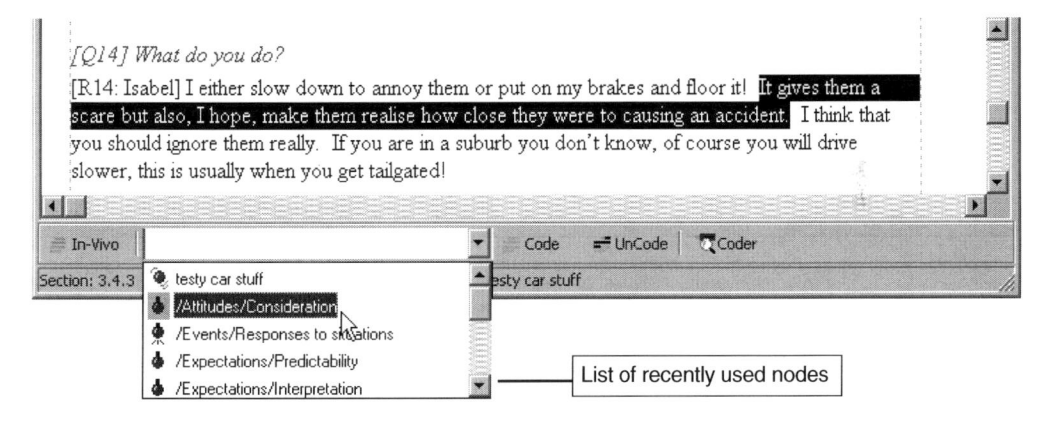

**Figure 7.5** Coding text in NVivo

Further, the researcher can create a 'data bite' for key words or phrases. A data bite is similar to attaching a Post-it note to a physical document. The researcher can write a reminder or indicate some connection to another part of the research. The data bite option is a valuable way for the researcher to make a quick notation without dropping out of the focal document and thereby losing the thread of the analysis (see figures 7.4 and 7.6).

7. *Use constant comparative analysis.* By being able to highlight different passages in a document in different colours and to move quickly between documents, the researcher's ability to compare concepts, ideas and themes is enhanced to a significant degree.

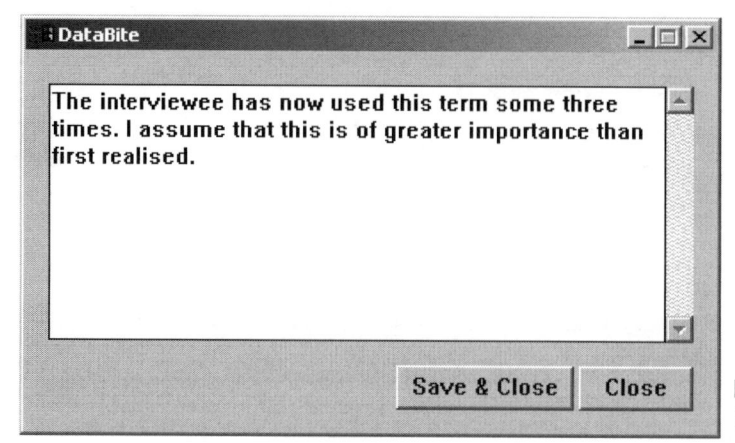

**Figure 7.6** Data bite in NVivo

8. *Create a data index.* NVivo automatically creates a reference to each passage that is highlighted. This record can be readily examined by switching to the node submenu (see figure 7.7).

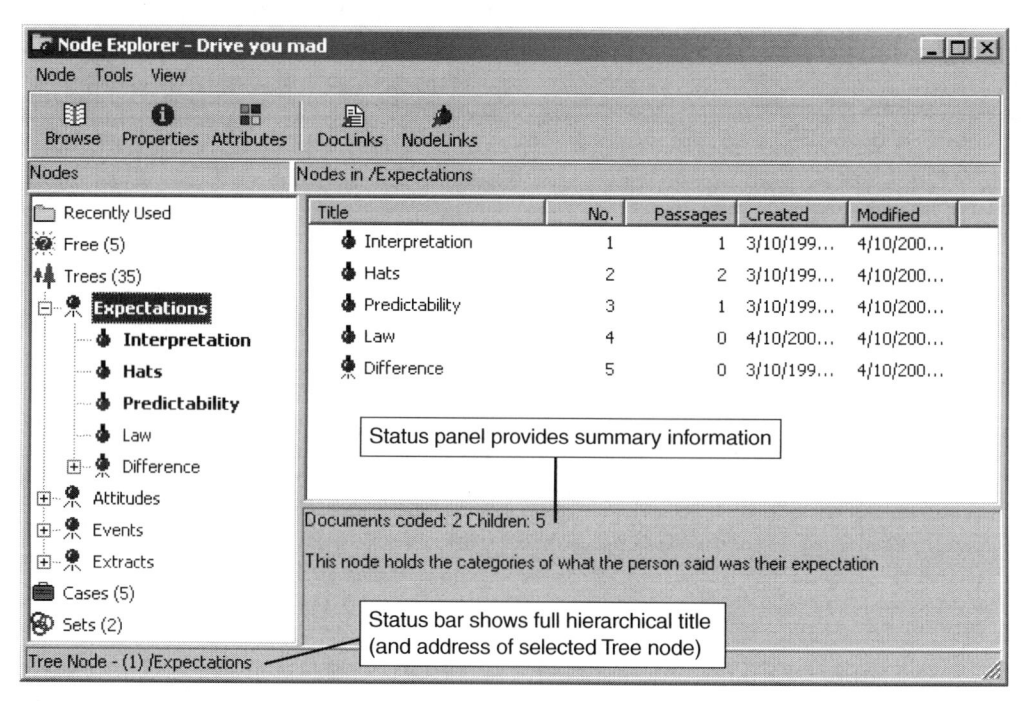

**Figure 7.7** Node Explorer in NVivo

9. *Transfer the indicated passages to a file.* NVivo automatically achieves this by creating nodes. Each passage that is highlighted and assigned to a node is added to that node. Further, the passage is automatically sourced to the document.
10. *Open coding.* Overall, NVivo provides the researcher with a variety of options to locate themes and assign codes.
11. *Axial coding.* Using the node submenu, the researcher has an equal variety of options to review the content of each node and to move quickly between nodes. A unique function of this feature is the ability to work in a category and to 'code-on' to finer dimensions.

12. *Identify rules for inclusion.* This is easily achieved by assigning attributes to each node or writing memos about the node.
13. *Selective coding.* Again, the ability to move between documents, between nodes, and between documents and nodes, and revisit the context provides a good decision support system for the researcher.
14. *Mapping.* The 'Modeler' in NVivo allows researchers to draw or represent visually their ideas (see figure 7.8).

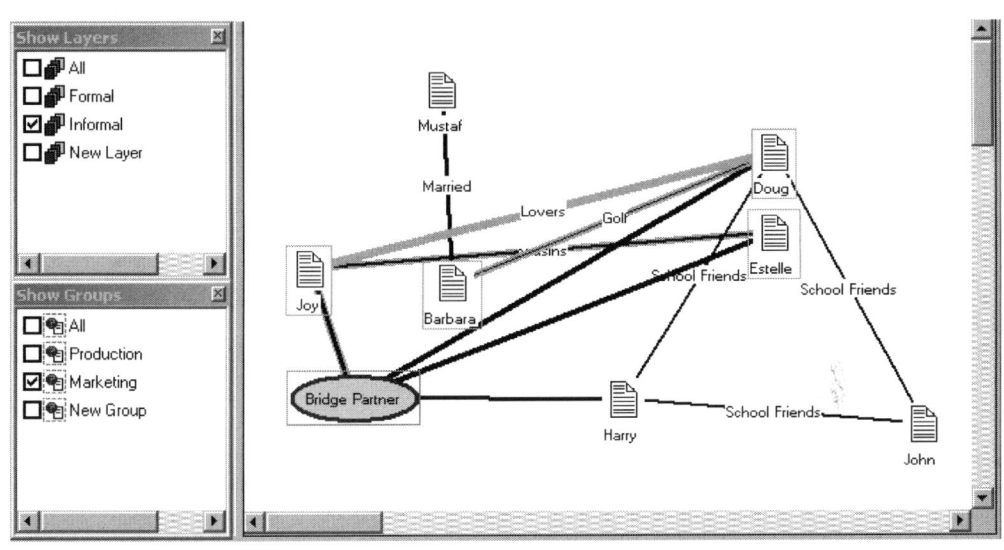

**Figure 7.8** Mapping in NVivo

15. *The researcher writes the report.* All the results of the analyses can be printed out and used as part of the report or as a basis for the report.

Overall, then, NVivo provides the researcher with a good support system. The procedures for identifying themes, assigning passages to categories and managing the data and the research processes are particularly user friendly. The package gives the researcher the additional benefit of obviating the need to physically transfer passages and create a category data index.

The above offers a very brief introduction to NVivo. The authors of the program have developed a support site on the Internet — see www.qsrinternational.com. In addition, the text by Bazeley and Richards (2000) is highly recommended for those who wish to use the NVivo package.

## SUMMARY

In this chapter we have seen that analysing qualitative data is different in at least two dimensions from analysing quantitative data. First, data analysis occurs while the data are being gathered. Second, no computer program can conduct the analysis for the researcher. The mind of the researcher is the analytic tool in qualitative research and a computer program can only support this process. If the data have been gathered using one of the structured methods (for example a structured interview), the cue questions form the basis for initial analysis. If a more unstructured data gathering method has been used, the researcher uses an analytic approach called content analysis. There are 15 steps in conducting a content analysis using the constant comparative method. Finally, to support these 15 steps, the use of a computer package called NVivo was described.

## DISCUSSION POINTS

1. What is the purpose of qualitative data analysis?
2. Explain the overlap between data gathering and data analysis in qualitative research.
3. How can the cue questions used in a focus group be used to analyse qualitative data?
4. List the 15 steps in content analysis.
5. Explain why all raw data should be source coded.
6. Describe what is meant by a theme coding system and give an example.
7. Explain constant comparative analysis.
8. What is the difference between open coding, axial coding and selective coding?
9. What is a 'rule for inclusion' and why is it used?
10. Explain why qualitative data analysis is such a rich, messy and complex process.
11. The following is an excerpt from an interview. Analyse the qualitative data using content analysis and constant comparative analysis.

> Hmm! Can knowledge be considered an organisational asset? Yes, I suppose it can in a way. On the other hand, of course, you can't put a dollar value on it so in some ways it's not. Then again, accountants put a dollar value on goodwill and you can't see that. I suppose knowledge is similar. When you think of it, an organisation doesn't work without knowledge. Workers have to have knowledge to make the machines work, and all the procedures we use are really knowledge in a distilled form — from all the experience of a lot of people in the past. Yes, it's an interesting question, isn't it? When someone starts here at the Service Centre, they may be a qualified technician but they don't know everything. You know, the way we do things, the funny quirks about some of our customers. We give them an orientation program to tell them all about that. Of course, because they are qualified, they have most of the technical knowledge, but I suppose that is why we pay them — for their knowledge, I mean. I suppose their wage gives a dollar value to their knowledge. And there's another thing. We don't always know how to fix a machine, because maybe we haven't come across the problem before and the manufacturers haven't thought about it. We then have to problem-solve, so I suppose you could say that our ability to problem-solve is another form of knowledge. Just don't ask me how we solve the problem — that seems to come out like magic sometimes. You know, if you think of knowledge as an asset you really have to wonder. I mean, you use some material or spare parts and you have less left. But you use knowledge and you still have it. Sometimes you have even more. Like when you fix a new problem, you use your old knowledge to help solve it partly, but sometimes you talk to someone else, and then when you fix it you have a lot of new knowledge. Funny, eh?

# part IV

# QUANTITATIVE BUSINESS RESEARCH

8 Measurement of variables
9 Scaling, reliability and validity
10 Questionnaire design
11 Sampling design
12 Experimental designs
13 Quantitative data analysis and interpretation

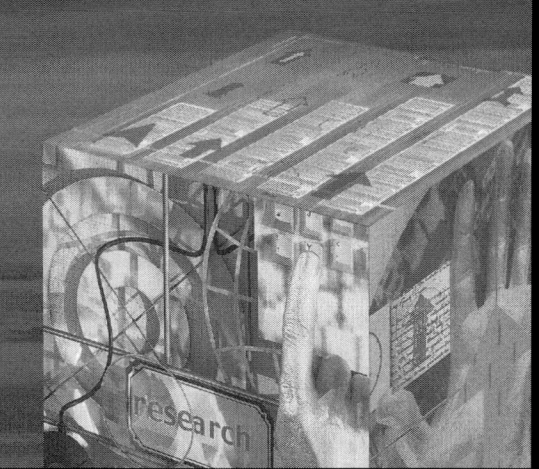

# chapter 8

# MEASUREMENT OF VARIABLES

## OUTLINE
HOW VARIABLES ARE MEASURED
OPERATIONAL DEFINITION: DIMENSIONS AND ELEMENTS
MEASUREMENT SCALES
SUMMARY
DISCUSSION POINTS
EXERCISES

## CHAPTER OBJECTIVES
After completing this chapter, you should be able to:
- operationally define (or operationalise) concepts
- explain the characteristics and power of the four types of measurement scale — nominal, ordinal, interval and ratio.

The previous two chapters have examined the gathering and analysis of qualitative data. You may recall from chapter 2 that qualitative research aims to discover how humans construct meanings in contextual settings so that people's values, interpretative schemes, belief systems and rules of living are revealed and understood. A high emphasis is placed on careful and detailed descriptions of social practices in an attempt to understand the participants' rich experiences.

Quantitative research, on the other hand, is broadly based on the ideals of positivism; it assumes that 'reality' is out there waiting to be discovered and that universal laws of nature operate according to rational, logical reasoning. Quantitative research values objective observation, precise measurements, statistical analysis and verifiable truths. The hallmarks of good quantitative research are reliability and validity.

Chapters 8 to 13 will examine quantitative research in detail.

Measurement of the variables in the theoretical framework is an integral part of research and an important aspect of quantitative research design (see shaded portions in figures 8.1 and 8.2). Unless the variables are measured in some way, we will not be able to test our hypotheses and find answers to complex research issues. In this chapter we will discuss how variables lend themselves to measurement.

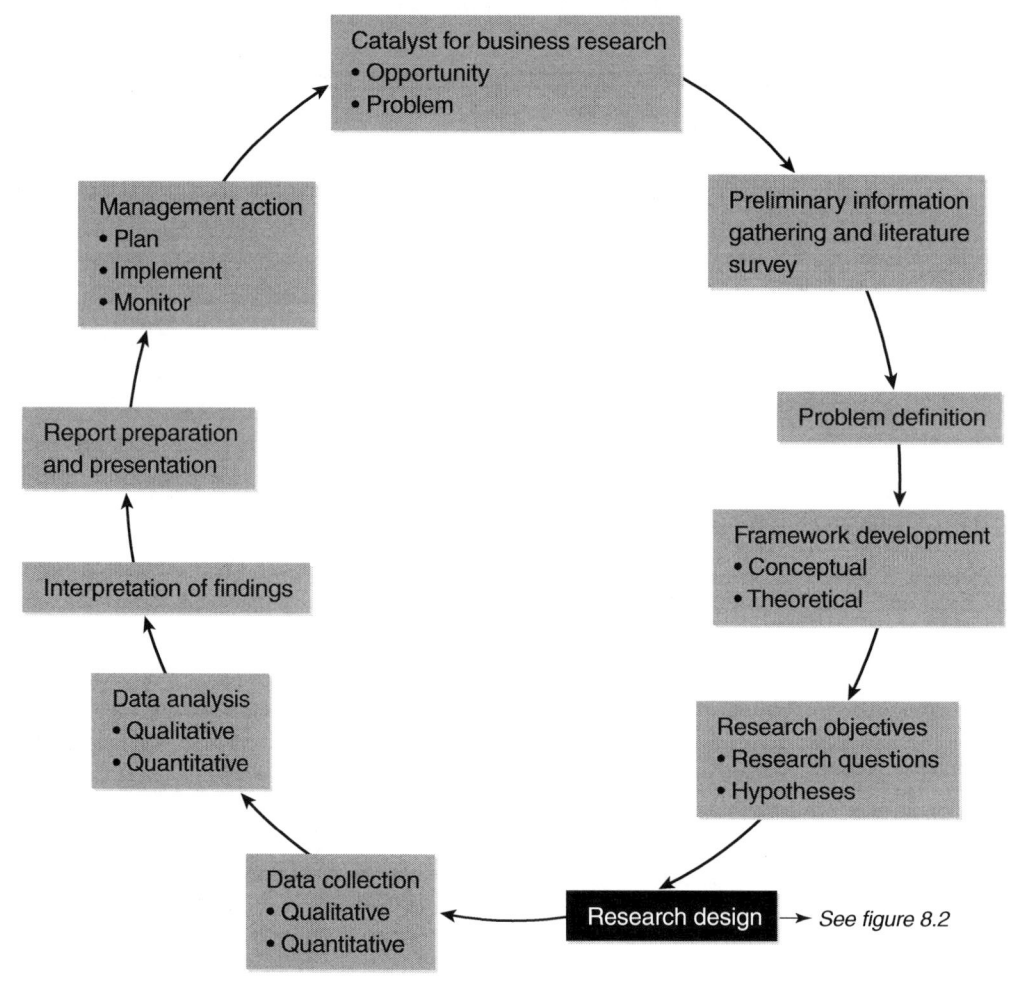

**Figure 8.1** The business research process: measurement and measures

**Research design**

| Purpose of the study | Types of investigation | Extent of researcher interference | **Measurement and measures** | Qualitative data collection |
|---|---|---|---|---|
| • Exploration<br>• Description<br>• Hypothesis testing<br>• Case study | • Clarification<br>• Causal<br>• Correlational<br>• Experimental | • Minimal: studying events as they normally occur<br>• Manipulation and/or control and/or simulation | • Operational definition<br>• Items (measure)<br>• Scaling | • Interviews<br>• Focus groups<br>• Observation |

Problem statement

Data analysis
• Qualitative
• Quantitative

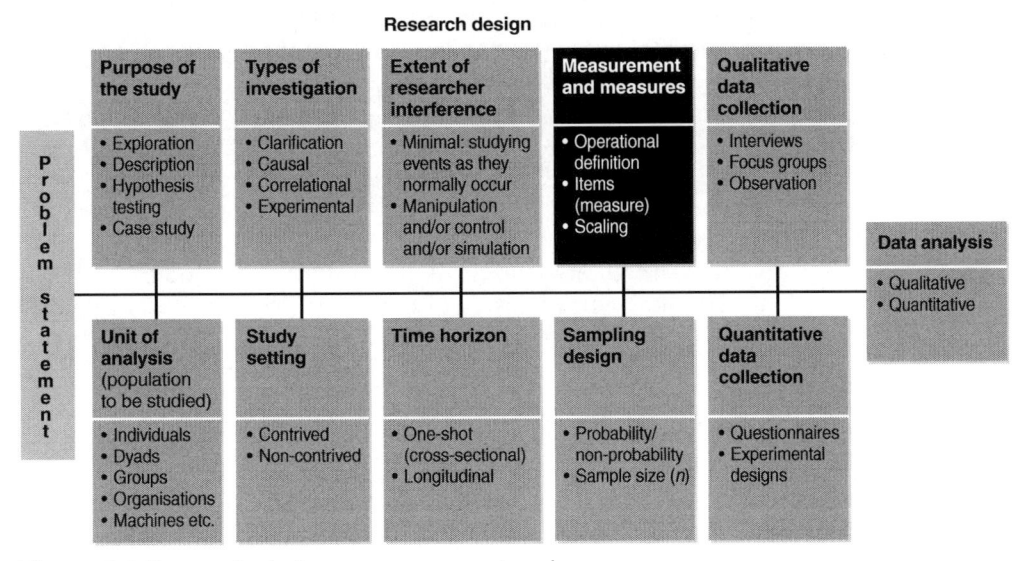

| Unit of analysis (population to be studied) | Study setting | Time horizon | Sampling design | Quantitative data collection |
|---|---|---|---|---|
| • Individuals<br>• Dyads<br>• Groups<br>• Organisations<br>• Machines etc. | • Contrived<br>• Non-contrived | • One-shot (cross-sectional)<br>• Longitudinal | • Probability/non-probability<br>• Sample size (n) | • Questionnaires<br>• Experimental designs |

**Figure 8.2** Research design: measurement and measures

# HOW VARIABLES ARE MEASURED

Objects that can be physically measured by calibrated instruments pose no measurement problems. For example, the length and width of an office table can be easily measured with a measuring tape or a ruler. The same is true for measuring the office floor area. Data representing several demographic characteristics of the office personnel are also easily obtained by asking employees simple, straightforward questions — for example:

- How long have you been working in this organisation?
- How long have you been working on this particular assignment?
- What is your job title?
- What is your marital status?

One can also check the company records to obtain or verify certain types of information — for example the absenteeism of employees or their objective performance in terms of product produced or rejected during the course of each month. However, even such objective data might, in some cases, call for careful interpretation when making managerial decisions. For example, the decision to fire a factory worker would depend on whether he was responsible for 10 rejects during a particular day. Perhaps he was running a high fever (which was beyond the control of the worker), or he may have accrued the 10 rejects over the course of a month because he is a slipshod worker (10 incidents of laxity). Though the number of rejects is the same, the number of incidents and the motivation of the worker are likely to play a part in decision making.

Certain human physiological phenomena such as blood pressure, pulse rates and body temperature, as well as certain physical attributes such as height and weight, lend themselves to measurement through the use of appropriate measuring instruments. However, when we get into the realm of people's subjective feelings, attitudes and perceptions, the measurement of these factors or variables becomes difficult. This is one of the aspects of organisational behaviour and management research that adds to the complexity of research studies.

There are at least two types of variables: one lends itself to objective and precise measurement; the other is more nebulous and does not lend itself to precise measurement because of its subjective nature. Despite the lack of objective physical devices to measure the latter type, there are ways of tapping the subjective feelings and perceptions of individuals. One technique is to reduce the abstract notions, or concepts such as motivation, involvement, satisfaction, buyer behaviour or stock market exuberance, to observable behaviour and characteristics. In other words, the abstract notions are broken down into observable characteristic behaviours. For instance, the concept of thirst is abstract; we cannot see thirst. However, we would expect a thirsty person to drink plenty of fluids. In other words, the expected behaviour of people who are thirsty is to drink fluids. If several people say they are thirsty, then we can measure the thirst levels of each of these individuals by measuring the quantity of fluids that they drink to quench their thirst. We will thus be able to measure their levels of thirst, even though the concept of thirst itself is abstract and nebulous.

Reduction of abstract concepts so that they can be measured in a tangible way is called operationalising the concepts. However, researchers must recognise that, by operationalising, some of the richness of the concept may be lost. The arguments on positivist, interpretivist and critical research, as covered in chapter 1, are relevant here. For the researcher, the purpose of the research usually defines the appropriate direction (see chapter 5). If the purpose is hypothesis testing or using some types of descriptive study, then operationalising the concept is the correct choice.

## OPERATIONAL DEFINITION: DIMENSIONS AND ELEMENTS

Operationalising, or operationally defining, a concept to render it measurable is achieved by looking at the behavioural dimensions, facets or properties denoted by the concept. These are then translated into observable and measurable elements so as to form an index of measurement of the concept. Operationally defining a concept involves a series of steps. An example will help to illustrate how this is done.

### EXAMPLE 8.1 OPERATIONALISING THE CONCEPT OF ACHIEVEMENT MOTIVATION

Let us try to operationally define achievement motivation, a concept of interest to educators, managers and students alike. What behavioural dimensions or facets or characteristics would we expect to find in people with high achievement motivation? They would probably have the following five typical broad characteristics, which we will call *dimensions*.

1. They would be driven by work; that is, they would be constantly working in order to derive the satisfaction of having 'achieved and accomplished'.
2. Many of them would generally find it hard to relax and devote their attention to other than work-related activity.
3. Because they always want to be achieving and accomplishing, they would prefer to work on their own rather than with others.
4. In order to derive a sense of accomplishment and achievement, they would rather engage in challenging jobs than easy, routine ones. However, they would not want to take on excessively challenging jobs because the expectation and probability of accomplishment and achievement in such jobs would not be very high.
5. They would like to know how they are progressing in their jobs as they go along. That is, they would want frequent feedback in direct and subtle ways from their superiors, colleagues and sometimes even their subordinates in order to confirm how they are performing.

Thus, we would expect those with high achievement motivation to drive themselves hard at work, find it difficult to relax, prefer to work alone, engage in challenging but not too challenging jobs, and seek feedback. Although breaking the concept into these five dimensions has reduced its level of abstraction, we have still not operationalised the concept into measurable elements of behaviour. This could be done by examining each of the five dimensions and breaking it down further into its elements, thus delineating the actual patterns of behaviour that would be exhibited. These should somehow be quantitatively measurable so that we can distinguish those who have high motivation from those who have low motivation. Let us see how this can be done.

**Elements of dimension 1**
It is possible to describe the behaviour of a person who is driven by work. Such a person will be constantly working, be reluctant to take time off from work and persevere even if there are setbacks. These types of behaviour would lend themselves to measurement.

For instance, we can count the number of hours employees engage themselves in work-related activities during work hours, beyond working hours at the workplace, and at home where they are likely to carry their unfinished assignments. Thus, merely observing and keeping track of the number of hours that they work would provide an indication of the extent to which work 'drives' them.

Next, keeping track of how frequently people continue to persevere with their job despite failures gives a good idea of how persevering people are in achieving their goals. A student who drops out of school because he could not pass the first exam is not representative of a highly persevering, achievement-oriented individual. However, a student who, despite getting D grades on three quizzes, works night after night in order to understand and master a course he considers difficult exhibits persevering and achievement-oriented behaviours. Achievement-motivated individuals are usually reluctant to give up on their tasks when confronted by failures. They have the perseverance to continue. Hence, the extent of perseverance can be measured by the number of setbacks people experience on the job yet continue to work. For example, an accountant finds that she is unable to balance the books. After trying to detect the error for an hour and failing to do so, she gives up and leaves the workplace. Another employee in the same position does not want to leave until the mistake has been detected and the books are balanced, even if it takes the whole evening to accomplish the task. In this case we can get an idea of who is the more persevering of the two merely by observing them.

Thus, if we can measure the number of hours per week individuals spend on work-related activities, how persevering they are in completing their daily tasks, and how frequently and for what reasons they take time off from their jobs, we will have a measure of the extent to which employees are driven by work. This variable, when thus measured, places individuals on a continuum ranging from those who are driven very little by work to those whose central life interest is their work. This, then, would give a partial indication of the extent of their achievement motivation.

Figure 8.3 schematically illustrates the dimensions (the several facets or main characteristics) and the elements (representative behaviours) of the concept of achievement motivation. Frequent reference to this figure will help you follow the ensuing discussions.

**Elements of dimension 2**
The extent of unwillingness to relax can be measured by asking individuals such questions as how often they think of work while away from the workplace, what are their hobbies and how do they spend their time when not at the workplace? Those

who are able to relax would indicate that they do not generally think about work or the workplace while at home, spend time on hobbies, engage in leisure-time activities, and spend their waking hours with their family or in other social or cultural activities.

Thus, we can place employees on a continuum ranging from those who relax very easily to those who relax very little. This dimension also then becomes measurable.

## Elements of dimension 3

Individuals with high achievement motivation are very impatient with ineffectiveness and are reluctant to work with others. Whereas achievement-motivated individuals in the organisation may rank very high on these behavioural predispositions, there may be others who are not achievement motivated. These people may not be concerned with ineffectiveness in either themselves or others, and may be quite willing to work with almost anyone. Thus, impatience with ineffectiveness can also be measured by observing behaviours.

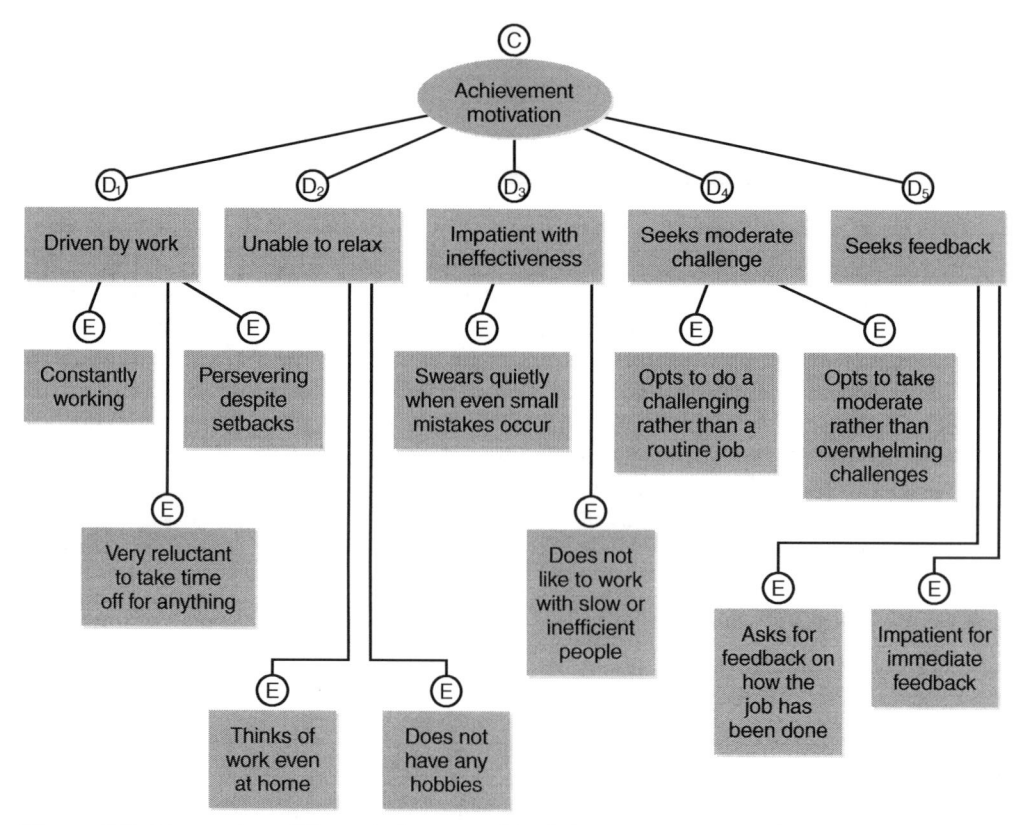

**Figure 8.3** Dimensions (D) and elements (E) of the concept (C) achievement motivation

## Elements of dimension 4

A measure of how eager people are to seek challenging jobs can be found by asking employees what kinds of jobs they prefer. A number of different job descriptions can be presented — some entailing stereotyped work of a routine nature, and others with gradations of challenges built into them. Employee preferences for different types of jobs can then be placed on a continuum ranging from those who prefer fairly routine jobs to those who prefer jobs with a progressive increase in challenge. Those opting for medium degrees of challenge are likely to be more achievement motivated than those who opt for either lower or higher degrees of challenge. Achievement-oriented individuals tend to be realistic and choose jobs that are reasonably challenging but possible to accomplish. Less conscientious and overconfident persons would perhaps choose the highly challenging jobs where success is more difficult to achieve, oblivious to whether or not the end results will be achieved. Those who are low in achievement motivation would perhaps choose the more routine type of jobs. Thus, those seeking moderate challenges can also be identified.

**Elements of dimension 5**
Those who desire feedback would seek it from their superiors, co-workers and sometimes even from their subordinates. They would want to know others' opinions on how well they are performing. Feedback, both positive and negative, would indicate to them how much they are accomplishing. If they receive messages suggesting a need for improvement, they will act on them. Hence, they would be constantly seeking feedback from several sources. By keeping track of how often individuals seek feedback from others during a certain period of time — say, over several months — employees can again be placed on a continuum ranging from those who seek extensive feedback from all sources to those who never seek any feedback from anyone at any time.

Having thus operationalised the concept of achievement motivation by reducing its level of abstraction to observable behaviours, it is possible to develop a good measure to tap the concept of achievement motivation. Its usefulness is that others could use the same measure, thus ensuring replicability. It should, however, be recognised that any **operational definition** is likely to exclude some of the important dimensions and elements arising from failure to recognise or conceptualise them, and also to include certain irrelevant features mistakenly thought to be relevant. You will recall that we pointed out earlier that management research cannot be 100 per cent scientific because we do not have the 'perfect' measuring instruments.

Operationally defining the concept, nevertheless, is the best way to measure it. However, actually observing and counting the number of times individuals behave in particular ways, even if practical, would be too laborious and time-consuming. So, instead of actually observing the behaviours of individuals, we could have them report their own behaviour patterns by asking them appropriate questions, which they can respond to on some scale that we provide. In example 8.2 we will look at the type of questions that can be asked to tap achievement motivation.

**EXAMPLE 8.2**

Answers from respondents to the following questions would be one way of tapping the level of achievement motivation.
1. To what extent would you say you push yourself to get the job done on time?
2. How difficult do you find it to continue to do your work in the face of initial failures or discouraging results?
3. How often do you neglect personal matters because you are preoccupied with your job?
4. How frequently do you think of your work when you are at home?
5. To what extent do you engage in hobbies?
6. How disappointed would you be if you did not achieve the goals you had set for yourself?

7. How much do you concentrate on achieving your goals?
8. How annoyed do you get when you make mistakes?
9. To what extent would you prefer to work with a friendly but incompetent colleague, rather than a difficult but competent one?
10. To what extent would you prefer to work by yourself rather than with others?
11. To what extent would you prefer a job that is difficult but challenging to one that is easy and routine?
12. To what extent would you prefer to take on extremely difficult assignments rather than moderately challenging ones?
13. During the past three months, how often have you sought feedback from your superiors on how well you are performing your job?
14. How often have you tried to obtain feedback on your performance from your co-workers during the past three months?
15. How often during the past three months have you checked with your subordinates that what you are doing is not interfering with their efficient performance?
16. To what extent would it frustrate you if people did not give you feedback on how you are progressing?

The foregoing example illustrates a possible way to measure variables relating to the subjective domain of people's attitudes, feelings and perceptions by first operationally defining the concept. Operational definition consists of the reduction of the concept from its level of abstraction by breaking it into its dimensions and elements, as discussed. By tapping the behaviours associated with a concept, we can measure the variable. Of course, the questions will require responses on some scale attached to them (such as *very little* to *very much*); we will discuss some of these scales in the next chapter.

## WHAT AN OPERATIONAL DEFINITION IS NOT

As important as it is to understand what an operational definition is, it is equally important to remember what it is not. An operational definition does not describe the correlates of the concept. For example, success in performance cannot be a dimension of achievement motivation, even though a motivated person is likely to meet with it in large measure. Thus, achievement motivation and performance and/or success may be highly correlated, but we cannot measure an individual's level of motivation through success and performance. Performance and success could have occurred as a consequence of achievement motivation, but in and of themselves, the two are not measures of achievement motivation. To elaborate, a person may have high achievement motivation, but for some reason, perhaps beyond her control, might have failed to perform the job successfully. Thus, if we judge the achievement motivation of this person by looking at performance, we would have measured the wrong concept. Instead of measuring achievement motivation — our variable of interest — we would have measured performance, another variable that we had neither intended to measure nor were interested in.

Thus, it is clear that operationally defining a concept does not consist of delineating the reasons, antecedents, consequences or correlates of the concept. Rather, it describes its observable characteristics in order to be able to measure the concept. This is important to remember because if we either operationalise the concepts incorrectly or confuse them with other concepts, then we will not have valid measures. This means that we will not have 'good' data, and our research will not be scientific.

Having seen what an operational definition is, and what it is not, let us now operationally define another concept relevant to the classroom: the concept of 'learning'.

> **EXAMPLE 8.3**
>
> **OPERATIONALISING THE CONCEPT OF LEARNING**
>
> Learning is an important concept in the educational setting. Teachers tend to measure student learning by giving exams. Students quite often feel, probably correctly, that exams do not really measure learning — at least not the multiple-choice questions that are asked in exams.
>
> How, then, might we measure the abstract concept called learning? As before, we need to define the concept operationally and break it down to observable and measurable behaviours. In other words, we should delineate the dimensions and elements of the concept of learning. The dimensions of learning may well be as follows:
> 1. Understanding   2. Retention   3. Application.

In other words, we can be reasonably certain that a student in the class is 'learning' when that individual (1) understands what is taught in the classroom, (2) retains (that is, remembers) what is understood, and (3) applies whatever has been understood and remembered.

Terms such as *understanding*, *remembering* and *applying* are still abstract, even though they have helped us to get a better grasp of what learning is all about. It is necessary to break these three dimensions into elements so that we can measure the concept of learning. A schematic diagram of the operational definition of the concept of learning is shown in figure 8.4. The diagram will facilitate our understanding of the discussion that follows.

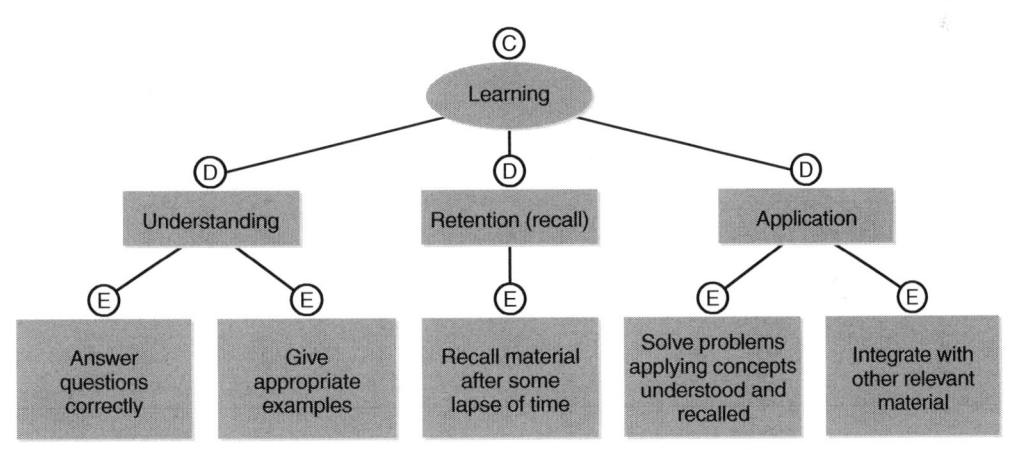

**Figure 8.4** Dimensions (D) and elements (E) of the concept (C) learning

A teacher can assess whether students have understood a concept that has just been taught by asking them to explain it and provide appropriate examples. If they answer correctly, the teacher can assume that the students have understood. By giving a test a week or a month later, the teacher can measure the extent to which they remember what has been taught. By asking them to apply the concepts learned in a new problem situation, the teacher can also measure how much they can apply what is understood. If they solve the problem successfully using the material taught to them in class, the teacher will be reasonably assured that learning has occurred. To the extent that they do not successfully apply the concepts taught, learning might not have progressed to the degree expected. Note that in this case, *application* of the relevant concepts subsumes both *understanding* and *retention*. That is, one cannot apply the concepts unless one has understood them *and* retained them in memory. In most multiple-choice questions, understanding and retention are likely to be tested; the application aspects often are not. Exams, when properly designed, can be a good instrument for assessing the learning that students acquire during the semester. In other words, it is possible to measure learning reliably when exam questions are well constructed to tap the students' understanding, retention and ability to apply what has been taught.

Again, it is very important to remember that learning does not represent the effort the teacher expends in explaining, or that put in by the student to understand, though both of these naturally tend to enhance understanding. Although both may be correlated to learning, they do not actually measure it.

## A MEASURE OF STUDENT LEARNING

An exam that measures *learning* in students (that is, whether they have grasped the concept of motivation) would include the following questions (the particular dimensions tapped are shown in parentheses).

1. Define the concept of motivation (*recall*).
2. State the various theories of motivation and explain them, giving examples (*understanding* and *recall*).
3. At the beginning of the semester, the class was split into two debate teams, one to argue for the manager's role as a motivator, and the other that it is not a manager's job to motivate the employees. State three important arguments put forward by each group (*understanding* and *recall*).
4. What is your viewpoint regarding the manager's role as motivator (*understanding* and *analysis*)?
5. Describe three different situations in which a manager of a work organisation would use equity theory, the expectancy theory and job design to motivate employees (*application*).
6. In the Lake Taupo Camp case, how could Bob have been motivated to take an interest in the camp's activities? Adequately defend your answer, citing the appropriate theories and why they are superior to some of the other possible solutions (*application*, which subsumes *understanding* and *retention*).
7. How does motivation relate to leadership? How are both these concepts related to a manager's job (*understanding, retention, application*)?

## REVIEW OF OPERATIONAL DEFINITION

We have thus far examined how to define concepts operationally and to ask questions that are likely to measure the concept. Operational definitions are necessary to measure abstract concepts such as those that usually fall into the subjective areas of feelings and attitudes. More objective variables such as age or educational level are easily measured through simple, straightforward questions and do not have to be operationally defined. Fortunately, measures for many concepts that are relevant in the business context have already been developed by researchers. While you review the literature in a given area, you might want to note particularly the reference that discusses the instrument used to tap the concept in the study, and read it. The article will give you an idea of when the measure was developed, by whom and for how long it has been in use. Only a well-developed instrument which has been carefully operationally defined will be accepted and frequently used by other researchers.

> Now do exercises 8.1 and 8.2 at the end of the chapter.

## MEASUREMENT SCALES

Now that we have learned how to operationalise concepts, we need to measure them in some way. The end product of operationalising concepts is a variable that can be measured. To this end, in this chapter we will examine the types of measurement scale that can be applied to measure different variables; in the next chapter we will see how we actually apply these scales.

A scale is a tool or mechanism by which individuals are distinguished on how they differ from one another on the variables of interest to our study. The scale or tool could be a gross one in the sense that it would only broadly categorise individuals on certain variables; or it could be a finetuned tool that would differentiate individuals on the variables with varying degrees of sophistication.

There are four basic types of measurement scale: nominal, ordinal, interval and ratio. The degree of sophistication to which the scales are finetuned increases progressively as we move from the nominal to the ratio scale. That is, information on the variables can be obtained with a greater degree of detail when we use an interval or a ratio scale rather than the other two scales. As the calibration or finetuning of the scale increases in sophistication, so does the power of the scale. With more powerful scales, increasingly sophisticated data analyses can be performed, which in turn means that more meaningful answers can be found to our research questions. Certain variables lend themselves more readily to more powerful scaling than others. Let us now examine each of these four scales.

## NOMINAL SCALE

A **nominal scale** is one that allows the researcher to assign subjects to certain categories or groups. For example, with respect to the variable of gender, respondents can be grouped into two categories — male and female. These two groups can be assigned code numbers 1 and 2. These numbers serve as simple and convenient category labels with no intrinsic value, other than to assign respondents to one of two non-overlapping or *mutually exclusive* categories. Note that the categories are also *collectively exhaustive*. In other words, there is no third category into which respondents would normally fall. Thus, nominal scales categorise individuals or objects into mutually exclusive and collectively exhaustive groups. The information that can be generated from nominal scaling is to calculate the percentage (or frequency) of males and females in our sample of respondents. For example, if we had interviewed 200 people, and assigned code number 1 to all male respondents and number 2 to all female respondents, then computer analysis of the data at the end of the survey might show that 98 of the respondents were men and 102 were women. This frequency distribution tells us that 49 per cent of the survey's respondents were men and 51 per cent women. Other than this marginal information, such scaling tells us nothing more about the two groups. Thus, the nominal scale gives some basic, categorical, gross information.

**EXAMPLE 8.4**

Let us take a look at another variable that lends intself to nominal scaling — the nationality of individuals. We could nominally scale this variable in the following mutually exclusive and collectively exhaustive categories.

| American | Japanese | Australian | Korean |
| Chinese | New Zealander | English | Samoan |
| Fijian | Tongan | Indian | Other |

Note that every respondent has to fit into one of the preceding categories and that the scale will allow computation of the numbers and percentage of respondents that fit into them.

> Now respond to exercise 8.3 at the end of the chapter.

## ORDINAL SCALE

An **ordinal scale** not only categorises the variables in such a way as to denote differences among the various categories, it also rank-orders the categories in some meaningful way. With any variable for which the categories are to be ordered according to some preference, the ordinal scale would be used. The preferences would be ranked (say, from best to worst; first to last) and numbered 1, 2 and so on. For example, respondents might be asked to indicate their preferences by ranking the importance they attach to five distinct characteristics in a job that the researcher might be interested in studying, as in example 8.5.

> **EXAMPLE 8.5**
>
> Rank the following five characteristics in a job in terms of how important they are for you. You should rank the most important item as 1, the next in importance as 2, and so on, until you have ranked each of them 1, 2, 3, 4 or 5.
>
> | Job characteristic | Ranking of importance |
> |---|---|
> | The opportunity provided by the job to: | |
> | 1. interact with others | — |
> | 2. use a number of different skills | — |
> | 3. complete a task from beginning to end | — |
> | 4. serve others | — |
> | 5. work independently. | — |

The ordinal scale helps the researcher to determine the percentage of respondents who consider interaction with others to be most important, those who consider using a number of different skills to be most important, and so on. Such knowledge might help in designing jobs that would be seen as most enriched by the majority of the employees.

We can now see that the ordinal scale provides more information than the nominal scale. The ordinal scale goes beyond differentiating the categories to providing information on how respondents distinguish among them by rank-ordering them. Note, however, that the ordinal scale does not give any indication of the the magnitude of the differences among the ranks. For instance, in the job characteristics example, the first-ranked job characteristic might be only marginally preferred over the second-ranked characteristic, whereas the characteristic that is ranked third might be preferred considerably more than the one ranked fourth. Thus, in ordinal scaling, even though we would know there are differences in the ranking of objects, persons or events investigated, we would not know the magnitude of these differences. This deficiency is overcome by interval scaling, which is discussed next.

> Now respond to exercise 8.4 at the end of the chapter.

## INTERVAL SCALE

An **interval scale** allows us to perform certain arithmetical operations on the data collected from the respondents. Whereas the nominal scale allows us to distinguish groups only qualitatively by categorising them into mutually exclusive and collectively exhaustive sets, and the ordinal scale to rank-order the preferences, the interval scale allows us to measure the distance between any two points on the scale. This helps us to compute the means and the standard deviations of the responses on the variables. In other words, the interval scale not only groups individuals according to certain categories and taps the order of these groups, it also measures the magnitude of the differences in the preferences among the individuals. If, for instance, employees think that (1) it is more important for them to have a variety of skills in their jobs than to complete a task from beginning to end, and (2) it is more important for them to serve people than to work independently on the job, then the interval scale would indicate whether the first preference is to the same extent, a lesser extent or a greater extent than the second. This can be done by now changing the scale from the ranking type in example 8.5 to make it appear as if there were several points on a scale that would represent the extent or magnitude of the importance of each of the five job characteristics. Such a scale could be indicated for the job design example as follows.

**EXAMPLE 8.6**

Indicate the extent to which you agree with the following statements as they relate to your job, by *circling* the appropriate number against each, using the response scale given below.

| Strongly disagree | Disagree | Neither agree nor disagree | Agree | Strongly agree |
|---|---|---|---|---|
| 1 | 2 | 3 | 4 | 5 |

The following opportunities offered by the job are very important to me:

| | | | | | |
|---|---|---|---|---|---|
| a. Interacting with others | 1 | 2 | 3 | 4 | 5 |
| b. Using a number of different skills | 1 | 2 | 3 | 4 | 5 |
| c. Completing a task from beginning to end | 1 | 2 | 3 | 4 | 5 |
| d. Serving others | 1 | 2 | 3 | 4 | 5 |
| e. Working independently | 1 | 2 | 3 | 4 | 5 |

Let us illustrate how the interval scale establishes the equality of the magnitude of differences in the scale points. Suppose that employees circle the numbers 3, 1, 2, 4 and 5 for the five items in example 8.6. They then indicate to us that the extent of their preference for skill utilisation over doing the task from beginning to end is the same as the extent of their preference for serving customers over working independently. That is, the magnitude of difference represented by the space between points 1 and 2 on the scale is the same as the magnitude of difference represented by the space between points 4 and 5, or between any other two points. Any number can be added to or subtracted from the numbers on the scale, still retaining the magnitude of the difference. For instance, if we add 6 to all five points on the scale, the interval scale will have the numbers 7 to 11 (instead of 1 to 5). The magnitude of the difference between 7 and 8 is still the same as the magnitude of the difference between 9 and 10. Thus, the origin, or starting point, could be any *arbitrary number*. The clinical thermometer is a good example of an interval-scaled instrument; it has an arbitrary origin and the magnitude of the difference between 98.6 degrees (supposed to be the normal body temperature) and 99.6 degrees is the same as the magnitude of the difference between 104 and 105 degrees. Note, however, that one may not be seriously concerned if one's temperature rises from 98.6 to 99.6, but one is likely to be so when the temperature goes from 104 to 105 degrees!

The interval scale, then, taps the differences, the order and the equality of the magnitude of the differences in the variable. As such, it is a more powerful scale than the nominal and ordinal scales, and has for its measure of central tendency the arithmetic mean. Its measures of dispersion are the range, the standard deviation and the variance.

Finally, it should be noted that, under the most strict definition, the response scales of 1, 2, 3, 4 and 5 in example 8.6 may not be considered an interval scale. We cannot be absolutely certain that the difference between 1 and 2 is the same as that between 2 and 3 and, also, between 4 and 5. However, in business research it has become conventional to accept that such response scales on questionnaires are interval scales.

> Now respond to exercises 8.5 and 8.6 at the end of the chapter.

## RATIO SCALE

The **ratio scale** overcomes the deficiency of the arbitrary origin point of the interval scale, in that it has an *absolute* (in contrast to an *arbitrary*) zero point, which is a meaningful measurement point. Thus, the ratio scale not only measures the magnitude of the differences between points on the scale but also taps the proportions in the differences. It is the most powerful of the four scales because it has a unique zero origin (not an arbitrary origin) and subsumes all the properties of the other three scales. The weighing balance is a good example of a ratio scale. It has an absolute (and not arbitrary) zero origin calibrated on it, which allows us to calculate the ratio of the weights of two individuals. For instance, a person weighing 120 kilograms is *twice* as heavy as one who weighs 60 kilograms. Note that multiplying or dividing both of these numbers (120 and 60) by any given number will preserve the ratio of 2:1. The measure of central tendency of the ratio scale could be either the arithmetic or the geometric mean and the measure of dispersion could be either the standard deviation, or variance, or the coefficient of variation. Some examples of ratio scales are those pertaining to age, income and the number of organisations individuals have worked for.

The properties of the scales, as finetuning is increasingly achieved, are summarised in table 8.1. We may also see from the table how the power of the statistic increases as we move away from the nominal scale (where we group subjects or items under categories), to the ordinal scale (where we rank-order the categories), to the interval scale (where we tap the magnitude of the differences), to the ratio scale (which allows us to measure the proportion of the differences).

**Table 8.1** Properties of the four measurement scales

| | Highlights | | | | | | |
|---|---|---|---|---|---|---|---|
| Scale | Difference | Order | Distance | Unique origin | Measures of central tendency | Measures of dispersion | Some tests of significance |
| Nominal | Yes | No | No | No | Mode | — | $X^2$ |
| Ordinal | Yes | Yes | No | No | Median | Semi-interquartile range | Rank-order correlations |
| Interval | Yes | Yes | Yes | No | Arithmetic mean | Standard deviation, variance, coefficient of variation | $t, F$ |
| Ratio | Yes | Yes | Yes | Yes | Arithmetic or geometric mean | Standard deviation, variance or coefficient of variation | $t, F$ |

*Note*: The interval scale has 1 as an arbitrary starting point. The ratio scale has the natural origin 0, which is meaningful.

You must have surmised by now that some variables such as gender can be measured only on the nominal scale, while others such as temperature can be measured on a nominal scale (high/low), an ordinal scale (high–medium–low) or the interval scale through the thermometer. Whenever it is possible to use a more powerful scale than a less powerful one, it is wise to do so.

Now that we have looked at the four types of scales, let us see, through the examples that follow, when and how they would be used.

> Now respond to exercise 8.7 at the end of the chapter.

### EXAMPLE 8.7 USE OF THE NOMINAL SCALE

The *nominal scale* is always used for obtaining personal data, such as gender or the department in which one works, where grouping of individuals or objects is useful, as shown below.

1. *Your gender*
   __ Male
   __ Female

2. *Your department*
   __ Production
   __ Sales
   __ Accounting
   __ Finance
   __ Human Resources
   __ R & D
   __ Other (specify)

### EXAMPLE 8.8 USE OF THE ORDINAL SCALE

The *ordinal scale* is used to rank the preferences or usage of various brands of a product by individuals and to rank-order individuals, objects or events, as in the examples below.

1. Rank the following personal computers with respect to their usage in your office, assigning the number 1 to the most used system, 2 to the next most used and so on. If a particular system is not used at all in your office, put a 0 next to it.
   __ Acer
   __ Toshiba
   __ Compaq
   __ Hewlett Packard
   __ Dell Computer
   __ IBM
   __ Gateway
   __ Other (specify)

2. Rank the cities listed below in the order that you consider suitable for opening a new plant. The city considered most suitable will be ranked 1, the next 2 and so on.
   __ Adelaide
   __ Melbourne
   __ Auckland
   __ Perth
   __ Brisbane
   __ Sydney
   __ Christchurch

### EXAMPLE 8.9 USE OF THE INTERVAL SCALE

The *interval scale* is used when responses to various items that measure a variable can be tapped on a five-point (or seven-point or any other number of points) scale, which can therefore be averaged across the items. See the example of a Likert scale that follows.

Using the scale below, please indicate your response to each of the items that follow by *circling* the number that best describes your feeling.

| Strongly disagree | Disagree | Neither agree nor disagree | Agree | Strongly agree |
|:---:|:---:|:---:|:---:|:---:|
| 1 | 2 | 3 | 4 | 5 |

| | Strongly disagree | Disagree | Neither agree nor disagree | Agree | Strongly agree |
|---|:---:|:---:|:---:|:---:|:---:|
| 1. My job offers me a chance to test myself and my abilities. | 1 | 2 | 3 | 4 | 5 |
| 2. Mastering this job means a lot to me. | 1 | 2 | 3 | 4 | 5 |
| 3. Doing this job well is a reward in itself. | 1 | 2 | 3 | 4 | 5 |
| 4. Considering the time spent on the job, I feel thoroughly familiar with my tasks and responsibilities. | 1 | 2 | 3 | 4 | 5 |

### EXAMPLE 8.10 USE OF THE RATIO SCALE

*Ratio scales* are usually used in business research when exact numbers on objective (as opposed to subjective) factors are called for, as in the following questions.
1. How many other organisations did you work for before joining this one? __
2. Please indicate the number of children you have in each of the following categories:
   __ below 3 years of age
   __ between 3 and 6 years
   __ over 6 years but under 12
   __ 12 years and over
3. How many retail outlets do you operate? __

The responses to the questions could range from 0 to any reasonable figure.

## REVIEW OF SCALES

The four scales that can be applied to the measurement of variables are the nominal, ordinal, interval and ratio scales. The nominal scale highlights the differences by classifying objects or persons into groups, and provides the least amount of information on the variable. The ordinal scale provides some additional information by rank-ordering the categories of the nominal scale. The interval scale not only ranks, but also provides us with information on the magnitude of the differences in the variable. The ratio scale indicates not only the magnitude of the differences but also their proportion. Multiplication or division would preserve these ratios. As we move from the nominal to the ratio scale, we obtain greater precision in quantifying the data and greater flexibility in using more powerful statistical tests. Hence, whenever possible and appropriate, a more powerful rather than a less powerful scale should be used to measure the variables of interest.

## SUMMARY

In this chapter we saw that any concept can be broken down to dimensions and elements so that it can be measured. We also examined the four types of measurement scale — nominal, ordinal, interval and ratio. We could see that knowledge of how to operationalise a concept and which type of scale to use for the purpose of categorising, rank-ordering and tapping variables to varying degrees of sophistication helps managers and researchers to undertake surveys on their own without difficulty. In the next chapter we will discuss the further development of measures and scales to tap concepts within the general area of business research.

## DISCUSSION POINTS

1. What is meant by operational definition and why is it necessary?
2. Operationally define the following:
   (a) Sexual harassment
   (b) Career success
3. Describe the four types of measurement scale.
4. How is the interval scale more sophisticated than the nominal and ordinal scales?
5. Why is the ratio scale considered to be the most powerful of the four measurement scales?

| | |
|---|---|
| Exercise 8.1 | Schematically depict the operational definition of the concept of **stress** and develop 10 questions that would measure stress. |
| Exercise 8.2 | Schematically depict the operational definition of the concept of enriched job and develop 12 items to measure it. |
| Exercise 8.3 | Suggest two variables that would be natural candidates for nominal scales, and set up mutually exclusive and collectively exhaustive categories for each. |
| Exercise 8.4 | Develop an ordinal scale for consumer preferences for different brands of beer. |
| Exercise 8.5 | Measure any three variables on an interval scale. |
| Exercise 8.6 | Example 8.2 lists 16 items directed towards tapping achievement motivation. Take items 6 to 9 and item 14, and use an interval scale to measure them. Reword the questions if you wish, without changing their meaning. |
| Exercise 8.7 | Identify one variable for each of the four scales in the context of a market survey, and explain how or why it would fit into the scale. |

# chapter 9

# SCALING, RELIABILITY AND VALIDITY

## OUTLINE

RATING SCALES

RANKING SCALES

GOODNESS OF MEASURES

RELIABILITY

VALIDITY

SUMMARY

DISCUSSION POINTS

EXERCISES

APPENDIX: EXAMPLES OF SOME MEASURES

## CHAPTER OBJECTIVES

After reading this chapter, you should be able to:
- know how and when to use the different forms of rating scales and ranking scales
- explain stability and consistency, and how they are established
- explain the different forms of validity
- discuss what 'goodness' of measures means, and why it is necessary to establish it in research.

In the previous chapter we discussed the four different types of measurement scale (nominal, ordinal, interval and ratio). They can be used to measure the operationally defined dimensions and elements of a variable. The position of measurement and scaling as part of research design was also highlighted in figures 8.1 and 8.2. Now we will examine the methods of scaling (that is, assigning numbers or symbols) to elicit the responses of subjects towards objects, events or persons. There are two main categories of response scale (not to be confused with the four different types of measurement scale) — the *rating scale* and the *ranking scale*. **Rating scales** have several response categories and are used to elicit responses with regard to the object, event or person studied. **Ranking scales**, on the other hand, make comparisons between or among objects, events or persons, and elicit the preferred choices and ranking among them. These response scales are discussed below.

## RATING SCALES

The following rating scales are often used in business research:
- dichotomous scale
- category scale
- Likert scale
- numerical scales
- semantic differential scale
- itemised rating scale
- fixed or constant sum rating scale
- Stapel scale
- graphic rating scale
- consensus scale.

Other scales, such as the Thurstone Equal Appearing Interval scale, and the multidimensional scale, are less frequently used. We will briefly describe each of the preceding attitudinal scales.

## DICHOTOMOUS SCALE

The **dichotomous scale** is used to elicit a *yes* or *no* answer, as in the example below. Note that a nominal measurement scale is used to elicit the response.

**EXAMPLE 9.1** *Do you own a car?* Yes   No

## CATEGORY SCALE

The **category scale** uses multiple items to elicit a single response, as in the following example. This also uses the nominal measurement scale.

**EXAMPLE 9.2** *Where in the Wellington region do you reside?*
   __ Wellington City
   __ Lower Hutt
   __ Upper Hutt
   __ Porirua
   __ Other

Category scales can also be expressed as ordinal measurement scales. However, the wording is very important for the usefulness of these scales. Figure 9.1 presents a range of selected category scales prepared by Zikmund (2000:292). In some cases numbers can be assigned to the different categories and as long as the interval between each category is regarded as equal, then the scales can be treated as interval scales for the purposes of subsequent data analysis.

| | | Quality | | |
|---|---|---|---|---|
| Excellent | Good | Fair | Poor | |
| Very good | Fairly good | Neither good nor bad | Not very good | Not good at all |

| | | Importance | | |
|---|---|---|---|---|
| Very important | Fairly important | Neutral | Not so important | Not at all important |

| | | Interest | | |
|---|---|---|---|---|
| Very interested | | Somewhat interested | | Not very interested |

| | | Satisfaction | | |
|---|---|---|---|---|
| Very satisfied | Somewhat satsified | Neither satisfied nor dissatisfied | Somewhat dissatisfied | Very dissatisfied |
| Very satisfied | Quite satisfied | | Somewhat dissatisfied | Not at all satisfied |

| | | Frequency | | |
|---|---|---|---|---|
| All of the time | Very often | Often | Sometimes | Hardly ever |
| Very often | Often | Sometimes | Rarely | Never |
| All of the time | Most of the time | | Some of the time | Just now and then |

| | | Truth | | |
|---|---|---|---|---|
| Very true | Somewhat true | | Not very true | Not at all true |
| Definitely true | More true than false | | More false than true | Definitely not true |

**Figure 9.1** Selected category scales

**Source:** Zikmund (2000:292).

# LIKERT SCALE

The **Likert scale** is designed to examine how strongly subjects agree or disagree with statements on a five-point (or seven-point) scale with the following anchors:

| Strongly disagree | Disagree | Neither agree nor disagree | Agree | Strongly agree |
|---|---|---|---|---|
| 1 | 2 | 3 | 4 | 5 |

The Likert scale always has an odd total of possible response points (it is usually a five-point or seven-point response scale), and the midpoint (e.g. the third in a five-point scale) is either neutral ('neither agree nor disagree') or a passing level (e.g. 'satisfactory').

The responses over a number of items tapping a particular concept or variable (as in the following example) are then totalled for every respondent. The interval measurement scale is used here, the differences in the responses between any two points on the scale remaining the same.

**EXAMPLE 9.3**

*Using the preceding Likert scale, indicate the extent to which you agree with each of the following statements:*

| | | | | | |
|---|---|---|---|---|---|
| My work is very interesting. | 1 | 2 | 3 | 4 | 5 |
| I am not engrossed in my work all day. | 1 | 2 | 3 | 4 | 5 |
| Life without my work would be dull. | 1 | 2 | 3 | 4 | 5 |

# SEMANTIC DIFFERENTIAL SCALE

Several bipolar attributes are identified at the extremes of the scale, and respondents are asked to indicate their attitudes, on what may be called a semantic space, towards a particular individual, object or event on each of the attributes. The bipolar adjectives used, for instance, would denote such ideas as Good–Bad; Strong–Weak; Hot–Cold. The **semantic differential scale** is used to assess respondents' attitudes towards a particular brand, advertisement, object or individual. The responses can be plotted to obtain a good idea of the perceptions of the respondents. This is treated as an interval scale. An example of the semantic differential scale follows.

**EXAMPLE 9.4**

| Responsive | - - - - - - - - - - - - - - - - - - - - - - | Unresponsive |
|---|---|---|
| Beautiful | - - - - - - - - - - - - - - - - - - - - - - | Ugly |
| Courageous | - - - - - - - - - - - - - - - - - - - - - - | Timid |

# NUMERICAL SCALE

The **numerical scale** is similar to the semantic differential scale, with the difference that numbers on a five-point or seven-point scale are provided, with bipolar adjectives at either end, as illustrated below. This is also an interval measurement scale.

**EXAMPLE 9.5**

*How pleased are you with your new real estate agent?*

| Extremely pleased | 7 | 6 | 5 | 4 | 3 | 2 | 1 | Extremely displeased |
|---|---|---|---|---|---|---|---|---|

## ITEMISED RATING SCALE

A five-point or seven-point scale with anchors, as needed, is provided for each item and the respondent states the appropriate number on the side of each item, or circles the relevant number against each item, as in the examples that follow. The responses to the items are then added up. This uses an interval measurement scale.

---

**EXAMPLE 9.6(i)** *Respond to each item using the scale below, and indicate your response number on the line by each item.*

| Very unlikely | Unlikely | Neither unlikely nor likely | Likely | Very likely |
|---|---|---|---|---|
| 1 | 2 | 3 | 4 | 5 |

1. I will be changing my job within the next 12 months. —
2. I will take on new assignments in the near future. —
3. It is possible that I will be out of this organisation within the next 12 months. —

Note that the above is a *balanced rating scale* with a *neutral* point.

---

**EXAMPLE 9.6(ii)** *Circle the number that is closest to how you feel about each item below.*

| Not at all interested | Somewhat interested | Moderately interested | Very much interested |
|---|---|---|---|
| 1 | 2 | 3 | 4 |

| | | | | |
|---|---|---|---|---|
| How would you rate your interest in changing current organisational policies? | 1 | 2 | 3 | 4 |

This is an **unbalanced rating scale** which does *not* have a neutral point.

---

The **itemised rating scale** provides the flexibility to use as many points in the scale as considered necessary (four, five, seven, nine or whatever), and it is also possible to use difference anchors (for example, *Very unimportant* to *Very important*; *Extremely low* to *Extremely high*). When a neutral point is provided, it is a balanced rating scale; when it is not, it is an unbalanced rating scale.

Research indicates that a five-point scale is as good as any, and that an increase from five to seven or nine points on a rating scale does not improve the reliability of the ratings (Elmore & Beggs 1975).

This scale is frequently used in business research, since it lends itself to adaptation as to the number of points used, as well as the nomenclature of the anchors, as is considered necessary to fit the needs of the researcher for tapping the variable.

## FIXED OR CONSTANT SUM RATING SCALE

Here the respondents are asked to distribute a given number of points across various items, as in the example below. The **constant sum rating scale** resembles an ordinal measurement scale.

**EXAMPLE 9.7** *In choosing a toilet soap, indicate the importance you attach to each of the following five aspects by distributing a total of 100 points among them.*

|  |  |
|---|---|
| Fragrance | — |
| Colour | — |
| Shape | — |
| Size | — |
| Texture of lather | — |
| Total points | 100 |

## STAPEL SCALE

The **Stapel scale** simultaneously measures both the direction and the intensity of the attitude towards the items under study. The characteristic of interest to the study is placed at the centre and a numerical scale ranging from, say, +3 to −3 is placed on either side of the item, as illustrated below. This gives an idea of how close or distant the individual response to the stimulus is, as in the example below. Since it does not have an absolute zero point, this is an interval measurement scale.

**EXAMPLE 9.8** *State how you would rate your supervisor's abilities with respect to each of the characteristics mentioned below, by circling the appropriate number.*

| +3 | +3 | +3 |
|---|---|---|
| +2 | +2 | +2 |
| +1 | +1 | +1 |
| Adopting modern technology | Product innovation | Interpersonal skills |
| −1 | −1 | −1 |
| −2 | −2 | −2 |
| −3 | −3 | −3 |

## GRAPHIC RATING SCALE

Here, a graphical representation helps the respondents to indicate their answers to a particular question by placing a mark at the appropriate point on the line, as in the following example. This is an ordinal measurement scale, though the following example might seem like an interval measurement scale.

**EXAMPLE 9.9** *On a scale of 1 to 10, how would you rate your supervisor?*

| 10 | Excellent |
|---|---|
| 5 | All right |
| 1 | Very bad |

The **graphic rating scale** is easy to respond to. The brief descriptions on the scale points are meant to serve as a guide in locating the rating rather than to represent discrete categories. The **faces scale**, which depicts faces ranging from smiling to sad (illustrated as example 10.6 in chapter 10, page 237), is also a graphic rating scale used to obtain responses regarding people's feelings with respect to some aspect (for example how they feel about their jobs).

## CONSENSUS SCALE

Scales are also developed by consensus — a panel of judges select certain items they feel measure the concept to be measured. The items are chosen particularly based on their relevance to the concept. Such a **consensus scale** is developed after the selected items are examined and tested for their validity and reliability. One such consensus scale is the **Thurstone Equal Appearing Interval scale**; here a concept is measured by a complex process followed by a panel of judges. Using a pile of cards on which are statements describing the concept, a panel of judges offer their inputs to indicate how close the statements are, or are not, to the concept under study. The scale is then developed based on the consensus reached. However, this scale is rarely used for measuring business concepts because of the time involved in developing it.

## OTHER SCALES

There are also some advanced scaling methods, such as **multidimensional scaling**, in which one can visually scale objects or people, or both, and a conjoint analysis is performed. This provides a visual image of the relationships in space among the dimensions of a construct.

It should be noted that the Likert scale or some form of category or numerical scale is most frequently used to measure attitudes and behaviours in business research.

## RANKING SCALES

As already mentioned, **ranking scales** are used to tap preferences between two or more objects or items (ordinal measurements in nature). However, such ranking may not give definitive clues to some of the answers sought. For instance, let us say there are four product lines and the manager desires to obtain information which would be helpful in deciding which product line should get the most attention. Let us also say that 35 per cent of the respondents choose the first product, 25 per cent choose the second, and 20 per cent choose each of products three and four as of importance to them. The manager cannot then decide that the first product is the most preferred since 65 per cent of the respondents did not choose that product! Alternative methods used are the *paired comparisons*, *forced choice* and *comparative scale*, which are discussed below.

## PAIRED COMPARISON

The *paired comparison scale* is used when, among a small number of objects, respondents are asked to choose between two objects at a time. This helps to assess preferences. If, for instance, in the previous example of **paired comparisons**, respondents consistently show a preference for product one over products two, three and four, that would provide the manager with a good indication of which product line is worth pursuing with vigour. However, as the number of objects to be compared increases, the number of paired comparisons also increases. The paired choices for $n$ objects will be $((n)(n-1)/2)$. The greater the number of objects or stimuli, the greater the number of paired comparisons presented to the respondents, and the greater the respondent fatigue. Hence, paired comparison is a good method when the number of stimuli presented is small.

## FORCED CHOICE

The *forced choice* offers respondents the opportunity to rank objects relative to one another, among the alternatives provided. This is easier for the respondents to do, particularly if the number of choices to be ranked is limited in number.

**EXAMPLE 9.10**

Rank your preferences among the following magazines which you would like to subscribe to, 1 being the most preferred choice and 5 being the least preferred.

Australian Financial Review  __
Business Review Weekly  __
Playboy  __
The Economist  __
Time  __

## COMPARATIVE SCALE

The **comparative scale** provides a benchmark or a point of reference to assess attitudes towards the current object, event or situation under study. An example of the use of the comparative scale follows.

**EXAMPLE 9.11**

In a volatile financial environment, compared with shares, how useful is it to invest in government bonds? Please circle the appropriate response.

| More useful | | About the same | | Less useful |
|---|---|---|---|---|
| 1 | 2 | 3 | 4 | 5 |

To summarise, nominal data lend themselves to dichotomous or category scales; ordinal data lend themselves to any one of the ranking scales — paired comparison, forced choice or comparative scales; and interval or interval-like data lend themselves to the other rating scales, as seen from the various examples above. The semantic differential and the numerical scales are not, strictly speaking, interval measurement scales, though they are often treated as such in data analysis.

Rating scales are used to measure most behavioural concepts. Ranking scales are used to make comparisons or rank the variables that have been tapped on a nominal measurement scale.

## GOODNESS OF MEASURES

Now that we have seen how to operationally define variables and apply different scaling techniques, it is important to make sure that the instrument we develop to measure a particular concept is indeed *accurately* measuring the variable and that we are *actually* measuring the concept that we set out to measure. The latter ensures that in operationally defining perceptual and attitudinal variables, we have not overlooked important dimensions and elements or included irrelevant ones. The scales developed could often be imperfect, and of course, there are always errors in measurement of attitudinal variables. The use of better instruments will ensure more accurate results, which in turn will enhance the scientific quality of the research. Hence, in some way we need to assess the 'goodness' of the measures developed. That is, we need to be reasonably sure that the instruments we use in our research do indeed measure the variables they are supposed to, and that they measure them accurately.

Let us now examine how we can ensure that the measures developed are reasonably good. First, an item analysis of the responses to the questions tapping the variable is carried out, then the reliability and validity of the measures are established as described in the following pages.

## ITEM ANALYSIS

Item analysis is done to see whether the items in the instrument belong there. Each item is examined to see if it is able to discriminate between those subjects whose total scores are high and those whose scores are low. In item analysis, the means between the high-score group and the low-score group are tested to detect significant differences through the $t$-values (see appendix I at the end of the book for an explanation of $t$-tests). Items with a high $t$-test (a test that is able to identify the highly discriminating items in the instrument) are then included in the instrument. Thereafter, tests for the reliability of the instrument are done. The validity of the measure is then established.

Briefly, reliability tests how *consistently* a measuring instrument measures a particular concept. Validity tests how *well* an instrument measures the particular concept it is supposed to measure. In other words, validity is concerned with whether we measure the right concept, and reliability is concerned with stability and consistency in measurement. Validity and reliability of the measure attest to the scientific rigour applied to the research study. These two criteria will now be discussed. The various forms of reliability and validity are illustrated in figure 9.2.

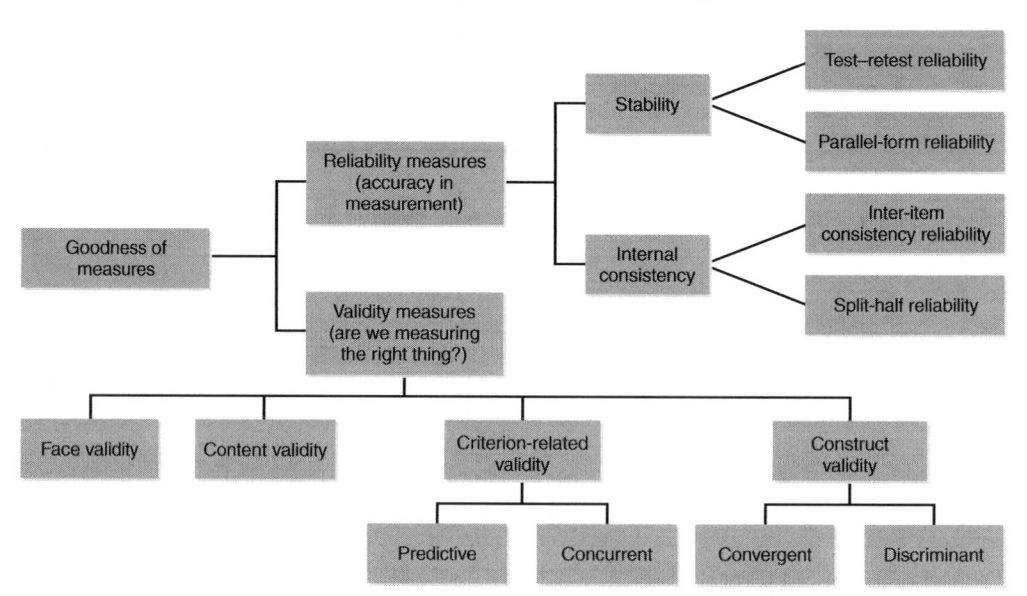

**Figure 9.2** Testing goodness of measures: forms of reliability and validity

## RELIABILITY

The reliability of a measure indicates the extent to which the measure is without bias (error free) and hence offers consistent measurement across time and across the various items in the instrument. In other words, the reliability of a measure indicates the stability and consistency with which the instrument measures the concept and helps to assess the 'goodness' of a measure.

### STABILITY OF MEASURES

The ability of a measure to maintain **stability** over time, despite uncontrollable testing conditions or the state of the respondents themselves, indicates its stability and low vulnerability to changes in the situation. This attests to the 'goodness' of the measure, inasmuch as it stably measures the concept, no matter when it is measured. Two tests of stability are test–retest reliability and parallel-form reliability.

### Test–retest reliability

The reliability coefficient obtained with a repetition of the same measure on a second occasion is called test–retest reliability. That is, when a questionnaire containing some items that are supposed to measure a concept is administered to a set of respondents now, and presented again to the same respondents, say, several weeks or six months later, then the correlation between the scores obtained at the two different times from the same set of respondents is called the test–retest coefficient. The higher it is, the better the test–retest reliability, and hence the better the stability of the measure across time.

### Parallel-form reliability

When responses on two comparable sets of measures tapping the same construct are highly correlated, we have parallel-form reliability. Both forms have similar items and the same response format, with only the wording and the ordering of questions changed. What we try to establish here is the error variability resulting from the wording and ordering of the questions. If two such comparable forms are highly correlated (say, 0.8 and above), we can be fairly certain that the measures are reasonably reliable, with minimal error variance caused by wording, ordering or other factors.

## INTERNAL CONSISTENCY OF MEASURES

The **internal consistency** of measures indicates the homogeneity of the items in the measure that tap the construct. In other words, the items should 'hang together as a set' and be capable of independently measuring the same concept so that the respondents attach the same overall meaning to each of the items. This can be seen by examining whether the items and the subsets of items in the measuring instrument are highly correlated. Consistency can be examined through the **inter-item consistency reliability** and split-half reliability tests.

### Inter-item consistency reliability

This is a test of the consistency of respondents' answers to all the items in a measure. To the degree that items are independent measures of the same concept, they will be correlated with one another. The most popular test of inter-item consistency reliability is the **Cronbach's coefficient alpha** (Cronbach 1946), which is used for multipoint-scaled items, and the Kuder-Richardson formulas (Kuder & Richardson 1937), used for dichotomous items. The higher the coefficients, the better the measuring instrument.

### Split-half reliability

**Split-half reliability** reflects the correlations between two halves of an instrument. Split-half reliability estimates would vary depending on how the items in the measure are split into halves. Split-half reliabilities could be higher than Cronbach's alpha only in the circumstance of there being more than one underlying response dimension tapped by the measure and when certain other conditions are met as well (for complete details, refer to Campbell 1976). Hence, in almost all cases, Cronbach's alpha can be considered a perfectly adequate index of the inter-item consistency reliability.

It should be noted that the consistency of the judgement of several raters on how they see a phenomenon or interpret responses is termed **inter-rater reliability**, and should not be confused with the reliability of a measuring instrument. As we noted earlier, inter-rater reliability is especially relevant when the data are obtained through observations, projective tests or unstructured interviews, all of which are liable to be subjectively interpreted.

It is important to note that reliability is a necessary but insufficient condition of the test of goodness of a measure. For example, one could very reliably measure a concept, establishing high stability and consistency, but it may not be the concept that one set out to measure. **Validity** ensures the ability of a scale to measure the intended concept. We will now discuss the concept of validity.

Figure 9.3 illustrates the concepts of reliability and validity in relation to a rifle sharpshooter taking shots at a target. Aiming at target 1, the sharpshooter is using an instrument (an old British smooth-bore musket!) that is neither reliable nor valid. At target 2, the sharpshooter tries out a rifle that proves to be reliable (stable and consistent), but unfortunately not valid (almost all the shots are off the target!). For target 3, the shooter tries out a new Australian rifle and hits the bullseye every time (the instrument is reliable and valid) (based on Davis 2000 and Zikmund 2000).

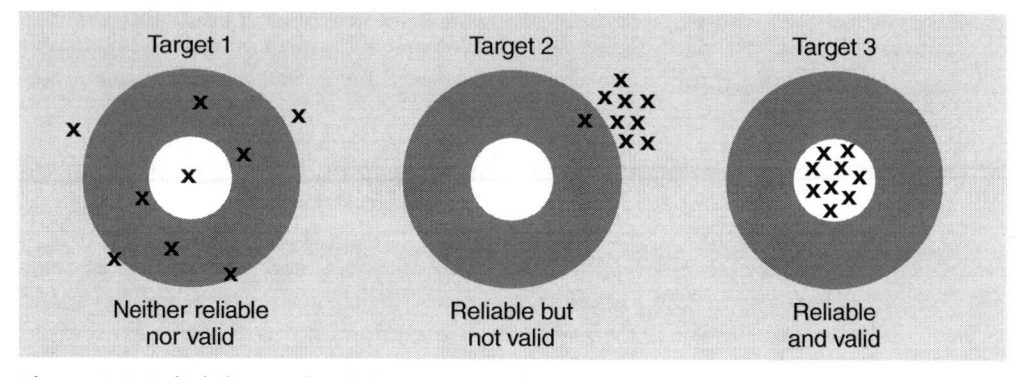

**Figure 9.3** Reliability and validity in target shooting

# VALIDITY

In chapter 12 we will examine the terms **internal validity** and **external validity** in the context of experimental designs. We are concerned about the issue of the authenticity of the cause and effect relationships (internal validity), and their generalisability to the external environment (external validity). Here we are going to examine the validity of the measuring instrument itself. When we ask a set of questions (that is, develop a measuring instrument) in the hope that we are tapping the concept, how can we be reasonably sure that we are measuring the concept we set out to measure and not something else? This can be determined by applying certain validity tests.

Several types of validity test are used to test the goodness of measures. Writers use different terms to denote these validity tests. For the sake of clarity, we can group validity tests under four broad headings: **face validity**, **content validity**, **criterion-related validity** and **construct validity**.

## FACE VALIDITY

*Face validity* is considered by some to be a basic and very minimal index of validity. It indicates that the items being presented on the questionnaire are clear and understandable to the subjects. Face validity is usually tested by giving the questionnaire to a sample of respondents to gauge their reaction to the items. Most researchers do not treat it as a valid component of content validity.

## CONTENT VALIDITY

*Content validity* ensures that the measures include an adequate and representative set of items that tap the concept. The more the scale items represent the domain or universe of the concept being measured, the greater the content validity. In other words, content validity is a function of how well the dimensions and elements of a concept have been delineated.

There are at least three ways to achieve content validity — from the literature, from qualitative research and from the judgement of a panel of experts. The researchers may identify specific points that describe the concept from the literature. Alternatively, these specific points may come from the analysis of qualitative data, for example from interviews. These specific points are then measured, for example as items in a questionnaire. To ensure that these specific points are representative of the concepts, a full list of the points is referred to a panel of experts. Kidder and Judd (1986) cite the example in which a test designed to measure degrees of speech impairment can be considered as having validity if it is so evaluated by a group of expert judges (professional speech therapists).

## CRITERION-RELATED VALIDITY

*Criterion-related validity* is established when the measure differentiates individuals on a criterion it is expected to predict. This can be done by establishing **concurrent validity** or **predictive validity**, as explained below.

*Concurrent validity* is established when the scale discriminates between individuals who are known to be different; that is, they should score differently on the instrument, as in the example that follows.

---

**EXAMPLE 9.12**

If a measure of work ethic is developed and administered to a group of welfare recipients, the scale should differentiate those who are enthusiastic about accepting a job and being off welfare from those who do not want to work even when offered a job. Obviously, those with a strong work ethic would not want to be on welfare and would be eager to accept a job as soon as possible. Those who are low on work ethic values, on the other hand, might exploit the opportunity to survive on welfare for as long as possible without having to work. If both types of individuals have the same score on the work ethic scale, then the test would not be a measure of work ethic, but of something else.

---

*Predictive validity* indicates the ability of the measuring instrument to differentiate among individuals on a future criterion. For example, if an aptitude or ability test administered to employees at the time of recruitment is expected to differentiate between individuals on their future job performance, then those who score low on the test should be poor performers and those who score high should be good performers.

## CONSTRUCT VALIDITY

*Construct validity* testifies to how well the results obtained from the use of the measure fit the theories around which the test is designed. Two specific forms of construct validity are **convergent** and **discriminant validity**. *Convergent validity* is established when the scores obtained by two different instruments measuring the same concept are highly correlated. *Discriminant validity* is established when, based on theory, two variables are predicted to be uncorrelated, and the scores obtained by measuring them are indeed empirically found to be so.

Validity can thus be established in different ways. Published measures for various concepts usually report the kinds of validity that have been established for the instrument, so that the user or reader can judge the 'goodness' of the measure. Table 9.1 summarises the kinds of validity discussed here.

Some of the ways in which the above forms of validity can be established are through (i) *factor analysis*, a multivariate technique discussed in appendix I at the back of the book that would confirm the dimensions of the concept that have been operationally defined, as well as indicate which of the items are most appropriate for each dimension (establishing construct validity); (ii) *correlational analysis* (establishing concurrent and predictive validity or convergent and discriminant validity); (iii) the *multitrait, multimethod matrix* of correlations derived from measuring concepts by different forms and different methods, additionally establishing the robustness of the measure. These are more fully discussed in the chapters that follow.

**Table 9.1** Types of validity

| Validity | Description |
| --- | --- |
| Face validity | Does a sample of respondents validate that items are clear and understandable? |
| Content validity | Does the measure adequately measure the concept as based on the relevant literature, previous research or the opinion of experts? |
| Criterion-related validity | Does the measure differentiate in a manner that helps to predict a criterion variable? |
| Concurrent validity | Does the measure differentiate in a manner that helps to predict a criterion variable concurrently? |
| Predictive validity | Does the measure differentiate individuals in a manner that helps to predict a future criterion? |
| Construct validity | Does the instrument tap the concept as theorised? |
| Convergent validity | Do two instruments measuring the concept correlate closely? |
| Discriminant validity | Does the measure have a low correlation with a variable that is supposed to be unrelated to this variable? |

In summary, the **goodness of measures** is established through the different kinds of validity and reliability depicted in figure 9.2. The results of any research can only be as good as the measures that tap the concepts in the theoretical framework. We need to use well-validated and reliable measures to ensure that we engage in scientific research. Fortunately, measures have been developed for many important concepts in business research, and their psychometric properties (that is, reliability and validity) established by the developers. Thus, researchers can use the instruments already reputed to be 'good', rather than laboriously develop their own measures. When using these measures, however, researchers should cite the source (the author and reference) so that the reader can seek more information, if necessary.

It is not unusual for two or more equally good measures to be developed for the same concept. For example, there are several different instruments for measuring the concept of job satisfaction. One of the most frequently used scales to measure job satisfaction, however, is the Job Descriptive Index (JDI) developed by Smith, Kendall and Hulin (1969). When more than one scale exists for any variable, it is preferable to use the measure that has better reliability and validity and is also more frequently used.

At times, we may also have to adapt an established measure to suit the setting. For example, a scale that is used to measure job performance, job characteristics or job satisfaction in the manufacturing industry may have to be modified slightly to suit a utility company or a health-care organisation. The work environment in each case is different and the wording in the instrument may have to be adapted. However, in doing this, we are tampering with an established scale, so it would be advisable to test the validity and reliability again.

A sample of a few measures used to tap some frequently researched concepts in the management and marketing areas is provided in the appendix to this chapter.

## SUMMARY

In this chapter we saw what kinds of response rating scales and ranking scales can be used in developing instruments after a concept has been operationally defined. We discussed how the goodness of measures is established by means of item analysis, and reliability and validity tests. We also noted that the Likert scale and other types of interval-type scale such as the numerical scale are extensively used in business research, since they lend themselves to more sophisticated data analysis. Finally, we discussed the goodness of measures in terms of reliability and validity and the various ways in which these can be established.

Knowledge of the different scales and scaling techniques helps managers and researchers to administer surveys by designing questions that use ranking or rating scales, as appropriate. Awareness of the fact that measures are already available for many business concepts further facilitates survey development.

In the next chapter we will discuss the design of questionnaires for data collection.

## DISCUSSION POINTS

1. Briefly describe the difference between attitude rating scales and ranking scales, and indicate when the two are used.

2. Why is it important to establish the 'goodness' of measures and how is this done?

3. Construct a semantic differential scale to assess the properties of a particular brand of coffee or tea.

4. 'Whenever possible, it is advisable to use instruments that have already been developed and repeatedly used in published studies, rather than develop our own instruments for our studies.' Do you agree? Discuss the reasons for your answer.

5. 'A valid instrument is always reliable, but a reliable instrument may not always be valid.' Comment on this statement.

Excercise 9.1   Develop and name the type of measuring instrument used to tap the following:
a. which brands of wine are consumed by how many individuals
b. among three types of exams — multiple choice, essay type and a mix of both — which is the one preferred by most by students
c. to what extent individuals agree with your definition of accounting principles
d. how much people like an existing organisational policy.

# APPENDIX

## EXAMPLES OF SOME MEASURES

Some of the measures used in behavioural research are found in the *Handbook of Organizational Measurement* by Price (1972) and in the *Michigan Organizational Assessment Package* published by the Institute of Survey Research in Ann Arbor, Michigan. Several measures can also be seen in *Psychological Measurement Yearbooks* and in other books and academic journals. A sample of measures from the management and marketing areas is provided here.

## MEASURES FROM MANAGEMENT RESEARCH

Below is a sample of scales used to measure a number of different variables related to management research.

### I. Job involvement

| | Strongly disagree | Disagree | Neither agree nor disagree | Agree | Strongly agree |
|---|---|---|---|---|---|
| 1. My job means a lot more to me than just money. | 1 | 2 | 3 | 4 | 5 |
| 2. The major satisfaction in my life comes from my job. | 1 | 2 | 3 | 4 | 5 |
| 3. I am really interested in my work. | 1 | 2 | 3 | 4 | 5 |
| 4. I would probably keep working even if I didn't need the money. | 1 | 2 | 3 | 4 | 5 |
| 5. The most important things that happen to me involve my work. | 1 | 2 | 3 | 4 | 5 |
| 6. I will do overtime to finish a job, even if I am not paid for it. | 1 | 2 | 3 | 4 | 5 |
| 7. For me, the first few hours at work really fly by. | 1 | 2 | 3 | 4 | 5 |
| 8. How much do you actually enjoy performing the daily activities that make up your job? | 1 | 2 | 3 | 4 | 5 |
| 9. How much do you look forward to coming to work each day? | 1 | 2 | 3 | 4 | 5 |

**Source:** J. K. White and R. R. Ruh 1973. 'Effects of personal values on the relationship between participation and job attitudes'. *Administrative Science Quarterly* 18 (4), 509. Reproduced with permission.

## II. Role conflict

| | Very false | | | | | | Very true |
|---|---|---|---|---|---|---|---|
| 1. I have to do things that should be done differently. | 1 | 2 | 3 | 4 | 5 | 6 | 7 |
| 2. I work under incompatible policies and guidelines. | 1 | 2 | 3 | 4 | 5 | 6 | 7 |
| 3. I receive an assignment without the manpower to complete it. | 1 | 2 | 3 | 4 | 5 | 6 | 7 |
| 4. I have to buck a rule or policy in order to carry out an assignment. | 1 | 2 | 3 | 4 | 5 | 6 | 7 |
| 5. I work with two or more groups who operate quite differently. | 1 | 2 | 3 | 4 | 5 | 6 | 7 |
| 6. I receive incompatible requests from two or more people. | 1 | 2 | 3 | 4 | 5 | 6 | 7 |
| 7. I do things that are apt to be accepted by one person and not accepted by others. | 1 | 2 | 3 | 4 | 5 | 6 | 7 |
| 8. I receive an assignment without adequate resources and materials to execute it. | 1 | 2 | 3 | 4 | 5 | 6 | 7 |
| 9. I work on unnecessary things. | 1 | 2 | 3 | 4 | 5 | 6 | 7 |

**Source:** J. R. Rizzo, R. J. House and S. I. Lirtzman, 1970. 'Role conflict and ambiguity in complex organisations'. *Administrative Science Quarterly* 15, 156. Reproduced with permission.

## III. Career salience

| Strongly disagree 1 | Disagree 2 | Slightly disagree 3 | Neutral 4 | Slightly agree 5 | Agree 6 | Strongly agree 7 |
|---|---|---|---|---|---|---|

| | |
|---|---|
| 1. My career choice is a good occupational decision for me. | — |
| 2. My career enables me to make significant contributions to society. | — |
| 3. The career I am in fits me and reflects my personality. | — |
| 4. My education and training are not tailored for this career. | — |
| 5. I don't intend changing careers. | — |
| 6. All the planning and thought I gave to pursuing this career are a waste. | — |
| 7. My career is an integral part of my life. | — |

**Source:** U. Sekaran 1986, *Dual-Career Families: Contemporary Organizational and Counseling Issues*. San Francisco: Jossey Bass. Reproduced with permission.

**IV. Least preferred co-worker scale (to assess whether employees are primarily people-oriented or task-oriented)**

Look at the words at both ends of the line before you put in your 'X'. Please remember that there are *no right or wrong answers*. Work rapidly; your first answer is likely to be the best. Please do not omit any items, and mark each item only once.

### LPC

Think of the person *with whom you can work least well*. He may be someone you work with now, or someone you knew in the past. He does not have to be the person you like least well, but should be the person with whom you had the most difficulty in getting a job done. Describe this person as he appears to you.

| Left | 8 | 7 | 6 | 5 | 4 | 3 | 2 | 1 | Right |
|---|---|---|---|---|---|---|---|---|---|
| Pleasant | : | : | : | : | : | : | : | : | Unpleasant |
| Friendly | 8 | 7 | 6 | 5 | 4 | 3 | 2 | 1 | Unfriendly |
| Rejecting | 1 | 2 | 3 | 4 | 5 | 6 | 7 | 8 | Accepting |
| Helpful | 8 | 7 | 6 | 5 | 4 | 3 | 2 | 1 | Frustrating |
| Unenthusiastic | 1 | 2 | 3 | 4 | 5 | 6 | 7 | 8 | Enthusiastic |
| Tense | 1 | 2 | 3 | 4 | 5 | 6 | 7 | 8 | Relaxed |
| Distant | 1 | 2 | 3 | 4 | 5 | 6 | 7 | 8 | Close |
| Cold | 1 | 2 | 3 | 4 | 5 | 6 | 7 | 8 | Warm |
| Cooperative | 8 | 7 | 6 | 5 | 4 | 3 | 2 | 1 | Uncooperative |
| Supportive | 8 | 7 | 6 | 5 | 4 | 3 | 2 | 1 | Hostile |
| Boring | 1 | 2 | 3 | 4 | 5 | 6 | 7 | 8 | Interesting |
| Quarrelsome | 1 | 2 | 3 | 4 | 5 | 6 | 7 | 8 | Harmonious |
| Self-assured | 8 | 7 | 6 | 5 | 4 | 3 | 2 | 1 | Hesitant |
| Efficient | 8 | 7 | 6 | 5 | 4 | 3 | 2 | 1 | Inefficient |
| Gloomy | 8 | 7 | 6 | 5 | 4 | 3 | 2 | 1 | Cheerful |
| Open | 8 | 7 | 6 | 5 | 4 | 3 | 2 | 1 | Guarded |

Source: Fred E. Fiedler 1967, *A Theory of Leadership Effectiveness*. New York: McGraw-Hill. Reproduced with permission.

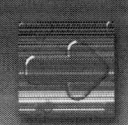

## V. Management priorities

Listed below are items that describe some *management priorities* in manufacturing. Please indicate the importance given to each item in your plant.

|  | Not important | Somewhat important | Quite important | Very important | Extremely important |
|---|---|---|---|---|---|
| 1. Production cost | 1 | 2 | 3 | 4 | 5 |
| 2. Labour productivity | 1 | 2 | 3 | 4 | 5 |
| 3. Capacity utilisation | 1 | 2 | 3 | 4 | 5 |
| 4. Conformance of final product to design specification | 1 | 2 | 3 | 4 | 5 |
| 5. Ability to introduce new products into production quickly | 1 | 2 | 3 | 4 | 5 |
| 6. Ability to adjust capacity rapidly within a short time period | 1 | 2 | 3 | 4 | 5 |
| 7. Ability to make design changes in the product after production has started | 1 | 2 | 3 | 4 | 5 |
| 8. Reducing inventory | 1 | 2 | 3 | 4 | 5 |
| 9. Reducing production lead time | 1 | 2 | 3 | 4 | 5 |

**Source:** P. T. Ward, J. K. McCreery, L. P. Ritzman and D. Sharma 1998, 'Competitive priorities in operations management'. *Decision Sciences* 29 (4), 1045.

## VI. Business strategy proactivity

The field within which the firm currently conducts its business is:

| Narrow (related areas with prospect of change) | 1 2 3 4 5 6 7 | Broad (diversified and continuing to develop) |
|---|---|---|

The main focus of concern in relation to the firm's technological process is:

| Having cost-efficient technologies | 1 2 3 4 5 6 7 | Having flexible and innovative technologies |
|---|---|---|

Planning in the firm is:

| Tremendously rigorous and predetermined | 1 2 3 4 5 6 7 | Tremendously open, impossible to complete before acting |
|---|---|---|

**Source:** J. A. Aragón-Correa 1998. 'Strategic proactivity and firm approach to the natural environment'. *Academy of Management Journal* 41 (5), 567.

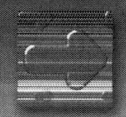

# MEASURES FROM MARKETING RESEARCH

Below is a sample of some scales used to measure commonly researched concepts in marketing. Bruner and Hensel have done extensive work since 1992 on documenting and detailing several scores of scales in marketing research. For each scale examined, they have provided the following information:
1. Scale description
2. Scale origin
3. Samples in which the scale was used
4. Reliability of the scale
5. Validity of the scale
6. How the scale was administered
7. Major findings of the studies using the scale.

The interested student should refer to the two volumes of *Marketing Scales Handbook* by G. C. Bruner and P. J. Hensel, published by the American Marketing Association. The first volume covers scales used in articles published in the 1980s, and the second volume covers scales used in articles published from 1990 to 1993. The third volume, covering the period between 1994 and 1997, was published in early 2000. Also refer to the website for the Office for Scale Research at Southern Illinois University: http://www.siu.edu/departments/coba/mktg/osr.

## I. Index of consumer sentiment towards marketing

1. Listed below are seven statements pertaining to product quality. For each statement, please 'X' the box which best describes how strongly you agree or disagree with the statement. For example, if you strongly agree that the quality of most products today is as good as can be expected, then 'X' the *Strongly agree* box. Remember to 'X' one box for each statement.

| Product quality | Strongly disagree | Somewhat disagree | Neither agree nor disagree | Somewhat agree | Strongly agree |
|---|---|---|---|---|---|
| The quality of most products I buy today is as good as can be expected. | ☐1 | ☐2 | ☐3 | ☐4 | ☐5 |
| I am satisfied with most of the products I buy. | ☐1 | ☐2 | ☐3 | ☐4 | ☐5 |
| Most products I buy wear out too quickly. | ☐1 | ☐2 | ☐3 | ☐4 | ☐5 |
| Products are not made as well as they used to be. | ☐1 | ☐2 | ☐3 | ☐4 | ☐5 |
| Too many of the products I buy are defective in some way. | ☐1 | ☐2 | ☐3 | ☐4 | ☐5 |
| The companies that make products I buy don't care enough about how well they perform. | ☐1 | ☐2 | ☐3 | ☐4 | ☐5 |
| The quality of products I buy has consistently improved over the years. | ☐1 | ☐2 | ☐3 | ☐4 | ☐5 |

2. Now we'd like to know how satisfied you are, in general, with the marketing of products. Please 'X' the one box which best describes your overall satisfaction with each aspect of marketing.

| | Very satisfied | Somewhat satisfied | Neither satisfied nor dissatisfied | Somewhat dissatisfied | Very dissatisfied |
|---|---|---|---|---|---|
| The *quality* of most products available to buy | ☐1 | ☐2 | ☐3 | ☐4 | ☐5 |
| The *prices* of most products | ☐1 | ☐2 | ☐3 | ☐4 | ☐5 |
| Most of the *advertising* you read, see and hear | ☐1 | ☐2 | ☐3 | ☐4 | ☐5 |
| The *selling conditions* at most of the stores in which you buy products | ☐1 | ☐2 | ☐3 | ☐4 | ☐5 |

3. Listed below are four questions which ask how often you have had problems with the products you buy, the prices you pay, the advertising you read, see and hear, and the stores at which you shop.

    After each statement, there are five numbers from 1 to 5. A high number means you have experienced the problem often. A lower number means you have experienced the problem less often.

    For each question, please 'X' the box which comes closest to how often the problem occurs. Remember to 'X' one box for each question.

| | Very seldom | | | | Very often |
|---|---|---|---|---|---|
| How *often* do you have problems with or complaints about the *products* you buy? | ☐1 | ☐2 | ☐3 | ☐4 | ☐5 |
| How *often* do you have problems with or complaints about the *prices* you pay? | ☐1 | ☐2 | ☐3 | ☐4 | ☐5 |
| How *often* do you have problems with or complaints about *advertising*? | ☐1 | ☐2 | ☐3 | ☐4 | ☐5 |
| How *often* do you have problems with or complaints about the *stores* at which you buy products? | ☐1 | ☐2 | ☐3 | ☐4 | ☐5 |

**Source:** J. F. Gaski and M. J. Etzel 1986. 'The index of consumer sentiment toward marketing'. *Journal of Marketing* 50, 71–81. Reproduced with permission of the American Marketing Association.

## II. SERVQUAL-P Battery (to assess the quality of service rendered)

**Reliability**
1. Provides the service as promised
2. Is dependable in handling customers' service problems
3. Performs the service right the first time
4. All _____'s employees are well-trained and knowledgeable.

**Responsiveness**
5. Employees of _____ give you prompt service.
6. Employees of _____ are always willing to help you.
7. Employees of _____ are always ready to respond to your requests.
8. _____ gives customers individual attention.

**Personalisation**
9. Everyone at _____ is polite and courteous.
10. The _____ employees display personal warmth in their behaviour.
11. All the persons working at _____ are friendly and pleasant.
12. The ____ employees take the time to know you personally.

**Tangibles**
13. _____ has modern-looking equipment.
14. _____'s physical facilities are visually appealing.
15. _____s employees have a neat and professional appearance.
16. Materials associated with the service (such as pamphlets or statements) are visually appealing at _____.

Source: B. Mittal and W. M. Lassar 1996, 'The role of personalization in service encounters'. *Journal of Retailing* 72, 95–109. Reproduced with permission of Jai Press, Inc.

## III. Role ambiguity (salesperson)

| Very false | | | | | | Very true |
|---|---|---|---|---|---|---|
| 1 | 2 | 3 | 4 | 5 | 6 | 7 |

1. I feel certain about how much authority I have in my selling position. ___
2. I have clearly planned goals for my selling job. ___
3. I am sure I divide my time properly while performing my selling tasks. ___
4. I know my responsibilities in my selling position. ___
5. I know exactly what is expected of me in my selling position. ___
6. I receive lucid explanations of what I have to do in my sales job. ___

Source: Adapted from J. R. Rizzo, R. J. House and S. I. Lirtzman 1970, 'Role ambiguity in complex organizations scale'. *Administrative Science Quarterly* 15, 156.

## IV. Brand image

How would you characterise your brand's image in this market? Please allocate 100 points to each of the following types of image. Allocate the most points to the most emphasised image (up to 100 points), and the fewest points to the least emphasised image (as little as zero points).

| | |
|---|---|
| Functional image (problem solving, problem prevention) | — |
| Social image (conveys status, social approval, accreditation) | — |
| Sensory image (provides variety, stimulation, sensory gratification) | — |
| | 100% |

**Source:** M. S. Roth 1995, 'The effects of culture and socioeconomics on the performance of global brand image strategies'. *Journal of Marketing Research* XXXII, May, 173.

# chapter 10

# QUESTIONNAIRE DESIGN

## OUTLINE

WHY ARE QUESTIONNAIRES IMPORTANT?
GUIDELINES FOR QUESTIONNAIRE DESIGN
PRINCIPLES OF WORDING
PRINCIPLES OF MEASUREMENT
GENERAL APPEARANCE OF THE QUESTIONNAIRE
PRE-TESTING QUESTIONNAIRES
GATHERING THE DATA
CROSS-CULTURAL RESEARCH
MULTIMETHODS OF DATA COLLECTION
SUMMARY
DISCUSSION POINTS
EXERCISES
APPENDIX

## CHAPTER OBJECTIVES

After reading this chapter, you should be able to:
- explain why it is important for managers or business researchers to know how to design good questionnaires
- identify the types of information included in a questionnaire
- design questionnaires to tap different variables
- evaluate questionnaires, distinguishing the 'good' and 'bad' questions therein
- identify and minimise the biases in collecting data with questionnaires
- discuss how a pilot study can be used to prove the structure of a questionnaire
- discuss the advantages and disadvantages of the different ways of administering questionnaires
- apply what you have learned to class assignments and projects.

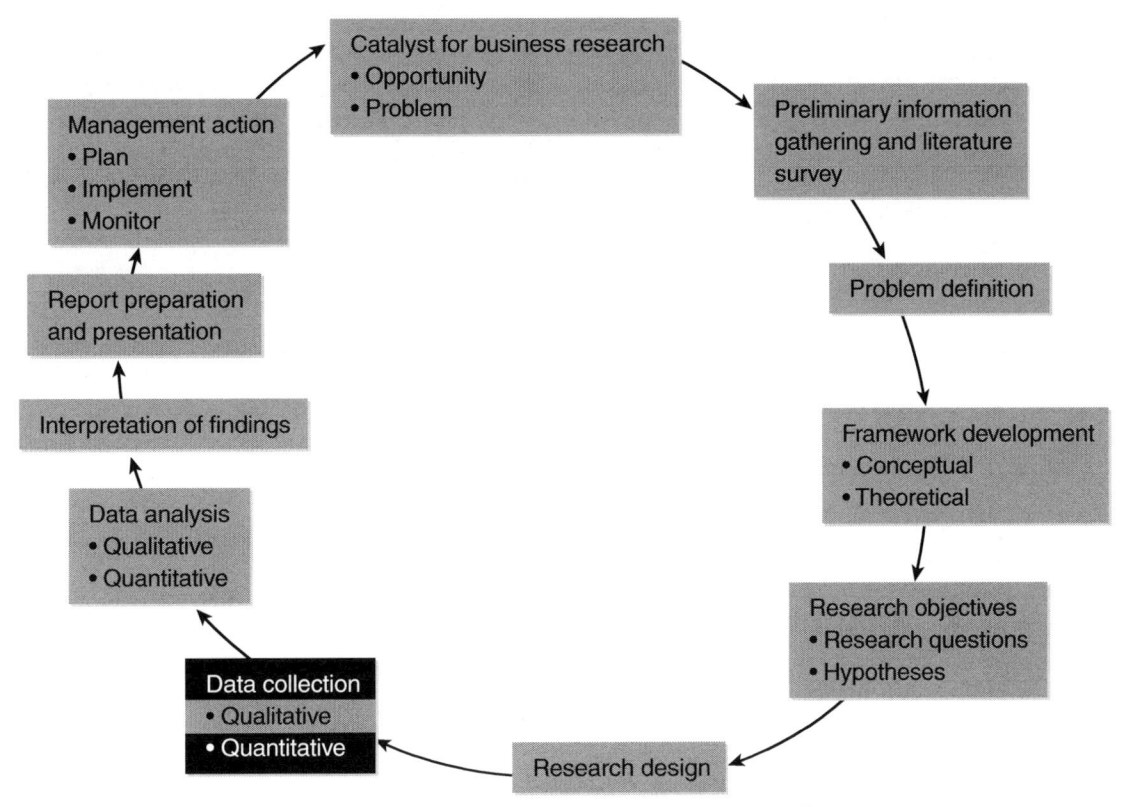

**Figure 10.1** The business research process: questionnaire design

Having examined how variables are measured, we will now discuss how data can be gathered by questionnaires for the purpose of analysis, testing of hypotheses and answering research questions. The manner in which data are collected could make a big difference to the rigour and effectiveness of the research project.

Questionnaire design is an integral part of the research project, as shown in the shaded portion in figure 10.1. In this chapter we will discuss the design of questionnaires to collect data, but first we will consider why questionnaires are important.

## WHY ARE QUESTIONNAIRES IMPORTANT?

A questionnaire? Yes, that sounds easy — jot down a few ideas, type them up and send the survey out to everyone. What could be more simple? Actually, designing business survey questionnaires properly is hard work and is based on a number of strict requirements.

Some business practitioners and managers often ask, 'Do we really need to know how to construct and use questionnaires properly?' The answer is a resounding 'Yes!' First, managers must have a working knowledge of the common business research processes, of which the use of questionnaires is one. Second, in the business environment, where litigation is becoming more common, a manager who uses a questionnaire without a reasonably professional knowledge of questionnaire design and analysis is running a grave risk. Third, if a decision is made to use a limited questionnaire — perhaps without a pilot study or perhaps only using a frequency analysis of single items — then the manager must be aware of the weaknesses of the resultant data from that limited questionnaire. These weaknesses mean that less confidence can be placed in the findings and that caution must be exercised when making decisions based on the findings. So, knowing the basics of questionnaire design and the analysis of quantitative data are essential for the professional manager. While managers may not necessarily be able to carry out some of the procedures — for example conducting the necessary statistical routines — they do need a level of knowledge that allows them to understand what is happening and, perhaps more important, when to call in experts to provide assistance.

A well-designed questionnaire will provide accurate and useable data that will allow you confidently to write the business report — which, remember, you are going to sign. Unlike the interview and the focus group, with questionnaires the researcher is not always present to make adjustments or answer queries from the respondents. Once a questionnaire is sent out, it is at the mercy of the respondents — whether they decide to complete it; whether they interpret the questions as intended; and whether they answer the questions honestly. Designing the questionnaire is about ensuring that these barriers are overcome — before the questionnaire is sent out.

A questionnaire allows the manager or business researcher to progress from gathering the ideas and suggestions of a few people at the qualitative stage to confirming whether the ideas and suggestions are widely held throughout the whole organisation or target population.

We define a questionnaire as a pre-formulated written set of questions to which respondents record their answers, usually within closely defined alternatives. An example of a questionnaire is provided in figure 10.2. We will be analysing the data collected from this questionnaire in appendix I at the back of the book.

---

## Business Research Class Questionnaire

The purpose of this short questionnaire is to collect some nominal, ordinal, interval and ratio data that can be used to demonstrate some of the basic statistical methods for analysing quantitative data. The individual responses will be anonymous and the data collected will be used only for class exercises.

*Please tick the appropriate box, provide the data requested or circle a number, where appropriate.*

1. What is your gender?
    Female ☐     Male ☐
2. Please indicate your height to the nearest centimetre (cm) _____
3. Please indicate your weight to the nearest kilogram (kg) _____
4. What is the colour of your eyes? (just tick one box please!)
    Blue ☐     Brown ☐     Other ☐
5. Please indicate the extent to which you disagree or agree with the following statements:

| | Strongly disagree | Disagree | Neutral | Agree | Strongly agree |
|---|---|---|---|---|---|
| *Statistics is interesting.* | 1 | 2 | 3 | 4 | 5 |
| *Statistics knowledge is useful in business.* | 1 | 2 | 3 | 4 | 5 |

Many thanks for your time and assistance with completing this questionnaire. We will now proceed to analyse the data collected!

---

**Figure 10.2** A sample questionnaire

However, for most business research, after the variables for the research have been identified and the measures found or developed, the questionnaire is a convenient data collection mechanism. Field studies, comparative surveys and experimental designs often use questionnaires to measure the variables of interest. Because questionnaires are in common use in surveys, it is necessary to know how to design them effectively.

As can be seen from figure 10.3, the design of a questionnaire cannot be considered in isolation from other parts of a business research survey. For example, the figure indicates that the research objectives, method of delivery, survey population, data input and processing methods, type of analysis and final report all have an impact on the design of the questionnaire, and vice versa. A set of guidelines for questionnaire design follows.

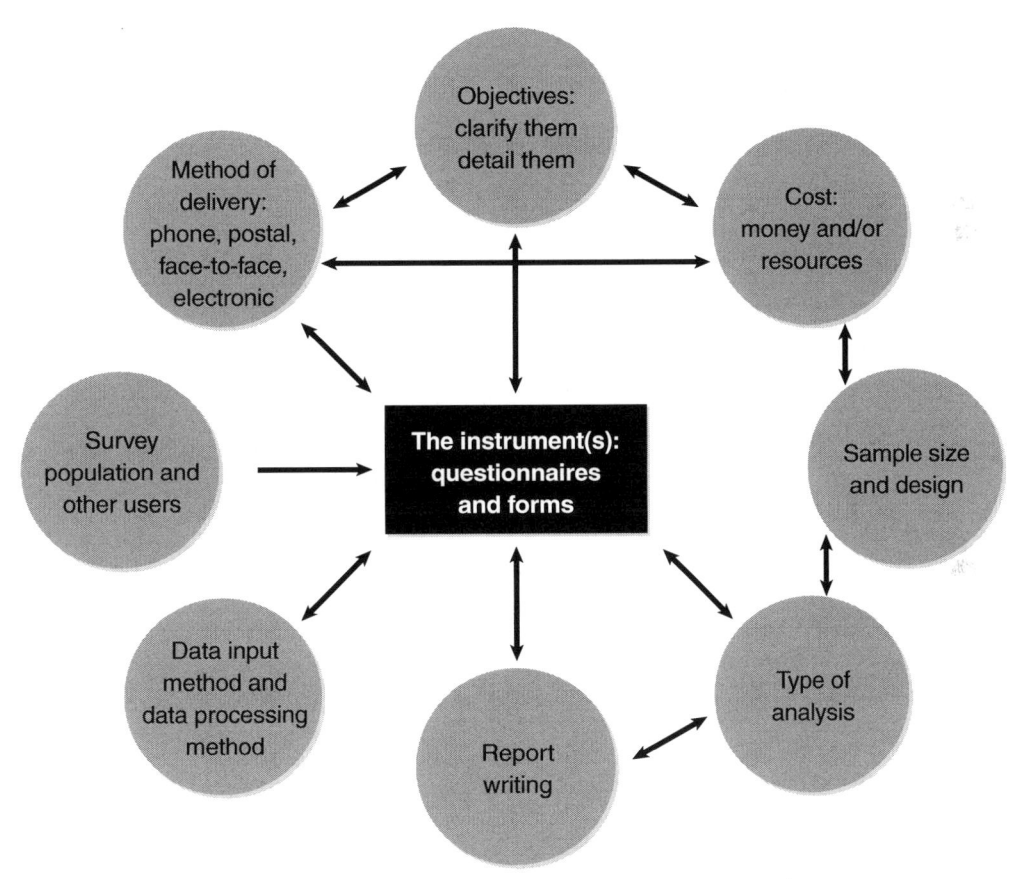

**Figure 10.3** Impact of other aspects of a survey on questionnaire design

**Source:** Statistics New Zealand (1995:42).

## GUIDELINES FOR QUESTIONNAIRE DESIGN

Sound questionnaire design principles should focus on three areas. The first relates to the wording of the questions. The second refers to planning issues — how the variables will be categorised, scaled and coded after receipt of the responses. The third pertains to the general appearance of the questionnaire. All three are important factors in questionnaire design because they can minimise biases in research. These issues are discussed below. The important aspects are illustrated in figure 10.4.

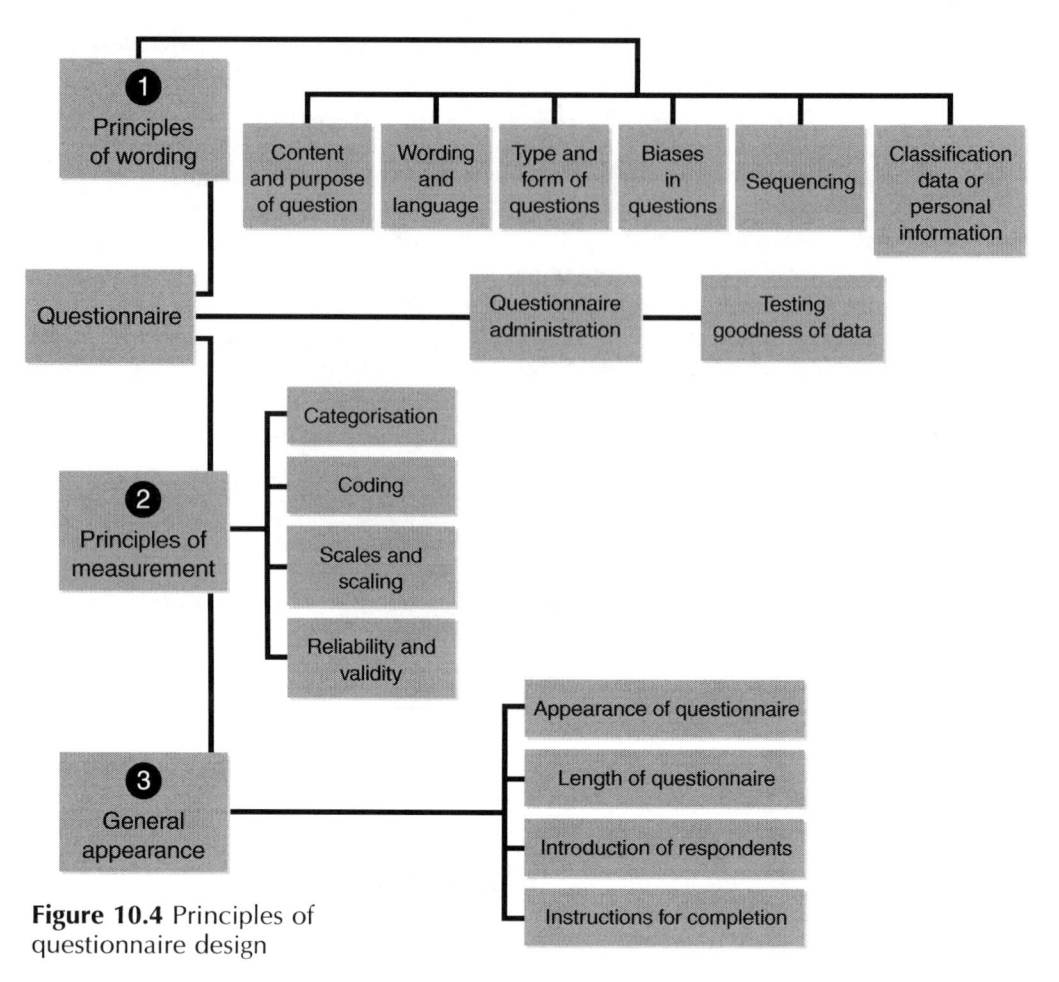

**Figure 10.4** Principles of questionnaire design

## PRINCIPLES OF WORDING

The principles of wording refer to such factors as:
- the appropriateness of the content of the questions
- how questions are worded and the level of sophistication of the language used
- the type and form of questions asked
- biases in question
- the sequencing of the questions
- the personal data sought from the respondents.

Each of these factors is explained below.

### CONTENT AND PURPOSE OF THE QUESTION

The nature of the variable tapped — subjective feelings or objective facts — will determine what kinds of question will be asked. If the variables tapped are of a subjective nature (for example satisfaction or involvement), where respondents' beliefs, perceptions and attitudes are to be measured, the questions should tap the dimensions and elements of the concept. Where objective variables such as age and educational levels of respondents are tapped, a single direct question — preferably one that has an ordinal scaled set of categories — would be appropriate. Thus, the purpose of each question should be carefully considered so that the variables are adequately measured and yet no superfluous questions are asked.

# LANGUAGE AND WORDING OF THE QUESTIONNAIRE

The language of the questionnaire should approximate the level of understanding of the respondents. The choice of words would depend on their educational level, the usage of terms and idioms in the culture, and the frames of reference of the respondents. For instance, even when English is the spoken or official language in two cultures, certain words may be alien to one culture. Comments such as *'Working here is a drag'* and *'She is a compulsive worker'* may not be interpreted the same way in different cultures. Because some blue-collar workers may not understand terminology such as 'organisational structure', it is essential to word questions in such a way that they are understood by the respondent. If some questions either are not understood or are interpreted differently by the respondent, the researcher will be obtaining the wrong answers to the questions, and responses will thus be biased. Hence, the questions asked and the language used should be appropriate to tap respndents' attitudes, perceptions and feelings.

# TYPE AND FORM OF QUESTIONS

*Type of question* refers to whether the question will be open-ended or closed. *Form* refers to positively and negatively worded questions.

## Open-ended versus closed questions

*Open-ended questions* allow respondents to answer in any way they choose. An example of an open-ended question is asking the respondent to state five things that are interesting and challenging in the job. Another example is asking what the respondents like about their supervisors or their work environment. A third example is to invite their comments on the investment portfolio of the firm.

A *closed question*, in contrast, would ask the respondents to make choices among a set of alternatives given by the researcher. For instance, instead of asking the respondent to state any *five* aspects of the job that are interesting and challenging, the researcher might list 10 or 15 characteristics that might seem interesting or challenging in jobs and ask the respondent to rank the first five among these. All items in a questionnaire using a nominal, ordinal, interval or ratio scale are considered closed.

Closed questions help the respondents to make quick decisions to choose among the several alternatives before them. They also help the researcher to code the information easily for subsequent analysis. Care has to be taken to ensure that the alternatives are mutually exclusive and collectively exhaustive. If there are overlapping categories, or if all possible alternatives are not given (that is, the categories are not exhaustive), the respondents may be confused and the advantage of their being able to make a quick decision thus lost.

Some respondents may find even well-delineated categories in a closed question confining, and might like the opportunity to make additional comments. This is the reason that many questionnaires end with open-ended questions that invite respondents to comment on topics that might not have been fully or adequately covered. The responses to such open-ended questions have to be edited and categorised for subsequent data analysis.

## Positively and negatively worded questions

Instead of phrasing all questions positively, it is advisable to include some negatively worded questions as well, so the tendency of respondents to mechanically circle the points towards one end of the scale is minimised. For example, let us say that a set of six questions are used to tap the variable 'perceived success' on a five-point scale, with 1 being 'very low' and 5 being 'very high' on the scale. A respondent who is not particularly interested in completing the questionnaire is more likely to stay involved and remain alert while answering the questions when positively and negatively worded questions are interspersed in it. For instance, if the respondent had circled 5 for a positively worded question such as *'I feel I have been able to accomplish a number of different things in my job'*, he cannot circle number 5 again to the negatively worded question *'I do not feel I am very effective in my job'*. The respondent is now shaken out of any likely tendency to respond mechanically at one end of the scale. If this still happens, the researcher has an opportunity to detect such biases. A good questionnaire should therefore include both positively and negatively worded questions. The use of double negatives and excessive use of the words *not* and *only* should be avoided in the negatively worded questions because they tend to confuse respondents. For instance, it is better to say *'Coming to work is no great fun'* than to say *'Not coming to work is greater fun than coming to work'*. Similarly, it is better to say *'The rich need no help'* than to say *'Only the rich do not need help'*.

## BIASES IN QUESTIONS

### Double-barrelled questions

A question that lends itself to different possible responses to its subparts is called a **double-barrelled question**. Such questions should be avoided and two or more separate questions asked instead. For example, the question 'Do you think there is a good market for the product and that it will sell well?' could bring a 'Yes' response to the first part (that is, there is a good market for the product) and a 'No' response to the latter part (that is, it will not sell well — for various other reasons). In this case, it would be better to ask two questions: (1) 'Do you think there is a good market for the product?' and (2) 'Do you think the product will sell well?' The answers might be 'Yes' to both, 'No' to both, 'Yes' to the first and 'No' to the second, or 'Yes' to the second and 'No' to the first. If we combined the two questions and asked a double-barrelled question, we would confuse the respondents and obtain ambiguous responses. Hence, double-barrelled questions should be avoided.

### Ambiguous questions

Even questions that are not double-barrelled may be ambiguously worded and the respondent may not be sure what exactly they mean. An example of such a question is 'To what extent would you say you are happy?' Respondents might be unsure whether the question refers to their state of feelings at the workplace, or at home, or in general. Because it is an organisational survey, she might presume that the question relates to the workplace. Yet the researcher might have intended to inquire about the general, overall degree of satisfaction that the individual experiences in everyday life — a general feeling not specific to the workplace alone. Thus, responses to **ambiguous questions** have built-in bias inasmuch as different respondents might interpret such items in the questionnaire differently. The result would be a mixed bag of ambiguous responses that do not accurately reflect the correct answer to the question.

### Recall-dependent questions

Some questions might require respondents to recall experiences from the past that are hazy in their memory. Answers to such questions might have bias. For instance, if an employee who has had 30 years' service to the organisation is asked to state when he first started working in a particular department and for how long, he may be unable to give the correct answer and may be way off in his responses. A better source for obtaining that information would be his personnel records.

## Leading questions

Questions should not be phrased in such a way that they lead the respondents to give the responses that the researcher would like or want them to give. An example of such a question is: *'Don't you think that in these days of escalating costs of living, employees should be given good pay rises?'* By asking such a question, we are signalling and pressuring respondents to say 'Yes'. Tagging the question to rising living costs makes it difficult for most respondents (unless they are the top managers in charge of budget and finances) to say 'No; not unless their productivity increases too!'. Another way of asking the question about pay rises to elicit less biased responses would be: *'To what extent do you agree that employees should be given pay rises?'* If respondents think that the employees do not deserve a higher pay rise, their response would be 'Strongly disagree'; if they think that respondents should definitely be given a pay rise, they would respond at the 'Strongly agree' end of the scale; and the in-between points would be chosen depending on the strength of their agreement or disagreement. In this case, the question is not framed in a suggestive manner, as is the previous instance.

## Loaded questions

Another type of bias in questions occurs when they are phrased in an emotionally charged manner. An example of such a **loaded question** is asking employees: *'To what extent do you think management is likely to be vindictive if the union decides to go on strike?'* The words *strike* and *vindictive* are emotionally charged terms polarising management and unions. Hence, asking a question such as the above would elicit strongly emotional and highly biased responses. If the purpose of the question is twofold — that is, to learn (1) the extent to which employees are in favour of a strike and (2) the extent to which they fear adverse reactions if they do go on strike — then these are the two specific questions that need to be asked. It may turn out that the employees do not strongly favour a strike but they also do not believe that management would retaliate if they did go on strike!

## Social desirability

Questions should not be worded in such a way that they elicit socially desirable responses. For instance, a question such as *'Do you think that older people should be retrenched?'* would elicit a 'No' response, mainly because society would frown on a person who would say that older people should be fired even if they are capable of performing their jobs. Hence, irrespective of the true feelings of the respondent, a socially desirable answer would be provided. If the purpose of the question is to gauge the extent to which organisations are seen as obligated to retain those above 65 years of age, a differently worded question with less pressure towards social desirability would be: *'There are advantages and disadvantages to retaining senior citizens in the work force. To what extent do you think companies should continue to keep the elderly on their payroll?'*

Sometimes certain items that tap **social desirability** are deliberately introduced at various points in the questionnaire, from which an index of each individual's social desirability tendency is calculated. This index is then applied to all other responses given by the individual in order to adjust for social desirability biases (Crowne & Marlow 1980; Edwards 1957).

## Length of questions

Finally, simple, short questions are preferable to long ones. As a rule of thumb, a question or a statement in the questionnaire should not exceed 20 words or one full line in print (Horst 1968; Oppenheim 1986). However, in some cases longer questions may be necessary in order to explain the question more clearly or in a more interesting way.

## SEQUENCING OF QUESTIONS

The sequence of questions in the questionnaire should be such that the respondent is led from questions of a general nature to those that are more specific, and from questions that are relatively easy to answer to those that are progressively more difficult. This *funnel* approach, as it is called (Festinger & Katz 1966), facilitates the easy and smooth progress of the respondent through the items in the questionnaire. The progression from general to specific questions might mean that the respondent is first asked questions of a global nature that pertain to the organisation or research objectives, and then is asked more incisive questions regarding the specific job, department and the like. Easy questions might relate to issues that do not involve much thinking; the more difficult ones might call for more thought, judgement and decision making in providing the answers.

In determining the sequence of questions, it is advisable not to juxtapose a positively worded and a negatively worded question tapping the same element or dimension of a concept. For instance, placing two questions such as the following, one immediately after the other, is not only awkward but might also seem insulting to the respondent.

1. *I have an opportunity to interact with my colleagues during work hours.*
2. *I have few opportunities to interact with my colleagues during work hours.*

First, there is no need to ask exactly the same question in a positive and a negative way. Second, if for some reason this is deemed necessary (for example to check the consistency of the responses), the two questions should be placed in different parts of the questionnaire, as far apart as possible.

The way questions are sequenced could also introduce certain biases, frequently referred to as the ordering effects. Though randomly placing the questions in the questionnaire would reduce any systematic biases in the response, it is very rarely done because of subsequent confusion while categorising, coding and analysing the responses.

In summary, the language and wording of the questionnaire focus on such issues as the type and form of questions asked (that is, open-ended and closed questions, and positively and negatively worded questions, as well as avoiding double-barrelled questions, ambiguous questions, **leading questions**, loaded questions, questions prone to tapping socially desirable answers and those soliciting distant recall. Questions should also not be unduly long. Using the funnel approach helps respondents to move through the questionnaire easily and comfortably.

## CLASSIFICATION DATA OR PERSONAL INFORMATION

**Classification data**, also known as personal information or demographic questions, consist of such information as age, educational level, marital status and income. Unless absolutely necessary, it is best not to ask for the name of the respondent. If, however, the questionnaire has to be identified with the respondents for any reason, then the questionnaire could be numbered and connected by the researcher to the respondent's name, in a separately maintained, private document. This procedure must be clearly explained to the respondent. The reason for using the numerical system in questionnaires is to ensure the anonymity of the respondent event if the questionnaires should fall into someone else's hands.

Whether questions seeking personal information should appear at the beginning or at the end of the questionnaire is a matter of choice for the researcher. Some people advocate asking for personal data at the end rather than the beginning (Oppenheim 1986). Their reasoning may be that by the time the respondent reaches the end of the questionnaire the individual would have been convinced of the genuineness of the questions posed by the researcher, and hence would be more open to sharing personal information. Researchers who prefer to elicit most of the personal information at the very beginning may feel that once respondents have said something about themselves at the very beginning, they may have psychologically identified themselves with the questionnaire and feel more committed to respond. Thus, whether one asks this information at the beginning or at the end of the questionnaire is a matter of individual choice. However, questions regarding details of income, or other highly sensitive information — if such information is absolutely necessary — are best placed at the very end of the questionnaire.

It is also a wise policy to ask for information regarding age, income and other sensitive personal questions by providing a range of response options. For example, the variables can be tapped as shown below.

**EXAMPLE 10.1**

| Age (years) | Annual income |
|---|---|
| ☐ Under 20 | ☐ Less than $20 000 |
| ☐ 20–30 | ☐ $20 000–30 000 |
| ☐ 31–40 | ☐ $30 001–40 000 |
| ☐ 41–50 | ☐ $40 001–50 000 |
| ☐ 51–60 | ☐ $50 001–70 000 |
| ☐ Over 60 | ☐ $70 001–90 000 |
| | ☐ Over $90 000 |

In business surveys, it is advisable to obtain certain demographic data such as age, gender, educational level, job level, department and number of years in the organisation, even if the theoretical framework does not necessitate or include these variables. Such data will help to describe the sample characteristics while writing the report after data analysis. However, when there are only a few respondents in a department, then asking information that could reveal their identity might be threatening to employees. For instance, if there is only one female in a department, she might not respond to the question on gender because it might reveal the source of the data, and this apprehension is understandable.

To sum up, certain principles of wording need to be followed when designing a questionnaire. The questions asked must be appropriate for tapping the variable. The language and wording of the questionnaire should be at a level that is meaningful to the respondents. The form and type of questions should be geared to minimising respondent biases. The sequencing of the questions should facilitate the smooth progression of the responses through the questionnaire. The personal data should be gathered with sensitivity to the respondents' feelings, and with respect for their privacy.

# PRINCIPLES OF MEASUREMENT

Just as there are guidelines that have to be followed to ensure that the wording of the questionnaire is appropriate to minimise bias, so also are there principles of measurement to be followed to ensure that the data collected are appropriate to test our hypotheses. These principles of measurement refer to the scales and scaling techniques used in measuring concepts, as well as the assessment of reliability and validity of the measures used, which were discussed in chapter 9.

As we have seen, appropriate scales have to be used according to the type of data that need to be obtained. The different scaling mechanisms, which help us to anchor our scales appropriately, should be properly used. Whenever possible, the interval and ratio scales should be used in preference to nominal or ordinal scales. Once data are obtained, the 'goodness of data' is assessed through tests of validity and reliability. Validity establishes how well a technique, instrument or process measures a particular concept, and reliability indicates how stably and consistently the instrument taps the variable. These tests will be discussed further later in the chapter, under 'Pre-testing questionnaires', and also in chapter 13 on data analysis. Finally, the data have to be obtained in a manner that makes for easy categorisation and coding, both of which are discussed in chapter 13.

# GENERAL APPEARANCE OF THE QUESTIONNAIRE

Not only is it important to address issues of wording and measurement in questionnaire design, but it is also necessary to pay attention to how the questionnaire looks. An attractive and neat questionnaire with appropriate introduction and instructions, and a well-arrayed set of questions and response alternatives, will make the respondents' task easier. A good introduction, well-organised instructions and neat alignment of the questions are all important. These elements are briefly discussed with examples.

## INTRODUCTION TO RESPONDENTS

A proper introduction that clearly discloses the identity of the researcher and conveys the purpose of the survey is absolutely necessary. It is also essential to establish rapport with the respondents and motivate them to respond to the questionnaire willingly and enthusiastically. Assuring respondents of the confidentiality of the information provided by them will ensure less biased answers. The introduction should end on a courteous note, thanking the respondent for taking the time to respond to the survey. The following is an example of an appropriate introduction.

---

**EXAMPLE 10.2**

School of Business and Public Management
Victoria University of Wellington
PO Box 600, Wellington
New Zealand

3 July 2000

Dear Participant,

   This questionnaire is designed to study aspects of life at work. The information you provide will help us better understand the quality of our work life. Because *you* are the only one who can give us a correct picture of how *you* experience your work life, we would be most grateful if you would respond to the questions frankly and honestly.

Your response will be kept *strictly confidential*. Only members of the research team will have access to the information you give. In order to ensure the utmost privacy, we have provided an identification number for each participant. This number will be used by us only for follow-up procedures. The numbers, names or completed questionnaires will not be made available to anyone other than the research team. A summary of the results will be mailed to you after the data are analysed, if you would like a copy.

Thank you very much for your time and cooperation. We greatly appreciate your organisation's and your help in assisting us with this research.

Yours sincerely

Janet Smith
Coordinator
VUW Work in Action Project Team

## INSTRUCTIONS AND ORGANISING QUESTIONS

Organising the questions logically and neatly in appropriate sections, and providing instructions on how to complete the items in each section, will help the respondents to answer them without difficulty. Questions should also be neatly and conveniently organised in such a way that the respondent can read and answer the questionnaire without eyestrain, and with a minimum amount of time and effort.

A specimen of the portion of a questionnaire incorporating the above points follows.

**EXAMPLE 10.3**

**SECTION TWO: ABOUT WORK LIFE**

The questions below relate to how you experience your work life. Think in terms of your everyday experiences and accomplishments on the job and put the most appropriate response number for you beside each item, using the scale below.

| Strongly disagree | Disagree | Slightly disagree | Neutral | Slightly agree | Agree | Strongly agree |
|---|---|---|---|---|---|---|
| 1 | 2 | 3 | 4 | 5 | 6 | 7 |

1. I do my work best when my job assignments are fairly difficult. ___
2. When I have a choice, I try to work in a group instead of by myself. ___
3. In my work assignments, I try to be my own boss. ___
4. I seek an active role in the leadership of a group. ___
5. I try very hard to improve on my past performance at work. ___
6. I pay a good deal of attention to the feelings of others at work. ___
7. I go my own way at work, regardless of the opinions of others. ___
8. I avoid trying to influence those around me to see things my way. ___
9. I take moderate risks, sticking my neck out to get ahead at work. ___
10. I prefer to do my own work, letting others do theirs. ___
11. I disregard rules and regulations that hamper my personal freedom. ___

## DEMOGRAPHIC DATA

Demographic or personal data could be organised as in the example that follows. Note the ordinal scaling of the age variable.

**EXAMPLE 10.4**

**SECTION ONE: ABOUT YOURSELF**

Please *circle* the numbers representing the most appropriate responses for you in respect of the following items.

| 1. Your age (years) | 2. Your highest completed level of education | 3. Your gender |
|---|---|---|
| 1 Under 20 | 1 Primary school | 1 Female |
| 2 20–35 | 2 Secondary school | 2 Male |
| 3 36–50 | 3 TAFE/Polytechnic qualification | |
| 4 51–65 | 4 University degree | |
| 5 Over 65 | 5 Other (please specify) | |

| 4. Your marital status | 5. Number of preschool children (under 5 years of age) | 6. Age of the eldest child in your care (years) |
|---|---|---|
| 1 Married | 1 None | 1 Under 5 |
| 2 Single | 2 One | 2 5–12 |
| 3 Widowed | 3 Two | 3 13–19 |
| 4 Divorced or separated | 4 Three or more | 4 Over 19 |
| 5 Other (please specify) | | 5 Not applicable |

| 7. Number of years worked in this organisation | 8. Number of other organisations worked for before joining this organisation | 9. Current work shift |
|---|---|---|
| 1 Less than 1 | 1 None | 1 First |
| 2 1–2 | 2 One | 2 Second |
| 3 3–5 | 3 Two | 3 Third |
| 4 6–10 | 4 Three | |
| 5 Over 10 | 5 Four or more | |

**10. Job status**

1 Top management
2 Middle management
3 First-level supervisor
4 Non-managerial

## SENSITIVE PERSONAL DATA

Though demographic information can be asked either at the beginning or at the end of the questionnaire, information of a very private and personal nature such as income or state of health, if considered absolutely necessary for the survey, should be asked at the end of the questionnaire rather than at the beginning. Also, such questions should be justified by explaining why this information might contribute to knowledge and problem solving, so that respondents do not perceive the questions to be of an intrusive or prying nature (see example below). Shifting such questions to the end would help reduce respondent bias in the event that the individual becomes irritated by the personal nature of the question.

**EXAMPLE 10.5**

Because many people believe that income is a significant factor in explaining the type of career decisions individuals make, the following two questions are very important for this research. Like all other items in this questionnaire, the responses to these two questions will be kept confidential. Please circle the number that describes your position.

Roughly, *my* total yearly income before taxes and other deductions is:

1 Less than $36 000
2 $36 001–50 000
3 $50 001–70 000
4 $70 001–90 000
5 Over $90 000

Roughly, the total yearly income before taxes and other deductions of my immediate *family* — including my own job income, income from other sources and the income of my spouse — is:

1 Less than $36 000
2 $36 001–50 000
3 $50 001–70 000
4 $70 001–90 000
5 $90 001–120 000
6 $120 001–150 000
7 Over $150 000

## OPEN-ENDED QUESTION AT END

The questionnaire could include at the end an open-ended question allowing respondents to comment on any aspect they choose. The questionnaire would end with sincere thanks to respondents. The last part of the questionnaire could look like the following.

**EXAMPLE 10.6**

The questions in the survey may not have allowed you to report some things you want to say about your job, organisation or yourself. Please make any additional comments you wish in the space provided.

How did you feel about completing this questionnaire? Tick the box below the face in the following diagram that best reflects your feelings.

## CONCLUDING THE QUESTIONNAIRE

The questionnaire ends on a courteous note, reminding the respondent to check that all the items have been completed, as in the example below.

**EXAMPLE 10.7**

I sincerely appreciate your time and cooperation. Please check to make sure that you have not skipped any questions, and then drop the questionnaire in the locked box, clearly marked for the purpose, at the entrance of your department.

# PRE-TESTING QUESTIONNAIRES

Once designed, and before using the questionnaire to gather data on which to make decisions or recommendations, the prudent researcher will conduct pre-tests. There are several types of pre-tests that can be carried out; among the most important are face validity, content validity (introduced in chapter 9) and a pilot study.

## FACE VALIDITY

**Face validity** addresses the concern of whether the questionnaire *appears* to measure the concepts being investigated (Burns 1994). Of particular interest is whether the respondents will find the wording of the items clear and understandable. Accordingly, the researcher should arrange for a small sample of respondents to answer the questionnaire and then interview them to see if any items caused confusion.

## CONTENT VALIDITY

**Content validity** relates to the **representativeness** or sampling adequacy of the questionnaire regarding the content or the theoretical constructs to be measured (Burns 1994). The researcher reports the origins or pedigree of each of the items, often based on the literature search.

A further test of content validity is to send the questionnaire to a group of experts, who examine each item and make a judgement on whether each item does measure the theoretical construct nominated. Other names for this process are panel or expert judgement validity.

## PILOT STUDY

If possible, a questionnaire should be piloted with a reasonable sample of respondents who come from the target population or who closely resemble the target population. Unfortunately, in a business research project a pilot study of a questionnaire is sometimes not possible because of the finite number of people in the target population. As we shall see, some of the analytic procedures in a pilot study demand a large number of respondents. If a significant number of respondents are 'used up' in the pilot study, then the investigator has very few people left from whom to gather data. As is often the case in the messy world of field research (research carried out in the real world as opposed to that conducted in experimental laboratories), the business researcher needs to acknowledge two considerations — the requirements of an ideal research design and the realities of what the field situation will allow. Let us look at the requirements of an ideal research design for a pilot study.

### Ideal research design

The first consideration is the number of respondents needed for a pilot study. If the questionnaire contains several opinion items which make up one or more theoretical scales (designed to measure one or more theoretical constructs), then a statistical procedure called *factor analysis* will be needed (discussed in appendix I at the back of the book). To conduct a factor analysis, an investigator needs a ratio of respondents to items of between 4:1 and 10:1. For example, if the questionnaire has

20 opinion items (do not count the factual and classification items), then the ideal number of respondents will be between 80 and 200 — quite a large number to find! However, if the questionnaire contains only factual items, then a pilot study of 30 respondents is common. Of course, opinion items, particularly those which form a theoretical scale, provide such rich data that a large number of business research projects incorporate them.

## Reality — less than ideal

So what does the business researcher do if there are insufficient numbers in the target population to carry out a pilot study as well as an investigation? Well, a less than perfect design will have to be used. The researcher may use fewer people in the pilot study — for example 20 instead of 80 — and accept that the results will be only indicative. As an alternative, the researcher may be able to find a population that has most of the important characteristics of the target population — for example general office staff if sales personnel are the target population. The characteristic that these two populations have in common is that neither are production staff and, providing this is the only important variable that could contaminate the result, the general office staff will provide a reasonable substitute. A final alternative is not to do a pilot study but rather to analyse the robustness of the questionnaire on the raw data gathered from the study itself. Recognise, however, that the further away from the ideal pilot study design the business researcher moves, the greater the risk that the questionnaire will not produce the desired result. However, such accommodations are the reality of a business researcher's life.

## Collecting and analysing the data

If a pilot study can be conducted, then the questionnaire is sent out to the respondents, returned to the researcher and the answers on completed questionnaires are entered into a database suitable for data and statistical analysis, such as the spreadsheet Excel or **SPSS (Statistical Package for the Social Sciences)**. Then a number of statistical analyses are conducted on the data by the researcher. These will be discussed in chapter 13 and appendix I at the back of the book.

# GATHERING THE DATA

Questionnaires are an efficient data collection mechanism when the researcher knows exactly what is required and how to measure the variables of interest. Questionnaires can be administered personally, mailed to the respondents or electronically distributed.

## PERSONALLY ADMINISTERED QUESTIONNAIRES

When the survey is confined to a local area, and the organisation is willing and able to assemble groups of employees to respond to the questionnaires at the workplace, personally administering the questionnaires is a good way to collect data. The main advantage of this is that the researcher or a member of the research team can collect all the completed responses within a short period of time. Any doubts the respondents might have regarding any question can be clarified on the spot. The researcher also has the opportunity to introduce the research topic and motivate the respondents to give frank answers.

Administering questionnaires to large numbers of individuals simultaneously is less expensive and less time-consuming than interviewing; it also does not require as much skill to administer the questionnaire as to conduct interviews. Wherever possible, it is best to administer questionnaires personally to groups of people because of these advantages. However, organisations are often unable or unwilling to allow use of work hours for data collection, and other ways of seeing that the questionnaires are completed and returned may have to be found. In such cases, employees may be given blank questionnaires which can be collected from them personally after a few days, or the respondents can be provided with self-addressed, stamped envelopes with a request to complete and mail them back by a certain date. Scanner sheets (the answer sheets that are usually provided for answering multiple-choice questions in exams) are usually sent with the questionnaire so that respondents can circle their answers to each question on the sheet, which can then be entered directly into the computer as data without someone having to code and then manually enter them into the computer. Disks containing the questions can also be sent to respondents who have personal computers.

## MAIL QUESTIONNAIRES

The main advantage of mail questionnaires is that a wide geographical area can be covered in the survey. They are mailed to the respondents, who can complete them at their own convenience in their homes, and at their own pace. However, the return rates of mail questionnaires are typically low. A 30 per cent response rate is considered acceptable. Another disadvantage of the mail questionnaire is that any doubts the respondents might have cannot be clarified. Also, with very low return rates it is difficult to establish the representativeness of the sample, because those responding to the survey may be different from the population they are supposed to represent. However, effective techniques exist for improving the rates of response to mail questionnaires. Sending follow-up letters, enclosing small monetary incentives or a free gift with the questionnaire, providing the respondent with self-addressed, stamped return envelopes, and keeping the questionnaire brief are all helpful.

Mail questionnaires are also expected to elicit a better response rate when respondents are notified in advance about the forthcoming survey and a well-known research organisation administers the questionnaire with its own introductory cover letter.

The choice of using the questionnaire as a data gathering method might be restricted if the researcher has to reach subjects with limited education. Adding pictures to the questionnaires, if feasible, might be helpful in such cases.

## ELECTRONIC QUESTIONNAIRES

On-line **electronic questionnaire** surveys are easily designed and administered when microcomputers are hooked up to computer networks. As noted, data disks can also be mailed to respondents, who can use their own personal computers for responding to the questions. These can, of course, be helpful only when the respondents know how to use the computer and feel comfortable responding in this manner.

CAPPA, which facilitates the preparation and administration of questionnaires, is particularly useful for marketing research. The CAPPA system includes 10 programs enabling the user to design a sophisticated computerised questionnaire, computerise the data collection process and analyse the data collected. More reliable data are likely to result since the respondent can go back and forth and easily change a response, and various on- and off-screen stimuli are provided to sustain respondents' interest.

A program that checks for syntactical or logical errors in the coding is designed into the CAPPA system. Even as the survey is in progress, descriptive summaries of the cumulative data can be obtained either on the screen or in printed form. After data collection is complete, a **data editing** program identifies missing or out-of-range data (for example a '6' in response to a question on a five-point scale). The researcher can set the parameters for either deleting the missing responses where there are too many, or computing the mean on other responses and substituting this figure for the missing response. CAPPA also includes data analytic programs such as cross-tabs, ANOVA, multiple regression and others (discussed later in this book). Randomisation of questions and the weighting of respondents to ensure more representative results (in cases where the sample either overrepresents or underrepresents certain population groups — discussed in chapter 11) are some of the attractive features of CAPPA.

Several programs have been developed to administer questionnaires electronically. Disks are inexpensive, so mailing them across the country is not a problem. Alternatively, these programs may be distributed electronically as attachments to e-mails. The PC medium non-response rates may not be any higher than the mail questionnaire rates. With increasing computer literacy, we can expect electronic questionnaire administration to play an increasing part in the future.

## CROSS-CULTURAL RESEARCH

So far we have discussed instrument development for eliciting responses from subjects within a country. With the globalisation of business operations, managers often want to compare the business effectiveness of their subsidiaries in different countries. Researchers engaged in **cross-cultural research** also endeavour to trace the similarities and differences in the behavioural and attitudinal responses of employees or respondents at various levels in different cultures. Such data collected through questionnaires and occasionally through interviews should also pay attention to cultural differences in the use of certain terms, and measuring instruments should be tailored to the different cultures, as discussed below.

### SPECIAL ISSUES IN INSTRUMENTATION

Certain special issues need to be addressed while designing instruments for collecting data from different countries. Since different languages are spoken in different countries, it is important to ensure that the translation of the instrument in the local language is equivalent to the original language in which the instrument was developed. For this purpose, the instrument should be first translated by a local expert. If a comparative survey is to be done between Japan and Australia, and the researcher is an Australian national, then the instrument must first be translated from English to Japanese. Then another bilinguist should translate it back to English. This *back translation*, as it is called, ensures *vocabulary equivalence* (that is, that the words used have the same meaning). *Idiomatic equivalence* could also become an issue when idioms unique to one language do not lend themselves to translation into another language. *Conceptual equivalence*, ensuring that the meanings of certain words do not differ in different cultures, is yet another important issue. As an example, the meaning of the concept 'love' may differ in different cultures. All these can be taken care of through good back translation by persons who are proficient in the relevant languages and are also knowledgeable about the cultures concerned.

## ISSUES IN DATA COLLECTION

At least three issues are important for cross-cultural data collection. These are response equivalence, timing of data collection and the status of the individual collecting the data. *Response equivalence* is ensured by adopting uniform data collection procedures in the different cultures. Identical methods of introducing the study, the researcher, task instructions and closing remarks in personally administered questionnaires would provide equivalence in motivation, goal orientation and response attitudes. *Timing of data collected* across cultures is also critical for cross-cultural comparison. Data collection should be completed within acceptable time frames in the different countries — say, within three to four months. If too much time elapses in collecting data in the different countries, much might change during the time lag in either country or all the countries.

As pointed out as early as 1969 by Mitchell, in *interview surveys*, the egalitarian-oriented interviewing style used in the west may be inappropriate in societies that have well-defined status and authority structures. Also, when a foreigner comes to collect data, the responses might be biased for fear of portraying the country in an 'adverse light' (Sekaran 1983). The researcher has to be sensitive to these cultural nuances when doing cross-cultural research.

There are other concerns that need to be addressed in cross-cultural research that relate to scaling and sampling. In chapter 9 we discussed scaling, which becomes a sensitive area in instrument development in cross-cultural research. For instance, a five-point or a seven-point scale may make no difference in Australia, but could be significant in the responses of subjects in other countries (see Sekaran & Martin 1982; Sekaran & Trafton 1978). Barry (1969), for instance, found that in some countries, a seven-point scale is more sensitive than a four-point scale in eliciting unbiased responses. We will examine the issues regarding sampling in the next chapter.

## MULTIMETHODS OF DATA COLLECTION

Because almost all data collection methods have biases associated with them, collecting data through multimethods and from multiple sources lends rigour to research. For instance, if the responses collected through interviews, questionnaires and observation strongly correlate with one another, then we will have more confidence about the goodness of the collected data. If there are discrepancies in how respondents answer the same question when interviewed, as opposed to how they answer the question in a questionnaire, then we would become suspicious and would be inclined to discard both sets of data as biased.

Similarly, if data obtained from several sources are highly similar, we would have more confidence in the goodness of the data. For example, if an employee rates his performance as '4' on a five-point scale, and his supervisor rates him the same way, we may be inclined to think that he is perhaps a better than average worker. In contrast, if he gives himself a '5' on the five-point scale and his supervisor gives him a rating of '2', then we will not know to what extent there is a bias or from which source it originates. Therefore, high correlations among data obtained on the same variable from different sources and through different data collection methods lend more credibility to the research instrument and to the data obtained through this instrument. Good research entails the collection of data from multiple sources using multiple data collection methods. Such research, though, is costly and time-consuming.

## COMPARISON OF DATA COLLECTION METHODS

Having discussed the various data collection methods, we will now briefly outline the advantages and disadvantages of the three most commonly used data collection methods — interviews, questionnaires and observation — and see when each method can be most profitably used.

### Face-to-face interviews

Face-to-face interviews provide rich data, offer the opportunity to establish rapport with the interviewees, and help to explore and understand complex issues. Many ideas that are ordinarily difficult to articulate can be uncovered and discussed during such interviews. Also, CAPI can be used and responses entered diirectly into a portable computer (laptop). On the negative side, face-to-face interviews have the potential for introducing interviewer bias and can be expensive if a large number of subjects are to be personally interviewed. Where several interviewers are involved, adequate training becomes a necessary first step.

Face-to-face interviews are best used at the exploratory stages of research when the researcher seeks an understanding of the concepts or situational factors.

### Telephone interviews

Telephone interviews help in contacting subjects dispersed over various geographic regions and obtaining responses from them immediately. This is an efficient way of collecting data when you have specific questions to ask, need quick responses and have the sample spread over a wide geographic area. On the negative side, the interviewer cannot observe the non-verbal responses of the respondents, and the interviewee can block a call.

Telephone interviews are best suited to asking structured questions when responses need to be obtained quickly from a sample that is geographically spread. These interviews can also be done using computer-assisted packages (CATI).

### Personally administered questionnaires

Personally administering questionnaires to groups of individuals allows you to (a) establish rapport with the respondents while introducing the survey, (b) provide clarifications sought by the respondents on the spot and (c) collect the questionnaires immediately after they are completed. In that sense, there is a 100 per cent response rate. On the negative side, administering questionnaires personally is expensive, especially if the sample is geographically dispersed.

Personally administered questionnaires are best suited when data are collected from organisations that are located in close proximity to one another and groups of respondents can be conveniently assembled in the company's conference (or other) rooms.

### Mail questionnaires

Mail questionnaires are advantageous when responses to many questions have to be obtained from a sample that is geographically dispersed, or it is difficult or impossible to conduct telephone interviews to obtain the same data without great expense. On the negative side, mailed questionnaires usually have a low response rate and one cannot be sure if the data obtained are biased because the non-respondents may be different from those who did respond.

The mailed questionnaire survey is best suited (and perhaps the only option open to the researcher) when a substantial amount of information is to be obtained through structured questions, at a reasonable cost, from a sample that is widely dispersed geographically.

## Electronic questionnaires

Electronic questionnaires are similar to mail questionnaires in that they are easy to administer and respondents can answer at their convenience. However, they also suffer from a fairly low response rate, and the responses could be biased because respondents may not be representative of the target population. Nevertheless, they can reach wide geographic locations (particularly in international surveys) very quickly and inexpensively.

A further disadvantage of electronic questionnaires is that respondents must be computer literate and have access to computers and e-mail (through the Internet or company intranet). Also, respondents must be willing to complete the survey. If they do, then data is entered directly into the computer by respondents, and packages are available to input and analyse the data in specialised computer programs.

However, some electronic questionnaires may be better printed off the computer, and filled out and returned by post. This may be the case if information is required that is not immediately accessible to the respondent.

## Observational studies

Observational studies help to clarify complex issues through direct observation (by a participant- or nonparticipant-observer). If possible, the observer can then ask questions to seek clarifications on certain issues. The data obtained are rich and uncontaminated by self-report biases. On the negative side, they are expensive, since long periods of observation (usually encompassing several weeks or even months) are required, and observer bias may well be present in the data.

Because of the costs involved, very few observational studies are undertaken in business. Henry Mintzberg's study of managerial work is one of the best-known published works that used an observational data collection method. Observational studies are best suited for research requiring non-self-report descriptive data; that is, when behaviours are to be understood without directly asking the respondents themselves. Observational studies can also capture 'in-the-stores buying behaviours'.

## Summary of multimethod data collection

The advantages and disadvantages of personal or face-to-face interviews, telephone interviews, personally administered questionnaires, mail questionnaires and questionnaires distributed through the electronic system are tabulated in table 10.1.

It should be pointed out that information obtained from respondents through interviews or questionnaires, being self-report data, could be biased. That is the reason why data should be collected from different sources and by different methods.

**Table 10.1** Advantages and disadvantages of interviews and questionnaires

| Mode of data collection | Advantages | Disadvantages |
|---|---|---|
| Personal or face-to-face interviews | • Can establish rapport and motivate respondents<br>• Can clarify the questions, clear doubts, add new questions<br>• Can read non-verbal cues<br>• Can use visual aids to clarify points<br>• Rich data can be obtained<br>• CAPI can be used and responses entered in a portable computer | • Take personal time<br>• Costs more when a wide geographic region is covered<br>• Respondents may be concerned about confidentiality of information given<br>• Interviewers need to be trained<br>• Can introduce interviewer biases |
| Telephone interviews | • Less costly and speedier than personal interviews<br>• Can reach a wide geographic area<br>• Greater anonymity than personal interviews<br>• Can be done using CATI | • Respondents can terminate the interview at any time<br>• Non-verbal cues cannot be read<br>• Interviews have to be kept short<br>• Obsolete telephone numbers could be contacted, and unlisted ones omitted from the sample |
| Personally administered questionnaires | • Can establish rapport and motivate respondent<br>• Doubts can be clarified<br>• Less expensive when administered to groups of respondents<br>• Almost 100% response rate assured<br>• Anonymity of respondent is high | • Organisations may be reluctant to give up company time for the survey with groups of employees assembled for the purpose |
| Mail questionnaires | • Anonymity is high<br>• Wide geographic regions can be reached<br>• Token gifts can be enclosed to seek compliance<br>• Respondent can take more time to respond at convenience<br>• Can be administered electronically, if desired | • Response rate is almost always low; 30 per cent rate is quite acceptable<br>• Cannot clarify questions<br>• Follow-up procedures for non-responses are necessary |

(*continued*)

| Mode of data collection | Advantages | Disadvantages |
|---|---|---|
| Electronic questionnaires | • Easy to administer<br>• Can reach out globally<br>• Very inexpensive<br>• Fast delivery<br>• Respondents can answer at their convenience, as with the mail questionnaire | • Computer literacy is essential<br>• Respondents must have access to the facility<br>• Respondent must be willing to complete the survey |

## MANAGERIAL PERSPECTIVE

As a manager, you will perhaps engage consultants to do research and may not be collecting data yourself through interviews, questionnaires or observation. However, during those instances when you will perforce have to obtain work-related information through interviews with clients, employees or others, you will know how to phrase unbiased questions to elicit the right types of useful responses. Moreover, as the sponsor of research, you will be able to decide at what level of sophistication you want data to be collected, based on the complexity and gravity of the situation. Also, as a constant participant observer of all that goes on around you at the workplace, you will be able to understand the dynamics operating in the situation. Finally, as a manager, you will be able to differentiate between good and bad survey questions.

## SUMMARY

In this chapter we have devoted a lot of attention to questionnaire design because questionnaires are one of the most common methods of collecting data in business. The principles of questionnaire design relate to how the questions are worded and the data measured, and how the entire questionnaire is organised. To minimise respondent biases and measurement errors, all the principles discussed have to be followed carefully.

Questionnaires are most useful as a data collection method when large numbers of people are to be reached in different geographical regions. Questionnaires are a popular method of collecting data because researchers can obtain data fairly easily, and the questionnaire responses are easily coded. When well-validated instruments are used, the findings of the study benefit the scientific community since the results can be replicated and additions to the theory base made.

There are several ways of administering questionnaires — they can be personally administered to respondents, inserted in magazines, periodicals or newspapers, mailed to respondents, or electronically distributed through e-mail — via either the Internet or an intranet. Software is also available to ask questions adapting to the subject's response to the preceding question. Companies' websites can also elicit survey responses — for example reactions to customer service, product utility and the like. Global research is now vastly facilitated by computer technology.

We also examined various data collection methods and different primary sources of data. Because of the inherent biases in each of the data collection methods, the collection of data from multiple sources and through multiple methods was recommended. The final decision would, of course, be governed by considerations of cost and the degree of rigour that the research goal would require.

In the next chapter we will discuss sampling designs and how data can be collected from samples to make the results generalisable to the population under study.

## DISCUSSION POINTS

1. As a manager, you have invited in a research team to study and offer suggestions on how to improve the performance of your staff. What steps would you take to allay their apprehensions even before the research team sets foot in your department?
2. Explain the principles of wording, stating how these are important in questionnaire design, citing examples not in the book.
3. What is the difference between factual data and opinion?
4. Discuss the reasons why a researcher would include classification items in a questionnaire.
5. Discuss the issues that need to be considered when deciding on the sequencing of items in a questionnaire.
6. How are multiple methods of data collection from multiple sources related to the reliability and validity of the measures?
7. 'Every data collection method has its own built-in biases. Therefore, resorting to multimethods of data collection is only going to compound the biases.' How would you critique this statement?
8. 'One way to deal with discrepancies found in the data obtained from multiple sources is to average the figures and take the mean as the value of the variable.' What is your reaction to this statement?
9. How have advances in technology helped data gathering?
10. 'The fewer the biases in measurement and in the data collection procedures, the more scientific the research.' Comment on this statement.

| | |
|---|---|
| Exercise 10.1 | A production manager wants to assess the reactions of the blue-collar workers in his department (including foremen) to the introduction of computer-integrated manufacturing (CIM) systems. He is particularly interested in knowing how they would perceive the effects of CIM on:<br>(a) their future jobs<br>(b) additional training that they will have to receive<br>(c) future job advancement.<br>Design a questionnaire for the production manager. |
| Exercise 10.2 | The CEO of Fox Publishing Co. suspects that most of the 500 male and female employees of the organisation are somewhat alienated from work. She is also of the view that those who are more involved (less alienated) are also the ones who experience greater satisfaction with their work lives. |

Design a questionnaire the CEO could use to test her hypothesis.

Exercise 10.3  Critically evaluate the questionnaire in the appendix at the end of this chapter.

Exercise 10.4  Rebecca Chapelli made the following decisions on a questionnaire that she was designing.
- All the 32 opinion items had come from the qualitative data of 28 interviews that Rebecca had conducted the previous month.
- There were four theoretical constructs to be tested, each made up of eight items.
- None of the opinion items had more than 20 words. There were three that she was doubtful about:
    Item 6   'Managers in this organisation feel concerned if they have to work more than 10 hours' overtime.'
    Item 15  'Managers should not show any negative emotions.'
    Item 26  'Managers should attend at least one management development course each year.'
- The items would be sequenced, with one item coming from each construct as item 1, item 2, item 3 and item 4, and this order would be repeated (i.e. item 5 — construct 1; item 6 — construct 2; item 7 — construct 3; item 8 — construct 4; item 9 — construct 1; item 10 — construct 2; item 11 — construct 3; item 12 — construct 4; and so on).
- A Likert scale of six points would be used for the response sets.
- Three classification items on age, gender and salary scale would be placed at the end of the questionnaire.

1. Discuss the decisions that Rebecca has made, making reference to good questionnaire design.
2. Are there any other critical decisions that Rebecca should have made? Justify your answer(s).

# APPENDIX

## MANAGEMENT'S BEST MBAs

In July, *Management* will publish a list of New Zealand's top educators. We'd like to know your opinion on one of the education and training industry's most popular products — the MBA. How do you rate an MBA's content, quality and value?

RATE MBA COURSES AND GO IN TO THE DRAW TO WIN A FABULOUS ERICSSON FREEDOM MOBILE PHONE VALUED AT $799.

### GENERAL INFORMATION

Rating: 1 = outstanding 2 = very good
3 = good 4 = average 5 = poor

a. Do you have an MBA? (i) yes (ii) no
b. How many employees have an MBA at your workplace? ...................................................
c. How many staff at your workplace? .........
d. What type of industry are you in? (please circle one)
   (i) Education and Training
   (ii) Manufacturing
   (iii) Professional Services
   (iv) Information Communication
   (v) Other (please state) ...........................
e. How valuable as a qualification is an MBA in terms of:
   (i) Career?              1  2  3  4  5
   (ii) Salary prospects?    1  2  3  4  5
   (iii) Job satisfaction?   1  2  3  4  5
f. How practical is an MBA as a qualifcation?
                            1  2  3  4  5
g. How sympathetic do you think MBA providers are to the needs of business?
                            1  2  3  4  5

### SPECIFIC INFORMATION

*Please circle one*

h. Which MBA offers its students the best theoretical content?
   a Otago          b Canterbury     c Victoria
   d Massey         e Waikato        f Auckland
   g Henley/AIT     h Asia Pacific Institute
   i Other (please state)................................
i. Which course offers the most current thinking in management practice?
   a Otago          b Canterbury     c Victoria
   d Massey         e Waikato        f Auckland
   g Henley/AIT     h Asia Pacific Institute
   i Other (please state)................................
j. Which course provides graduates with the best practical skills in terms of hands-on management?
   a Otago          b Canterbury     c Victoria
   d Massey         e Waikato        f Auckland
   g Henley/AIT     h Asia Pacific Institute
   i Other (please state)................................
k. Which course is best tailored for working students — and therefore least disruptive to management?
   a Otago          b Canterbury     c Victoria
   d Massey         e Waikato        f Auckland
   g Henley/AIT     h Asia Pacific Institute
   i Other (please state)................................
l. Which of the following gives the best business grounding?
   a An MBA?
   b Bachelor of Commerce degree?
   c A specialist course at an international university
   d Other (please state)................................
m. If you could send a student to any MBA course in the world, which college/university would you choose? (Please state) ...............................
n. If you could enrol a student in any MBA course in New Zealand, which university/polytechnic/private provider would you choose?
   a Otago          b Canterbury     c Victoria
   d Massey         e Waikato        f Auckland
   g Henley/AIT     h Asia Pacific Institute
   i Other (please state)................................
o. What improvements could be made to an MBA to design it better for the work force?
   a more practical    b more theoretical
   c more international perspective
   d Other (please state)................................
Name..............................................................
Position..........................................................
Company Name................................................
Telephone......................................................
Are you willing to be contacted by one of our writers for further comment?
   Yes   No

PLEASE COMPLETE THIS FORM AND RETURN TO PROFILE PUBLISHING LIMITED, FAX: 09 358 5462 OR PO BOX 5544, WELLESLEY ST AUCKLAND, BY 15 MAY 1995 AND GO IN THE DRAW TO WIN A FABULOUS ERICSSON FREEDOM MOBILE PHONE. This personal information is being collected by Profile Publishing in relation to an article about MBAs. We may pass the information to others, but only for that same purpose.

# SAMPLING DESIGN

## OUTLINE

POPULATION, ELEMENT, SAMPLING FRAME, SAMPLE AND SUBJECT

SAMPLING

PROBABILITY AND NON-PROBABILITY SAMPLING

PROBABILITY SAMPLING

NON-PROBABILITY SAMPLING

EXAMPLES OF SAMPLING DESIGNS

SAMPLING IN CROSS-CULTURAL RESEARCH

ISSUES OF PRECISION AND CONFIDENCE IN DETERMINING SAMPLE SIZE

SAMPLE DATA, PRECISION AND CONFIDENCE IN ESTIMATION

TRADE-OFF BETWEEN PRECISION AND CONFIDENCE

DETERMINING THE SAMPLE SIZE

IMPORTANCE OF SAMPLING DESIGN AND SAMPLE SIZE

EFFICIENCY IN SAMPLING

SUMMARY

DISCUSSION POINTS

EXERCISES

## CHAPTER OBJECTIVES

After reading this chapter, you should be able to:
- define sampling, sample, population, element, subject and sampling frame
- describe and discuss the different sampling designs
- identify the use of appropriate sampling designs for different research purposes
- discuss precision and confidence
- estimate sample size
- discuss the factors to be taken into consideration in determining sample size
- discuss efficiency in sampling
- discuss generalisability in the context of sampling designs
- apply the material learned in this chapter to class assignments and projects.

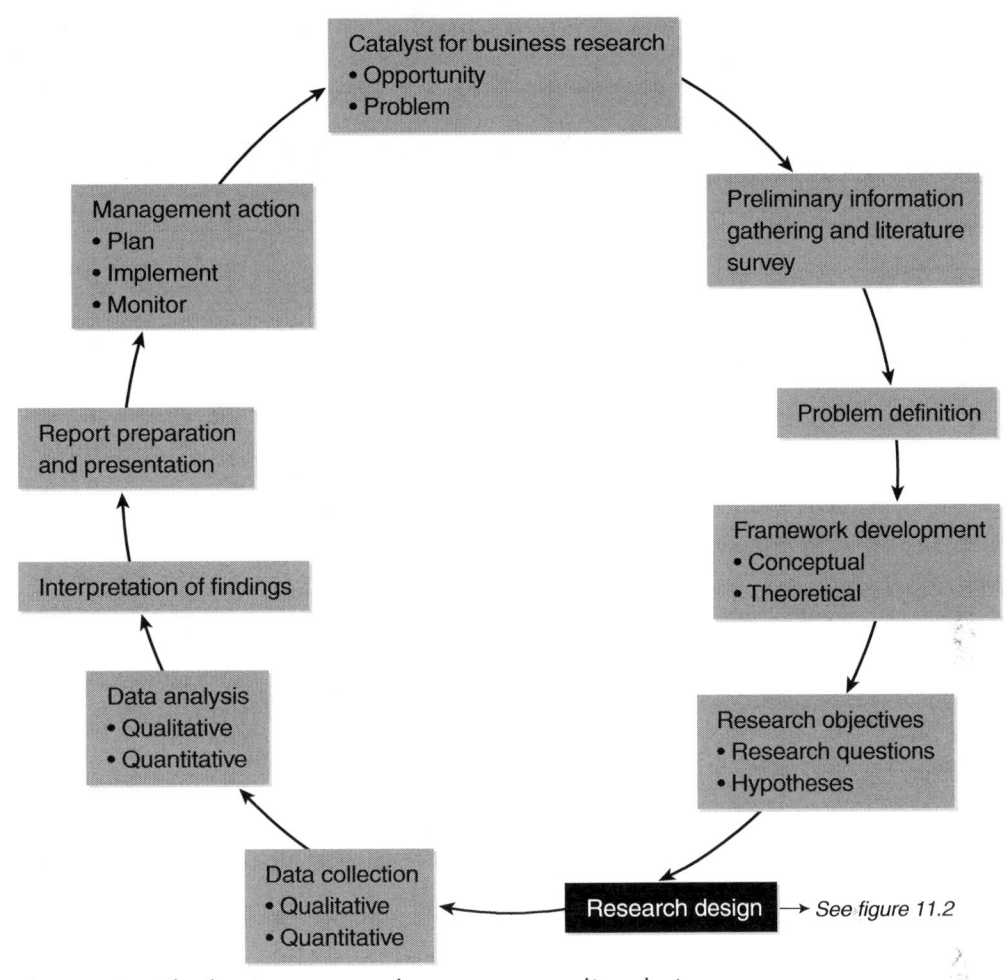

**Figure 11.1** The business research process: sampling design

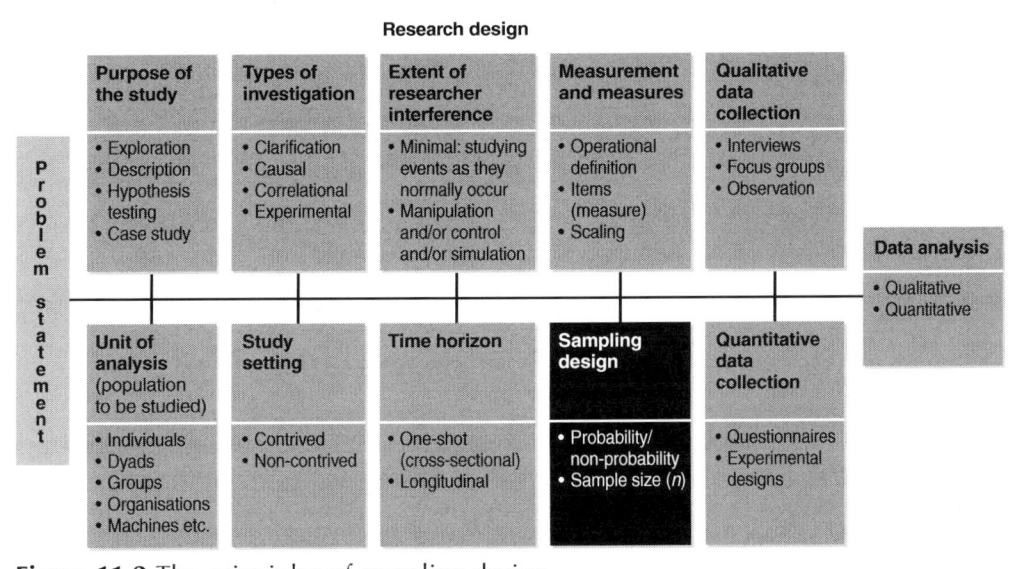

**Figure 11.2** The principles of sampling design

Surveys are useful and powerful for finding answers to research questions, but they can do more harm than good if not correctly targeted. That is, if data are not collected from the people or objects that can provide the correct answers to solve the problem, the survey will be in vain. We will now examine sampling (the shaded portions in figures 11.1 and 11.2) in some detail. Note, however, that it may be useful to review the Descriptive Statistics section of appendix I at the back of the book either before you start or as you are progressing through this chapter.

## POPULATION, ELEMENT, SAMPLING FRAME, SAMPLE AND SUBJECT

In understanding how representative data can be collected, a few terms first have to be understood. These are described below.

### Population

Population (or target population) refers to the entire group of people, events or things of interest that the researcher wishes to investigate. For instance, if the CEO of a computer firm wants to know the kinds of advertising strategies adopted by computer firms in Melbourne, then all computer firms situated there will constitute the population. If a banker is interested in investigating the savings habits of blue-collar workers in the Australian mining industry, then all blue-collar workers in that industry throughout the country will form the population. If an organisational consultant is interested in studying the effects of a four-day work week on the white-collar workers in a telephone company in Victoria, then all white-collar workers in that company will make up the population. If regulators want to know how patients in nursing homes run by Thirdage Australia are cared for, then all the patients in all the nursing homes run by Thirdage Australia will form the population. If, however, the regulators are interested only in a particular nursing home in Victoria run by Thirdage Australia, then only the patients in that specific nursing home will form the population.

### Element

An **element** is a single member of the population. If 1000 blue-collar workers in a particular organisation happen to be the population of interest to a researcher, each single blue-collar worker therein is an element. If 500 pieces of machinery are to be approved after inspecting a few, there would be 500 elements in this population. Incidentally, the census is a count of all the elements in the population.

### Sampling frame

The **sampling frame** is a listing of all the elements in the population from which the sample is drawn. The sampling frame is sometimes referred to as the **population frame** or working population. The payroll of an organisation would serve as the sampling frame if its members were to be studied. Similarly, the university registry containing a listing of all students, faculty, administrators and support staff in the university during a particular academic year or semester could serve as the sampling frame for a study of the university population. A roster of class students could be the sampling frame for the study of students in a class. The telephone directory is also frequently used as a sampling frame for some types of studies, even though it has an inherent bias inasmuch as some numbers are unlisted and others may have become obsolete by the time of the study.

Although the sampling frame is useful in providing a listing of each element in the population, it may not always be a current, updated document. For instance, the names of members who have just left the organisation or dropped out of the university, as well as members who have just joined the organisation or the university, may not appear in the organisation's payroll or the university registers on a given day. The most recently installed or disconnected telephones also will not be shown in the current telephone directory. Hence, although the sampling frame may be available in many cases, it may not always be correct. However, the researcher might recognise this problem and not be overly concerned about it, because a few additions to and deletions from the telephone directory might not make any significant difference to the study. Even if the researcher is concerned about it, and spends time and effort trying to obtain an updated sampling frame, there is no guarantee that the new sampling frame will give an accurate listing of *all* the elements either, for the reasons already discussed.

## Sample

A sample is a subset of the population. It comprises some members selected from the population. In other words, some, but not all, elements of the population would form the sample. If 200 members are drawn from a population of 1000 blue-collar workers, these 200 members form the sample for the study. That is, by studying these 200 members, the researcher would draw conclusions about the entire population of 1000 blue-collar workers. Similarly, if there are 145 in-patients in a hospital and 40 of them are to be surveyed by the hospital administrator to assess their level of satisfaction with the treatment received, then these 40 members will be the sample.

A sample is thus a subgroup or subset of the population. By studying the sample, the researcher is able to draw conclusions that are generalisable to the population of interest.

## Subject

A subject is a single member of the sample, just as an element is a single member of the population. If 200 members from the total population of 1000 blue-collar workers formed the sample for the study, then each blue-collar worker in the sample is a subject. As another example, if a sample of 50 machines from a total of 500 machines is to be inspected, then every one of the 50 machines is a subject, just as every single machine in the total population of 500 machines is an element.

**EXAMPLE 11.1**  For example, the Wellington Regional Council is interested in the attitudes of Wellington residents to a proposed new highway development out of Wellington, called the Transmission Gully project. The population would consist of all adult residents in the Wellington region (about 300 000 people) and the sampling frame might be the Wellington telephone directory. The sample would consist of 383 people (based on table 11.4 in this chapter). An illustration of how these terms are connected is provided in figure 11.3.

## SAMPLING

Sampling is the *process* of selecting a sufficient number of elements from the population so that by studying the sample, and understanding the properties or characteristics of the sample subjects, it would be possible to generalise the properties or characteristics to the population elements. The characteristics of the population, such as µ (the population mean), σ (the population standard deviation) and σ² (the population variance), are referred to as the *parameters* of the population. The central tendencies, the dispersions and other statistics in the sample of interest to the researchers are treated as approximations of the central tendencies, dispersions and other parameters of the population. As such, all conclusions drawn about the sample under study are generalised to the population. In other words, the sample statistics — $\bar{X}$ (the sample mean), $S$ (standard deviation) and $S^2$ (the variance in the sample) — are used as estimates of the population parameters µ, σ and σ². Figure 11.4 shows the relationship between the sample and the population.

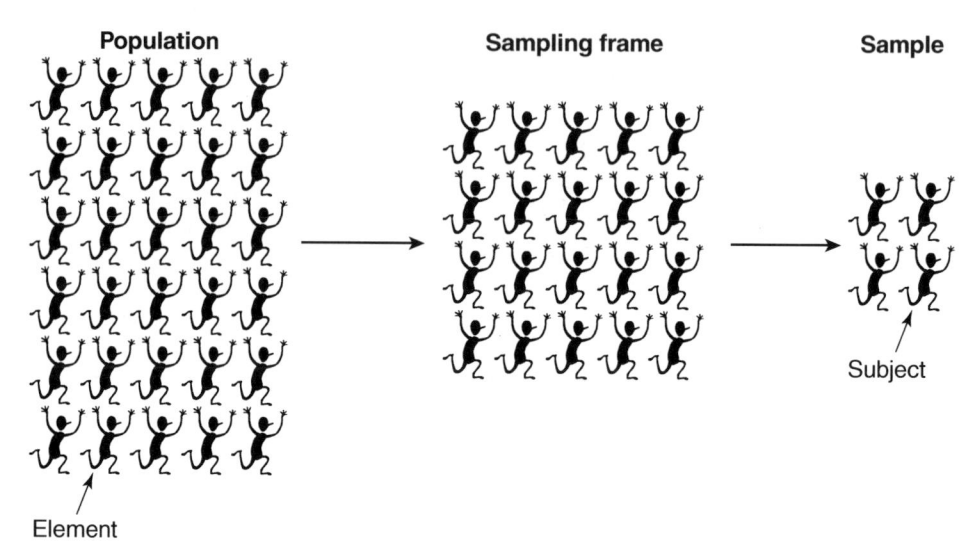

**Figure 11.3** The relationship between population, sampling frame and sample

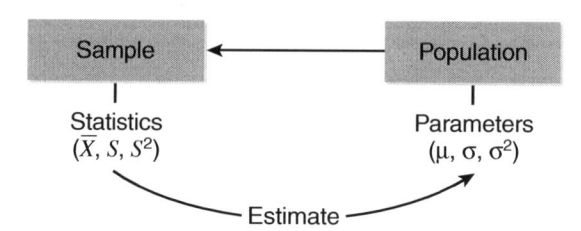

**Figure 11.4** The relationship between sample statistics and population parameters

# REASONS FOR SAMPLING

The reasons for using a sample rather than collecting data from the entire population are fairly obvious. In research investigations involving several hundreds and even thousands of elements, it would be practically impossible to collect data from, or test or examine, every element. Even if it were possible, it would be prohibitive in terms of time, cost and other human resources. Studying a sample rather than the entire population is also sometimes likely to lead to more reliable results, mostly because fatigue is reduced, resulting in fewer errors in collecting data, especially when the elements involved are large in number. In a few cases, it would also be impossible to use the entire population to learn about or test something. Consider, for instance, the case of electric bulbs. In testing the life of a batch of bulbs, if we were to burn every bulb produced, there would be none left to sell! This is known as destructive sampling.

# REPRESENTATIVENESS OF SAMPLES

The need to choose the right sample for a research investigation cannot be overemphasised. We know that a sample will rarely be the exact replica of the population from which it is drawn. For instance, very few sample means ($\bar{X}$) are likely to be exactly equal to the population means ($\mu$). Neither is the standard deviation of the sample ($S$) going to be the same as the standard deviation of the population ($\sigma$). However, if we choose the sample in a scientific way, we can be reasonably sure that the sample statistic (for example, $\bar{X}$, $S$ or $S^2$) is fairly close to the population parameter (that is, $\mu$, $\sigma$ or $\sigma^2$). To put it differently, it is possible to choose the sample in such a way that it is representative of the population. There is always the slight probability, however, that sample values might fall outside the population parameters.

Attributes or characteristics in the population are generally normally distributed. That is, attributes such as height and weight are such that most people will be clustered around the mean, and there will be only a small number at the extremes who are either very tall or very short, very heavy or very light, and so on, as indicated in figure 11.5. If we are to estimate the population characteristics from the characteristics represented in a sample with reasonable accuracy, the sample has to be chosen in such a way that the distribution of the characteristics of interest follows the same type of normal distribution in the sample as it does in the population. From the central limit theorem, we know that the sampling distribution of the sample mean is normally distributed. As the sample size *n* increases, the means of the random samples taken from practically any population approach a normal distribution with mean $\mu$ and standard deviation $\sigma$. In sum, irrespective of whether or not the attributes in the population are normally distributed, if we take a sufficiently *large number* of samples and *choose* them with care, we will have a sampling distribution of the means that has normality. This is the reason that the two important issues in sampling are the sample size (*n*) and the sampling design, as discussed later.

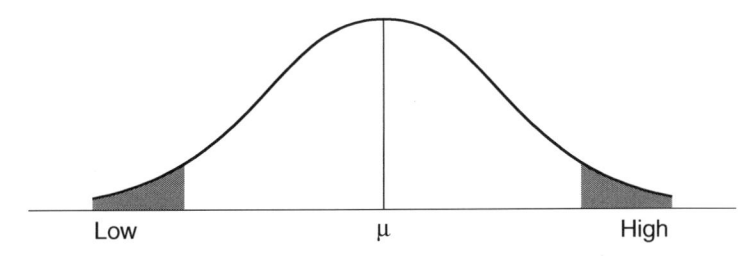

**Figure 11.5** Normal distribution in a population

When the properties of the population are not overrepresented or underrepresented in the sample, we will have a representative sample. When a sample consists of elements in the population that have extremely high values on the variables we are studying, the sample mean $\bar{X}$ will be far higher than the population mean $\mu$. If in contrast, the sample subjects consist of elements in the population with extremely low values on the variable of interest, the sample mean $\bar{X}$ will be much lower than the true population mean $\mu$. If our sampling design and sample size are right, however, the sample mean $\bar{X}$ will be within close range of the true population mean $\mu$. Thus, through appropriate sampling designs, we can ensure that the sample subjects are not chosen from the extremes, but are representative of the true properties of the population. The more representative the sample is of the population, the more generalisable are the findings of the research. Recall that generalisability is one of the hallmarks of scientific research, as we saw in chapter 2.

Although in view of our concern about generalisability, we may be particular about choosing representative samples for most research, in some cases we may be less concerned about generalisability. For instance, at the exploratory stages of fact finding, we may be interested only in 'getting a handle' on the situation, and therefore we may interview only the most conveniently available people. The same is true when time is of the essence, and urgency in getting information takes priority over high accuracy. For instance, a film agency might want to find out quickly the impact on the viewers of a newly released film exhibited the previous evening. The interviewer might question the first 20 people leaving the theatre after seeing the film and obtain their reactions. On the basis of their replies, she may form an opinion as to the likely success of the film. As another example, a restaurant manager might want to learn the reactions of customers to a new item added to the menu, so as to determine whether or not it has been a worthwhile addition. For this purpose, the first 15 people who ordered the special item might be interviewed, and their reactions found. In such cases, eliciting quick information may be more important than getting the most representative facts. It should be noted, however, that the results of such convenience samples are not reliable and can never be generalised to the population. We will discuss the different types of sampling designs now, bearing in mind the points to be considered while making such choices (see figure 11.6).

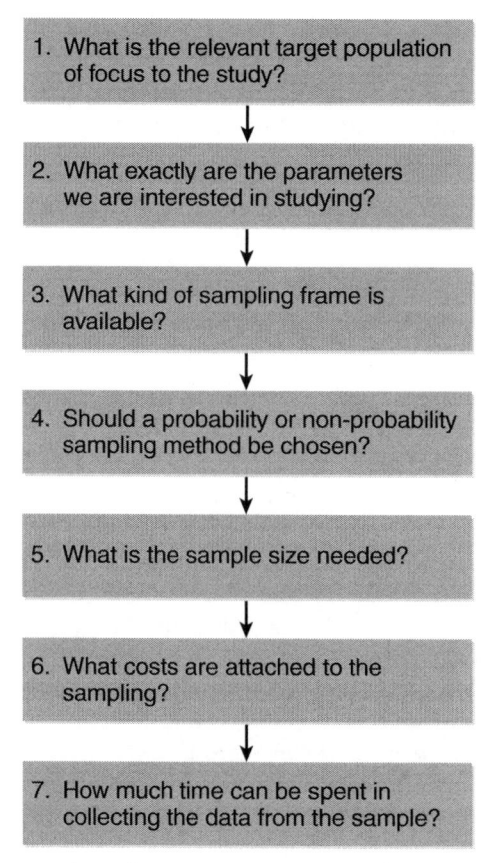

1. What is the relevant target population of focus to the study?
2. What exactly are the parameters we are interested in studying?
3. What kind of sampling frame is available?
4. Should a probability or non-probability sampling method be chosen?
5. What is the sample size needed?
6. What costs are attached to the sampling?
7. How much time can be spent in collecting the data from the sample?

**Figure 11.6** Points to consider when preparing a sampling design

# PROBABILITY AND NON-PROBABILITY SAMPLING

There are two major types of sampling designs: probability and non-probability sampling. In probability sampling, the elements in the population have some known chance or probability of being selected as sample subjects. In non-probability sampling, the elements do not have a known or predetermined chance of being selected as subjects. **Probability sampling** designs are used when the representativeness of the sample is of importance in the interests of wider generalisability. When time or other factors rather than generalisability become critical, non-probability sampling is generally used.

Each of these two major designs has different sampling strategies. Depending on the extent of generalisability desired, the availability of time and other resources, and the purpose of the study, different types of probability and non-probability sampling designs are chosen. These are discussed next.

# PROBABILITY SAMPLING

When elements in the population have a known chance of being chosen as subjects in the sample, we resort to a probability sampling design. Probability sampling can be either unrestricted (simple random sampling) or restricted (**complex probability sampling**) in nature.

## SIMPLE RANDOM SAMPLING

In the **unrestricted probability sampling** design, more commonly known as simple random sampling, every element in the population has a *known and equal* chance of being selected as a subject. Let us say there are 1000 elements in the population, and we need a sample of 100. Suppose we were to drop pieces of paper into a hat, each bearing the name of one of the elements, and we were to draw 100 of these from the hat with our eyes closed. We know that each one of those elements has a 100/1000 chance of being drawn. In other words, we know that the probability of any one of them being chosen as a subject is 0.1 (or 10 per cent), and we also know that each single element in the hat has the same or an equal probability of being chosen. We know, of course, that computers can generate random numbers and one does not have to go through the tedious process of pulling out names from a hat!

When we thus draw the elements from the population, it is likely that the distribution patterns of the characteristics we are interested in investigating in the population are also similarly distributed in the subjects we draw for our sample. This sampling design, known as **simple random sampling**, has the least bias and offers the most generalisability. However, this sampling process could become cumbersome and expensive; in addition, an entirely updated listing of the population may not always be available. For these and other reasons, other probability sampling designs are often chosen instead.

## COMPLEX PROBABILITY SAMPLING

As an alternative to the simple random sampling design, several complex probability sampling (**restricted probability**) designs can be used. These probability sampling procedures offer a viable and sometimes more efficient alternative to the unrestricted design we just discussed. Efficiency is improved in that more information can be obtained for a given sample size using some of the complex probability sampling procedures than the simple random sampling design. The five most common complex probability sampling designs — **systematic sampling, stratified random sampling, cluster sampling, area sampling** and **double sampling** — will now be discussed.

## Systematic sampling

The systematic sampling design involves drawing every *n*th element in the population starting with a randomly chosen element between 1 and *n*. The procedure is illustrated below.

> **EXAMPLE 11.2**
>
> If we want a sample of 35 households from a total population of 260 houses in a particular locality, then we could sample every seventh house starting from a random number from 1 to 7. Let us say that the random number is 7, then houses numbered 7, 14, 21, 28 and so on would be sampled until the 35 houses are selected.

The one problem to be borne in mind in the systematic sampling design is the probability of a systematic bias creeping into the sample. In the preceding example, for instance, let us say that every seventh house happens to be a corner house. If the focus of the research study conducted by the construction industry is to control 'noise pollution' experienced by residents through the use of appropriate filtering materials, then the residents of corner houses may not be exposed to as much noise as the houses in between. Information on noise levels gathered from corner house dwellers might therefore bias the researcher's data. The likelihood of drawing incorrect conclusions from such data is therefore high. In view of the scope for such systematic bias, the researcher must consider the plans carefully and make sure that the systematic sampling design is appropriate for the study, before deciding on it.

For market surveys, consumer attitude surveys and the like, the systematic sampling design is often used, and the telephone directory frequently serves as the sampling frame for this sampling design.

## Stratified random sampling

While sampling helps to estimate population parameters, identifiable subgroups of elements within the population may be expected to have different parameters on a variable of interest to the researcher. For example, to the human resources manager interested in assessing the extent of training that the employees in the system feel they need, the entire organisation will form the population for study. But the extent, quality and intensity of training desired by middle-level managers, lower-level managers, first-line supervisors, computer analysts, clerical workers and so on will be different for each group. Knowledge of the kinds of differences in needs that exist for the different groups will help the manager to develop useful and meaningful training programs for each group in the organisation. Data will therefore have to be collected in a manner that would help the assessment of needs at each subgroup level in the population. The unit of analysis then would be at the group level. The stratified random sampling process will then come in handy.

Stratified random sampling, as its name implies, involves a process of stratification or segregation, followed by random selection of subjects from each stratum. The population is first divided into mutually exclusive groups that are relevant, appropriate and meaningful in the context of the study. For instance, if the CEO of a company is concerned about low motivational levels or high absentee rates among the employees, it makes sense to stratify the population of organisational members according to their job levels. When the data are collected and the analysis completed, we may find that contrary to expectations, it is the middle-level managers who are not motivated. This information will help the CEO to focus on action at the right level and devise better ways to motivate this group. Tracing the differences in the parameters of the subgroups within a population would not have been possible without the stratified random sampling procedure. If either the simple random sampling or the systematic sampling procedure was used in a case such as this, the high motivation at some job levels and the low motivation at other levels would have cancelled each other out, thus masking the real problems that exist at a particular level or levels.

Stratification also helps when research questions such as the following are to be answered:
1. Are machinists more accident prone than clerical workers?
2. Are people raised in New Zealand more loyal to the organisation than recent immigrants?

Stratifying customers on the basis of life stages, income levels and the like to study buying patterns, and stratifying companies according to size, industry, profits and so forth to study share market reactions, are common examples of the use of stratification as a sampling design technique.

Stratification is an *efficient* research sampling design; that is, it provides more information for a given sample size. Stratification should follow the lines appropriate to the research question. If we study consumer preferences for a product, stratification of the population could be by geographic areas, market segments, consumer age, consumer gender or various combinations of these. If an organisation contemplates budget cuts, the effects of these cuts on employee attitudes can be studied with stratification by department, function or region. Stratification ensures homogeneity within each stratum (that is, very few differences or dispersions on the variable of interest within each stratum), but heterogeneity (that is, wide differences and variability) between strata. In other words, there will be more between-group differences than within-group differences.

### Proportionate and disproportionate stratified random sampling

Once the population has been stratified in some meaningful way, a sample of members from each stratum can be drawn using either a simple random sampling or a systematic sampling procedure. The subjects drawn from each stratum can be either proportionate or disproportionate to the number of elements in the stratum. For instance, if an organisation employs 10 top managers, 30 middle managers, 50 lower-level managers, 100 supervisors, 500 clerks and 20 secretaries, and a stratified sample of about 140 people is needed for some scientific survey, the researcher might decide to include in the sample 20 per cent of members from each stratum. That is, members represented in the sample from each stratum will be proportionate to the total number of elements in the respective strata. This would mean that two from the top, six from the middle and 10 from the lower levels of management will be included in the sample. In addition, 20 supervisors, 100 clerks and 4 secretaries will be represented in the sample, as shown in the third column of table 11.1. This type of sampling is called a **proportionate stratified random sampling** design.

In situations like the one above, researchers might sometimes be concerned that obtaining information from just two members at the top and six from the middle levels would not truly reflect how all members at those levels would respond. Therefore, a researcher might decide instead to use a **disproportionate stratified random** sampling procedure. The number of subjects from each stratum will now be altered, while keeping the sample size unchanged. Such a sampling design is illustrated in the far right-hand column in table 11.1. The idea here is that the 60 clerks might be considered adequate to represent the population of 500 clerks; 7 out of 10 managers at the top level would also be considered representative of the top managers, and similarly 15 out of the 30 managers at the middle level. This redistribution of the numbers in the strata would be considered more appropriate and representative for the study than the previous proportionate sampling design.

**Table 11.1** Proportionate and disproportionate stratified random sampling

| Job level | Number of elements | Number of subjects in the sample | |
| --- | --- | --- | --- |
| | | Proportionate sampling (20% of the elements) | Disproportionate sampling |
| Top management | 10 | 2 | 7 |
| Middle-level management | 30 | 6 | 15 |
| Lower-level management | 50 | 10 | 20 |
| Supervisors | 100 | 20 | 30 |
| Clerks | 500 | 100 | 60 |
| Assistants | 20 | 4 | 10 |
| Total | 710 | 142 | 142 |

Disproportionate sampling decisions are made either when a stratum or some strata are too small or too large, or when there is more variability suspected within a particular stratum. As an example, the educational levels among supervisors, which may be thought of as influencing perceptions, may range from high school to master's degrees. Here, more people will be sampled at the supervisor's level. Disproportionate sampling is also sometimes done when it is easier, simpler and less expensive to collect data from one or more strata than from others.

In summary, stratified random sampling involves stratifying the elements into meaningful levels and taking proportionate or disproportionate samples from the strata. This sampling design is more efficient than the simple random sampling design because, for the same sample size, each important segment of the population is better represented, and more valuable and differentiated information is obtained with respect to each group.

## Cluster sampling

Groups or chunks of elements that ideally would have heterogeneity among the members within each group are chosen for study in cluster sampling. This is in contrast to choosing some elements from the population, as in simple random sampling; or stratifying and then choosing members from the strata, as in stratified random sampling; or choosing every nth element in the population, as in systematic sampling. When several groups with intragroup heterogeneity and intergroup homogeneity are found, then a random sampling of the clusters or groups can ideally be done and information gathered from each of the members in the randomly chosen clusters. Ad hoc organisational committees drawn from various departments to offer inputs to the company CEO to enable him or her to make decisions in product development, budget allocations, marketing strategies and the like are good examples of different clusters. Each of these clusters or groups contains a heterogeneous collection of members with different interests, orientations, values, philosophy and vested interests, drawn from different departments to offer a variety of perspectives. Drawing on their individual and combined insights, the CEO is able to make final decisions on strategic moves for the company. Cluster samples offer more heterogeneity within groups and more homogeneity among groups — the reverse of what we find in stratified random sampling, where there is homogeneity within each group and heterogeneity across groups.

The unit costs of cluster sampling are much lower compared with the other probability sampling designs of simple or stratified random sampling or systematic sampling. However, cluster sampling lends itself to greater biases and is the least generalisable of all the probability sampling designs, because most naturally occurring clusters in the organisational context do not contain heterogeneous elements. In other words, the conditions of intracluster heterogeneity and intercluster homogeneity are often not met.

For these reasons, the cluster sampling technique is not very common in business research since, as in the case of the committee example cited previously, duplication of members in several clusters is also possible. Moreover, for marketing research activities, naturally occurring clusters, such as clusters of residents, buyers, students or shops, do not have much heterogeneity among the elements. As stated earlier, there is more intracluster homogeneity than heterogeneity in such clusters. Hence, cluster sampling, though less costly, does not offer much **efficiency** in terms of precision or confidence in the results. However, cluster sampling offers convenience. For example, it is easier to inspect an assortment of units packed inside, say, four boxes (that is, all the elements in four clusters) than to open 30 boxes in a shipment in order to inspect a few units from each at random.

### Single-stage and multistage cluster sampling

We have thus far discussed single-stage cluster sampling, which involves the division of the population into convenient clusters, randomly choosing the required number of clusters as sample subjects, and investigating all the elements in each of the randomly chosen clusters. Cluster sampling can also be done in several stages, and is then called **multistage cluster sampling**. If we were to carry out a national survey of average monthly bank deposits, for instance, cluster sampling would first be used to select the urban, semi-urban and rural geographical locations for study. At the next stage, particular areas in each of these locations would be chosen. At the third stage, banks within each area would be chosen. In other words, multistage cluster sampling involves a probability sampling of the primary sampling units; from each of these primary units, a probability sample of the secondary sampling units is then drawn; a third level of probability sampling is done from each of these secondary units — and so on, until we have reached the final stage of breakdown for the sample units, when we will sample every member in those units.

## Area sampling

The area sampling design constitutes geographic clusters; that is, when the research pertains to populations within identifiable geographic areas such as states, city blocks or particular boundaries within a locality, area sampling can be done. Thus, area sampling is a form of cluster sampling within an area. Sampling the needs of consumers before opening a 24-hour convenience store in a particular part of the town would involve area sampling. Retail store location plans, advertisements focused specifically on local populations, and TV and radio programs beamed at specific areas could all use an area sampling design to gather information on the interests, attitudes, predispositions and behaviours of the local people.

Area sampling is less expensive than most other probability sampling designs, and it is not dependent on a population frame. A city map showing the blocks of the city would be adequate information to allow a researcher to take a sample of the blocks and obtain data from the residents therein.

## Double sampling

This plan is resorted to when further information is needed from a subset of the group from which some information has already been collected. A sampling design in which a sample is used in a study to collect some preliminary information of interest, and later a subsample of this primary sample is used to examine the matter in more detail, is called double sampling. For example, a structured interview might indicate that a subgroup of respondents has more insight into the problems of the organisation. These respondents might be interviewed again with additional questions. This research would have adopted a double sampling procedure.

## REVIEW OF PROBABILITY SAMPLING DESIGNS

There are two basic probability sampling plans: the unrestricted or simple random sampling, and the restricted or complex probability sampling plans. In the simple random sampling design, every element in the population has a known and equal chance of being selected as a subject. The complex probability plan consists of five different sampling designs. Of these five, the cluster sampling design is probably the least expensive, as well as the least dependable, but is used when no list of the population elements is available. The stratified random sampling design is probably the most efficient, in the sense that, for the same number of sample subjects, it offers precise and detailed information. The systematic sampling design has the built-in hazard of possible systematic bias. Area sampling is a popular form of cluster sampling, and double sampling is used when information in addition to that already obtained by using a primary sample has to be collected using a subgroup of the sample.

## NON-PROBABILITY SAMPLING

In non-probability sampling designs, the elements in the population have no probabilities attached to their being chosen as sample subjects. This means that the findings from the study of the sample cannot be confidently generalised to the population. As stated earlier, however, researchers may at times be less concerned about generalisability than they are about obtaining some preliminary information in a quick and inexpensive way. They would then resort to non-probability sampling. Some of the non-probability sampling plans are more dependable than others and could offer important leads to potentially useful information with regard to the population. The non-probability sampling designs, which fit into the broad categories of convenience sampling and **purposive sampling**, are dicussed next.

## CONVENIENCE SAMPLING

As its name imples, **convenience sampling** involves collecting information from members of the population who are conveniently available to provide it. One would expect that the Pepsi Challenge contest was administered on a convenience sampling basis. Such a contest, with the purpose of determining whether people prefer one product to another, might be held at a shopping centre visited by many shoppers. Those inclined to take the test might form the sample for the study of how many people prefer Pepsi over Coke or product X over product Y. Such a sample is a convenience sample.

Consider another example. A convenience sample of five managers, who attended the competitor's showcase demonstration at the trade convention the previous evening, offered the general manager of marketing of the company information on the 'new' products of the competitor and their pricing strategies, which helped the general manager to formulate some ideas on the next steps to be taken by the company.

Convenience sampling is most often used during the exploratory phase of a research project and is perhaps the best way of collecting basic information quickly and efficiently.

## PURPOSIVE SAMPLING

Instead of obtaining information from those who are most conveniently available, it might sometimes become necessary to obtain information from specific target groups. Here the sampling is confined to specific types of people who can provide the desired information, either because they are the only ones who possess it, or because they conform to some criteria set by the researcher. This type of sampling design is called purposive sampling, and the three major types of purposive sampling — judgement sampling, snowball sampling and quota sampling — will now be explained.

### Judgement sampling

**Judgement sampling** involves the choice of subjects who are in the best position to provide the information required. For instance, if a researcher wants to find out what it takes for women managers to make it to the top, the only people who can give first-hand information are the women who have risen to the positions of CEO and general manager and important top-level executives in work organisations. By virtue of having gone through the experiences and processes themselves, they might be expected to have expert knowledge and perhaps be able to provide good data or information to the researcher. Thus, the judgement sampling design is used when a limited number or category of people have the information that is sought. In such cases, any type of probability sampling across a cross-section of the entire population is purposeless and useless.

Judgement sampling may curtail the generalisability of the findings because we are using a sample of experts who are conveniently available to us. However, it is the only viable sampling method for obtaining the type of information that is required from very specific pockets of people who alone possess the needed facts and can give the information sought. In business settings, and particularly for market research, opinion leaders who are very knowledgeable are included in the sample. Enlightened opinions, views and knowledge constitute a rich data source.

Judgement sampling calls for special efforts to locate and gain access to the individuals who do have the requisite information. As already stated, this sampling design may be the only useful one for answering certain types of research questions.

### Snowball sampling

**Snowball sampling** is frequently used when the elements in the population have specific characteristics or knowledge, but they are very difficult to locate and contact.

The initial sample group can be selected by probability or non-probability methods, but new subjects are selected based on recommendations and information provided by the initial subjects. This method is used to locate members of 'rare' or 'private' populations — for example members of confidential societies, or groups in society of which it is difficult to get access to sufficient numbers. The name is derived from the 'snowball' effect of accumulating more subjects as the study proceeds.

An example of a snowball sample occurred recently during a survey of stakeholders' attitudes towards a road toll system for the proposed major roading project in the Wellington region (the Transmission Gully project we looked at earlier in example 11.1). The transport policy manager at the Wellington Regional Council identified one stakeholder from each stakeholder group (for example from Transit New Zealand, an environmental group, a Maori *iwi* group, the Public Transport Users Association, the New Zealand Police, the Transmission Gully Action Group, the *Evening Post* and the Commercial Road Users Association). This initial sample group was identified using judgement sampling methods. These people were interviewed and asked to provide the names of additional people from their stakeholder group to obtain further subjects for interviewing so the desired sample size could be achieved.

A limitation of this method is that bias can occur, as subjects may refer the researcher on to additional subjects who hold similar views to themselves. Also, snowball sampling may limit the generalisability of the findings, based on the representativeness of the initial set of subjects and the range of people located through the referral networks. A problem may occur in determining how well this group represents the views of the target population. Nevertheless, it is an extremely useful method for gaining access to information from people who are very hard to locate under normal circumstances.

## Quota sampling

**Quota sampling**, another type of purposive sampling, ensures that certain groups are adequately represented in the study through the assignment of a quota. Generally, the quota fixed for each subgroup is based on the total numbers of each group in the population. However, since this is a non-probability sampling plan, the results are not generalisable to the population.

Quota sampling can be considered a form of proportionate stratified sampling, in which a predetermined proportion of people are sampled from different groups, but on a convenience basis. For instance it may be surmised that the work attitudes of blue-collar workers in an organisation are quite different from those of white-collar workers. If there are 60 per cent blue-collar workers and 40 per cent white-collar workers in this organisation, and if a total of 30 people are to be interviewed to find the answer to the research question, then a quota of 18 blue-collar workers and 12 white-collar workers will form the sample, because these numbers represent 60 and 40 per cent of the sample size. The first 18 conveniently available blue-collar workers and 12 white-collar workers will be sampled according to this quota. Obviously, the sample may not be totally representative of the population; hence, the generalisability of the findings will be restricted. However, the convenience it offers in terms of effort, costs and time makes quota sampling attractive for some research efforts. Quota sampling also becomes a necessity when a subset of the population is underrepresented in the organisation — for example particular identity groups, foremen and so on. In other words, quota sampling ensures that all the subgroups in the population are adequately represented in the sample. Quota samples are basically stratified samples from which subjects are selected nonrandomly.

In a workplace (and society) that is becoming increasingly heterogeneous because of changing demographics, quota sampling may be expected to be used more frequently in the future. For example, quote sampling can be used to identify the buying predispositions of various ethnic groups and for getting a sense of how employees from different nationalities perceive the organisational culture.

Although quota sampling is not as generalisable as stratified random sampling, it does offer some information based on which further investigation, if necessary, can proceed. That is, it is possible that the first stage of research will use the non-probability design of quota sampling, and once some useful information has been obtained, a probability design will follow. The converse is also possible. A probability sampling design might indicate new areas for research, and non-probability sampling designs might be used to explore their feasibility.

## REVIEW OF NON-PROBABILITY SAMPLING DESIGNS

There are two main types of non-probability sampling designs: convenience sampling and purposive sampling. Convenience sampling is the least reliable of all sampling designs in terms of generalisability, but sometimes it may be the only viable alternative when quick and timely information is needed, or for exploratory research purposes. Purposive sampling plans fall into three main categories: judgement, snowball and quota sampling designs. Judgement sampling, although restricted in generalisability, may sometimes be the best sampling design choice, especially when there is a limited population that can supply the necessary information. Snowball sampling is frequently used when subjects who have the desired characteristics or knowledge are hard to find and contact. Quota sampling is often used for considerations of cost and time, and the need to adequately represent minority elements in the population.

Although the generalisability of non-probability sampling designs is very restricted, they have certain advantages and are sometimes the only viable alternative for the researcher.

Table 11.2 summarises the probability and non-probability sampling designs discussed thus far, along with their advantages and disadvantages. Figure 11.7 offers some decision choice points as to which design might be useful for specific research goals.

## EXAMPLES OF SAMPLING DESIGNS

### 1. Simple random sampling

This sampling design is best when the generalisability of the findings to the whole population is the main objective of the study. Consider the following two examples.

**EXAMPLE 11.3**

The human resources manager of a company with 82 people on its payroll has been asked by the general manager to consider formulating an implementable flexitime policy. The HR manager feels that such a policy is not necessary because everyone seems happy with the nine to five hours, and no one has complained. Formulating such a policy now, in the opinon of the HR manager, runs the risk of creating problems on the home front for the staff and scheduling problems for the company. She wants, however, to resort to a simple random sampling procedure to do an initial survey, and with the results convince the GM that there is no need for flexitime, and urge him to drop the matter. Since simple random sampling offers the greatest generalisability of the results to the entire population, and the general manager needs to be convinced of their validity, it is important to use this sampling design.

**EXAMPLE 11.4**

The regional director of sales operations of a medium-sized company, having 20 retail stores in each of its four geographical regions of operation, wants to know what types of sales promotion worked best for the company overall during the past year. This is to help formulate some general policies for the company *as a whole* and prioritise sales promotion strategies for the coming year.

Instead of studying each of the 80 stores, some *dependable* (that is, *representative* and *generalisable*) information can be had based on the study of a few stores drawn through a simple random sampling procedure. That is, each one of the 80 stores would have an equal chance of being chosen in the sample, and the results of the study would be the most generalisable.

A simple random sampling procedure is recommended in this case since the policy is to be formulated for the company as a whole. This implies that the most representative information has to be obtained that can be generalised to the entire company. This is best accomplished through this design.

Table 11.2 Probability and non-probability sampling designs

| Sampling design | Description | Advantages | Disadvantages |
|---|---|---|---|
| **Probability sampling** | | | |
| 1. Simple random sampling | All elements in the population are considered and each element has an equal chance of being chosen as the subject. | High generalisability of findings | Not as efficient as stratified sampling |
| 2. Systematic sampling | Every *n*th element in the population is chosen starting from a random point in the sampling frame. | Easy to use if sampling frame is available | Systematic biases are possible |
| 3. Stratified random sampling (Str.R.S.) Proportionate Str.R.S. in the population. Disproportionate Str.R.S. | Population is first divided into meaningful segments; thereafter subjects are drawn:<br>• in proportion to their original numbers<br>• based on criteria other than their original population numbers. | Most efficient among all probability designs. All groups are adequately sampled and comparisons among groups are possible. | Stratification *must* be meaningful. More time-consuming than simple random sampling or systematic sampling. Sampling frame for *each* stratum is essential. |
| 4. Cluster sampling | Groups that have heterogeneous members are first identified, then some are chosen at random; all the members in each of the randomly chosen groups are studied. | In geographic clusters, costs of data collection are low. | The least reliable and efficient among the probability sampling designs since subsets of clusters are more homogeneous than heterogeneous |
| 5. Area sampling | Cluster sampling is done within a particular area or locality. | Cost-effective. Useful for decisions relating to a particular location | Takes time to collect data from an area |
| 6. Double sampling | The same sample or a subset of the sample is studied twice. | Offers more detailed information on the topic of study | Original biases, if any, will be carried over. Individuals may not be happy responding a second time. |

| Sampling design | Description | Advantages | Disadvantages |
|---|---|---|---|
| **Non-probability sampling** | | | |
| 7. Convenience sampling | The most easily accessible members are chosen as subjects. | Quick, convenient, inexpensive | Not generalisable at all |
| 8. Judgement sampling | Subjects are selected on the basis of their expertise in the subject investigated. | Sometimes the only meaningful way to investigate | Generalisability is questionable; not generalisable to entire population |
| 9. Snowball sampling | Initial sample is identified, then more subjects are selected from referrals. | Useful when subjects have required characteristics but are hard to find and contact | Not normally generalisable |
| 10. Quota sampling | Subjects are conveniently chosen from targeted groups according to some predetermined number or quota. | Very useful where minority participation in a study is critical | Not easily generalisable |

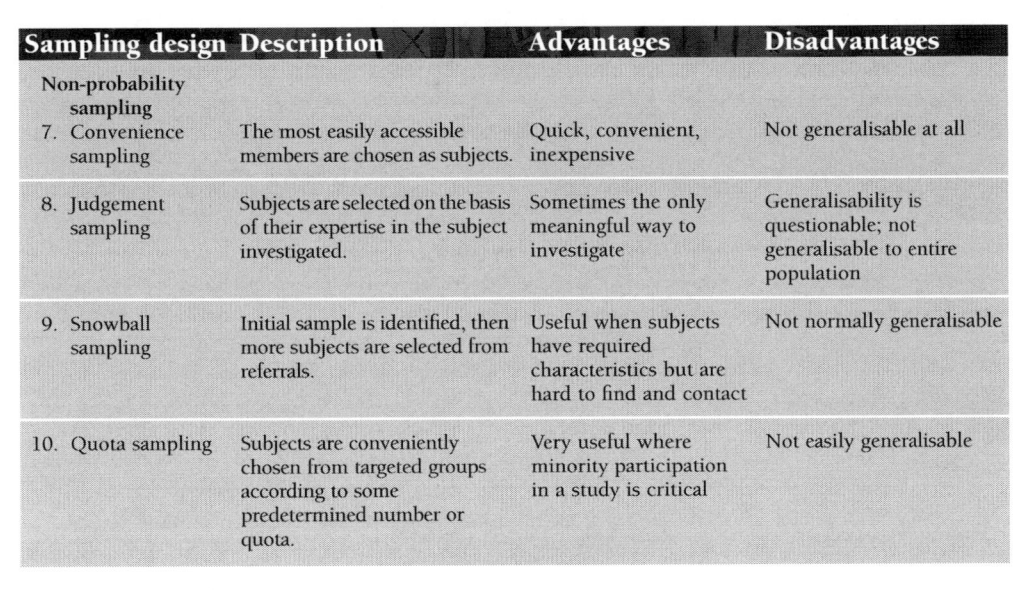

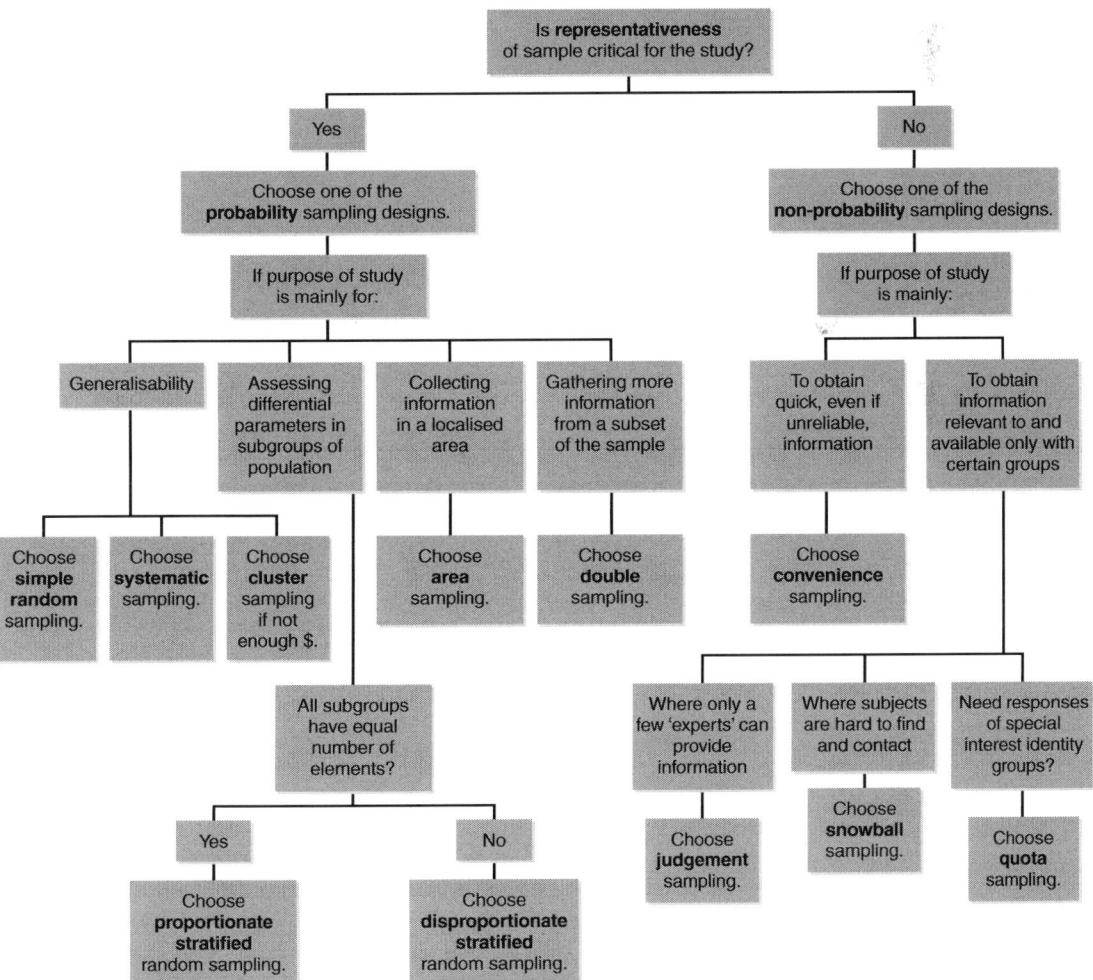

**Figure 11.7** Choice points in sampling design

It has to be noted that in some cases where *cost* is a primary consideration (that is, resources are limited), and the number of elements in the population is very large and/or geographically dispersed, the simple random sampling design may not be the most desirable, because it could become quite expensive. Thus, both the criticality of generalisability and cost considerations come into play in the choice of this sampling design.

## 2. Stratified random sampling

This sampling design, which is the most efficient, is a good choice when differentiated information is needed regarding various strata within the population which are known to differ in their parameters. (See examples 11.5 and 11.6.)

**EXAMPLE 11.5**

The human resources manager of a manufacturing firm wants to offer stress management seminars to the personnel exposed to high levels of stress. She conjectures that three groups are most prone to stress: the workmen who constantly handle dangerous chemicals, the foremen who are held responsible for production quotas and the counsellors who listen to the problems of the employees throughout the day, internalise them and offer them counsel, without knowing to what extent they have actually helped the clients.

To understand the experienced level of stress within each of the three groups and the rest of the firm, the HR manager would stratify the sample into four distinct categories:
1. the workmen handling the dangerous chemicals
2. the foremen
3. the counsellors
4. all the rest.

She would then choose a *disproportionate random sampling procedure* (since group 3 can be expected to be very small, and groups 2 and 1 are much smaller than group 4).

This is the only sampling design that would allow the designing of stress management seminars in a meaningful way, targeted at the right groups.

**EXAMPLE 11.6**

If in example 11.4 the regional director had wanted to know which sales promotion activity offered the best results for *each* geographic area so that different sales promotion strategies (according to regional preferences) could be developed, then first the 80 stores would be stratified on the basis of geographic region. Then a representative sample of stores would be drawn from each of the geographic regions (strata) through a simple random-sampling procedure. In this case, since each of the regions has 20 stores, a *proportionate stratified random sampling* process (say, five stores from each region) would be appropriate. If, however, the northern region had only three stores, the southern had 15, and the eastern and western regions had 24 and 38 stores, respectively, then a *disproportionate stratified random sampling* procedure would be the right choice, with all three stores in the northern region being studied, because of the small number of elements in that population.

If the sample size is retained at 20, then the north, south, east and west regions would probably have samples, respectively, of three, four, five and eight.

It is interesting to note that sometimes when stratified random sampling might seem logical, it might not really be necessary. For example, when test-marketing results show that Cook Islanders, Samoans and Tongans perceive and consume a particular product the same way, there is no need to segment the market and study each of the three groups using a stratified sampling procedure.

### 3. Systematic sampling

If the sampling frame is large, and a listing of the elements is conveniently available in one place (as in the telephone directory, company payroll or chamber of commerce listings), then a systematic sampling procedure will offer the advantages of ease and speed in developing the sample, as illustrated in the following two examples.

**EXAMPLE 11.7**

An administrator wants to assess the reactions of employees to a new and improved superannuation scheme that requires a modest increase in the premiums to be paid by employees for their families. The administrator can assess the enthusiasm for the new scheme by using a systematic sampling design. The company's records will provide the sampling frame, and every $n$th employee can be sampled. A stratified plan is not called for here since the policy is for the entire company.

**EXAMPLE 11.8**

If customers' interest in a highly sophisticated telephone is to be gauged by an entrepreneur, a systematic sampling procedure with the telephone directory as the sampling frame will be the easiest and quickest way to obtain the information, while still ensuring representativeness of the population studied.

Note that systematic sampling is inadvisable where systematic biases can be anticipated, if data are collected in this manner. For example, systematic sampling from the personnel directory of a company (especially one that has an equal number of employees in each department), which lists the names of the individuals according to department, with the head of the department listed first, and the personal assistant listed next, has inherent biases. The possibility of systematic biases creeping into the data cannot be ruled out in this case, since the selection process may end up picking each of the heads of the departme2nt or the departmental assistants as the sample subjects. The results from such a sample will clearly be biased and not generalisable, despite the use of a probability sampling procedure. Systematic sampling will have to be scrupulously avoided in cases where known systematic biases are possible.

### 4. Cluster sampling

This sampling design would be most useful when a heterogeneous group is to be studied at one time. Two examples are offered below.

**EXAMPLE 11.9**

A human resources manager is interested in knowing why staff resign. Cluster sampling design will be useful in this case for conducting exit interviews of all members completing their final papers in the HR department on the same day (cluster), before resigning. The clusters chosen for interviews will be based on a simple random sampling of the various clusters of personnel resigning on different days.

The interviews would help an understanding of the reasons for turnover of a heterogeneous group of individuals (that is, from various departments), and the study could be conducted at a low cost.

**EXAMPLE 11.10**

A financial analyst wishes to study the lending practices of pawnbrokers in New South Wales. All the pawnbrokers in each city would form a cluster. By randomly sampling the clusters, the analyst would be able to draw conclusions on the lending practices.

### 5. Area sampling

Area sampling is best suited when the goal of the research is confined to a particular locality or area, as in the example that follows.

> **EXAMPLE 11.11**
> A telephone company wants to install a public telephone outlet in a locality where crime is most rampant so that victims can have access to a telephone. Studying the crime statistics and interviewing residents in a particular area will help the company to choose the right location for installation of the phone.

### 6. Double sampling

This design provides further information at minimal additional expenditure (see example 11.12).

> **EXAMPLE 11.12**
> In example 11.9 (exit interview example), some individuals (a subset of the original cluster sample) might have indicated that they were resigning because of philosophical differences with the company's policies. The researcher might want to do an in-depth interview with these individuals to obtain further information regarding the nature of the policies disliked, the actual philosophical differences and why these particular issues were central to the individuals' value systems. Such additional detailed information from the target group through the double sampling design could help the company to find ways of retaining employees in the future.

### 7. Convenience sampling

This non-probability design, which is not generalisable at all, is sometimes used to obtain 'quick' information to get a 'feel' for the phenomenon or variables of interest. (See example 11.13.)

> **EXAMPLE 11.13**
> The accounts executive has established a new accounting system that maximally utilises computer technology. Before making further changes, she would like to get a feel for how the accounting clerks react to the new system without making it seem that she has doubts about their acceptability. She may then 'casually' talk to the first five accounting personnel who walk into her office, in order to gauge their reactions.

Note that convenience sampling should be used in the interests of expediency, with the full knowledge that the results are not at all generalisable.

### 8. Judgement sampling

Judgement sampling design is used when the collection of 'specialised informed inputs' on the topic area researched is vital, and the use of any other sampling designs would not offer opportunities to obtain the specialised information, as in the example that follows.

> **EXAMPLE 11.14**
> A pharmaceutical company wants to trace the effects of a new drug on patients with specific health problems (namely, muscular dystrophy, sickle-cell anaemia or rheumatoid arthritis). It contacts such individuals and, with the group of voluntarily consenting patients, tests the drug. This is a judgement sample because data are collected from appropriate special groups.

### 9. Snowball sampling

This non-probability sampling design is used to collect information from subjects who are difficult to locate and contact.

**EXAMPLE 11.15**

The district governor of a New Zealand Lions district expresses concern at the increasing average age of the district's membership and the lack of replacement. He requests a study to investigate why younger members of the community are not joining Lions (or similar community groups). However, he is particularly interested to limit the study to those people in the 30 to 50 age group, who appear to have a stable situation and sufficient spare time and interest to stick with the movement for the next 20 years. Now, while there might be many people in the district who satisfy the age criteria, it would certainly be more difficult to find people who meet all the criteria outlined!

A snowball sample is considered the most appropriate. First, a number of current Lions members are selected by simple random sampling (probability methods), and they are asked to identify suitable people they know who might be suitable for the study. When these subjects are contacted, they are asked to recommend other people in similar positions to themselves, and this 'snowball' procedure is followed until the required number of subjects are identified for the sample.

### 10. Quota sampling

This sampling design allows for the inclusion of all groups in the system researched. Thus, groups that are small in numbers are not neglected, as in the example below.

**EXAMPLE 11.16**

A company is considering operating an on-site kindergarten facility. But before taking further steps, it wants to get the reactions of four groups to the idea: (1) employees who are parents of kindergarten-age children, and who both work outside the home; (2) employees who are parents of kindergarten-age children, but one of them is *not* working outside of home; (3) single parents with children at kindergarten; and (4) all those without children of kindergarten age. If the four groups are expected to represent 60, 7, 23 and 10 per cent, respectively, in the population of 420 employees in the company, then a quota sampling will be appropriate to represent the four groups.

*Note:* The last group should also be included in the sample since there is a possibility that they may perceive this as a facility that favours the parents with children at kindergarten only, and may resent the idea. Hence, using quota sampling would be important.

## REVIEW OF SAMPLING PLAN DECISIONS

In effect, as can be seen from the discussions on sampling designs so far, decisions on which design to use depend on many factors, including the following:
1. the extent of prior knowledge in the area of research undertaken
2. the main objective of the study: generalisability, efficiency, knowing more about subgroups within a population, obtaining some quick (even if unreliable) information and so on
3. cost considerations: Is exactitude and generalisability worth the extra investment of time, cost and other resources in using a more sophisticated sampling design than a less sophisticated one? Even if it is, is suboptimisation because of cost or time constraints required? (See also figure 11.7.)

Choosing the appropriate sampling plan is one of the important research design decisions the researcher has to make. The choice of a specific design will depend largely on the goal of research, the characteristics of the population and cost considerations.

## SAMPLING IN CROSS-CULTURAL RESEARCH

It is appropriate here to point out that, as in instrument development and data collection, one has to be sensitive to the issue of selecting *matched samples* in the different countries while conducting cross-cultural research. Taking into consideration the nature and types of organisations studied, whether subjects are from rural or urban areas, their ethnicity and similar issues will enable true comparisons.

Apart from ensuring functional equivalence of the concepts investigated for the populations concerned (that is, the problems faced in the cultures are perceived and reacted to in the same manner in all the countries studied), how should the samples be chosen? With the multicultural work force that exists in various countries — for example Vietnamese, Australian, Indian or other nationals in Australian organisations, and Indian, Malay and Singaporeans in countries such as Malaysia and Singapore — one cannot be sure which subjects truly represent the central tendencies of the nation. A good way to address this problem is to study *matched* samples. For example, if a comparison is to be made between Malaysia and Singapore, it is advisable to study matched samples of Malays, Singaporeans and Indians in both countries to detect any intergroup and intragroup differences. Similarly, if Australia and Vietnam are to be compared, it is better first to draw a matched sample of Vietnamese in both countries, and then to draw a representative sample from both cultures for further examination.

## ISSUES OF PRECISION AND CONFIDENCE IN DETERMINING SAMPLE SIZE

Having discussed the various probability and non-probability sampling designs, we now need to focus attention on the second aspect of the sampling design issue — sample size. Suppose we select 30 people from a population of 3000 through a simple random sampling procedure. Will we be able to generalise our findings to the population with confidence, since we have chosen a probability design that has the most generalisability? What sample size would be required to make reasonably precise generalisations with confidence? What do precision and confidence mean? These issues will be considered now.

A reliable and valid sample should enable us to generalise the findings from the sample to the population under investigation. In other words, the sample statistics should be good estimates and reflect the population parameters as closely as possible within a narrow margin of error. No sample statistic ($\bar{X}$, for instance) is going to be *exactly* the same as the population parameter ($\mu$), no matter how sophisticated the probability sampling design may be. Remember that the very reason for a probability sampling design is to increase the probability that the sample statistics will be as close as possible to the population parameters! Although the point estimate $\bar{X}$ may not accurately reflect the population mean $\mu$, an interval estimate can be made within which $\mu$ will lie, with probabilities attached — that is, at particular confidence levels. The issues of confidence interval and confidence level are addressed in the following discussions on precision and confidence.

# PRECISION

Precision refers to how close our estimate is to the true population characteristic. Usually, we would estimate the population parameter to fall within a range, based on the sample estimate. For example, let us say that from a study of a simple random sample of 50 of the total 300 employees in a workshop, we find that the average daily production rate per person is 50 pieces of a particular product ($\bar{X} = 50$). We might then (by doing certain calculations, as we will see later) be able to say that the true average daily production of the product ($\mu$) would lie anywhere between 40 and 60 for the population of employees in the workshop. In saying this, we offer an interval estimate, within which we expect the true population mean production to be ($\mu = 50 \pm 10$). The narrower this interval, the greater the precision. For instance, if we are able to estimate that the population mean will fall anywhere between 45 and 55 pieces of production ($\mu = 50 \pm 5$) rather than 40 and 60 ($\mu = 50 \pm 10$), then we will have more precision. That is, we will now estimate the mean to fall within a narrower range, which means that we can estimate with greater exactitude or precision.

Precision is a function of the extent of variability in the sampling distribution of the sample mean. That is, if we take a number of different samples from a population, and take the mean of each of these, we will usually find that they are all different, are normally distributed and have a dispersion associated with them. The smaller this dispersion or variability, the greater the probability that the sample mean will be closer to the population mean. We need not necessarily take several different samples to estimate this variability. Even if we take only one sample of 30 subjects from the population, we will still be able to estimate the variability of the sampling distribution of the sample mean. This variability is called the standard error, denoted by $S_{\bar{X}}$. The standard error is calculated by the following formula (Sandy 1989:278; Zikmund 2000:385–6):

$$S_{\bar{X}} = \frac{S}{\sqrt{n}}$$

where $S$ is the standard deviation of the sample, $n$ is the sample size, and $S_{\bar{X}}$ indicates the standard error or the standard deviation of the sample mean.

Note that the standard error varies inversely with the square root of the sample size. Hence, if we want to reduce the standard error given a particular standard deviation in the sample, we need to increase the sample size. Another noteworthy point is that the smaller the variation in the population, the smaller the standard error, which in turn implies that the sample size need not be large. Thus, low variability in the population requires a smaller sample size.

In summary, the closer we want our sample results to reflect the population characteristics, the greater will be the precision we would aim for. The greater the precision required, the larger the sample size needed, especially when the variability in the population itself is large.

# CONFIDENCE

Whereas precision denotes how close we estimate the population parameter to be based on the sample statistic, **confidence** denotes how *certain* we are that our estimates will actually hold true for the population. In the previous example of production rate, we know we are more precise when we estimate the true mean production ($\mu$) to fall somewhere between 45 and 55 pieces, than somewhere between 40 and 60. However, we may have more confidence in the latter estimation than in the former. After all, anyone can say with 100 per cent certainty or confidence that the mean production (µ) will fall anywhere between zero and infinity! Other things being equal, the narrower the range, the lower the confidence. In other words, there is a trade-off between precision and confidence for any given sample size, as we will see later in this chapter.

In essence, confidence reflects the level of certainty with which we can state that our estimates of the population parameters, based on our sample statistics, will hold true. The level of confidence can range from 0 to 100 per cent. A 95 per cent confidence is the conventionally accepted level for most business research, most commonly expressed by denoting the significance level as p ≤ .05. In other words, we say that at least 95 times out of 100 our estimate will reflect the true population characteristic.

## SAMPLE DATA, PRECISION AND CONFIDENCE IN ESTIMATION

Precision and confidence are important issues in sampling because when we use sample data to draw inferences about the population, we hope to be fairly 'on target' and have some idea of the extent of possible error. Because a point estimate provides no measure of possible error, we do an interval estimation to ensure a *relatively accurate* estimation of the population parameter. Statistics that have the same distribution as the sampling distribution of the mean are used in this procedure, usually a $z$ statistic (for samples ≥ 30) or a $t$ statistic (for small samples < 30) (Sandy 1989: 282).

For example, we may want to estimate the mean dollar value of purchases made by customers when they shop at department stores. From 49 customers sampled through a systematic sampling design procedure, we may find that the sample mean $\bar{X} = 105$ (i.e. $105), and the sample standard deviation $S = 10$ (i.e. $10). $\bar{X}$, the sample mean, is a point estimate of µ, the population mean. We could construct a confidence interval around $\bar{X}$ to estimate the range within which µ would fall. The standard error $S_{\bar{X}}$ and the percentage or level of confidence we require will determine the width of the interval, which can be represented by the following formula, where $K$ is the $z$ statistic for the level of confidence desired. We can use the $z$ statistic here rather than the $t$ statistic, since the sample size involved is greater than 30.

$$\mu = \bar{X} \pm KS_{\bar{X}}$$

We already know that:

$$S_{\bar{X}} = \frac{S}{\sqrt{n}}$$

Here,

$$S_{\bar{X}} = \frac{10}{\sqrt{49}} = 1.43$$

From the table of critical values for $z$ in any statistics book (see table I, appendix II, at the end of this book), we know that:
- for a 90 per cent confidence level, the $K$ value (i.e. $z$ score) is 1.645
- for a 95 per cent confidence level, the $K$ value (i.e. $z$ score) is 1.96
- for a 99 per cent confidence level, the $K$ value (i.e. $z$ score) is 2.576.

If we desire a 90 per cent confidence level in the preceding case, then, $\mu = 105 \pm 1.645 * 1.43$ (that is, $\mu = 105 \pm 2.352$). $\mu$ would thus fall between 102.65 and 107.35. These results indicate that using a sample size of 49, we could state with 90 per cent confidence that the true population mean value of purchases for all customers would fall anywhere between $102.65 and $107.35. If we now want to be 99 per cent confident of our results without increasing the sample size, we would necessarily have to sacrifice precision, as may be seen from the calculation $\mu = 105 \pm 2.576 * 1.43$. The value of $\mu$ now falls between $101.32 and $108.68. In other words, the width of the interval has increased and we are now less precise in estimating the population mean, although we are a lot more confident about our estimation. It is not difficult to see that if we want to maintain our original precision while increasing confidence, or maintain the confidence level while increasing precision, or we want to increase both the confidence and the precision, we need a larger sample size.

In summary, the sample size, $n$, is a function of:
- the variability in the population
- precision or accuracy needed
- confidence level desired
- type of sampling plan used — for example simple random sampling versus stratified random sampling.

## TRADE-OFF BETWEEN PRECISION AND CONFIDENCE

We have noted that if we want more precision or more confidence, or both, the sample size needs to be increased — unless, of course, there is very little variability in the population itself. However, if the sample size ($n$) cannot be increased, for whatever reason — say, we cannot afford the costs of increased sampling — then, with the same $n$, the only way to maintain the same level of precision would be by surrendering the confidence with which we can predict our estimates. That is, we reduce the confidence level or the certainty of our estimate. This trade-off between precision and confidence is illustrated in figures 11.8a and b. Figure 11.8a indicates that 50 per cent of the time the true mean will fall within the narrow range indicated in the figure, the 0.25 in each tail representing the 25 per cent non-confidence, or the probability of making errors, in our estimation on either side. Figure 11.8b indicates that 99 per cent of the time we would expect the true mean $\mu$ to fall within the much wider range indicated in the figure, and there is only a 0.5 per cent chance that we would be making an error on either side. That is, in figure 11.8a we have more precision but less confidence (our confidence level is only 50 per cent). In figure 11.8b we have high confidence (99 per cent), but then we are far from being precise — that is, our estimate falls within a broad interval range.

It thus becomes necessary for researchers to consider at least four aspects while making decisions on the sample size needed to do the research.
1. How much precision is really needed in estimating the population characteristics of interest — that is, what is the *margin* of admissible error?
2. How much confidence is really needed — that is, how much *chance* can we take of making errors in estimating the population parameters?
3. To what extent is there variability in the population on the characteristics investigated?
4. What is the *cost–benefit analysis* of increasing the sample size?

(a) More precision but less confidence

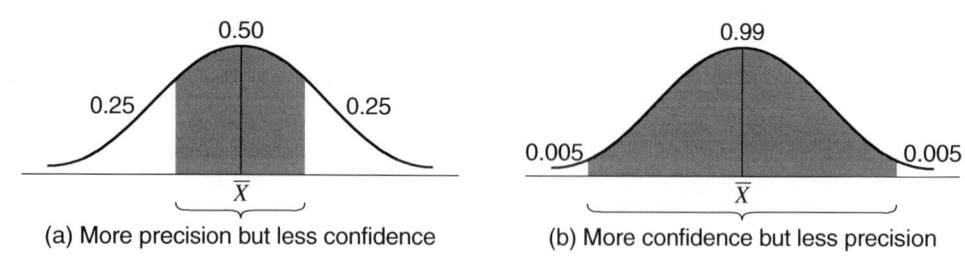

(b) More confidence but less precision

**Figure 11.8** The trade-off between precision and confidence

## DETERMINING THE SAMPLE SIZE

Now that we are aware of the fact that the sample size is governed by the extent of precision and confidence desired, how do we determine the sample size required for our research? The procedure can be illustrated through an example.

Suppose a manager wants to be 95 per cent confident that the expected monthly withdrawals from a bank will be within a confidence interval of ±$500. Let us say that a study of a sample of clients indicates that the average withdrawals made by them have a standard deviation of $3500. What would be the sample size needed in this case?

We noted earlier that the population mean can be estimated by using the formula:

$$\mu = \bar{X} \pm K\, S_{\bar{X}}$$

Now the expression $K\, S_{\bar{X}}$ is equivalent to the level of precision required or the margin of admissible error. Let us call this term E. Therefore,

$$E = KS_{\bar{X}}$$

We already know that $S_{\bar{X}} = \dfrac{S}{\sqrt{n}}$, so we can substitute this into the formula for E:

$$E = K \times \dfrac{S}{\sqrt{n}}$$

By rearranging these terms, we arrive at a formula for the sample size ($n$), as follows:

$$n = \left(\dfrac{K \times S}{E}\right)^2$$

Now, in our banking example above, we can substitute the appropriate values for K, S and E. Since the confidence level needed here is 95 per cent, the applicable K value is 1.96 (from the normal ($z$) table in appendix II, assuming a large sample). The sample standard deviation (S), is $3500 and the level of precision required (E) is ±$500.

Hence, the sample size

$$n = \left(\dfrac{1.96 \times 3500}{500}\right)^2$$

$$= 13.72^2 \text{ or } (13.72)^2$$

$$= 188.$$

Let us now consider some variations with this banking example. Initially, we will consider the effect on sample size if the number of customers is finite. Then we will consider the effects of changes to the levels of precision or confidence levels required on the sample size.

### (a) Correcting for a finite number of bank customers

The sample size needed in the preceding example was 188. Let us say that this bank has a total clientele of only 185. This means we cannot sample 188 clients. We can in this case apply the finite population correction formula and see what sample size would be needed to have the same level of precision and confidence, given the fact that we have a total of only 185 clients. The standard error modified by the correction formula is as follows (Sandy 1989:278).

$$S_{\bar{X}} = \frac{S}{\sqrt{n}} \times \sqrt{\frac{N-n}{N-1}}$$

where $N$ is the total number of elements in the population, $n$ is the sample size to be estimated, $S_{\bar{X}}$ is the standard error of the sample mean, and $S$ is the sample standard deviation of the sample mean. Note that this correction factor is required when you are dealing with a finite population and samples are taken without replacement. However, it is normally applied only when the sample size is 5 per cent or more of the population (i.e. $n/N \geq 0.05$) (Sandy 1989:237).

Applying the correction formula, we find that:

$$E = K \times \frac{S}{\sqrt{n}} \times \sqrt{\frac{N-n}{N-1}}$$

$$\text{or } 500 = 1.96 \times \frac{3500}{\sqrt{n}} \times \sqrt{\frac{185-n}{185-1}}$$

By rearranging and solving it, it can be shown that $n = 94$. We would now sample 94 of the total 185 clients.

### (b) Effect of changes in precision and confidence levels

To understand the impact of precision and/or confidence on the sample size, let us try changing the confidence level required in the bank withdrawal exercise, which needed a sample size of 188 for a confidence level of 95 per cent. Let us say that the bank manager now wants to be 99 per cent (i.e. $K = 2.576$) sure that the expected monthly withdrawals will be within the interval of ± $500. What sample size will now be needed?

Applying the formula

$$n = \left(\frac{K \times S}{E}\right)^2$$

$$= \left(\frac{2.576 \times 3500}{500}\right)^2$$

$$= 325.$$

The sample has now to be increased by 73 per cent (from 188 to 325) to increase the confidence level from 95 to 99 per cent!

Try calculating the sample size if the precision has to be narrowed down from $500 to $300 for a 95 and a 99 per cent confidence level. Your answers should show the sample sizes needed as 523 and 903, respectively. These results are summarised in table 11.3. They dramatically highlight the effects on the required sample size of increased precision, confidence or both. Naturally, the higher the sample size, the higher the associated costs of collecting data. It is therefore advisable to think through how much precision and confidence one really needs before determining the sample size for the research project.

**Table 11.3** Calculations of sample size for banking example

| Precision required | Confidence level | |
|---|---|---|
| | 95% | 99% |
| ±$500 | 188 | 325 |
| ±$300 | 523 | 903 |

So far we have discussed sample size in the context of precision and confidence with respect to one variable only. In research, however, the theoretical framework has several variables of interest, and the question arises of how one should come up with a sample size when all the factors are taken into account. Krejcie and Morgan (1970) greatly simplified the sample size decision by providing a table that ensures a good decision model. Table 11.4 provides generalised scientific guidelines for sample size decisions. The interested student is advised to read Krejcie and Morgan (1970) as well as Cohen (1969) for decisions on sample size.

**Table 11.4** Sample size for a given population size

| N | S | N | S | N | S |
|---|---|---|---|---|---|
| 10 | 10 | 220 | 140 | 1 200 | 291 |
| 15 | 14 | 230 | 144 | 1 300 | 297 |
| 20 | 19 | 240 | 148 | 1 400 | 302 |
| 25 | 24 | 250 | 152 | 1 500 | 306 |
| 30 | 28 | 260 | 155 | 1 600 | 310 |
| 35 | 32 | 270 | 159 | 1 700 | 313 |
| 40 | 36 | 280 | 162 | 1 800 | 317 |
| 45 | 40 | 290 | 165 | 1 900 | 320 |
| 50 | 44 | 300 | 169 | 2 000 | 322 |
| 55 | 48 | 320 | 175 | 2 200 | 327 |
| 60 | 52 | 340 | 181 | 2 400 | 331 |
| 65 | 56 | 360 | 186 | 2 600 | 335 |
| 70 | 59 | 380 | 191 | 2 800 | 338 |
| 75 | 63 | 400 | 196 | 3 000 | 341 |
| 80 | 66 | 420 | 201 | 3 500 | 346 |
| 85 | 70 | 440 | 205 | 4 000 | 351 |
| 90 | 73 | 460 | 210 | 4 500 | 354 |
| 95 | 76 | 480 | 214 | 5 000 | 357 |
| 100 | 80 | 500 | 217 | 6 000 | 361 |
| 110 | 86 | 550 | 226 | 7 000 | 364 |
| 120 | 92 | 600 | 234 | 8 000 | 367 |
| 130 | 97 | 650 | 242 | 9 000 | 368 |
| 140 | 103 | 700 | 248 | 10 000 | 370 |
| 150 | 108 | 750 | 254 | 15 000 | 375 |
| 160 | 113 | 800 | 260 | 20 000 | 377 |
| 170 | 118 | 850 | 265 | 30 000 | 379 |
| 180 | 123 | 900 | 269 | 40 000 | 380 |
| 190 | 127 | 950 | 274 | 50 000 | 381 |
| 200 | 132 | 1000 | 278 | 75 000 | 382 |
| 210 | 136 | 1100 | 285 | 1 000 000 | 384 |

# IMPORTANCE OF SAMPLING DESIGN AND SAMPLE SIZE

It is now possible to see how both sampling design and sample size are important to establish the representativeness of the sample for generalisability. If the appropriate sampling design is not used, a large sample size will not, in itself, allow the findings to be generalised to the population. Similarly, unless the sample size is adequate for the desired level of precision and confidence, no sampling design, however sophisticated, can be useful to the researcher in meeting the objectives of the study. Hence, sampling decisions should consider both the sampling design and the sample size. Too large a sample size, however (say, over 500), could also become a problem inasmuch as we would be prone to committing Type II errors — that is, we would accept the findings of our research when in fact we should reject them (this is discussed further in appendix I). In other words, with too large a sample size, even weak relationships (say, a correlation of 0.10 between two variables) might reach significance levels, and we would be inclined to believe that these significant relationships found in the sample are indeed true of the population, when in fact they may not be. Thus, neither too large nor too small a sample size helps research projects.

Another point to consider (even with the appropriate sample size) is whether statistical significance is more relevant than practical significance. For instance, a correlation of 0.25 may be statistically significant, but since this explains only about 6 per cent of the total variance (0.25 squared), how meaningful is it in terms of practical usefulness?

Roscoe (1975) proposes the following rules of thumb for determining sample size.
1. Sample sizes larger than 30 and smaller than 500 are appropriate for most research.
2. Where samples are to be broken into subsamples (e.g. males/females, juniors/seniors and so on), a minimum sample size of 30 for each category is usually necessary.
3. In multivariate research (including multiple regression analyses), the sample size should be several times (preferably 10 times or more) as large as the number of variables in the study.
4. For simple experimental research with tight experimental controls (e.g. matched pairs), successful research is possible with samples as small as 10 to 20.

# EFFICIENCY IN SAMPLING

Efficiency in sampling is attained when for a given level of precision (standard error), the sample size could be reduced, or for a given sample size ($n$), the level of precision could be increased. Some probability sampling designs are more efficient than others. The simple random sampling procedure is not always the most efficient plan to adopt; some other probability designs are often more efficient. A stratified random sampling plan is often the most efficient, and in many cases a disproportionate stratified random sampling design has been shown to be more efficient than a proportionate sampling design. Cluster sampling is less efficient than simple random sampling because there is generally more homogeneity among the subjects in the clusters than is found in the elements in the population. Multistage cluster sampling is more efficient than single-stage cluster sampling when there is more heterogeneity found in the earlier stages. There is often a trade-off between time and cost efficiencies (as achieved in non-probability sampling designs) and precision efficiencies (as achieved in probability sampling plans). The choice of a sampling plan thus depends on the objectives of the research, as well as on the extent and nature of efficiency desired.

## REVIEW OF SAMPLE SIZE DECISIONS

We can summarise the factors affecting decisions on sample size as (1) the extent of precision desired (the confidence interval); (2) the acceptable risk in predicting that level of precision (confidence level); (3) the amount of variability in the population itself; (4) the cost and time constraints; and, in some cases, (5) the size of the population itself.

As a rule of thumb, sample sizes between 30 and 500 could be effective depending on the type of sampling design used and the research question investigated. Qualitative studies typically use small sample sizes because of the intensive nature of such studies. When qualitative studies are undertaken for exploratory purposes, the sampling design will generally be convenience sampling.

## SUMMARY

Sampling design decisions are important aspects of research design and include both the sampling plan to be used and the sample size that will be needed. Probability sampling plans lend themselves to generalisability, and non-probability sampling designs (though not generalisable) offer convenience and timely information. Some probability plans are more efficient than others. Although non-probability sampling plans have limitations in terms of generalisability, they are often the only designs available for certain types of investigation, as in the case of exploratory research, or where information is needed quickly, or is available only with certain special groups.

The sample size is determined by the level of precision and confidence desired in estimating the population parameters, as well as the variability in the population itself. Cost considerations could also play a part. The generalisability of the findings from a study of the sample to the population is dependent on its representativeness — that is, the sophistication of the sampling design used and the sample size. Sample data are used for estimating population parameters.

Care should be taken not to overgeneralise the results of any study to populations that are *not* represented by the sample. This is a problem common in some research studies.

Awareness of sampling designs and sample size helps managers to understand why a particular method of sampling is used by researchers. It also facilitates understanding of the cost implications of different designs, and the trade-off between precision and confidence vis-à-vis the costs. This enables managers to undestand the risk they take in implementing changes, based on the results of the research study. While reading journal articles, this knowledge also helps managers to assess the generalisability of the findings and analyse the implications of trying out the recommendations in their own organisations.

In chapter 13 we will see how the data gathered from a sample of respondents in the population are analysed to test the hypotheses generated, and to find answers to the research questions. Appendix I at the back of the book will enhance understanding of the statistical tests used.

## DISCUSSION POINTS

1. Identify the relevant population for the following research opportunities, and suggest the appropriate sampling design to investigate the issues, explaining *why* they are appropriate. Wherever necessary, identify the sampling frame as well.
   (a) A hospital administrator wants to find out if the single parents working in the hospital have a higher rate of absenteeism than parents who are not single.
   (b) A researcher would like to assess the extent of pilferage in the materials storage warehouses of manufacturing firms on the Gold Coast.
   (c) The director of human resources wants to investigate the relationship between drug abuse and dysfunctional behaviour among blue-collar workers in a particular plant.
   (d) A gun manufacturing firm would like to know the types of guns possessed by various age groups in Queensland.

2. (a) Explain why cluster sampling is a probability sampling design.
   (b) What are the advantages and disadvantages of cluster sampling?
   (c) Describe a situation in which you would consider the use of cluster sampling.

3. (a) Explain what precision and confidence are and how they influence sample size.
   (b) There is a trade-off between precision and confidence under certain conditions. Discuss what is meant by this statement.

4. 'The use of a convenience sample in organisational research is correct because all members share the same organisational stimuli and go through almost the same kinds of experiences in their organisational lives.' Comment.

5. 'Using a sample of 5000 is not necessarily better than using one of 500.' How would you react to this statement?

6. 'Double sampling is probably the least used of all sampling designs in business research.' Do you agree? Provide reasons for your answer.

7. 'Non-probability sampling designs ought to be preferred to probability sampling designs in some cases.' Explain with examples.

8. 'Because there seems to be a trade-off between accuracy and confidence for any given sample size, accuracy should always be considered more important than precision.' Explain with reasons why you would or would not agree.

9. 'Overgeneralisations give rise to much confusion and other problems for researchers who try to replicate the findings.' Explain what is meant by this.

For the situations presented in exercises 11.1 to 11.6, indicate what would be the relevant population and the most appropriate sampling design. Make sure you discuss the reasons for your answers.

Exercise 11.1    A medical inspector wants to estimate the overall average monthly occupancy rates of the cancer wards in different hospitals that are evenly located in the northern, southern, western and eastern suburbs of Sydney.

Exercise 11.2    The Association of Victoria University Women (AVUW) is a semi-formal liaison group at Victoria University of Wellington. The group meets regularly and makes submissions about equality issues related to women staff members and female students. AVUW provides input on promotions, university procedures and appointments of senior managers at the university. At a lunchtime meeting of the group, it suddenly occurred to the convenor that it would be a good idea to get the opinion of members of this group on how effective they perceived AVUW to be in enhancing the role of women on campus. She thought she could ask a few quick questions as the audience left the meeting room. What should be her sampling design and how should she proceed?

Exercise 11.3    A magazine article suggested that 'Consumers aged 35 to 44 will soon be the nation's biggest spenders, so advertisers must learn how to appeal to this over-the-thrill crowd'. If this suggestion appeals to an apparel manufacturer, what should be the sampling design to assess the tastes of this group?

Exercise 11.4    Dunedin is a university town with about 17 000 students, including more than 1100 international students from various parts of the world. For instance, more than 500 Malaysian students and over 500 students from about 50 other countries attend Otago University in Dunedin.
   June McIntosh, a talented and adventurous seamstress, wishes to open a tailoring shop (so rare these days!) in Dunedin, close to the university, where she lives. She has a good sewing machine and would start her business immediately if she knew there would be adequate demand for her services. To assess the market potential, June would like to talk to a few women to estimate how many clients she might attract.

While the New Zealand women buy ready-made clothes from the university shopping centre, she believes that the international women, particularly the Malays, prefer to buy plain material from the shopping centre and either stitch their own blouses or get them stitched at home. How should June go about selecting a sample of 45 individuals to estimate the demand that might exist

**Exercise 11.5**

Waiwhetu Vacuum Specialists Ltd produces special vacuum cleaners for conveniently cleaning the inside of cars. About a thousand of these are produced every month with stamped serial numbers and are stored serially in a stockroom. Once a month an inspector does a quality control check on 50 of these. When he certifies them as to quality, the units are released from the stockroom for sale. The production and sales managers, however, are not satisfied with the quality control check since, quite often, the units sold are returned by customers because of various types of defects. What would be the most useful sampling plan to test the 50 units?

**Exercise 11.6**

A consultant had administered a questionnaire to some 285 employees using a simple random sampling procedure. As she looked at the responses, she suspected that two questions might not have been clear to the respondents. She would like to know if her suspicion is well-founded.

**Exercise 11.7**

In an article in the *Wall Street Journal* titled 'Kellogg to Study Work of Salaried Staff, Setting Stage for Possible Job Cutbacks', it was stated that Kellogg's earnings remained under heavy competitive pressure and its cereal market continued to slip. It was also stated that Kellogg was seeking to regain its lost momentum through the first three strategies listed below, to which we add the last two.
1. Increasing production efficiencies.
2. Developing new products.
3. Increasing product promotion through advertising effectiveness.
4. Tapping creative ideas from organisational members at different levels.
5. Assessing perceptions of organisational health and vitality.

Discuss in as much detail as possible the sampling designs you would use for each of the five strategies. Give reasons for your choice.

# chapter 12

# EXPERIMENTAL DESIGNS

## OUTLINE

INTRODUCTION TO EXPERIMENTAL DESIGNS
LABORATORY EXPERIMENTS
FIELD EXPERIMENTS
VALIDATION ISSUES
TYPES OF EXPERIMENTAL DESIGNS
SIMULATION
ETHICAL ISSUES IN EXPERIMENTAL RESEARCH
MANAGERIAL IMPLICATIONS
SUMMARY
DISCUSSION POINTS
APPENDIX: FURTHER EXPERIMENTAL DESIGNS

## CHAPTER OBJECTIVES

After reading this chapter, you should be able to:
- understand the role and scope of experimental research in business
- distinguish between causal and correlational analysis
- explain the difference between laboratory and field experiments
- explain the following terms: extraneous variables, manipulation, experimental and control groups, treatment effect, matching and randomisation
- discuss internal and external validity in experimental designs
- discuss the seven possible threats to internal validity in experimental designs
- describe the different types of experimental designs
- discuss the Solomon four-group design and its implications for internal validity
- explain the role of simulation in experimental research
- describe the ethical issues involved in experimental research
- apply what has been learned to class assignments.

This chapter, which examines experimental designs, incorporates aspects of both the research design and quantitative data collection stages of the business research process (see the shaded area of figure 12.1).

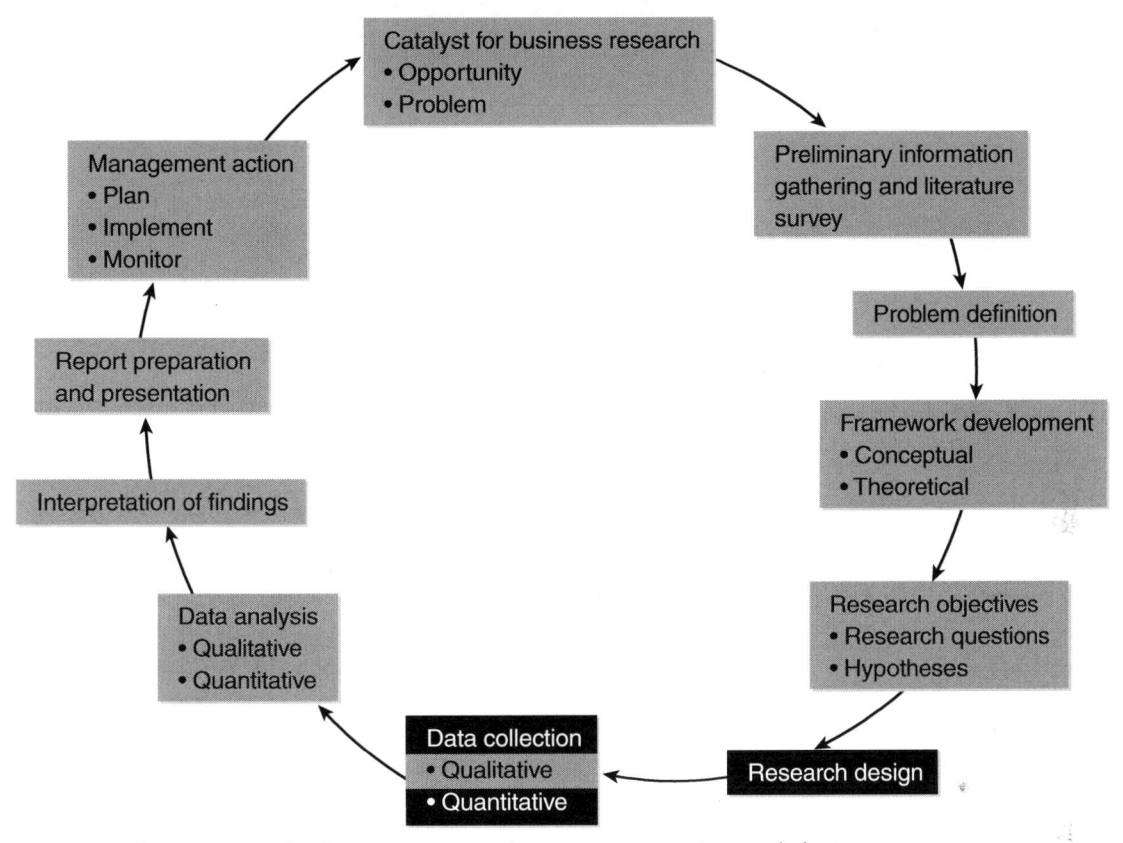

**Figure 12.1** The business research process: experimental designs

# INTRODUCTION TO EXPERIMENTAL DESIGNS

Consider the following two scenarios.

*Scenario A*

For some time now there has been the feeling that individual companies and the economy would be better served if executive compensation contracts were entered into that made the CEOs accountable for performance. Currently, the top executives are compensated irrespective of their performance, making them permanent corporate fixtures.

A change to the new mode is likely to annoy the CEOs, but it is definitely worth a try. How can we be sure that it would work?

*Scenario B*

A study of absenteeism and the steps taken to curb it indicates that companies use the following incentives to reduce it.
- 14 per cent give bonus days.
- 39 per cent offer cash.
- 39 per cent give out recognition awards.
- 4 per cent give prizes.
- 4 per cent pursue other strategies.

Asked about the effectiveness of offering incentives for reducing absenteeism, 22 per cent of the companies said they were very effective; 66 per cent said they were somewhat effective; and 12 per cent said they were not at all effective.

What does the preceding information tell us? How do we know what kinds of incentives *cause* people not to absent themselves? What particular incentive(s) were used by the 22 per cent of companies that found their strategies to be 'very effective'? Is there a direct causal connection between one or two specific incentives and absenteeism?

The answers to the questions raised in scenarios A and B might be found by using experimental designs in researching the issues.

In this chapter we will discuss both lab experiments and field experiments. We will also briefly discuss simulation experiments. Experimental designs, as we know, are set up to examine possible cause and effect relationships among variables, in contrast to correlational studies, which examine the relationships among variables without necessarily trying to establish if one variable causes another.

To establish that a change in variable X *causes* a change in variable Y, *all three* of the following conditions should be met.
1. Both X and Y should co-vary — that is, when one goes up, the other should also go up (or down).
2. The independent variable X (the presumed causal factor) should precede the dependent variable Y. In other words, there must be a time sequence in which the two occur.
3. No other factor should possibly cause the change in the dependent variable Y.

It may therefore be seen that to establish causal relationships between two variables in a business setting, several variables that might co-vary with the dependent variable have to be controlled. This would then allow us to say that changes in the independent variable X and variable X alone cause the changes in dependent variable Y. Useful as it is to know the cause and effect relationships, establishing them is not easy, because several other variables that co-vary with the dependent variable have to be controlled. It is not always possible to control all the co-variates while manipulating the causal factor (the independent variable that is causing the dependent variable) in business settings, where events flow or occur naturally and normally. It is, however, possible first to isolate the effects of a variable in a tightly controlled artificial setting (the lab setting), and after testing and establishing the cause and effect relationship under these tightly controlled conditions, see how generalisable such relationships are to the field setting.

Let us illustrate this with an example. Suppose a manager believes that staffing the corporate planning department completely with personnel with MBA (Master of Business Administration) degrees will increase its productivity; it is well nigh impossible to transfer all those without the MBA degree currently in the department to other departments and recruit fresh MBA degree holders to take their place. Such a course of action is bound to disrupt the work of the entire organisation inasmuch as many new people will have to be trained, work will slow down, employees will be upset, and so on. However, the hypothesis that possession of an MBA would *cause* increases in productivity can be tested in an artificially created setting (that is, not at the regular workplace) in which a business analysis and planning job can be given to three groups of people: those with an MBA, those without an MBA, and a mixed group of those with and without an MBA (as is the case in the present work setting). If the first group performs exceedingly well, the second group poorly and the third group falls somewhere in the middle, there will be evidence to indicate that the MBA degree qualification might indeed *cause* productivity to rise. If such evidence is found, then planned and systematic efforts can be made to gradually transfer those without the MBA in the corporate planning department to other departments and recruit others with such a degree to this department. It is then possible to see to what extent productivity does, in fact, go up in the department because all the staff members will be MBA degree holders.

Experimental research in business falls into two main categories: experiments done in an artificial or contrived environment, known as **lab experiments**, and those done in the natural environment in which activities regularly take place, known as **field experiments**. (We shall also briefly consider simulation experiments later in this chapter.)

## LABORATORY EXPERIMENTS

As stated earlier, when a cause and effect relationship between an independent and a dependent variable of interest is to be clearly established, then all other variables that might contaminate or confound the relationship have to be tightly controlled. In other words, the possible effects of other variables on the dependent variable have to be accounted for in some way, so that the actual causal effects of the investigated independent variable on the dependent variable can be determined. It is also necessary to manipulate the independent variable so that the extent of its causal effects can be established. The controls and manipulations are best done in an artificial setting — the laboratory — where the causal effects can be tested. When controls and manipulations are introduced to establish cause and effect relationships in an artificial setting, we have laboratory experimental designs, also known as lab experiments.

Because we use the terms *control* and *manipulation*, let us examine what these concepts mean. We shall also use other concepts relevant to lab experiments, including selecting subjects and internal and external validity.

## CONTROLLING THE EXTRANEOUS VARIABLES

When we postulate cause and effect relationships between two variables, X and Y, it is possible that some other factor, say A, might also influence the dependent variable Y. In such a case, it will not be possible to determine the extent to which Y occurred only because of X, and to what extent Y was additionally influenced by the presence of the other factor, A. Note that here we are not referring to an intervening or moderating variable (see chapter 4), as these would be included in the experiment. Factor A, as described here, is an extraneous variable that is totally outside our interest to investigate. This is illustrated diagrammatically as:

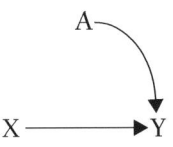

$$
\begin{array}{c}
A \\
\downarrow \\
X \longrightarrow Y
\end{array}
$$

A research design is needed that excludes factor A.

For instance, a human resource development manager might arrange for special training in creating web pages to a set of newly recruited personal assistants, to prove to the CEO (his boss) that such training would *cause* them to function more effectively. However, some of the new personal assistants might function more effectively than others, possibly because they have had previous intermittent experience with the Web. In this case, the manager cannot prove that the special training alone *caused* greater effectiveness, since the previous intermittent experience of some personal assistants with the Web is a contaminating factor, or extraneous variable. If the true effect of the training on learning is to be assessed, then the learners' previous experience has to be controlled. This might be done by *not* including in the experiment those who already have had some experience with the Web. This is what is meant by having to control the contaminating factor, or extraneous variables, and we will later see how this is done by a process of selecting and assigning subjects for the experiment.

## MANIPULATING THE INDEPENDENT VARIABLE

In order to examine the causal effects of an independent variable on a dependent variable, certain manipulations need to be tried. Manipulation simply means that we *create* different levels of the independent variable to assess the impact on the dependent variable. For example, we may want to test the theory that depth of knowledge of various manufacturing technologies is *caused* by rotating the employees on all the jobs on the production line and in the design department over a four-week period. Then we can *manipulate* the independent variable, 'rotation of employees', by rotating one group of production workers and exposing them to all the systems during the four-week period, rotating another group of workers only partially during the four weeks (that is, exposing them to only half of the manufacturing technologies), and leaving the third group to do what they are currently doing, without any special rotation. By measuring the depth of knowledge of these three groups both before and after the manipulation (or 'treatment'), it would be possible to assess the extent to which the treatment *caused* the effect, after controlling the contaminating factors or extraneous variables. If deep knowledge is indeed caused by rotation and exposure, the results would show that the third group had the lowest increase in depth of knowledge, the second group had some significant increase, and the first group had the greatest gains!

Let us look at another example on how causal relationships are established by manipulating the independent variable. Let us say we want to test the effects of lighting on worker production levels among sewing machine operators. To establish a cause and effect relationship, we must first measure the production levels of all the operators over a 15-day period with the usual amount of light they work with — say, 60-watt lamps. We might then want to split the group of 60 operators into three groups of 20 members each, and while allowing one subgroup to work under the same conditions as before (60-watt electric lightbulbs), we might want to manipulate the intensity of the light for the other two subgroups by making one group work with 75-watt and the other with 100-watt lightbulbs. After the different groups have worked with these varying degrees of light exposure for 15 days, each group's total production for these 15 days may be analysed to see if the difference between the pre-experimental and the post-experimental production among the groups is directly related to the intensity of the lighting to which they have been exposed. If our hypothesis that better lighting increases the production levels is correct, then the subgroup that had no change in the lighting (called the **control group**) should have no increase in production, and the two other groups should show increases, with the ones having the most light (100 watts) showing greater increases than those that had the 75-watt lighting.

In this case the independent variable, lighting, has been manipulated by exposing different groups to different degrees of changes in the lighting. This manipulation of the independent variable is also known as the **treatment**, and the results of the treatment are called *treatment effects*.

Let us illustrate how variable X can be both controlled and manipulated in the lab setting through example 12.1.

---

**EXAMPLE 12.1**

Let us say an entrepreneur — the owner of a toy shop — is somewhat disappointed with the number of imitation Tele Tubbies (greatly in demand) produced by his workers, who are paid at an hourly rate. He might wonder whether paying them piece rates would increase their production levels. However, before implementing the piece-rate system, he would want to make sure that switching over to the new system would indeed achieve the objective.

In a case like this, the researcher might first want to test the causal relationships in a lab setting, and if the results are encouraging, conduct the experiment later in a field setting. In designing the lab experiment, the researcher should first think of possible factors that would affect the production level of the workers, and then try to control these. Besides piece rates, previous job experience might also influence the rate of production because familiarity with the job makes it easy for people to increase their productivity levels.

---

In some cases, where the jobs are very strenuous and require muscular strength, gender differences may affect productivity. Let us say that for the type of production job discussed earlier, age, gender and prior experience of the employees are the factors that would influence the production levels of the employees. The researcher needs to control these three variables. Let us see how this can be done.

Suppose the researcher intends to set up four groups of 15 people each for the lab experiment — one to be used as the control group, and the other three subjected to three different pay manipulations (as in table 12.1). Now, the variables that may affect the cause and effect relationship can be controlled in two different ways — by selecting and assigning subjects to each group either by '**matching** the groups' or through '**randomisation**'. These concepts are explained before we proceed further.

## SELECTING AND ASSIGNING SUBJECTS

### Matching groups

One way of controlling the contaminating or extraneous variables is to match the various groups by taking the confounding characteristics and deliberately spreading them across groups. For instance, if there are 20 women among the 60 members, then each group will be assigned 5 women, so that the effects of gender are distributed across the four groups. Similarly, age and experience factors can be matched across the four groups, so that each group has a similar mix of individuals in terms of gender, age and experience. Because the suspected contaminating factors or extraneous variables are matched across the groups, we may take comfort in saying that variations in variable X alone cause variations in variable Y, if such is the result of the study. But here we are not sure that we have controlled *all* the extraneous factors, since we may not be aware of them all. A safer bet is to randomise.

### Randomisation

Another way of controlling the contaminating or extraneous variables is to assign the 60 members randomly (that is, with no predetermination) to the four groups. Every member would have a known and equal chance of being assigned to any of these four groups. For instance, we might throw the names of the 60 members into a hat, and draw their names. The first 15 names drawn may be assigned to the first group, the second 15 to the second group and so on, or the first person drawn might be assigned to the first group, the second person drawn to the second group and so on. Thus, in randomisation, the process by which individuals are drawn is random (that is, everyone has a known and equal chance of being drawn), and the assignment of the individual to any particular group is also random (each individual could be assigned to any one of the groups set up). By thus randomly assigning members to the groups we would be distributing the confounding variables among the groups equally. That is, the variables of age, gender and previous experience — the controlled variables — will have an equal probability of being distributed among the groups. The process of randomisation would ideally ensure that each group is comparable to the other, and that all variables, including the effects of age, gender and previous experience, are controlled. That is, each group will have some members who have more experience mingled with those who have less or no experience. All groups will have members of different age and gender composition. Thus, randomisation would ensure that if these variables do indeed have a contributory or confounding effect, we would have controlled their confounding effects (along with those of other unknown factors) by distributing them across groups. This is achieved because, when we manipulate the independent variable of piece rates by having no piece rate system whatsoever for one group (control) and having different piece rates for the other three groups (experimental), we can determine the causal effects of the piece rates on production levels. Any errors or biases caused by age, gender and previous experience are now distributed evenly among all four groups. Any causal effects found would be over and above the effects of the confounding or extraneous variables.

To make it clear, let us illustrate this with some actual figures, as in table 12.1. Note that because the effects of experience, gender and age have been controlled in all four groups in productivity, it can be safely concluded from the results that the percentage increases in production are a result of the piece rate (treatment effects). In other words, piece rates are the cause of the increase in the number of toys produced. We cannot now say that the cause and effect relations have been confounded by other extraneous variables, because they have been controlled through the process of randomly assigning members to the groups. Here, we have high *internal validity* or confidence in the cause and effect relationship.

**Table 12.1** Cause and effect relationship after randomisation

| Groups | Treatment | Treatment effect (% increase in production over pre–piece rate system) |
| --- | --- | --- |
| Experimental group 1 | $1.00 per piece | 10 |
| Experimental group 2 | $1.50 per piece | 15 |
| Experimental group 3 | $2.00 per piece | 20 |
| Control group (no treatment) | Old hourly rate | 0 |

## Differences between matching and randomisation

The difference between matching and randomisation is that in the former individuals are deliberately and consciously matched to control the differences among group members, whereas in the latter we expect that the process of randomisation will distribute the inequalities among the groups based on the laws of normal distribution. Thus, we need not be particularly concerned about any confounding factors.

Compared with randomisation, matching may be less effective, because we may not know all the extraneous factors that could possibly contaminate the cause and effect relationship in any given situation, and hence fail to match some critical factors across all groups while conducting an experiment. Randomisation, however, will take care of this, since all the known and unknown contaminating factors will be spread across all groups. Moreoever, even if we know the confounding variables, we may be unable to find a match for all such variables. For instance, if gender is a confounding variable, and if there are only two women in a four-group experimental design, we will not be able to match all the groups with respect to gender. Randomisation solves these dilemmas as well. Thus, lab experimental designs involve controlling the contaminating or extraneous variables through the process of either matching or randomisation, and the manipulation of the treatment.

# INTERNAL VALIDITY

Internal validity refers to the confidence we place in the cause and effect relationship. In other words, it addresses the question, 'To what extent does the research design permit us to say that independent variable A *causes* a change in dependent variable B?'. As Kidder and Judd (1986) note, in research with high internal validity, we are relatively better able to argue that the relationship is causal, whereas in studies with low internal validity, causality cannot be inferred at all. In lab experiments where cause and effect relationships are substantiated, internal validity can be said to be high.

So far we have talked about establishing cause and effect relationships within the laboratory setting, which is an artificially created and controlled environment. You may have been a subject taking part in one of the lab experiments conducted by the psychology or other departments on campus at some time. You may not have been told specifically what cause and effect relationships the experimenter was looking for, but you would have been told what is called a 'cover story'. That is, you would have been briefed in general terms on some reason for the study and your role in it, without its true purpose being divulged. After the end of the experiment you would also have been debriefed and given a full explanation of the experiment, and any questions you had would have been answered. This is how lab experiments are usually conducted: subjects are selected and assigned to different groups through matching or randomisation; they are moved to a lab setting; they are given some details of the study and a task to perform; and some kind of questionnaire or other tests are administered both before and after the task is completed. The results of these studies would indicate the cause and effect relationship between the variables under investigation.

# EXTERNAL RELIABILITY

To what extent would the results found in the lab setting be transferable or generalisable to the actual organisational or field settings? In other words, if we do find a cause and effect relationship after conducting a lab experiment, can we then say with confidence that the same cause and effect relationship will also hold true in the organisational setting?

Consider the following situation. If in a lab experimental design the groups are given the simple production task of screwing nuts and bolts onto a plastic frame, and the results indicate that the groups that were paid piece rates were more productive than those that were paid hourly rates, to what extent can we say that this would be true of the sophisticated nature of the jobs performed in organisations? The tasks in organisational settings are far more complex, and there may be several confounding or extraneous variables that cannot be controlled — for example experience. Under such circumstances, we cannot be sure that the cause and effect relationship found in the lab experiment is necessarily likely to hold true in the field setting. To test the causal relationships in the organisational or business setting, field experiments are done. These will now be briefly discussed.

## FIELD EXPERIMENTS

A field experiment, as the name implies, is an experiment done in the natural environment in which work goes on as usual, but treatments are given to one or more groups. Thus, in the field experiment, even though it might not be possible to control all the extraneous variables because members cannot be either randomly assigned to groups or matched, the treatment could still be manipulated. Control groups could also be set up in field experiments. The experimental and control groups in the field experiment could be made up of the people working at several plants within a certain radius, or from the different shifts in the same plant, or in some other way. If there are three different shifts in a production plant, for instance, and the effects of the piece-rate system are to be studied, one of the shifts could be used as the control group, and the two other shifts given two different treatments or the same treatment — that is, difference piece rates or the same piece rate. Any cause and effect relationship found under these conditions would have wider generalisability to other similar production settings, even though we might not be sure to what extent the piece rates alone were the cause of the increase in productivity, because some of the other confounding or extraneous variables could not be controlled.

## VALIDATION ISSUES

### VALIDATION COMPARISON: LAB AND FIELD EXPERIMENTS

What we have just discussed can be referred to as an issue of external validity versus internal validity. **External validity** refers to the extent of generalisability of the results of a causal study to other settings, people or events, and **internal validity** refers to the degree of our confidence in the causal effects (that is, that variable X causes variable Y). Field experiments have more external validity (the results are more generalisable to other similar organisational settings), but less internal validity (we cannot be certain of the extent to which changes in variable X alone cause changes in variable Y). Note that in the lab experiment, the reverse is true. The internal validity is high but the external validity is rather low. In other words, in lab experiments we can be sure that changes in variable X cause changes in variable Y because we have been able to keep the other confounding extraneous variables under control, but we have so tightly controlled several variables to establish the cause and effect relationship that we do not know to what extent the results of our study can be generalised, if at all, to field settings. In other words, since the lab setting does not reflect the 'real-world' setting, we do not know to what extent the lab findings validly represent the realities in the outside world.

# TRADE-OFF BETWEEN INTERNAL AND EXTERNAL VALIDITY

There is a trade-off between internal validity and external validity. If we want high internal validity, we should be willing to settle for lower external validity, and vice versa. To ensure both types of validity, researchers usually try first to test the causal relationships in a tightly controlled artificial or lab setting, and once the relationship has been established, they try to test the causal relationship in a field experiment. Lab experimental designs in the management area have thus far been done to assess such things as gender differences in leadership styles, managerial aptitudes and so on. However, gender differences and other factors found in the lab settings are frequently not found in field studies (Osborn & Vicars 1976). These problems of external validity usually limit the use of lab experiments in the management area. Field experiments are also seldom undertaken because of the resultant unintended consequences — personnel becoming suspicious, rivalries and jealousies being created among departments, and the like.

# FACTORS AFFECTING INTERNAL VALIDITY

Even the best-designed lab studies could be influenced by factors that might affect the internal validity of the lab experiment. That is, some confounding factors might still be present that could offer rival explanations of what is causing variations in the dependent variable. These possible confounding factors pose a *threat to internal validity*. The seven major threats to internal validity are the effects of *history, maturation, testing, instrumentation, selection, statistical regression* and *mortality*; these are explained below with examples.

## History effects

Certain events or factors that would have an impact on the independent variable–dependent variable relationship might unexpectedly occur while the experiment is in progress, and this history of events would confound the cause and effect relationship between the two variables, thus affecting the internal validity. For example, let us say that the manager of a Dairy Products Division wants to test the effects of the 'Buy one, get one free' sales promotion on the sale of the company-owned brand of packaged cheese for a week. She carefully records the sales of the packaged cheese during the preivous two weeks to assess the effect of the promotion. However, on the very day that her sales promotion goes into effect, the Dairy Farmers' Association unexpectedly launches a multimedia advertisement on the benefits of consuming dairy products, especially cheese. The sales of all dairy products, including cheese, increase in all the stores, including the one where the experiment was in progress. Here, because of the unexpected advertisement, one cannot be sure how much of the increase in sales of the packaged cheese in question was due to the sales promotion and how much it was due to the advertisement of the Dairy Farmers' Association! The effects of *history* have reduced the internal validity or the faith that can be attached to the conclusion that the sales promotion caused the increase in sales. The **history effects** in this case are illustrated in figure 12.2.

To give another example, let us say a bakery is studying the effects of adding to its bread a new ingredient that is expected to enrich it and offer more nutritional value to children under 14 years of age within 30 days, subject to a certain daily intake. At the start of the experiment the bakery takes a measure of the health of 30 children through some yardsticks. Thereafter, the children are given the prescribed daily intakes of bread. Unfortunately, on the twentieth day of the experiment, a flu virus hits the city in epidemic proportions, affecting most of the children studied. This unforeseen and uncontrollable effect of history, flu, has contaminated the cause and effect relationship study for the bakery.

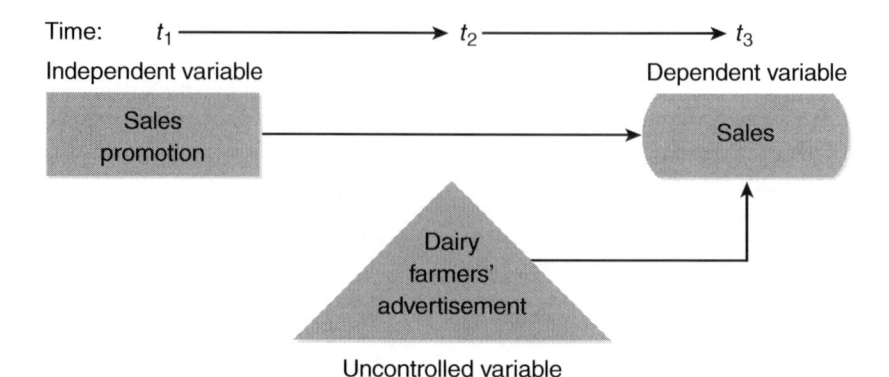

**Figure 12.2** History effects in experimental design

## Maturation effects

Cause and effect inferences can also be contaminated by the effects of the passage of time — another uncontrollable variable. Such contamination is called **maturation effects**. The maturation effects are a function of the processes — both biological and psychological — operating within the respondents as a result of the passage of time. Examples of maturation processes could include *growing older, getting tired, feeling hungry* and *getting bored*. In other words, there could be maturation effect on the dependent variable purely because of the passage of time. For instance, let us say that an R & D director contends that increases in the efficiency of workers would result within three months' time if advanced technology was introduced in the work setting. In other words, there could be a maturation effect on the dependent variable purely because of the passage of time. If at the end of the three months, increased efficiency is indeed found, it would be difficult to claim that the advanced technology (and it *alone*) increased the efficiency of workers, because with the passage of time, employees would also have gained experience, resulting in better job performance and therefore in improved efficiency. Thus, the internal validity is also reduced owing to the effects of maturation inasmuch as it is difficult to pinpoint how much of the increase is attributable to the introduction of the enhanced technology alone. Figure 12.3 illustrates the maturation effects in the preceding example.

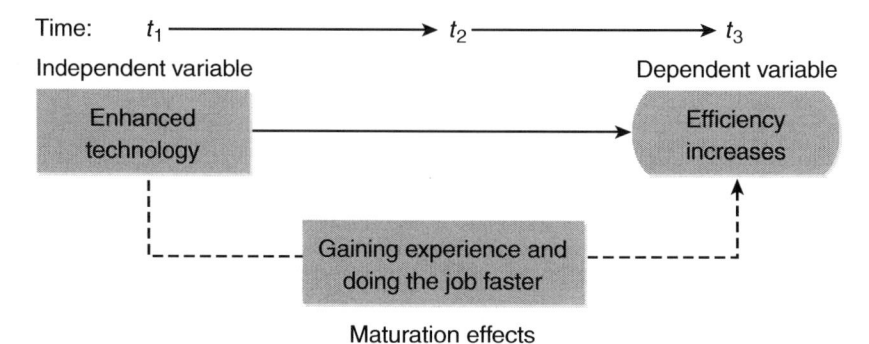

**Figure 12.3** Maturation effects on the cause and effect relationship

## Testing effects

Frequently, to test the effects of a treatment, subjects are given what is called a **pre-test** (for example, a short questionnaire eliciting their feelings and attitudes). That is, first a measure of the dependent variable is taken (the pre-test), then the treatment is given, and after that a second test, called the **post-test**, is administered. The difference between the post-test and the pre-test scores is then attributed to the treatment. However, the very fact that respondents were exposed to the pre-test might influence their responses on the post-test, which would adversely affect internal validity.

For example, if a challenging job is expected to cause increases in job satisfaction, and a pre-test on job satisfaction is administered asking for employees' level of satisfaction with their current jobs, it might sensitise people to the issue of job satisfaction. When a challenging job is introduced and a further job satisfaction questionnaire is administered subsequently, the respondents might now react and respond to the post-test with a different frame of reference than if they had not originally been sensitised to the issue of job satisfaction through the pre-test.

This kind of sensitisation through previous testing is called the testing effect, which also affects the internal validity of experimental designs. In the preceding case, although increases in job satisfaction can legitimately be measured through pre- and post-tests, the pre-test could confound the cause and effect relationship by sensitising the respondents to the post-test. Thus, testing effects are another threat to internal validity.

## Instrumentation effects

Instrumentation effects are another source of threat to internal validity. These effects might arise because of a change in the measuring instrument between pre-test and post-test, and not because of the treatment's differential impact at the end (Cook & Campbell 1979). For instance, an observer who is involved in observing a particular pattern of behaviours in respondents before a treatment might start concentrating on a different set of behaviours after the treatment. The frame of measurement of behaviours (in a sense, the measuring instrument) has now changed and will not reflect the change in behaviours that can be attributed to the treatment. This is also true in the case of physical measuring instruments like the spring balance or other finely calibrated instruments that might lose their accuracy owing to loss of tension with constant use, resulting in erroneous final measurement.

In organisations, instrumentation effects in experimental designs are possible when the pre-test is done by the experimenter, treatments are given to the **experimental groups** and the post-test on measures such as performance is done by different managers. One manager might measure performance by the final units of output, a second manager might assess performance taking into account the number of rejects as well, and a third manager might also take into consideration the amount of resources expended in getting the job done. Here, there are at least three different measuring instruments, if we treat each manager as a performance measuring instrument.

Thus, instrumentation effects also pose a threat to internal validity in experimental designs.

## Selection bias effects

The threat to internal validity could also come from improper or unmatched selection of subjects for the experimental and control groups. For example, if a lab experiment is set up to assess the impact of working environment on employees' attitudes towards work, and if one of the experimental conditions is to have a group of subjects work for about two hours in a room with some mild stench, an ethical researcher might disclose this condition to prospective subjects, who might decline to participate in the study. However, some volunteers might be lured through incentives (say, a payment of $70 for the two hours of participation in the study). The volunteers so selected may be quite different from the others (inasmuch as they may come from an environment of deprivation) and their responses to the treatment might be quite different. Such bias in the selection of the subjects might contaminate the cause and effect relationships and pose a threat to internal validity as well. Hence, newcomers, volunteers and others who cannot be matched with the control groups would pose a threat to internal validity in certain types of experiments.

## Statistical regression

Statistical regression occurs when the members chosen for the experimental group have extreme scores on the dependent variable to begin with. For instance, if a manager wants to test if he can increase the 'salesmanship' repertoire of the sales personnel through Dale Carnegie–type programs, he should not choose those with extremely low or extremely high abilities for the experiment. This is because we know from the laws of probability that those with very low scores on a variable (in this case, current sales abilities) have a greater probability of showing improvement and scoring closer to the mean on the post-test after being exposed to the treatment. This phenomenon of low scorers tending to score closer to the mean is known as 'regressing towards the mean' (statistical regression). Similarly, those with very high abilities would also have a greater tendency to regress towards the mean — they will score lower on the post-test than on the pre-test. Thus, those who are at either end of the continuum with respect to a variable would not 'truly' reflect the cause and effect relationship. The phenomenon of statistical regression is therefore yet another threat to internal validity.

## Mortality

Another confounding factor affecting the cause and effect relationship is the mortality or attrition of the members in the experimental or control group or both, as the experiment progresses. When the group composition changes over time across the groups, comparison between the groups becomes difficult, because those who have dropped out of the experiment may confound the results. Again, we would not be able to say how much of the effect observed arises from the treatment, and how much is attributable to the members who dropped out, since those who stayed with the experiment could be quite different from those who dropped out (see example 12.2).

---

**EXAMPLE 12.2**

A sales manager had heard glowing reports about three different programs that train salespersons in effective sales strategies. All three were of six weeks' duration. The manager was curious to know which one would offer the best results for the company. The first program took the trainees on daily field trips and demonstrated effective and ineffective sales strategies through practical experience. The second program trained groups on the same strategies but indoors in a classroom type of setting, lecturing, role playing and answering questions from the members. The third program used mathematical models and simulations to increase sales effectiveness.

The manager chose eight trainees each for the three different programs and sent them on training. By the end of the fourth week, three trainees from the first group, one from the second group, and two from the third group had dropped out of the training programs for a variety of reasons, including ill health, family exigencies, transportation problems and a car accident. This attrition from the various groups has now made it impossible to compare the effectiveness of the various programs.

Thus, mortality can also lower the internal validity of an experiment.

# SCENARIO CASE: IDENTIFYING THREATS TO INTERNAL VALIDITY

Let us examine each of the possible seven threats to internal validity in the context of the following scenario.

> A business consultant wanted to demonstrate to the CEO of a company, through an experimental design, that the democratic style of leadership best enhances the morale of employees. She set up three experimental groups and one control group for the purpose and assigned members to each of the groups randomly. The three experimental groups were headed by an autocratic leader, a democratic leader and a laissez-faire leader, respectively.
>
> The members in the three experimental groups were administered a pre-test. Since the control group was not exposed to any treatment, they were not given a pre-test. As the experiment progressed, two members in the 'democratic' treatment group became very excited and started moving around to the other members saying that the participative atmosphere was 'great' and 'performance was bound to be high in this group'. Two members from each of the 'autocratic' and 'laissez-faire' groups left after the first hour, saying they had to go and could no longer participate in the experiment. After two hours of activities, a post-test was administered to all the participants, including the control group members, on the same lines as the pre-test.

## History effects

The two members in the 'participative' group, by unexpectedly moving around in an excited manner and remarking that participative leadership is 'great' and the 'performance is bound to be high in this group', may have boosted the morale of all the members in the group. It would be difficult to separate out how much of the increase in morale was due to the 'participative' condition alone and how much to the sudden enthusiasm displayed by the two members.

## Maturation

It is doubtful that maturation will have any effects on morale in this situation, since the passage of time, in itself, may not be related to the increase or decrease in morale.

## Testing

The pre-tests are likely to have sensitised the respondents to the post-test. Thus, testing effects would exist. If, however, *all* the groups had been given both the pre- and the post-tests, the testing effects across all groups would have been taken care of (that is, nullified) and the post-tests of each of the experimental groups could have been compared with that of the control group to detect the effects of the treatment. Unfortunately, the control group was not given the pre-test, and thus this group's post-test scores were not biased by the pre-test — a phenomenon that could have occurred in the experimental groups. Hence, the experimental groups' scores cannot even be compared with those of the control group.

## Instrumentation

Because the same questionnaire has measured morale both before and after the treatment for all members, we do not expect instrumentation bias.

## Selection bias

Because members have been randomly assigned to all groups, we do not expect selection bias to exist.

## Statistical regression
Though not specifically stated, we can presume that all the members participating in the experiment were selected randomly from a normally distributed population, in which case the issue of statistical regression contaminating the experiment does not arise.

## Mortality
Because members dropped out of two experimental groups, the effects of mortality could affect internal validity.

In effect, three of the seven threats to internal validity do exist in this case. The history, testing and mortality effects are of concern, and hence the internal validity will not be high.

# INTERNAL VALIDITY IN CASE STUDIES
If there are several threats to internal validity even in a tightly controlled lab experiment, it should become quite clear why we cannot draw conclusions about causal relationships from case studies that describe the events that occurred during a particular time. Unless a well-designed experimental study that randomly assigns members to experimental and control groups, and successfully manipulates the treatment indicates possible causal relationships, it would be impossible to say which factor causes another to vary. For example, there are several causes attributed to the fact that Slice, the soft drink introduced by Pepsico Inc., did not take off after its initial success. Among the reasons given are (1) a cutback in advertisement for Slice, (2) operating on the mistaken premise that the juice content in Slice would appeal to health-conscious buyers, (3) Pepsico's attempts to milk the brand too quickly, (4) several strategic errors made by Pepsico and (5) underestimation of the time taken to build a brand. While all the above reasons could provide the basis for developing a theoretical framework for explaining the variance in the sales of a product such as Slice, conclusions about cause and effect relationships cannot be determined from anecdotal events.

# FACTORS AFFECTING EXTERNAL VALIDITY
Whereas internal validity raises questions about whether it is the treatment alone or some additional extraneous factor that causes the effects, external validity raises issues about the generalisability of the findings to other settings. For instance, the extent to which the experimental situation differs from the setting to which the findings are expected to be generalised is directly related to the degree of threat it poses to external validity. To illustrate, subjects in a lab experiment might be given a pre-test and a post-test. Those findings, however, cannot be generalised to the business world, where a pre-test is rarely administered to employees to be followed up by a post-test. Thus, the effects of the treatment will not be the same in the field, which reduces the external validity. Another threat is the selection of the subjects. In a lab setting, the types of subjects selected for the experiment could be very different from the types of employees recruited by the organisations. For example, students in a university might be given a task that could be manipulated to study the effects on their performance. The findings from this experiment cannot be generalised to the real world of work, however, where the employees and the nature of the jobs would both be quite different. Thus, subject selection and its interaction with the treatment would also pose a threat to external validity. These are just some of the factors that restrict generalisability. Maximum external validity can be obtained by ensuring that the lab experimental conditions are as close and compatible as possible to the

real-world situation. It is in this sense that field experiments have greater external validity than lab experiments. That is, the effects of the treatment can be generalised to other settings similar to the one in which the field experiment was conducted. We discussed generalisability as a function of sampling design in chapter 11.

## REVIEW OF FACTORS AFFECTING INTERNAL AND EXTERNAL VALIDITY

In summary, at least seven contaminating factors exist that might affect the internal validity of experimental designs. These are the effects of history, maturation, testing, instrumentation, selection, statistical regression and mortality. However, it is possible to reduce the biases by enhancing the level of sophistication of the experimental design. Whereas some of the more sophisticated designs, discussed below, would help increase the internal validity of the experimental results, they could also become expensive and time-consuming.

Threats to external validity can be combated by creating experimental conditions that are as close as possible to the situations to which the results of the experiment are to be generalised. For more extensive discussions on validity, see Cook and Campbell (1979).

The different *types* of experimental designs and the extent to which internal validity is met in each are discussed next.

## TYPES OF EXPERIMENTAL DESIGNS

Let us consider some of the commonly used experimental designs and determine the extent to which they guard against the seven factors that could contaminate the internal validity of experimental results. It is obvious that the shorter the time span of the experiments, the less the chances of encountering history, maturation and mortality effects. Experiments lasting an hour or two do not usually encounter many of these problems. It is only when experiments take place over an extended period (say, several months) that the possibility of encountering more of the confounding factors increases.

## QUASI-EXPERIMENTAL DESIGNS

Some studies expose an experimental group to a treatment and measure its effects. Such an experimental design is the weakest of all designs, and it does not measure the true cause and effect relationship. This is because there is no comparison between groups or any recording of the status of the dependent variable as it was prior to the experimental treatment and how it changed after the treatment. In the absence of such control, the study is of no scientific value in determining cause and effect relationships. Hence, such a design is referred to as a quasi-experimental design. The following two designs are quasi-experimental.

### Pre-test and post-test experimental group design

An experimental group (without a control group) may be given a pre-test, exposed to a treatment, and then given a post-test to measure the effects of the treatment. This can be illustrated as in table 12.2, where $O$ refers to some process of observation or measurement, $X$ represents the exposure of a group to an experimental treatment, and the $X$ and $O$s in the row are applied to the same specific persons. Here, the effects of the treatment can be obtained by measuring the difference between the post-test and the pre-test ($O_2 - O_1$). Note, however, that **testing** and **instrumentation effects** might contaminate the interval validity. If the experiment is extended over a period of time, history effects and maturation effects may also confound the results.

**Table 12.2** Pre-test and post-test experimental group design

| Group | Pre-test | Treatment | Post-test |
|---|---|---|---|
| Experimental group | $O_1$ | X | $O_2$ |

Treatment effect = $(O_2 - O_1)$

## Post-tests only with experimental and control groups

Some experimental designs are set up with an experimental and a control group, the former alone being exposed to a treatment and not the latter. The effects of the treatment are studied by assessing the difference in the outcomes — that is, the post-test scores of the experimental and control groups. This is illustrated in table 12.3. Here is a case where the testing effects have been avoided because there is no pre-test, only a post-test. Care has to be taken, however, to make sure that the two groups are matched for all the possible contaminating extraneous variables. Otherwise, the true effects of the treatment cannot be determined by merely looking at the difference in the post-test scores of the two groups. Randomisation would take care of this problem.

There are at least two possible threats to validity in this design. If the two groups are not matched or randomly assigned, *selection biases* could contaminate the results. That is, the differential recruitment of the persons making up the two groups would confound the cause and effect relationship. **Mortality** (the dropout of individuals from groups) can also confound the results, and thus pose a threat to internal validity.

**Table 12.3** Post-test only with experimental and control groups

| Group | Treatment | Outcome |
|---|---|---|
| Experimental group | X | $O_1$ |
| Control group |   | $O_2$ |

Treatment effect = $(O_1 - O_2)$

## TRUE EXPERIMENTAL DESIGNS

Experimental designs, which include both the treatment and control groups and record information both before and after the experimental group is exposed to the treatment, are known as *post facto* experimental designs. These are discussed below.

## Pre-test and post-test experimental and control group designs

This design can be visually depicted as in table 12.4. Two groups — one experimental and the other control — are both exposed to the pre-test and the post-test. The only difference between the two groups is that the former is exposed to a treatment whereas the latter is not. Measuring the difference between the differences in the post- and pre-test scores of the two groups would give the net effects of the treatment. Both groups have been exposed to both the pre- and post-tests, and both groups have been randomised; thus, we could expect that the history, maturation, testing and instrumentation effects have been controlled. This is because whatever happened with the experimental group (for example maturation, history, testing and instrumentation) also happened with the control group, and in measuring the net effects (the difference in the differences between the pre- and post-test scores) we have controlled these contaminating factors. Through the process of randomisation, we have also controlled the effects of selection biases and statistical regression. Mortality could, however, pose a problem in this design. In experiments that take several weeks, as in the case of assessing the impact of training on skill development, or measuring the impact of technology advancement on effectiveness, some of the subjects in the experimental group may drop out before the end of the experiment. It is possible that those who drop out are in some way different from those who stay on until the end and take the post-test. If so, mortality could offer a plausible rival explanation for the difference between $O_2$ and $O_1$.

**Table 12.4** Pre-test and post-test experimental and control groups

| Group | Pre-test | Treatment | Post-test |
|---|---|---|---|
| Experimental group | $O_1$ | X | $O_2$ |
| Control group | $O_3$ | | $O_4$ |

Treatment effect = $[(O_2 - O_1) - (O_4 - O_3)]$

## SOLOMON FOUR-GROUP DESIGN

To gain more confidence in internal validity in experimental designs, it is advisable to set up two experimental groups and two control groups for the experiment. One experimental group and one control group can be given both the pre-test and the post-test, as shown in table 12.5. The other two groups will be given only the post-test. Here the effects of the treatment can be calculated in several different ways, as indicated in the figure. To the extent that we come up with almost the same results in each of the different calculations, we can attribute the effects to the treatment. This increases the internal validity of the results of the experimental design. This design, known as the **Solomon four-group design**, is probably the most comprehensive and the one with the least problems with internal validity.

**Table 12.5** Solomon four-group design

| Group | Pre-test | Treatment | Post-test |
|---|---|---|---|
| 1. Experimental | $O_1$ | X | $O_2$ |
| 2. Control | $O_3$ | | $O_4$ |
| 3. Experimental | | X | $O_5$ |
| 4. Control | | | $O_6$ |

Treatment effect (E) could be judged by:
$E_1 = (O_2 - O_1)$
$E_2 = (O_2 - O_4)$
$E_3 = (O_5 - O_6)$
$E_4 = (O_5 - O_3)$
$E_5 = (O_2 - O_1) - (O_4 - O_3)$
If all Es are similar, the cause and effect relationship is highly valid.

## Solomon four-group design and threats to internal validity

Let us examine how the threats to internal validity are taken care of in the Solomon four-group design. It is important to note that subjects have been randomly selected and randomly assigned to groups. This removes the **statistical regression** and selection biases. Group 2, the control group that was exposed to both the pre- and post-test, helps us to see whether or not history, maturation, testing, instrumentation, regression or mortality threats to validity exist. If scores $O_3$ and $O_4$ (pre- and post-test scores of group 2) remain the same, then it is established that neither history, nor maturation, nor testing, nor instrumentation, nor statistical regression, nor mortality has had an impact.

Group 3, the experimental group that was not given a pre-test, helps to establish whether or not testing effects have affected internal validity in a given experiment. The difference, if any, between $O_2$ (the post-test score of group 1, which was exposed to a treatment and also took a pre-test) and $O_5$ (the post-test score of group 3, which was exposed to a treatment but did not take the pre-test) can be attributed to the testing effects. If, however, $O_2$ and $O_5$ are equal, then internal validity has not been thwarted by testing effects.

Group 4 (which has only the post-test score, without pre-test and without having been exposed to any treatment) helps us to see whether or not changes in the post-test scores for our experimental group are a function of the combined effects of history and maturation by comparing $O_6$ (the post-test score of the control group without the pre-test) with $O_1$ (the pre-test score of the experimental group that was exposed to a pre-test) and $O_3$ (the pre-test score of the control group that was exposed to a pre-test as well). If all three scores are similar, maturation and history effects have not been a problem.

Thus, the Solomon four-group experimental design ensures the maximum internal validity, ruling out many other rival hypotheses. Where establishing cause and effect relationships is critical for the survival of businesses — for example for pharmaceutical companies, which often face lawsuits for questionable products — the Solomon four-group design is extremely useful. However, because of the number of subjects that need to be recruited, the care with which the study has to be designed, the time that needs to be devoted to the experiment, and other reasons, the cost of conducting such an experiment is high. The experimental set-up shown in table 12.3, with one experimental and one control group, exposing both to the post-test only, is a viable alternative because it has many of the advantages of the Solomon four-group design and requires only half the number of subjects.

Table 12.6 summarises the threats to internal validity covered by the different experimental designs. If the subjects have all been randomly assigned to the groups, then selection biases and statistical regression are avoided in all cases.

**Table 12.6** Major threats to internal validity in different experimental designs (when members are randomly selected and assigned)

| Types of experimental designs | Major threats to internal validity |
| --- | --- |
| 1. Pre-test and post-test with one experimental group only | Testing, history, maturation |
| 2. Post-tests only with one experimental and one control group | Maturation |
| 3. Pre-test and post-test with one experimental and one control group | Mortality |
| 4. Solomon four-group design | Mortality |

## DOUBLE-BLIND STUDIES

When extreme care and rigour are needed in experimental designs, as in the case of discovery of new medicines which could affect human lives, blind studies are conducted to avoid any bias that might creep in. For example, pharmaceutical companies experimenting with the efficacy of newly developed drugs in the prototype stage ensure that the subjects in the experimental and control groups are not made aware of who are given the drug and who the placebo. Such studies are called blind studies.

When Aviron tested and announced the Flu-mist vaccine, neither the subjects nor the researchers who administered the vaccine to them were aware of the 'true' versus the 'placebo' treatment. The entire process was conducted by an outside testing agency, which alone knew who got what treatment. Since both the experimenter and the subjects are blinded, such studies are called **double-blind studies**. Since there is no tampering with the treatment in any way, such experimental studies are the least biased.

Managers rarely undertake the study of cause and effect relationships in organisations using experimental designs because of the inconveniences and disruptions they cause to the system.

## EX POST FACTO DESIGNS

Cause and effect relationships are sometimes established through what is called the **ex post facto design**. Here, there is no manipulation of the independent variable in the lab or field setting, but subjects who have already been exposed to a stimulus and those not so exposed are studied. For example, training programs might have been introduced in an organisation two years earlier. Some might already have gone through the training, whereas others might not. To study the effects of training on work performance, performance data might now be collected for both groups. Since the study is not conducted immediately after the training, but much later, it is an ex post facto design.

More advanced experimental designs such as the completely randomised design, the randomised block design, the Latin square design and the factorial design are described for the interested student in the appendix to this chapter.

## SIMULATION

An alternative to lab and field experimentation currently being used in business research is simulation. Simulation uses a model-building technique to determine the effects of changes, and computer-based simulations are becoming popular in business research. A simulation can be thought of as an experiment conducted in a specially created setting that resembles the natural environment in which activities are usually carried out. In that sense, the simulation lies somewhere between a lab and a field experiment, insofar as the environment is artificially created but not very different from 'reality'. Participants are exposed to real-world experiences over a period of time lasting anywhere from several hours to several weeks, and they can be randomly assigned to different treatment groups. If managerial behaviour as a function of a specific treatment is to be studied, subjects will be asked to operate in an environment very much like an office, with desks, chairs, cabinets, telephones and so on. Members will be randomly assigned the roles of managers, directors, clerks and so on, and specific stimuli will be presented to them. Thus, the researcher would retain control over the assignment and manipulation, but the subjects would be free to operate as in a real office. In essence, some factors will be built into or incorporated in the simulated system and others left free to vary (participants' behaviours, within the rules of the game). Data on the dependent variable can be obtained through observation, videotaping, audio recording, interviews or questionnaires.

Causal relationships can be tested because both manipulation and control are possible in simulations. Two types of simulations can be carried out: one (called experimental simulation) in which the nature and timing of simulated events are totally determined by the researcher and the other (called free simulation) in which the course of activities is at least partly governed by the participants' reactions to the various stimuli as they interact among themselves. Looking Glass, the free simulation developed by Lombardo, McCall and DeVries (1983) to study leadership styles, has been quite popular in the management area.

Cause and effect relationships are better established in experimental simulations, where the researcher exercises greater control. In simulations involving several weeks, however, there can be a high rate of attrition of members. Experimental and free simulations are both expensive, since creating real-world conditions in an artificial setting and collecting data over extended periods of time involve the deployment of many types of resources. Simulations can be done in specially created settings using subjects, with computers and mathematical models. Steufert, Pogash and Piasecki (1988), who assessed managerial competence through a six-hour computer-assisted simulation, believe that simulation technology may be the only viable method to simultaneously study several types of executive styles. Computer-based simulations are frequently used in the business area. For example, the effectiveness of various analytic review procedures in detecting errors in account balances has been tested through simulations (Knechel 1986). In the finance area, risk management has been studied through simulations. Simulations have also been used to understand the complex relationships in the financing of pension plans in the US and for making important investment decisions (Perrier & Kalwarski 1989). It is possible to vary several variables (work force demographics, inflation rates and so on) singly or simultaneously in such models.

An illustration of computer simulation for experimentation is provided in figure 12.5. The model is used as a vehicle for experimentation, often by 'trial and error', to demonstrate the likely effects of various policies. Thus, those that produce the best results in the model would be implemented in the real system (Pidd 1992:5).

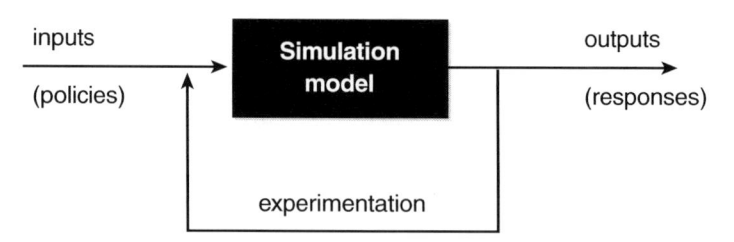

**Figure 12.4** Simulation as experimentation

**Source:** Pidd (1992:5).

Prototypes of machines and instruments are often the result of simulated models. Simulation has been used by many companies to test the robustness and efficacy of various products. We are also familiar with flight simulators, driving simulators and even nuclear reactor simulators. Here, the visual patterns presented keep changing in response to the reactions of the individual (the pilot, the driver or the emergency handler) to the previous stimulus presented, and not in any predetermined order. Entire business operations, from office layout to profitability, can be simulated using different prospective scenarios. An illustration of a management flight simulator for analysing quality management decisions is provided in figure 12.5. This has been developed using the system dynamics approach to computer simulation. (Forrester 1961; Coyle 1996; Maani & Cavana 2000; Sterman 2000).

With increasing access to sophisticated PC technology, and advances in mathematical models, simulation is becoming an important managerial decision-making tool. Simulation is now being used as a managerial tool to enhance motivation, leadership and the like. Simulation can also be applied as a problem-solving managerial tool in other behavioural and administrative areas. Programmed, computer-based simulation models in behavioural areas are likely to become more effective in managerial decision making.

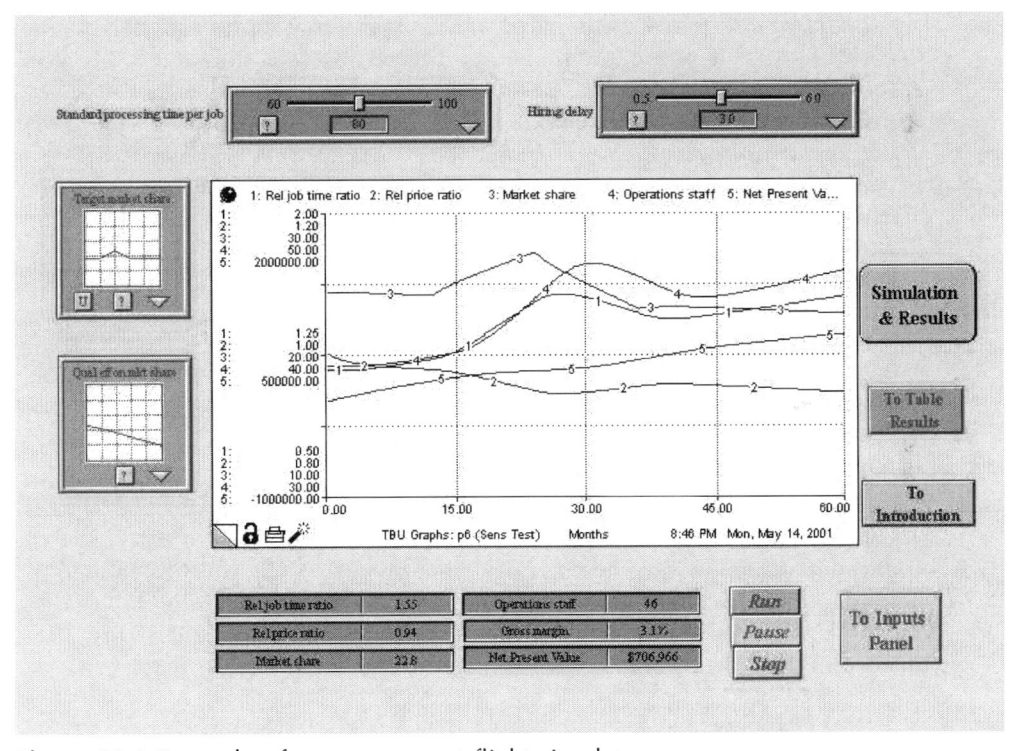

**Figure 12.5** Example of a management flight simulator

**Source:** Maani and Cavana (2000:116).

# ETHICAL ISSUES IN EXPERIMENTAL RESEARCH

It is appropriate at this point to briefly discuss a few of the many ethical issues involved in doing research, some of which are particularly relevant for conducting lab experiments. The following practices are considered *unethical*:
- pressuring individuals to participate in experiments through coercion or applying social pressure

- giving out menial tasks and asking demeaning questions that diminish the subject's self-respect
- deceiving subjects by deliberately misleading them as to the true purpose of the research
- exposing participants to physical or mental stress
- not allowing subjects to withdraw from the research when they want to
- using the research results to disadvantage the participants, or for purposes that they would not like
- not explaining the procedures to be followed in the experiment
- exposing respondents to hazardous and unsafe environments
- not debriefing participants fully and accurately after the experiment is over
- not preserving the confidentiality of the information given by the participants
- withholding benefits from control groups.

There is some controversy over whether the last item should be considered an ethical dilemma, especially in business research. If three different incentives are offered for three experimental groups and none is offered to the control group, then the control group has participated in the experiment with absolutely no benefit. Similarly, if four different experimental groups receive four different levels of training but the control group does not, the other four groups have gained expertise that the control group has been denied. But is this an ethical dilemma *preventing* experimental designs with control groups in business research? Perhaps not, for at least three reasons. One is that several others in the system who did not participate in the experiment also did not benefit. Second, even in the experimental groups, some would have benefited more than the others (depending on the extent to which the causal factor is manipulated). Finally, if a cause and effect relationship is found, the system will in all probability implement the new-found knowledge sooner or later, and everyone will ultimately stand to gain. The assumption that the control group did not benefit from participating in the experiment may not be a sufficient reason not to use lab or field experiments.

Many universities and polytechnics have a 'human ethics committee' to protect the rights of those participating in any type of research activity involving people. The basic function of these committees is to discharge the moral and ethical responsibilities of the university system by studying the procedures outlined in the research proposals and giving their stamp of approval to the studies if appropriate. The human ethics committee might require the investigators to modify their procedures or inform the subjects fully.

## MANAGERIAL IMPLICATIONS

Before using experimental designs in research studies, it is essential to consider whether they are necessary at all, and if so, at what level of sophistication. This is because experimental designs call for special efforts and varying degrees of interference with the natural flow of activities. Below are some questions that need to be addressed in making these decisions.

1. Is it necessary to identify causal relationships, or would it suffice if the correlates that account for the variance were identified?
2. If it is important to trace the causal relationships, is there a greater need for internal validity or external validity, or are both needed? If internal validity alone is important, a carefully designed lab experiment would be required; if generalisability is the more important criterion, then a field experiment would be called

for; if both are equally important, then first a lab study should be undertaken, followed by a field experiment — if the results of the former warrant the latter.
3. Is cost an important factor in the study? If so, would a less sophisticated rather than a more sophisticated experimental design suffice?

These decision points are illustrated in the chart in figure 12.6.

Though many managers may not be interested in cause and effect relationships, a good knowledge of experimental designs could encourage some pilot studies to be undertaken to determine whether factors like bonus systems, piece rates and rest pauses lead to positive outcomes such as better motivation and job performance and other favourable results at the workplace. Marketing managers would be able to use experimental designs to study the effects on sales of advertisements, sales promotions, pricing and the like. Awareness of the usefulness of simulation as a research tool can also result in creative research endeavours in the management area, as it currently does in the manufacturing side of businesses.

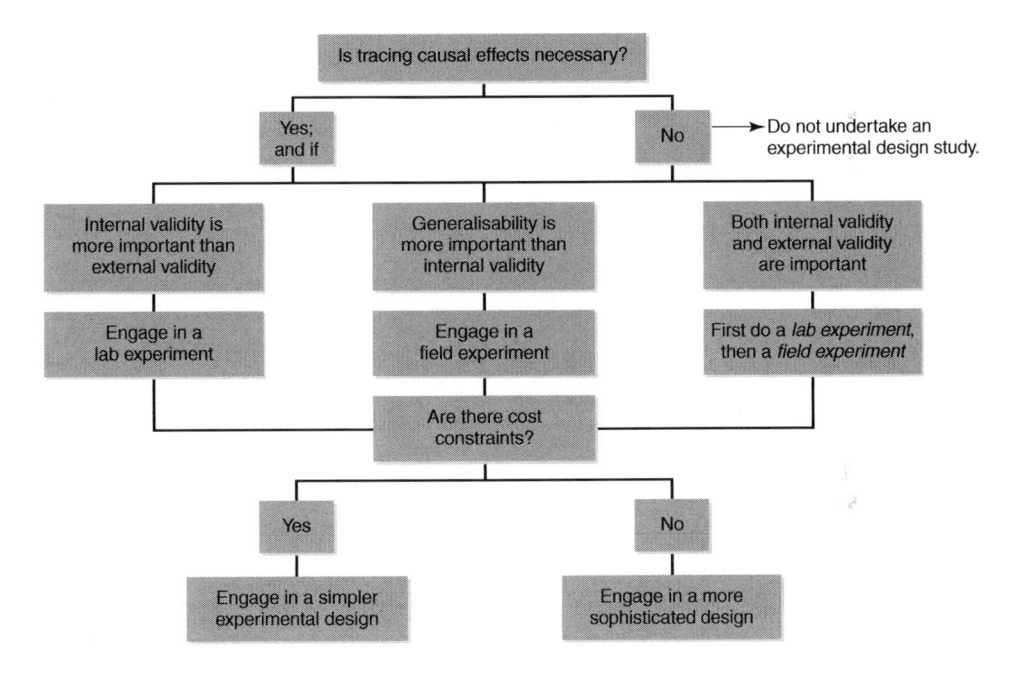

**Figure 12.6** Decision points for embarking on an experimental design

# SUMMARY

This chapter has covered experimental designs with particular reference to laboratory and field experiments. We examined how the contaminating variables in detecting the cause and effect relationship can be controlled through the processes of matching and randomisation. Issues of internal and external validity and the seven factors that could affect internal validity were discussed. Also, some types of experimental designs that can be used to test cause and effect relationships and their usefulness in the context of validity and practicality were examined. Simulation, as an alternative to lab and field experiments, was also briefly discussed. Finally, we described the ethical issues involved in conducting experimental research and the implications for managers in using experimental designs.

## DISCUSSION POINTS

1. What are the differences between causal and correlational studies?
2. In what ways do lab experiments differ from field experiments?
3. Define the terms *control* and *manipulation*. Describe a possible lab experiment in which you would need to control a variable. Further, include a possible variable over which you would have no control but which could affect your experiment.
4. Explain the possible ways in which you can control extraneous variables.
5. What is internal validity and what are the threats to internal validity?
6. Explain the concept of 'trade-off between internal validity and external validity'.
7. Explain fully how you would demonstrate to machine operators and convince them that thorough knowledge of the operating policies and procedures (by reading the manual) will eliminate almost all on-the-job accidents.
8. 'If a control group is a part of an experimental design, one need not worry about controlling other extraneous variables.' Discuss this statement.
9. A researcher wants to set up a lab experiment to test the effects of different kinds of leadership styles on followers' attitudes. The three particular kinds of leadership style she is interested in testing are autocratic, democratic and participative. You are asked to enlist some students to play the part of followers. What cover story would you give the participants?
10. 'Because the external validity of lab experiments is not usually high, they are useless for investigating cause and effect relationships in organisations.' Comment on this statement.
11. 'Co-variance (that is, two variables varying together either positively or negatively) and control are integral aspects of experimental designs.' Discuss.
12. 'The Solomon four-group design is the answer to all our research questions pertaining to cause and effect relationships because it guards against all the threats to internal validity.' Comment on this statement.
13. Discuss the role of simulation, as an alternative form of experimental research, compared with laboratory and field experiments.
14. Below is a note on self-esteem. After reading it, apply what you have learned in this chapter and design a study after sketching the theoretical framework.

---

**The role of self-esteem in efficacy**

One often wonders why some people earn more than others. Economists focused on the importance of education, basic skills and work experience — what they called human capital — on increased productivity, reflected in greater earning power. Researchers found that self-esteem was also instrumental in acquiring human capital.

# APPENDIX

## FURTHER EXPERIMENTAL DESIGNS

In this chapter we discussed different types of experimental designs in which groups were subjected to one or more treatments and the effects of the manipulation were measured. However, the simultaneous effects of two or more variables on a dependent variable may sometimes need to be assessed, which would call for more complex designs. Among the many advanced experimental designs that are available, we will examine here the completely randomised design, the randomised block design, the Latin square design and the factorial design.

It would be useful to understand some terms before describing the various designs. The term *factor* is used to denote an independent variable — for example, price. The term *level* is used to denote various gradations of the factor — for example high price, medium price or low price — while making it clear what these gradations signify (for example, high price is anything over $2 per piece; medium is $1–$2 per piece; low price is anything less than $1 per piece). *Treatment* refers to the various levels of the factors. A *blocking factor* (or extraneous variable) is a pre-existing variable in a given situation that might have an effect on the dependent variable in addition to the treatment, the impact of which would be important to assess. In effect, a blocking factor is an independent variable that has an effect on the dependent variable, but that already exists in a given situation — for example the number of women and men in an organisation; or teenagers, middle-aged men, and senior citizens as customers of a store.

## THE COMPLETELY RANDOMISED DESIGN

Let us say that a bus transportation company manager wants to know the effects of a fare reduction by 5 cents, 7 cents and 10 cents on the average daily increase in the number of passengers using the bus as a means of transportation. He may take 27 routes that the buses usually ply, and randomly assign nine routes for each of the treatments (that is, a reduction of fares by 5, 7 and 10 cents) for a two-week period. His experimental design would be as shown in table 12.7, where the Os on the left indicate the number of passengers that used the bus for the two weeks preceding the treatment; $X_1$, $X_2$ and $X_3$ indicate the three different treatments (fare reductions of 5c, 7c and 10c per mile), and the Os on the right indicate the number of passengers that used the bus as the transportation mode during the two weeks when the fares were reduced. The manager will be able to assess the impact of the three treatments by deducting each of the three Os on the left from its corresponding O to the right. The results of this study would provide the answer to the bus company manager's question.

**Table 12.7** A completely randomised design

| Routes | Number of passengers before | Treatment | Number of passengers after |
|---|---|---|---|
| Group 1 of nine routes | $O_1$ | $X_1$ | $O_2$ |
| Group 2 of nine routes | $O_3$ | $X_2$ | $O_4$ |
| Group 3 of nine routes | $O_5$ | $X_3$ | $O_6$ |

# RANDOMISED BLOCK DESIGN

In the previous case the bus company manager was simply interested in the effects of different levels of price reduction on the increase in the number of passengers in general. However, he may be more interested in targeting the price reduction on specific routes or sectors. For example, it is possible that the reduction in fares will be more valuable to senior citizens and to individuals living in crowded urban areas, where driving is stressful, than to car owners living in the suburbs, who may not be equally sensitive to price reduction. Thus, reduction in fares would attract more passengers if targeted to the right groups (that is, the right blocking factor — the residential areas). In this case, the bus company manager would first segregate the routes according to the three blocks — whether they are in suburbs, crowded urban areas or retirement areas. Thus, the 27 routes would be assigned to one of three blocks and then randomly assigned, within blocks, to the three treatments. The experimental design would now resemble table 12.8.

Through the above randomised block design, not only can the direct effect of each treatment (that is, the main effect of the level, which is the effect of each type of fare reduction) be assessed, but so, too, can the joint effects of price and the residential area route (the interaction effect). For example, the general effect of a 5-cent reduction for all routes will be known by the increase in passengers across all three residential areas, and the general effect of a 5-cent reduction on those in the suburbs alone will also be known by seeing the effects in the first cell. If the highest average daily number of increased passengers is 75 for a 7-cent decrease for the crowded urban area route, followed by an increase of 30 for the retirement areas for the 10-cent decrease, and an increase of five passengers for a 5-cent reduction for the suburbs, the bus company manager can work out a cost–benefit analysis and decide on the course of action to be taken. Thus, the randomised block design is a more powerful technique, providing more information for decision making. However, the costs of this experimental design will be higher.

**Table 12.8** A randomised block design

| Fare reduction | Blocking factor: residential areas | | |
|---|---|---|---|
| | Suburbs | Crowded urban areas | Retirement areas |
| 5c | $X_1$ | $X_1$ | $X_1$ |
| 7c | $X_2$ | $X_2$ | $X_2$ |
| 10c | $X_3$ | $X_3$ | $X_3$ |

Note that the Xs above indicate only various levels of the blocking factor, and the Os (the number of passengers before and after each treatment at each level) are not shown, although these measures will be taken.

# LATIN SQUARE DESIGN

Whereas the randomised block design helps the experimenter to minimise the effects of one extraneous variable (variation among the rows) in evaluating the treatment effects, the Latin square design is very useful when two extraneous blocking factors (that is, variations across both the rows and the columns) are to be controlled. Each treatment appears an equal number of times in any one ordinal position in each row. For instance, in studying the effects of bus fare reduction on passengers, two extraneous blocking factors could be (1) the day of the week: (a) midweek (Tuesday through Thursday), (b) weekend, and (c) Monday and Friday; and (2) the (three) residential localities of the passengers. A three by three Latin square design can be created in this case, to which will be randomly assigned the three treatments (5c, 7c and 10c fare reduction), so that each treatment occurs only once in each row and column intersection. The Latin square design would resemble table 12.9. After the experiment is carried out and the net increase in passengers under each treatment calculated, the average treatment effects can be gauged. The price reduction that offers the best advantage can also be assessed.

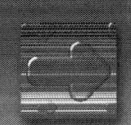

A problem with the Latin square design is that it presupposes the absence of interaction between the treatments and blocking factors, which may not always be the case. We also need as many cells as there are treatments. Furthermore, it is an uneconomical design compared with some others.

**Table 12.9** The Latin square design

| Residential area | Day of the week | | |
|---|---|---|---|
| | Midweek | Weekend | Monday/Friday |
| Suburbs | $X_1$ | $X_2$ | $X_3$ |
| Urban | $X_2$ | $X_3$ | $X_1$ |
| Retirement | $X_3$ | $X_1$ | $X_2$ |

## FACTORIAL DESIGN

Thus far we have discussed experimental designs in the context of examining a cause and effect relationship between one independent variable and the dependent variable. The factorial design enables us to test the effects of *two or more manipulations* at the same time on the dependent variable. In other words, two treatments can be simultaneously manipulated and their single and joint (known as main and interaction) effects assessed. For example, the manager of the bus company might be interested in knowing passenger increases if he used three different types of buses (Luxury Express, Standard Express, Regular) and simultaneously manipulated both the fare reduction and the type of vehicle used. Table 12.10 illustrates the 3 × 3 factorial design that will be used for the purpose.

Here, two factors are used with three levels of each. The design is completely randomised, since the fares are randomly assigned to one of nine treatment combinations. A wealth of information can be obtained from this design. For example, the bus company manager would know the increase in passengers for each fare reduction, for each type of vehicle and for the two in combination. Thus, the main effects of the two independent variables as well as the interactions among them can be assessed. For this reason, the factorial design is more efficient than several single-factor randomised designs.

It is also statistically possible to control one or more variables through *co-variance analysis*. For example, it may be suspected that even after randomly assigning members to treatments, there is a further extraneous blocking factor. It is possible to statistically block such factors while analysing the data.

Several other complex experimental designs are also available and are treated in books devoted to experimental designs.

**Table 12.10** A 3 × 3 factorial design

| Type of bus | Bus fare reduction rates | | |
| --- | --- | --- | --- |
| | 5c | 7c | 10c |
| Luxury Express | $X_1Y_1$ | $X_2Y_1$ | $X_3Y_1$ |
| Standard Express | $X_2Y_2$ | $X_1Y_2$ | $X_3Y_2$ |
| Regular | $X_3Y_3$ | $X_2Y_3$ | $X_1Y_3$ |

# chapter 13

# QUANTITATIVE DATA ANALYSIS AND INTERPRETATION

## OUTLINE

GETTING DATA READY FOR ANALYSIS

DATA ANALYSIS

GETTING A FEEL FOR THE DATA

TESTING GOODNESS OF DATA

HYPOTHESIS TESTING

CASE: RESEARCH DONE IN WOLLONGONG ENTERPRISES

USE OF EXPERT SYSTEMS

SUMMARY

DISCUSSION POINTS

APPENDIX: DATA ANALYSIS USING EXCEL

## CHAPTER OBJECTIVES

After completing this chapter, you should be able to:
- edit questionnaire and interview responses
- handle blank responses
- set up the coding key for the data set and code the data
- categorise data
- create a data file
- use SPSS, Excel or other software programs for data entry and data analysis
- get a 'feel' for the data
- test the goodness of data
- statistically test each hypothesis
- interpret the computer results and prepare recommendations based on the quantitative data analysis.

After data have been collected from a representative sample of the population, the next step is to analyse them to test the research hypotheses or answer specific research questions. Data analysis is now routinely managed with PC software programs such as SPSS, SAS, STATPAK, SYSTAT or Excel. All are user-friendly and interactive, and have the capability to interface seamlessly with different databases. Excellent graphs and charts can also be produced by most of these software programs. Some of the charts generated by Excel's Chart Wizard may be seen in the next chapter.

The activities in the research process identified as quantitative data analysis and interpretation are illustrated by the shaded boxes in figure 13.1.

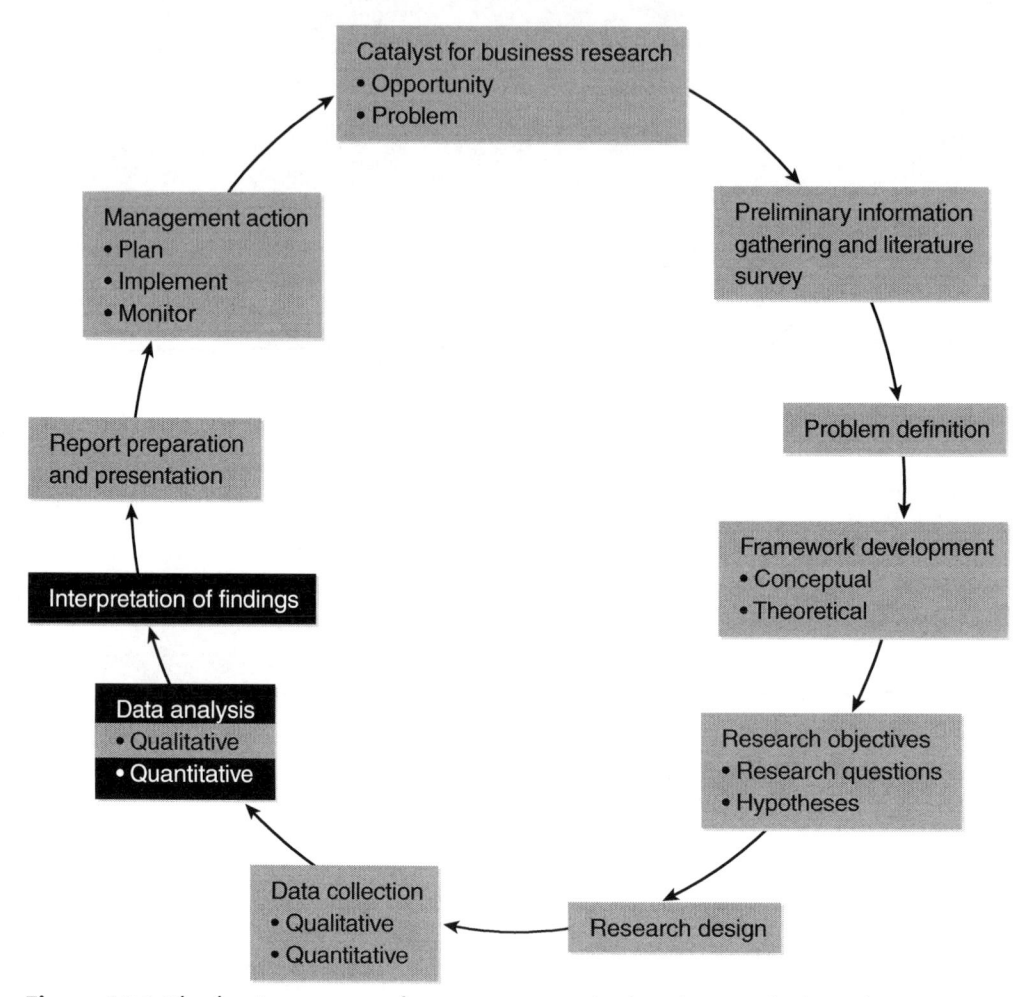

**Figure 13.1** The business research process: quantitative data analysis and interpretation

Before we start analysing the data and testing hypotheses, however, some preliminary steps need to be completed. These steps help to prepare the data for analysis, ensuring that the data obtained are reasonably good. Figure 13.2 identifies the four steps in quantitative data analysis: (1) getting data ready for analysis, (2) getting a feel for the data, (3) testing the goodness of data and (4) testing the hypotheses. We will now examine each of these steps.

# GETTING DATA READY FOR ANALYSIS

After data have been obtained through questionnaires, interviews, observation or secondary sources, they need to be edited. The blank responses, if any, have to be handled in some way; the data then have to be coded, and a categorisation scheme has to be set up. The data will then have to be keyed in, and a software program used to analyse the data. Each of these stages of data preparation will now be discussed.

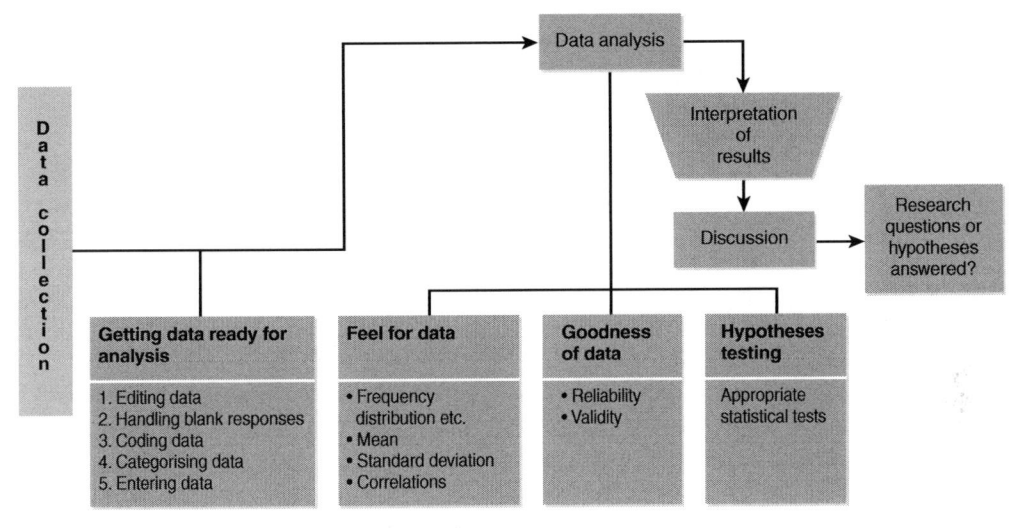

**Figure 13.2** The quantitative data analysis process

# EDITING DATA

Data have to be edited, especially when they relate to responses to open-ended questions of interviews and questionnaires, or unstructured observations. In other words, information that may have been written down in a hurry by the interviewer, observer or respondent must be clearly deciphered so that it may be coded systematically in its entirety. Lack of clarity at this stage will result in later confusion. In an earlier chapter, it was recommended that such editing should be done on the very same day that the data are collected so that the respondents (if not anonymous) may be contacted for any further information or clarification, as needed. The edited data should be identifiable through the use of a different colour pencil or ink so that the original information is still available in case of later doubts.

Incoming mailed questionnaire data have to be checked for incompleteness and inconsistencies by designated members of the research staff. Inconsistencies that can be logically corrected should be rectified and edited at this stage. For instance, the respondent might have inadvertently neglected to answer the item on a questionnaire about her marital status. Against the column asking for the number of years married, she might have responded 12 years; in the number of children column, she might have marked 2, and for ages of children, she might have answered 8 and 4. The latter three responses would indicate that the respondent is in all probability married. The unanswered response to the marital status question could then be edited by the researcher to read 'yes'. It is possible, however, that the respondent deliberately omitted responding to the item because she is either a recent widow or has just been separated, or for some other reason. If such is the case, we would be introducing a bias in the data by editing the data to read 'yes'. Hence, whenever possible it is better to follow up with the respondent and get the correct data while editing. The example we gave is a clear case for editing, but some others may not be so simple, or omissions could be unnoticed and not rectified. There may be other biases that could affect the goodness of the data, over which the researcher may have no control. The validity and the replicability of the study could thus be impaired.

As indicated in previous chapters, much of the editing is taken care of automatically in the case of computer-assisted telephone interviews and electronically administered questionnaires, even as the respondent is answering the questions.

## HANDLING BLANK RESPONSES

Not all respondents answer every item in the questionnaire. Answers may have been left blank because the respondent did not understand the question, did not know the answer, was unwilling to answer or was simply indifferent to responding to the entire questionnaire. In the last situation, the respondent may have left many of the items blank. If a substantial number of questions — say, 25 per cent of the questionnaire — have been left unanswered, it may be advisable to throw out the questionnaire and not include it in the data set for analysis. It is important to mention the number of returned responses that are unused because of excessive missing data in the final report submitted to the sponsor or client of the study. If, however, only two or three items are left blank in a questionnaire with, say, 30 or more items, a decision must be made about how these blank responses are to be handled.

One way to handle a blank response to an interval-scaled item with a midpoint is to assign the midpoint in the scale as the response to that particular item. Another way is to allow the computer to ignore the blank responses when the analyses are done. This, of course, will reduce the sample size whenever that variable is involved in the analyses. A third way is to assign to the item the mean value of the responses of all those who have responded to that particular item. A fourth is to give the item the mean of the responses of this particular respondent to all other questions measuring this variable. A fifth way of dealing with it is to give the missing response a random number within the range for that scale. It should also be noted that SPSS uses linear interpolation from adjacent points as a linear trend to replace missing data. There are at least seven different ways of handling missing data.

The computer can be programmed to handle missing and 'don't know' responses in any manner we decide to deal with them. The best way to handle missing data to enhance the validity of the study, especially if the sample size is big, is to omit the case where the data relating to a particular analysis are missing. Although an item with a 'don't know' response can be treated as a missing value and ignored in the analysis, if many of the respondents have answered 'don't know' to a particular item or items, it may be worthwhile to investigate further. The question might not have been clear, or some organisational aspect could have precluded them from answering, which then might need further probing.

## CODING

The next step is to code the responses. In chapter 10 we discussed the convenience of using scanner sheets for collecting questionnaire data; such sheets facilitate the entry of the responses directly into the computer without manually keying in the data. However, if for some reason this cannot be done, then it is perhaps better to use a coding sheet first to transcribe the data from the questionnaire and then key in the data. This method, in contrast to flipping through each questionnaire for each item, avoids confusion, especially when there are many items in the questionnaire and the number of questionnaires is also large. The easiest way to illustrate a coding scheme is through an example. Let us take the correct answer to exercise 10.2 in chapter 10 — the questionnaire design exercise to test the job involvement – job satisfaction hypothesis in the Fox Publishing Co. case — and see how it can be coded.

### EXAMPLE 13.1 — CODING THE FOX PUBLISHING CO. DATA

In the Fox Publishing Co. questionnaire we have six demographic variables and 16 items measuring involvement and satisfaction, as shown in figure 13.3. The responses to the demographic variables can be coded from 1 to 5 for age, and from 1 to 6 for the variables of education and job level, depending on which box in the columns was checked by the respondent. Gender can be coded as 1 or 2 depending on whether the response was from a male or a female. Work shift can be coded 1 to 3, and employment status as either 1 or 2.

**Figure 13.3** Coding of Fox Publishing Co. questionnaire

1. Age (years)
   - [1] Under 25
   - [2] 25–35
   - [3] 36–45
   - [4] 46–55
   - [5] Over 55

2. Education
   - [1] High school
   - [2] TAFE or polytechnic diploma
   - [3] Bachelor's degree
   - [4] Master's degree
   - [5] Doctoral degree
   - [6] Other (specify)

3. Job level
   - [1] Manager
   - [2] Supervisor
   - [3] Clerk
   - [4] Secretary
   - [5] Technician
   - [6] Other (specify)

4. Gender
   - [1] M
   - [2] F

5. Work shift
   - [1] First
   - [2] Second
   - [3] Third

6. Employment status
   - [1] Part time
   - [2] Full time

*Here are some questions that ask you to tell us how you experience your life in general. Please circle the appropriate number on the scales below.*

To what extent would you agree with the following statements, on a scale of 1 to 7, 1 denoting very low agreement, and 7 denoting very high agreement?

| | |
|---|---|
| 7. The major happiness in my life comes from my job. | 1 2 3 4 5 6 7 |
| 8. Time at work flies by quickly. | 1 2 3 4 5 6 7 |
| 9. I live, eat and breathe my job. | 1 2 3 4 5 6 7 |
| 10. My work is fascinating. | 1 2 3 4 5 6 7 |
| 11. My work gives me a sense of accomplishment. | 1 2 3 4 5 6 7 |
| 12. My supervisor praises good work. | 1 2 3 4 5 6 7 |
| 13. The opportunities for advancement are very good here. | 1 2 3 4 5 6 7 |
| 14. My co-workers are very stimulating. | 1 2 3 4 5 6 7 |
| 15. People can live comfortably with their pay in this organisation. | 1 2 3 4 5 6 7 |
| 16. I get a lot of cooperation in the workplace. | 1 2 3 4 5 6 7 |
| 17. My supervisor is not very capable. | 1 2 3 4 5 6 7 |
| 18. Most things in life are more important than work. | 1 2 3 4 5 6 7 |
| 19. Working here is a drag. | 1 2 3 4 5 6 7 |
| 20. The promotion policies here are very unfair. | 1 2 3 4 5 6 7 |
| 21. My pay is barely adequate to take care of my expenses. | 1 2 3 4 5 6 7 |
| 22. My work is not the most important part of my life. | 1 2 3 4 5 6 7 |

It is easy to see that when some thought is given to it at the time of designing the questionnaire, coding can become an easy job. For example, since numbers were given within the boxes for all the above items (instead of simply putting in a box for marking the appropriate one), it would be easy to transfer the numbers to the code sheet or key in the data directly.

Items numbered 7 to 22 on the questionnaire can be coded by using the actual number circled by the respondents. If, for instance, 3 has been circled for the first question, then the response will be coded as 3; if 4 was circled, we would code it as 4, and so on.

Although it is possible to key in the data directly from the questionnaires, it will mean flipping through several questionnaires, page by page, with the likelihood of committing errors and omitting items. Hence, entering the data onto a code sheet first is helpful.

Human errors can occur while coding. Therefore, at least 10 per cent of the coded questionnaires should be checked for coding accuracy. Questionnaires may be selected using a systematic sampling procedure. That is, every $n$th one coded will be verified for accuracy. If many errors are found in the sample, all items may have to be checked.

## CATEGORISING

At this point it is useful to set up a scheme for categorising the variables so that the several items measuring a concept are all grouped together. Responses to some of the negatively worded questions have to be reversed so that all answers are in the same direction. Note that with respect to negatively worded questions, a response of 7 on a seven-point scale, with 7 denoting 'strongly agree', really means 'strongly disagree', which is actually a 1 on the seven-point scale. Thus, the item has to be reversed so as to be in the same direction as the positively worded questions. This can be done in SPSS on the computer through a Recode, as will be described later. In the Fox Publishing Co. data, items 17 to 22 will have to be recoded so that scores of 7 are read as 1; 6 as 2; 5 as 3; 3 as 5; 2 as 6; and 1 as 7.

If the questions measuring a concept are not contiguous but are scattered over various parts of the questionnaire, care has to be taken to include all the items without any omission or wrong inclusion.

## ENTERING DATA

If questionnaire data are not collected on scanner answer sheets, which can be entered directly into the computer as a data file, the raw data will have to be manually keyed into the computer. Raw data can be entered through any software program. For instance, the SPSS Data Editor, which looks like a spreadsheet (see appendix I for examples), can enter, edit and view the contents of the data file. Each row of the editor represents a case, and each column represents a variable. All missing values will appear with a full point (dot) in the cell. It is easy to add, change or delete values after the data have been entered. Similarly, questionnaire data can be entered directly into a spreadsheet like Excel, but missing values will appear as a blank in each cell.

It is also easy in SPSS to compute the new variables that were categorised earlier, using the Compute dialogue box, which opens when the Transform icon is chosen. After the missing values, the recodes and the computing of new variables are taken care of, the data are ready for analysis.

## DATA ANALYSIS

In the rest of this chapter we will elaborate on the various statistical tests, and the interpretation of the results of the analyses, using SPSS for Windows, a menu-driven software program. In the appendix to this chapter, we also show the results of data analysis using Excel. Use of these two programs is illustrated mainly because they are easily available in business settings. Note that other software programs can be used which produce similar results, with the data interpreted in the same manner.

In data analysis we have three objectives: getting a feel for the data, testing the goodness of data and testing the hypotheses developed for the research. The feel for the data will give preliminary ideas of how good the scales are, how well the coding and entering of data have been done and so on. Suppose an item tapped on a seven-point scale has been improperly coded and/or entered as 8; this will be highlighted by the maximum values on the descriptive statistics and the error can be rectified. The second objective — testing the goodness of data — can be accomplished by submitting the data for the factor analysis, obtaining the Cronbach's alpha or the split-half reliability of the measures, and so on. The third objective — hypotheses testing — is achieved by choosing the appropriate menus of the software programs to test each of the hypotheses using the relevant statistical test. The results of these tests will determine whether or not the hypotheses are substantiated. We will now discuss data analysis in detail with respect to each of these three objectives. However, before you continue with the rest of this chapter, you may wish to refer to appendix I at the back of the book for a refresher on some of the statistical terms and tests used in this chapter. Appendix I also provides further examples of statistical analysis using SPSS.

## GETTING A FEEL FOR THE DATA

We can acquire a feel for the data by checking the central tendency and the dispersion. The mean, the range, the standard deviation and the variance in the data will give the researcher a good idea of how the respondents have reacted to the items in the questionnaire and how good the items and measures are. If the response to each individual item in a scale does not have a good spread (range) and shows very little variability, then the researcher would suspect that the particular question was probably improperly worded and respondents did not fully understand the intent of the question. Biases, if any, could also be detected if the respondents have tended to respond similarly to all items — that is, stuck to only certain points on the scale. The maximum and minimum scores, mean, standard deviation, variance and other statistics can be easily obtained, and these will indicate whether the responses range satisfactorily over the scale. Remember that if there is no variability in the data, then no variance can be explained! Researchers go to great lengths to obtain the central tendency, the range, the dispersion and other statistics for every single item measuring the dependent and independent variables, especially when the measures for a concept are newly developed.

A frequency distribution of the nominal variables of interest should be obtained. Visual displays of this using histograms/bar charts and so on can also be provided through programs that generate charts. In addition to the frequency distributions and the means and standard deviations, it is helpful to know how the dependent and independent variables in the study are related to each other. For this purpose, a correlation matrix of these variables should also be obtained.

It is always prudent to obtain (1) the frequency distributions for the demographic variables; (2) the mean, standard deviation, range and variance on the other dependent and independent variables; and (3) a correlation matrix of the variables, irrespective of whether or not the hypotheses are directly related to these analyses. These statistics give a *feel for the data*. In other words, examination of the measure of central tendency, and how clustered or dispersed the variables are, gives a good idea of how well the questions were framed for tapping the concept. The correlation matrix will give an indication of how closely related or unrelated are the variables under investigation. If the correlation between two variables happens to be high — say, over 0.75 — we would wonder whether they are really two different concepts or whether they are measuring the same concept. If two variables that are theoretically stated to be related do not seem to be significantly correlated to each other in our sample, we would wonder whether we have measured the concepts validly and reliably. Recall our discussions on convergent and discriminant validity in chapter 9.

Establishing the goodness of data lends credibility to all subsequent analyses and findings. Hence, getting a feel for the data becomes the necessary first step in all data analysis. Based on this initial feel, further detailed analyses may be done to test the goodness of the data.

## TESTING GOODNESS OF DATA

The reliability and validity of the measures can now be tested.

## RELIABILITY

As discussed in chapter 9, the reliability of a measure is established by testing for both consistency and stability. Consistency indicates how well the items measuring a concept hang together as a set. Cronbach's alpha is a reliability coefficient that indicates how well the items in a set are positively correlated to one another. Cronbach's alpha is computed in terms of the average intercorrelations among the items measuring the concept. SPSS conducts this analysis quite simply when the investigator nominates the items to be included and provides a statistic called *Cronbach's alpha coefficient*. This coefficient can hold a value of zero to 1. Generally, an alpha coefficient of 0.8 or higher is accepted (Bryman & Cramer 1990:71), although some texts (for example Nunnally 1978) suggest 0.6 and above is acceptable, especially for initial investigations. Again, the researcher would have to decide on the quality of outcome that is desirable and the degree of risk that he or she is willing to take.

Another measure of consistency reliability used in specific situations is the **split-half reliability** coefficient. Since this reflects the correlations between two halves of a set of items, the coefficients obtained will vary depending on how the scale is split. Sometimes split-half reliability is obtained to test for consistency when more than one scale, dimension or factor is assessed. The items across each of the dimensions or factors are split, based on some predetermined logic (Campbell 1976). In almost every case, Cronbach's alpha is an adequate test of internal consistency reliability. You will see later in this chapter how Cronbach's alpha is obtained through computer analysis.

As discussed in chapter 9, the stability of a measure can be assessed through **parallel-form reliability** and **test–retest reliability**. When a high correlation between two similar forms of a measure (see chapter 9) is obtained, parallel form reliability is established. In test–retest reliability (sometimes called temporal reliability), the researcher has a group of people (preferably 30 or more) complete the questionnaire twice, with a reasonable time period between the completions. A reasonable time period is usually considered to be at least a week. This process tests whether the respondents complete the questionnaire differently the second time around — in other words, whether the questionnaire measures the constructs consistently over time. Obviously, various incidents could occur between the two completions that could affect an individual's response. However, the assumption is that, everything else being equal, people's opinions tend to remain relatively constant over a reasonable period of time. When the second completion has been finished, the data are entered into the database. The researcher can then score each construct (that is, add up all the scores for each person for each construct). Each score for each person can then be compared. For example, if respondent no. 1 scored 22 on the first completion and 21 on the second completion for a particular construct, we would say that the temporal reliability for that construct was consistent over time. If, however, a respondent scored 22 on the first completion and 11 on the second completion, we would have to suspect that the construct was not reliable for that respondent. Of course, making such judgements for each person for each construct would strain the mental capacity, if not the concentration, of the researcher. Once again, a statistical package such as SPSS can come to the rescue.

The procedure used this time is called *correlation analysis*. A correlation analysis will compare each of the two completions for each person for each of the constructs, examine all the results and come up with a statistic, called a correlation coefficient, for each theoretical construct. A **correlation coefficient** has a value of −1 to +1. A +1 value means that the second completion by each respondent had exactly the same first score for each respondent on that construct. A −1 value means that all the respondents scored exactly the opposite of their first score. A zero value means that there was no relationship between the first and the second completions; that is, every respondent scored completely differently on the second time around. Again, the rule of thumb is a value of +0.8 and above for the correlation coefficient (Bryman & Cramer 1990:71), and texts are very uniform on this recommendation.

However, with correlation analysis, another statistical consideration must be taken into account. The concern is the likelihood that the correlation coefficient value may have been achieved by chance. Fortunately, the statistical packages also provide an estimate of this occurring and provide a statistic in the form of a probability statement or significance level. So, as well as ensuring that the correlation coefficient value is 0.8 or higher, the researcher checks to see that the probability statement or significance level is less than 0.05 (there was less than a 5 per cent probability that the correlation coefficient value was achieved by chance).

# VALIDITY

**Factorial validity** can be established by submitting the data for factor analysis. The results of factor analysis (a multivariate technique) will confirm whether or not the theorised dimensions emerge. Recall from chapter 8 that measures are developed by first delineating the dimensions so as to operationalise the concept. Factor analysis would reveal whether the dimensions are indeed tapped by the items in the measure, as theorised. **Criterion-related validity** can be established by testing for the power of the measure to differentiate individuals who are known to be different (refer to discussions regarding concurrent and predictive validity in chapter 9). **Convergent validity** can be established when there is a high degree of correlation between two difference sources responding to the same measure (for example, both supervisors and subordinates respond similarly to a *perceived reward system* measure administered to them). **Discriminant validity** can be established when two distinctly different concepts are not correlated to each other (as, for example, courage and honesty; leadership and motivation; attitudes and behaviour). Convergent and discriminant validity can be established through the multitrait, multimethod matrix, a full discussion of which is beyond the scope of this book. However, a brief outline of factor analysis and how this is used for construct and content validity is provided in appendix I. The student interested in knowing more about factor analysis and the multitrait, multimethod matrix is referred particularly to Gorsuch (1974) and Campbell and Fiske (1959). When well-validated measures are used, there is no need, of course, to re-establish their validity for each study. The reliability of the items, however, can be tested.

# HYPOTHESIS TESTING

Once the data are ready for analysis (out-of-range/missing responses and so on are cleaned up), and the goodness of the measures is established, the researcher is ready to test the hypotheses already developed for the study. In appendix I at the end of the book, the statistical tests that would be appropriate for different hypotheses and for data obtained on different scales are discussed. We will now examine the results of analyses of data obtained from a company, and how they are interpreted.

# CASE: RESEARCH DONE IN WOLLONGONG ENTERPRISES

Data analysis and interpretation of results may be most meaningfully explained by referring to a business research project. After a brief description of the background of the company in which the research was carried out and the sample, we will discuss the analysis done to obtain a feel for the data, establish reliability and test each hypothesis. We will also discuss how the results are interpreted.

Wollongong Enterprises is a medium-sized company manufacturing and selling instruments and supplies needed by the health care industry, including blood pressure instruments, surgical instruments and dental accessories. The company, with a total of 360 employees working three shifts, is doing reasonably well but could do far better if it did not experience employee turnover at almost all levels and in all the departments. The CEO of the company called in a research team to study the situation and to make recommendations on the turnover problem.

Since access to those who had left the company would be difficult, the research team suggested to the CEO that they would talk to the current employees and, based on their input and a literature survey, try to determine the factors influencing employees' intentions to stay with or leave the company. Since past research has shown that intention to leave (ITL) is an excellent predictor of actual turnover, the CEO concurred.

The team first conducted an unstructured interview with about 50 employees at various levels and from different departments. Their broad statement was:

> We are here to find out how you experience your work life. Tell us whatever you consider is important for you in your job as issues relate to your work, the environment, the organisation, supervision and whatever else you think is relevant. If we get a good handle on the issues involved, we may be able to make appropriate recommendations to management to enhance the quality of your work life. We would like just to talk to you now, and administer a questionnaire later.

Each interview typically lasted about 45 minutes, and notes on the responses were written down by the team members. When the responses were tabulated it became clear that the issues most frequently raised by the respondents in one form or another related to three main areas: *the job* (employees said their jobs were dull or too complex; or complained of a lack of freedom to do the job as they wanted to), *perceived inequities* (with remarks such as, 'Other companies pay more for the kind of jobs we do' or 'Compared with the work we do, we are not adequately paid'); and *burnout* (comments such as, 'There is so much work to be done that by the end of the day we are physically and emotionally exhausted' or 'We frequently feel a need to take time off because of exhaustion').

A literature survey confirmed that these variables were good predictors of intention to leave and subsequent turnover. In addition, *job satisfaction* was also found to be a useful predictor. A theoretical framework was developed based on the interviews and the literature survey, and five hypotheses (stated later) were developed.

Next, a questionnaire was designed incorporating well-validated and reliable measures for the four independent variables of job characterstcs, perceived inequity, burnout and job satisfaction, and the dependent variable of intention to leave. Demographic variables such as age, education, gender, tenure, job title, department and work shift were also included in the questionnaire.

The questionnaire was administered personally to 174 employees who were chosen on a disproportionate stratified random sampling basis. The responses were entered into the computer. Thereafter, the data were submitted for analysis to test the following hypotheses, which were formulated by the researchers.

1. Men will perceive less equity than women (or women will perceive more equity than men).
2. The job satisfaction of individuals will vary depending on the shift they work.
3. Employees' intentions to leave (ITL) will vary according to their job title. In other words, there will be significant differences in the ITL of top managers, middle-level managers, supervisors, and clerical and blue-collar employees.
4. There will be a relationship between the shifts that people work (first, second and third shift) and the part-time versus full-time status of employees. In other words, these two factors will not be independent.
5. The four independent variables of job characteristics, distributive justice, burnout and job satisfaction will significantly explain the variance in intention to leave.

It may be pertinent to point out here that the five hypotheses derived from the theoretical framework are particularly relevant for finding answers to the turnover issue in direct and indirect ways. For example, if men perceived more inequity (as could be conjectured from the interview data), it would be important to set right their (mis)perceptions so that they are less inclined to leave (if indeed a positive correlation between perceived inequities and ITL is found). If work shift has an influence on job satisfaction (irrespective of its influence on ITL), the matter will have to be further examined, since job satisfaction is also an important outcome variable for the organisation. If employees at particular levels have greater intentions of leaving, further information has to be gathered on what can be done for these groups. If there is a pattern to the part-time/full-time employees working for particular shifts, this might offer some suggestions for further investigation, such as, 'Do part-time employees on the night shift have some special needs that are not currently addressed?' The results of testing the last hypothesis, of course, will offer insights into how much of the variance in ITL will be explained by the four independent variables, and what corrective action, if any, needs to be taken.

The researcher submitted the data for computer analysis using the SPSS for Windows software program. We will now discuss the results of these analyses and their interpretation. In particular, we will examine:
1. the establishment of Cronbach's alpha for the measures
2. the frequency distribution of the variables
3. descriptive statistics such as the mean and standard deviation
4. the Pearson correlation matrix
5. the results of hypotheses testing.

## SOME PRELIMINARY STEPS

It is useful to know that recent versions of the Student Version of SPSS for Windows comes with an on-line tutorial, which can be very useful in that it takes one through all the steps necessary to perform whatever analysis is needed. To have some idea of how the Main Menu in SPSS 10 is set up, the main bar lists several items, two of which are used frequently during data analysis — the Transform and the Analyze menus. The Transform menu is used to *compute*, *recode*, *categorise* variables and *replace missing values*. Once these preliminaries are taken care of, the reliability of measures can be checked. The graphs on the menu bar can be used to generate several types of graphs, including bar charts, line charts, histograms and scattergrams.

## CHECKING THE RELIABILITY OF MEASURES: CRONBACH'S ALPHA

The inter-item consistency reliability or the Cronbach's alpha reliability coefficients of the five independent and dependent variables were obtained. They were all above 0.80. A sample of the result obtained for Cronbach's alpha test for the dependent variable, Intention to Leave, together with instructions on how it is obtained, is shown in output 13.1.

The result indicates that the Cronbach's alpha for the six-item Intention to Leave measure is 0.82. The closer the reliability coefficient gets to 1.0, the better. In general, reliabilities of less than 0.60 are considered to be poor, those in the 0.7 range are acceptable, and those over 0.8 are good. Cronbach's alpha for the other four independent variables ranged from 0.81 to 0.85. Thus, the internal consistency reliability of the measure used in this study can be considered to be good.

It is important to note that all the negatively worded items in the questionnaire should first be reversed before the items are submitted for reliability tests. Unless all the items measuring a variable are in the same direction, the reliabilities obtained will be incorrect.

**Output 13.1**
Reliability analysis
1. From the menus, choose:
    *Analyze*
     *Scale*
      *Reliability analysis . . .*
2. Select the variables constituting the scale.
3. Choose model *Alpha*.

**Reliability output**
Reliability coefficients    6 items
Alpha = 0.8172    Standardised item alpha = 0.8168

# OBTAINING DESCRIPTIVE STATISTICS

A range of descriptive statistics are available with SPSS. We shall present the results for the frequency distributions, measures of central tendencies (averages) and dispersion (spread) of some of the main variables considered in this case.

## Frequency distributions

Frequency distributions were obtained for all the personal data or classification variables. The frequencies for the number of individuals in the various departments for this sample are shown in output 13.2. From this it may be seen that the greatest number of individuals in the sample came from the Production Department (28.1 per cent), followed by the Sales Department (25.3 per cent). Only three individuals (1.7 per cent) came from Public Relations, and five individuals each from the Finance, Maintenance and Accounting departments (2.9 per cent from each). The low numbers in the sample in some of the departments are a function of the total population (very few members) in those departments.

From the frequencies obtained for the other variables (results not shown here), it was found that 86 per cent of the respondents are men and 14 per cent are women; about 68 per cent worked the first shift, 19 per cent the second shift and 13 per cent the third shift. Sixteen per cent of the respondents worked part time and 84 per cent full time. About 8 per cent had elementary school education, 28 per cent a high school qualification, 23 per cent a bachelor's degree, 30 per cent a master's degree and 11 per cent had doctoral degrees. About 21 per cent of the respondents had worked for the organisation for less than a year, 20 per cent for one to three years, 20 per cent for four to six years and the balance of 39 per cent for over six years, including 8 per cent who had worked for more than 20 years.

We thus have a profile of the employees in this organisation, which is useful to describe the sample in the Methods section of the written report (see next chapter). The frequencies can also be visually displayed as bar charts, histograms or pie charts by clicking on Graphs in the SPSS menu.

## Measures of central tendencies and dispersion

Descriptive statistics such as maximum, minimum, means, standard deviations and variance were obtained for the interval-scaled independent and dependent variables. The results of the computer output are shown in output 13.3. It may be mentioned that all variables, excepting ITL, were tapped on a five-point scale. ITL was measured on a four-point scale. From the results, it may be seen that the mean on perceived equity (termed distributive justice) is rather low (2.38 on a five-point scale), as also is the mean on experienced burnout (2.67). Job satisfaction is about average (3.12 on a five-point scale), and the job is perceived as somewhat enriched (3.47). The mean of 2.21 on a four-point scale for ITL indicates that most of the respondents are neither bent on leaving nor set on staying. The minimum of 1 indicates that there are some who do not intend to leave at all, and the maximum of 4 indicates that some are seriously considering leaving.

**Output 13.2**
Frequencies
1. From the menus, choose:
    *Analyze*
        *Descriptive statistics*
            *Frequencies . . .*
2. Select the relevant variables.

3. Choose as needed:
   *Statistics* ...
   *Charts* ...
   *Format* (for the order in which the results are to be displayed).

Frequencies output

### Respondent's department

|  | Frequency | Percent | Valid Percent | Cumulative Percent |
|---|---|---|---|---|
| Marketing | 13 | 7.5 | 7.5 | 7.5 |
| Production | 49 | 28.1 | 28.1 | 35.6 |
| Sales | 44 | 25.3 | 25.3 | 60.9 |
| Finance | 5 | 2.9 | 2.9 | 63.8 |
| Servicing | 34 | 19.5 | 19.5 | 83.3 |
| Maintenance | 5 | 2.9 | 2.9 | 86.2 |
| Personnel | 16 | 9.2 | 9.2 | 95.4 |
| Public Relations | 3 | 1.7 | 1.7 | 97.1 |
| Accounting | 5 | 2.9 | 2.9 | 100.0 |
| Total | 174 | 100.0 | 100.0 | 100.0 |

The *variance* for burnout, job satisfaction and the job characteristics is not high. The variance for ITL and perceived equity (distributive justice) is only slightly higher, indicating that most respondents are very close to the mean on all the variables.

## Output 13.3

Descriptive statistics: central tendencies and dispersions
1. From the menus, choose:
   *Analyze*
      *Descriptive statistics*
         *Descriptives* ...
2. Select the variables.
      *Options* ...
3. Choose the relevant statistics needed.

Descriptives output

### Descriptive statistics

|  | N | Minimum | Maximum | Mean | Standard Deviation | Variance |
|---|---|---|---|---|---|---|
| Dist Just | 173 | 1.00 | 5.00 | 2.379 | .756 | .570 |
| Burnout | 173 | 1.00 | 5.00 | 2.671 | .521 | .271 |
| Job Sat | 170 | 1.00 | 5.00 | 3.117 | .507 | .257 |
| Job Char | 167 | 2.00 | 5.00 | 3.474 | .518 | .268 |
| ITL | 174 | 1.00 | 4.00 | 2.212 | .673 | .453 |

In summary, the perceived equity is rather low, not much burnout is experienced, the job is perceived to be fairly enriched, there is average job satisfaction, and there is neither a strong intention to stay with the organisation nor a strong determination to leave it.

# INFERENTIAL STATISTICS: PEARSON CORRELATION

The Pearson correlation matrix obtained for the five interval-scaled variables is shown in output 13.4. From the results, we see that the intention to leave is, as would be expected, significantly negatively correlated to perceived distributive justice (equity), job satisfaction and enriched job. That is, the intention to leave is low if equitable treatment and job satisfaction are experienced, and an enriched job is there. However, when individuals experience burnout (physical and emotional exhaustion), their intention to leave also increases (positive correlation of 0.33). Job satisfaction is also positively correlated to perceived equity and to enriched job. It is negatively correlated to burnout and ITL. The correlations are all in the expected direction.

As discussed in appendix I, the Pearson correlation coefficient is appropriate for interval- and ratio-scaled variables, and the Spearman Rank or the Kendall's Tau coefficients are appropriate when variables are measured on an ordinal scale. Any bivariate correlation can be obtained by clicking the relevant menu, identifying the variables, and seeking the appropriate parametric or non-parametric statistics.

## Output 13.4
Pearson correlations matrix

1. From the menus, choose:
   >Analyze
   >>Correlate
   >>>Bivariate ...
2. Select relevant variables.
   >Options ...
3. Select:
   >a. Type of correlation coefficient: select relevant one (e.g. Pearson, Kendall's Tau, Spearman)
   >b. Test of significance — two-tailed, one-tailed.

### Correlations

| | | Dist Just | Burnout | Job Sat | Job Char | ITL |
|---|---|---|---|---|---|---|
| Pearson Correlation | Dist Just | 1.000 | −.374** | .588** | .169* | −.357** |
| | Burnout | −.374** | 1.000 | −.474** | −.299** | .328** |
| | Job Sat | .588** | −.474** | 1.000 | .328** | −.535** |
| | Job Char | .169* | −.299** | .328** | 1.000 | −.274** |
| | ITL | −.357** | .328** | −.535** | −.274** | 1.000 |
| Significance (2-tailed) | Dist Just | | .000 | .000 | .015 | .000 |
| | Burnout | .000 | | .000 | .000 | .000 |
| | Job Sat | .000 | .000 | | .000 | .000 |
| | Job Char | .015 | .000 | .000 | | .000 |
| | ITL | .000 | .000 | .000 | .000 | |
| N | Dist Just | 172 | 173 | 169 | 166 | 173 |
| | Burnout | 172 | 173 | 169 | 166 | 173 |
| | Job Sat | 169 | 169 | 173 | 163 | 167 |
| | Job Char | 166 | 166 | 163 | 173 | 167 |
| | ITL | 173 | 173 | 167 | 167 | 172 |

\* Significant at $p < 0.001$.        \*\* Correlation at 0.0001 (2-tailed).

It is important to note that no correlation exceeded 0.59 for this sample. If correlations were higher (say, 0.75 and above), we might have to question whether the correlated variables are two different and distinct variables, and doubt the validity of the measures.

## HYPOTHESIS TESTING

Five hypotheses were generated for this study, as stated earlier. These call for the use of a *t*-test (for hypothesis 1), an ANOVA (for hypotheses 2 and 3), a chi-square test (for hypothesis 4) and a multiple regression analysis (for hypothesis 5). The results of these tests and their interpretation are discussed below.

## Hypothesis 1: use of *t*-test

Hypothesis 1 can be stated in the null and alternate as follows:

$H1_0$: There will be no difference between men and women in their perceived inequities.

Statistically expressed, $H1_0$ is $\mu_W \leq \mu_M$

where $\mu_W$ is the equity perceived by women and $\mu_M$ is the equity perceived by men.

$H1_A$: Women will perceive more equity than men (or men will perceive less equity than women).

Statistically expressed, $H1_A$ is: $\mu_W > \mu_M$

A *t*-test will indicate if the perceived differences are significantly different for women than for men. The results of the *t*-test done are shown in output 13.5. As can be seen, the difference in the means of 2.43 and 2.34 with standard deviations of 0.75 and 0.76 for the women and men on perceived equity (or distributive justice) is not significant (see table showing *t*-test for Equality of Means). For example, if equal variances are assumed for males and females, then the mean difference is 0.03 with a significance level of 0.461 (or 46.1 per cent). Since this significance level is much greater than the acceptable level of 0.05 (or 5 per cent), we do not reject the null hypothesis ($H1_0$). Thus, *hypothesis 1 is not substantiated* (i.e. the null hypothesis was accepted).

## Hypothesis 2: use of ANOVA

The second hypothesis can be stated in the null and alternate as follows:

$H2_0$: The job satisfaction of individuals will be the same irrespective of the shift they work (1, 2 or 3).

Statistically expressed, $H2_0$ is: $\mu_1 = \mu_2 = \mu_3$

where $\mu_1$, $\mu_2$ and $\mu_3$ signify the means on the job satisfaction of employees working in shifts 1, 2 and 3, respectively.

$H2_A$: The job satisfaction of individuals will *not* be the same (will vary) depending on which shift they work.

Statistically expressed, $H2_A$ is: $\mu_1 \neq \mu_2 \neq \mu_3$

Because there are more than two groups (three different shifts) and job satisfaction is measured on an interval scale, ANOVA is appropriate to test this hypothesis. The results of ANOVA, testing this hypothesis, are shown in output 13.6.

The *df* in the fourth column refers to the **degrees of freedom**, and each source of variation has associated degrees of freedom (*df*). For the between-groups variance, $df = (K - 1)$, where K is the total number of groups or levels. Because there were three shifts, we have $(3 - 1) = 2$ *df*. The *df* for the within-groups sum of squares equals $(N - K)$, where N is the total number of respondents and K is the total number of groups. If there were no missing responses, $(N - K)$ should be $(174 - 3) = 171$. In this case, however, there were 12 missing responses, and hence the associated $df$ is $(162 - 3) = 159$.

The mean square for each source of variation (column 5 of the results) is derived by dividing the sum of squares by its associated $df$. Finally, the $F$ value itself equals the explained mean square divided by the residual mean square.

$$F = \frac{\text{MS explained}}{\text{MS residual}}$$

## Output 13.5
*t*-Test for differences between two groups
(Independent samples test)
1. Choose:
   Analyze
      Compare means
         Independent-samples t-test ...
2. Select a single grouping variable and click *Define groups* to specify the two codes to be compared.
      Options ...
         (specify significance level required — 0.05, 0.01 etc.).

*t*-Test output

### Group statistics

|  |  |  | N | Mean | Standard Deviation | Std. Error Mean |
|---|---|---|---|---|---|---|
| Dist Just | Treatment | Male | 149 | 2.43 | .75 | .052 |
|  |  | Female | 25 | 2.34 | .76 | .154 |

### Independent samples test

|  | Levene's Test for Equality of Variance | | *t*-Test for Equality of Means | | | | | | |
|---|---|---|---|---|---|---|---|---|---|
|  |  |  |  |  |  |  |  | 95% Confidence Interval of the Mean | |
|  | F | Significance | t | df | Significance (2-tailed) | Mean Difference | Std. Error Difference | Lower | Upper |
| Dist Just Equal variance assumed | 1.31 | .352 | .74 | 171 | .461 | .03 | .10 | .30 | .91 |
| Equal variance not assumed |  |  | .67 | 29 | .506 | .03 | .09 | .29 | .89 |

## Output 13.6
ANOVA
1. Choose:
   Analyze
      Compare means
         One-way ANOVA ...
2. Select the dependent variable/s and one independent factor variable.

One-way ANOVA output

ANOVA

|  |  | Sums of Squares | df | Mean Square | F | Sig. |
|---|---|---|---|---|---|---|
| Job Sat | Between groups | 1.659 | 2 | .831 | 3.327 | .038 |
|  | Within groups | 39.645 | 159 | .249 |  |  |
|  | Total | 41.304 | 161 |  |  |  |

*Note:* For post-hoc test to determine in which of the multiple groups the differences lie (as discussed in the text), click on:

Post Hoc ...

(Select as appropriate from among the many tests such as Bonferroni, Scheffe, Tukey or Duncan.)

In this case, $F = 3.327$ (0.831/0.249). This F value is significant at the 0.004 level. This implies that *hypothesis 2 is substantiated*. That is, there are significant differences in the mean satisfaction levels of workers in the three shifts, and the null hypothesis can be rejected.

The *F test* used here is called the overall or omnibus F test. To determine among which groups the true differences lie, other tests need to be done, as discussed in appendix I. The Duncan Multiple Range test was performed for the purpose (output not shown). The results showed that the mean job satisfaction for the three groups was 3.15 for the first shift, 2.91 for the second shift and 3.23 for the third shift. The second shift with the low job satisfaction is the one that is significantly different from groups 1 and 3 at the $p < 0.05$ (i.e. at the 5 per cent significance level).

## Hypothesis 3: use of ANOVA

Hypothesis 3 can be stated in the null and the alternate as follows:

H3$_0$: There will be no difference in the intention to leave of employees at the five different job levels.

Statistically expressed, H3$_0$ is: $\mu_1 = \mu_2 = \mu_3 = \mu_4 = \mu_5$

where the five $\mu$s represent the five means on ITL of employees at the five different job levels.

H3$_A$: The ITL of members at the five different job levels will vary significantly.

Statistically expressed, H3$_A$ is: $\mu_1 \neq \mu_2 \neq \mu_3 \neq \mu_4 \neq \mu_5$

The results of this ANOVA test, shown in output 13.7, do not indicate any significant differences in the intention to leave among the five groups ($F = 1.25$; $p = 0.29$). Thus, *hypothesis 3 was not substantiated* (i.e. the null hypothesis was accepted).

**Output 13.7**
ANOVA with ITL as the dependent variable

One-way ANOVA output

ANOVA

|  |  | Sums of Squares | df | Mean square | F | Sig. |
|---|---|---|---|---|---|---|
| ITL | Between groups | 2.312 | 4 | .578 | 1.254 | .288 |
|  | Within groups | 75.143 | 163 | .461 |  |  |
|  | Total | 77.455 | 167 |  |  |  |

## Hypothesis 4: use of chi-square test

Hypothesis 4 can be stated in the null and alternate as follows:

$H4_0$: Shifts worked and employment status (part time vs. full time) will be independent (i.e., will not be related).

$H4_A$: There will be a relationship between the shifts that people work and their part-time vs. full-time status.

Since both variables are nominal, a chi-square ($\chi^2$) test was done, the results of which are shown in output 13.8. The cross-tabulation *count* indicates that, of the full-time employees, 103 work the first shift, 25 the second shift and 18 the third shift. Of the part-time employees, 16 work the first shift, 8 the second shift and 4 the third shift.

It may be seen that the $\chi^2$ value of 2.31, with two degrees of freedom, is not significant (i.e. $p > 0.05$). From table III in appendix II, we can see that at the 5 per cent level of significance, and with two degrees of freedom, the criterion $\chi^2$ value is 5.99. Clearly, the calculated $\chi^2$ value of 2.31 is below this, hence we do not reject the null hypothesis $H4_0$. In other words, the part-time/full-time status and the shifts worked are not related. Hence, *hypothesis 4 has not been substantiated* (i.e. we accept the null hypothesis).

### Output 13.8

**Chi-square test**
Choose:
> Analyze
> > Descriptive statistics
> > > Crosstabs ...
> > > > (enter variables in the *Rows* and *Columns* boxes)
> > > > > Statistics ...
> > > > > > Select Chi-square

**Crosstabs Output**

**Employment status*shift Cross-tabulation**

| Employment status | Shift | | | Total |
|---|---|---|---|---|
| | First | Second | Third | |
| Full time | 103 | 25 | 18 | 146 |
| Part time | 16 | 8 | 4 | 28 |
| Total | 119 | 33 | 22 | 174 |

**Chi-square tests**

| | Value | df | Asymp. Sig. (2-sided) |
|---|---|---|---|
| Pearson chi-square | 2.312 | 2 | .314 |
| Likelihood ratio | 2.163 | 2 | .339 |
| Linear-by-linear | 1.103 | 1 | .294 |
| No. of valid cases | 174 | | |

## Hypothesis 5: use of multiple regression analysis

The last hypothesis can be stated in the null and alternate as follows:

$H5_0$: The four independent variables will *not* significantly explain the variance in intention to leave.

$H5_A$: The four independent variables will significantly explain the variance in intention to leave.

To test this hypothesis, multiple regression analysis was carried out. The results of regressing the four independent variables against Intention to Leave can be seen in output 13.9.

The first table in the output titled 'Model Summary' shows the four independent variables that are entered into the regression model, the R (0.548), which is the correlation of the four independent variables with the dependent variable, after all the intercorrelations among the four independent variables are taken into account, and the R Square (0.30). This is the explained variance and is actually the square of the multiple R $(0.548)^2$.

**Output 13.9**
Multiple Regression Analysis
Choose:
    Analyze
        Regression
            Linear . . .
                (enter dependent and independent variables)
**Regression output**

Model summary[3, 4]

| Model | | Variables Entered | Variables Removed | R | R Square | Adjusted R Square | Std. Error of the Estimate |
|---|---|---|---|---|---|---|---|
| Model | 1 | Job Char<br>Dist Just<br>Burnout<br>Job Sat[1, 2] | | .548 | .300 | .282 | .578 |

1 Indep. vars: (constant) Job Char, Dist Just, Burnout, Job Sat
2 All requested variables entered.
3 Dependent variable: ITL
4 Method: Enter

ANOVA[2]

| Model | | | Sum of Squares | df | Mean Square | F | Significance |
|---|---|---|---|---|---|---|---|
| Model | 1 | Regression | 22.366 | 4 | 5.591 | 16.717 | .000[1] |
| | | Residual | 52.180 | 156 | .335 | | |
| | | Total | 74.546 | 160 | | | |

1 Indep. vars: (constant) Job Char, Dist Justice, Burnout, Job Sat
2 Dependent variable: ITL

Coefficients[1]

| Model | | Unstandardised Coefficients | | Standardised Coefficients | | |
|---|---|---|---|---|---|---|
| | | B | Std. error | Beta | t | Sig. |
| 1 | (Constant) | 4.048 | .603 | | 6.713 | .000 |
| | Job Char | −.112 | .095 | −.084 | −1.173 | .243 |
| | Dist Just | −.115 | .078 | −.121 | −1.461 | .146 |
| | Burnout | .143 | .103 | .109 | 1.393 | .166 |
| | Job Sat | −.498 | .121 | −.371 | −4.121 | .000 |

1 Dependent variable: ITL

The *ANOVA* table shows that the F value of 16.72 is significant at the 0.001 level. In the column *df* (degree of freedom) in the table, the first number represents the number of independent variables (4), the second number (156) is the total number of complete responses for all the variables in the equation (N) minus the number of independent variables (K) minus 1 ($N - K - 1$) (($161 - 4 - 1$) = 156). The F statistic produced ($F = 16.72$) is significant at the .001 level.

What the results mean is that 30 per cent of the variance (R-square) in intention to leave has been significantly explained by the four independent variables. Thus, *hypothesis 5 is substantiated* (i.e. the null hypothesis is rejected).

The next table, titled Coefficients, helps us to see which among the four independent variables is the most important in explaining the variance in ITL. If we look at the column Beta under Standardised coefficients, we see that the highest number in the **beta** ($\beta$) is −0.37 for job satisfaction, which is significant at the 0.001 level. It may also be seen that this is the only independent variable that is significant (i.e. $p \leq 0.05$). The negative beta weight indicates that if ITL is to be reduced, enhancing the job satisfaction of employees is necessary.

# OVERALL INTERPRETATION AND RECOMMENDATIONS

Of the five hypotheses tested, two were substantiated and three were not. From the results of the multiple regression analysis, it is clear that job satisfaction is a critical factor in explaining employees' intentions to stay with the organisation. Hence, whatever is done to increase job satisfaction will help employees to think less about leaving.

It is also clear from the results that ITL does not differ by job level. That is, employees at all levels feel neither too strongly inclined to stay with the organisation nor too strongly inclined to leave it. Hence, if retention of employees is a top priority for the CEO, it is important to pay attention to employees at all levels and formulate policies and practices that help enhance the job satisfaction of all. Also, since job satisfaction is found to be significantly lower for employees working the evening shift, further interviews with them might shed some light on the factors that are causing them dissatisfaction. Corrective action can then be taken.

It is informative to find that the perceived equity (or distributive justice), though not significantly different for men and women as originally hypothesised, is nevertheless rather low for all (see output 13.3). The Pearson correlation matrix (output 13.4) indicates that perceived equity (or distributive justice) is positively correlated to job satisfaction and negatively correlated to ITL. Hence, the CEO will be well advised to rectify inequities in the system, if they do exist, or clear misperceptions of inequities, if this is the case.

Increasing job satisfaction will help to reduce employees' intentions to quit, but the fact that only 30 per cent of the variance in intention to leave was significantly explained by the four independent variables considered in this study still leaves 70 per cent to be explained. In other words, there are other additional variables that are important in explaining ITL and that have not been considered in this study. So further research might be necessary to explain more of the variance in ITL, if the CEO wishes to pursue the matter further.

We have seen how different hypotheses can be tested by applying the appropriate statistical tests in data analysis. Based on the interpretation of the results, the research report is then written, making necessary recommendations and discussing the pros and cons of each, together with a cost–benefit analysis. Limitations to the study are also specifically stated so that the reader is made aware of the biases that might have crept into the study. This also gives a professional touch to the study, attesting to its scientific orientation.

## USE OF EXPERT SYSTEMS

As we know, an Expert System employs unique programming techniques to model the decisions that experts make. A considerable body of knowledge fed into the system, and some good software and hardware, help the individual using it to make sound decisions about the problem that he or she is concerned about solving. In sum, an Expert System can be thought of as an 'adviser', clarifying or resolving problematic issues that are confusing to the individual.

Expert Systems relating to data analysis help the perplexed researcher to choose the most appropriate statistical procedure for testing different types of hypotheses. The *Statistical Navigator* is an Expert System that recommends one or more statistical procedures after seeking information on the *goals* (that is, the purpose of the analysis — say, to understand the relationship between two variables) and the *data* (that is, categories, measurement scales).

The *Statistical Navigator* is a useful guide for those who are not well versed in statistics but want to ensure that they use the appropriate statistical techniques.

Incidentally, Expert Systems can also be used for making decisions with respect to various aspects of the research design — *nature of study, time horizon, type of study, study setting, unit of analysis, sampling designs, data collection methods* and so on.

Other applications of Expert Systems for business decisions using available data include *Auditor* (for decisions on allowing for bad debts), and *Tax Advisor* (which helps audit firms to advise clients on estate planning). As suggested by Luconi, Malone and Morton (1986), Expert Systems can be used for making decisions with respect to operational control (accounts receivable, inventory control, cash management, production scheduling), management control (budget analysis, forecasting, variance analysis, budget preparation) and strategic planning (warehouse and factory location, mergers and acquisitions, new product planning). Thus, the scope for developing and using Expert Systems to aid managerial problem solving and decision making appears unlimited!

## SUMMARY

In this chapter we have covered the procedures for analysing data after they are collected. We followed the steps necessary to get the data ready for analysis — editing, coding and categorising. Through the example of the research on Wollongong Enterprises, we considered various statistical analyses and tests used to examine different hypotheses to answer the research question. We also saw how the computer results generated by SPSS are interpreted. An important point to note is that data analysis should follow the testing of hypotheses that have already been formulated. It would be incorrect to change our original hypotheses to suit the results of data analyses. It is, however, acceptable to develop inductive hypotheses and later test them through further research.

The appendix to this chapter illustrates the use of Excel in data analysis, demonstrated by Professors Barclay and York. In the next chapter we will learn how to write a research report after the data are analysed and the results interpreted.

## DISCUSSION POINTS

1. What kinds of biases do you think could be minimised or avoided during the data analysis stage of research?

2. When we collect data on the effects of treatment in experimental designs, which statistical test would be most appropriate to test the treatment effects?

3. A tax consultant wonders if he should be more selective about the class of clients he serves, so as to maximise his income. He usually deals with four categories of clients: the very rich, rich, upper middle class and middle class. He has records of each and every client served, the taxes paid by them and how much he has charged them. Since many factors with respect to the clients vary (for example, number of dependants and business deductibles) irrespective of the category they belong to, he would like an appropriate analysis to be done to see which among the four categories of clientele he should choose to serve in the future.
*What kind of analysis should be done in the preceding case and why?*

4. Below are tables 13A to 13D, summarising the results of data analyses of research conducted in a sales organisation that operates in 50 different cities of the United States, with a total sales force of about 500. The number of salespeople sampled for the study was 150. *You are to:*
   a. Interpret the information contained in each of the tables in as much detail as possible.
   b. Summarise the results for the CEO of the company.
   c. Make recommendations based on your interpretation of the results.

**Table 13A** Means, standard deviations, minimum and maximum

| Variable | Mean | Std. Deviation | Minimum | Maximum |
|---|---|---|---|---|
| Sales (in $000s) | 75.1 | 8.6 | 45.2 | 97.3 |
| No. of salespeople | 25 | 6 | 5 | 50 |
| Population (in 00s) | 5.1 | 0.8 | 2.78 | 7.12 |
| Per capita income (in 000s) | 20.3 | 20.1 | 10.1 | 75.9 |
| Advertisement (in $000s) | 10.3 | 5.2 | 6.1 | 15.7 |

**Table 13B** Correlations among the variables

| | Sales | Salespeople | Population | Income | Advertisement |
|---|---|---|---|---|---|
| Sales | 1.0 | | | | |
| No. of salespeople | .76 | 1.0 | | | |
| Population | .62 | .06 | 1.0 | | |
| Income | .56 | .21 | .11 | 1.0 | |
| Ad. expenditure | .68 | .16 | .36 | .23 | 1.0 |

All figures above 0.15 are significant at $p = 0.05$.
All figures above 0.35 are significant at $p \leq 0.001$.

**Table 13C** Results of one-way ANOVA: sales by level of education

| Source of Variation | Sums of Squares | df | Mean Squares | F | Signficance of F |
|---|---|---|---|---|---|
| Between groups | 50.7 | 4 | 12.7 | 3.6 | .01 |
| Within groups | 501.8 | 145 | 3.5 | | |
| Total | 552.5 | 150 | | | |

**Table 13D** Results of regression analysis

| | |
|---|---|
| Multiple R | .65924 |
| R square | .43459 |
| Adjusted R square | .35225 |
| Standard error | .41173 |
| df | (5,144) |
| F | 5.278 |
| Sig. | .000 |

| Variable | Beta | t | Sig. t |
|---|---|---|---|
| Training of salespeople | .28 | 2.768 | .0092 |
| No. of salespeople | .34 | 3.55 | .00001 |
| Population | .09 | 0.97 | .467 |
| Per capita income | .12 | 1.200 | .089 |
| Advertisement | .47 | 4.54 | .00001 |

# APPENDIX

## DATA ANALYSIS USING EXCEL
By Lizabeth A. Barclay and Kenneth M. York
School of Business Administration, Oakland University, Rochester, Michigan

## ANALYSIS OF THE ACCOUNTING CHAIR DATA SET USING EXCEL

### Background information

This project involved exploratory research undertaken to obtain a feel for the role of Accounting Department chairs before launching a longitudinal study of 'burnout' in the same population.

The environment of higher education is undergoing change. Universities are seeking new sources of revenue, course delivery is changing, and professors and department chairs are increasingly being asked to engage in activities not traditional to the university job. Universities expect chairs to engage in fund-raising and friend-making at an increasingly intense level. At the same time, chairs are still expected to engage in traditional administrative duties as well as conduct research and teach classes.

The researchers designed a questionnaire tapping demographic information on gender, educational level, tenure status, budget, job title and accreditation status of the chair's business school. The survey also asked for the number of full-time and part-time faculty in the department, and whether they had the terminal degree. The chair's perceptions of time availability, working relationships and salary comparisons were also obtained. The questionnaire was mailed to 684 current Accounting Department chairs. Accounting chairs were selected because that position has entailed traditional chair duties as well as external relationship building to a greater extent than other chair positions.

Two hundred and eight questionnaires were returned (response rate = 31 per cent). Data were entered into an Excel spreadsheet and analysed using the data analysis procedures found under the Tools menu.

This study tested the following hypotheses.
1. The more faculty with a PhD degree in the department, the higher the chair's compensation vis-à-vis other business school chairs.
2. The proportion of AACSB-accredited schools responding to the survey will be higher than the proportion of AACSB Accounting-accredited schools responding.
3. Male chairs will have a higher number of research articles than female chairs.
4. There will be a relationship between years spent as chair and scores on the Working Relationships Scale.
5. Soft dollars, budget discretion and the one-item Hours in the Day Scale will significantly predict chairs' number of publications.

### ANALYSIS USING EXCEL

A discussion of the results of these analyses using Excel and their interpretation follows. Statistical analysis using a spreadsheet like Excel is different from using a statistical package like SPSS. With Excel, the data and the analysis are both visible to the researcher, whereas SPSS has a separate data file, and at any given time, both the data set and the output cannot be simultaneously displayed.

The data analyses included:
1. the establishment of Cronbach's alpha for the relevant scales
2. the frequency distribution for several of the measures
3. measures of central tendency and dispersion
4. Pearson correlation matrix
5. hypothesis testing.

A sample output for each of the preceding, with brief interpretations, follows. Note that all computer output has been rounded down to a maximum of 3 decimal places for ease of interpretation and presentation, and only some data have been shown.

## 1. Reliability of chair time scale: Cronbach's alpha

The alpha coefficient for the 'Chair Time Scale' is shown in output A1. Because the Excel Analysis ToolPak does not directly compute Cronbach's alpha, the researchers calculated it using a formula; the Data Analysis Tool Correlation was used to calculate the item intercorrelations. The results indicate that Cronbach's alpha for the five-item scale is only 0.53, as shown in output A1. Therefore, the reliability of this scale would be considered poor. The researchers should consider not using these items as a scale because of their poor reliability.

### Output A1
### Reliability

What is the reliability of the Chair Time Scale?
Chair Time Scale (5-item scale)

| Item16 | Item17 | Item18 | Item19 | Item28 |
|---|---|---|---|---|
| 3 | 5 | 3 | 4 | 5 |
| 4 | 2 | 2 | 2 | 3 |
| 3 | 2 | 3 | 2 | 4 |
| 4 | 4 | 3 | 2 | 4 |
| 1 | 5 | 3 | 2 | 4 |
| 4 | 5 | 4 | 3 | 4 |
| 3 | 3 | 2 | 4 | 5 |
| 4 | 3 | 3 | 4 | 3 |
| 4 | 3 | 2 | 2 | 5 |
| 1 | 3 | 3 | 4 | 5 |
| 4 | 1 | 1 | 1 | 5 |
| 4 | 3 | 2 | 2 | 2 |
| 3 | 2 | 3 | 2 | 2 |
| 5 | 5 | 5 | 5 | 5 |
| 4 | 4 | 4 | 4 | 3 |
| 4 | 3 | 2 | 2 | 5 |
| 2 | 4 | 2 | 5 | 5 |
| 4 | 4 | 2 | 2 | 5 |
| 5 | 5 | 2 | 2 | 4 |
| 3 | 3 | 1 | 2 | 3 |
| 5 | 5 | 3 | 2 | 5 |
| 4 | 4 | 3 | 4 | 5 |
| 5 | 3 | 3 | 1 | 5 |
| 3 | 3 | 5 | 4 | 4 |
| 4 | 2 | 4 | 2 | 5 |

|  | Item16 | Item17 | Item18 | Item19 | Item28 |
|---|---|---|---|---|---|
| Item16 | 1 | | | | |
| Item17 | 0.295 | 1 | | | |
| item18 | 0.094 | 0.073 | 1 | | |
| item19 | 0.193 | 0.209 | 0.244 | 1 | |
| Item28 | 0.233 | 0.197 | 0.134 | 0.140 | 1 |

$$\text{Cronbach's alpha} = \frac{N * \text{mean\_inter-item\_correlation}}{(1 + \text{mean\_inter\_item\_correlation} * (N - 1))}$$

N = 5
mean_interitem_correlation = 0.181
Cronbach's alpha = 0.53

Steps:
1. From the Tools menu, select Data Analysis, Correlation.
2. In the Correlation dialogue box:
    Enter the Input Range as A7:E213
    Check Grouped by Columns
    Check Labels in first row
    Enter the Output Range as G7.
3. Calculate the mean inter-item correlation
    Calculate the average correlation in the matrix created in step 2.
    Do not include the correlation of each item with itself (all are 1).
4. Create a formula to calculate Cronbach's alpha using the mean inter-item correlation and the number of items in the scale.

## 2. Frequency distribution

Output A2 shows the frequency distribution obtained for the item 'At the end of your current term as chair, which is most appealing to you?'. This item assesses which type of career options a current chair might choose. In Excel, frequencies can be generated using the Data Analysis option. After the frequencies are obtained, the Chart Wizard can be used to generate a bar chart.

The results show that most of the current accounting chairs wish to 'return to faculty status' (48.0 per cent), followed by those who want to 'remain as chair' (33.8 per cent). Only 3.9 per cent of chairs aspire to 'a higher administrative position' at their current school, while 5.4 per cent would like such a position at a different school.

### Output A2
### Frequency distribution

What is the frequency distribution for Appeal?
Item4: At the end of your current term as Chair, which is most appealing to you?

| Appeal | Bin Range | Bin | Frequency | |
|---|---|---|---|---|
| 2 | | | | |
| 1 | Return to Faculty | 1 | Return to Fac | 98 | 48.04% |
| 1 | Remain as Chair | 2 | Remain as Ch | 69 | 33.82% |
| 2 | Become chair other university | 3 | Become chair | 2 | 0.98% |
| 6 | Seek higher admin position | 4 | Seek higher a | 8 | 3.92% |
| 5 | Seek higher admin position elsewhere | 5 | Seek higher a | 11 | 5.39% |
| 2 | Retire | 6 | Retire | 13 | 6.37% |
| 1 | Other | 7 | Other | 3 | 1.47% |
| 2 | | | More | 0 | |
| 1 | | | | | |
| 3 | | | | | |
| 2 | Steps: | | | | |
| 2 | 1. From the Tools menu, select Data Analysis, Histogram. | | | | |
| 1 | 2. In the Histogram dialogue box: | | | | |
| 2 |      Enter Input Range as A8:A211 | | | | |
| 1 |      Enter Bin Range as E9:E15 | | | | |
| 5 |      Uncheck Labels | | | | |
| 2 |      Enter Output Range as F8 | | | | |
| 6 |      Click OK. | | | | |
| 1 | 3. Copy cells D9 to D15 into cells F9 to F15. | | | | |
| 1 | 4. Select column F, then from the Format menu select Autofit. | | | | |
| 1 | 5. On the menu bar, select Chart Wizard. | | | | |
| 1 | 6. Write formulas to calculate frequency per cent: | | | | |
| 2 |      In cell H9 enter =G9/sum($G$9:$G$15). | | | | |
| 2 |      Copy the formula in cell H9 to cells H10 to H15. | | | | |
| 1 |      Select cells H9 to H15, then from the Format menu, Cells, Percentage, 2 decimal places. | | | | |
| 6 | 7. For Chart Type, select Column, click Next. | | | | |
| 2 | 8. For Source Data, enter Data Range as F9:G15, check Series in Columns. | | | | |
| 1 | 9. For Chart Options, under Titles tab: | | | | |
| 1 |      Enter Chart Title as Most Appealing After Current Term. | | | | |
| 2 |      Enter Value (Y) axis as Frequency. | | | | |
| 6 | 10. For Chart Options, under Legend tab, uncheck Show legend. | | | | |
| 1 | 11. For Chart Options, under Data labels tab check Show value, click Next. | | | | |
| 1 | 12. For Chart Location, select As object in worksheet, click Finish. | | | | |
| | 13. Resize chart to make all variable labels readable. | | | | |

## 3. Measures of central tendency and dispersion

The results in output A3 were obtained using the Data Analysis Tool in Excel, which calculates such statistics as the mean, standard deviation, skewness and kurtosis. The 'Descriptive Statistics' option under the Data Analysis menu is selected to obtain these measures. Output A3 shows these descriptive statistics for the amount of time (hours per week) spent by the chairs on administrative tasks, teaching, research and external activities.

The results indicate that the chairs spend most of their time each week on administrative activities, but the variance is large. The mean number of hours spent on teaching, research and external contact activities are 14.0, 5.6 and 6.8 respectively, with a variance of 51.2, 24.3 and 23.3 hours.

### Output A3
### Measures of Central Tendency and Dispersion

*What is the central tendency and dispersion of hours spent on university-related activities?*

| Hours Admin | Hours Teaching | Hours Research | Hours External | Admin | | Teaching | | Research | | External | |
|---|---|---|---|---|---|---|---|---|---|---|---|
| 30 | 20 | | 1 | Mean | 21.786 | Mean | 13.971 | Mean | 5.574 | Mean | 6.764 |
| 20 | 15 | 5 | 10 | Std. Error | 0.715 | Std. Error | 0.498 | Std. Error | 0.364 | Std. Error | 0.353 |
| 15 | 25 | 5 | 5 | Median | 20 | Median | 12 | Median | 5 | Median | 5 |
| 20 | 10 | 10 | | Mode | 20 | Mode | 10 | Mode | 5 | Mode | 5 |
| 30 | 20 | 3 | 3 | Std. Dev. | 10.244 | Std. Dev. | 7.153 | Std. Dev. | 4.929 | Std. Dev. | 4.830 |
| 15 | 15 | 10 | 20 | Sample Var. | 104.934 | Sample Var. | 51.170 | Sample Var. | 24.295 | Sample Var. | 23.326 |
| 20 | 20 | 15 | 5 | Kurtosis | 0.252 | Kurtosis | 0.155 | Kurtosis | 1.448 | Kurtosis | 3.548 |
| 15 | 15 | 5 | | Skewness | 0.331 | Skewness | 0.738 | Skewness | 1.295 | Skewness | 1.616 |
| 25 | 6 | | 10 | Range | 58 | Range | 35 | Range | 20 | Range | 29 |
| 20 | 8 | 8 | 4 | Minimum | 2 | Minimum | 0 | Minimum | 0 | Minimum | 1 |
| 3 | 12 | 1 | 4 | Maximum | 60 | Maximum | 35 | Maximum | 35 | Maximum | 30 |
| 30 | 5 | | 5 | Sum | 4466 | Sum | 2878 | Sum | 1020.1 | Sum | 1264.9 |
| 20 | 30 | | 3 | Count | 205 | Count | 206 | Count | 183 | Count | 187 |
| 30 | 5 | 5 | 5 | | | | | | | | |
| 20 | 15 | 3 | 20 | | | | | | | | |
| 30 | 10 | 2 | 4 | | | | | | | | |
| 40 | 10 | 1 | 2 | Steps: | | | | | | | |
| 20 | 5 | 10 | 15 | 1. From the Tools menu, select Data Analysis, Descriptive Statistics, click OK. | | | | | | | |
| 2 | 10 | | 1 | 2. In the Descriptive Statistics dialogue box: | | | | | | | |
| 10 | 20 | 10 | 2 |     Enter the Input Range as A7:D213 | | | | | | | |
| 25 | 15 | 15 | 5 |     Check Grouped by columns | | | | | | | |
| 20 | 18 | 0 | 25 |     Check Labels in first row | | | | | | | |
| 4 | 30 | 0 | 6 |     Enter Output Range as F7 | | | | | | | |
| 30 | 6 | 3 | 5 |     Check Summary Statistics | | | | | | | |
| 30 | 10 | | 5 |     Click OK. | | | | | | | |
| 20 | 10 | 8 | 5 | 3. Select columns F to M, then from the Format menu, select Column, Autofit to make the output easier to read. | | | | | | | |
| 20 | 12 | 4 | 4 | | | | | | | | |
| 22 | 10 | 0 | 8 | | | | | | | | |
| 40 | 15 | 0 | 5 | | | | | | | | |
| 30 | 12 | 8 | | | | | | | | | |
| 30 | 4 | 20 | | | | | | | | | |
| 25 | 10 | 2 | 3 | | | | | | | | |

Not all of the respondents answered each item, as evidenced by the reported sample sizes (labelled Count). This *may* mean that some chairs do not engage in any research or external activities.

## 4. Pearson correlation

Output A4 shows the intercorrelations among four variables. The Pearson correlation matrix shown in output A4 was obtained through the Data Analysis Tool Correlation, in the Tools menu.

Excel does not give the number of cases for each correlation, neither does it give the probability value for each correlation. To determine statistical significance you must first determine the critical value in the Pearson Correlation Table for a correlation at 121 degrees of freedom ($df$ = number of pairs −2) at the 0.05 level for a two-tailed test. In this case, the critical value is 0.178. If the obtained correlation is equal to or greater than the critical value, it is significant. For example, the correlation between the number of faculty with PhDs and the number of faculty without PhDs is 0.03, which is less than the critical value of 0.178; therefore, the correlation is not statistically significant.

### Output A4
### Pearson Correlation

*What is the correlation between number of PhD, non-PhD, and part-time faculty and chair compensation?*

| Faculty PhD | Faculty No PhD | Faculty Part-time | Salary Compare |
|---|---|---|---|
| 3 | 3 | 1 | 2 |
| 4 | 2 | 0 | 2 |
| 3 | 1 | 1 | 2 |
| 6 | 2 | 1 | 2 |
| 7 | 16 | 1 | 2 |
| 11 | 1 | 2 | 1 |
| 1 | 5 | 2 | 2 |
| 11 | 1 | 3 | 2 |
| 2 | 12 | 14 | 1 |
| 3 | 2 | 1 | 3 |
| 3 | 5 | 2 | 2 |
| 15 | 4 | 9 | 1 |
| 13 | 2 | 12 | 1 |
| 6 | 5 | 8 | 2 |
| 12 | 3 | 1 | 2 |
| 10 | 5 | 2 | 2 |
| 14 | 2 | 5 | 2 |
| 6 | 2 | 2 | 2 |

|  | PhD | No PhD | Part-time | Compare |
|---|---|---|---|---|
| PhD | 1 | | | |
| No PhD | 0.032 | 1 | | |
| Part-time | 0.387 | 0.106 | 1 | |
| Compare | −0.303 | 0.072 | −0.050 | 1 |

$df = N−2$   121

**Steps:**
1. From the Tools menu, select Data Analysis, Correlation, then click OK.
2. In the Correlation dialogue box:
    Enter the Input Range as A7:D130
    Check Grouped by columns
    Check Labels in first row
    Enter Output Range as F7
    Click OK.
3. Write a formula to calculate the degrees of freedom for the correlations.
    In cell F13 enter =count(A8:A130)−2

# 5. Hypothesis testing

Five hypotheses were generated in this research. These call for the use of a Pearson correlation (for hypothesis 1), a chi-square (for hypothesis 2), a $t$-test (for hypothesis 3), an ANOVA (for hypothesis 4) and multiple regression (for hypothesis 5). The results of these tests and their interpretation are discussed below.

## Hypothesis 1: Pearson correlation

Hypothesis 1 can be stated in the null and alternate form as follows:

$H1_0$: There will be no relationship between the number of PhD faculty in a department and chair compensation relative to other business school chairs.

$H1_A$: There will be a relationship between the number of PhD faculty in a department, and the chair compensation relative to other business school chairs.

From the results in output A4, we can see that the greater the number of PhD faculty, the higher the chair's compensation vis-à-vis other business school chairs. In this study, the respondents indicated that their salary was higher than other chairs by picking '1'; therefore, the correlation is a negative –0.30. At 121 degrees of freedom and a significance level of 0.05, the correlation must be 0.178 or greater to be statistically significant; therefore, the null hypothesis is rejected and hypothesis 1 is substantiated.

## Hypothesis 2: use of chi-square test

Hypothesis 2 can be stated in the null and alternate as follows:

$H2_0$: The percentage of AACSB-accredited schools responding to the survey will be no different from the percentage of AACSB Accounting-accredited schools responding.

$H2_A$: The percentage of AACSB-accredited schools responding to the survey will be different from the percentage of AACSB Accounting-accredited schools responding.

The results shown in output A5 indicate that of the 205 schools responding, 109 hold AACSB accreditation, while 48 hold the AACSB Accounting accreditation. The chi-square value of 38.4 with 1 degree of freedom is significant, with $p < 0.05$. Therefore, hypothesis 2 is substantiated.

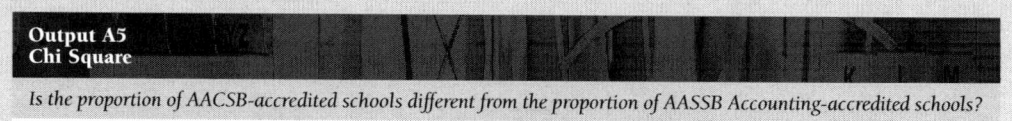

**Output A5**
**Chi Square**

Is the proportion of AACSB-accredited schools different from the proportion of AASSB Accounting-accredited schools?

| Accredited AACSB | Yes | Accredited ACC | Yes | | AACSB | ACC | Total |
|---|---|---|---|---|---|---|---|
| 2 | | 2 | | Yes | 109 | 48 | 157 |
| 2 | | 2 | | No | 96 | 157 | 253 |
| 1 | 1 | 1 | 1 | | | | |
| 2 | | 2 | | Total | 205 | 205 | 410 |
| 1 | 1 | 1 | 1 | %Yes | 53.17% | 23.41% | |
| 2 | | 2 | | | | | |
| 1 | 1 | 2 | | | | | |
| 2 | | 2 | | | | 64113760250 | |
| 2 | | 2 | | | | 1669275025 | |
| 2 | | 2 | | Chi square | | 38.41 | |
| 1 | 1 | 1 | 1 | df | | 1 | |
| 2 | | 2 | | p-value (2-tail) | | 5.73923E–10 | |
| 2 | | 2 | | | | | |
| 1 | | 2 | | | | | |
| 1 | 1 | 1 | 1 | Chi square = $\dfrac{N(AD-BC)^2}{(A+B)(C+D)(A+C)(B+D)}$ | | A | B |
| 2 | | 2 | | | | C | D |
| 2 | | 2 | | | | | |

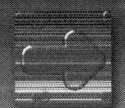

| | | | | |
|---|---|---|---|---|
| 2 | | 2 | | |
| 1 | 1 | 1 | 1 | |
| 2 | | 2 | | |
| 1 | 1 | 1 | 1 | |
| 1 | 1 | 2 | | |
| 1 | 1 | 2 | | |
| 2 | | 2 | | |
| 2 | | 2 | | |
| 1 | 1 | 2 | | |
| 2 | | 2 | 1 | |
| 1 | 1 | 1 | | |
| 1 | 1 | 2 | | |
| 2 | | 2 | | |
| 2 | | 2 | | |
| 1 | 1 | 2 | 1 | |
| 1 | 1 | 1 | | |
| 1 | 1 | 2 | 1 | |
| 1 | 1 | 1 | | |
| 2 | | 2 | | |
| 2 | | 2 | 1 | |
| 2 | 1 | 1 | | |
| 2 | | 2 | | |
| 1 | 1 | 2 | | |
| 2 | | 2 | | |
| 2 | | 2 | | |
| 1 | 1 | 2 | | |
| 2 | | 2 | | |
| 2 | | 2 | | |
| 2 | | 2 | | |
| 1 | 1 | 2 | 1 | |
| 1 | 1 | 1 | | |
| 1 | 1 | 2 | | |
| 2 | | 2 | | |
| 1 | 1 | 2 | | |

Steps:
1. Write a formula to identify Yes responses on Accredited AACSB:
   In cell B8 enter formula =if(A8=1,1,"")
   Copy formula in cell B8 to cells B9 to B212
2. Write a formula to identify Yes responses on Accredited ACC:
   In cell D8 enter formula =if(C8=1,1,"")
   Copy formula in cell D8 to cells D9 to D212
3. Write formulas to count the number of responess:
   In cell A214 enter formula =count(A8:A212)
   In cell B214 enter formula =count(B8:B212)
   In cell B215 enter formula =A214–B214
   In cell C214 enter formula =count(C8:C212)
   In cell D214 enter formula =count(D8:D212)
   In cell D215 enter formula =C214–D214
4. Create a 2X2 table to store the results of step 3:
   In cell G7 enter formula +B214
   In cell G8 enter formula +B215
   In cell H7 enter formula +D214
   In cell H8 enter formula +D215
5. Write formulas to calculate the total number of observations for each variable:
   In cell G10 enter formula =sum(G7:G8)
   In cell H10 enter formula =sum(H7:H8)
   In cell J7 enter formula =sum(G7:H7)
   In cell J8 enter formula =sum(G8:H8)
   In cell J10 enter formula =sum(G7:H8)
6. Write formulas to calculate the percentage of Yes for each variable:
   In cell G11 enter formula =G7/G10
   In cell H11 enter formula =H7/H10
7. Write a formula to calculate the chi square
   In cell H13 enter formula =J10*(G7*H8–H7*G8)^2
   In cell H14 enter formula
   =(G7+H7)*(G8+H8)*(G7+G8)*(H7+H8)
   In cell H15 enter formula = H13/H14
8. Write a formula to calculate the degrees of freedom for the chi square:
   In cell H16 enter formula =(COUNT(G7:H7)–1)
   *(COUNT(G7:G8)–1)
9. Write a formula to calculate the probability value of the chi square with 1 degree of freedom:
   In cell H17 enter formula =CHIDIST(H15,1)

## Hypothesis 3: use of *t*-test

Hypothesis 3 can be stated in the null and alternate as follows:

**H3$_0$:** There will be no difference between men and women in the number of research articles reported.

**H3$_A$:** There will be a difference between male and female chairs in the number of research articles reported.

The results of this *t*-test are shown in output A6. The *t*-test used is for two samples assuming unequal variance. The *t* value of –0.152 is not significant, so the null hypotheses is accepted. Thus, this hypothesis is *not* substantiated. Although women have more publications on average (1.13 vs. 1.05) there is no statistically significant difference between males and females in the number of research articles.

### Output A6
### t-Test

*Is there a difference in scholarly activity by gender?*

| Gender | Publications research |
|---|---|
| 1 | 0 |
| 1 | 0 |
| 1 | 3 |
| 1 | 0 |
| 1 | 0 |
| 1 | 1 |
| 1 | 4 |
| 1 | 0 |
| 1 | 0 |
| 1 | 2 |
| 1 | 0 |
| 1 | 0 |
| 1 | 2 |
| 1 | 1 |
| 1 | 0 |
| 1 | 0 |
| 1 | 0 |
| 1 | 2 |
| 1 | 0 |
| 1 | 0 |
| 1 | 0 |
| 1 | 4 |
| 1 | 0 |
| 1 | 0 |
| 1 | 2 |
| 1 | 2 |
| 1 | 11 |

**t-Test: Two-Sample Assuming Unequal Variances**

|  | Variable 1 | Variable 2 |
|---|---|---|
| Mean | 1.049 | 1.125 |
| Variance | 4.027 | 5.158 |
| Observations | 103 | 24 |
| Hypothesised Mean Difference | 0 | |
| df | 32 | |
| t Stat | −0.152 | |
| P(T<=t) one tail | 0.440 | |
| t Critical one-tail | 1.694 | |
| P(T<=t) two-tail | 0.880 | |
| t Critical two-tail | 2.037 | |

Steps:
1. Sort the data by gender:
   Select cells A7 to B134
   From the Data menu, select Sort, check Header row, select Sort by Gender, check Ascending
   Click OK
2. From the Tools menu, select Data Analysis, t-Test: Two Sample Assuming Unequal Variances, click OK:
   From the t-Test menu enter Input Variable 1 range as B8:B110
   Enter Input Variable 2 Range as B111:B134
   Uncheck labels
   Enter Alpha as 0.05
   Enter Output Range as D7
3. Reformat output to make it easier to read:
   Select columns E to G, and from the Format menu, select Column, Autofit.

## Hypothesis 4: use of ANOVA

The fourth hypothesis can be stated in the null and alternate forms as follows:

**H4$_0$:** Scores on the Working Relationships scale will be the same irrespective of the number of years a person has served as chair.

**H4$_A$:** Working Relationships scale scores will vary depending on the number of years an individual has served as chair.

Because there are more than two groups (service as chair was categorised as 1–2 years, 3–6 years and 7 or more years) and the working relationship scale is interval in nature, an ANOVA is the appropriate test.

The Excel results can be seen in output A7. The F-Ratio of 5.028, with 2 and 200 degrees of freedom, is statistically significant at $p = 0.007$. That is, there are significant differences in perceived working relationships based on length of time in office. This hypothesis has been substantiated.

### Output A7
### ANOVA

Is there an effect of years spent as chair on working relationships?

Years as Chair

| 1 to 2 | 3 to 6 | 7 or more |
|---|---|---|
| 23 | 27 | 19 |
| 21 | 20 | 24 |
| 26 | 20 | 27 |
| 23 | 28 | 23 |
| 23 | 23 | 28 |
| 26 | 17 | 20 |
| 23 | 20 | 28 |
| 24 | 28 | 25 |
| 18 | 13 | 28 |
| 20 | 22 | 21 |
| 21 | 17 | 25 |
| 21 | 19 | 23 |
| 23 | 25 | 23 |
| 26 | 2 | 24 |
| 21 | 21 | 28 |
| 20 | 21 | 24 |
| 22 | 25 | 28 |
| 20 | 28 | 26 |
| 20 | 22 | 26 |
| 22 | 22 | 21 |
| 22 | 14 | 23 |
| 22 | 27 | 21 |
| 20 | 21 | 22 |
| 16 | 24 | 24 |
| 23 | 18 | 13 |
| 28 | 23 | 24 |
| 29 | 29 | 24 |
| 16 | 22 | 21 |

Anova: Single Factor
SUMMARY

| Groups | Count | Sum | Average | Variance |
|---|---|---|---|---|
| 1 to 2 | 58 | 1285 | 22.155 | 10.239 |
| 3 to 6 | 92 | 2043 | 22.207 | 12.628 |
| 7 or more | 53 | 1267 | 23.906 | 10.972 |

ANOVA

| Source of Variation | SS | df | MS | F | P-value | F crit |
|---|---|---|---|---|---|---|
| Between Groups | 115.817 | 2 | 57.908 | 5.028 | 0.007 | 3.041 |
| Within Groups | 2303.207 | 200 | 11.516 | | | |
| Total | 2419.025 | 202 | | | | |

Steps:
1. From the Tools menu, select Data Analysis, ANOVA: Single Factor.
2. In the ANOVA: Single Factor dialogue box:
   Enter Input range as A7:C99
   Check Grouped by Columns
   Check Labels in first row
   Set Alpha at 0.05
   Enter Output Range as E7
   Click OK.
3. Make the ANOVA output easier to read:
   Select columns E to K
   From the Format menu, select Columns, Width, and enter 15.

## Hypothesis 5: use of multiple regression analysis

The last hypothesis can be stated in the null and alternate forms as follows:

**H5$_0$:** The three independent variables of soft money, budget discretion and hours in the day will not significantly predict the number of research publications by the chair.

**H5$_A$:** The three independent variables will significantly predict the number of research publications by the chair.

To test this hypothesis, multiple regression analysis was carried out. The results of regressing the three independent variables against the number of research publications can be seen in output A8. The Multiple R (0.356) is the multiple correlation among the three independent variables and the dependent variable, and the R Square (0.127) is the variance in the dependent variable accounted by the three independent variables. The F-Ratio of 4.59 at 3 and 95 degrees of freedom is statistically significant at the 0.005 level.

In effect, this hypothesis is substantiated with 12.7 per cent of the variance in the number of the research publications explained by the three independent variables. However, it should be noted that the variance explained is small, and other variables should be explored in this context.

To determine which variables in the regression equation are significant predictors of the number of research publications by the chair, Excel provides the unstandardised regression coefficients, and a t-statistic and associated probability value for these regression coefficients. For the regression analysis shown in output A8, both discretionary budget money and soft money are significant predictors of the number of research publications by the chair, but the hours-in-the-day scale is not. Excel does not provide standardised regression coefficients (Beta weights).

## Overall interpretation

This was an exploratory study. The authors hoped to learn something about the chair job before starting a longitudinal study on 'burnout' in the chair position. They have learned that one of their scales is not a reliable scale and should be substituted with a better scale. They have also learned that chairs with more PhD faculty think they are more highly paid than other business school chairs. Some of the anticipated gender differences in research publications were not substantiated by the results. The time spent as chair of the department also does not seem to be related to working relationships within the department and the school. The variables examined to predict the number of research publications explained only a small part of the variance. Other variables have to be examined in this connection. Some of the measures will have to be refined before launching the next phase of the research effort.

### Output A8
### Multiple Regression

Does the amount of discretionary funds and soft dollars in the budget and reported time in the day predict the number of publications by chairs?

| Publications Research | Budget Discretionary | Budget Soft $ | Hours in Day Scale |
|---|---|---|---|
| 0 | 3 | 4 | 5 |
| 0 | 3 | 2 | 4 |
| 3 | 2 | 1 | 4 |
| 0 | 1 | 1 | 3 |
| 0 | 3 | 3 | 5 |
| 4 | 4 | 4 | 5 |
| 0 | 2 | 1 | 5 |
| 2 | 5 | 3 | 3 |
| 10 | 1 | 4 | 4 |
| 0 | 3 | 1 | 5 |
| 0 | 3 | 1 | 4 |
| 0 | 3 | 3 | 4 |
| 1 | 4 | 1 | 5 |
| 0 | 5 | 4 | 4 |
| 1 | 2 | 1 | 5 |
| 0 | 2 | 1 | 4 |
| 0 | 4 | 4 | 4 |
| 2 | 1 | 3 | 4 |
| 2 | 2 | 1 | 5 |
| 0 | 1 | 1 | 3 |
| 1 | 4 | 1 | 5 |
| 0 | 4 | 4 | 4 |
| 4 | 1 | 1 | 4 |
| 0 | 2 | 1 | 5 |
| 2 | 3 | 4 | 4 |
| 2 | 5 | 2 | 4 |
| 2 | 5 | 5 | 3 |
| 0 | 1 | 1 | 4 |
| 4 | 2 | 3 | 5 |
| 0 | 5 | 4 | 5 |
| 3 | 1 | 1 | 4 |
| 0 | 1 | 1 | 2 |
| 0 | 4 | 3 | 5 |

SUMMARY OUTPUT

*Regression statistics*

| | |
|---|---|
| Multiple R | 0.356 |
| R Square | 0.127 |
| Adusted R square | 0.099 |
| Standard error | 2.227 |
| Observations | 99 |

ANOVA

| | df | SS | MS | F | Significance F |
|---|---|---|---|---|---|
| Regression | 3 | 68.294 | 22.765 | 4.588 | 0.005 |
| Residual | 95 | 471.343 | 4.962 | | |
| Total | 98 | 539.636 | | | |

| | Co-efficients | Standard error | t Stat | P-value | Lower 95% | Upper 95% |
|---|---|---|---|---|---|---|
| Intercept | 1.343 | 1.194 | 1.125 | 0.263 | −1.026 | 3.713 |
| Discretionary | −0.488 | 0.192 | −2.541 | 0.013 | −0.870 | −0.107 |
| Soft $ | 0.652 | 0.181 | 3.590 | 0.001 | 0.291 | 1.012 |
| Day scale | −0.012 | 0.273 | −0.072 | 0.942 | −0.561 | 0.521 |

Steps:
1. From the Tools menu, select Data Analysis, Regression.
2. In the Regression dialogue box:
    Enter Input Y range as A7:A106
    Enter Input X range as B7:D106
    Check Labels
    Enter Output Range as F7
    Click OK.
3. Make the output easier to read:
    Select columns F to N
    From the Format menu, select Column, Width, and enter 15.

# part V

## RESEARCH REPORTING AND MANAGERIAL DECISION MAKING

14 Research reporting

15 Managerial decision making and evaluating research

# chapter 14

# RESEARCH REPORTING

## OUTLINE

**THE WRITTEN REPORT**

**INTEGRAL PARTS OF THE REPORT**

**ORAL PRESENTATION**

**SUMMARY**

**DISCUSSION POINTS**

**EXERCISES**

**APPENDIX**
- REPORT 1: EXAMPLE OF A REPORT INVOLVING A DESCRIPTIVE STUDY
- REPORT 2: EXAMPLE OF A REPORT WHERE AN IDEA HAS TO BE 'SOLD'
- REPORT 3: EXAMPLE OF A REPORT OFFERING ALTERNATIVE SOLUTIONS AND EXPLAINING THE PROS AND CONS OF EACH ALTERNATIVE
- REPORT 4: EXAMPLE OF AN ABRIDGED BASIC RESEARCH REPORT
- REPORT 5: EXAMPLE OF AN ABRIDGED APPLIED BUSINESS RESEARCH REPORT

## CHAPTER OBJECTIVES

After reading this chapter, you should be able to:
- understand the contents and structure of a business research report
- tailor the report format to meet the needs of different types of research (basic and applied), different research goals that need reports of varying lengths, and different audiences
- write a good executive summary or abstract, introductory section, methods section, data analysis section and interpretation of the results, using tables and pictorial representations wherever appropriate
- give your conclusions, recommendations and suggestions for implementation, as necessary
- write the report summary and acknowledgements
- provide the appropriate references
- include appropriate materials in the appendix
- identify the components of, and make, a good oral presentation.

Once the data analyses are completed and conclusions drawn from the findings, the researcher is ready to present the results of the research study and make suitable recommendations. This is usually done in the form of a written report, frequently followed up by an oral presentation. (This step in the resesrach process is illustrated by the shaded box in figure 14.1.)

It is important that the results of the study and the recommended solutions to the problem are effectively communicated to the sponsors or client, so that the suggestions made are accepted and implemented. Otherwise, all the effort expended on the investigation would be in vain. Writing the report concisely, convincingly and with clarity is perhaps even more important than conducting a perfect research study. Hence, a well-thought-out written report and oral presentation are critical.

The contents and organisation of both modes of communication — the written report and the oral presentation — depend on the purpose of the research study and the audience at which it is targeted. The relevant aspects of the written and oral reports are discussed in this chapter.

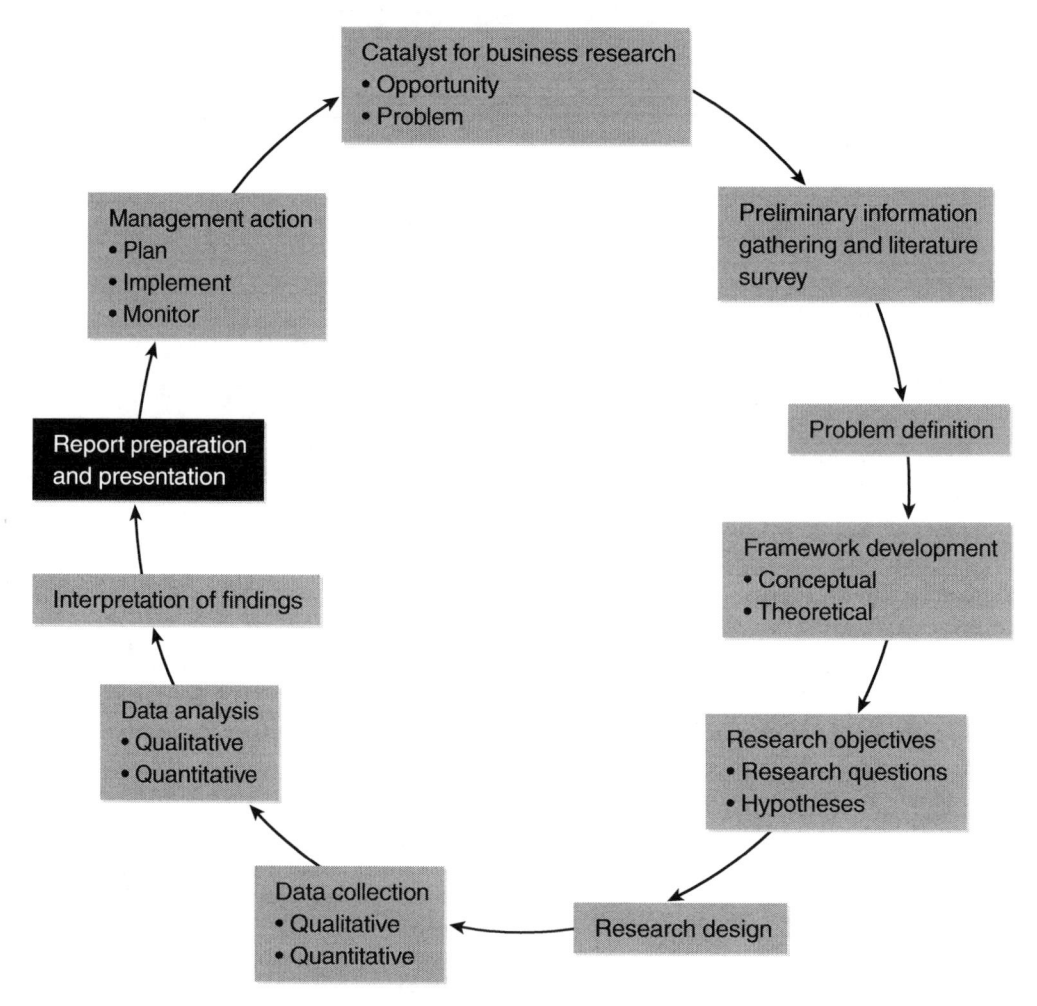

**Figure 14.1** The business research process: research reporting

# THE WRITTEN REPORT

The written report enables the manager to weigh the facts and arguments presented therein and implement the acceptable recommendations, with a view to closing the gap between the existing state of affairs and the desired state. To achieve its goal, the written report has to focus on the following issues.

## THE WRITTEN REPORT AND ITS PURPOSE

Reports can be written for different purposes, so the form of the written report will vary according to the situation. It is important to identify the *purpose* of the report so that it can be tailored accordingly. If the purpose is simply to offer *details on some specific factors* requested by a manager, the report can be very narrowly focused and provide the desired information to the manager in a brief format, as in example 14.1. If, on the other hand, the report is intended to '*sell an idea*' to management, then it has to be more detailed and convincing as to why the proposed idea is an improvement and should be adopted. Here the emphasis should be on presenting all the relevant information, backed by the necessary data, to persuade the reader to 'buy into the idea'. An illustration of the purpose of such a report and its contents can be seen in example 14.2. A variation will be provided in cases where a manager asks for *several alternative solutions or recommendations* to rectify a problem in a given situation. The researcher provides the requested information and the manager chooses from among the alternatives and makes the final decision. In this case, a more detailed report surveying past studies, the methodology used for the present study, different perspectives generated from interviews and current data analysis, and alternative solutions based on the conclusions drawn from the results of data analyses, will have to be provided. How each alternative will help to improve the problem situation must also be discussed. The advantages and disadvantages of each of the proposed solutions, together with a cost–benefit analysis in terms of dollars and/or other resources, will also have to be presented to help the manager make the decision. A situation such as in example 14.3 would warrant this kind of a report. Such a report can also be found in Report 3 in the appendix to this chapter.

Still another type of report might require the researcher to *identify the problem and provide the final solution* as well. That is, the researcher might be called in to study a situation, determine the nature of the problem, and offer a report of the findings and recommendations. Such a report has to be very detailed, following the format of a full-fledged study, as detailed later in this chapter. A fifth kind of research report is the more scholarly publication presenting the *findings of a basic or applied study* that one usually finds published in academic journals.

---

### EXAMPLE 14.1 — A SIMPLE DESCRIPTIVE REPORT

If a study is undertaken to understand in detail certain factors of interest in a given situation (for example variations in production levels or composition of employees), then a report describing the phenomena of interest, in the manner desired, is all that is called for. For instance, let us say a human resources manager wants to know how many employees have been recruited during the past 18 months in the organisation, their gender composition, their educational level and the average proportion of days that these individuals have absented themselves since recruitment. A simple report giving the desired information is all that would be necessary.

In this report, a statement of the *purpose* of the study will be first given (for example, it was desired that a profile of the employees recruited during the past 18 months in the company and an idea of their rate of absenteeism be provided). The *methods* or *procedures* adopted to collect the data would then be given (say, the company payroll and the personal records of the employees were examined). Finally, a narration of the actual *results*, reinforced by visual tabular and graphical forms of representation of the data, will be provided. Frequency distributions, cross-tabulations and other data will be presented in a tabular form, and illustrations will include bar charts (for gender), pie charts (to indicate the proportions of individuals at various educational levels) and so on. This section will summarise the data, and may look as follows.

A total of 80 employees have been recruited during the past 18 months, of whom 45 per cent are women and 55 per cent are men. Twenty per cent have a master's degree, 68 per cent a bachelor's degree, and 12 per cent a high school qualification. The average proportion of days that these employees remained absent during the past 18 months is 16 per cent.

These details provide the required information to the manager. It may, however, also be advisable to provide a further gender breakdown of the mean proportion of days of absence of the employees in an appendix, even though this information might not have been specifically requested. If considered relevant, a similar breakdown can also be offered for people at different job levels.

A short, simple report of the type discussed previously is provided in Report 1 in the appendix to this chapter.

### EXAMPLE 14.2 DETAILS OF A REPORT TO 'SELL' AN IDEA

The purpose of a report may be to sell an idea to top management. For example, the Information Technology (IT) manager might want to convince the top executives that a Web-based *executive information system (EIS)* would greatly enhance the effectiveness of top executives of a multinational organisation with branches throughout Australasia and the Pacific, by virtue of the speed and timeliness of the electronic information delivery system. With up-to-the-minute information available at the fingertips of executives — something the current reporting system lacks — informed decisions could be made with much greater confidence. When the executives realise that they can perform their information-intensive activities with ease and speed, and simultaneously enhance the quality of their decisions, they will readily buy into the data. But then the research report for this purpose will have a different thrust and focus in greater detail on:

- explaining in clear and simple terms what a Web-based EIS is, and how it would be a powerful executive tool for effective decision making
- how an EIS would save time (for example by giving immediate access to the specific information executives need in the different branches throughout the region)
- how it would be infinitely better than the current system (since all information would be on the Web, the EIS would provide executives with all the current data needed — something that would enhance the quality of the decisions made)
- how it would save resources in the long run (backed by a detailed cost–benefit analysis). For instance, compare the costs of training executives to use the system and updating information on a daily basis, *versus* the benefits of savings accrued through more informed and timely decisions, as in the case of the establishment of a viable 'just-in-time' inventory system, which would save a lot of money for the organisation.
- giving examples from past company history (within the past six months, if possible) of how a Web-based EIS system would have helped the executives make more informed decisions in those instances, and how it could have saved the system money and/or resources
- a final convincing recommendation to adopt a Web-based EIS as a way of organisational decision making.

A specimen of the type of report discussed above with respect to recommending sabbatical leave for managers is provided in Report 2 in the appendix to this chapter.

**EXAMPLE 14.3**

## A CASE FOR A COMPREHENSIVE REPORT OFFERING ALTERNATIVE SOLUTIONS

The CEO of a tyre company wants recommendations on how the future growth of the company should be planned, taking into consideration manufacturing, marketing, accounting and financial perspectives. In this case, only a broad objective is stated: corporate growth. There may currently be several impediments that retard growth. One has to carefully examine the situation to determine the obstacles to expansion and how these may be overcome through strategic planning from the production, marketing, management, financial and accounting perspectives. Identifying the problems or impediments in the situation would require intensive interviewing, a literature review, industry analysis, formulation of a theoretical perspective, the generation of several hypotheses to come up with different alternative solutions, data gathering, data analyses and exploration of alternative ways of attaining corporate growth through diifferent strategies. To enable the CEO to assess the alternatives proposed, the pros and cons of implementing each of the alternative solutions, and a statement of the costs and benefits attached to each, would follow.

This report will be more elaborate than the previous two, detailing each step in the study, emphasising the results of data analysis and providing a strong basis for the various recommendations. The alternatives generated and the pros and cons of each in a report such as this are likely to follow the format of Report 3 in the appendix to this chapter.

As we have seen, the contents and format of a report will depend on the purpose of the study and the needs of the audience to whom it is submitted.

Examples of basic and applied business research projects are provided in Reports 4 and 5 in the appendix to this chapter. Report 4 is an example of a published basic research study that looks at the factors influencing the upward mobility of women in accounting firms, and Report 5 presents an applied business research report investigating staff attitudes towards the system of academic titles used in New Zealand universities.

# THE WRITTEN REPORT AND ITS AUDIENCE

The organisation of a report, its length, focus on details, data presentation and illustrations, will in part be a function of the audience for whom it is intended. The letter of transmittal of the report would clearly indicate to whom the report is being sent. An executive summary placed at the beginning would offer busy executives just the right amount of vital details — usually in less than three pages. The executive summary will help the business managers to quickly grasp the essentials of the study and its findings, and turn to the pages that offer more detailed information on aspects that are of particular interest to them.

Some managers are distracted by data presented in the form of tables and feel more comfortable with graphs and charts, while others want to see 'facts and figures' (Williams 1990). Whereas both tables and figures are visual forms of representation and need to be presented in reports, which ones are predominantly displayed within the body of the report and which are relegated to an appendix depends on an awareness of the idiosyncracies of the ultimate consumer of the report. If a report were to be handled by different executives with different orientations, it should be packaged in such a way that the individuals know where to find the information that meets their preferred mode of information processing. For example, in addition to mentioning market share in the text, it can be illustrated through a pie chart, while the raw data can also be presented in tabular form.

The length, organisation and presentation modes of the report will depend partly on the target audience. Some businesses might prescribe their own format for report writing. In all cases, good reporting is a function of knowing who the audience is and the purpose of the report. As we have seen, some reports may have to be long and detailed, others brief and specific.

Sometimes the findings of a study could be unpalatable to the executive (for example, the organisational policies are outdated and the system is too bureaucratic) or could reflect poorly on management, tending to make them react defensively (for example, the system has an ineffective top-down approach). In such cases, tact should be exercised in presenting the conclusions without compromising the actual findings. That is, although there is no need to suppress the unpalatable findings, they can be presented in a non-judgemental and non-accusatory way, using objective data and facts that forcefully lead to and convince the managers of the correctness of the conclusions drawn. If this is not done, the report will be read defensively, the recommendations will not be accepted and the problem will remain unsolved.

Tact and diplomacy, combined with honesty and objectivity, are essential in report writing and presentation. Although this is true for both internal and external research teams, the internal team's research report writing in such cases becomes even more difficult. Being a part of the very system on which such findings are reported, the internal team might be perceived as challenging the authority of the hierarchy. Hence, it is easy to be intimidated by power and authority, but the internal research team, while being polite, should package its findings in a professional, unbiased and tactful manner, thereby preserving the integrity of the findings.

As an example of such a presentation, if the system has outmoded policies (or is highly bureaucratic), the report can convey the following. After presenting the data to support the facts, it might state that these policies (and the system) were perhaps appropriate at the time they were formulated, but the current goals of the present management, coupled with the passage of time, call for a change. It can also highlight the fact that the present system is receptive to changes and changing the policies (or the structure) of the organisation will not, therefore, pose difficult problems. A similar appropriate strategy can be followed to change the top-down approach to a bottom-up management style.

## CHARACTERISTICS OF A WELL-WRITTEN REPORT

Despite the fact that report writing is a function of the purpose of the study and the type of audience to which it is presented, and has accordingly to be tailored to meet both, certain basic features are integral to all written reports. Clarity, conciseness, coherence, proper emphasis on important aspects, meaningful organisation of paragraphs, smooth transitions from one topic to the next, apt choice of words and specificity are all important features of a good report. The report should be free of technical or statistical jargon as far as possible, unless it happens to be of a technical or statistical nature. Care should also be taken to eliminate grammatical and spelling errors.

Any assumptions made by the researcher should be clearly stated in the report, and facts, rather than opinions, provided. The report should be organised in a manner that enhances the meaningful and smooth flow of materials, as the reader goes through it. The importance of the appearance of the report and its readability cannot be overemphasised.

Appropriate headings and subheadings help to organise the report in a logical manner and help the reader to follow the transitions easily. A one-and-a-half- or double-spaced, typed report with wide margins on all sides enables the reader to make notes or comments while going through the contents.

## CONTENTS OF THE RESEARCH REPORT

It is obvious that the research report should bear a *title* that indicates in a succinct manner what the study is about. It should have at the beginning a *table of contents*, where appropriate a copy of the *authorisation* to conduct the study (in response to the original research proposal), and an *executive summary* (in the case of applied research) or a **synopsis** (in the case of basic research). An *abstract* is provided for a thesis, dissertation or published paper. Note that sometimes the authorisation is placed as the first appendix, and the executive summary is presented before the table of contents.

All reports should have an introductory section detailing the purpose of the study, giving some background on what it relates to and stating the problem studied, setting the stage for what the reader can expect in the rest of the report. The body of the report should contain details regarding the framework of the study, hypotheses if any, sampling design, data collection methods, analysis of data and the results obtained. The final part of the report would present the findings and draw conclusions. Also, every professional report would point out the limitations of the study (in sampling, data collection and so on). If recommendations have been called for, they would be included, with a cost–benefit analysis provided with respect to each. Such information would clarify the net advantages of implementing each of the recommendations. The details provided in the report should convince the reader of the thoroughness of the study, and offer a sense of confidence in accepting the results and the recommendations made.

Good descriptions and lucid explanations, smooth and easy flow of materials, recommendations that flow logically from the results of data analysis and an explicit statement of any limitations to the study offer a scientific authenticity to the report. The transmittal letter (that is, a cover note to the client or manager accompanying the report) is best written with a personal touch, where appropriate.

To summarise, a rigorous, well-conducted study loses its value when it is not properly presented. To be useful, a report should provide a good rationale for the study, clearly present the problem studied, present the results of data analyses fully and adequately, and interpret the data in a manner that is comprehensible to the reader. The conclusion drawn from the findings should indicate a clear solution to the problem or opportunity.

The report can be organised in parts, sections or chapters, and should be tailored to meet the needs of the situation. Good, crisp and clear writing; figures, charts and tables that succinctly support or highlight the salient issues; and attractive packaging are some of the essential characteristics of a good report. The writing style should be simple, interesting, precise and comprehensible. Unbiased and objective presentation of the findings and specific reference to the limitations of the study lend credibility to the research work. Tact and diplomacy are required in presenting unpalatable findings without distortion, and in an objective, non-threatening and useful manner that would not offend the sponsor or client. The format and style of reporting should be tailored to the audience and meet the purpose of the study.

The report would end with a summary and conclusions, and acknowledge the help received from various individuals and sources. A list of references cited in the report would then follow. Appendices, if any, would be attached to the back of the report. We will now discuss the different parts of the report.

# INTEGRAL PARTS OF THE REPORT

## THE TITLE PAGE OF THE RESEARCH REPORT

The title of the report should indicate succinctly what the study is about. Examples of good report titles are:

1. A Study of Customer Satisfaction with Pizzarama in Perth, Western Australia
2. Factors Influencing the Burnout of Nurses in Wellington Hospital
3. Antecedents and Consequences of White-Collar Employees' Resistance to Mechanisation in Service Industries
4. Factors Affecting the Upward Mobility of Women in Accounting Firms
5. A Study of Portfolio Balancing and Risk Management in Investment Firms.

The first two projects will involve applied research, whereas the last three will be in the realm of basic research.

In addition to the title of the project, the title page will indicate the name of the sponsor or client of the study, the names of the researchers and their affiliations, and the date the final report is prepared.

## TABLE OF CONTENTS

The table of contents with page references usually lists the important headings and subheadings in the report. For larger reports, a separate list of tables and figures should follow the table of contents.

The table of contents, following the title page and the letter of transmittal, would look something like the example below, with some variations. Note that the actual table of contents would depend on the size and nature of the study/research report and the client or sponsor for the research.

**Table of Contents**

*Authorisation letter*

*Executive summary*

*Introduction*
- Problem studied
- Background information
- Research objectives

*Preliminary details*
- Unstructured and structured interviews
- Literature survey
- Theoretical framework
- Hypotheses formulated

*Research design*
- Type and nature of the study
- Sampling design
- Data collection methods
- Data analytic techniques used

*Results of data analysis*
- Descriptive statistics
- Hypothesis tests

*Conclusions*
- Summary and conclusions
- Limitations of the study
- Recommendations

*Acknowledgements*

*References*

*Appendices*

## AUTHORISATION LETTER

A copy of the letter of authorisation from the sponsor or client of the study, approving the investigation and detailing its scope, is sometimes attached at the beginning of the report (or more generally in the first appendix). This letter would have been given by the sponsor (or client) in response to the research proposal submitted by the researcher soon after the initial interviews and the identification of the problem. The authorisation makes clear to the reader the goals of the study.

# THE EXECUTIVE SUMMARY OR SYNOPSIS

The executive summary (or synopsis) is a brief account of the research study that provides an overview and highlights the following important information related to the study: the problem statement, the sampling design, the data collection methods used, results of data analysis, the findings, conclusions and recommendations, with suggestions for their implementation. The executive summary (or synopsis) will be brief — usually less than three pages in length. Sometimes the executive summary is presented before the table of contents.

An example of an executive summary of the study of customer satisfaction with Pizzarama in Perth follows.

---

**EXAMPLE 14.6** **EXECUTIVE SUMMARY OF PIZZARAMA STUDY**

*Introduction and relevant details*
At the request of the manager of Pizzarama in a Perth suburb, a survey was conducted to assess customer satisfaction. The sample comprised 240 customers, who were administered a short questionnaire during a two-month period from 15 July to 14 September. Each day, four customers who walked into Pizzarama at 12:00 noon, 3:00 p.m., 6:00 p.m., and 9:00 p.m. were asked to respond to a short questionnaire on site, after they had eaten the pizza. The questionnaire, requiring fewer than three minutes for completion, asked respondents to give information on their gender and age, and to indicate on a five-point scale, the extent of their satisfaction with (1) the flavour and texture of the pizza, (2) its taste, (3) nutritional value, (4) price, (5) the quality of service, and (6) the ambience of the eating place. An open-ended question also asked them to offer additional comments they might wish to make. Customers placed their responses in a locked drop box kept near the exit.

*Results of data analysis*
Analysis of the data indicated that about 60 per cent of the respondents were men and 40 per cent women. Most of them were over 25 years of age. Customers expressed greatest satisfaction with the taste of the pizza (a mean of 4.5 on a five-point scale), followed by its flavour and texture (mean of 4). They were neither pleased nor displeased with the price or the quality of service (3 on a five-point scale). However, they were not particularly happy with the ambience or the nutritional value (mean of 2.5 for each). The comments offered in the open-ended question indicated that some 25 individuals thought that the amount of cheese in the pizza might increase their cholesterol level to the detriment of their health.

*Conclusions and recommendations*
These results indicate that customers do like the pizza and have no specific complaints about the price or the service. Should the manager be concerned about the displeasure of the customers with the ambience or the nutritional value, these can be handled fairly easily. It is possible, for instance, to improve the ambience with flowers and hanging baskets of plants. Lighted candles on the tables in the evenings would also enhance the atmosphere.

As for dissatisfaction with the nutritional value, information about the use of only low-fat cheese in the pizza as a health safeguard could be disseminated through the menu card and advertisements. The option of pizza with non-fat cheese might also be offered to customers.

If enhancement of the level of customer satisfaction is desired, a short training program could be introduced for the waiters for the purpose, and their service thereafter supervised until the 'service with a smile' motto is internalised by them.

## THE INTRODUCTORY SECTION

The introductory section starts with a statement of the problem investigated. The research objective, together with background information of why and how the study was initiated, will also be stated. In the case of basic research the introductory section will offer an idea of the topic researched, and why it is important to study it. The arguments would focus on the relevance, timeliness and appropriateness of the research, in the context of current factors and trends in society and/or organisations.

The research objectives and the problem statement to be studied are clearly set out in this section.

## THE BODY OF THE REPORT

In this part, the details of the interviews conducted, the literature survey, the theoretical framework and the hypotheses are provided. The design details, such as sampling and data collection methods, as well as the nature and type of study, the time horizon, the field setting and the unit of analysis, will be described.

Next, the details of the types of data analyses carried out to test the hypotheses and the findings will be provided. Tabular and graphical illustrations of the results of data analysis will find a place here. A few of the various ways in which data can be graphically presented in written reports and oral presentations are illustrated in figure 14.2 opposite.

## THE FINAL PART OF THE REPORT

The final part of the report will contain the conclusions drawn from the findings. In most cases (depending on the scope of the project), a list of recommendations for implementation will follow. Frequently, a cost–benefit analysis will also be provided. Any limitations to the study — for example flaws in sampling due to circumstances beyond one's control — will find a place here. A brief summation paragraph will also be provided at the end (or with the conclusions).

## ACKNOWLEDGEMENTS

Next, the help received from others is acknowledged. Usually, the people who assisted in the study by collecting the questionnaires, acting as liaisons, helping in data analysis and so on are recognised and thanked. The organisation is thanked for the facilities provided, and organisational members are thanked for responding to the survey.

It should now be easy to see, given the variety of information covered in the report, why it is important to have appropriate headings and subheadings throughout. This enables the reader to progress through the report smoothly, easily and quickly, and leaving wide margins on all sides enables the reader to jot down points or make notes, where considered necessary, while reading the report.

## REFERENCES

Immediately after the acknowledgements, starting on a fresh page, a list of the references cited in the literature review and at other places in the report will be given. The format of the references has been discussed and illustrated in section 3 of the appendix to chapter 3. Footnotes, if there are any in the text, are referenced either separately at the end of the report, or at the bottom of the page where the footnote occurs.

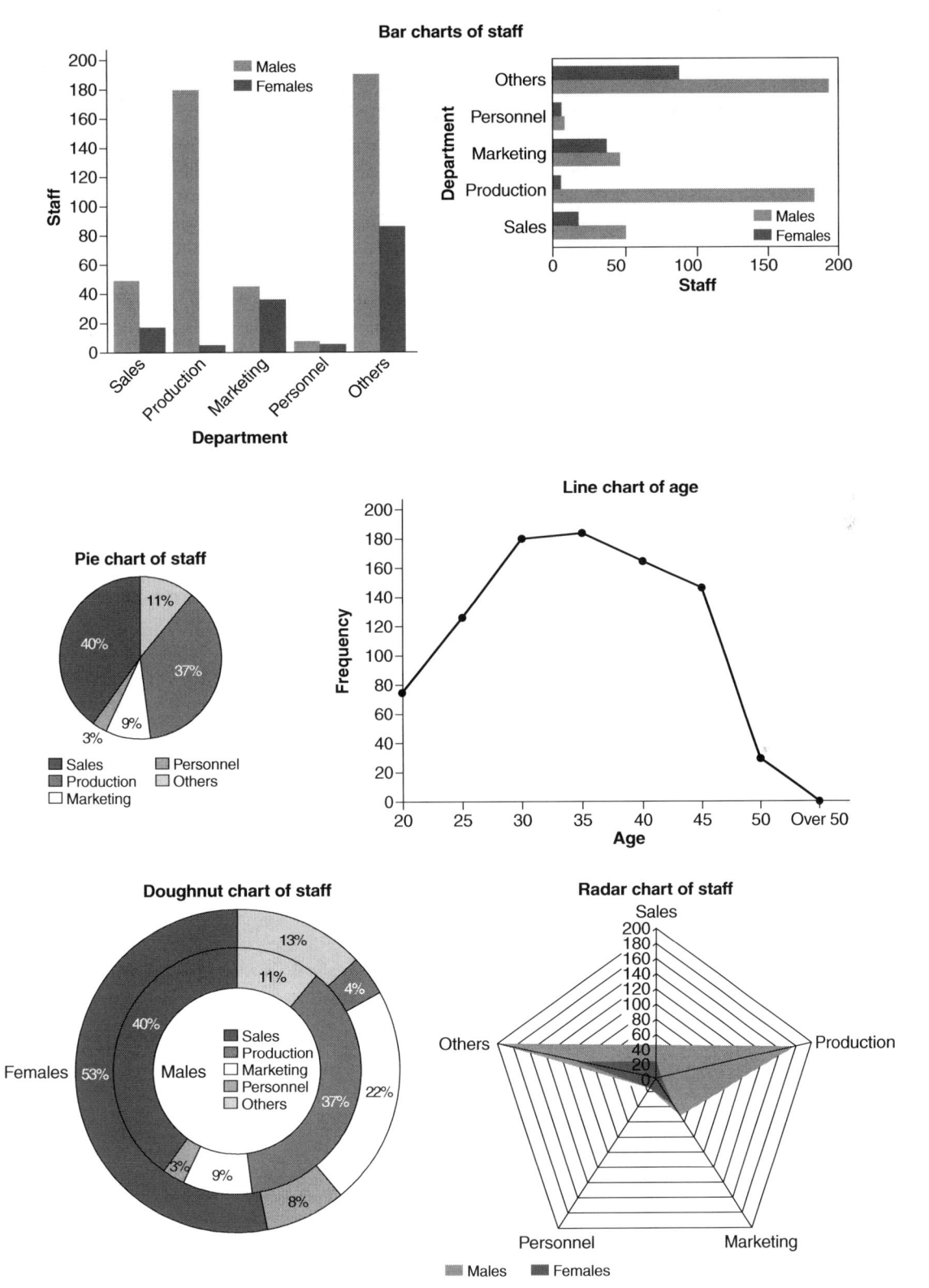

**Figure 14.2** Pictorial representations of data

## APPENDICES

The appendices, which come last, are the appropriate place for the organisation chart, newspaper clippings or other materials that substantiate the text of the report, detailed verbatim narration of interviews with members and anything else that would help the reader follow the text. The appendices should also contain a copy of the questionnaire administered to the respondents and the detailed statistical calculations, if relevant. If there are several appendices, they could be referenced as appendix A, appendix B and so on, and appropriately labelled.

## ORAL PRESENTATION

Most organisations (and class instructors) require about a 20-minute oral presentation of the research project, followed by a question-and-answer session.

The oral presentation requires considerable planning. A study that spanned several months has to be presented in 20 minutes to a live audience! Those who have only superficially read the report, or not read it at all, have to be convinced that the recommendations made in the study would prove to be beneficial to the organisation. All this will have to be accomplished effectively in a very short space of time.

The challenge is to present the important aspects of the study in an interesting manner while still providing statistical and quantitative information that many in the audience may find rather dull. Different visual stimuli (overheads, slides, charts, pictorial and tabular illustrations) have to be used creatively to sustain the audience's interest throughout the presentation. To make all this possible, time and effort have to be expended in planning, organising and rehearsing the presentation.

Slides, overheads, charts, graphs, handouts — all in large, bold print, and preferably in colour — help the presenter to sustain the interest of the audience. They also help to communicate and explain the research project coherently, without *reading* from prepared notes. See Delahaye and Smith (1998), chapters 20 and 21, for advice on giving presentations.

Factors irrelevant to the written report, such as dress, mannerisms, gestures, voice modulation and the like, take on added importance in oral presentations. Speaking audibly, clearly, without distracting mannerisms, and with the right voice intonation to communicate to the audience, is vital for holding their attention. Varying the length of the sentences, establishing eye contact, tone variations, voice modulation and the rate of flow of information make all the difference to audience receptivity. Using small prompt cards helps smooth transitions during the presentation. Thus, both the content of the presentation and the style of delivery should be well planned.

## DECIDING ON THE CONTENT

Because a lot of material has to be compressed into a 20-minute presentation, it is necessary to decide what points will be focused on and how much importance will be given to each. Remembering that the listener absorbs only a small proportion of all that he or she has heard, it is important to determine what the presenter would like the listener to walk away with, and then organise the presentation accordingly.

Obviously, the problem investigated, the results found, the conclusions drawn, the recommendations made and the ways they can be implemented are of most interest to organisational members, and need to be emphasised during the presentation. The design aspects of the study, details of the sample, data collection methods, details of data analysis and the like can be mentioned in passing, to be picked up at the question-and-answer session by the interested members.

Depending on the type of audience, however, it may become necessary to place more stress on the data analysis aspects. For example, if the presentation is made to a group of statisticians in the company, or in a research methods class, the data analyses and results will receive more time than if the project is presented to a group of managers whose main interest lies in the solution to the problem and implementation of the recommendations. Thus, the time and attention devoted to the various components of the study will require adjustment, depending on the audience.

## VISUAL AIDS

Graphs, charts and tables help to drive home the points you wish to make much faster and more effectively, true to the adage that a picture is worth a thousand words. Visual aids provide sensory stimuli that sustain the attention of the audience. Modern technology makes it possible for colour graphics to be produced on personal computers and projected onto the screen. Slides, transparencies, flipcharts, the chalkboard and handout materials also help the audience to follow the points of the speaker's presentation. The selection of specific visual modes of presentation will depend on such things as the size of the room, the availability of a good screen for projection, and the cost constraints of developing sophisticated visuals. All visuals should be produced with a view to easy visibility from the back of the presentation room. Large, easily readable visuals that are properly labelled in big bold letters help the audience to focus on the presentation. Visuals that present side-by-side comparisons of the existing and potential state of affairs via graphs or pie charts drive home the points much more forcefully than elaborate and laborious verbal explanations.

Integrated multimedia presentations using videotapes, videodiscs, CD-ROMs and the visuals described earlier are common in this technological age. Digital whiteboards facilitate digital storage of intricate diagrams that can be used in conjunction with electronic projective systems to serve as electronic flipcharts. When planning a presentation using PowerPoint or integrated multimedia, it is important to ensure before the presentation starts that the related equipment is properly hooked up and tested so that the presentation can proceed smoothly without interruptions.

## THE PRESENTER

An effective presentation also depends on how 'unstressed' the presenter is. The speaker should establish eye contact with the audience, speak audibly and clearly, and be sensitive to the non-verbal reactions of the audience. Strict adherence to the time frame and concentration on the points of interest to the audience are critical aspects of good presentation. Extreme nervousness throughout the presentation, stumbling over words, fumbling with notes or audiovisuals, speaking inaudibly and/or with distracting mannerisms, straying away from the main focus of the study and exceeding the time limit all detract from effectiveness. Dress, posture and self-confidence also contribute importantly to the impression created on the audience. Such simple things as covering the materials on the visuals until they need to be exhibited help the audience to focus on the discussion.

## THE PRESENTATION

The opening remarks set the stage for capturing the attention of the audience. Introducing the problem or opportunity investigated, the findings, the conclusions drawn, the recommendations made and their implementation are important aspects of the presentation. The speaker should drive home these points at least three times — once at the beginning, again when each of these areas is covered, and finally while summarising and concluding the presentation.

## HANDLING QUESTIONS

Concentrated and continuous investigation of the research topic over a considerable period of time makes the presenter more knowledgeable about the project than anyone in the audience. Hence, it is not difficult to handle questions from the audience with confidence and poise. It is important not to be defensive when questions that appear to find fault with some aspect of the research are posed. Openness to suggestions also helps, since the audience might occasionally come up with excellent ideas or recommendations the researcher has not thought of. Such ideas must always be acknowledged graciously. If a question or a suggestion from a member of the audience happens to be flawed, it should be addressed in a non-judgemental fashion.

The question-and-answer session, when handled well, leaves the audience with a sense of involvement and satisfaction. Questions should be encouraged and responded to with care. This interactive session offers an exciting experience to both audience and presenter.

As may readily be understood, a 20-minute presentation followed by a short question-and-answer session call for substantial planning, anticipation of audience concerns, psychological preparedness and management skills.

Reporting has to be done in an honest and straightforward manner. It is unethical to suppress findings that are unpalatable to the sponsors (or client), or reflect poorly on management. As suggested earlier, it is possible to be tactful in presenting such findings, without withholding or distorting information to please the sponsors (or client). Internal researchers, in particular, will have to find ways of presenting unpopular information in a tactful manner. It is also important to state the limitations of the study — and almost every study has some limitations — so as not to mislead the audience.

## SUMMARY

The components of various types of written research reports were discussed in this chapter. It was emphasised that the purpose of the report and the intended audience are critical factors in deciding what aspects of the study should be stressed the most. Examples of different kinds of reports were offered, and additional examples can be found in the appendix to this chapter.

We also discussed ways of making effective oral presentations, stressing the importance of both the content of the presentation and the style of delivery.

The appendix to this chapter contains samples from five business research projects that have different purposes and audiences.

## DISCUSSION POINTS

1. Why is it necessary to have the letter of authorisation in the report?
2. Discuss the purpose and contents of the executive summary.
3. What are the similarities and differences between basic and applied research reports?
4. How have technological advances helped in writing and presenting research reports?
5. Why is it necessary to specify the limitations of the study in the research report?
6. What aspects of a class research project would you stress in the written report and in the oral presentation?

# APPENDIX

## REPORT 1: EXAMPLE OF A REPORT INVOLVING A DESCRIPTIVE STUDY

SEKRAS COMPANY

To: L. Raiburn, Chair
Strategic Planning Committee

From: Joanne Williams
Public Relations Officer

Subject: Report requested by Mr Raiburn

Date: 3 July 1998

Attached is the report requested by Mr Raiburn

If any further information or clarification is needed, please contact me.

Encl: Report

### REPORT FOR THE STRATEGIC PLANNING COMMITTEE

*Introduction*

Vice-President Raiburn, Chair of the Strategic Planning Committee, requested two pieces of information — namely:
1. the sales figures of the top five retailers in the country in 1997 and in 1988
2. customers' ideas of what improvements can be made at Sekras to enhance their satisfaction.

For this purpose, he asked that a quick survey of the company's customers be done to elicit their opinions.

*Method used for obtaining the requisite information*

Figures of sales of the top five retailers in the country for 1997 and 1988 were obtained from *Business Week*, which periodically publishes many kinds of industry statistics.

To obtain customers' inputs on improvements that could be made by the company, a short questionnaire (specimen in appendix I) was mailed to 300 of our credit card customers — 100 who had most frequently used the card in the last 18 months, 100 who most infrequently used it during the same period, and 100 average users. Questionnaires in three different colours were sent to the three groups. Respondents were given a US$2 bill as an 'incentive' to complete the questionnaire!

The questionnaire asked for responses to three questions.
1. What are some of the things you like best about shopping at Sekras?
2. What are some of the things you dislike and would like to see improved at Sekras? Please explain in as much detail as possible.
3. What are your specific suggestions for making improvements so as to enhance the quality of our service to customers like you?

*Findings*

*I. Sales figures of the top five retailers in 1997 and 1988*

Information regarding sales of the top five retailers in 1997 and 1988 is provided in table 14.1. It is evident that the top five retailers are the same across the two time periods. Wal-Mart, however, had jumped from third place in 1988 to first place in 1997, Sears had dropped from first place to the second, and Kmart slid from second position to third during the same period. JC Penney and Dayton Hudson continued to retain fourth and fifth positions, respectively.

It is interesting that Wal-Mart had increased its sales a spectactular five and a half times during this period, while the others had increased theirs between 1.4 and 2.2 times.

**Table 14.1** Comparative sales figures of the five top retail companies during 1997 and 1988

| Top retailers in 1997 | | | Top retailers in 1988 | | |
|---|---|---|---|---|---|
| Company | Sales in billions of $ | Share among top five | Company | Sales in billions of $ | Share among top five |
| Wal-Mart Stores | 113.4 | 47% | Sears, Roebuck | 30.2 | 29% |
| Sears, Roebuck | 41.5 | 17% | Kmart | 27.3 | 26% |
| Kmart | 32.1 | 13% | Wal-Mart Stores | 20.6 | 20% |
| JC Penney | 29.2 | 12% | JC Penney | 15.2 | 14% |
| Dayton Hudson | 26.9 | 11% | Datyon Hudson | 12.2 | 11% |

| Increase in sales from 1988 to 1997 | |
|---|---|
| Company | Increase (times) |
| Wal-Mart Stores | 5.5 |
| Sears, Roebuck | 1.4 |
| Kmart | 1.2 |
| JC Penney | 1.9 |
| Dayton Hudson | 2.2 |

## II. Customer suggestions for improvements

Of the 300 surveys sent out, 225 were returned — a 75 per cent response rate. Of the 100 most frequent users of our credit card to whom questionnaires were sent, 80 responded; among the most infrequent users, 60 responded; and among the average users, 85 responded.

About 75 per cent of the respondents were women. The majority of the customers were between the ages of 35 and 55 (62 per cent).

The responses to the three open-ended questions were analysed. The information needed by the Committee on the Suggested Improvements is tabulated (see table 14.2). Responses to the other two questions on features liked by the customers, and their specific suggestions for improvement are provided in the two tables in the appendix. The following are suggestions received from one or two respondents only.
1. More water fountains are needed on each floor.
2. The pushcarts could be lighter, so they will be easier to push.
3. More seats for resting after long hours of shopping would help.
4. Prices of luxury items are too high.

From table 14.2, it can be seen that the most dissatisfaction stems from (a) out-of-stock small appliances, and (b) inability to locate the store assistants who could guide customers in finding what they want (44 per cent each). The need for child-care services is expressed by 38 per cent of the customers. Twenty per cent also indicate that the cafeteria should cater to the international spicy type of foods. The next two important items pertain to the temperature (18 per cent), and billing mistakes (16 per cent). Some customers (16 per cent) also wish the store would be open 24 hours. The rest of the suggestions are offered by fewer than 10 per cent of the customers, and hence can perhaps be attended to later.

Table 14.2 Suggested areas for improvement

| Features | Frequent users (no.) | Medium users (no.) | Infrequent users (no.) | Total (no.) | Total (%) |
|---|---|---|---|---|---|
| 1. Small appliances such as mixers and blenders are often not in stock. This is irritating. | 30 | 48 | 22 | 100 | 44 |
| 2. The cafeteria serves only bland, uninteresting food. How about some spicy international food? | 26 | 14 | 5 | 45 | 20 |
| 3. Often, we are unable to locate the items we want! | 3 | 6 | 14 | 23 | 10 |
| 4. It would be nice if you could have a child-care service so we can shop without distractions. | 28 | 32 | 25 | 85 | 38 |
| 5. It is often difficult to locate an assistant who can help us with answers to our questions. | 29 | 49 | 22 | 100 | 44 |
| 6. I wish it was a 24-hour store. | 17 | 13 | 7 | 37 | 16 |
| 7. Sometimes there is a mistake in billing. We have to make some telephone calls before charges are corrected. This is a waste of our time. | 4 | 12 | 14 | 20 | 16 |
| 8. Allocate some floor space for kids to play video games. | 2 | — | 4 | 6 | 2 |
| 9. Import more Eastern apparel like the kimono, saris and sarongs. | — | 8 | 4 | 12 | 5 |
| 10. Regulate the temperature better; often it is too cold or too hot. | 15 | 12 | 17 | 44 | 18 |

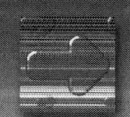

A note of caution is in order at this juncture. We are not sure how representative our sample is. We thought that a mix of high, average and infrequent users of our credit card would provide some useful insights. If a more detailed study obtaining information from a sample of *all* the customers who come to the store is considered necessary, we will initiate it quickly. In the meantime, we are also interviewing a few of the customers who shop here daily. If we find anything of significance from these interviews, we will inform you.

### III Improvements indicated by these suggestions

Based on the current sample of customers who have responded to our survey, the following improvements and actions seem to be called for.

1. Small appliances need to be adequately stocked (44 per cent of respondents complained about this). An effective reorder inventory system has to be developed for this department to minimise customer dissatisfaction and avoid loss of sales for want of stock.
2. Customers seem to have trouble locating store items and would appreciate help from store assistants (44 per cent expressed this need). If providing assistance is a primary concern, it would be a good idea to have liveried store personnel wear badges to indicate they are there to assist customers. During idle hours, if any (when there are no customers seeking help), these individuals can be deployed as shelf organisers.
3. Need for child-care facilities has been expressed by more than a third of our customers (38 per cent). It would be a good idea to earmark a portion of the front of the building for parents to drop off their kids while shopping. The children will have to be supervised by a trained child-care professional recruited by the organisation. An assistant could later be recruited if there is a need. From the cost–benefit analysis in exhibit 7, it may be seen that these additional expenditures will pay off many times over in sales revenues, and at the same time create a fund of goodwill for the company.
4. Adding to the variety of foods served in the cafeteria (a need expressed by 20 per cent) is at once a simple and a complex matter. We need further ideas and details as to what types of food need to be added. This information can be obtained through a short survey, if Mr Raiburn so wishes.
5. Billing errors should not occur (16 per cent indicated this). Our billing department should be warned that such mistakes should be avoided and should not recur. Their performance assessment should be tied to such mistakes.
6. Regulation of temperature (16 per cent identified this) is easy. This, in fact, could be immediately attended to by our Engineering Department personnel.

I hope this report contains all the information sought by Mr Raiburn. As stated earlier, if the non–credit card customers have also to be sampled, it can be easily arranged.

# REPORT 2: EXAMPLE OF A REPORT WHERE AN IDEA HAS TO BE 'SOLD'

MUELLER PHARMACEUTICALS

To: The Board of Directors
From: Harry Wood, GM
(through: CEO Michael Osborn)
Subject: Sabbatical for Managers
Date: 15 June 2001

Enclosed is a brief report on the need for a sabbatical policy for our managers and R & D personnel, for discussion at our next board meeting. We will also plan on a more detailed presentation at that time.

## WHY SABBATICALS FOR MANAGERS ARE NECESSARY
### Introduction
At the company's board meeting last month, the members were concerned that no new products have been developed during the past four years and that the profits of the company are down considerably. One of the board members suggested that a 'sabbatical' (that is, leave for study, travel and battery 'recharge'), given to the managers and key staff of our company, might rejuvenate them and help creativity flow again. At that time the matter was treated casually and not given any further consideration. Sensing the need to consider this option seriously, I have since talked to a few companies that do offer this benefit to their managers. I have also obtained some data from them, which demonstrate the efficacy of sabbaticals.

Based on the available information, there is a strong case for introducing a sabbatical policy in our company. Details of my discussions with other companies and their data are presented below.

### Gist of telephone conversations with general managers and CEOs of companies
I talked to the CEOs, general managers and directors of Telstra, NZ Telecom, News Corp, Westpac, Fletcher Challenge, Mobil and Caltex. All these companies have had sabbatical policies for at least the past seven years. Some CEOs to whom I spoke said they had initiated the policy because they found that their own productivity increased after they had some time away from their jobs doing different kinds of things. Some said that they introduced the sabbatical because they felt that their managerial staff experienced burnout and became ineffective after long years of non-stop work at a hectic pace.

Without exception, everyone said that it makes good business sense to offer managers a chance to refurbish their lives and recharge their batteries every six years or so, so that they come back to work with renewed vigour. Among the many advantages recounted by those to whom I spoke are:
- more enthusiasm and zest for work
- better working relationships with staff
- a fresh approach to problem solving with less competitiveness among the different departments

- a more creative flow of ideas, new marketing strategies and product development ideas
- a more dynamic workplace in terms of interpersonal interaction, interdepartmental collegiality and joint problem solving.

### Some hard data

The appendix, which contains the information provided by two companies, shows that the number of new products developed quadrupled in one company and increased five-fold in the other during the years since the introduction of the sabbatical. As they themselves acknowledge, the increase cannot be attributed to the sabbatical alone, but they have also documented that most of the new products developed were under the leadership of the managers after their return from a three-month sabbatical. You will note that new product development statistics for these managers, before and after their sabbatical, are indeed compelling! Reinforcing our theory is also the decline in the figures in the fourth or fifth year after their return from sabbatical and the pick-up again after the next sabbatical. Noteworthy, too, is that the 'pick-up' years were no different from the others in terms of the economic environment, technology advances or other factors that might have a direct impact on innovation!

I have also placed in the appendix a copy of the article on executive life that appeared in the *Business Review Weekly* of 3 June 2000, which you have probably already read. Is it not incredible that many of the executives who try something new during the sabbatical ultimately want to get back to their old jobs? The case cited of the law firm partner Smithies, who missed the rigours of his old job and could just not shake off the lawyer in him when he tried to be a rabbi-in-training during his sabbatical, is particularly interesting.

### Benefits of sabbatical

The benefits of sabbaticals to the managers are obvious: they refresh themselves trying their hand at new things or doing the things they have dreamed of (such as learning to play the flute or paint or write). These activities seem to offer them a new lease on their professional lives, but the benefits to the corporation seem to be even greater, as experienced by the companies that already have this scheme in place. Apple Computers' revenues are stated to have quadrupled under the leadership of John Sculley, who took nine-week sabbaticals. Again, no one is attributing a cause and effect relationship, but a strong correlation is possible there! Mr Lerman, partner of Wilmer, Cutler & Pickering, strongly affirms that when managers come back from sabbatical, they are more effective and invigorated.

### Recommendation

Given the qualitative and quantitative evidence generated from a number of organisations that have implemented the sabbatical policy, I strongly recommend that we also establish a sabbatical policy in our company. The suggestion is to offer a paid, three-month sabbatical for all our R & D scientists, and managerial and executive staff, after every six years of service. The costs of implementing this with respect to our senior scientists, managers and executives are worked out and shown in exhibit 4. The likely benefits within 10 years of our initiating such a policy in terms of new product development, increased sales and joint problem-solving endeavours due to higher energy levels of department heads are also shown in the same exhibit.

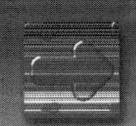

I will ask the HRM Director to collect information from more companies having sabbatical policies and make a presentation to the board at our next meeting. In the meantime, if you need more information or clarification, feel free to give me a call.

In conclusion, our company is at the crossroads and our scientists and managers need to be energised to enhance their performance and productivity. Constant pressure and ceaseless toil are wearing them out. Many are frustrated by the demands imposed by the jobs. 'All work and no play' has eroded their zest for work and drained them of their creative ideas. It is high time we injected some vitality into our system through sabbaticals.

## REPORT 3: EXAMPLE OF A REPORT OFFERING ALTERNATIVE SOLUTIONS AND EXPLAINING THE PROS AND CONS OF EACH ALTERNATIVE

To:    Charles Orient, CEO
        Lunard Manufacturing Company

From:  Alexis Ventura, Senior Researcher
        Mr Bean Research Team

Subject: Suggestions on alternative ways of cutting costs in anticipation of recession

Date:   16 February 1999

Enclosed is the report requested by Mr Orient. If any additional information or clarification is needed, please let me know.

Encl: report

### REPORT ON ALTERNATIVE WAYS OF HANDLING RECESSIONARY TIMES WITHOUT MASSIVE LAY-OFFS

*Introduction*
The Mr Bean Research Team was asked to suggest alternative ways of tiding over the anticipated recession during the next several months, when a slowdown of the economy is expected. A recent article in *Business Review Weekly* titled 'Downsizing in a Hurry' indicated that executives in a large number of companies are slashing costs, mostly through lay-offs and restructuring. Mr Orient wanted the Mr Bean Research Team to suggest alternatives besides lay-offs.

This report provides five alternatives, citing the advantages and disadvantages of each.

*Method used for developing the alternatives*
The team studied the economic indicators and the published industry analyses, read the Governor of the Reserve Bank of Australia's speeches, examined the many ways in which companies cut costs during non-recessionary periods as well as recessions and, based on these, suggested the following five alternatives.

*Alternatives suggested*
1. A moratorium on all capital expenditure
2. A hiring freeze

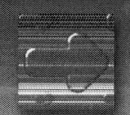

3. Recovery of bad debts through sustained efforts
4. Trimming of operating expenditures, with substantial reduction in travel and entertainment expenditures
5. Discontinuance of the manufacture of low-profit-margin products.

*Advantages and disadvantages of each of the above*
Itemised details of the cost–benefit analysis for each of the preceding suggestions are furnished in the appendix, which may be referred to. We give only the net benefits for each alternative here.

*1. Moratorium on all capital expenditure*
It makes good sense to desist from all capital expenditure since manufacture of most items will slow down during recession. Except for parts for existing machines, there is no need to buy capital equipment, and all proposals in this regard should be shelved.

This strategy will cut down expenditure to the extent of 7 to 10 per cent of revenue. See appendix for full details. A reserve fund can be created to catch up with future orders when the economy returns to normal.

*2. Hiring freeze*
The annual increase in the strength of our staff during the past four years has been about 15 per cent. With a slowdown of the economy, a hiring freeze in all our branch offices will save more than $10 million annually.

This may initially result in some extra workload for the staff and cause some job dissatisfaction. But once they get used to it, and the impact of the recession hits them, employees will be thankful for the job they have. It is advisable to explain in advance the reasons for the hiring freeze to the employees so that they understand the motive behind the company's policy and appreciate having been informed.

*3. Recovery of bad debts through aggressive efforts*
Bad debts have been on the increase over the past three years, and no intensive efforts to recover them seem to have been made hitherto.

We suggest that collection agents who have successfully recovered bad debts for other companies be hired immediately. Such agents may have to be paid more than other collection agents, but the extra cost will be well worth it. About a billion dollars can be collected within a few weeks of their being on the job, and this will help the financial cash flow of the company.

*4. Trimming of operating expenditures*
Several operating expenses can be trimmed — the travel expenses of managers in particular — as shown in exhibit 4 of the appendix. Video-conferencing is inexpensive and should be encouraged for most of the meetings and negotiations. This alone will result in savings of more than $175 000 per month.

Another way of curtailing expenditure considerably is to restrict entertainment expenses to such purposes and managers as actively promote the business of the company and are essential for public relations.

These changes will have a negative impact on morale, but managers understand the economic situation and will adjust to the new system once the initial resistance wears off.

### 5. Eliminating the manufacture of low-margin products

The team found from a detailed study of the company records of manufacturing, sales and profits figures for the various products that all the items listed in exhibit 5 of the appendix have very low profit margins. It is evident from the data provided that considerable time and effort are expended in manufacturing and selling these items.

It will be useful to phase out the manufacture of these items, and divert the resources to the high-profit items suggested in exhibit 6. From the cost–benefit analysis in exhibit 7, it may be seen that several billions can be saved through this strategy.

It is possible to put into effect all of the five preceding alternatives and handle the onslaught of the recession with confidence.

## REPORT 4: EXAMPLE OF AN ABRIDGED BASIC RESEARCH REPORT

### FACTORS AFFECTING THE UPWARD MOBILITY OF WOMEN IN PUBLIC ACCOUNTING

#### Introduction

A substantial number of women have entered the public accounting profession in the past 15 years or so. However, fewer than 4 per cent of the partners in the Big Eight accounting firms are women, indicating a lack of upward mobility for women in the accounting profession. Given the fact that women students perform significantly better during their academic training than their male counterparts, it is unfortunate that their intellectual ability and knowledge remain underutilised during their professional careers. The recent costly litigation and discrimination suits filed make it imperative for us to study the factors that affect the upward mobility of women and examine how the situation can be rectified.

#### A Brief literature survey

Studies of male and female accounting majors indicate that the percentage of women accounting students has increased several-fold since 1977 (Kurian 1998). Based on the analysis of longitudinal data collected over a 15-year period, Mulcher, Turner and Williams (1997) found that women students' grades in senior accounting courses were significantly higher than those of male students. This higher level of academic performance has been theorised as due to the higher need and desire that women have to achieve and overcome stereotypes (Messing 1989), having higher career aspirations (Tinsley et al. 1983) or having a higher aptitude for accounting (Riley 1984; Jones & Alexander 1996). Empirical studies by Fraser, Lytle and Stolle (1978), and Johnson and Meyer (1995), however, found no significant differences in personality predispositions or behavioural traits between male and female accounting majors.

Several surveys of women accountants in the country pinpoint three major factors that hinder women's career progress in the public accounting field (see, for example, Kaufman 1986; Larson 1994; Walkup & Fenman 1997). They are: (1) the long hours of work demanded by the profession (a factor that conflicts with family demands), (2) failure to be entrusted with responsible assignments, and (3) discrimination. In sum, the lack of upward mobility seems to be due to factors over which the organisation has some control.

## Research question
Do long work hours, failure to be handed greater responsibilities and discrimination account for the lack of upward mobility of women in public accounting?

## Theoretical framework
The variance in the dependent variable, *upward mobility*, can be explained by the three independent variables: long hours of work, not handling greater responsibilities and discrimination. As women are expected to, and do indeed, take on responsibility for household work and child rearing, they are unable to work beyond regular work hours at the workplace. This creates a mistaken impression among managers in the organisation that women are less committed to their work. Because of this perception, they are not entrusted with significant responsibilities. This further hinders their progress, because they are not afforded the same exposure to the intricacies of accounting practices as men. Hence, women are overlooked at the time of promotion.

Deliberate discriminatory practices due to sex-role stereotypes, as evidenced in the well-known case of *Hopkins v Price Waterhouse & Co.*, also arrest women's progress. If women are not valued for their potential and are expected to conform to sex-typed behaviour (which confines them to inconspicuous roles), their chances of moving up the career ladder are significantly reduced.

Thus, the three independent variables considered here significantly explain the variance in the upward mobility of women in public accounting. The impracticability of putting in long hours of work, lack of opportunities to handle greater responsibilities and sex-role stereotyping all negatively impact on upward mobility.

## Hypotheses
1. If women spend more hours on the job after regular work hours, they will be given greater responsibilities.
2. If women are entrusted with higher levels of responsibilities, they will have more opportunities to move up in the organisation.
3. If women are not expected to conform to stereotypical behaviour, their chances for upward mobility will increase.
4. All three independent variables will significantly explain the variance in women CPAs' upward mobility.

## METHOD SECTION

### Study design
In this cross-sectional correlational field study, data on the three independent variables and the dependent variable were collected from women CPAs in several public accounting organisations in the country through mail questionnaires.

### Population and sample
The population for the study comprised all women CPAs in the country. A systematic sampling procedure was first used to select 30 cities from the various regions of the

country from which a sample of accounting firms would be drawn. Then, through a simple random sampling procedure, five CPA firms from each of the cities were chosen for the study. Data were collected from all the women in each of the firms so chosen. The total sample size was 300 and responses were received from 264 women CPAs, for an 88 per cent response rate for the mail questionnaires. The unit of analysis was the individuals who responded to the survey.

All respondents had, as expected, the CPA degree. Their ages ranged from 28 to 66. About 60 per cent of the women were over 45 years of age. The average number of children in the house below the age of 13 was two. The average number of years of work in the organisation was 15, and the average number of organisations worked for was two. The average number of hours spent at home on office-related matters was 2.8.

*Variables and measures*
All demographic variables, such as age, number of years in the organisation, number of other organisations in which the individual had worked, number of hours spent at home on office-related matters, and number of children in the house and their ages, were tapped by direct single questions.

*Upward mobility.* This dependent variable indicates the extent to which individuals expected to progress in their career during the succeeding 3 to 10 years. Hall (1986) developed four items to measure this variable, an example item being: *I see myself being promoted to the next level quite easily.* The measure is reported to have convergent and discriminant validity, and the Cronbach's alpha for the four items for this sample was 0.86.

*Sex-role stereotyping.* This independent variable was measured using Hall and Humphrey's (1972) 8-item measure. An example item is: *Men in this organisation do not consider women's place to be primarily in the home.* Cronbach's alpha for the measure for this sample was 0.82.

*Responsibilities assigned.* This was tapped by three items from Sonnenfield and McGrath (1983), which asked respondents to indicate their levels of assigned responsibility to (a) make important decisions, (b) handle large accounts, and (c) account for the annual profits of the firm. Cronbach's alpha for the three items was 0.71 for this sample.

*Data collection method*
Questionnaires were mailed to 300 women CPAs in the United States. After two reminders, 264 completed questionnaires were received within a period of six weeks. The high return rate of 88 per cent can be attributed to the shortness of the questionnaire and perhaps the motivation of the women CPAs to respond to a topic close to their hearts.

Questionnaires were not electronically administered for various reasons, including the advantage it afforded to the respondents to reply without switching on the computer.

*Data analysis and results*
After determining the reliabilities (Cronbach's alpha) for the measures for this sample, frequency distributions for the demographic variables were obtained. These

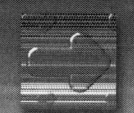

may be seen in exhibit 1. Then a Pearson correlation matrix was obtained for the four independent and dependent variables. This may be seen in exhibit 2. It should be noted that no correlation exceeded 0.6.

Each hypothesis was then tested. The correlation matrix provided the answer to the first three hypotheses. The first hypothesis stated that the number of hours put in beyond work hours on office-related matters will be positively correlated to the responsibilities assigned. The correlation of 0.56 ($p < 0.001$), between the number of hours spent on office work beyond regular work hours and the entrusted responsibilities, substantiates this hypothesis.

The second hypothesis stated that if women are given higher responsibilities, their upward mobility will improve. The positive correlation of 0.59 ($p < 0.001$) between the two variables substantiates this hypothesis. That is, the greater the entrusted responsibilities, the greater the perceived chances of being promoted.

The third hypothesis indicated that sex-role stereotyping would be negatively correlated to upward mobility. The correlation of $-0.54$ ($p < 0.001$) substantiates this hypothesis as well. That is, the greater the expected conformity to stereotyped behaviour, the lower the chances of upward mobility.

To test the fourth hypothesis, that the number of hours spent beyond regular work hours on job-related matters, assignment of higher responsibilities and expectations of conformity with stereotyped behaviour will significantly explain the variance in perceived upward mobility, the three independent variables were regressed against the dependent variable. The results shown in exhibit 3 indicate that this hypothesis is also substantiated. That is, the $R^2$ value of 0.43 at a significance level of $p < 0.001$, with $df(3, 238)$, confirms that 43 per cent of the variance in upward mobility is significantly explained by the three independent variables.

## Discussion of results

The results of this study confirm that the variables considered in the theoretical framework are important. By focusing solely on the number of hours worked, ignoring the quality of work done, the organisation is perhaps not harnessing the full potential and encouraging the development of the talents of the women CPAs adequately. It seems worthwhile to investigate and remedy this situation.

It would be useful if the top executive were to assign progressively higher levels of responsibilities to women. This will help to utilise their abilities fully, and in turn, enhance the effectiveness of the firm. If executives are helped to modify their mental attitudes and sex-role expectations, they would tend to expect less stereotypical behaviour, and encourage the upward mobility of women CPAs. Knowing that women bring a different kind of perspective to organisational matters (Smith 1989; Vernon 1998), it is quite possible that having them as partners of the firm will enhance the organisational effectiveness as well.

## Recommendations

It is recommended that a system be set up to assess the value of the contributions of each individual in discharging the duties, and use that, rather than the number of hours of work put in, as a yardstick for promotion.

Second, women CPAs should be given progressively more responsibilities after they have served three to five years in the system. Assigning a mentor to train them will make for smooth functioning of the firm. Third, a short seminar could be organised for executives to sensitise them to the adverse effects of sex-role stereotyping in the workplace. This will help them to utilise the talents of women CPAs. If viewed as professionals with career goals and aspirations, rather than in stereotyped ways, women CPAs will be enabled to handle more responsibilities and advance in the system. The organisation will also stand to benefit by their contributions.

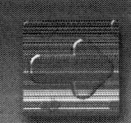

In conclusion, it would be worthwhile for public accounting firms to modify their mental orientations towards and expectations of women CPAs. It is a national waste not to utilise their abilities.

## REPORT 5: EXAMPLE OF AN ABRIDGED APPLIED BUSINESS RESEARCH REPORT

Attitudes towards Reclassifying Academic Titles in New Zealand Universities*

*Prepared for*
Nick Park, AUS Academic Vice-President,
Association of University Staff of New Zealand (Inc.),
PO Box 11–767, Wellington, New Zealand

*Prepared by*
Bob Cavana, Rob Crozier & Perumal Pillai, Victoria University of Wellington,
PO Box 600, Wellington, New Zealand

December 1994

### CONTENTS

| | Page |
|---|---|
| EXECUTIVE SUMMARY | 3 |
| 1 INTRODUCTION | 4 |
| 1.1 Problem statement | 4 |
| 1.2 Research objectives | 4 |
| 1.3 Background | 4 |
| 2 METHODOLOGY | 5 |
| 2.1 Research design | 5 |
| 2.2 Data collection methods | 6 |
| 2.3 Sample characteristics | 6 |
| 2.4 Responses | 7 |
| 2.5 Data analysis | 7 |
| 3 RESULTS | 7 |
| 4 QUALITATIVE ANALYSIS OF COMMENTS | 9 |
| 4.1 Classification of comments | 9 |
| 4.2 Implications | 11 |
| 5 CONCLUSIONS | 14 |
| ACKNOWLEDGEMENTS | 14 |
| REFERENCES | 14 |
| APPENDICES | |
| *Appendix A*  Academic titles preference questionnaire | 15 |
| *Appendix B*  Summarised results by university | 16 |

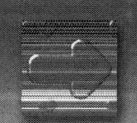

# EXECUTIVE SUMMARY

This report presents the results of a survey of academic staff at New Zealand universities to determine their attitudes towards the current British system of academic titles compared with the US system. A questionnaire was developed and sent to a stratified random sample of 1340 academic staff selected from the seven universities in New Zealand. A total of 671 valid responses were received. The responses were analysed statistically by university, faculty, designation, qualifications, gender, age and overseas experience. The comments were also analysed qualitatively.

The overall results indicated that 44 per cent of the respondents preferred the current system of titles, 39 per cent preferred the alternative US system and 17 per cent did not have a preference. However, the differences between the preferences for the two systems were not significant at the 95 per cent (or 90 per cent) confidence level. The analysis by university revealed that although academic staff at Auckland and Victoria Universities generally preferred the alternative US system and academic staff at Canterbury, Lincoln and Otago Universities generally preferred the current system of academic titles, only responses from Massey and Waikato Universities indicated a statistically significant preference for the current system. Staff in the 'professional' faculties (e.g. Agriculture, Commerce and Law) generally preferred the alternative US system, compared with academics from the more 'traditional' academic areas (e.g. Humanities/Arts and Social Sciences), who tended to prefer the current British system. However, the only statistically significant differences were recorded by Medical/Dental academic staff, who overwhelmingly indicated a preference for the current system. The results also indicated that staff who were born or had their main overseas academic experiences in generally non-Commonwealth countries (e.g. in Asia, Europe (excluding the UK) and North America) preferred the alternative US system. Professors and assistant/junior lecturers showed a statistically significant preference for the current system whereas, overall, senior lecturers tended to prefer the alternative system (although not statistically significant).

Generally, the results indicate that there is not a majority support for either the British or the US systems of academic titles and there is a considerable level of dissatisfaction with the current system. Consequently, it is concluded that a sustained effort is required to develop policy and form some agreement on an appropriate mix of academic titles and rewards for academic staff at New Zealand universities.

# 1. INTRODUCTION

## 1.1 Problem statement

At a 1994 meeting of academic members of the Association of University Staff (AUS) held at the University of Waikato, a new salary scale incorporating US academic titles was unanimously rejected (AUS 1994:8). The main features of this 'alternative system' were the new US titles (assistant professor, associate professor and professor), a reduction in the number of steps in the equivalent lecturer grade, and a new associate professor grade which had a lower commencing salary than the current senior lecturer grade. However, it was not clear whether academics were opposed to the change to the US system of academic titles from the current British titles (assistant lecturer, lecturer, senior lecturer, associate professor/reader and professor), or whether they were opposed to other aspects of the salary package.

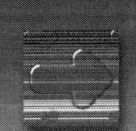

## 1.2 Research objectives

This dilemma led to the current research project to investigate whether academic staff in New Zealand universities preferred the current British system of academic titles or the alternative US system (the main characteristics of the two systems are summarised in table 1, although information on the proposed Waikato salary scale was not provided to respondents to this study). In addition, the AUS required information about the characteristics of academic staff who preferred each system, as this would help the AUS to better represent their members in future negotiations over academic staff salaries and conditions with the universities.

**Table 1** Comparison of current and alternative systems of academic titles

| Current system (1) | | Alternative system (2) | |
| --- | --- | --- | --- |
| Level | Salary range | Level | Salary range |
| Assistant/Junior Lecturer | $31 200–$35 880 | Assistant Professor | $37 500–$49 088 |
| Lecturer | $37 440–$49 088 | | |
| Senior Lecturer | $52 000–$67 080 | Associate Professor | $51 000–$75 920 |
| Associate Professor/ Reader | $69 680–$75 920 | | |
| Professor | $80 080–$99 840 | Professor | $72 000–$99 840 |

**Sources:** (1) Pers. comm., AUS National Office, Wellington. (2) Waikato proposal outlined in the *AUS Bulletin* (AUS 1994:8).

## 1.3 Background

A review of the literature showed that little work has been done in this precise area. However, straw polls undertaken at AUS meetings at various times in the past had indicated that there was often more resentment at the fact that (seemingly) under-qualified staff in disciplines where recruitment is difficult may be appointed at higher ranks in order to provide a competitive salary than at the higher salary level *per se*. For example, a person without a terminal degree (i.e. a PhD or equivalent) may have to be appointed at the senior lecturer rank in order to arrive at a salary level sufficient to recruit them. There is a perception then that there is a degree of 'psychic income' in the status of academic staff.

The Association has, in the past, argued for a series of overlapping scales in order to avoid this level of resentment building up. To date, neither the New Zealand Vice-Chancellors' Committee nor the individual Vice-Chancellors have supported this concept although Waikato University has raised the issue as a means of solving the problem of integrating former College of Education staff into the university salary scale.

An informal survey undertaken by AUS in 1990 as part of a wider survey concerning the content of a possible national award for academic staff indicated that 58 per cent of respondents preferred to retain the British system of academic titles. (Canterbury University was not included in the survey.)

Halsey and Trow (1971) have devoted a chapter to the status and style of life of academic staff and noted elsewhere that 'the maintenance of a style of life depends, at least in the long run, on a set of material conditions'. Their book was written at a time when, in the words of the authors:

> university teaching is a traditionally gentlemanly profession informed by the norms of a democratically self-governing guild which is in the process of adapting itself to internal and external pressures towards bureaucracy and specialisation.

In their words:

> A gentleman is not subjected to wages, hours and conditions of work. He has no employer, no trade union and no machinery of negotiation, arbitration and conciliation. He may receive remuneration but never a rate of pay. He may follow a career or vocation, or better still dedicate himself to a hobby, but he does not have a job.

The prestige of an academic appointment thus brought about its own rewards in terms of its status in society. Nevertheless, conditions have changed dramatically over the last 20 years. This is reflected in the discussion by Halsey (1992) of what he sees as the 'proletarisation' of the academic profession brought about by the worldwide trend to increased participation in higher education.

## 2. METHODOLOGY

### 2.1 Research design

This is a descriptive research project, as its major purpose was to gain a better understanding of the attitudes of academic staff towards the system of academic titles used in New Zealand universities. Survey-based methods were used to collect detailed information regarding the characteristics of academic staff, faculties and universities and their preferences for each system.

### 2.2 Data collection methods

Following discussions with a number of academic staff from a wide range of disciplines at Victoria University of Wellington, a questionnaire was prepared which asked academics to state their preference for the current British system of academic titles or the alternative US system, or to indicate no preference. (Note, however, that no information was provided about salary levels and other conditions of employment.) In addition, a range of demographic questions were asked from each university, including questions on the respondent's faculty, designation, highest qualification, membership of the Association of University Staff (AUS), age group, gender, place of birth and experience at academic institutions overseas. General comments were also requested. The draft questionnaire was pre-tested and then the final version was sent to the secretaries of randomly selected departments at each university, where they were distributed to staff members. The questionnaire, which was contained on one side of an A4 page with an introductory letter by the AUS

Academic Vice-President on the back, took about 10 minutes to complete (see appendix A). The completed questionnaires were then sent by internal mail by 16 September 1994 to the AUS branch organiser at each university and then returned for analysis at Victoria University.

## 2.3 Sample characteristics

A stratified random sample of 1340 academic staff was selected from the total of 4100 academic staff from all seven universities in New Zealand. Following Sekaran (1992:253), a total of 351 valid responses was required to provide a 95 per cent confidence level in the results of the main analysis. In addition, where the sample is required to be broken into subgroups (e.g. males/females, university), Roscoe (1975) suggests that 'a minimum sample size of 30 in each category is necessary'. A total of 671 valid responses were received, which represented nearly a 50 per cent response rate (or 16 per cent of the total population of academic staff). Between 48 and 163 valid responses were received from each university, thus satisfying Roscoe's criteria. Details of the sample characteristics by university are provided in table 2.

**Table 2** Sample characteristics by university

| University | Academic staff[1] (no.) | Staff surveyed (no.) | Proportion of staff surveyed (%) | Valid responses (no.) | Proportion of valid responses (%) |
|---|---|---|---|---|---|
| Auckland | 966 | 330 | 34 | 163 | 49 |
| Canterbury | 451 | 160 | 35 | 74 | 46 |
| Lincoln | 211 | 100 | 47 | 48 | 48 |
| Massey | 686 | 240 | 35 | 105 | 44 |
| Otago | 774 | 270 | 35 | 120 | 44 |
| Victoria | 464 | 160 | 34 | 101 | 63 |
| Waikato | 537 | 130 | 24 | 60 | 46 |
| Total | 4089 | 1390 | 34 | 671 | 48 |

[1]University full-time equivalent academic staff as at 31 July 1993 (Ministry of Education 1993).

## 2.4 Responses

A total of 690 questionnaires were returned but 19 were regarded as invalid since the question that related to academic title preference was not answered, or two or more important demographic questions were left unanswered. Hence, the analysis was based on 671 valid responses. However, a total of 148 (or 22 per cent) of the respondents did not complete the gender question. This may have been because they inadvertently missed it out on the questionnaire or, alternatively, because they objected to answering it. During the questionnaire pre-test, a number of staff members indicated that they thought the gender question was irrelevant. However, the question was retained because of the valuable demographic information it would provide. Overall at New Zealand universities, women comprise about 25 per cent of total academic staff, and 26 per cent of the respondents (where gender was specified) were females. A chi-square test indicated that there were no significant statistical differences between the male/female survey response numbers and the numbers expected based on the academic staff at all universities in New Zealand. Currently, there are still large gender differences in the New Zealand universities, with 59 per cent of female academic staff in the survey occupying the positions of assistant/junior lecturers or lecturers compared with 25 per cent of men, and 8 per cent of females in the senior positions of associate professor or professor compared with 31 per cent of men. However, 47 per cent of the females in the survey were under 40 years of age compared with 26 per cent of the males.

## 2.5 Data analysis

The questionnaire responses were loaded into an Excel spreadsheet (Microsoft Corporation 1992) for preliminary analysis and then imported into the JMP statistical package (SAS 1989) on the Macintosh personal computer for further statistical analysis. Responses to the main question regarding preference for current (British) or alternative (US) systems of academic titles were analysed by subgroup (e.g. by university, faculty, designation etc.). Chi-square tests were undertaken to examine the hypothesis that there was no difference in the responses between each category of the subgroups. Also, chi-square tests were prepared to test whether there was any significant statistical difference between the responses for the current system compared with the alternative system for each category of each subgroup. For the second set of chi-square tests, the null hypothesis that there are no differences in the preferences between the current system and the alternative system would be rejected if the calculated chi-square (with 1 degree of freedom) was greater than 3.841 (at the 95 per cent confidence level) and 2.706 (at the 90 per cent confidence level) (Sekaran 1992:411–2).

## 3. RESULTS

The main results of the analysis of the academic titles survey are summarised in table 3. This includes the number and percentages of responses for each category of each subgroup, the percentage of respondents indicating a preference for the current British system of academic titles or the alternative US system or indicating no preference. The chi-square results (as discussed in the previous section) are also presented. Detailed results for each university are provided in appendix B.

The overall results indicated that of the 671 valid responses, 44 per cent (298) of the respondents preferred the current system of titles, 39 per cent (262) preferred the alternative US system and 17 per cent (111) did not have a preference. However, a chi-square test indicated that there was no statistical difference between the preferences for the current and alternative systems at the 95 per cent (or 90 per cent) confidence level. The analysis by university revealed that although academic staff at

Auckland and Victoria Universities generally preferred the alternative US system and academic staff at Canterbury, Lincoln and Otago Universities generally preferred the current system of academic titles, only responses from Massey and Waikato Universities indicated a statistically significant preference for the current system. The reason why Waikato University staff may have been so strongly opposed to the US system, is that the earlier offer to change to the US system had also incorporated unfavourable changes to the salary scales (AUS 1994:8).

**Table 3** Summary results of the academic titles survey

| | Responses (no.) | (%) | Preference for academic titles | | | Chi-square |
| | | | Current system (%) | Alternative system (%) | No preference ($) | |
| --- | --- | --- | --- | --- | --- | --- |
| University | | | | | | 26.9† |
| Auckland | 163 | 24 | 38.7 | 48.5 | 12.9 | 1.8 |
| Canterbury | 74 | 11 | 48.7 | 37.8 | 13.5 | 1.0 |
| Lincoln | 48 | 7 | 43.8 | 39.6 | 16.7 | 0.1 |
| Massey | 105 | 16 | 51.4* | 25.7 | 22.9 | 9.0 |
| Otago | 120 | 18 | 44.2 | 35.8 | 20.0 | 1.1 |
| Victoria | 101 | 15 | 34.7 | 47.5 | 17.8 | 2.0 |
| Waikato | 60 | 9 | 60.0* | 30.0 | 10.0 | 6.0 |
| Total | 671 | 100 | 44.4 | 39.1 | 16.5 | 2.3 |

\* Indicates the preferred system, statistically significant at the 95 per cent confidence level.

† Indicates that there are significant differences between the categories at the 95 per cent confidence level.

## 4. QUALITATIVE ANALYSIS OF COMMENTS

### 4.1 Classification of comments

The quotations in the following come from the 671 respondents (academics at New Zealand universities) to the survey. The conflicts between their different value positions are summarised here under five headings which classify the reasons they gave according to:
- clarity and meaning in the nomenclature
- elitism vs. egalitarianism
- pomposity and claims to the status of academic work
- titles and reward systems
- detachment from the question.

When respondents gave the reasons for their positions, they were not, of course, confined by these classifications, so the correspondence between the system we apply and what they say cannot be exact. Behind most reasons are usually a number of facts (beliefs about what is) and some values (beliefs about what ought to be). These are not always openly expressed, so it has to be granted that most interpretation of what is common ground, and what is not, is likely to be mistaken at a number of points. However, the only way to test where there are agreements is through seeking reasoned response through a public platform.

Points of agreement are, of course, interesting. So, too, are points of disagreement — particularly those which use the same set of facts, and seem to suggest an aspiration to the same set of outcomes (which are based upon apparent belief in a similar set of normative values) and yet place considerable stress upon different policies, or different processes, to secure those outcomes. The following classification reveals that some differences among the respondents were of just this sort.

### Titles and reward systems

There are some who see status separated out from the payment issues.

> *Supporter of US system:*
> Would give us the status, without costing more in salaries.
>
> *Supporter of US system:*
> Have for many years believed that the alternative would significantly improve morale and performance at no expense.

One supporter of change would probably not be satisfied with any change in titles that might be offered if these did not address some other (perceived) fundamental difficulties in the promotion system.

> *Supporter of US system:*
> The hypocrisy of calling people lecturers but judging them solely on research must go. Researcher and senior researcher would be more honest.

But another, rather trusting to hard work and talent reaping its own reward, thought that the conservative system was best.

> *Supporter of British system:*
> Leave the system as it is — we do not need to imitate the USA! Besides, titles do not engender respect — reputations do.

And a different supporter of the status quo had a worry about insufficient salary and overwork.

> *Supporter of British system:*
> No point changing our titles but not upgrading our salary and working conditions! I don't wish to have a better title and yet still be so overworked!

There is a line of argument that suggests that the central issue should not be about the meaning of words or about academic careers, but should simply be a matter of what will secure the largest personal rewards.

> *Unspecified support:*
> I prefer the system which will pay me the most!

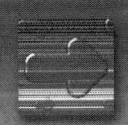

## 4.2 Implications

The argument between elitism and egalitarianism has extreme positions. However, there is considerable support for some sort of hierarchy or different levels of recognition. This means that those who suggest an indifference of one sort are out of tune with all those who see these as matters of considerable importance.

Nevertheless, very few reasons are furnished around the number of titles proposed. Few people seriously comment upon why five titles rather than three. In fact, a common approach applied by managers to solve problems which emerge from the rationing of cash rewards is to substitute a complex number of titles. Reich (1993:182–3) provides an interesting commentary on the way titles are created. One of the supporters of the traditional system (above) wishes to avoid the trend. But the traditional system has already proliferated a much larger variety of titles than the five mentioned in the traditional list. Universities also have graduate assistants, fellowships, tutors, senior tutors, research assistants, researchers and senior researchers in their academic employ. In addition, they institute and maintain a number of bars in their scales and now seem bent upon applying an even more complex system of differentials using ranges of rates.

Earlier we quoted Kogan et al. (1994), who drew attention to the tendency of universities to proliferate titles and roles. Accompanying this has been a widening of the gap between the 'haves' and 'have nots' in the university community.

This then takes us back to the key need for reform, and that is to institute a fairer system of employment. For the system in which some are favoured and have a lot and others, by comparison, are considerably disadvantaged and have nothing like the same rewards and opportunities is unjust. And unjust systems of employment are not likely to be good for morale and can contribute to dysfunctional patterns of behaviour.

So a central question does surely ask just how many levels of hierarchy are useful. Here it is possible to reduce the words of one of the current system's supporters:

> *Supporter of British system:*
> *To have too many variations ... is in my opinion very affected, and absolutely ludicrous.*
> *Unspecified support:*
> *The current system is patently out of line with North American terminology and so stupid. The alternative system is preferred if the following is adopted. Professor 30 per cent, Associate Professor 40 per cent and Assistant Professor 30 per cent. You need to define the break points.*

It may be that there are no matters affecting tertiary education which are more important than this. Perhaps those who think university staff have a serious morale and performance problem are right. Perhaps a system which explained them better to the world might also make it possible to justify themselves better to each other.

Since there has been a continuing egalitarian effect upon the proportions of the population proceeding to university, perhaps it is time to acknowledge that this has had some effect, not only upon the workloads of staff, but also upon the standards demanded of students in their work, and even upon the performance of staff as they cope with heavier workloads.

This survey presents a strong case for a serious look at the structuring of academic titles and the associated reward structures.

## 5. CONCLUSIONS

This report has presented the results of a survey of academic staff at universities in New Zealand to determine their attitudes towards the current British system of academic titles compared with the alternative US system. Generally, the results indicate that there is not a majority support for either the British or the US systems of academic titles and there is a considerable level of dissatisfaction with the current system. Consequently, it is concluded that a sustained effort is required to develop policy and form some agreement on an appropriate mix of academic titles and rewards for academic staff at New Zealand universities. This may result in a compromise situation between the British and US systems, but it is hoped that a new system will alleviate many of the grievances identified by the participants in this study and also provide opportunities for professional development and advancement of all academic staff in New Zealand universities.

## ACKNOWLEDGEMENTS

The authors gratefully acknowledge all the assistance received in the preparation of this report. In particular, we would like to thank Charlotte Fitzgerald of the Association of University Staff (AUS) in New Zealand for her help with the questionnaire design and data collection, and Barrie Davis of Telecom New Zealand Ltd for his help with the original research project. We would also like to thank Nick Park, AUS Academic Vice-President, for his contributions to the qualitative analysis in this report. However, the opinions and interpretations contained within this report are the authors' own.

* See Cavana et al. (1996) for the published version of the full report.

# chapter 15

# MANAGERIAL DECISION MAKING AND EVALUATING RESEARCH

## OUTLINE

SCIENTIFIC RESEARCH AND MANAGERIAL DECISION MAKING

EVALUATING BUSINESS RESEARCH

A FINAL COMMENT

DISCUSSION POINTS

EXERCISES

## CHAPTER OBJECTIVES

After reading this chapter, you should be able to:
- appreciate the importance of both qualitative and quantitative investigations in business research
- appreciate the many ways in which scientific research can help managers to make good decisions
- critique business research reports and published studies.

# SCIENTIFIC RESEARCH AND MANAGERIAL DECISION MAKING

Managers wrestle with a multitude of problems, big and small, in their everyday work life. The difference between a successful and a not so successful organisation lies in the quality of decisions made by the managers in the system. We have seen that scientific thinking equips managers with an awareness and comprehension of the multiplicity of factors operating in their work environment. It also gears managers to problem solving with objectivity after taking calculated risks, and making good decisions after weighing the alternatives. Does this mean that, once the manager applies scientific research results to decision making, the decisions so made are *always* going to be right?

No, for various reasons. First, there is always a chance (usually 5 per cent) of making a Type I error; that is, rejecting the null hypothesis when it should be accepted. Second, though research results may offer the directions for change, sound common sense should be the guiding light for good decision making. For example, research results may indicate that operating costs have to be cut. The recommendations made to achieve this might be to cut down on staff, close a couple of departments and so on. Does the manager then make the decision to follow these recommendations? A great amount of thought would have to centre on the implications of following the recommended suggestions. Questions such as the immediate and long-term effects of following these strategies to cut costs, and the ripple effects on the rest of the system if mass lay-offs and closing certain operations were resorted to would loom large in the mind of the manager. These, and other important factors, will then have to be carefully weighed by the manager, before a final decision is made in choosing the right alternative to cut costs. Thus, good decision making entails a commonsense approach to applying research results.

However, if management action is taken on the basis of the business research undertaken, then this will involve the managerial activities of planning, implementation and control — that is, to introduce the recommendations and to monitor progress when the recommendations have been implemented (see the shaded box in figure 15.1). After a period of time the research cycle is complete and management can determine whether the problem or opportunity that was the catalyst for the original business research project has in fact been resolved satisfactorily. If not, the business research cycle can commence again, this time with previous research and experiences to call upon!

To sum up, research is the scientific path that leads the manager to decision making, and experience and common sense are the beacons that guide managers to solve problems sensibly. Experience is the cumulative knowledge gained from the outcomes of past problem-solving endeavours — a treasure filed away in a part of the brain, to be readily recalled whenever necessary. Such experience might be the result of a trial-and-error mode of operation in the past, leading to an understanding of what works and what does not. The question then arises, why not be guided by past experience and common sense alone? Why go through the rigorous scientific process of research?

Scientific research is important for several reasons. It is only through a scientific and systematic thinking process that we come to understand, and take into consideration, the complex set of factors that operates in any given problem situation. A viable and parsimonious model of theory building is enabled by the preliminary interviews and the literature review processes. We test the relevance of the model for solving the issue at hand by scientifically testing the various research questions and/ or hypotheses that logically flow from it. For this purpose, we collect data in a scientific manner, using the sampling design that is appropriate for the situation. The results of our data analysis then tell us how good our conceptualised theory is, and how the problem at hand can be solved, using a combination of alternatives generated by the results of data analysis. It is at this stage that the manager exercises good judgement both by using the research findings and by drawing on the personal, invaluable resources of past experiences. In sum, research indicates the direction to problem solving; experience and common sense, in conjunction with scientific research results, contribute to good managerial decision making. One without the other is not completely effective.

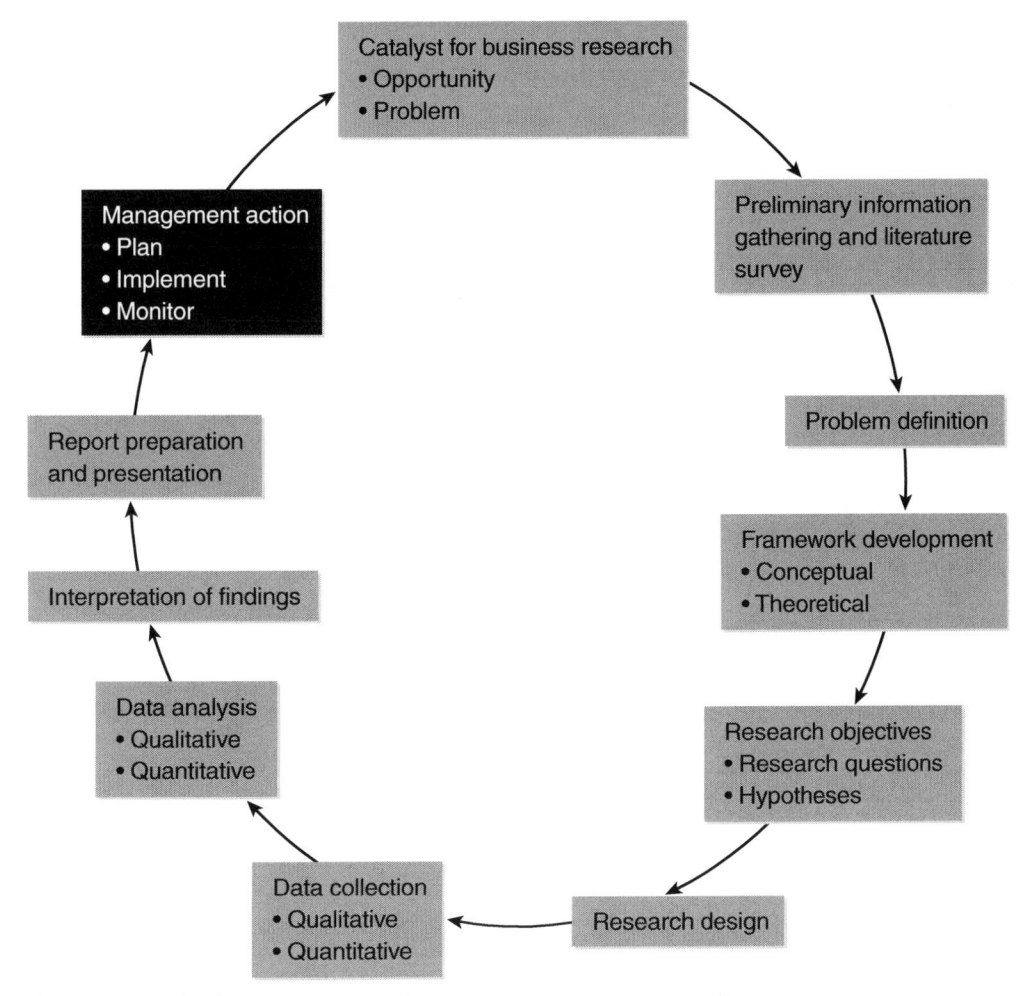

**Figure 15.1** The business research process: management action

Research also exposes us to the ever-increasing advances in technology. Today, the manager can find facts material to the business — national and global — by simply sitting in front of the computer and using the Internet. Vast masses of company data also become available to managers on practically any aspect of the company's multifarious operations, through a good Information System and Data Warehouse installed in the company's Information Technology system. Managers also solve simple, repetitive problems by using the menu-driven Expert System. Such technology was not readily available even a couple of decades ago.

True, managers cannot solve every problem by doing scientific research themselves. Often, internal research teams help in conducting research to find the answers to problems, or outside researchers are hired for the purpose. In either case, knowledge of research and the scientific thinking process help the manager to understand each step taken by the researcher, and enhance the quality of the decisions made. This is primarily because the contents of the research report, on submission, are meaningfully grasped, and intelligent and useful dialogues had transpired between the manager and the researcher throughout the duration of the study. As a matter of fact, a good research report itself may very well be, at least in part, the result of a knowledgeable manager interacting effectively with the researcher. With all the requisite information provided at the beginning, and throughout the duration of the study, the researcher has a better understanding of the problem situation and the constraints, and is enabled to conduct a good study.

Good decision making, as we have seen, is a function of thoroughly understanding and using the findings of the research, carefully weighing the various recommendations made, taking experience as a guide, and recognising the organisational culture and the values of the system. Ethical behaviour dictates that the manager applies research findings for the benefit of the organisation, even if they clash with his or her own personal goals and ambitions. As an example, it would be difficult to deny oneself the prospect of an imminent promotion to a higher position when research findings recommend an immediate temporary halt of all organisational changes. Governed by a sense of fairness and ethics, the manager instituting the study must, in such a case, subordinate him- or herself to organisational interests.

# PURPOSIVE RESEARCH

It is necessary for us to recall at this point that purposive research can be of different types, depending on the nature of the problem investigated. Sometimes descriptive studies are called for, and at other times, **analytical** or predictive **studies** may be necessary. Also, some situations lend themselves only to qualitative studies and others to quantitative analysis. Though one would like to conduct scientific studies that satisfy the hallmarks of science, this may not always be possible in applied business research, mainly because sufficient prior knowledge does not exist in that realm. In such cases, one may have to rely mainly on qualitative studies until sufficient knowledge is gained to conceptualise theoretical models that can be subsequently tested.

# DECISION-MAKING PROCESSES AND DIFFERENT TYPES OF RESEARCH

Results of data analysis of **descriptive studies** do provide information of interest to the manager. Based on such information, the manager might contemplate some future course of action. For example, the manager might consider creating opportunities for more challenging work, if a descriptive study were to indicate that employees are bored with their jobs. No complex decision making is called for in such cases.

Results of analysis of **hypothesis-testing studies** provide alternative choices for solving problems. The manager has to make a decision on the choice of alternative or combination of alternatives, and their implementation to solve the problem. Here, experience and sound judgement come into play in the decision-making process.

**Qualitative studies** may either describe events or offer solutions. However, in the absence of hard empirical statistical results, there is perhaps a higher element of unmeasured risk in implementing the solutions proposed in this kind of a study. The manager has to consider and judge if the recommendations made would solve the problems, and to what extent changes would be worthwhile. There is always an undetermined element of risk that the manager takes in making the proposed changes. Experience-based personal judgement, with a touch of intuition, will play a big part in decision making in the case of qualitative research.

We have given several examples of scientific research conducted as qualitative and quantitative research projects throughout this book, while discussing the process and design aspects of research.

To conclude, and as a basic summary of this book, we present a method of evaluating and critiquing business research. This suggested method can be used by clients/sponsors of business research or by researchers themselves in the process of ensuring good business research.

## EVALUATING BUSINESS RESEARCH

An essential part of the research process is the ability to critically evaluate a research report or published research article. This is equally important whether you are the client or consumer of a business research report, reviewing a published article for inclusion in your literature review, or preparing a business research report or article for publication or presentation at a conference or meeting.

As discussed in chapter 14, a range of different purposes for business research reports have been identified, including:
- offering details on some specific factors requested by a manager
- selling an idea to management
- providing a manager with alternative solutions or recommendations to rectify a problem
- identifying a problem and providing a solution to it
- preparing a paper for a trade or academic journal with the findings of an applied or basic business research study.

We will now offer some guidelines on helping you to evaluate business research studies. The amount of detail you include in your evaluation depends to a large extent on the intended purpose and audience for the report or article. Initially, you should comment on your reasons for undertaking the critique, and the general paradigm or conceptual approach of the research — that is, conceptual/overview questions. Then, following Katzer et al. (1991), we suggest that you breakdown the analysis of the report or article (and appendices) into three major categories — framework questions, method questions and results or conclusions questions. In addition, we also suggest you complete your evaluation with a reader's abstract.

Within each of the above categories certain general criteria and questions are useful for evaluating a research report (Beck 1990). These criteria and questions were originally prepared for nursing students and academics engaged in research, and have been modified in order to relate them more specifically to business and management research (Leedy 1997; Katzer et al. 1991). We have also added a few extra questions where appropriate.

## CONCEPTUAL/OVERVIEW QUESTIONS

The following questions relate to the conceptual and overall level of the business research report or article, identifying mainly the key assumptions guiding the approach to the research.

1. What are your reasons for undertaking this critique?
2. Who is the research prepared for?
3. What are the general philosophical bases or paradigms guiding the research — for example, is it positivist, interpretivist or critical research?
4. Are the research methods used primarily quantitative, qualitative or a mixture of both?
5. What are the backgrounds or biases of the researchers or authors of the business research project or article?
6. What is the effect of the language used in the article or report?

## FRAMEWORK QUESTIONS

These are the questions that appear at the beginning of most business research reports or published articles. The framework questions include everything prior to the method section, including the problem statement, literature review, outline of the theoretical or conceptual framework for the research, research variables and hypotheses.

*Step 1: The problem*
1. Is the problem clearly and concisely stated?
2. Is the problem adequately narrowed down into a researchable form?
3. Is the problem significant enough to warrant a formal research effort?
4. Is the relationship of the identified problem to previous research clear?

*Step 2: Literature review*
1. Is the literature review logically organised?
2. Does the literature review provide a critique of the relevant studies?
3. Are gaps in knowledge about the research problem identified?
4. Are important relevant references omitted?

*Step 3: Theoretical or conceptual framework*
1. Is the theoretical framework easily linked with the problem, or does it seem forced?
2. If a conceptual framework is used, are the concepts clearly defined and are possible relationships among these concepts explored?

*Step 4: Research variables*
1. Are the independent and dependent variables operationally defined?
2. Are any extraneous or intervening variables identified?

*Step 5: Research objectives*
For research questions:
Are the research questions specific enough to provide direction?

For hypotheses:
1. Is a predicted relationship between two or more variables included in each hypothesis?
2. Are the hypotheses clear, testable and specific?
3. Do the hypotheses flow logically from the theoretical or conceptual framework?

# METHOD QUESTIONS

These questions relate to the overall methodology of the research and are likely to be found in the middle sections of business reports or articles. The method questions consist of a detailed description of how the data were obtained and include questions related to sampling, research design and data collection methods.

*Step 6: Sampling*
1. Is the sample size adequate?
2. Is the sample representative of the defined population?
3. Is the method for selection of the sample appropriate?
4. Are the sample criteria for inclusion into the study identified?
5. Is there any sampling bias in the chosen method?

*Step 7: Research design*
1. Is the research design adequately described?
2. Is the design appropriate for the research objectives?
3. Does the research design control for threats in internal and external validity of the study?

*Step 8: Data collection methods*
1. Are the data collection methods appropriate for the study?
2. Are the data collection methods described adequately?
3. For qualitative research, are the methods trustworthy and accurate, or for quantitative research are the reliability and validity of the measurement tools adequate?

# RESULTS AND CONCLUSIONS QUESTIONS

The final set of questions relate to the latter parts of a business research report or paper. The results or conclusions consist of what the researcher found out during the research and how these findings were interpreted. These questions include the analysis and interpretation of the data collected, discussions of the research findings, conclusions, recommendations and implementation plans.

*Step 9: Data analysis*
1. Is the results section clearly and logically organised?
2. Is the type of analysis appropriate for the type of data collected?
3. Are the tables and figures clear and understandable?
4. If quantitative research, are the statistical tests the correct ones for answering the research questions?

*Step 10: Interpretation and discussion of the findings*
1. Are the interpretations based on the data obtained?
2. Does the researcher clearly distinguish between actual findings and interpretations?
3. Does the researcher answer the questions asked?
4. Are the findings discussed in relation to previous research and to the conceptual or theoretical framework?
5. How important are the findings?
6. Are unwarranted generalisations made beyond the study sample?
7. Are the limitations of the results identified?
8. Are the implications of the results for business and management practice discussed?
9. Are recommendations for future research identified?
10. Are the conclusions justified?

## READER'S ABSTRACT

Finally, we suggest you prepare a reader's abstract. This should include the main items that are normally found in an abstract or executive summary — outline of problem statement and research/study objectives, overview of methodology used in the research, the main findings or results, conclusions and recommendations. However, this summary should be in your own words. In addition, you should include a brief summary of your critique of the business report or article, particularly in terms of 'your assessment of the factual accuracy of the findings and their generalisability to your situation' (Katzer et al. 1991:201). This abstract should appear at the end of your critique.

## A FINAL COMMENT

After having gone through the different steps in the research process and research design of scientific research studies, we came full circle in understanding and acknowledging the role of both qualitative and quantitative studies in research. Hence, we end this final chapter with the observation that both qualitative and quantitative studies are integral parts of scientific investigations — each having its distinct role to play. In the ultimate analysis, the induction–deduction process — an issue we examined at the beginning of the book — is what leads to problem solving.

## DISCUSSION POINTS

1 Briefly describe a situation in which, given the results of a hypothesis-testing study, the manager has to apply extensive experience and common sense in making the final decision.

2 Which involves a more difficult decision-making situation for a manager — applying the results of a qualitative study or those of a hypothesis-testing study? Why?

3 Describe and depict through a diagram the cycle of the research process, from the point when the area is investigated for the first time, to finding definitive answers to the problems encountered in that area.

4 Why should managers develop the capacity to critically evaluate business reports and published business articles?

| | |
|---|---|
| Exercise 15.1 | Critique Report 4 in the appendix of chapter 14. Discuss it in terms of good and bad research, suggesting how the study could be improved, what aspects of it are good, and how scientific it is. |
| Exercise 15.2 | Critically evaluate Report 5 in the appendix of chapter 14. Prepare a report using the evaluation guidelines provided in this chapter. |

# REFERENCES

Aaker, D.A., Kumar. V., and Day, G.S. 1995, *Marketing Research*, 5th edition. New York: John Wiley & Sons.

Abbott, C. C. 1966, *Basic Research in Finance: Needs and Prospects*. Charlottesville, VA: University Press.

Abdel-Khalik, A. R., and Ajinkya, B. B. 1979, *Empirical Research in Accounting: A Methodological Viewpoint*. Sarasota, FL: American Accounting Association.

Angell, R. C., and Freedman, R. 1966, 'The use of documents, records, census materials, and indices'. In L. Festinger and D. Katz (eds), *Research Methods in the Behavioral Sciences*. New York: Holt, Rinehart and Winston.

Aragon-Correa, J. A. 1998, 'Strategic proactivity and firm approach to the natural environment'. *Academy of Management Journal* 41 (5), 556–67.

Baker, R. L., and Schultz, R. E. (eds) 1972, *Instructional Product Research*. New York: Van Nostrand.

Bales, R. 1950, *Interaction Process Analysis*. Reading, MA: Addison-Wesley.

Balsley, H. L., and Clover, V. T. 1988, *Research for Business Decisions: Business Research Methods*, 4th edition. Columbus, OH: Publishing Horizons.

Barry, H. 1969, 'Cross-cultural research with matched pairs of societies'. *Journal of Social Psychology* 79, 25–33.

Beck, C. T. 1990, 'The Research Critique: General Criteria for Evaluating a Research Report'. *Journal of Gynecology and Neonatal Nursing* 19 (Jan–Feb), 18–22.

Bendig, A. W. 1954, 'Transmitted information and the length of rating scales'. *Journal of Experimental Psychology* 47, 303–8.

Benne, K. D., and Sheats, P. 1948, 'Functional roles of group members'. *Journal of Social Issues* 4 (2), 41–9.

Bentley, T. J., and Forkner, I. H. 1983, *Making Information Systems Work for You: How to Make Better Decisions Using Computer-tigenerated Information*. Englewood Cliffs, NJ: Prentice Hall.

Bibby, M. 1997, 'Introduction: Education research and morality'. In M. Bibby (ed.), *Ethics and Education Research*. Coldstream, Vic.: AARE.

Billings, R. S., and Wroten, S. P. 1978, 'Use of path analysis in industrial/organizational psychology: Criticisms and suggestions'. *Journal of Applied Psychology* 63 (6), 677–88.

Blank, G. 1989, 'Finding the right statistic with statistical navigator'. *PC Magazine*, March 14, 97.

Boot, J. C. G., and Cox, E. B. 1970, *Statistical Analysis for Managerial Decisions*. New York: McGraw-Hill.

Bordens, K. S., and Abbott, B. B. 1988, *Research Design and Methods: A Process Approach*. Mountain View, CA: Mayfield Publishing.

Brazeley, P., and Richards, L. 2000, *The NVivo Qualitative Project Book*. London: Sage.

Brown, L. D., and Vasarhelyi, M. A. 1985, *Accounting Research Directory: The Database of Accounting Literature*. New York: Markus Wiener Publishing.

Bruce, W. M., and Reed, C. M. 1991, *Dual-Career Couples in the Public Sector*. New York: Quorum Books.

Bruner, G. C., and Hensel, P. J. 1994, *Marketing Scales Handbook*. New York: American Marketing Association.

Bryman, A., and Cramer, D. 1990, *Quantitative Data Analysis for Social Scientists*. London: Routledge.

Bryman, A., and Cramer, D. 1997, *Quantitative Data Analysis with SPSS for Windows: A Guide for Social Scientists*. London: Routledge.

Burns, R. B. 1994, *Introduction to Research Methods*, 2nd edition. Melbourne: Longman Cheshire.

*Business Week* (1998, January 26). 'Digital Whitebands'. Special Advertising Section.

*Business Week* (1998, March 23). 'Connections: Competitive strategies for the age of e-business'. Special Advertising Section.

Campbell, A. A., and Katona, G. 1966, 'The sample survey: A technique for social science research'. In L. Festinger and D. Katz (eds), *Research Methods in the Behavioral Sciences*. New York: Holt, Rinehart and Winston.

Campbell, D. T. 1976, 'Psychometric theory'. In M. D. Dunnette (ed.), *Handbook of Industrial and Organizational Psychology*. Chicago, IL: Rand-McNally.

Campbell, D. T., and Fiske, D. W. 1959, 'Convergent and discriminant validation by the multitrait–multi-method matrix'. *Psychological Bulletin* 56, 81–105.

Campbell, D. T., and Stanley, J. C. 1966, *Experimental and Quasi-experimental Designs for Research*. Chicago, IL: Rand-McNally.

Cannell, C. F., and Kahn, R. L. 1966, 'The collection of data by interviewing'. In L. Festinger and D. Katz (eds), *Research Methods in Behavioral Sciences*. New York: Holt, Rinehart and Winston.

Carlsmith. M., Ellsworth, P. C., and Aronson, E. 1976, *Methods of Research in Social Psychology*. Reading, MA: Addison-Wesley.

Cattell, R. B. 1966, 'The screen test for the number of factors'. *Multivariate Behavioral Research* 1, 245–76.

Cavana, R. Y., Crozier, R. A., Park, N. S., and Pillai, A. P. 1996, 'Attitudes towards Reclassifying Academic Titles in New Zealand Universities'. *Journal of Higher Education Policy and Management* 18 (1), 93–106.

Chein, I. 1959, 'An introduction to sampling'. In C. Selltiz, M. Jahoda, M. Deutsch and S. W. Cook (eds), *Research Methods in Social Relations*. New York: Holt, Rinehart and Winston.

*The Chicago Manual of Style* 1993, 14th edition. Chicago: University of Chicago Press.

Churchill, G. A. 1987, *Marketing Research: Methodological Foundations*. Chicago, IL: Dryden Press.

Coakes, S. J., and Steed, L. G. 2001, *SPSS Analysis without Anguish: Version 10.0 for Windows*. Brisbane: John Wiley & Sons.

Cohen, J. 1969, *Statistical Power Analysis for the Behavioral Sciences*. New York: Academic Press.

Cohen, J. 1990, 'Things I have learned (so far)'. *American Psychologist*, 1304–12.

Cohen, L., and Manion, L. 1989, *Research Methods in Education*, 3rd edition. London: Routledge.

Cook, T. D., and Campbell, D. T. 1979, *Quasi-Experimentation: Design and Analysis Issues for Field Settings*. Boston, MA: Houghton-Mifflin.

Cook, T. D., and Campbell, D. T. 1979, 'Four kinds of validity'. In R. T. Mowday and R. M. Steers (eds), *Research in Organizations: Issues and Controversies*. Santa Monica, CA: Goodyear Publishing.

Coombs, C. H. 1966, 'Theory and methods of social measurement'. In L. Festinger and D. Katz (eds), *Research Methods in the Behavioral Sciences*. New York: Holt, Rinehart and Winston.

Cormier, W. H., and Cormier, L. S. 1991, *Interviewing Strategies for Helpers*, 3rd edition. Pacific Grove, CA: Brooks/Cole.

Coyle, R. G. 1996, *System Dynamics Modelling: A Practical Approach*. London: Chapman and Hall.

Creswell, J. W. 1994, *Research Design: Qualitative & Quantitative Approaches*. Thousand Oaks, CA: Sage.

Cronbach, L. J. 1946, 'Response sets and test validating'. *Educational and Psychological Measurement* 6, 475–94.

Cronbach, L. J. 1990, *Essentials of Psychological Testing*, 5th edition. New York: Harper & Row.

Crowne, D. P., and Marlowe, D. 1980, *The Approval Motive: Studies in Evaluative Dependence*. Westport, CT: Greenwood Press.

Davies, G. R., and Yonder, D. 1937, *Business Statistics*. New York: John Wiley & Sons.

Davies, J., Smith, D., and Underhill, M. 1989, A Guide to Preparing a Research Proposal. An unpublished paper, Victoria University of Wellington, NZ.

Davis, D. 2000, *Business Research for Decision Making*, 5th edition. Pacific Grove, CA: Duxbury, Thomson Learning.

Davis, D., and Cosenza, R. M. 1988, *Business Research for Decision Making*, 2nd edition. Boston, MA: PWS-Kent Publishing.

Davis, D., and Cosenza, R. M. 1993, *Business Research for Decision Making*, 3rd edition. Belmont, CA: Wadsworth.

Delahaye, B. L. 1982, 'The structure of an interview'. *Update*, Issue 29, March. Brisbane: Australian Institute of Management.

Delahaye, B. L. 2000, *Human Resource Development: Principles and Practice*. Brisbane: John Wiley & Sons.

Delahaye, B. L., and Smith, B. J. 1998, *How to Be an Effective Trainer*, 3rd edition. New York: John Wiley & Sons.

Dick, R. 1990, *Convergence Interviewing*. Chapel Hill, Qld: Interchange.

Drenkow, G. 1987, 'Data acquisition software that adapts to your needs'. *Research and Development*, April, 84–87.

Dunphy, D. C., with Dick, R. 1981, *Organizational Change by Choice*. Sydney: McGraw-Hill.

Edwards, A. L. 1957, *Manual for the Edwards Personal Preference Schedule*. New York: Psychological Corporation.

Egan, G. 1994, *The Skilled Helper: A Problem-Management Approach to Helping*, 5th edition. Pacific Grove, CA: Brooks/Cole.

Ehrich, L. C. 2000, 'Principals as morally accountable leaders'. *International Journal of Educational Reform* 9 (2), April, 120–7.

Eisner, E. 1991, *The Enlightened Eye: Qualitative Inquiry and the Enhancement of Educational Practice*. New York: Macmillan.

Elmore, P. E., and Beggs, D. L. 1975, 'Salience of concepts and commitment to extreme judgments in response pattern of teachers'. *Education* 95 (4), 325–34.

Emory, C. W. 1985, *Business Research Methods*, 3rd edition. Homewood, IL: Richard D. Irwin.

Ferris, K. R. 1988, *Behavioral Accounting Research: A Critical Analysis*. Columbus, OH: Century VII Publishing.

Fern, E. F. 1982, 'The use of focus groups for idea generation: The effects of group size, acquaintanceship and moderator on response quantity and quality'. *Journal of Marketing Research* 19, 1–13.

Festinger, L. 1966, 'Laboratory experiments'. In L. Festinger and D. Katz (eds), *Research Methods in the Behavioral Sciences*. New York: Holt, Rinehart and Winston.

Festinger, L., and Katz, D. 1966, *Research Methods in the Behavioral Sciences*. New York: Holt, Rinehart and Winston.

Fiedler, F. 1967, *A Theory of Leadership Effectiveness*. New York: McGraw-Hill.

Fishbein, M. 1967, *Readings in Attitude Theory and Meaurement*. New York: John Wiley & Sons.

Fontana, A., and Frey, J. H. 1998, 'Interviewing: The art of science'. In N. K. Denzin and Y. S. Lincoln (eds), *Collecting and Interpreting Qualitative Data*. Thousand Oaks, CA: Sage.

Forrester, J. W. 1961, *Industrial Dynamics*. Cambridge, MA: MIT Press.

Forsyth, D. R. 1990, *Group Dynamics*, 2nd edition. Pacific Grove, CA: Brooks/Cole.

Fowler, F. J., and Mangione, T. W. 1990, *Standardized Survey Interviewing: Minimising Interviewer-related Error*. Newbury Park, CA: Sage.

Fraser, D. 1999, *QSR NUD*IST Vivo: Reference Guide*. Bundoora, Vic.: QSR.

French, J. R. P. 1966, 'Experiments in field settings'. In L. Festinger and D. Katz (eds), *Research Methods in the Behavioral Sciences*. New York: Holt, Rinehart and Winston.

Friedman, D. E. 1986, 'Child care for employees' kids'. *Personnel Administrator* 32 (8), 36–8.

Gaski, J. F., and Etzel, M. J. 1986, 'The index of consumer sentiment toward marketing'. *Journal of Marketing* 50, April, 71–81.

Gephart, R. 1999, Paradigms and Research Methods. *Research Methods Forum*, Vol. 4, Summer. Academy of Management, Research Methods Division. (Web address: http://www.aom.pace.edu/rmd/1999_RMD_Forum_Paradigms_and_Research_Methods.htm.)

Glaser, B. G., and Strauss, A. L. 1967, *The Discovery of Grounded Theory*. Chicago: Aldine.

Gorsuch, R. L. 1974, *Factor Analysis*. Philadelphia, NY: Saunders.

Gorsuch, R. L. 1983, *Factor Analysis*, 2nd edition. Philadelphia, NY: Saunders.

Green, P. E., Kedia, P. K., and Nikhil, R. S. 1985, *Electronic Questionnaire Design and Analysis with CAPPA*. Palo Alto, CA: The Scientific Press.

Groebner, D. F., and Shannon, P. W. 1989, *Business Statistics: A Decision-Making Approach*. Colombus, OH: Merrill.

Guba, E. G. 1978, *Toward a Methodology of Naturalistic Inquiry in Educational Evaluation*. CSE monograph series in evaluation, no. 8. Los Angeles: Center for the Study of Evaluation, University of California.

Harnett, D. L., and Horrell, J. F. 1998, *Data, Statistics, and Decision Models with Excel*. New York: John Wiley & Sons.

Hempel, C. G. 1952, *Fundamentals of Concept Formation in Empirical Science*. Chicago, IL: University of Chicago Press.

Hoel, P. G., and Jessen, R. J. 1971, *Basic Statistics for Business and Economics*. New York: John Wiley & Sons.

Horst, P. 1968, *Personality: Measurement of Dimensions*. San Francisco: Jossey-Bass.

Huberman, A. M., and Miles, M. B. 1998, 'Data management and analysis methods'. In N. K. Denzin and Y. S. Lincoln (eds), *Collecting and Interpreting Qualitative Materials*. Thousand Oaks, CA: Sage.

Jackson, W. 1995, *Methods: Doing Social Research*. Toronto, Ontario: Prentice Hall.

Kanuk, L., and Berenson, C. 1975, 'Mail surveys and response rates: A literature review'. *Journal of Marketing Research* 12, 440–53.

Kaplan, A. 1979, *The Conduct of Inquiry: Methodology for Behavioral Sciences*. New York: Harper & Row.

Katz, D. 1966, *Research Methods in the Behavioral Sciences*. New York: Holt, Rinehart and Winston.

Katzer, J., Cook, K. H., and Crouch, W. W. 1991, *Evaluating Information: A Guide for Users of Social Science Research*. New York: McGraw-Hill.

Kelly, F. J., Beggs, D. L., McNeil, K. A., Eichelberger, T., and Lyon, J. 1969, *Research Design in the Behavioral Sciences: Multiple Regression Approach*. Carbondale, IL: Southern Illinois University Press.

Kerlinger, R. N. 1986, *Foundations of Behavioral Research*, 3rd edition. New York: Holt, Rinehart and Winston.

Kidder, L. H., and Judd, C. H. 1986, *Research Methods in Social Relations*. New York: Holt, Rinehart and Winston.

Kilmer, B., and Harnett, D. L. 1998, *KADD-STAT: Statistical Analysis Plug-in to Microsoft Excel*. New York: John Wiley & Sons.

Kirk, R. E. 1982, *Experimental Design: Procedures for the Behavioral Sciences*. Belmont, CA: Brooks/Cole.

Kish, L. 1965, *Survey Sampling*. New York: John Wiley & Sons.

Kish, L. 1966, 'Selection of the sample'. In L. Festinger and D. Katz (eds), *Research Methods in the Behavioral Sciences*. New York: Holt, Rinehart and Winston.

Knechel, W. R. 1986, 'A simulation study of the relative effectiveness of altenrative analytical review procedures'. *Decision Sciences* 17 (3), 376–94.

Kornhauser, A., and Sheatsley, P. B. 1959, 'Questionnaire construction and intreview procedure'. In C. Sellitz, M. Jahoda, M. Deutsch and S. W. Cook (eds), *Research Methods in Social Relations*. New York: Holt, Rinehart and Winston.

Krejcie, R., and Morgan, D. 1970, 'Determining sample size for research activities'. *Educational and Psychological Measurement* 30, 607–10.

Krippendorff, K. 1980, *Content Analysis: An Introduction to Its Methodology*. Beverley Hills, CA: Sage.

Kruger, R. A. 1994, *Focus Groups: A Practical Guide for Applied Research*, 2nd edition. Thousand Oaks, CA: Sage.

Kuder, G. F., and Richardson, M. W. 1937, 'The theory of the estimation of test reliability'. *Psychometrika* 2, 151–60.

Labaw, P. 1980, *Advanced Questionnaire Design*. Cambridge, MA: Abt Books.

Lawson, E. 1997, 'Deception in research: After thirty years of controversy'. In M. Bibby (ed.), *Ethics and Education Research*. Coldstream, Vic.: AARE.

Lazarsfeld, P. F. 1935, 'The art of asking why'. *National Marketing Research* 1, 26–38.

Leedy, P. D. 1985, *Practical Research: Planning and Design*, 3rd edition. New York: Macmillan.

Leedy, P. D. 1997, *Practical Research: Planning and Design*, 6th edition. Englewood Cliffs, NJ: Prentice Hall.

Likert, R. 1932, 'A technique for the measurement of attitudes'. *Archives of Psychology* 140.

Lincoln, Y. S., and Guba, E. G. 2000, 'Paradigmatic Controversies, Contradictions, and Emerging Confluences'. In N. K. Denzin and Y. S. Lincoln (eds), *Handbook of Qualitative Research*, 2nd edition. Thousand Oaks, CA: Sage.

Lincoln, Y., and Guba, E. 1985, *Naturalistic Inquiry*. Beverly Hills, CA: Sage.

Lombardo, M. L., McCall, M., and DeVries, D. L. 1983, *Looking Glass*. Glenview, IL: Scott Foresman.

Luconi, F. L., Malone, T. W., and Scott Morton, M. S. 1986, 'Expert systems: The next challenge for managers'. *Sloan Management Review* 27 (4), 3–14.

Luftman, J. N. 1996, *Competing in the Information Age: Strategic Alignment in Practice*. New York: Oxford University Press.

Maani, K. E., and Cavana R. Y. 2000, *Systems Thinking and Modelling: Understanding Change and Complexity*. Auckland: Prentice Hall.

Marascuilo, L. A., and McSweeney, M. 1977, *Nonparametric and Distribution-free Methods for the Social Sciences*. Monterey, CA: Brooks/Cole.

Martin, M. H. 1998, 'Smart managaing: Best practices, careers, and ideas'. *Fortune*, February 2, 149.

Maykut, P., and Morehouse, R. 1994, *Beginning Qualitative Research: A Philosophic and Practical Guide*. London: The Falmer Press.

McClave, J. T., and Benson, P. G. 1988, *Statistics for Business and Economics*, 4th edition. San Francisco: Dellen Publishing.

McNeil, K. A., Kelly, F. J., and McNeil, J. T. 1975, *Testing Research Hypotheses Using Multiple Linear Regression*. Carbondale, IL: Southern Illinois University Press.

Meltzer, M. E. 1981, *Information: The Ultimate Management Resource*. New York: Amacom.

Merton, R. K., and Kendall, P. L. 1955, 'The focused interview'. In P. F. Lazarsfeld and M. Roseberg (eds), *The Language of Social Research*. New York: The Free Press.

Meuhling, D. D. 1987, 'An investigation of factors underlying attitude-toward-advertising-in-general'. *Journal of Advertising* 16 (1), 32–40.

Miles, M. B., and Huberman, A. M. 1994, *Qualitative Data Analysis: A Sourcebook of New Methods*, 2nd edition. Thousand Oaks, CA: Sage.

Minichiello, V., Aroni, R., Timewell, E., and Alexander, L. 1990, *In-depth Interviewing: Researching People*. Melbourne: Longman Cheshire.

Mitchell, R. E. 1969, 'Survey materials collected in developing countries: Sampling, measurement, and interviewing obstacles to intra- and inter-national comparisons'. In J. Boddewyn (ed.), *Comparative Management and Marketing*. Glenview, IL: Scott Foresman, 232–52.

Mittal, B., and Lassar, W. M. 1996, 'The role of personalization in service encounters'. *Journal of Retailing* 72 (2), 95–109.

Morgan, D. L. 1997, *Focus Groups as Qualitative Research*, 2nd edition. Thousand Oaks, CA: Sage.

Murdick, P. G., and Cooper, D. R. 1982, *Business Research: Concepts and Guides*. Columbus, OH: Grid Publishing.

Namboodiri, N. K., Carter, L. F., and Blalock, H. M. 1975, *Applied Multivariate Analysis and Experimental Designs*. New York: McGraw-Hill.

Napier, R. W., and Gershenfeld, M. K. 1993, *Groups: Theory and Experience*. Boston: Houghton Mifflin.

Neuman, W. L. 1997, *Social Research Methods: Qualitative and Quantitative Approaches*, 3rd edition. Boston, MA: Allyn and Bacon.

Norusis, M. H. 1998, *SPSS 8.0 Guide to Data Analysis*. Englewood Cliffs, NJ: Prentice Hall.

Nunnally, J. C. 1978, *Psychometric Theory*, 2nd edition. New York: McGraw-Hill.

Oppenheim, A. N. 1986, *Questionnaire Design and Attitude Measurement*. UK: Gower Publishing.

Osborn, R. N., and Vicars, W. M. 1976, 'Sex stereotypes: An artifact in leader behavior and subordinate satisfaction analysis?' *Academy of Management Journal* 19, 439–49.

Parker, M., Peltier, S., and Wolleat, P. 1981, 'Understanding dual career couples'. *Personnel and Guidance Journal* 60 (1), 14–8.

Patton, M. Q. 1990, *Qualitative Evaluation and Research Methods*. Newbury Park, CA: Sage.

Payne, S. L. 1951, *The Art of Asking Questions*. Princeton, NJ: Princeton University Press.

Peak, H. 1966, 'Problems of objective observation'. In L. Festinger and D. Katz (eds), *Research Methods in the Behavioral Sciences*. New York: Holt, Rinehart and Winston.

Pedhazur, E. J. 1982, *Multiple Regression in Behavioral Research: Explanation and Prediction*, 2d edition. New York: CBS College Publishing.

Pelosi, M. K., Sandifer, T. M., and Letkowski, J. J. 1998, *Doing Statistics with Excel 97: Software instruction and exercise activity supplement*. New York: John Wiley & Sons.

Perrier, C., and Kalwarski, G. 1989, 'Stimulating simulations: Technique shows relationship between risk, funding'. *Pensions and Investment Age*, October 30, 41–3.

Pidd, M. 1992, *Computer Simulation in Management Science*, 3rd edition. Chichester, UK: John Wiley & Sons.

Pierce, J. 1998, The Dual Career Couple: A Human Resource Management Perspective. Unpublished doctoral thesis, Queensland University of Technology, Brisbane.

Price, J. L. 1972, *Handbook of Organizational Measurement*. Lexington, MA: D. C. Heath.

*Publications Manual of the American Psychological Association*, 4th edition (1994). Washington, DC: American Psychological Association.

Rao, C. R. 1973, *Linear Statistical inference and Its Applications*, 2nd edition. New York: John Wiley & Sons.

Resta, P. A. 1972, *The Research Report*. New York: American Book Company.

Reynolds, P. D. 1971, *A Primer in Theory Construction*. Indianapolis: Bobby-Merrill.

Richards, L. 1999, *Using NVivo in Qualitative Research*. Bundoora, Vic.: QSR.

Riley, M. W., and Nelson, E. E. 1974, *Sociological Observation: A Strategy for New Social Knowledge*. New York: Basic Books.

Rizzo, J. R., House, R. J., and Lirtzman, S. I. 1970, 'Role conflict and role ambiguity in complex organizations'. *Administrative Science Quarterly* 15, 150–63.

Roscoe, J. R. 1975, *Fundamental Research Statistics for the Behavioral Sciences*, 2nd edition. New York: Holt, Rinehart and Winston.

Roth, M. S. 1995, 'The effects of culture and socioeconomics on the performance of global brand image strategies'. *Journal of Marketing Research* XXXII, May, 163–75.

Runkel, P. J., and McGrath, J. E. 1972, *Research on Human Behavior: A Systematic Guide to Method*. New York: Holt, Rinehart and Winston.

Salvia, A. A. 1990, *Introduction to Statistics*. Philadelphia: Saunders.

Sandy, R. 1989, *Statistics for Business and Economics*. New York: McGraw-Hill.

Schein, E. H. 1969, *Process Consultation*, 1st edition. Reading, MA: Addison-Wesley.

Schmitt, N. W., and Klimoski, R. J. 1991, *Research Methods in Human Resources Management*. Cincinnati, OH: South-Western Publishing.

Seidman, I. E. 1991, *Interviewing as Qualitative Research*. New York: Teacher's College Press.

Sekaran, U. 1983, 'Methodological and theoretical issues and advancements in cross-cultural research'. *Journal of International Business*, Fall, 61–73.

Sekaran, U. 1986, *Dual-career Families: Contemporary Organizational and Counseling Issues*. San Francisco: Jossey-Bass.

Sekaran, U., and Martin, H. J. 1982, 'An examination of the psychometric properties of some commonly researched individual differences, job and organizational variables in two cultures'. *Journal of International Business Studies*, Spring/Summer, 551–66.

Sekaran, U., and Trafton, R. S. 1978, 'The dimensionality of jobs: Back to square one'. *Twenty-fourth Midwest Academy of Management Proceedings*, 249–62.

Selltiz, C., Jahoda, M., Deutsch, M., and Cook, S. W. 1959, *Research Methods in Social Rel.ations* (rev. ed.). New York: Holt, Rinehart and Winston.

Selltiz, C., Wrightsman, L. S., and Cook, S. W. 1981, *Research Methods in Social Relations*, 4th edition. New York: Holt, Rinehart and Winston.

Shurter, R. L., Williamson, J. P., and Broehl, W. G., Jr. 1965, *Business Research and Report Writing*. New York: McGraw-Hill.

Smith, C. B. 1981, *A Guide to Business Research: Developing, Conducting, and Writing Research Projects*. Chicago, IL: Nelson-Hall.

Smith, P. C., Kendall, L., and Hulin, C. 1969, *The measurement of Satisfaction in Work and Retirement*. Chicago: Rand-McNally, 79–84.

SQM 1994, *Service Quality Microworld* ™. Cambridge, MA: Microworlds, 21–22.

Statistics New Zealand 1995, *A Guide to Good Survey Design*. Wellington, NZ: Statistics New Zealand.

Sterman, J. D. 2000, *Business Dynamics: Systems Thinking and Modeling for a Complex World*. Boston, MA: Irwin McGraw-Hill.

Steufert, S., Pogash, R., and Piasecki, M. 1988, 'Simulation-based assessment of managerial competence: Reliability and validity'. *Personnel Psychology* 41 (3), 537–57.

Stolz-Loike, M. 1992, *Dual Career Couples: New Perspectives in Counseling*. Alexandria, VA: American Association for Counseling and Development.

Stone, E. 1978, *Research Methods in Organizational Behavior*. Santa Monica, CA: Goodyear Publishing.

Strauss, A., and Corbin, J. 1990, *Basics of Qualitative Research: Grounded Theory Procedures and Techniques*. Newbury Park, CA: Sage.

Ticehurst, G. W., and Veal, A. J. 1999, *Business Research Methods: A Managerial Approach*. Sydney: Longman.

Tomeski, E. A. 1970, *The Computer Revolution: The Executive and the New Information Technology*. New York: Macmillan.

Tregoe, B. J. 1983, 'Questioning: The key to effective problem solving and decision making'. In B. Taylor and G. Lippitt (eds), *Management Development and Training Handbook*, 2nd edition. London: McGraw-Hill.

Turabian, K. L. 1996, *A Manual for Writers of Term Papers, Theses, and Dissertations*, 6th edition, revised by John Grossman and Alice Bennett. Chicago, IL: University of Chicago Press.

Turban, E., McLean, E., and Wetherbe, J. 1998, *Information Technology for Management: Making Connections for Strategic Advantage*. New York: John Wiley & Sons.

Van Maanen, J. 1983, *Qualitative Methodology*. London: Sage.

Ward, P. T., McCreery, J. K, Ritzman, L. P., and Sharma, D. 1998, 'Competitive priorities in operations management'. *Decision Sciences* 29 (4), 1035–46.

Webb, E. J., Campbell, D. T., Schwartz, P. D., and Sechrest, L. 1966, *Unobtrusive Measures: Non-reactive Research in the Social Sciences*. Chicago, IL: Rand-McNally.

Wetherbe, J. C. 1983, *Computer-based Information Systems*. Englewood Cliffs, NJ: Prentice Hall.

White, J. K., and Ruh, P. A. 1973, 'Effects on personal values on the relationship between participation and job attitudes'. *Administrative Science Quarterly* 18 (4), 506–14.

Wildstrom, S. H. 1998, 'Web sites made simpler'. *Business Week*, January 26.

Williams, C. T., and Wolfe, G. K. 1979, *Elements of Research: A Guide for Writers*. Sherman Oaks, CA: Alfred Publishing.

Williams, J. 1990, Visual decision support: Choice of representation form by managers. Unpublished paper, Department of Management, Southern Illinois University, Carbondale.

Zetterberg, H. 1955, 'On axiomatic theories in sociology'. In P. F. Lazarsfeld and M. Rosenberg (eds), *The Language of Social Research*. New York: The Free Press.

Zikmund, W. G. 2000, *Business Research Methods*, 6th edition. Orlando, FL: The Dryden Press, Harcourt College Publishers.

Zima, J. P. 1991, *Interviewing: Key to Effective Management*. New York: Macmillan.

# GLOSSARY OF STATISTICAL SYMBOLS

| | |
|---|---|
| $\alpha$ | (alpha) significance level or probability of a Type I error |
| $\beta$ | (beta) probability of a Type II error |
| $df$ | degrees of freedom |
| CV | coefficient of variation |
| F | F test or value of F distribution |
| $H_A$ | alternate hypothesis |
| $H_0$ | null hypothesis |
| $n$ | number of observations in a sample |
| N | number of elements in the population |
| $p$ | probability or significance level |
| $r$ | simple correlation coefficient |
| $r_s$ | Spearman's rank correlation coefficient (called Spearman's rho) |
| R | multiple regression coefficient |
| $R^2$ | R square or coefficient of determination |
| S | sample standard deviation |
| $S^2$ | sample variance |
| $S_{\bar{X}}$ | standard error of the sample mean |
| $\sigma$ | population standard deviation |
| $\sigma^2$ | population variance |
| $\Sigma$ | Summation (the sum of) |
| $t$ | $t$-test or value of $t$ distribution |
| $\mu$ | (mu) population mean |
| $\chi^2$ | chi-square statistic |
| X | independent variable |
| $\bar{X}$ | (X-bar) sample mean |
| Y | dependent variable |
| $\hat{Y}$ | (Y-hat) estimated value of the dependent variable, Y |
| $z$ | $z$ score or value for normal distribution |

# appendix 1

## A REFRESHER ON SOME STATISTICAL TERMS AND TESTS

### OUTLINE

INTRODUCTION
DESCRIPTIVE STATISTICS
INFERENTIAL STATISTICS
OTHER TESTS AND ANALYSES
MANAGERIAL RELEVANCE
SUMMARY
DISCUSSION POINTS

### APPENDIX OBJECTIVES

This appendix is provided as a 'refresher' of some statistical terms and tests that you may have previously learned about on a statistics course. We provide examples of SPSS computer output to illustrate the use of statistics to analyse quantitative data collected by questionnaires, structured interviews and so on. We do not provide full details of all the mathematical features of the statistical tests, neither do we provide detailed instructions on how to use SPSS (or any other statistical or spreadsheet package you may be using). However, we hope that we have provided sufficient background material here to help you undertake a fairly rigorous quantitative analysis of the survey data you have collected. This appendix should be read in conjunction with chapter 13 on Quantitative Data Analysis and Interpretation.

# INTRODUCTION

To many, the very mention of the word *statistics* creates anxiety. You may wonder when, if ever, you would use statistics in real life. But when you think about it, we use statistics every day without even realising it. For example, you might be interested in how many hours a week, on average, you spend in reading a particular subject, what are the highest and lowest marks obtained by students in a specific exam, and where you stand in the class relative to others. You might even wonder if the time and effort you spend in studying for a particularly difficult class are worth it, considering the grades you get in that class. In answering each of these questions, you do indeed apply the concepts of central tendencies and dispersions and correlations — all related to statistics!

Knowledge about the use of appropriate statistical tests in data analysis will prove to be a boon to managers who seek to understand the implications of the findings of a study conducted to solve a problem. *The purpose of this appendix is to refresh your memory about the various terms and statistical tests that you might have studied earlier.* After reading this appendix, you should be able to explain what types of analysis are appropriate, under what conditions and for what objectives. This will help you to follow with relative ease the data analyses discussed in chapter 13.

In research, we seek scientific data, which on analysis provide answers to the research questions. *Data* refer to the available raw information gathered through interviews, questionnaires, observations or secondary databases. By organising the data in some fashion, analysing them and making sense of the results, we find the answers we seek.

In most quantitative business research, at the very minimum it is of interest to know how frequently certain phenomena occur (frequencies), and the mean or average score of a set of data collected, as well as the extent of variability in the set (that is, the central tendencies and dispersions of the dependent and independent variables). These are known as **descriptive statistics** (statistics that describe the phenomena of interest). Beyond this, we might want to know how variables relate to each other, whether there are any differences between two or more groups, and the like. These are called **inferential statistics** (that is, statistical results that let us draw inferences from a sample to the population, as discussed in chapter 12). Inferential statistics can be categorised as **parametric** or **non-parametric**. The use of parametric statistics is based on the assumption that the population from which the sample is drawn is normally distributed and data are collected on an interval or ratio scale. Non-parametric statistics, on the other hand, make no explicit assumption regarding the normality of distribution in the population and are used when the data are collected on a nominal or ordinal scale. Refer to table 8.1 on page 198, which summarises some of the statistical properties of the four measurement scales.

Both descriptive and inferential statistics can be obtained by using PC software programs designed to enter data, edit and analyse them, and produce results for various types of data analysis. Programs such as SPSS, Minitab and Excel are used in social science and business research. Before discussing data analysis, it would be useful to quickly refresh your memory regarding some of the statistical concepts and their applications.

We will briefly explain some of the terms and tests such as **frequencies, measures of central tendencies and dispersions,** *correlation,* **chi-square test,** *t*-**test, analysis of variance (ANOVA), regression analysis** and *factor analysis.* The idea is to give an overview of these and their relevance, rather than offer a tutorial in statistical formulas and interpretations, which you might have studied earlier in a course on statistics. However, we will provide some formulas where we feel this helps to clarify the concepts being discussed.

Also, we will provide examples of SPSS computer files and output to further illustrate some of the statistical concepts discussed in this appendix. We will use the data collected from the Business Research Class Questionnaire (BRCQ), presented as figure 10.2 on page 226. These data were originally input into an Excel spreadsheet, but we have now imported them into SPSS for further statistical analysis. In the SPSS data file, presented as table A1, each row shows the responses to each question by each respondent (or '**case**'); and each column shows the responses to each question (or 'variable') by all respondents. There were 34 responses (cases) to this questionnaire, which had five questions, although question 5 had two parts; hence we have six variables. Each completed questionnaire was given a separate number (identifier), mainly to prevent the same questionnaire being entered into the computer twice, but also to facilitate data entry checking later. Table A2 summarises the labels and values given to each variable. In SPSS each variable must have eight or fewer alphanumeric characters.

**Table A1** Responses from the Business Research Class Questionnaire

| ID | GENDER | HEIGHT | WEIGHT | EYE_COL | STAT_INT | STAT_USE |
|----|--------|--------|--------|---------|----------|----------|
| 1  | 1 | 175 | 76 | 2 | 3 | 2 |
| 2  | 1 | 173 | 70 | 3 | 2 | 2 |
| 3  | 1 | 174 | 75 | 2 | 4 | 2 |
| 4  | 1 | 175 | 77 | 1 | 2 | 2 |
| 5  | 1 | 173 | 70 | 1 | 1 | 2 |
| 6  | 0 | 165 | 58 | 2 | 3 | 2 |
| 7  | 1 | 185 | 85 | 1 | 2 | 1 |
| 8  | 1 | 172 | 84 | 2 | 3 | 2 |
| 9  | 1 | 175 | 85 | 3 | 5 | 2 |
| 10 | 1 | 179 | 73 | 3 | 4 | 2 |
| 11 | 1 | 175 | 82 | 3 | 3 | 3 |
| 12 | 0 | 178 | 70 | 2 | 2 | 1 |
| 13 | 1 | 183 | 82 | 1 | 1 | 2 |
| 14 | 1 | 178 | 73 | 1 | 2 | 2 |
| 15 | 0 | 165 | 58 | 1 | 3 | 2 |
| 16 | 0 | 167 | 55 | 3 | 3 | 4 |
| 17 | 1 | 168 | 70 | 2 | 4 | 3 |
| 18 | 1 | 182 | 91 | 1 | 5 | 2 |
| 19 | 1 | 168 | 75 | 2 | 4 | 2 |
| 20 | 0 | 163 | 70 | 3 | 3 | 2 |
| 21 | 1 | 183 | 75 | 3 | 5 | 5 |
| 22 | 1 | 183 | 77 | 3 | 5 | 1 |
| 23 | 0 | 160 | 78 | 1 | 3 | 1 |
| 24 | 1 | 188 | 95 | 1 | 2 | 2 |
| 25 | 0 | 160 | 60 | 2 | 5 | 2 |
| 26 | 1 | 168 | 54 | 2 | 1 | 2 |
| 27 | 1 | 180 | 75 | 2 | 5 | 4 |
| 28 | 1 | 173 | 73 | 1 | 2 | 1 |
| 29 | 1 | 165 | 65 | 2 | 3 | 2 |
| 30 | 1 | 178 | 77 | 2 | 2 | 1 |
| 31 | 0 | 163 | 56 | 1 | 2 | 2 |
| 32 | 1 | 173 | 89 | 1 | 2 | 2 |
| 33 | 1 | 175 | 75 | 1 | 4 | 3 |
| 34 | 1 | 185 | 93 | 2 | 3 | 3 |

**Table A2** Variable names, labels and values in the data set in table A1

| Variable name | Labels (variable definition) | Values for variable |
|---|---|---|
| id | Identifier for each respondent | |
| gender | Female or male | 0 = Female<br>1 = Male |
| height | Height in centimetres | |
| weight | Weight in kilograms | |
| eye_col | Eye colour | 1 = Blue<br>2 = Brown<br>3 = Other |
| stat_int | Statistics is interesting | 1 = Strongly disagree<br>2 = Disagree<br>3 = Neutral<br>4 = Agree<br>5 = Strongly agree |
| stat_use | Statistics is useful | |

Examples of different SPSS Data Editor views of this input data are provided in figures A1 and A2. Figure A1 shows the data in numeric form, which is particularly suitable for statistical analysis. These data can also be shown displaying all the alphanumeric values for each variable by clicking on the 'tag'-shaped icon the second from the right below the menu bar. The variable view for these data is presented in figure A2, where the name, type, label (description), values and measurement scale for each variable can be specified.

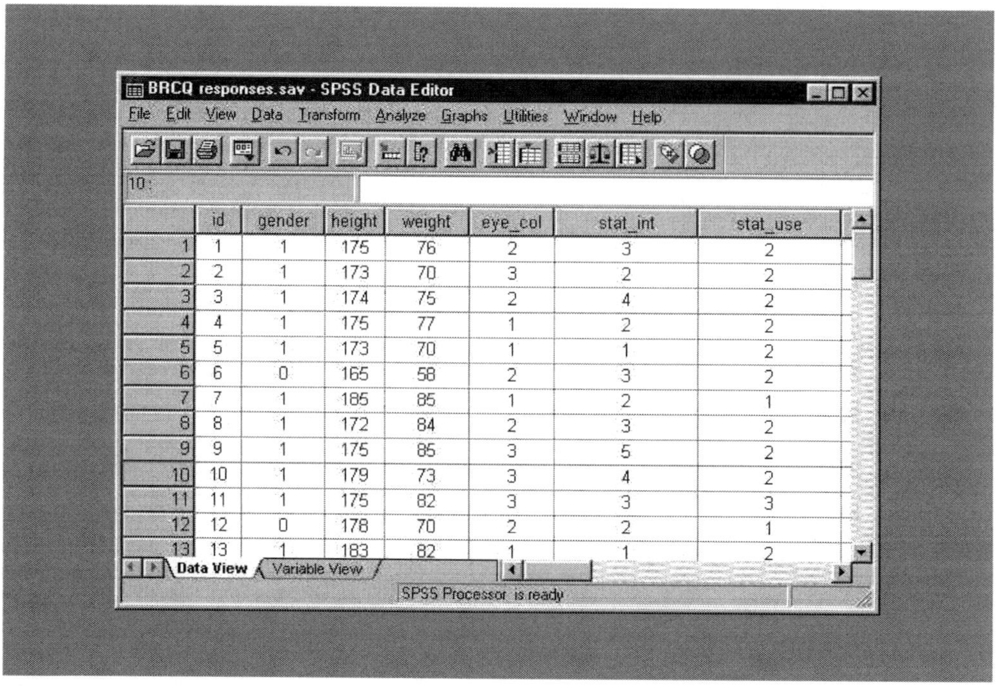

| id | gender | height | weight | eye_col | stat_int | stat_use |
|---|---|---|---|---|---|---|
| 1 | 1 | 175 | 76 | 2 | 3 | 2 |
| 2 | 1 | 173 | 70 | 3 | 2 | 2 |
| 3 | 1 | 174 | 75 | 2 | 4 | 2 |
| 4 | 1 | 175 | 77 | 1 | 2 | 2 |
| 5 | 1 | 173 | 70 | 1 | 1 | 2 |
| 6 | 0 | 165 | 58 | 2 | 3 | 2 |
| 7 | 1 | 185 | 85 | 1 | 2 | 1 |
| 8 | 1 | 172 | 84 | 2 | 3 | 2 |
| 9 | 1 | 175 | 85 | 3 | 5 | 2 |
| 10 | 1 | 179 | 73 | 3 | 4 | 2 |
| 11 | 1 | 175 | 82 | 3 | 3 | 3 |
| 12 | 0 | 178 | 70 | 2 | 2 | 1 |
| 13 | 1 | 183 | 82 | 1 | 1 | 2 |

**Figure A1** Example of SPSS Data Editor input data — 'Data View'

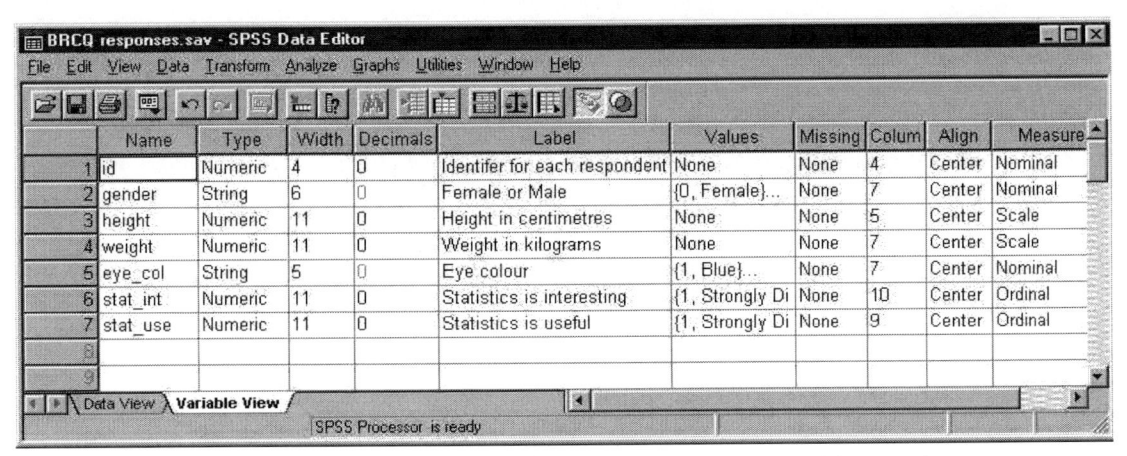

**Figure A2** Example of SPSS Data Editor input data — 'Variable View'

## DESCRIPTIVE STATISTICS

Descriptive statistics involve transformation of raw data into a form that would provide information to describe a set of factors in a situation. This is done through ordering and manipulation of the raw data collected. Descriptive statistics are provided by frequencies, measures of central tendency and dispersion. These are now described.

### FREQUENCIES

Frequencies simply refer to the number of times various subcategories of a certain phenomenon occur, from which the percentage and the cumulative percentage of their occurrence can be easily calculated. An example will make this clear.

Let us consider the responses to the item 'Statistics is interesting', included in the business research class questionnaire. This item is represented by the variable 'stat_int' in the data set shown in table A1 and figure A1. What might the researcher be interested in? Well, perhaps the number of respondents who had circled each of the scale points. This is fairly easy — simply go through the data and count the number of people who have circled '1', '2', '3', '4' and '5'. This statistical procedure goes by the name of *frequency analysis*, and the SPSS package has a program called 'Frequencies' to perform just this task. If you look at figure A3, you will see a table at the top that shows the number of people who circled each point on the response scale (under the heading 'Frequency'). Another heading, 'Percent', converts these figures into a percentage for each point — so, the three respondents who circled '1' (Strongly disagree) represent 8.8 per cent of the total respondents. This table is a typical output that can be produced by most statistical analysis packages. Further, the frequencies can be converted to a visual representation, such as bar charts. Figure A3 also shows the results of a frequency analysis in a bar chart. Bar charts are particularly suitable for displaying data measured on nominal or ordinal scales.

Frequencies are used to examine three parts of the questionnaire. First, the researcher will see how many respondents there are in each category of the classifications and compare these numbers with the number of questionnaires sent to the respondents in each category. Has one category returned fewer questionnaires than the other categories? If so, the researcher will need to find out why, to ensure that the problem is remedied before the main analysis of the data.

|  |  | Frequency | Percent | Valid Percent | Cumulative Percent |
|---|---|---|---|---|---|
| Valid | Strongly disagree | 3 | 8.8 | 8.8 | 8.8 |
|  | Disagree | 10 | 29.4 | 29.4 | 38.2 |
|  | Neutral | 10 | 29.4 | 29.4 | 67.6 |
|  | Agree | 5 | 14.7 | 14.7 | 82.4 |
|  | Strongly agree | 6 | 17.6 | 17.6 | 100.0 |
|  | Total | 34 | 100.0 | 100.0 |  |

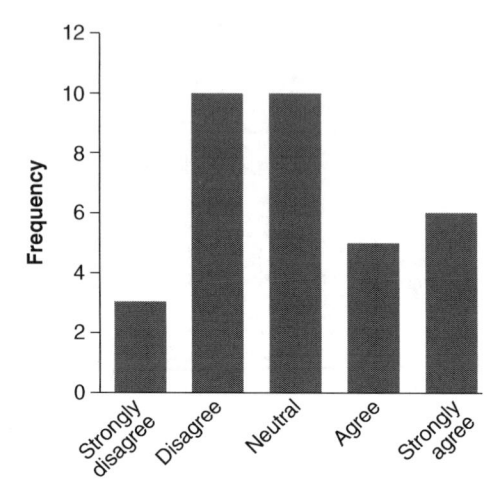

**Figure A3** Responses to the statement 'Statistics is interesting'

Second, the researcher will examine the frequencies for the factual data. What is the range (the highest and lowest scores)? Is this range within the expected? If categories of factual data were used, were the categories adequate? For example, if all of the respondents in a pilot study ticked 'More than 10 hours', a new set of categories might be needed — perhaps 'Less than 10 hours', '10–14 hours', '15–19 hours' or '20 hours or more', rather than the original categories '0–2 hours', '3–5 hours', '5–10 hours' or 'More than 10 hours'.

Third, frequencies are used for an initial examination of the opinion items. By examining the frequencies and bar charts for each opinion item, the researcher can see how the respondents have answered each scale. Is it a fairly even distribution, high in the middle and lower at the two ends? Or is there a hump at one end? Have more people responded for one point than the others?

Examples of other instances where frequency distributions would be useful are when (1) a marketing manager wants to know how many units (and what proportions or percentages) of each brand of coffee are sold in a particular region during a given period, (2) a tax consultant desires to keep count of the number of times different sizes of firms (small, medium, large) are audited by the Australian Taxation Office or the Inland Revenue Department, and (3) a financial analyst wants to keep track of the number of times the shares of manufacturing, industrial and utility companies lose or gain more than 10 points on the Australian Stock Exchange over a six-month period.

In all the above cases, it may be noted that we wish to obtain the frequencies on a **nominally or ordinally scaled** variable. That is, these variables will be grouped into various non-overlapping subcategories, such as the different brands of coffee, sizes of firms and types of companies. The number of occurrences under each category and their respective percentages will then be determined.

In business research, frequencies are generally obtained for nominal variables such as gender and educational level, and ordinal variables such as attitudes or opinions. However, for 'continuous' data collected an interval or ratio scale then a histogram can be used to display frequencies (rather than a bar chart for 'discrete' data). First, class intervals have to be established for the continuous data, then the data need to be sorted into these class intervals. In SPSS, the 'Recode' procedure is used, initially to define a new variable, then to transform the data into new class intervals. For example, for our business research class data, we transformed the heights of the 34 respondents into six groups (class intervals). These are shown in figure A4, which displays the frequency table and the histogram for the variable 'height group'. In the histogram, '1' represents the class interval for height 164 centimetres and below, '2' represents the interval for the heights of respondents between 165 and 169 centimetres, and so on.

We have also selected the option in SPSS to generate a normal curve (discussed on page 410) based on the data. As can be seen from figure A4, the height data follow a bimodal distribution rather than a normal curve. This suggests that either the sample data are biased or the population from which this sample was drawn did not display features of a 'normal' population (that is, a bell-shaped distribution, symmetrical about the mean). This result is hardly surprising since the sample consisted of both male and female respondents, and there has been plenty of evidence to suggest that the heights of males and females are generally different (although this is a very good hypothesis to test when we consider the 'mean differences between two groups' below)!

Height group (cm)

| | | Frequency | Percent | Valid Percent | Cumulative Percent |
|---|---|---|---|---|---|
| Valid | 164 and below | 7 | 20.6 | 20.6 | 20.6 |
| | 165–169 | 4 | 11.8 | 11.8 | 32.4 |
| | 170–174 | 6 | 17.6 | 17.6 | 50.0 |
| | 175–179 | 9 | 26.5 | 26.5 | 76.5 |
| | 180–184 | 5 | 14.7 | 14.7 | 91.2 |
| | 185 and above | 3 | 8.8 | 8.8 | 100.0 |
| | Total | 34 | 100.0 | 100.0 | |

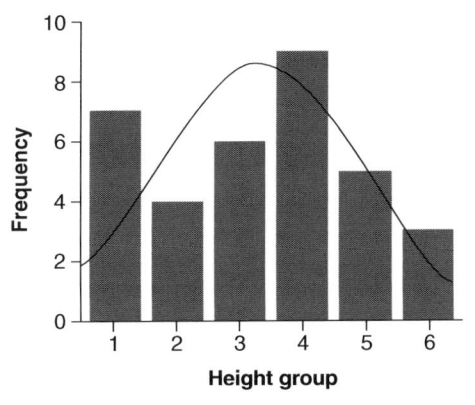

**Figure A4** Example of SPSS frequency and histogram output

# MEASURES OF CENTRAL TENDENCIES

It is often useful to describe a series of observations in a data set in a summarised and meaningful way, which would enable individuals to get an idea of, or a 'feel' for, the basic characteristics of the data. Measures of central tendencies and dispersions enable us to achieve this goal. There are three measures of central tendencies: the mean, the median and the mode.

## The mean

The **mean** or *average* is a measure of central tendency that offers a general picture of the data without unnecessarily inundating one with each of the observations in a data set. For example, the Production Department might keep detailed records on how many units of a product are being produced each day. However, to estimate the raw materials inventory, all that the manager might want to know is how many units per month, *on average*, the department has been producing over the past six months. This measure of central tendency — that is, the *mean* — might offer the manager a good idea of the quantity of materials that need to be stocked.

Similarly, a marketing manager might want to know how many cans of soup are being sold, *on average*, each week, or a banker might be interested in the number of new accounts that are opened each month, *on average*. The mean or average of a set of, say, 10 observations, is the sum of the 10 individual observations divided by 10 (the total number of observations).

Since the mean is one of the most widely used statistical measures, it is useful to provide the formula for it. It is defined for a sample of $n$ observations as the sum of all the values divided by $n$. Thus, if the values are denoted by $X_1, X_2, X_3, \ldots X_n$, then the mean ($\bar{X}$, called X-bar) is:

$$\bar{X} = \frac{(X_1 + X_2 + \ldots + X_n)}{n} = \frac{1}{n}\sum X_i$$

For example, the mean of the values 25, 22, 53, 11, 6 and 0 is:

$$\frac{25 + 22 + 53 + 11 + 6 + 0}{6} = \frac{117}{6} = 19.5$$

## The median

The **median** is the *central item* in a group of observations when they are arrayed in either ascending or descending order. Let us take an example to examine how the median is determined as a measure of central tendency. Let us say the salaries of nine employees in a department are $65 000, $30 000, $25 000, $64 000, $35 000, $63 000, $32 000, $60 000 and $61 000. The mean salary here works out to be about $48 333, but the median is $60 000. That is, when arrayed in the ascending order the figures will be as follows: $25 000, $30 000, $32 000, $35 000, $60 000, $61 000, $63 000, $64 000, $65 000. The figure in the middle is $60 000. If there is an even number of employees, then the median will comprise the average of the middle two salaries.

## The mode

In some cases, a set of observations would not lend itself to a meaningful representation through either the mean or the median, but could be described by the *most frequently occurring phenomenon*. For instance, in an academic department where there are 10 lecturers, 24 senior lecturers, three associate professors and two professors, the most frequently occurring group — the **mode** — is the senior lecturers. Neither a mean nor a median can be calculated in this case, nor is there any way of indicating any measure of dispersion.

As is evident from the above, nominal data lend themselves to description only by the mode as a measure of central tendency. It is possible that a data set could contain bimodal observations. For example, using the foregoing scenario, if 14 new lecturers were recruited to cope with additional work, then we would have two modes, 'lecturers' and 'senior lecturers'.

We have illustrated how the mean, median and mode can be useful measures of central tendencies, based on the type of data we have. We will now examine dispersions.

# MEASURES OF DISPERSION

Apart from knowing that the measure of central tendency is the mean, median or mode (depending on the type of available data), one would also like to know about the variability that exists in a set of observations. Like the measure of central tendency, the measure of dispersion also depends on the measurement scale used. Measures of dispersion include the *range*, the *standard deviation* and the *variance* (where the measure of central tendency is the mean), and the **interquartile range** (where the measure of central tendency is the median).

Two sets of data might have the same mean, but the dispersions could be different. For example, if company A sold 30, 40 and 50 units of a product during the months of April, May and June, respectively, and company B sold 10, 40 and 70 units during the same period, the average units sold per month by both companies is the same — 40 units — but the variability or the *dispersion* in the latter company is larger.

The three measurements of dispersion connected with the mean are the range, the variance and the standard deviation, which are explained below.

## Range

**Range** refers to the extreme values in a set of observations. The range is between 30 and 50 for company A (a dispersion of 20 units), and between 10 and 70 units (a dispersion of 60 units) for company B. The range is very easy to calculcate and interpret, but is not a very satisfactory measure since it is too dependent on extreme values — intermediate values are ignored.

## Variance

The sample **variance** is calculated by subtracting the mean from each of the observations in the data set, taking the square of this difference and dividing the total of these by the number of observations less one. In the preceding example, the sample variances for the two companies are as follows:

$$\text{Sample variance for company A} = \frac{(30-40)^2 + (40-40)^2 + (50-40)^2}{2} = 100$$

$$\text{Sample variance for company B} = \frac{(10-40)^2 + (40-40)^2 + (70-40)^2}{2} = 900$$

The formula for the sample variance (referred to as $S^2$) is

$$S^2 = \frac{1}{n-1}\sum(X_i - \bar{X})^2$$

where: $n$ = number of sample observations
$X_i$ = value of the *i*th variable
$\bar{X}$ = mean of variable $X$

As we can see, the variance is much larger in company B than in company A. It is more difficult for the manager of company B to estimate the quantity of goods to stock than it is for the manager of company A. Thus, variance gives an indication of how dispersed the data in a data set are.

## Standard deviation

The **standard deviation**, which is another measure of dispersion for interval and ratio scaled data, offers an indication of the spread of a distribution or the variability in the data. It is a very commonly used measure of dispersion, and is simply the square root of the variance. It is given by the formula

$$S = \sqrt{\text{variance}}$$

$$= \sqrt{\frac{1}{n-1} \sum (X_i - \bar{X})^2}$$

where $S$ represents the sample standard deviation and is expressed in the same units as the underlying data. In the case of the preceding two companies, the standard deviation of products sold for companies A and 1B would be $\sqrt{100}$ and $\sqrt{900}$, or 10 and 30 units respectively.

The mean and standard deviation are the most widely used descriptive statistics. The standard deviation, in conjunction with the mean, is a very useful tool because of the following statistical rules, in a normal distribution.

1. Most observations (more than 99 per cent) fall within three standard deviations of the average or mean.
2. More than 95 per cent of the observations are within two standard deviations of the mean.
3. About 68 per cent of the observations are within one standard deviation of the mean.

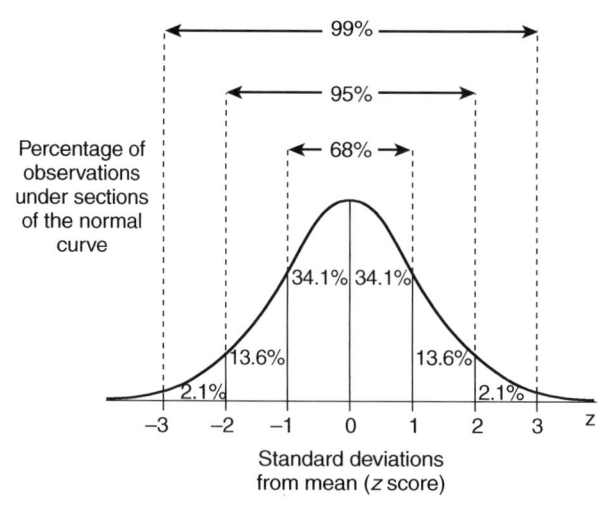

**Figure A5** Area under the normal curve

Applying this to the case of companies A and B, what is indicated to the manager of company A is that when the average is 40 units, and the standard deviation is 10, very simplistically (that is, with 95 per cent confidence and assuming the data are based on large sample sizes), he would need anywhere between 20 and 60 units for the next month (40 ± (2 × 10)). In other words, in all probability he would need no more than 60 units. For company B, on the other hand, the demand could be as high as 100 units. The demand could vary anywhere between 0 and 100 (40 ± (2 × 30)) — a much wider spread.

As can readily be seen, if an estimate has to be made of the optimum number of units to be manufactured for the next month based on the three months' sales data, the manager of company B will be in a greater predicament than that of company A, even though both companies sold 40 units per month on an average. Rather than try to estimate how many units should be produced based on the average of the past three months, the manager of company B might opt to trace the trends during the same months of the previous years and make them the basis of her estimation since there is so much variability in the sales.

In the foregoing example, the calculations of the *mean* (or the *average*) and the *standard deviation* were rendered possible since the observations pertained to values measured on a ratio scale — that is, they were not nominal or ordinal in nature. Whenever observations are measured either on an interval or a ratio scale, it is possible to calculate the mean. Refer to the discussion on scales and table 8.1, where the mean is shown to be appropriate as a measure of central tendency, and the variance and standard deviation are indicated as appropriate indicators of the dispersion, when either the interval or the ratio scale is used as the basis of measurement.

## Other measures of dispersion

When the *median* is the measure of central tendency, percentiles, deciles and quartiles become meaningful. Just as the median divides the total realm of observations into two equal halves, the *quartile* divides it into four equal parts, the *decile* into 10, and the *percentile* into 100 equal parts. The percentile is useful when huge masses of data, such as the GMAT scores, are handled. When the area of observations is divided into 100 equal parts, there are 100 percentile points. Any given score has a probability of 0.01 (or 1 per cent) that it will fall in any one of those points. If John's score is in the sixteenth percentile, it indicates that 84 per cent of those who took the exam scored better than he did, whereas 15 per cent did worse.

Often we are interested in knowing where we stand in comparison with others — are we in the middle, in the upper 10 or 25 per cent, or in the lower 20 or 25 per cent, or what? For instance, if in a company-administered test Mr Smith scores 78 out of a total of 100 points, he would be unhappy if he were in the bottom 10 per cent among his colleagues (the test-takers) but would be reasonably pleased if he were in the top 10 per cent, despite the fact that his score remains the same. His standing in relation to the others can be determined by the central tendency median, and the percentile he falls in.

The measure of dispersion for the median, the *interquartile range*, consists of the middle 50 per cent of the observations — that is, observations excluding the bottom and top 25 per cent quartiles. The interquartile range could be very useful when comparisons are to be made among several groups. For instance, telephone companies can compare long-distance charges of customers in several areas by taking samples of customer bills from each of the cities to be compared. By plotting the first and third quartiles and comparing the median and the spread, they can get a good idea of where billings tend to be highest, to what extent customers vary in the frequency of use of long-distance calls, and so on. This is done by the box-and-whisker plot for each area. The box-and-whisker plot is a graphic device that portrays central tendencies, percentiles and variability. A box is drawn extended from the lower quartile (LQ) to the upper quartile (UQ) and lines are drawn from either side of the box to the extreme scores, as shown in figure A6(a). Figure A6(b) has the median represented by a line within each box. Side-by-side comparisons of the various plots clearly indicate the highest value, the range, and the spread for each area or city.

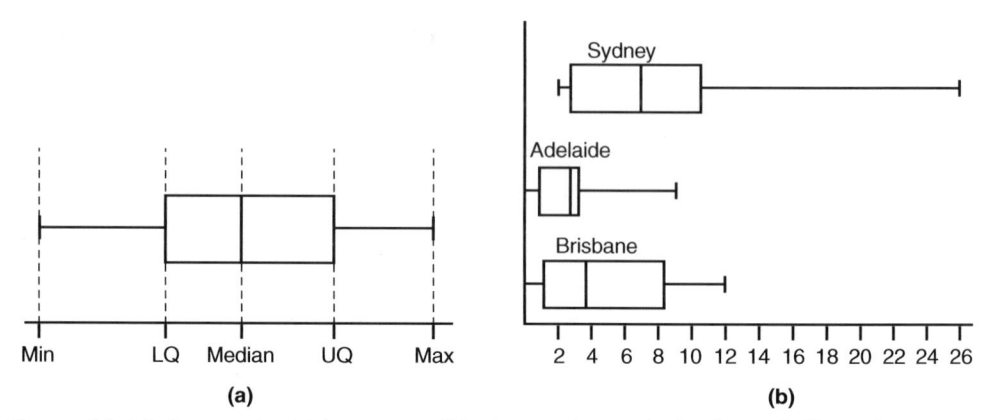

**Figure A6 (a)** Box and whisker plot  **(b)** Comparison of telephone bills in three cities

Note that it is also common practice to show the 'outliers' outside the upper and lower 'whiskers'. Typically, the outliers are defined as being the data points either the whole or half the value of the interquartile range above (or below) the upper (or lower) quartiles. This feature is available within SPSS.

A range of skewed distributions, compared with the normal curve, are presented in figure A7. Note the relationships between the mode, median and mean for these distributions. The mean is most influenced by the 'outliers' or the direction the distribution is skewed.

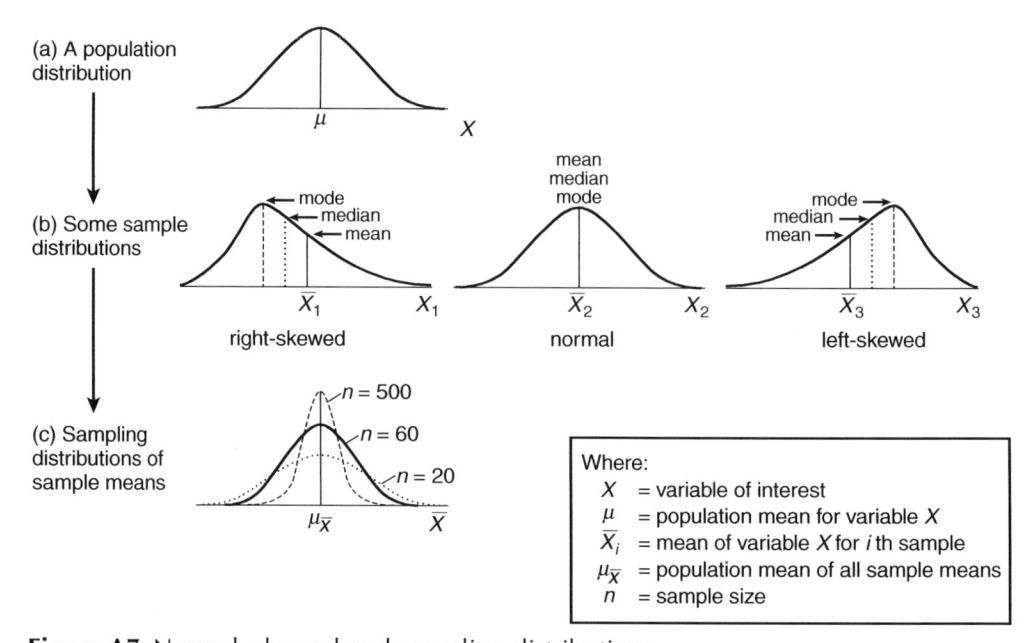

Where:
$X$ = variable of interest
$\mu$ = population mean for variable $X$
$\bar{X}_i$ = mean of variable $X$ for $i$th sample
$\mu_{\bar{X}}$ = population mean of all sample means
$n$ = sample size

**Figure A7** Normal, skewed and sampling distributions

**Source:** Adapted from Zikmund (2000:381).

## Standard error of the mean

The other important measure of dipersion is the **standard error** of the mean. When a number of samples are taken from the population, the sample means form a distribution. The standard deviation of these sample means is called the standard error of the mean. As the sample size increases, the standard error gets smaller (illustrated in figure A7(c)). In the following section on inferential statistics, we will be using the standard error and the mean to make inferences about the population from the sample, as we are more concerned about making inferences based on 'average' behaviour or observations, rather than from 'individual' behaviour or observations. This statistic is discussed on pages 273 in chapter 11. It is given by the formula

$$S_{\bar{x}} = \frac{S}{\sqrt{n}}$$

where $S$ is the sample standard deviation, and $n$ is the number of responses.

## Summary of descriptive statistics

In summary, we have illustrated how the mean, median and mode can be useful measures of central tendencies, depending on the type of available data. Similarly, we have shown how the standard deviation (and variance, which is the square of standard deviation), standard error and the interquartile range are useful measures of dispersion. Clearly, there is no measure of dispersion associated with the mode.

Figure A8 below provides an example of the Descriptive Statistics procedure in SPSS for the continuous, numeric variables in the business research class questionnaire data. The variables height and weight are measured on the continuous scale (ratio data). However, the variables 'Statistics is interesting' and 'Statistics is useful' are classified as ordinal data, although they can be analysed as interval data also (if the gap between the response categories on the scale are regarded as equal intervals). A 'Results Coach' is available under the Help menu in the SPSS package and provides the following advice.

> The Descriptive Statistics table provides summary statistics for continuous, numeric variables. Summary statistics include measures of central tendency such as the mean, measures of dispersion (spread of the distribution) such as the standard deviation, and measures of distribution, such as skewness and kurtosis, which indicate how much a distribution varies from a normal distribution. In general, a skewness value greater than one indicates a distribution that differs significantly from a normal, symmetric distribution.
>
> Transformations such as a log transformation can make a skewed distribution more normal. Since many statistical tests assume data are normally distributed, it's a good idea to check the distribution of your data, ... and either apply appropriate transformations or use nonparametric tests that don't require normally distributed data. (Results Coach, SPSS v. 10).

Kurtosis refers to the 'pointedness' or shape of the peak of a distribution compared with the standard normal curve.

| | N | Minimum | Maximum | Mean | | Std. Dev | Skewness | | Kurtosis | |
|---|---|---|---|---|---|---|---|---|---|---|
| | Statistic | Statistic | Statistic | Statistic | Std. Error | Statistic | Statistic | Std. Error | Statistic | Std. Error |
| Height in centimetres | 34 | 160 | 188 | 173.74 | 1.30 | 7.59 | −.088 | .403 | −.831 | .788 |
| Weight in kilograms | 34 | 54 | 95 | 74.15 | 1.84 | 10.72 | −.133 | .403 | −.318 | .788 |
| Statistics is interesting | 34 | 1 | 5 | 3.03 | .21 | 1.24 | .243 | .403 | −.901 | .788 |
| Statistics is useful | 34 | 1 | 5 | 2.15 | .15 | .89 | 1.329 | .403 | 2.579 | .788 |
| Valid N (listwise) | 34 | | | | | | | | | |

**Figure A8** Example of SPSS output of descriptive statistics

# INFERENTIAL STATISTICS

Thus far we have discussed descriptive statistics. Many times, however, we would be interested in inferential statistics. That is, we might be interested to know, or infer from the data through analysis, (1) the relationship between two variables (e.g. between advertisement and sales); (2) differences in a variable among different subgroups (e.g. whether women or men buy more of a product); and (3) how several independent variables might explain the variance in a dependent variable (e.g. how investments in the stock market are influenced by the level of unemployment, perceptions of the economy, disposable incomes and dividend expectations). We will now discuss some of these inferential statistics. However, before we do that we will outline the process we use for testing statistical hypotheses in this book.

## STATISTICAL HYPOTHESIS TESTING

In figure A9, we have outlined a process we recommend for the testing of statistical hypotheses when you are analysing the survey data with an appropriate computer package (e.g. SPSS, SAS or Excel). A number of processes are available and you are advised to examine a statistics book for these alternative approaches. We will demonstrate this approach with a number of examples in this appendix.

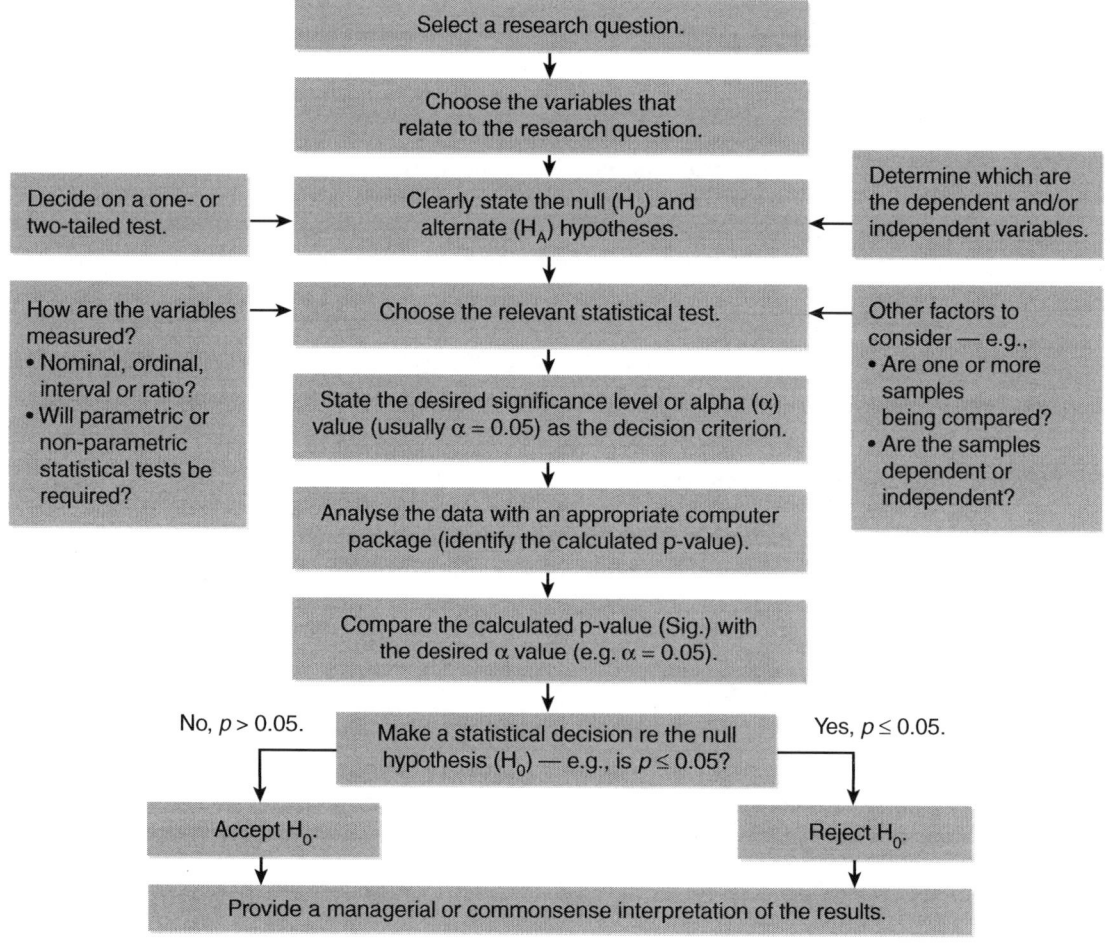

```
                        Select a research question.
                                   ↓
                    Choose the variables that
                    relate to the research question.
                                   ↓
Decide on a one- or     Clearly state the null ($H_0$) and      Determine which are
two-tailed test.    →   alternate ($H_A$) hypotheses.      ←   the dependent and/or
                                                               independent variables.
                                   ↓
How are the variables                                          Other factors to
measured?           →   Choose the relevant statistical test. ← consider — e.g.,
• Nominal, ordinal,                                            • Are one or more
  interval or ratio?                                             samples
• Will parametric or    State the desired significance level     being compared?
  non-parametric        or alpha ($\alpha$) value (usually     • Are the samples
  statistical tests be  $\alpha = 0.05$) as the decision         dependent or
  required?             criterion.                               independent?
                                   ↓
                    Analyse the data with an appropriate computer
                    package (identify the calculated p-value).
                                   ↓
                    Compare the calculated p-value (Sig.) with
                    the desired $\alpha$ value (e.g. $\alpha = 0.05$).
                                   ↓
   No, $p > 0.05$.  Make a statistical decision re the null    Yes, $p \leq 0.05$.
        ←           hypothesis ($H_0$) — e.g., is $p \leq 0.05$?    →
        ↓                                                           ↓
   Accept $H_0$.                                              Reject $H_0$.
        ↓                                                           ↓
            Provide a managerial or commonsense interpretation of the results.
```

**Figure A9** Process for statistical hypothesis testing using a computer package

## The null and alternate hypotheses

Initially, you start with the research question and choose the variables that relate to that question. Normally, you will have already developed a theoretical framework for your research and developed some appropriate hypotheses for testing. We recommend that you now refer back to the material on hypothesis development outlined in chapter 4 (on pages 98–103). You will recall that we discussed the differences between the null and alternate hypotheses there. Also, we discussed the differences between directional and non-directional hypotheses. We now test a non-directional hypothesis with a two-tailed statistical test, and a directional hypothesis with a one-tailed test. As also discussed in chapter 4 in the section on developing the theoretical framework (pages 82–90), you will have to determine which are the dependent and/or independent variables.

## Choosing a statistical test

The choice of the appropriate statistical test to use can be problematic, but the SPSS Statistics Coach can be a great friend here! Initially, it involves determining whether parametric or non-parametric tests are required. As discussed earlier in this appendix, parametric tests can be applied to interval and ratio data (and also ordinal data where they are expressed in numeric form and 'interval' features are present). Non-parametric tests are applied to categorical data — that is, nominal and most ordinal data. A full discussion of these measurement scales was provided in chapter 8. Table A3 summarises a range of statistical techniques and tests classified according to type, number and measurement scale of variables. Table A4 summarises the use of some non-parametric tests. We will demonstrate the use of only some of the more widely used statistical tests in this appendix. These include correlation, the chi-square test, the $t$-test, analysis of variance (ANOVA), regression analysis and factor analysis. We will briefly outline some of the main features of these statistical tests, then apply the hypothesis-testing process outlined in figure A9 to the data collected for the business research class questionnaire, and analyse these data with SPSS.

## Significance level

The most common **significance level** for testing hypotheses in business and management research is at the 5 per cent level. For example, this means that the null hypothesis ($H_0$ will be rejected if the difference between the sample statistic (e.g. the sample mean) and the hypothesised population parameter (e.g. the population mean) is so large that this or a larger difference would occur, on average, only five times or fewer in every 100 samples (assuming the hypothesised population parameter is correct). In other words, assuming the hypothesis to be true, the significance level indicates the percentage of sample means that would be outside the cut-off limits based on chance alone. This is also called the critical value, and the probability of this occurring is called $\alpha$ (**alpha**).

The significance level ($\alpha$) and the confidence level are related concepts. For example, a significance level of 5 per cent ($\alpha = 0.05$) indicates that the confidence level is 95 per cent. A higher significance level (e.g. $\alpha = 0.10$ or 10 per cent) indicates a lower confidence level (90 per cent) for the decision. (The relationship is: $\alpha$ + confidence level = 1.0 — that is, 100 per cent.)

There is no precise rule for selecting the significance level (or $\alpha$ value). The most frequently used values in business and social research are the 1 per cent, 5 per cent and 10 per cent levels. It is possible to test a hypothesis at any significance level. However, the significance level is also the risk (or probability) associated with rejecting the null hypothesis when it is true. This is also known as a **Type I error**.

Conversely, the risk of accepting (not rejecting) a null hypothesis when it is false is called a **Type II error**, and the probability of this occurring is called β (**beta**). These errors are summarised in table A5. There is a trade-off between Type I and Type II errors. The probability of one type of error can only be reduced if the decision maker or researcher is prepared to accept an increase in the other type of error. This is illustrated graphically in figure A10 on page 418.

> From this figure it can be seen that as the significance level increases the acceptance region becomes quite small [0.50 of the area under the curve in figure A10c]. With an acceptance region this small, rarely will a null hypothesis be accepted when it is not true; but at a cost of being this sure, the probability that a null hypothesis will be rejected when it is true will increase. In other words, in order to lessen the probability of committing a Type II error, the probability of committing a Type I error necessarily has to be increased (Aaker et al. 1995, pp. 471, 473).

**Table A3** Statistical techniques and tests classified according to type, number and measurement scale of variables

| Independent variables | | | Dependent variable | | |
|---|---|---|---|---|---|
| | | | Nominal | Ordinal | Interval/Ratio |
| One | Nominal | | • Chi-square test for independence<br>• Cochran Q test<br>• Fisher exact probability | • Sign test<br>• Median test<br>• Mann-Whitney U test<br>• Kruskal-Wallis one-way analysis of variance | • Analysis of variance (ANOVA)<br>• T-test |
| | Ordinal | | | • Spearman's rank correlation<br>• Kendall's rank correlation | Analysis of variance with trend analysis |
| | Interval ratio | | Analysis of variance (ANOVA) | | • Simple regression analysis<br>• Pearson correlation |
| Two or more | Nominal | | | Friedman two-way analysis of variance | Analysis of variance (factorial design) |
| | Ordinal | | | | |
| | Interval ratio | | Multiple discriminant analysis | | Multiple regression analysis |

**Source:** Adapted from R. L. Baker and R. E. Schultz (eds) 1972, *Instructional Product Research*. New York: Van Nostrand Co.

**Table A4** Use of some non-parametric tests

| Test | When used | Function |
|---|---|---|
| Chi-square | With *nominal* data for one sample or two or more independent samples | Tests for independence of variables |
| Cochran Q | With more than two related samples measured on *nominal* scale | Helps when data fall into two natural categories |
| Fisher Exact Probability | With two independent samples measured on *nominal* scale | More useful than $\chi^2$ when expected frequencies are small |
| Sign test | With two related samples measured on *ordinal* scale | A good test for ranked data |
| Median test | With one sample, to see if randomly drawn measurements are from a population with a specified median | In a symmetric distribution, the mean and median will be the same. |
| Mann-Whitney U test | With two independent samples on *ordinal* data | Analogue of the two independent sample *t*-tests |
| Kruskal-Wallis one-way ANOVA | With more than two independent samples on an *ordinal* scale | An alternative to one-way ANOVA where normality of distributions cannot be assumed |
| Friedman two-way ANOVA | With more than two related samples on *ordinal* data | A good alternative to two-way ANOVA where normality cannot be assumed |
| Kolmogorov-Smirnov | With one sample or two independent samples measured on an *ordinal* scale | Is a more powerful test than $\chi^2$ or Mann-Whitney U |

**Table A5** Hypothesis testing and statistical decision making

| | | Statistical decision | |
|---|---|---|---|
| | | Accept $H_0$ | Reject $H_0$ |
| True state of the situation | $H_0$ is true | Correct (Probability = $1-\alpha$) | Type I error (Probability = $\alpha$) |
| | $H_0$ is false | Type II error (Probability = $\beta$) | Correct (Probability = $1-\beta$) |

To resolve this trade-off, researchers generally decide the appropriate level of significance by examining the costs or penalties attached to both types of errors. For example, Zikmund (2000:464) has provided an example of the trade-off between Type I and Type II errors occurring in the legal profession.

> Although most attorneys and judges do not concern themselves with the statistical terminology of Type I and Type II errors, they do follow this logic. For example, our legal system is based on the concept that a person is innocent until proven guilty. Assume that the null hypothesis is that the person is innocent. If we make a Type I error, we send an innocent person to prison. Our legal system takes many precautions to avoid Type I errors. A person is innocent until proven guilty. A Type II error would occur when a guilty party is set free (the null hypothesis is accepted). Our society places such a high value on avoiding Type I errors that Type II errors are more likely to occur.

There is also a tendency in business research to emphasise Type I errors, although one must be wary of arbitrarily increasing the sample size to test a hypothesis as this will also increase the probability of making Type I errors.

We will now consider a number of commonly used statistical tests for testing hypotheses and relationships between variables in business research.

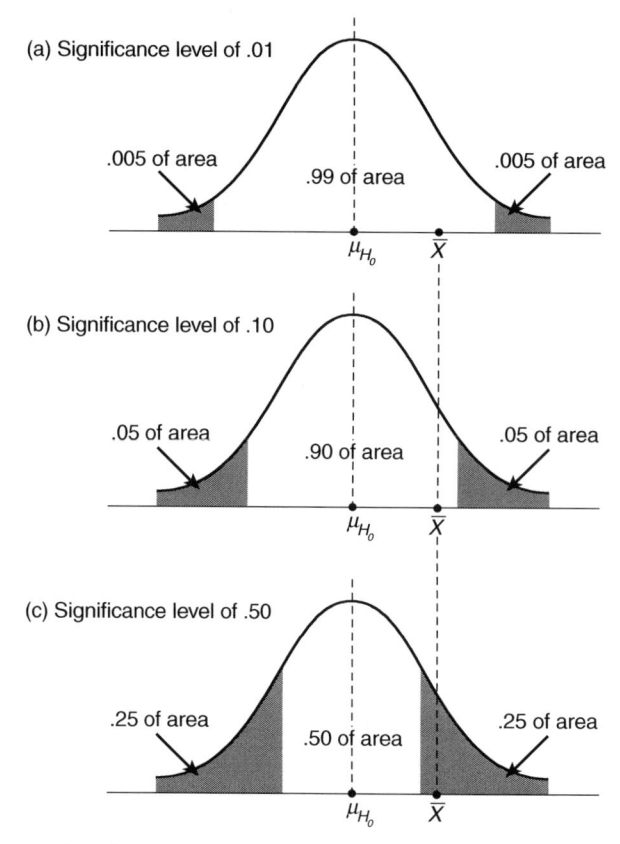

**Figure A10** Relationship between Type I and Type II errors

**Source**: D. A. Aaker, V. Kumar and G. S. Day 1995, *Marketing Research*, 5th edition. New York: John Wiley & Sons, p. 473.

# CORRELATIONS

In a research project that includes several variables, beyond knowing the means and standard deviations of the dependent and independent variables, we would often like to know how one variable is related to another. That is, we would like to see the nature, direction and significance of the *bivariate* relationships of the variables used in the study (the relationship between any two variables among the variables tapped in the study). A Pearson correlation matrix will provide this information — that is, it will indicate the direction, strength and significance of the bivariate relationships of all the interval or ratio variables in the study.

The correlation is derived by assessing the variations in one variable as another variable also varies. For the sake of simplicity, let us consider the data on height and weight collected from the business research class questionnaire.

Figure A11 indicates a discernible pattern of how the two factors vary simultaneously (the trend of the scatter is that of an upward straight line). The scatter diagram would suggest there is a direct positive correlation between height and weight for the students in the class.

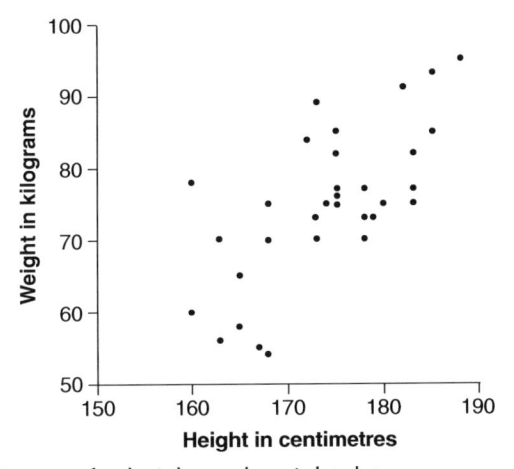

**Figure A11** Scatter diagram for height and weight data

A Pearson's correlation coefficient ($r$) that indicates the strength and direction of the relationship can be computed by applying the following formula that takes into consideration the two sets of figures.

Given $n$ paired observations $(X_1, Y_1), \ldots (X_n, Y_n)$ on variables $X$ and $Y$, the sample Pearson's correlation coefficient between $X$ and $Y$ is defined as:

$$r = \frac{\sum (X_i - \bar{X})(Y_i - \bar{Y})}{\sqrt{\sum (X_i - \bar{X})^2 \cdot \sum (Y_i - \bar{Y})^2}}$$

Theoretically, there could be a perfect positive correlation ($r$) between two variables, which is represented by 1.0 (plus 1), or a perfect negative correlation, which would be −1.0 (minus 1) (illustrated in figure A12). However, neither of these is likely to be found in reality when assessing correlations between any two variables expected to be different from each other. Figure A12 provides some further examples.

While the correlation could range between −1.0 and +1.0, we need to know if any correlation found between two variables is significant (that is, if it has occurred by chance alone or if there is a high probability of its actual existence). As we have previously discussed, a significance of $p = 0.05$ is the generally accepted conventional level in social science and business research. This indicates that 95 times out of 100 we can be sure that there is a true or significant correlation between the two variables, and there is only a 5 per cent chance that the relationship does not truly exist. Since there is a correlation of 0.70 (denoted as $r = 0.70$) between the two variables, height and weight, with $p < 0.01$, then we know that there is a positive relationship between the two variables and the probability of this not being true is 1 per cent or less. That is, more than 99 per cent of the time we would expect this correlation to exist. The correlation of 0.70 also indicates that the variables would explain the variance in one another to the extent of 49 per cent ($0.70^2$). These results can be seen in the SPSS output for the correlations analysis of our business research class data in figure A13.

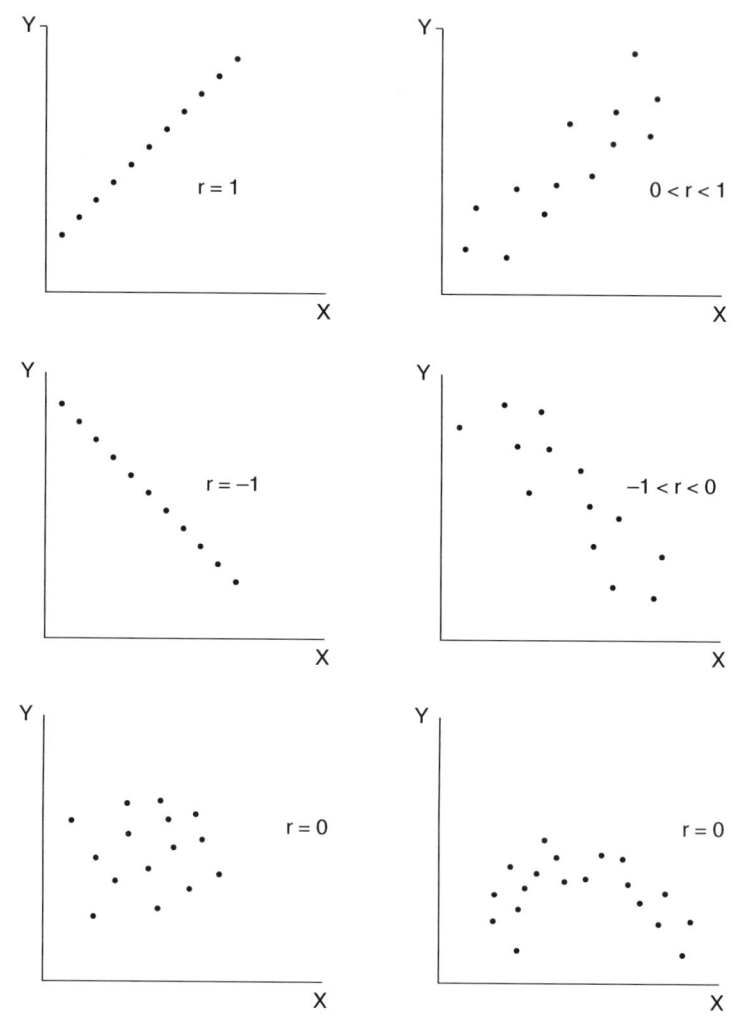

**Figure A12** Scatter diagrams of two variables with different correlation coefficients

We would not know which variable *causes* which, but we would know that the two variables are associated with each other. Thus, a hypothesis that postulates a significant positive (or negative) relationship between two variables can be tested by examining the correlation between the two. A bivariate correlation analysis, which indicates the strength of relationship ($r$) between the two variables, can be generated for variables measured on an interval or ratio scale.

Non-parametric tests are also available to assess the relationship between variables not measured on an interval or ratio scale. Spearman's rank correlation and Kendall's rank correlation are used to examine relationships between two ordinal variables.

The formula for the Spearman's rank correlation coefficient (called Spearman's rho) is

$$r_S = 1 - \frac{6 \sum d^2}{N(N^2 - 1)}$$

where $r_S$ refers to Spearman's rho, $d$ is the difference in the ranks of the two sets of rankings, and $N$ is the number of pairs of ranks. This statistic can also take on values between −1 and +1.

In our business research class example, all the students have been ranked first in terms of their weight (the heaviest given a rank of 1, the second heaviest given a rank of 2, and so on with the lightest given a rank of 34). The students have then been ranked according to their height. $d$ is the difference between a student's ranking for height and weight (for example, a height ranked as 10 but weight ranked as 4 gives a difference $d$ of 6). The difference is squared to avoid the negative signs. The Spearman's rank correlation for the business class data (see figure A13) is 0.65 and is significant at the 1 per cent level. Note that the numeric values for the Pearson's correlation coefficient (0.70) and the Spearman's rank correlation (0.65) should not be compared as they are calculated quite differently. However, what could be compared is their significance level, and our SPSS output indicates that the relationship between height and weight of the students in this business research class was highly correlated (with the significance level of $p$ less than 1 per cent in both cases), confirmed using both parametric and non-parametric approaches.

Correlations

Correlations

|  |  | Height in centimetres | Weight in kilograms |
|---|---|---|---|
| Height in centimetres | Pearson Correlation | 1.000 | .702** |
|  | Sig. (2-tailed) | . | .000 |
|  | N | 34 | 34 |
| Weight in kilograms | Pearson Correlation | .702** | 1.000 |
|  | Sig. (2-tailed) | .000 | . |
|  | N | 34 | 34 |

** Correlation is significant at the 0.01 level (2-tailed).

Non-parametric correlations

Correlations

|  |  |  | Height in centimetres | Weight in kilograms |
|---|---|---|---|---|
| Spearman's rho | Height in centimetres | Correlation Coefficient | 1.000 | .650** |
|  |  | Sig. (2-tailed) | . | .000 |
|  |  | N | 34 | 34 |
|  | Weight in kilograms | Correlation Coefficient | .650** | 1.000 |
|  |  | Sig. (2-tailed) | .000 | . |
|  |  | N | 34 | 34 |

** Correlation is significant at the 0.01 level (2-tailed).

**Figure A13** SPSS output for correlations between height and weight variables

# RELATIONSHIP BETWEEN TWO NOMINAL VARIABLES: CHI-SQUARE TEST

We might sometimes want to know whether there is a relationship between two nominal variables or whether they are independent of each other. As examples: (1) Is viewing a television advertisement of a product (yes/no) related to the buying of that product by individuals (buy/don't buy)? (2) Is the type of job done by individuals (white-collar jobs vs. blue-collar jobs) a function of their highest education level (tertiary vs. secondary)? Such comparisons are possible by organising data by groups or categories (called cross-tabulations (crosstabs) or contingency tables) and seeing if there are any statistically significant relationships. For example, we might collect data from a sample of 55 individuals whose education level and jobs, culled from a frequency count, might be illustrated as in table A6 in a two-by-two contingency table. Just by looking at table A6, a clear pattern seems to emerge that those with a tertiary education hold white-collar jobs. Only a few of the secondary educated staff hold white-collar jobs. Thus, there does seem to be a relationship between education level and type of job handled; the two do not seem to be independent. This can be statistically confirmed by the chi-square ($\chi^2$) test — a non-parametric test — which would indicate whether or not the observed pattern is due to chance. As we know, non-parametric tests are used when normality of distributions cannot be assumed, as in nominal or ordinal data. The $\chi^2$ test compares the expected frequency (based on probability) and the observed frequency, and the $\chi^2$ statistic is obtained by the formula

$$\chi^2 = \sum \frac{(O_i - E_i)^2}{E_i}$$

where $\chi^2$ is the chi-square statistic; $O_i$ is the observed frequency of the $i$th cell; and $E_i$ is the expected frequency. The $\chi^2$ statistic with its level of significance can be obtained for any set of nominal data through computer analysis.

**Table A6** Contingency table of education level and job type

| Education level | Job type | | Total |
| --- | --- | --- | --- |
| | White collar | Blue collar | |
| Tertiary | 30 | 5 | 35 |
| Secondary | 2 | 18 | 20 |
| Total | 32 | 23 | 55 |

Thus, in testing for differences in relationships among nominally scaled variables, the $\chi^2$ (chi-square) statistic comes in handy. The null hypothesis would be set to state that there is no significant relationship between two variables (education level and nature of the job, in the preceding example), and the alternate hypothesis would be that there is a significant relationship.

The chi-square statistic is associated with the degrees of freedom ($df$), which denotes whether or not a significant relationship exists between two nominal variables. Degrees of freedom is given by the formula

$$df = (c - 1)(r - 1)$$

where   $c$ = no. of columns
and      $r$ = no. of rows

Hence, for the example in table A6 we can calculate the degrees of freedom as:
$$df = (2-1)(2-1)$$
$$= 1$$

The chi-square statistic for various $df$ can be found in table III in appendix II.

The $\chi^2$ statistic can also be used for multiple levels of two nominal variables. For instance, one might be interested in knowing if four groups of employees — production, sales, marketing and R & D personnel — react to a policy in four different ways (that is, with no interest at all, with mild interest, with moderate interest or with intense interest). Here, the $\chi^2$ value for the test of independence will be generated by cross-tabulating the data in 16 cells (classifying the data in terms of the four groups of employees and the four categories of interest). The degrees of freedom here will be $(4-1) \times (4-1) = 9$.

The $\chi^2$ test of significance thus helps us to see whether or not two nominal (or categorical) variables are related. Besides the $\chi^2$ test, other tests such as the Fisher exact probability test, and the Cochran Q test are used to determine the relationship between two nominally scaled variables (see tables A3 and A4).

## SPSS example of a chi-square test

We will illustrate the use of SPSS for testing a hypothesis using a chi-square test by analysing the relationship between the nominal variables 'gender' and 'eye colour' in the business research class questionnaire data set. Now admittedly, this is rather a silly example, but it does demonstrate the approach well. Following the procedure outlined in figure A9, we undertake the hypotheses test as follows:

*Step 1: Formulating the hypotheses*
$H_0$: There is no relationship between gender and eye colour of students in the class.
$H_A$: There is a relationship between gender and eye colour of students in the class (gender and eye colour are related).

*Step 2: Decision criterion*
We will set the significance level at 5 per cent ($\alpha = 0.05$). In other words, we will reject $H_0$ (the null hypothesis) if the calculated $p$-value (significance level) is less than 0.05.

*Step 3: Analyse data with computer package*
We have analysed the data with the SPSS package and the output appears as figure A14. The frequencies for males and females by their eye colour is summarised in a cross-tabulation table. The 'count' in each cell is the 'observed' frequency. The 'expected count' is based on the proportion that would be 'expected' in that cell if $H_0$ was true. For example, the expected number of females with blue eyes would equal (13/34) * 8 (the fraction of the total number of students with blue eyes multiplied by the number of females) = 3.1 (as shown in the first cell). Note that the expected count (frequency) for each cell is almost the same number as the observed count. Given the nature of this example, that is hardly surprising!

The calculated value of the chi-square statistic is 0.013, with a significance level of 0.994. Note that three cells have an expected count of less than five. Normally, 'there should not be more than one fifth of the cells of the table with "expected frequencies" of less than five, and none with an expected frequency of less than one' (Ticehurst &

Veal 1999:208). If this rule is broken, then you should use the significance level reported for the Likelihood Ratio (rather than the Pearson chi-square).

*Step 4: Make a statistical decision*

We now compare our calculated *p*-value (called 'Sig.' in the SPSS output) of 0.994 with our desired significance level ($\alpha$ value) of 0.05. Clearly *p* is much greater than 0.05, hence we do not reject $H_0$. This is normally referred to as 'accepting $H_0$'. (If we did reject $H_0$, then a *p*-value of 0.994 indicates that there would be a 99.4 per cent chance of rejecting $H_0$ when $H_0$ is true!) In other words, we have demonstrated that there is no statistical relationship between gender and eye colour for the students in the business research class.

*Step 5: Interpret the decision.*

Fortunately, the statistical decision accords with common sense! However, in more general cases in business research it is important to confirm that the statistical decision does match up with managerial judgement and common sense. If not, the differences need to be reconciled before a managerial decision can be made on the basis of your research results.

Crosstabs

Case processing summary

|  | Cases | | | | | |
|---|---|---|---|---|---|---|
|  | Valid | | Missing | | Total | |
|  | N | Percent | N | Percent | N | Percent |
| Female or Male * Eye colour | 34 | 100.0 | 0 | .0% | 34 | 100.0 |

Female or male * eye colour cross-tabulation

|  |  |  | Eye colour | | | Total |
|---|---|---|---|---|---|---|
|  |  |  | Blue | Brown | Other |  |
| Female or Male | Female | Count | 3 | 3 | 2 | 8 |
|  |  | Expected Count | 3.1 | 3.1 | 1.9 | 8.0 |
|  | Male | Count | 10 | 10 | 6 | 26 |
|  |  | Expected Count | 9.9 | 9.9 | 6.1 | 26.0 |
| Total |  | Count | 13 | 13 | 8 | 34 |
|  |  | Expected Count | 13.0 | 13.0 | 8.0 | 34.0 |

Chi-square tests

|  | Value | df | Asymp. Sig. (2-sided) |
|---|---|---|---|
| Pearson chi-square | .013[a] | 2 | .994 |
| Likelihood ratio | .012 | 2 | .994 |
| No. of valid cases | 34 |  |  |

[a] 3 cells (50.0%) have expected count less than 5. The minimum expected count is 1.88.

**Figure A14** Example of SPSS output for Crosstabs and chi-square tests

# SIGNIFICANT MEAN DIFFERENCES BETWEEN TWO GROUPS: THE t-TEST

There are many instances in which we would be interested to know whether two groups are different from each other on a particular interval-scaled or ratio-scaled variable of interest. For example, would men and women express their need for the introduction of flexitime at the workplace to the same extent, or would their needs be different? Do MBAs perform better in organisational settings than business students who have only a bachelor's degree? Do individuals in urban areas have a different savings investment pattern from those in semi-urban areas? Do chartered accountants perform better than non-qualified accountants in accounting tasks? To find answers to such questions, a t-test is done to see if there are any significant differences in the means for two groups in the variable of interest. That is, a *nominal* variable that is split into two subgroups (for example, smokers and non-smokers; employees in the marketing department and those in the accounting department; younger and older employees) is tested to see if there is a significant mean difference between the two split groups on a dependent variable, which is measured on an *interval* or *ratio* scale (for instance extent of wellbeing, pay or comprehension level).

The t-test takes into consideration the means and standard deviations of the two groups on the variable and tests whether the numerical difference in the means is significantly different from 0 (zero), as postulated in our null hypothesis.

Thus, when we compare the mean differences between two different groups on a variable, we have a t-test done on two independent samples. The t-test can also be used to examine the differences in the same group before and after a treatment. For example, would a group of employees who have undergone training perform better after receiving the training than they did before? In this case, the formula for the t-test is adjusted to take into account a correlation between the two scores, if any. In other words, the adjusted t-test for the matched sample, or other types of dependent samples, reflects the true mean differences.

Table II in appendix II shows the t values, denoting the symmetrical bell-shaped distribution with mean = 0 for varying degrees of freedom (that is, the number of observations or the sample size less the number of constraints).

The t distribution is defined as

$$t = \frac{(\bar{X} - \mu)}{S_{\bar{X}}} = \frac{(\bar{X} - \mu)}{S/\sqrt{n}}$$

where $\mu$ (called mu) is the population mean, $\bar{X}$ is the sample mean and $S_{\bar{X}}$ is the standard error of the sample mean (note that $S$ is the sample standard deviation and $n$ is the sample size). The t distribution is suitable for analysing the means of small samples, drawn from a population that is normally distributed. The shape of the t distribution depends on the degrees of freedom ($df$) (that is, the number in the sample less the number of constraints or calculated parameters). The t distribution is identical to the normal curve ($z$ distribution) when the number of degrees of freedoms is infinitely large. A t distribution from a single sample has $n - 1$ degrees of freedom. Comparisons between the t distribution and the normal curve are provided in figure A15.

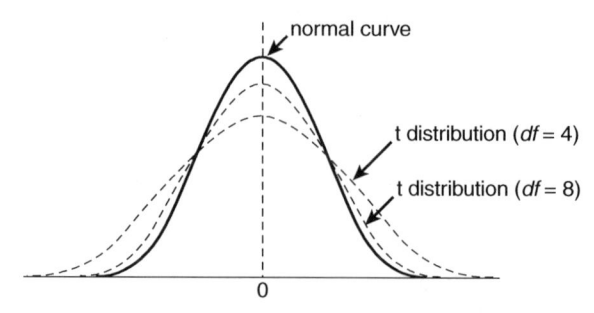

**Figure A15** Comparison of the *t* distribution and normal curve

The Mann-Whitney U test is a non-parametric test for examining significant differences when the dependent variable is measured on an ordinal scale and the independent variable on a nominal scale. However, when an ordinal scale is used and the intervals between each point on the scale are equal, you can usually use a *t*-test to compare differences in the mean values.

## SPSS example of some *t*-tests

Because of the widespread use of *t*-tests in business research, we will demonstrate two different types of *t*-test by further analysing the data set obtained from our business research class questionnaire. However, there are in fact three main types of *t*-tests. These are:
- comparing a single sample mean with a population mean
- comparing the means from two independent samples
- comparing the means from two dependent (same) samples.

We will demonstrate the first two types here, and leave the third type as a student exercise! We will also present a number of different hypotheses and test them using the procedures outlined in figure A9.

### (a) Comparing a single sample mean with a population mean

We will consider the responses to the variables 'Statistics is interesting' and 'Statistics knowledge is useful in business'. We are interested in whether the students' responses indicated whether they were 'neutral' on average on those variables, or whether they weren't neutral. Hence, we will test the variables as 'non-directional hypotheses' (that is, as two-tailed tests) and label them as hypotheses 1 and 2, respectively. Since the students were mature post-experience people from the Wellington business community, we will consider the population to be members of the wider Wellington business community.

*Step 1: Formulating the hypotheses*
Hypotheses 1 can be presented as:

$H1_0$: The students are generally neutral in their interest towards statistics.

$H1_A$: The students are generally not neutral in their interest towards statistics.

This can be expressed statistically as

$H1_0: \mu_1 = 3$ (or $\mu_1 - 3 = 0$)
$H1_A: \mu_1 \neq 3$ (or $\mu_1 - 3 \neq 0$)

where $\mu_1$ is the mean attitude of the business community towards interest in statistics, and '3' is the neutral response (see table A2).

Similarly, hypothesis 2 can be presented as:

H2$_0$: The students are generally neutral towards whether they think statistics knowledge is useful in business.

H2$_A$: The students are generally not neutral towards whether they think statistics knowledge is useful in business.

Or:

H2$_0$: $\mu_2 = 3$     (or $\mu_2 - 3 = 0$)

H2$_A$: $\mu_2 \neq 3$     (or $\mu_2 - 3 \neq 0$)

*Step 2: Decision criterion*

We will set the significance level at 5 per cent ($\alpha = 0.05$). In other words, we will reject H$_0$ (the null hypothesis) if the calculated *p*-value (significance level) is less than 0.05. This would indicate that the sample mean is statistically significantly different from the hypothesised population mean.

*Step 3: Analyse data with computer package*

We have analysed the data with the SPSS package, and the output appears as figure A16. For a single sample *t*-test, two tables can be generated by SPSS. The first contains the descriptive statistics for each of the variables tested. This shows that the average response for the 'Statistics is interesting' variable is about 3 (or neutral), and the average response for the 'Statistics is useful' variable is about 2.2 or very close to the 'disagree' category! Hence, we could make some inferences about these results, but let us now examine the *p*-values represented by the term Sig. in the second part of the table.

The significance value for the 'Statistics is interesting' variable is 0.89 and for the 'Statistics is useful' variable is 0.00. (Also, for the 'Statistics is useful' variable we notice that the 95 per cent confidence interval for the difference between the sample and hypothesised population mean does not contain zero (0) — that is, the difference is between −1.16 and −0.54. This also suggests we should reject H2$_0$.)

*Step 4: Make a statistical decision*

We now compare our calculated *p*-values with our desired significance level ($\alpha$ value) of 0.05.

*Hypothesis 1:* Clearly the calculated significance level of 0.89 is much greater than 0.05. Hence we accept H1$_0$, the null hypothesis, that the students are generally neutral in their interest towards statistics.

*Hypothesis 2:* The calculated significance level of 0.00 is much less than 0.05. Hence we reject H2$_0$ and accept the alternative hypothesis (H2$_A$) that the students are generally not neutral towards whether they think statistics knowledge is useful in business. In fact, with the significance level of these results, we would conclude that students generally disagreed with the statement that 'statistics knowledge is useful in business'. This result was of some concern to the lecturer trying to teach these students how useful statistics was to business research!

*Step 5: Interpret the decision*

While these *t*-tests results seem quite plausible, they were based on the data collected from post-experience mature business students at the beginning of the module on business statistics, and also at the stage in the evening when most students wanted to leave. These conditions may have created some 'bias' in their responses, which consequently may not totally reflect the population of people working in the Wellington business community (at least we hope this is the case, particularly as far as hypothesis 2 is concerned!). Nevertheless, we hope you now understand how to test single sample hypotheses with the *t*-test. We shall now consider a two-sample test.

*t*-Test (single sample, test value = 3)

One-sample statistics

|  | N | Mean | Std. Deviation | Std. Error Mean |
|---|---|---|---|---|
| Statistics is interesting | 34 | 3.03 | 1.24 | .21 |
| Statistics is useful | 34 | 2.15 | .89 | .15 |

One-sample test

| | Test Value = 3 | | | | | |
|---|---|---|---|---|---|---|
| | | | | | 95% Confidence Interval of the Difference | |
| | *t* | df | Sig. (2-tailed) | Mean Difference | Lower | Upper |
| Statistics is interesting | 0.138 | 33 | 0.891 | 2.94E-02 | −0.40 | 0.46 |
| Statistics is useful | −5.575 | 33 | 0.000 | −0.85 | −1.16 | −0.54 |

**Figure A16** Example of SPSS output for single-sample *t*-tests

### (b) Comparing the means from two independent samples

We shall now consider height differences between the men and women in the business research class. It is appropriate to use the independent samples *t*-test here since the groups 'men' and 'women' are clearly independent (at least respondents had to fill in only one gender box on the questionnaire!).

*Step 1: Formulating the hypotheses*
We shall consider a one-tailed test or directional hypothesis here, since it is a well-supported view that men are taller than women on average. However, we will test this hypothesis with the assistance of SPSS.

Hypothesis 3 can be presented as:

H3$_0$: Male students are not taller then female students on average.

H3$_A$: Male students are taller than female students on average.

This can be expressed statistically as

H3$_0$: $\mu_M \leq \mu_F$   (or $\mu_M - \mu_F \leq 0$)
H3$_A$: $\mu_M > \mu_F$   (or $\mu_M - \mu_F > 0$)

where: H3$_0$ represents the null hypothesis
H3$_A$ represents the alternate hypothesis
$\mu_M$ is the mean height of males
$\mu_F$ is the mean height of females.

Note that for a directional hypothesis, the mean height of males in the null hypothesis is expressed as less than or equal to the mean female height, rather than equal to it. This is because the alternate hypothesis is expressed in directional form.

*Step 2: Decision criterion*
Since SPSS provides significance levels only for two-tailed tests, we will need to double our normal desired significance level to 10 per cent (giving a 90 per cent confidence interval for a two-sided test). This is equivalent to a 5 per cent significance level in each tail of a two-sided *t*-test. Hence, we will set the significance level at 10 per cent ($\alpha = 0.10$).

In other words we will reject H3$_0$ (the null hypothesis) if the calculated *p*-value (significance level) is less than 0.10. This would indicate that the mean height for males is statistically significantly higher than the mean height for females.

*Step 3: Analyse data with computer package*
We have analysed the data with the SPSS package, and the output appears as figure A17. For an independent sample *t*-test, two tables are generated by SPSS. The first contains the descriptive statistics for each of the variables tested. This table shows that the average height for females in the sample is about 165 centimetres and the average height for males is about 176 centimetres, which certainly indicates that men in the sample are taller than women on average. However, we have to check that this result isn't due to chance alone, and that in fact men and women do come from the same 'biological' population, at least in terms of height! We will need to examine the calculated significance levels for this.

We also notice from the SPSS output (group statistics tables) that the standard deviations for males and females are about the same, hence the variances (the standard deviation squared) are also similar. This is confirmed by the Levene's test for equality of variances, which accepts the hypothesis that the variances are the same ($p = 0.39$, which is much greater than 0.05). If the variances were significantly different, then the calculated *p*-value would be less than 0.05. Hence, we can use the results for the *t*-test with equal variances assumed.

*Step 4: Make a statistical decision*
We now compare our calculated *p*-values with our desired significance level (α value) of 0.10.

The calculated significance level of 0.00 is much less than 0.10, hence we reject H3$_0$ and accept the alternate hypothesis (H3$_A$) that males are taller than females.

Also, note that the 90 per cent confidence interval for the height differences does not contain zero (0). The 90 per cent confidence interval indicates that 90 per cent of the time the specified interval will contain the true differences between the population means. This further supports our statistical decision to reject the null hypothesis (H3$_0$).

*t*-Test

Group statistics

|  | Female or Male | N | Mean | Std. Deviation | Std. Error Mean |
|---|---|---|---|---|---|
| Height in centimetres | Male | 26 | 176.38 | 5.97 | 1.17 |
|  | Female | 8 | 165.13 | 5.74 | 2.03 |

Independent samples test

|  |  | Levene's Test for Equality of Variances | | t-Test for Equality of Means | | | | | | |
|---|---|---|---|---|---|---|---|---|---|---|
|  |  | F | Sig. | t | df | Sig. (2-tailed) | Mean Difference | Std. Error Difference | 90% Confidence Interval of the Difference | |
|  |  |  |  |  |  |  |  |  | Lower | Upper |
| Height in centimetres | Equal variances assumed | .747 | .394 | 4.701 | 32 | .000 | 11.26 | 2.40 | 7.20 | 15.32 |
|  | Equal variances not assumed |  |  | 4.803 | 12.062 | .000 | 11.26 | 2.34 | 7.08 | 15.44 |

**Figure A17** Example of SPSS output for an independent sample *t*-test

*Step 5: Interpret the decision*

These statistical results are extremely significant, and they are consistent with the generally held view (and other statistical evidence!) that males are taller than females on average. However, the purpose of this exercise was not to demonstrate differences between males and females, but to show how the independent samples *t*-test can be used with the assistance of SPSS.

We suggest you now try out an exercise to compare the means of a dependent or 'paired' sample. Use the data from the business research class questionnaire to compare the mean (average) attitudes of all respondents to the two variables 'Statistics is interesting' and 'Statistics is useful'. Good luck!

## SIGNIFICANT MEAN DIFFERENCES AMONG MULTIPLE GROUPS: ANOVA

Whereas the *t*-test would indicate whether or not there is a significant mean difference in a dependent variable between two groups, an **analysis of variance (ANOVA)** helps to examine the significant mean differences among more than two groups on an interval- or ratio-scaled dependent variable. For example, would there be a significant difference in the sales by the following four groups of salespersons: those who are sent to training schools; those who are given on-the-job training during field trips; those who have been tutored by the sales manager; and those who have had none of the above? As another example, is the rate of promotion significantly different for those who have assigned mentors, those who choose their own mentors and those who have no mentors in the organisational system?

The results of ANOVA show whether or not the means of the various groups are significantly different from one another, as indicated by the F statistic. The F statistic shows whether two sample variances differ from each other or if they are from the same population. The F distribution is a probability distribution of sample variances and the family of distributions changes with the changes in the sample size. The F statistic is the ratio of the variance between groups divided by the variance within groups. The greater the likelihood of between-group variance compared with within-group variance, the greater the probability that the means of the groups will be different. Details of the F statistic can be seen in table IV in appendix II.

When significant mean differences among the groups are indicated by the F statistic, there is no way of knowing from the ANOVA results alone where they lie — that is, whether the significant difference is between groups A and B, or between B and C, or A and C, and so on. It would therefore be unwise to use multiple *t*-tests, taking two groups at a time, because the greater the number of *t*-tests done, the less confidence we can place on our results. For example, simultaneously doing three *t*-tests decreases the confidence level from 95 per cent to 86 per cent $(0.95)^3$. However, several tests, such as Scheffe's test, Duncan Multiple Range test, Tukey's test and Student-Newman-Keul's test, are available and can be used to detect where exactly the mean differences lie.

The Kruskal-Wallis one-way analysis of variance is the non-parametric test used when the dependent variable is on an ordinal scale, and the independent variable is nominally scaled. Tables A3 and A4 provide information regarding the statistical techniques and tests used, as well as information on the different non-parametric tests.

# SPSS example of a one-way ANOVA

We will now use the business research class data to demonstrate the use of the one-way analysis of variance (ANOVA) procedure within SPSS. We will consider the height groups as the independent variable and then consider the differences in the mean 'weight' of the students in the different groups, and also their mean attitudes towards the variable 'Statistics is interesting'. We have specified six height groups (see the histogram in figure A4). We will use our hypothesis-testing procedure outlined in figure A9.

*Step 1: Formulating the hypotheses*

Hypothesis 1 can be presented as:

   H1$_0$: The average weights of the students in each group are equal.

   H1$_A$: The average weights of the students in each group are not equal.

This can be expressed statistically as

   H1$_0$: $\mu_{11} = \mu_{12} = \mu_{13} = \mu_{14} = \mu_{15} = \mu_{16}$

   H1$_A$: $\mu_{11} \neq \mu_{12} \neq \mu_{13} \neq \mu_{14} \neq \mu_{15} \neq \mu_{16}$

where $\mu_{1t}$ is the mean weight for each group.

   Similarly, hypothesis 2 can be presented as:

   H2$_0$: The mean attitudes towards the 'Statistics is interesting' variable are the same for each height group.

   H2$_A$: The mean attitudes towards the 'Statistics is interesting' variable are not the same for each height group.

Or:

   H2$_0$: $\mu_{21} = \mu_{22} = \mu_{23} = \mu_{24} = \mu_{25} = \mu_{26}$

   H2$_A$: $\mu_{21} \neq \mu_{22} \neq \mu_{23} \neq \mu_{24} \neq \mu_{25} \neq \mu_{26}$

where $\mu_{2t}$ is the mean attitude towards the 'Statistics is interesting' variable for each group.

*Step 2: Decision criterion*

We will set the significance level at 5 per cent ($\alpha = 0.05$). In other words, we will reject H$_0$ (the null hypothesis) if the calculated *p*-value (significance level) is less than 0.05. This would indicate that at least one of the sample means is statistically significantly different from the other means.

*Step 3: Analyse data with computer package*

We have analysed the data with the SPSS package, and the output appears as figure A18. The calculated significance level for the mean differences in weights between the height groups is $p = 0.00$ (indicating significant differences in one or more of the mean weights). The significance level for the F test examining the mean responses to the variable 'Statistics is interesting' is $p = 0.19$, which does not indicate significant differences in the mean values.

*Step 4: Make a statistical decision*

We now compare our calculated *p*-values with our desired significance level ($\alpha$ value) of 0.05.

*Hypothesis 1:* The calculated significance level of 0.00 is much less than 0.05, hence we reject H1$_0$. Therefore, we accept the alternate hypothesis that the average weight for students is different based on their height group.

*Hypothesis 2:* The calculated significance level of 0.19 is outside the limit of 0.05, hence we do not reject H2$_0$. We accept the null hypothesis that there is no difference in the mean attitudes of students towards 'Statistics is interesting' based on their height groups.

*Step 5: Interpret the decision*
These statistical decisions appear perfectly sensible: we would expect the mean weight of groups to be different based on their classification by height. The post-hoc procedure within SPSS would help in determining which particular groups had the most significant mean differences. Also, we would expect that the mean attitudes of students to the variable 'Statistics is interesting' would not vary depending on which height group they were in!

We will further briefly consider the role of analysis of variance (ANOVA) in the context of regression modelling.

**One-way analysis of variance**

ANOVA

|  |  | Sum of Squares | df | Mean Square | F | Sig. |
|---|---|---|---|---|---|---|
| Weight in kilograms | Between groups | 2350.495 | 5 | 470.099 | 9.117 | .000 |
|  | Within groups | 1443.770 | 28 | 51.563 |  |  |
|  | Total | 3794.265 | 33 |  |  |  |
| Statistics is interesting | Between groups | 11.313 | 5 | 2.263 | 1.598 | .193 |
|  | Within groups | 39.657 | 28 | 1.416 |  |  |
|  | Total | 50.971 | 33 |  |  |  |

**Figure A18** Example of SPSS output for one-way between-groups ANOVA

# REGRESSION ANALYSIS

Whereas the simple correlation coefficient $r$ indicates the strength of relationship between two variables, it gives us no idea of how much of the variance in the dependent or criterion variable will be explained when several independent variables are theorised to influence it *simultaneously*. For example, when the variance in a dependent variable $X$ (say, performance) is expected to be explained by four independent or predictor variables correlated to the dependent variable to varying degrees, but that they might also be intercorrelated (that is, related among themselves). For example, task difficulty is likely to be related to supervisory support, pay might be correlated to task difficulty, and all three — task difficulty, supervisory support and pay — might influence the organisational culture. When these variables are jointly regressed against the dependent variable in an effort to explain the variance in it, the individual correlations are collapsed into what is called a *multiple R*, or multiple correlation. The square of multiple R, **R square** or $R^2$ as it is commonly known, is the amount of variance explained in the dependent variable by the predictors. Such analysis, where more than one predictor is jointly regressed against the criterion variable, is known as **multiple regression analysis**. When the R-square value, the F statistic and its significance level are known, we can interpret the results. For example, if the $R^2$ is 0.63 with an F value of, say, 25.56 and a significance level of $p < 0.001$, then we can say that 63 per cent of the variance has been significantly explained by the set of predictors. There is less than a 0.1 per cent chance of this not holding true.

In summary, multiple regression analysis is done to examine the simultaneous effects of several independent variables on a dependent variable that is interval scaled. In other words, multiple regression analysis helps us understand how much of the variance in the dependent variable is explained by a set of predictors. If we want to know which, among the set of predictors, is the most important in explaining the variance, which the next, and so on, a stepwise multiple regression analysis can be used. If we want to know whether a set of job-related variables (say, job challenge, job variety and job stress) would significantly *add* to the variance explained in the dependent variable (say, job satisfaction), over and above that explained by a set of organisational factors (such as participation in decision making, communication and supervisory relationship), a hierarchical regression analysis can be done.

Multiple regression analysis is also used to trace the sequential antecedents that *cause* the dependent variable through what is known as *Path analysis*. As stated in an earlier chapter, this tracing of sequential antecedents is possible even in crosssectional data. Although a detailed discussion of these types of analysis is beyond the scope of this book, we will briefly outline some of the characteristics of regression analysis and provide a couple of examples using SPSS to illustrate these points. First, we will consider simple regression, in which a dependent variable is explained by a single independent variable; then we will consider multiple regression, which examines the situation where a dependent variable is simultaneously influenced by a number of independent variables.

## Simple regression

If a scatter diagram (see figures A11 and A12) or the value of the correlation coefficient indicates a strong linear relationship between two variables, then it would make sense to fit a line to the data points to predict one variable when values of the other are given. This line is called a regression line: it is the line going through the data points that minimises the sum of squared vertical differences (referred to as 'errors' in regression analysis) between the line and the sample points. An example is provided in figure A19, where a regression line has been fitted between two variables from the business research class data set. In this case, we have used SPSS to estimate the straight line relationship between weight and height. It is assumed that weight (the dependent variable) is influenced by height (the independent variable).

(a) SPSS fitted regression line

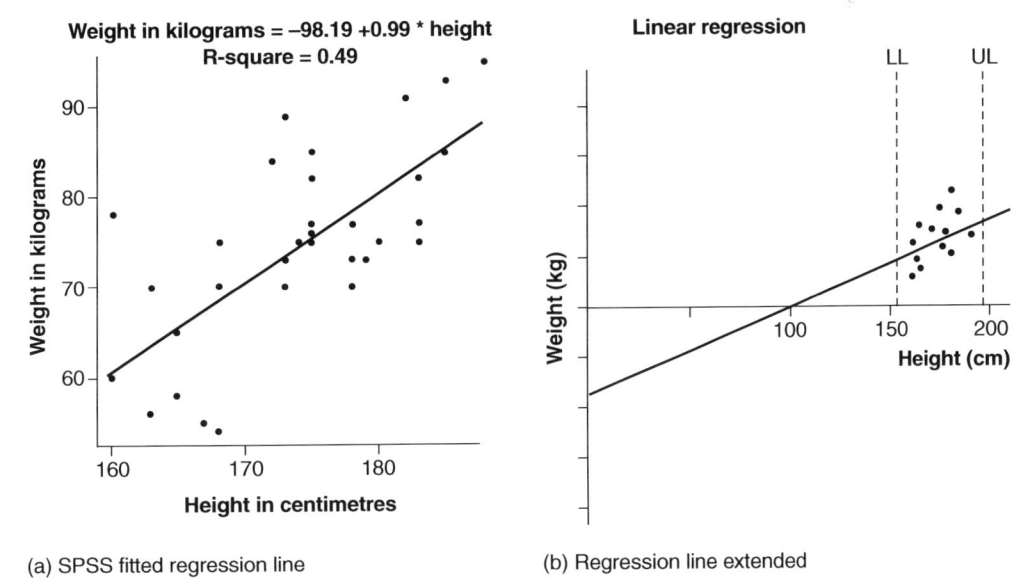

(b) Regression line extended

**Figure A19** A simple regression model

The general form of a simple regression line is given by the formula
$$Y = a + bX$$
where:  $Y$ is the dependent variable
$X$ is the independent variable
a is the intercept of the regression line on the $Y$ (vertical) axis
b is the slope of the regression line (or the increase in $Y$ for a unit increase in $X$).

Fortunately, we don't have to calculate the values of a and b manually any more. We have a wide variety of computer packages to do that. For our example in figure A19, the regression line formed between height and weight is given by the equation
$$\text{weight} = -98.19 + 0.99 * \text{height}$$
where: $Y$ = weight in kilograms
$X$ = height in centimetres
and the regression coefficients are a = $-98.19$ and b = 0.99.

To predict the $Y$-value for given $X$-values, all we need to do is substitute the $X$-values into the regression equation. For example, the predicted weight ($\hat{Y}$, called Y-hat) of a student who is 170 centimetres tall is:
$$\hat{Y} = -98.19 + 0.99 * 170 = 70.11 \text{ kilograms.}$$

Hence, we predict that a person who is 1 cm taller will be 0.99 kg heavier on average (based on our sample statistics)!

However, please note that in general, better predictions will be obtained for values of $X$ inside the sample range (interpolation) than for values outside the range (extrapolation). The relationship between the two variables may be approximately linear over the range covered by the sample, but you cannot extend the regression line indefinitely without risking a considerable divergence.

For example, if the regression line in figure A19(a) was extended back to the y axis it would intercept it at the point $-98.19$ (clearly nonsensical if height was zero!). We have indicated the region where the regression line is probably reasonably good, by the two vertical lines in figure A19(b) (that is, the lower limit (LL) and the upper limit (UL)). However, we can now check the SPSS output in figure A20 to determine how well the line fits the data. Fortunately, we have met most of the terms and statistical concepts in this output earlier in this appendix, including $r$ (correlation coefficient), standard error, $F$ statistic, Sig. (or the calculated level of significance, alternatively called the $p$-value), $df$ (degrees of freedom) and $t$-test.

We will not reiterate the meanings of all these statistical terms and tests here. However, we will briefly comment on some of the new terms and different ways these tests are used in the SPSS output in figure A20. The following definitions are mainly derived from the Results Coach in SPSS.

### Regression coefficients

The unstandardised coefficients are the coefficients of the estimated regression model. For example, these are the values of the coefficients a and b as discussed in the weight/height regression equation above.

### Beta coefficients

Generally, the independent variables are measured in different units (such as dollars, years or units). The standardised coefficients, or Betas, are an attempt to make the regression coefficients more comparable. If you transformed the data to $z$ scores prior to your regression analysis, you would get the Beta coefficients as your unstandardised coefficients. By looking at the beta values you can see immediately which independent variables contribute most to explaining the variation in the dependent variable. This is more useful when you examine the output from multiple regression models with a number of independent variables.

### *t* statistic

The *t* statistic in a regression model can help you determine the relative importance of each independent variable in the model. Generally, if a coefficient has a *t* value well below −2 or above +2, then you keep that independent variable in the equation. Of course, you can also determine this by looking at the significance or p-values for these coefficients. Generally, if the *p*-value is less than 0.05 (or our specified $\alpha$ level), we conclude that the coefficient is significantly different from zero, and hence we keep the variable in the equation.

The *t* value for the coefficient for height in figure A20 indicates a $p < 0.01$, which suggests that height is a very significant independent variable in the regression equation.

### Regression ANOVA

The analysis of variance (ANOVA) table provides details of the variation explained by the regression model compared with the unexplained variation. A model with a large regression sum of squares in comparison with the residual sum of squares indicates that the model accounts for most of the variation in the dependent variable. A very high residual sum of squares indicates that the model fails to explain a lot of the variation in the dependent variable, and you may want to look for additional variables that help account for a higher proportion of the variation in the dependent variable.

The *F* statistic is the regression mean square (MSR) divided by the residual mean square (MSE). The regression degrees of freedom (*df*) is the numerator *df* and the residual degrees of freedom is the denominator *df* for the *F* statistic. The total number of degrees of freedom is the number of cases (observations) minus 1.

If the significance or *p*-value of the *F* statistic is small (smaller than, say, 0.05 or your specified $\alpha$ level), then the independent variables collectively do a good job explaining the variation in the dependent variable. If the significance value of *F* is larger than 0.05 (or your specified $\alpha$ level), then the independent variables as a group do not explain the variation in the dependent variable to the level of confidence that you may require.

In figure A20, we see that the *F* statistic is highly significant, and the independent variable (height) does explain a significant amount of the variation in the dependent variable — that is, weight!

### *R* square

The *R* square value (also called the coefficient of determination) is the square of the correlation coefficient (*R*). It is the proportion of the total variation around the mean for the data that is explained by the regression model. Whereas *R* can take on a value from −1 to +1, depending on whether the association between the two variables is positive or negative, the value of *R* square can fall between 0 and 1. Clearly, a model with an *R* square value close to one indicates that the model fits the data very well. Conversely, a low *R* square value (close to 0) indicates the model is not very good.

The *R* square is calculated as the Regression Sum of Squares (RSS) divided by the Total Sum of Squares (TSS). In figure A20, we can calculate *R* square as: RSS/TSS = 1868/3794 = 0.492 (that is, the value in the Model Summary table).

The Adjusted R Square is the R square value adjusted for the degrees of freedom. Although technically it is the more correct measure to use in regression analysis, it is generally not as widely used (nor as well understood) as the R square measure.

## Standard error of the estimate

The standard error of the estimate is another measure of how well the model fits the data. It is particularly useful in constructing confidence intervals for predicted values of the dependent variable. (Refer to chapter 11, pages 274–6 for a discussion of confidence intervals.)

For example, for the results in figure A20 we can construct an approximate 95 per cent confidence interval for our predicted weight for the student weighing 170 centimetres in the business research class. We could represent this confidence interval as:

$\hat{Y}$ estimate +/– 2 * standard error of estimate
= 70.11 +/– 2 * 7.76 (kg)
= (70.11 – 15.52) to (70.11 + 15.52) (kg)
= 54.59 to 85.63 kg

Note that 2 is used as a proxy for a $z$ score or $t$ value for a reasonably large sample ($n \geq 30$) for a 95 per cent confidence interval. However, SPSS does calculate more accurate confidence intervals to be used with predictions using regression analysis.

## Variables entered/removed and method

A number of regression methods are provided in SPSS, but a discussion of these is outside the scope of this book. However, if the stepwise regression method is used, some independent variables are entered and removed from the regression equation to get a better-fitting model — that is, a set of independent variables that better explains the variation in the dependent variable.

By now, you will have realised that regression analysis can be quite a complicated process, although extremely powerful and useful. However, to perform regression analysis a number of assumptions must be made. These are summarised in the box below. If these assumptions are violated, then it is questionable whether regression analysis is the appropriate method to use to analyse your data.

> **Regression analysis — assumptions**
> 1. Errors are normally distributed.
> 2. Errors have a zero mean (or expected value).
> 3. Errors have a constant variance over all values of the dependent variable and in each time period.
> 4. Errors are not correlated (that is, errors in one time period are not related to one another).
>
> Assumptions (1) to (4) are required to obtain unbiased estimates and to use probability theory to test the reliability of estimates.
>
> Other assumptions for multiple regression analysis include:
> 5. The number of independent or explanatory variables in the regression must be smaller than the number of observations.
> 6. There must not be perfect linear correlation among the independent variables.

Before we leave our discussion of regression analysis, we will briefly discuss some SPSS output generated using multiple regression.

## Regression

Variables entered/removed[b]

| Model | Variables Entered | Variables Removed | Method |
|---|---|---|---|
| 1 | Height in centimetres[a] | . | Enter |

[a] All requested variables entered.
[b] Dependent variable: Weight in kilograms

### Model summary

| Model | R | R Square | Adjusted R Square | Std. Error of the Estimate |
|---|---|---|---|---|
| 1 | .702[a] | .492 | .476 | 7.76 |

[a] predictors: (constant) height in centimetres

### ANOVA[b]

| Model | | Sum of Squares | df | Mean Square | F | Sig. |
|---|---|---|---|---|---|---|
| 1 | Regression | 1868.153 | 1 | 1868.153 | 31.037 | .000[a] |
| | Residual | 1926.112 | 32 | 60.191 | | |
| | Total | 3794.265 | 33 | | | |

[a] Predictors: (constant), Height in centimetres
[b] Dependent variable: Weight in kilograms

### Coefficients[a]

| Model | | Unstandardised Coefficients | | Standardised Coefficients | t | Sig. |
|---|---|---|---|---|---|---|
| | | B | Std. Error | Beta | | |
| 1 | (Constant) | −98.189 | 30.963 | | −3.171 | .003 |
| | Height in centimetres | .992 | .178 | .702 | 5.571 | .000 |

[a] Dependent variable: Weight in kilograms

**Figure A20** Example of SPSS output for simple regression analysis

## Multiple regression

In figure A21, we have examined some data that come with the SPSS package. They are related to salaries for a sample size of about 474 people. Data have been collected on a range of variables. However, here we are testing to see whether the independent variables gender, education level (years) and previous experience (months) explain the variation observed in the salaries (the dependent variable).

The output in figure A21 is much the same as in figure A20, except that there are three independent variables in figure A21 compared with one in figure A20. However, SPSS can generate a lot more diagnostics and statistics, and we have limited the amount of output to facilitate discussion here. Nevertheless, we would like to remind you to closely examine the descriptive statistics for these variables *first*, before you embark on regression analysis. This will give you an overall 'feel' for the data.

Also, we suggest that you produce a correlation matrix, particularly to see if 'multi-collinearity' is present — that is, if any of the independent variables are highly correlated. If they are, one or more of them should be removed from the regression equation, otherwise the regression conditions will be violated and the regression coefficients are unlikely to be meaningful. For example, they may be calculated with coefficients of the wrong sign or the wrong quantity.

We should note at this stage that the variable *gender* has been introduced into the equation as a 'dummy variable', which has a value of '0' if the case (respondent) is a female and a value '1' if the case represents a male. The following multiple regression equation can be obtained from the SPSS output:

Current salary = −16219.9 + 8347.122*gender + 3407.795*education level + 1.248 * previous experience

We will now leave it to you to perform an analysis of the figure A21 output similar to the one we did for the simple regression output outlined in figure A20. Some questions to think about follow.

- How good is the overall model?
- Are all the coefficients significant?
- How do we interpret the Beta values?
- What is the relevance of the standard error of the estimate?
- What does the $F$ result tell us?
- Does the model explain a reasonable proportion of the variation?
- Do you think that there are any important variables left out?
- Is a linear relationship between these variables reasonable?

You may think of other questions yourself.

**Figure A21** Example of SPSS output for multiple regression analysis

**Regression**

Variables entered/removed[b]

| Model | Variables Entered | Variables Removed | Method |
|---|---|---|---|
| 1 | Previous Experience (months), Gender, Educational Level (years)[a] | . | Enter |

[a] All requested variables entered.
[b] Dependent variable: Current Salary

Model summary

| Model | R | R Square | Adjusted R Square | Std. Error of the Estimate |
|---|---|---|---|---|
| 1 | .69[a] | .489 | .486 | $12 242.79 |

[a] Predictors: (constant), Previous Experience (months), Gender, Educational Level (years)

ANOVA[b]

| Model | | Sum of Squares | df | Mean Square | F | Sig. |
|---|---|---|---|---|---|---|
| 1 | Regression | 6.75E+10 | 3 | 2.249E+10 | 150.048 | .000[a] |
|   | Residual | 7.04E+10 | 470 | 149 885 906.2 | | |
|   | Total | 1.38E+11 | 473 | | | |

[a] Predictors: (constant), Previous Experience (months), Gender, Educational Level (years)
[b] Dependent variable: Current Salary

Coefficients[a]

| Model | | Unstandardised Coefficients | | Standardised Coefficients | t | Sig. |
|---|---|---|---|---|---|---|
| | | B | Std. Error | Beta | | |
| 1 | (Constant) | −16 219.9 | 3041.402 | | −5.333 | .000 |
| | Gender | 8347.122 | 1259.233 | .244 | 6.629 | .000 |
| | Educational Level (years) | 3407.795 | 221.822 | .576 | 15.363 | .000 |
| | Previous Experience (months) | 1.248 | 5.797 | .008 | .215 | .830 |

[a] Dependent variable: Current Salary

Coefficient correlations[a]

| Model | | | Previous Experience (months) | Gender | Educational Level (years) |
|---|---|---|---|---|---|
| 1 | Correlations | Previous Experience (months) | 1.000 | −.282 | .337 |
| | | Gender | −.282 | 1.000 | −.417 |
| | | Educational Level (years) | .337 | −.417 | 1.000 |
| | Co-variances | Previous Experience (months) | 33.607 | −2056.099 | 433.951 |
| | | Gender | −2056.099 | 1585668 | −116363.278 |
| | | Educational Level (years) | 433.951 | −116 363 | 49 205.186 |

[a] Dependent variable: Current Salary

## FACTOR ANALYSIS

With the opinion items in a questionnaire, the researcher is interested in whether the planned structure has held true; in other words, whether the respondents saw the specific items that made up each theoretical construct as, in fact, clustering together. The statistical technique to test this clustering is called **factor analysis**. Factor analysis examines the way in which each respondent completed all the opinion items and compares this with the way in which every other respondent completed each and every item, and then suggests that certain items have come together on particular factors (or clusters, if you like). Table A7 shows an example of the output of a factor analysis on a questionnaire called the 'Evaluation questionnaire'.

The figures under factor A, factor B and factor C (for example 0.22346, −0.07300 and 0.56741 for item 1) are called *loadings*. When examining the output of a factor analysis, the first activity is to highlight or underline all the loadings that are greater than 0.3. Some texts recommend only using loadings greater than 0.4 but, in the early stages of the analysis, if you highlight those greater than 0.3, you can come back and decide whether you wish to be more parsimonious. As you can see in table A7, items 1, 2, 3 and 9 all load on factor C; items 4, 5, 7, 8 and 10 load on factor A; and items 6, 13, 14 and 15 load on factor B. It is said that these items *load cleanly* — they load on that factor and that factor only.

**Table A7** Output of a factor analysis for the evaluation questionnaire

| Item | Factor A | Factor B | Factor C |
|---|---|---|---|
| 01 | 0.22346 | −0.07300 | 0.56741 |
| 02 | 0.22173 | 0.11086 | 0.72553 |
| 03 | −0.11021 | −0.13279 | 0.81159 |
| 04 | 0.61291 | −0.18332 | −0.11947 |
| 05 | 0.66958 | 0.02347 | 0.20299 |
| 06 | 0.07750 | −0.61141 | 0.20597 |
| 07 | 0.72003 | −0.00131 | 0.00424 |
| 08 | 0.77667 | 0.19312 | 0.12914 |
| 09 | 0.01284 | −0.24331 | 0.58230 |
| 10 | 0.62759 | −0.26720 | −0.10879 |
| 11 | 0.43661 | −0.15479 | 0.39083 |
| 12 | 0.48110 | −0.44660 | 0.03393 |
| 13 | 0.03974 | −0.70698 | 0.17139 |
| 14 | −0.00829 | −0.81637 | 0.12066 |
| 15 | −0.06771 | −0.93732 | −0.08814 |

Item 11 loads on factor A and factor C, while item 12 loads on factor A and factor B. This is called *leakage* — they are leaking across two factors and are not loading cleanly. Leakage indicates that the respondents were confused about the item and the researcher has the choice of deleting these items from the final questionnaire or designing two substitute, but more understandable, items. Preferably, if new items are included, then another pilot study is conducted. However, in reality, some researchers will take the risk of including two or three new items in the final questionnaire rather than using resources to conduct a new pilot study. Once again, the researcher has a choice!

This evaluation questionnaire, which was used to collect the data factors analysed in table A7, was constructed originally from material in textbooks. This gave *content validity* to the questionnaire. Remember, content validity describes the intended theoretical constructs (see chapter 9, pages 212–5). The evaluation questionnaire was designed to measure three theoretical constructs — the trainer (items 4, 5, 6, 7, 8, 9 and 10), the benefits to the trainees (11, 12, 13, 14 and 15) and the management of the course (1, 2 and 3).

A factor analysis is used to examine another type of validity — *construct validity*. Construct validity is used to examine the actual constructs as perceived by the respondents. Once the factor analysis is completed, the researcher compares the factors (the construct validity) with the intended structure (content validity). As you can see in figure A22, the construct validity mirrors the content validity, except for four items.

## FACTOR A

4. The trainer has provided adequate feedback on student performance.
5. The trainer has provided an adequate flow of ideas in this course.
7. The trainer seems to know when trainees did not understand the material.
8. The trainer made a major contribution to the value of this course.
10. The trainer has been creative in developing materials for this course.

## FACTOR B

6. This course has been adapted to trainees' needs.
13. I learned a lot in this course.
14. This course generally fulfilled my goals.
15. This course stimulated me to want to take more work in the same or related area.

## FACTOR C

1. Class time was well spent.
2. The course was well organised.
3. There was considerable agreement between announced objectives and what was taught.
9. The goals and objectives for this course have been clearly stated.

## THE LEAKING ITEMS

11. The teaching methods used in this course have been suitable.
12. This course stimulated interest in the subject content.

**Figure A22** Items under each factor for the evaluation questionnaire

Items 6 and 9, meant to be part of the 'trainer' construct, have moved — item 6 to measure the 'benefits to the trainees' construct and item 9 to the 'management of the course' construct. In addition, items 11 and 12 caused confusion. So, not only has the researcher to decide whether to delete items 11 and 12 or redesign them, he or she has to decide whether to stay with the content validity (items 6 and 9 stay with the 'trainer' construct) or accept the construct validity version. As a general rule, researchers tend to go with the construct validity as this is the way that the respondents perceive the structure of the questionnaire.

## OTHER TESTS AND ANALYSES

We will now briefly describe three multivariate techniques — *multivariate analysis of variance* (MANOVA), *discriminant analysis* and *canonical correlations*. We will also briefly describe some of the other multivariate techniques, such as *cluster analysis* and *multidimensional scaling*, and more on *factor analysis*. Multivariate analyses examine several variables and their relationships simultaneously, in contrast to bivariate analyses, which examine relationships between two variables, and univariate analyses where one variable at a time is examined for generalisation from the sample to the population. The multivariate techniques are now presented superficially to give you some idea of their use.

## MANOVA

MANOVA is similar to ANOVA, with the difference that ANOVA tests the mean differences of more than two groups on *one* dependent variable, whereas MANOVA tests mean differences among groups across *several* dependent variables simultaneously by using sums of squares and cross-product matrices. Just as multiple $t$-tests would bias the results (as explained earlier), multiple ANOVA tests, using one dependent variable at a time, would also bias the results, since the dependent variables are likely to be interrelated. MANOVA circumvents this bias by simultaneously testing all the dependent variables, cancelling out the effects of any intercorrelations among them.

In MANOVA tests, the independent variable is measured on a nominal scale and the dependent variables on an interval or ratio scale.

The null hypothesis tested by MANOVA is $\mu_1 = \mu_2 = \mu_3 = \ldots \mu_n$.

The alternate hypothesis is $\mu_1 \neq \mu_2 \neq \mu_3 \neq \ldots \mu_n$.

## Discriminant analysis

Discriminant analysis helps to identify the independent variables that discriminate a nominally scaled dependent variable of interest — say, those who are high on a variable from those who are low on it. The linear combination of independent variables indicates the discriminating function showing the large difference that exists in the two group means. In other words, the independent variables measured on an inverval or ratio scale discriminate the groups of interest to the study.

## Canonical correlation

Canonical correlation examines the relationship between two or more dependent variables and several independent variables; for example, the correlation between a set of job behaviours (such as engrossment in work, timely completion of work and number of absences) and their influence on a set of performance factors (such as quality of work, number of items produced and rate of rejects). The focus here is on delineating the job behaviour profiles associated with performance which result in the production of good quality products.

Other types of statistical analyses such as *factor analysis, cluster analysis* and *multidimensional scaling* help us to understand how the variables under study form a pattern or structure, in contrast to focusing on predicting the dependent variable or tracing relationships.

## Factor analysis

Factor analysis helps to reduce a vast number of variables (for example all the questions tapping several variables of interest in a questionnaire) to a meaningful, interpretable and manageable set of factors. A principal component analysis transforms all the variables into a set of composite variables that are not correlated to one another. Suppose we have measured in a questionnaire the four concepts of mental health, job satisfaction, life satisfaction and job involvement, with seven questions tapping each. When we factor analyse these 28 items, we should find four factors with the right variables loading on each factor, confirming that we have measured the concepts correctly. We provided more details on this statistical method in the previous section above, because of its importance in helping to determine the construct validity of questionnaires.

## Cluster analysis

*Cluster analysis* is used to classify objects or individuals into mutually exclusive and collectively exhaustive groups with high homogeneity within clusters and low homogeneity between clusters. In other words, cluster analysis helps to identify objects that are similar to one another, based on some specified criterion. For instance, if our sample consists of a mix of respondents with different brand preferences for a product, cluster analysis will cluster individuals by their preferences for each of the different brands.

## Multidimensional scaling

Multidimensional scaling groups objects in multidimensional space. Objects that are perceived by respondents to be different are distanced; the greater the perceptual differences, the greater the distance between the objects in the multidimensional space. In other words, multidimensional scaling provides a spatial description of respondents' perception of products, services or other items of interest, and portrays the perceived similarities and differences.

In summary, multivariate techniques such as MANOVA, Discriminant Analysis and Canonical Correlation help us to analyse the influence of independent variables on the dependent variable in different ways. Other multivariate techniques, such as factor analysis, cluster analysis and multidimensional scaling offer meaningful insights into the data set by forming patterns of the data in one form or another.

It is most convenient that several univariate, bivariate and multivariate techniques are available to analyse sample data, so we can generalise the results obtained from the sample to the population at large. It is important, however, to pay attention to each hypothesis, and use the correct statistical technique to test it rather than apply advanced inappropriate techniques.

## MANAGERIAL RELEVANCE

Managers make decisions every day, some of which are routine and some critical for the organisation. The ability to understand the different types of analysis as well as the probabilities associated with each projected outcome helps managers to take calculated risks (or avoid them), based on their own natural inclinations as well as the gravity of the problem situation. If, for instance, the manager decides that a confidence level of 0.90 (or even 0.80) in the data analytic results is acceptable, then he or she is aware that the probability of making a wrong decision is 10 per cent (or 20 per cent). Such knowledge is extremely important for decision making on various matters of differing complexity and consequence.

Knowledge of analysis such as multiple regression reminds the manager that multiple factors influence outcomes and attention must be paid to all the critical variables indicated by the results of the analysis. The manager also develops a new appreciation of a scientific, data-based information system that would lend itself to different types of analysis to solve problems in a sophisticated and reliable manner. More advanced multivariate analyses, when comprehended, offer managers valuable insights into developing strategies for organisational and business growth.

## SUMMARY

In this appendix we examined the use of descriptive statistics such as the mean, median and mode as measures of central tendency and the range, standard deviation, variance, standard error and interquartile range as measures of dispersion. These descriptive statistics help managers to understand and describe the nature of the phenomena encountered in a situation, whether they relate to people, stocks, production, events or any other factor of interest.

We also saw the need for generating frequency distributions in the case of some nominal demographic data, such as educational level and number of organisations in which individuals have worked. Organisations might also like frequency distributions for certain types of occurrences such as machine breakdowns due to different specific reasons, or types of accounting errors made, or the investment portfolio during a given period.

While discussing inferential statistics, we examined (1) how correlational analysis can test the relationship between two variables; (2) how the $\chi^2$ test can detect whether two nominal variables are dependent or independent; (3) how to trace significant differences between two groups on a dependent variable, using the $t$-test; (4) how to trace differences among several groups using ANOVA; (5) how to explain and predict the variance in the dependent variable when multiple independent variables are theorised to influence it, using multiple regression analysis; and (6) how to use factor analysis to test the construct validity of questionnaire. We discussed the roles of the $\chi^2$, $t$ and F statistic as tests of significance for different types of data analyses. We also briefly described the use of multivariate analyses such as MANOVA, Discriminant Analysis and Canonical Correlation. In addition, we saw that techniques such as factor analysis, cluster analysis and multidimensional scaling help to detect patterns in the collected data.

After having revisited some statistical terms and tests, and demonstrated the use of some of them with SPSS, discussions on how the data are actually analysed will be more easily understood.

## DISCUSSION POINTS

1 Which measures of central tendency and dispersion are appropriate in the following cases, and why?
   (a) The ages of individuals who are grouped as follows:
      Under 25    3
      25–35     120
      36–55      80
      Over 55    22
   (b) The performance ratings (on a 100-point scale) given by the head of the department to the top six performers:
      Top scorer   87 per cent
      Second       82 per cent
      Third        81 per cent
      Fourth       76 per cent
      Fifth        74 per cent
      Sixth        68 per cent
   (c) The weights of eight boxes of raw materials purchased:
      275, 263, 298, 197, 275, 287, 263 and 243 kilograms.

2 What is the chi-square test? State a research hypothesis (not in the examples given in the book) that would call for a $\chi^2$ test.

3  If you want to know whether three groups of employees — those who have been with the organisation between four and six years, between seven and nine years, and between 10 and 12 years — are different in the number of trips they have taken outside of the city on business work, what statistical test would you use and why?

4  Explain in your own words what multiple regression analysis is. Give a business situation that would call for the use of multiple regression analysis.

5  Analyse the regression output provided in figure A21 and address the questions provided on page 438.

6  The CEO of Spedding International was perplexed by the rate of turnover in the company during the past 18 months or so. She suspected that three possible factors contributed to this — the lower salaries paid to staff compared with the industry average, the location of the company and the extent of bureaucracy that pervaded the system. She was not sure if there were any differences among the four categories of employees — managers, clerical staff, machine operators and secretarial staff — in their intentions to quit in the next six months. 'It would be nice to know how many of each category of staff are currently in the organisation, and to have a profile of their ages, educational qualifications and experience with the organisation,' she thought. Furthermore, she wanted to know if the older or the younger employees were more disgruntled. She directed her assistant, who had taken a course on Research Methods, to gather the necessary data and give her the needed information.

Indicate the variables on which the assistant would gather data, and what kinds of analyses he will be submitting the data to, to produce a report for the CEO. (It would help you first to list the information that the CEO wants and then to proceed with the exercise.)

# appendix II

## STATISTICAL TABLES

TABLE I     AREAS UNDER THE STANDARD NORMAL DISTRIBUTION
TABLE II     VALUES OF THE $t$ DISTRIBUTION FOR SELECTED PROBABILITIES
TABLE III     VALUES OF THE CHI SQUARE ($\chi^2$) DISTRIBUTION FOR SELECTED PROBABILITIES
TABLE IV     VALUES OF THE $F$ DISTRIBUTION
                (a) UPPER 5% PROBABILITY
                (b) UPPER 1% PROBABILITY

## TABLE I
Areas under the standard normal distribution

To illustrate: 19.85 per cent of the area under a normal curve lies between the mean, $\mu_X$, and a point 0.52 standard deviation units away.

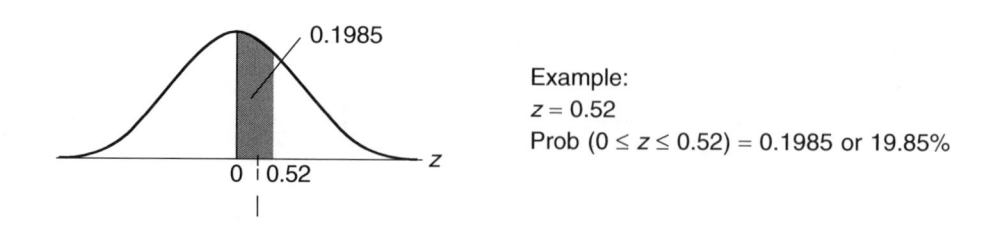

Example:
$z = 0.52$
Prob $(0 \leq z \leq 0.52) = 0.1985$ or $19.85\%$

| Z | .00 | .01 | .02 | .03 | .04 | .05 | .06 | .07 | .08 | .09 |
|---|---|---|---|---|---|---|---|---|---|---|
| 0.0 | .0000 | .0040 | .0080 | .0120 | .0160 | .0199 | .0239 | .0279 | .0319 | .0359 |
| 0.1 | .0398 | .0438 | .0478 | .0517 | .0557 | .0596 | .0636 | .0675 | .0714 | .0753 |
| 0.2 | .0793 | .0832 | .0871 | .0910 | .0948 | .0987 | .1026 | .1064 | .1103 | .1141 |
| 0.3 | .1179 | .1217 | .1255 | .1293 | .1331 | .1368 | .1406 | .1443 | .1480 | .1517 |
| 0.4 | .1554 | .1591 | .1628 | .1664 | .1700 | .1736 | .1772 | .1808 | .1844 | .1879 |
| 0.5 | .1915 | .1950 | .1985 | .2019 | .2054 | .2088 | .2123 | .2157 | .2190 | .2224 |
| 0.6 | .2257 | .2291 | .2324 | .2357 | .2389 | .2422 | .2454 | .2486 | .2517 | .2549 |
| 0.7 | .2580 | .2611 | .2642 | .2673 | .2704 | .2734 | .2764 | .2794 | .2823 | .2852 |
| 0.8 | .2881 | .2910 | .2939 | .2967 | .2995 | .3023 | .3051 | .3078 | .3106 | .3133 |
| 0.9 | .3159 | .3186 | .3212 | .3238 | .3264 | .3289 | .3315 | .3340 | .3365 | .3389 |
| 1.0 | .3413 | .3438 | .3461 | .3485 | .3508 | .3531 | .3554 | .3577 | .3599 | .3621 |
| 1.1 | .3643 | .3665 | .3686 | .3708 | .3729 | .3749 | .3770 | .3790 | .3810 | .3830 |
| 1.2 | .3849 | .3869 | .3888 | .3907 | .3925 | .3944 | .3962 | .3980 | .3997 | .4015 |
| 1.3 | .4032 | .4049 | .4066 | .4082 | .4099 | .4115 | .4131 | .4147 | .4162 | .4177 |
| 1.4 | .4192 | .4207 | .4222 | .4236 | .4251 | .4265 | .4279 | .4292 | .4306 | .4319 |
| 1.5 | .4332 | .4345 | .4357 | .4370 | .4382 | .4394 | .4406 | .4418 | .4429 | .4441 |
| 1.6 | .4452 | .4463 | .4474 | .4484 | .4495 | .4505 | .4515 | .4525 | .4535 | .4545 |
| 1.7 | .4554 | .4564 | .4573 | .4582 | .4591 | .4599 | .4608 | .4616 | .4625 | .4633 |
| 1.8 | .4641 | .4649 | .4656 | .4664 | .4671 | .4678 | .4686 | .4693 | .4699 | .4706 |
| 1.9 | .4713 | .4719 | .4726 | .4732 | .4738 | .4744 | .4750 | .4756 | .4761 | .4767 |
| 2.0 | .4772 | .4778 | .4783 | .4788 | .4793 | .4798 | .4803 | .4808 | .4812 | .4817 |
| 2.1 | .4821 | .4826 | .4830 | .4834 | .4838 | .4842 | .4846 | .4850 | .4854 | .4857 |
| 2.2 | .4861 | .4864 | .4868 | .4871 | .4875 | .4878 | .4881 | .4884 | .4887 | .4890 |
| 2.3 | .4893 | .4896 | .4898 | .4901 | .4904 | .4906 | .4909 | .4911 | .4913 | .4916 |
| 2.4 | .4918 | .4920 | .4922 | .4925 | .4927 | .4929 | .4931 | .4932 | .4934 | .4936 |
| 2.5 | .4938 | .4940 | .4941 | .4943 | .4945 | .4946 | .4948 | .4949 | .4951 | .4952 |
| 2.6 | .4953 | .4955 | .4956 | .4957 | .4959 | .4960 | .4961 | .4962 | .4963 | .4964 |
| 2.7 | .4965 | .4966 | .4967 | .4968 | .4969 | .4970 | .4971 | .4972 | .4973 | .4974 |
| 2.8 | .4974 | .4975 | .4976 | .4977 | .4977 | .4978 | .4979 | .4979 | .4980 | .4981 |
| 2.9 | .4981 | .4982 | .4982 | .4983 | .4984 | .4984 | .4985 | .4985 | .4986 | .4986 |
| 3.0 | .4987 | .4987 | .4987 | .4988 | .4988 | .4989 | .4989 | .4989 | .4990 | .4990 |

**Source:** D. F. Groebner and P. W. Shannon 1981, *Business Statistics: A Decision-making Approach*, 3rd Edition. Colombus, OH: Merrill Publishing Co., appendix C, p. A-34.

## TABLE II
Values of the *t* distribution for selected probabilities

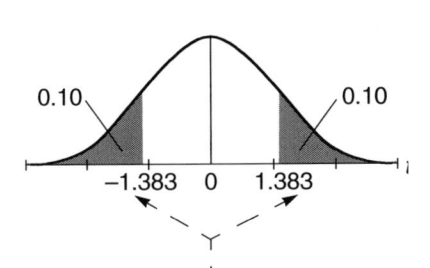

Example:
*df* (number of degrees of freedom) = 9
- One tail above *t* = 1.383 or below *t* = −1.383 represents 0.10 or 10% of the area under the curve.
- Two tails above *t* = 1.383 and below *t* = −1.383 represent 0.20 or 20% of the area.

**SELECTED PROBABILITIES**

| df | One tail = 0.40<br>Two tails = 0.80 | 0.25<br>0.50 | 0.10<br>0.20 | 0.05<br>0.10 | 0.025<br>0.05 | 0.01<br>0.02 | 0.005<br>0.01 | 0.001<br>0.002 |
|---|---|---|---|---|---|---|---|---|
| 1 | .325 | 1.000 | 3.078 | 6.314 | 12.706 | 31.821 | 63.657 | 318.31 |
| 2 | .289 | .816 | 1.886 | 2.920 | 4.303 | 6.965 | 9.925 | 22.326 |
| 3 | .277 | .765 | 1.638 | 2.353 | 3.182 | 4.541 | 5.841 | 10.213 |
| 4 | .271 | .741 | 1.533 | 2.132 | 2.776 | 3.747 | 4.604 | 7.173 |
| 5 | .267 | .727 | 1.476 | 2.015 | 2.571 | 3.365 | 4.032 | 5.893 |
| 6 | .265 | .718 | 1.440 | 1.943 | 2.447 | 3.143 | 3.707 | 5.208 |
| 7 | .263 | .711 | 1.415 | 1.895 | 2.365 | 2.998 | 3.499 | 4.785 |
| 8 | .262 | .706 | 1.397 | 1.860 | 2.306 | 2.896 | 3.355 | 4.501 |
| 9 | .261 | .703 | −1.383 | 1.833 | 2.262 | 2.821 | 3.250 | 4.297 |
| 10 | .260 | .700 | 1.372 | 1.812 | 2.228 | 2.764 | 3.169 | 4.144 |
| 11 | .260 | .697 | 1.363 | 1.796 | 2.201 | 2.718 | 3.106 | 4.025 |
| 12 | .259 | .695 | 1.356 | 1.782 | 2.179 | 2.681 | 3.055 | 3.930 |
| 13 | .259 | .694 | 1.350 | 1.771 | 2.160 | 2.650 | 3.012 | 3.852 |
| 14 | .258 | .692 | 1.345 | 1.761 | 2.145 | 2.624 | 2.977 | 3.787 |
| 15 | .258 | .691 | 1.341 | 1.753 | 2.131 | 2.602 | 2.947 | 3.733 |
| 16 | .258 | .690 | 1.337 | 1.746 | 2.120 | 2.583 | 2.921 | 3.686 |
| 17 | .257 | .689 | 1.333 | 1.740 | 2.110 | 2.567 | 2.898 | 3.646 |
| 18 | .257 | .688 | 1.330 | 1.734 | 2.101 | 2.552 | 2.878 | 3.610 |
| 19 | .257 | .688 | 1.328 | 1.729 | 2.093 | 2.539 | 2.861 | 3.579 |
| 20 | .257 | .687 | 1.325 | 1.725 | 2.086 | 2.528 | 2.845 | 3.552 |
| 21 | .257 | .686 | 1.323 | 1.721 | 2.080 | 2.518 | 2.831 | 3.527 |
| 22 | .256 | .686 | 1.321 | 1.717 | 2.074 | 2.508 | 2.819 | 3.505 |
| 23 | .256 | .685 | 1.319 | 1.714 | 2.069 | 2.500 | 2.807 | 3.485 |
| 24 | .256 | .685 | 1.318 | 1.711 | 2.064 | 2.492 | 2.797 | 3.467 |
| 25 | .256 | .684 | 1.316 | 1.708 | 2.060 | 2.485 | 2.787 | 3.450 |
| 26 | .256 | .684 | 1.315 | 1.706 | 2.056 | 2.479 | 2.779 | 3.435 |
| 27 | .256 | .684 | 1.314 | 1.703 | 2.052 | 2.473 | 2.771 | 3.421 |
| 28 | .256 | .683 | 1.313 | 1.701 | 2.048 | 2.467 | 2.763 | 3.408 |
| 29 | .256 | .683 | 1.311 | 1.699 | 2.045 | 2.462 | 2.756 | 3.396 |
| 30 | .256 | .683 | 1.310 | 1.697 | 2.042 | 2.457 | 2.750 | 3.385 |
| 40 | .255 | .681 | 1.303 | 1.684 | 2.021 | 2.423 | 2.704 | 3.307 |
| 60 | .254 | .679 | 1.296 | 1.671 | 2.000 | 2.390 | 2.660 | 3.232 |
| 120 | .254 | .677 | 1.289 | 1.658 | 1.980 | 2.358 | 2.617 | 3.160 |
| ∞ | .253 | .674 | 1.282 | 1.645 | 1.960 | 2.326 | 2.576 | 3.090 |

**Source:** Condensed from table 12 of the *Biometrika Tables for Statistics*, Vol. 1, 1st edition, edited by E. S. Pearson and H. O. Hartley, 1954. Cambridge, UK: Cambridge University Press, for the Biometrika Trustees.

## TABLE III
Values of the chi-square ($\chi^2$) distribution for selected probabilities

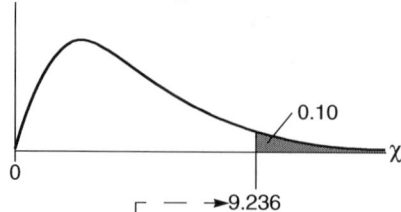

Example:
df (number of degrees of freedom) = 5
The tail above $\chi^2 = 9.236$ represents 0.10 or 10% of the area under the curve.

### SELECTED PROBABILITIES

| df  | .25     | .10     | .05     | .025    | .01     | .005    | .001    |
|-----|---------|---------|---------|---------|---------|---------|---------|
| 1   | 1.323   | 2.706   | 3.842   | 5.024   | 6.635   | 7.879   | 10.828  |
| 2   | 2.772   | 4.605   | 5.991   | 7.378   | 9.210   | 10.597  | 13.816  |
| 3   | 4.108   | 6.251   | 7.815   | 9.348   | 11.345  | 12.838  | 16.266  |
| 4   | 5.386   | 7.779   | 9.488   | 11.143  | 13.277  | 14.860  | 18.467  |
| 5   | 6.626   | 9.236   | 11.070  | 12.833  | 15.086  | 16.750  | 20.515  |
| 6   | 7.841   | 10.645  | 12.592  | 14.449  | 16.812  | 18.548  | 22.458  |
| 7   | 9.037   | 12.017  | 14.067  | 16.013  | 18.475  | 20.278  | 24.322  |
| 8   | 10.219  | 13.362  | 15.507  | 17.535  | 20.090  | 21.955  | 26.125  |
| 9   | 11.389  | 14.684  | 16.919  | 19.023  | 21.666  | 23.589  | 27.877  |
| 10  | 12.549  | 15.987  | 18.307  | 20.483  | 23.209  | 25.188  | 29.588  |
| 11  | 13.701  | 17.275  | 19.675  | 21.920  | 24.725  | 26.757  | 31.264  |
| 12  | 14.845  | 18.549  | 21.026  | 23.337  | 26.217  | 28.300  | 32.909  |
| 13  | 15.984  | 19.812  | 22.362  | 24.736  | 27.688  | 29.819  | 34.528  |
| 14  | 17.117  | 21.064  | 23.685  | 26.119  | 29.141  | 31.319  | 36.123  |
| 15  | 18.245  | 22.307  | 24.996  | 27.448  | 30.578  | 32.801  | 37.697  |
| 16  | 19.369  | 23.542  | 26.296  | 28.845  | 32.000  | 34.267  | 39.252  |
| 17  | 20.489  | 24.769  | 27.587  | 30.191  | 33.409  | 35.719  | 40.790  |
| 18  | 21.605  | 25.989  | 28.869  | 31.526  | 34.805  | 37.156  | 42.312  |
| 19  | 22.716  | 27.204  | 30.144  | 32.852  | 36.191  | 38.582  | 43.820  |
| 20  | 23.828  | 28.412  | 31.410  | 34.170  | 37.566  | 39.997  | 45.315  |
| 21  | 24.935  | 29.615  | 32.671  | 35.479  | 38.932  | 41.401  | 46.797  |
| 22  | 26.039  | 30.813  | 33.924  | 36.781  | 40.289  | 42.796  | 48.268  |
| 23  | 27.141  | 32.007  | 35.173  | 38.076  | 41.638  | 44.181  | 49.728  |
| 24  | 28.241  | 33.196  | 36.415  | 39.364  | 42.980  | 45.559  | 51.179  |
| 25  | 29.339  | 34.382  | 37.653  | 40.647  | 44.314  | 46.928  | 52.620  |
| 26  | 30.435  | 35.563  | 38.885  | 41.923  | 45.642  | 48.290  | 54.052  |
| 27  | 31.528  | 36.741  | 40.113  | 43.194  | 46.963  | 49.645  | 55.476  |
| 28  | 32.621  | 37.916  | 41.337  | 44.461  | 48.278  | 50.993  | 56.892  |
| 29  | 33.711  | 39.088  | 42.557  | 45.722  | 49.588  | 52.336  | 58.302  |
| 30  | 34.800  | 40.256  | 43.773  | 46.979  | 50.892  | 53.672  | 59.703  |
| 40  | 45.616  | 51.805  | 55.759  | 59.342  | 63.691  | 66.766  | 73.402  |
| 50  | 56.334  | 63.167  | 67.505  | 71.420  | 76.154  | 79.490  | 86.661  |
| 60  | 66.981  | 74.397  | 79.082  | 83.298  | 88.379  | 91.952  | 99.607  |
| 70  | 77.577  | 85.527  | 90.531  | 95.023  | 100.425 | 104.215 | 112.317 |
| 80  | 88.130  | 96.578  | 101.879 | 106.629 | 112.329 | 116.321 | 124.839 |
| 90  | 98.650  | 107.565 | 113.145 | 118.136 | 124.116 | 128.299 | 137.208 |
| 100 | 109.141 | 118.498 | 124.342 | 129.561 | 135.807 | 140.169 | 149.449 |

**Source:** Adapted from table 8 of the *Biometrika Tables for Statisticians*, Vol. 1, 1st edition, edited by E. S. Pearson and H. O. Hartley, 1954. Cambridge, UK: Cambridge University Press, for the Biometrika Trustees.

**TABLE IV** Values of the F distribution
(a) Upper 5% probability

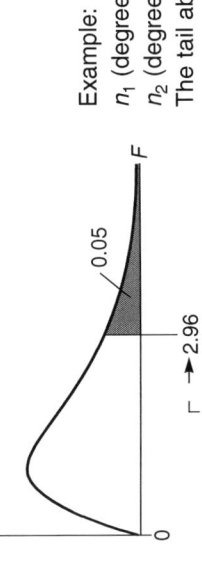

Example:
$n_1$ (degrees of freedom for numerator of F ratio) = 5,
$n_2$ (degrees of freedom for denominator) = 14:
The tail above $F = 2.96$ represents 0.05 or 5% of the area under the curve.

| $n_2$\$n_1$ | 1 | 2 | 3 | 4 | 5 | 6 | 7 | 8 | 9 | 10 | 12 | 15 | 20 | 24 | 30 | 40 | 60 | 120 | ∞ |
|---|---|---|---|---|---|---|---|---|---|---|---|---|---|---|---|---|---|---|---|
| 1 | 161.4 | 199.5 | 215.7 | 224.6 | 230.2 | 234.0 | 236.8 | 238.9 | 240.5 | 241.9 | 243.9 | 245.9 | 248.0 | 249.1 | 250.1 | 251.1 | 252.2 | 253.3 | 243.3 |
| 2 | 18.51 | 19.00 | 19.16 | 19.25 | 19.30 | 19.33 | 19.35 | 19.37 | 19.38 | 19.40 | 19.41 | 19.43 | 19.45 | 19.45 | 19.46 | 19.47 | 19.48 | 19.49 | 19.50 |
| 3 | 10.13 | 9.55 | 9.28 | 9.12 | 9.01 | 8.94 | 8.89 | 8.85 | 8.81 | 8.79 | 8.74 | 8.70 | 8.66 | 8.64 | 8.62 | 8.59 | 8.57 | 8.55 | 8.53 |
| 4 | 7.71 | 6.94 | 6.59 | 6.39 | 6.26 | 6.16 | 6.09 | 6.04 | 6.00 | 5.96 | 5.91 | 5.86 | 5.80 | 5.77 | 5.75 | 5.72 | 5.69 | 5.66 | 5.63 |
| 5 | 6.61 | 5.79 | 5.41 | 5.19 | 5.05 | 4.95 | 4.88 | 4.82 | 4.77 | 4.74 | 4.68 | 4.62 | 4.56 | 4.53 | 4.50 | 4.46 | 4.43 | 4.40 | 4.36 |
| 6 | 5.99 | 5.14 | 4.76 | 4.53 | 4.39 | 4.28 | 4.21 | 4.15 | 4.10 | 4.06 | 4.00 | 3.94 | 3.87 | 3.84 | 3.81 | 3.77 | 3.74 | 3.70 | 3.67 |
| 7 | 5.59 | 4.74 | 4.35 | 4.12 | 3.97 | 3.87 | 3.79 | 3.73 | 3.68 | 3.64 | 3.57 | 3.51 | 3.44 | 3.41 | 3.38 | 3.34 | 3.30 | 3.27 | 3.23 |
| 8 | 5.32 | 4.46 | 4.07 | 3.84 | 3.69 | 3.58 | 3.50 | 3.44 | 3.39 | 3.35 | 3.28 | 3.22 | 3.15 | 3.12 | 3.08 | 3.04 | 3.01 | 2.97 | 2.93 |
| 9 | 5.12 | 4.26 | 3.86 | 3.63 | 3.48 | 3.37 | 3.29 | 3.23 | 3.18 | 3.14 | 3.07 | 3.01 | 2.94 | 2.90 | 2.86 | 2.83 | 2.79 | 2.75 | 2.71 |
| 10 | 4.96 | 4.10 | 3.71 | 3.48 | 3.33 | 3.22 | 3.14 | 3.07 | 3.02 | 2.98 | 2.91 | 2.85 | 2.77 | 2.74 | 2.70 | 2.66 | 2.62 | 2.58 | 2.54 |
| 11 | 4.84 | 3.98 | 3.59 | 3.36 | 3.20 | 3.09 | 3.01 | 2.95 | 2.90 | 2.85 | 2.79 | 2.72 | 2.65 | 2.61 | 2.57 | 2.53 | 2.49 | 2.45 | 2.40 |
| 12 | 4.75 | 3.89 | 3.49 | 3.26 | 3.11 | 3.00 | 2.91 | 2.85 | 2.80 | 2.75 | 2.69 | 2.62 | 2.54 | 2.51 | 2.47 | 2.43 | 2.38 | 2.34 | 2.30 |
| 13 | 4.67 | 3.81 | 3.41 | 3.18 | 3.03 | 2.92 | 2.83 | 2.77 | 2.71 | 2.67 | 2.60 | 2.53 | 2.46 | 2.42 | 2.38 | 2.34 | 2.30 | 2.25 | 2.21 |
| 14 | 4.60 | 3.74 | 3.34 | 3.11 | 2.96 | 2.85 | 2.76 | 2.70 | 2.65 | 2.60 | 2.53 | 2.46 | 2.39 | 2.35 | 2.31 | 2.27 | 2.22 | 2.18 | 2.13 |
| 15 | 4.54 | 3.68 | 3.29 | 3.06 | 2.90 | 2.79 | 2.71 | 2.64 | 2.59 | 2.54 | 2.48 | 2.40 | 2.33 | 2.29 | 2.25 | 2.20 | 2.16 | 2.11 | 2.07 |
| 16 | 4.49 | 3.63 | 3.24 | 3.01 | 2.85 | 2.74 | 2.66 | 2.59 | 2.54 | 2.49 | 2.42 | 2.35 | 2.28 | 2.24 | 2.19 | 2.15 | 2.11 | 2.06 | 2.01 |
| 17 | 4.45 | 3.59 | 3.20 | 2.96 | 2.81 | 2.70 | 2.61 | 2.55 | 2.49 | 2.45 | 2.38 | 2.31 | 2.23 | 2.19 | 2.15 | 2.10 | 2.06 | 2.01 | 1.96 |
| 18 | 4.41 | 3.55 | 3.16 | 2.93 | 2.77 | 2.66 | 2.58 | 2.51 | 2.46 | 2.41 | 2.34 | 2.27 | 2.19 | 2.15 | 2.11 | 2.06 | 2.02 | 1.97 | 1.92 |
| 19 | 4.38 | 3.52 | 3.13 | 2.90 | 2.74 | 2.63 | 2.54 | 2.48 | 2.42 | 2.38 | 2.31 | 2.23 | 2.16 | 2.11 | 2.07 | 2.03 | 1.98 | 1.93 | 1.88 |
| 20 | 4.35 | 3.49 | 3.10 | 2.87 | 2.71 | 2.60 | 2.51 | 2.45 | 2.39 | 2.35 | 2.28 | 2.20 | 2.12 | 2.08 | 2.04 | 1.99 | 1.95 | 1.90 | 1.84 |
| 21 | 4.32 | 3.47 | 3.07 | 2.84 | 2.68 | 2.57 | 2.49 | 2.42 | 2.37 | 2.32 | 2.25 | 2.18 | 2.10 | 2.05 | 2.01 | 1.96 | 1.92 | 1.87 | 1.81 |
| 22 | 4.30 | 3.44 | 3.05 | 2.82 | 2.66 | 2.55 | 2.46 | 2.40 | 2.34 | 2.30 | 2.23 | 2.15 | 2.07 | 2.03 | 1.98 | 1.94 | 1.89 | 1.84 | 1.78 |
| 23 | 4.28 | 3.42 | 3.03 | 2.80 | 2.64 | 2.53 | 2.44 | 2.37 | 2.32 | 2.27 | 2.20 | 2.13 | 2.05 | 2.01 | 1.96 | 1.91 | 1.86 | 1.81 | 1.76 |
| 24 | 4.26 | 3.40 | 3.01 | 2.78 | 2.62 | 2.51 | 2.42 | 2.36 | 2.30 | 2.25 | 2.18 | 2.11 | 2.03 | 1.98 | 1.94 | 1.89 | 1.84 | 1.79 | 1.73 |
| 25 | 4.24 | 3.39 | 2.99 | 2.76 | 2.60 | 2.49 | 2.40 | 2.34 | 2.28 | 2.24 | 2.16 | 2.09 | 2.01 | 1.96 | 1.92 | 1.87 | 1.82 | 1.77 | 1.71 |
| 26 | 4.23 | 3.37 | 2.98 | 2.74 | 2.59 | 2.47 | 2.39 | 2.32 | 2.27 | 2.22 | 2.15 | 2.07 | 1.99 | 1.95 | 1.90 | 1.85 | 1.80 | 1.75 | 1.69 |
| 27 | 4.21 | 3.35 | 2.96 | 2.73 | 2.57 | 2.46 | 2.37 | 2.31 | 2.25 | 2.20 | 2.13 | 2.06 | 1.97 | 1.93 | 1.88 | 1.84 | 1.79 | 1.73 | 1.67 |
| 28 | 4.20 | 3.34 | 2.95 | 2.71 | 2.56 | 2.45 | 2.36 | 2.29 | 2.24 | 2.19 | 2.12 | 2.04 | 1.96 | 1.91 | 1.87 | 1.82 | 1.77 | 1.71 | 1.65 |
| 29 | 4.18 | 3.33 | 2.93 | 2.70 | 2.55 | 2.43 | 2.35 | 2.28 | 2.22 | 2.18 | 2.10 | 2.03 | 1.94 | 1.90 | 1.85 | 1.81 | 1.75 | 1.70 | 1.64 |
| 30 | 4.17 | 3.32 | 2.92 | 2.69 | 2.53 | 2.42 | 2.33 | 2.27 | 2.21 | 2.16 | 2.09 | 2.01 | 1.93 | 1.89 | 1.84 | 1.79 | 1.74 | 1.68 | 1.62 |
| 40 | 4.08 | 3.23 | 2.84 | 2.61 | 2.45 | 2.34 | 2.25 | 2.18 | 2.12 | 2.08 | 2.00 | 1.92 | 1.84 | 1.79 | 1.74 | 1.69 | 1.64 | 1.58 | 1.51 |
| 60 | 4.00 | 3.15 | 2.76 | 2.53 | 2.37 | 2.25 | 2.17 | 2.10 | 2.04 | 1.99 | 1.92 | 1.84 | 1.75 | 1.70 | 1.65 | 1.59 | 1.53 | 1.47 | 1.39 |
| 120 | 3.92 | 3.07 | 2.68 | 2.45 | 2.29 | 2.17 | 2.09 | 2.02 | 1.96 | 1.91 | 1.83 | 1.75 | 1.66 | 1.61 | 1.55 | 1.50 | 1.43 | 1.35 | 1.25 |
| ∞ | 3.84 | 3.00 | 2.60 | 2.37 | 2.21 | 2.10 | 2.01 | 1.94 | 1.88 | 1.83 | 1.75 | 1.67 | 1.57 | 1.52 | 1.46 | 1.39 | 1.32 | 1.22 | 1.00 |

**Source:** Abridged from table 18 of the *Biometrika Tables for Statisticians*, Vol. 1, 1st edition, edited by E. S. Pearson and H. O. Hartley, 1954. Cambridge, UK: Cambridge University Press, for the Biometrika Trustees.

(b) Upper 1% probability

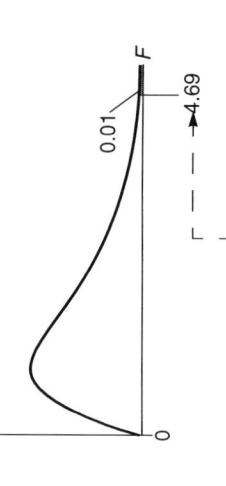

**Example:**
$n_1$ (degrees of freedom for numerator of F ratio) = 5,
$n_2$ (degrees of freedom for denominator) = 14:
The tail above $F = 4.69$ represents 0.01 or 1% of the area under the curve.

| $n_2$ \ $n_1$ | 1 | 2 | 3 | 4 | 5 | 6 | 7 | 8 | 9 | 10 | 12 | 15 | 20 | 24 | 30 | 40 | 60 | 120 | ∞ |
|---|---|---|---|---|---|---|---|---|---|---|---|---|---|---|---|---|---|---|---|
| 1 | 4052 | 4999.5 | 5403 | 5625 | 5764 | 5859 | 5928 | 5982 | 6022 | 6056 | 6106 | 6157 | 6209 | 6235 | 6261 | 6287 | 6313 | 6339 | 6366 |
| 2 | 98.50 | 99.00 | 99.17 | 99.25 | 99.30 | 99.33 | 99.36 | 99.37 | 99.39 | 99.40 | 99.42 | 99.43 | 99.45 | 99.46 | 99.47 | 99.47 | 99.48 | 99.49 | 99.50 |
| 3 | 34.12 | 30.82 | 29.46 | 28.71 | 28.24 | 27.91 | 27.67 | 27.49 | 27.35 | 27.23 | 27.05 | 26.87 | 26.69 | 26.60 | 26.50 | 26.41 | 26.32 | 26.22 | 26.13 |
| 4 | 21.20 | 18.00 | 16.69 | 15.98 | 15.52 | 15.21 | 14.98 | 14.80 | 14.66 | 14.55 | 14.37 | 14.20 | 14.02 | 13.93 | 13.84 | 13.75 | 13.65 | 13.56 | 13.46 |
| 5 | 16.26 | 13.27 | 12.06 | 11.39 | 10.97 | 10.67 | 10.46 | 10.29 | 10.16 | 10.05 | 9.89 | 9.72 | 9.55 | 9.47 | 9.38 | 9.29 | 9.20 | 9.11 | 9.02 |
| 6 | 13.75 | 10.92 | 9.78 | 9.15 | 8.75 | 8.47 | 8.26 | 8.10 | 7.98 | 7.87 | 7.72 | 7.56 | 7.40 | 7.31 | 7.23 | 7.14 | 7.06 | 6.97 | 6.88 |
| 7 | 12.25 | 9.55 | 8.45 | 7.85 | 7.46 | 7.19 | 6.99 | 6.84 | 6.72 | 6.62 | 6.47 | 6.31 | 6.16 | 6.07 | 5.99 | 5.91 | 5.82 | 5.74 | 5.65 |
| 8 | 11.26 | 8.65 | 7.59 | 7.01 | 6.63 | 6.37 | 6.18 | 6.03 | 5.91 | 5.81 | 5.67 | 5.52 | 5.36 | 5.28 | 5.20 | 5.12 | 5.03 | 4.95 | 4.86 |
| 9 | 10.56 | 8.02 | 6.99 | 6.42 | 6.06 | 5.80 | 5.61 | 5.47 | 5.35 | 5.26 | 5.11 | 4.96 | 4.81 | 4.73 | 4.65 | 4.57 | 4.48 | 4.40 | 4.31 |
| 10 | 10.04 | 7.56 | 6.55 | 5.99 | 5.64 | 5.39 | 5.20 | 5.06 | 4.94 | 4.85 | 4.71 | 4.56 | 4.41 | 4.33 | 4.25 | 4.17 | 4.08 | 4.00 | 3.91 |
| 11 | 9.65 | 7.21 | 6.22 | 5.67 | 5.32 | 5.07 | 4.89 | 4.74 | 4.63 | 4.54 | 4.40 | 4.25 | 4.10 | 4.02 | 3.94 | 3.86 | 3.78 | 3.69 | 3.60 |
| 12 | 9.33 | 6.93 | 5.95 | 5.41 | 5.06 | 4.82 | 4.64 | 4.50 | 4.39 | 4.30 | 4.16 | 4.01 | 3.86 | 3.78 | 3.70 | 3.62 | 3.54 | 3.45 | 3.36 |
| 13 | 9.07 | 6.70 | 5.74 | 5.21 | 4.86 | 4.62 | 4.44 | 4.30 | 4.19 | 4.10 | 3.96 | 3.82 | 3.66 | 3.59 | 3.51 | 3.43 | 3.34 | 3.25 | 3.17 |
| 14 | 8.86 | 6.51 | 5.56 | 5.04 | 4.69 | 4.46 | 4.28 | 4.14 | 4.03 | 3.94 | 3.80 | 3.66 | 3.51 | 3.43 | 3.35 | 3.27 | 3.18 | 3.09 | 3.00 |
| 15 | 8.68 | 6.36 | 5.42 | 4.89 | 4.56 | 4.32 | 4.14 | 4.00 | 3.89 | 3.80 | 3.67 | 3.52 | 3.37 | 3.29 | 3.21 | 3.13 | 3.05 | 2.96 | 2.87 |
| 16 | 8.53 | 6.23 | 5.29 | 4.77 | 4.44 | 4.20 | 4.03 | 3.89 | 3.78 | 3.69 | 3.55 | 3.41 | 3.26 | 3.18 | 3.10 | 3.02 | 2.93 | 2.84 | 2.75 |
| 17 | 8.40 | 6.11 | 5.18 | 4.67 | 4.34 | 4.10 | 3.93 | 3.79 | 3.68 | 3.59 | 3.46 | 3.31 | 3.16 | 3.08 | 3.00 | 2.92 | 2.83 | 2.75 | 2.65 |
| 18 | 8.29 | 6.01 | 5.09 | 4.58 | 4.25 | 4.01 | 3.84 | 3.71 | 3.60 | 3.51 | 3.37 | 3.23 | 3.08 | 3.00 | 2.92 | 2.84 | 2.75 | 2.66 | 2.57 |
| 19 | 8.18 | 5.93 | 5.01 | 4.50 | 4.17 | 3.94 | 3.77 | 3.63 | 3.52 | 3.43 | 3.30 | 3.15 | 3.00 | 2.92 | 2.84 | 2.76 | 2.67 | 2.58 | 2.49 |
| 20 | 8.10 | 5.85 | 4.94 | 4.43 | 4.10 | 3.87 | 3.70 | 3.56 | 3.46 | 3.37 | 3.23 | 3.09 | 2.94 | 2.86 | 2.78 | 2.69 | 2.61 | 2.52 | 2.42 |
| 21 | 8.02 | 5.78 | 4.87 | 4.37 | 4.04 | 3.81 | 3.64 | 3.51 | 3.40 | 3.31 | 3.17 | 3.03 | 2.88 | 2.80 | 2.72 | 2.64 | 2.55 | 2.46 | 2.36 |
| 22 | 7.95 | 5.72 | 4.82 | 4.31 | 3.99 | 3.76 | 3.59 | 3.45 | 3.35 | 3.26 | 3.12 | 2.98 | 2.83 | 2.75 | 2.67 | 2.58 | 2.50 | 2.40 | 2.31 |
| 23 | 7.88 | 5.66 | 4.76 | 4.26 | 3.94 | 3.71 | 3.54 | 3.41 | 3.30 | 3.21 | 3.07 | 2.93 | 2.78 | 2.70 | 2.62 | 2.54 | 2.45 | 2.35 | 2.26 |
| 24 | 7.82 | 5.61 | 4.72 | 4.22 | 3.90 | 3.67 | 3.50 | 3.36 | 3.26 | 3.17 | 3.03 | 2.89 | 2.74 | 2.66 | 2.58 | 2.49 | 2.40 | 2.31 | 2.21 |
| 25 | 7.77 | 5.57 | 4.68 | 4.18 | 3.85 | 3.63 | 3.46 | 3.32 | 3.22 | 3.13 | 2.99 | 2.85 | 2.70 | 2.62 | 2.54 | 2.45 | 2.36 | 2.27 | 2.17 |
| 26 | 7.72 | 5.53 | 4.64 | 4.14 | 3.82 | 3.59 | 3.42 | 3.29 | 3.18 | 3.09 | 2.96 | 2.81 | 2.66 | 2.58 | 2.50 | 2.42 | 2.33 | 2.23 | 2.13 |
| 27 | 7.68 | 5.49 | 4.60 | 4.11 | 3.78 | 3.56 | 3.39 | 3.26 | 3.15 | 3.06 | 2.93 | 2.78 | 2.63 | 2.55 | 2.47 | 2.38 | 2.29 | 2.20 | 2.10 |
| 28 | 7.64 | 5.45 | 4.57 | 4.07 | 3.75 | 3.53 | 3.36 | 3.23 | 3.12 | 3.03 | 2.90 | 2.75 | 2.60 | 2.52 | 2.44 | 2.35 | 2.26 | 2.17 | 2.06 |
| 29 | 7.60 | 5.42 | 4.54 | 4.04 | 3.73 | 3.50 | 3.33 | 3.20 | 3.09 | 3.00 | 2.87 | 2.73 | 2.57 | 2.49 | 2.41 | 2.33 | 2.23 | 2.14 | 2.03 |
| 30 | 7.56 | 5.39 | 4.51 | 4.02 | 3.70 | 3.47 | 3.30 | 3.17 | 3.07 | 2.98 | 2.84 | 2.70 | 2.55 | 2.47 | 2.39 | 2.30 | 2.21 | 2.11 | 2.01 |
| 40 | 7.31 | 5.18 | 4.31 | 3.83 | 3.51 | 3.29 | 3.12 | 2.99 | 2.89 | 2.80 | 2.66 | 2.52 | 2.37 | 2.29 | 2.20 | 2.11 | 2.02 | 1.92 | 1.80 |
| 60 | 7.08 | 4.98 | 4.13 | 3.65 | 3.34 | 3.12 | 2.95 | 2.82 | 2.72 | 2.63 | 2.50 | 2.35 | 2.20 | 2.12 | 2.03 | 1.94 | 1.84 | 1.73 | 1.60 |
| 120 | 6.85 | 4.79 | 3.95 | 3.48 | 3.17 | 2.96 | 2.79 | 2.66 | 2.56 | 2.47 | 2.34 | 2.19 | 2.03 | 1.95 | 1.86 | 1.76 | 1.66 | 1.53 | 1.38 |
| ∞ | 6.63 | 4.61 | 3.78 | 3.32 | 3.02 | 2.80 | 2.64 | 2.51 | 2.41 | 2.32 | 2.18 | 2.04 | 1.88 | 1.79 | 1.70 | 1.59 | 1.47 | 1.32 | 1.00 |

**Source:** Abridged from table 18 of the *Biometrika Tables for Statisticians*, Vol. 1, 1st edition, edited by E. S. Pearson and H. O. Hartley, 1954. Cambridge, UK: Cambridge University Press, for the Biometrika Trustees.

# GLOSSARY

**alpha (α):** the probability of making a Type I error

**alternate hypothesis:** an educated conjecture that sets the parameters one expects to find. The alternate hypothesis is 'tested' by determining whether the null hypothesis is to be accepted or rejected.

**ambiguous questions:** questions that are not clearly worded and likely to be interpreted by respondents in different ways

**analysis of variance (ANOVA):** tests for significant mean differences in variables among multiple groups

**analytical study:** a study that tries to explain why or how certain variables influence the dependent variable of interest to the researcher

**applied research:** research conducted in a particular setting with the specific objective of solving an existing problem in the situation

**area sampling:** cluster sampling within a specified area or region; a probability sampling design

**attitudinal factors:** people's feelings, dispositions and reactions towards the organisation, its products and services, and the wider environment

**axial coding:** the second pass through the raw qualitative data, when the researcher reviews and examines the initial coding (see open coding)

**basic research:** research conducted to generate knowledge and understanding of phenomena (in the work setting) that would add to the existing body of knowledge about organisations and management theory

**behavioural factors:** people's actual responses to a situation — e.g. the actual behaviour of employees on the job, such as being late, working hard, remaining absent or quitting work

**beta (β):** the probability of making a Type II error

**bias:** any error that creeps into the data. Biases can be introduced, for example, by the researcher, the respondent, the measuring instrument or the sample.

**bibliography:** a listing of books, articles and other relevant materials, alphabetised according to the last name of the authors, referencing the titles of their works and indicating where they can be located

**broad problem area:** a situation in which one senses a possible need for research and problem solving, even though the specific problem is not clear

**browser:** software that facilitates viewing and navigating through Web applications

**case:** the term given in SPSS to a particular respondent to a questionnaire or interview (also called observation)

**case study:** a comprehensive description and analysis of a single situation or case — e.g. a detailed study of an individual, group or organisation

**category scale:** a scale that uses multiple items to seek a single response

**causal analysis:** analysis done to detect cause and effect relationship between two or more variables

**causal study:** a research study conducted to establish cause and effect relationships among variables

**chi-square test:** a non-parametric test that establishes the independence or otherwise between two nominal variables

**clarification investigation:** a research study conducted to gain a clearer understanding of the concepts involved in the research problem

**classification data:** personal information or demographic details of the respondents such as age, marital status and educational level

**closed questions**: questions with a clearly delineated set of alternatives that confine the respondents' choice to one of them

**cluster sampling**: a probability sampling design in which the sample comprises groups or chunks of elements with intra-group heterogeneity and intergroup homogeneity

**comparative scale**: a scale that provides a benchmark or point of reference to assess attitudes, opinions and the like

**comparative study**: a study conducted by collecting data from several settings or organisations

**complex probability sampling**: several probability sampling designs (such as systematic and stratified random), which offer more efficient or effective alternatives to the simple random sampling design

**computer-assisted telephone interviews (CATI)**: interviews in which questions are prompted on a PC monitor that is networked into the telephone system, to which respondents provide their answers

**conceptual framework**: a model or structure of understanding based on concepts

**concurrent validity**: relates to criterion-related validity, which is established at the same time the test is administered

**confidence**: the probability estimate of how much reliance can be placed on the findings; the usual accepted level of confidence in social science research is 95 per cent

**consensus scale**: a scale developed through consensus or the unanimous agreement of a panel of judges, as to the items that measure a concept

**consequentialist view**: focuses on what is good or bad by concentrating on the consequences of the actions

**constant comparative analysis**: the process of separating themes in qualitative data

**constant sum rating scale**: a scale by which the respondents distribute a fixed number of points across several items

**construct**: an abstract representation of a phenomenon, used for special theoretical purposes

**construct validity**: testifies to how well the results obtained from the use of the measure fit the theories around which the test was designed

**content analysis**: the process of identifying, coding and categorising the primary patterns in qualitative data

**content validity**: establishes the representative sampling of a set of items that measures a concept, and reflects how well the dimensions and elements thereof are delineated

**contextual factors**: factors relating to the organisation under study such as the background and environment of the organisation, including its origin and purpose, size, resources, financial standing and the like

**contrived setting**: an artificially created or 'lab' environment in which research is conducted

**control group**: the group that is not exposed to any treatment in an experiment

**controlled variable**: any exogenous or extraneous variable that could contaminate the cause and effect relationship, but the effects of which can be controlled through the process of either matching or randomisation

**convenience sampling**: a non-probability sampling design in which information or data for the research are gathered from members of the population who are conveniently accessible to the researcher

**convergent validity**: that which is established when the scores obtained by two different instruments measuring the same concept, or by measuring the concept by two different methods, are highly correlated

**corporate accountability:** ethical responsibility to the sponsor or client of the research project

**correlational analysis:** analysis undertaken to assess the level of association (or co-variation) between variables

**correlation coefficient:** a number between −1 and +1 that reflects the level of association between two (or more) variables

**correlational study:** a research study conducted to identify the important factors associated with the variables of interest

**criterion-related validity:** that which is established when the measure differentiates individuals on a criterion that it is expected to predict

**criterion variable:** the variable of primary interest to the study; also known as the dependent variable

**Cronbach's alpha:** the most popular test of inter-item (internal) consistency reliability, used for multi-point scaled items; the coefficient ranges from 0 to 1.0, with a higher value indicating a better measuring instrument.

**cross-cultural research:** studies done across two or more cultures to understand, describe, analyse or predict phenomena

**cross-sectional study:** research for which data are gathered just once (stretched though it may be over a period of days, weeks or months) to answer the research question

**data editing:** the process of going over the data and ensuring that they are complete and acceptable for data analysis

**data index:** a list of abbreviations and a brief description of the conceptual themes identified in qualitative raw data

**data mining:** helps to trace patterns and relationships in the data stored in the data warehouse

**data warehouse:** a central repository of all information gathered by the company

**deduction:** the process of arriving at conclusions based on the interpretation of the meaning of the results of data analysis

**degrees of freedom ($df$):** equal to the number of observations (cases) less the number of constraints or assumptions needed to calculate a statistical term

**deontological view:** asserts that the end cannot justify the means and proposes absolute moral strictness that can never be violated

**dependent variable:** *see* criterion variable

**descriptive statistics:** statistics such as frequencies, the mean and the standard deviation, which provide descriptive information of a set of data

**descriptive study:** a research study that describes the variables in a situation of interest to the researcher

**dichotomous scale:** scale used to elicit a Yes/No response, or an answer to two different aspects of a concept

**directional hypothesis:** an educated conjecture as to the direction of the relationship, or differences among variables, which could be positive or negative, or more or less, respectively

**discriminant validity:** that which is established when two variables are theorised to be uncorrelated, and the scores obtained by measuring them are indeed empirically found to be so

**disproportionate stratified random sampling:** a probability sampling design that involves a procedure in which the number of sample subjects chosen from various strata is not directly proportionate to the total number of elements in the respective strata

**double-barrelled question:** refers to the improper framing of a question that should be posed as two or more separate questions, so that the respondent can give clear and unambiguous answers

**double-blind study:** a study in which neither the experimenter nor the subjects are aware of who is given the real treatment and who the placebo (i.e. the control group)

**double sampling:** a probability sampling design that involves the process of collecting information from a set of subjects twice — such as using a sample to collect preliminary information, and later using a subsample of the primary sample for more information

**dynamic panel:** consists of a changing composition of members in a group who serve as the sample subjects for a research study conducted over an extended period of time

**efficiency in sampling:** attained when the sampling design chosen either results in a cost reduction to the researcher or offers a greater degree of accuracy in terms of the sample size

**electronic mail (e-mail):** the most useful Internet service, which allows one to send and receive messages electronically from all over the world

**electronic questionnaire:** on-line questionnaire administered when the microcomputer is hooked up to computer networks

**element:** a single member of the population

**ethics:** code of conduct or expected societal norms of behaviour

**exogenous variable:** a variable not subject to control that exerts an influence on the cause and effect relationship between two variables in some way

**experimental design:** a study design in which the researcher might create an artificial setting, control some variables, and manipulate the independent variable to establish cause and effect relationships

**experimental group:** the group exposed to a treatment in an experimental design

**expert system:** an inference engine that uses stored knowledge and rules of IF–THEN relationships to solve problems

**exploratory study:** a research study in which very little knowledge or information is available on the subject under investigation

**ex post facto design:** studying subjects who have already been exposed to a stimulus and comparing them with those not so exposed, so as to establish cause and effect relationships (in contrast to establishing cause and effect relationships by manipulating an independent variable in a lab or a field setting)

**external consultants:** research experts outside the organisation who are hired to study specific problems and to find solutions

**external validity:** the extent of generalisability of the results of a causal study to other field settings

**$F$ test:** a statistical test, based on the analysis of variances, that is used to test for differences in the means between sample groups

**faces scale:** a particular representation of the graphic scale, depicting faces with expressions that range from smiling to sad

**face-to-face interview:** information gathering when the interviewer and interviewee meet in person

**face validity:** an aspect of validity examining whether the item on the scale, on the face of it, reads as if it indeed measures what it is supposed to measure

**factor analysis:** a statistical technique used for reducing a large number of variables to a meaningful, interpretable and manageable set of factors; also used to examine construct validity

**factorial validity:** that which indicates, through the use of factor-analytic techniques, whether a test is a pure measure of some specific factor or dimension

**field experiment:** an experiment to detect cause and effect relationships in the natural environment in which events normally occur

**field study:** a study conducted in the natural setting, with a minimal amount of researcher interference with the flow of events in the situation

**fixed rating scale:** *see* constant sum rating scale

**focus group:** a group consisting of about 8 to 10 randomly chosen members who discuss a product or any given topic for about two hours with a moderator present, so that their opinions can serve as the basis for further research

**forced choice:** elicits the ranking of objects relative to one another

**frequencies:** the number of times various subcategories of a phenomenon occur, from which the percentage and cumulative percentage of any occurrence can be calculated

**fundamental research:** *see* basic research

**funnel sequence:** the questioning technique that consists of initially asking general and broad questions, and gradually narrowing the focus thereafter to more specific themes

**generalisability:** the applicability of research findings in one setting to others

**goodness of measures:** attests to the reliability and validity of measures

**graphic rating scale:** a scale that graphically illustrates the responses that can be provided, rather than specifying any discrete response categories

**group video-conferencing:** video transmittal technology that enables remote groups of people to participate in a conference using video cameras and monitors

**history effects:** a threat to the internal validity of the experimental results, when factors unexpectedly occur while the experiment is in progress and contaminate the cause and effect relationship

**human-as-an-instrument:** in qualitative research, the researcher intervenes through speech and actions to understand the 'web of meaning' the respondent attributes to the phenomena under investigation

**hypothesis:** an educated conjecture about the logically developed relationship between two or more variables, expressed in the form of testable statements

**hypothesis testing:** a means of testing if the IF–THEN statements generated from the theoretical framework hold true when subjected to rigorous examination

**hypothesis-testing method of research:** a seven-step process of observing, preliminary data gathering, theorising, hypothesising, collecting further data, analysing data and interpreting the results to arrive at conclusions

**independent variable:** a variable that influences the dependent or criterion variable and accounts for (or explains) some of its variance

**induction:** the process by which general propositions based on observed facts are established

**indwelling:** in qualitative research, being at one with the respondent by understanding the respondent's point of view from an empathic rather than a sympathetic position

**inferential statistics:** statistics that help to establish relationships among variables and draw conclusions from them

**information system:** the system that acquires, stores and retrieves all relevant information for a specific group of functions (e.g. manufacturing information system)

**inkblot tests:** a motivational research technique that uses coloured patterns of inkblots to be interpreted by the subjects

**instrumentation effects:** the threat to internal validity in experimental designs caused by changes in the measuring instrument between the pre-test and the post-test

**inter-item consistency reliability:** a test of the consistency of responses to all the items in a measure to establish that they hang together as a set

**internal consistency:** homogeneity of the items in the measure that tap a construct

**internal consultants:** research experts within the organisation who investigate and find solutions to problems

**internal validity of experiments:** attests to the confidence that can be placed in the cause and effect relationship found in experimental designs

**Internet:** a vast network of computers and communication systems connecting people and information worldwide

**interquartile range:** the measure of dispersion for the median; the difference between the upper and lower quartile values

**inter-rater reliability:** the consistency of the judgement of several raters on how they see a phenomenon or interpret the activities in a situation

**interval scale:** a multipoint scale that taps the differences, the order and the equality of the magnitude of the differences in the responses

**intervening variable:** a variable that surfaces as a function of the independent variable, and helps in conceptualising and explaining the influence of the independent variable on the dependent variable

**interviewing:** a data collection method in which the researcher asks for information verbally from the respondents

**intranet:** a computer network that connects people and resources within the organisation

**in vivo:** using a term drawn directly from the qualitative raw data to name a conceptual theme

**itemised rating scale:** a scale that offers several categories of responses, out of which the respondent picks the one most relevant for answering the question

**judgement sampling:** a purposive, non-probability sampling design in which the sample subject is chosen on the basis of the individual's ability to provide the type of special information needed by the researcher

**lab experiment:** an experimental design set up in an artificially contrived setting where controls and manipulations are introduced to establish cause and effect relationships among variables of interest to the researcher

**latent content:** the symbolism underlying the physically present data (*see* manifest content)

**leading questions:** questions phrased in such a manner as to lead the respondent to give the answers that the researcher would like to obtain

**Likert scale:** an interval scale that specifically uses five anchors such as Strongly disagree, Disagree, Neither disagree nor agree, Agree and Strongly agree

**literature review:** the documentation of a comprehensive review of the published work from secondary sources of data in the areas of specific interest to the researcher

**literature survey:** *see* literature review

**loaded questions:** questions that would elicit highly biased emotional responses from subjects

**longitudinal study:** a research study for which data are gathered at several points in time to answer a research question

**management information system (MIS):** a generic term for information within an enterprise, facilitated by software and technology

**manifest content:** the data that is physically present and accountable in the qualitative data (*see* latent content)

**manipulation:** the researcher exposes the subjects to the independent variable to determine cause and effect relationships in experimental designs

**matching:** a method of controlling known contaminating factors in experimental studies by deliberately spreading them equally across the experimental and control groups so as not to confound the cause and effect relationship

**maturation effects:** a threat to internal validity that is a function of the biological, psychological and other processes taking place in the respondents as a result of the passage of time

**mean:** the average of a set of figures

**measure of central tendency:** descriptive statistics of a data set such as the mean, median or mode

**measure of dispersion:** the variability in a set of observations, represented by the range, variance, standard deviation and the interquartile range

**median:** the central item in a group of observations arranged in ascending or descending order

**mode:** the most frequently occurring number in a data set

**moderating variable:** a variable on which the relationship between two other variables is contingent — that is, if the moderating variable is present, the theorised relationship between the two variables will hold good, but not otherwise

**moral accountability:** ethical responsibility to the subjects in the research project

**mortality:** the loss of research subjects during the course of the experiment, which confounds the cause and effect relationship

**motivational research:** a particular data gathering technique directed towards uncovering information, ideas and thoughts either that are not easily verbalised, or that remain at the unconscious level in the respondents

**multiple regression analysis:** *see* regression analysis

**multistage cluster sampling:** a probability sampling design that is a stratified sampling of clusters

**nominal scale:** a scale that categorises individuals or objects into mutually exclusive and collectively exhaustive groups, and offers basic, categorical information on the variable of interest

**non-contrived setting:** research conducted in the natural environment where activities take place in the normal manner (i.e. the field setting)

**non-directional hypothesis:** an educated conjecture of a relationship between two variables, the directionality of which cannot be guessed

**non-parametric statistics:** statistics used to test hypotheses when the population from which the sample is drawn cannot be assumed to be normally distributed

**nonparticipant observer:** a researcher who collects observational data without becoming an integral part of the system

**nuisance variable:** a variable that contaminates the cause and effect relationship

**null hypothesis:** the conjecture that postulates no differences or no relationship between or among variables

**numerical scale:** a scale with bipolar attributes, with usually five or seven points indicated on the scale

**NVivo program:** a computer program that helps the researcher analyse qualitative data

**objectivity:** interpretation on the basis of the results of data analysis, as opposed to subjective or emotional interpretations

**observational study:** collection of data by observing people or events in the work environment and recording the information

**observations:** perceptions of reality can be expressed in the form of 'facts' or 'opinions'

**one-shot study:** *see* cross-sectional study

**open coding:** the first pass through the raw qualitative data, when the researcher locates conceptual themes

**open questions:** questions that the respondent can answer in a free-flowing format without restricting the range of choices to a set of specific alternatives suggested by the researcher

**operational definition:** definition of a construct in measurable terms by reducing it from its level of abstraction through the delineation of its dimensions and elements

**ordinal scale:** a scale that not only categorises the qualitative differences in the variable of interest, but also allows for the rank-ordering of these categories in a meaningful way

***p*-value:** the probability or chance that the null hypothesis is true

**paired comparisons:** respondents choose between two objects at a time, with the process repeated with a small number of objects

**panel studies:** studies conducted over a period of time to determine the effects of certain changes made in a situation, using a panel or group of subjects as the sample base

**parallel-form reliability:** that form of reliability which is established when responses to two comparable sets of measures tapping the same construct are highly correlated

**parametric statistics:** statistics used to test hypotheses when the population from which the sample is drawn is assumed to be normally distributed

**paraphrasing:** an interviewer repeats back to the interviewee, in a concise form, the essential message of the interviewee's reply.

**parsimony:** efficient explanation of the variance in the dependent variable of interest through the use of a smaller, rather than a larger number of independent variables

**participant observer:** a researcher who collects observational data by becoming a member of the system from which data are collected

**pattern of an interview:** the structure of a well-planned interview

**perspectival view:** in qualitative research, discovering the subjective perspective of the respondent

**population:** the entire group of people, events or things that the researcher desires to investigate

**population frame:** *see* sampling frame

**post-test:** a test given to the subjects to measure the dependent variable after exposing them to a treatment

**precision:** the degree of closeness of the estimated sample characteristics to the population parameters; determined by the extent of the variability of the sampling distribution of the sample mean

**predictive study:** a study that enables the prediction of the relationships among the variables in a particular situation

**prediction validity:** the ability of the measure to differentiate among individuals as to a criterion predicted for the future

**predictor variable:** *see* independent variable

**pre-test:** a test given to the subjects to measure the dependent variable before exposing them to a treatment

**primary data:** data collected first-hand for subsequent analysis to find solutions to the problem being researched

**probability sampling:** the sampling design in which the elements of the population have some known chance or probability of being selected as sample subjects

**probing:** a questioning technique that combines the funnel sequence of questions with paraphrasing

**problem definition:** a precise, succinct statement of the question or issue that is to be investigated

**problem statement:** *see* problem defintion

**projective tests:** ways of eliciting difficult-to-obtain responses through such means as word association, sentence completion and thematic apperception tests

**proportionate stratified random sampling:** a probability sampling design in which the number of sample subjects drawn from each stratum is proportionate to the total number of elements in the respective strata

**pure research:** *see* basic research

**purposiveness in research:** the situation in which research is focused on solving a well-identified and defined problem, rather than aimlessly looking for answers to vague questions

**purposive sampling:** a non-probability sampling design in which the required information is gathered from special or specific targets or groups of people on some rational basis

**qualitative data:** data that are not immediately quantifiable unless they are coded and categorised in some way

**qualitative study:** research involving analysis of data/information that are descriptive in nature and not quantified

**questionnaire:** a preformulated written set of questions to which the respondent records the answers, usually within rather closely delineated alternatives

**quota sampling:** a form of purposive sampling in which a predetermined proportion of people from different subgroups is sampled

**R square ($R^2$):** also known as the coefficient of determination; the proportion of the total variance around the mean for the data that is explained by the regression model

**randomisation:** the process of controlling the nuisance variables by randomly assigning members among the various experimental and control groups, so that the confounding variables are randomly distributed across all groups

**range:** the extreme values in a set of observations, the difference between which indicates the spread

**ranking scale:** scale used to tap preferences between two or among more objects or items

**rapport zone:** where the interviewee will disclose information honestly and openly. It consists of six steps — ritual, pass time, reason, rules, preview and activity no. 1.

**rating scale:** scale with several response categories that evaluate an object

**ratio scale:** a scale that has an absolute zero origin, and hence indicates not only the magnitude but also the proportion of the differences

**recall-dependent questions:** questions that elicit from the respondents information that involves recall of experiences from the past that may be hazy in their memory

**referential adequacy:** commenting, describing and citing in sufficient detail so that the reader is confident that the raw data has been reported accurately and the themes extracted are valid

**regression analysis:** a statistical method that develops an equation (usually a linear model) that relates a dependent variable to one or more independent (predictor or explanatory) variables

**reliability:** the internal consistency and stability over time of the measuring instrument

**replicability:** the repeatability of similar results when identical research is conducted at different times or in different organisational settings

**representativeness of the sample:** the extent to which the sample selected possesses the same characteristics as the population from which it is drawn

**research:** an organised, systematic, critical scientific inquiry or investigation into a specific problem, undertaken with the objective of finding answers or solutions

**research objective:** the aim of the research

**research proposal:** a written report that outlines a plan for the research study, including who should conduct the research, how it should be undertaken, how long it should take and how much it will cost

**research question:** the research objective for qualitative research and quantitative research that does not involve hypothesis testing

**researcher interference:** the extent to which the person conducting the research interferes with the normal course of work at the study site

**restricted probability:** *see* complex probability sampling

**rigour:** the theoretical and methodological precision adhered to in conducting research

**sample:** a subset or subgroup of the population

**sample size:** the actual number of subjects chosen as a sample to represent the population characteristics

**sampling:** the process of selecting items from the population so that the sample characteristics can be generalised to the population. Sampling involves both design choice and sample size decisions.

**sampling frame:** a listing of all the elements in the population from which the sample is drawn

**scale:** a tool or mechanism by which individuals, events or objects are distinguished on the variables of interest in some meaningful way

**scientific investigation:** a step-by-step, logical, organised and rigorous effort to solve problems

**search engine:** software program designed to search and locate information through 'keywords', typically in documents on the World Wide Web

**secondary data:** data that have already been gathered by researchers, data published in statistical and other journals, and information available from any published or unpublished source available either within or outside the organisation, all of which might be useful to the researcher

**selection bias effects:** the threat to internal validity that is a function of improper or unmatched selection of subjects for the experimental and control groups

**selective coding:** the third reading of the raw qualitative data, when the researcher justifies the themes and also compares and contrasts the themes (*see* open and axial coding)

**semantic differential scale:** usually a seven-point scale with bipolar attributes indicated at its extremes

**significance level:** the probability of rejecting the null hypothesis when it is true; also called the critical value, and the probability of this occurring is called $\alpha$ (alpha)

**simple random sampling:** a probability sampling design in which every single element in the population has a known and equal chance of being selected as a subject

**simulation:** a model-building technique for assessing the possible effects of changes that might be introduced in a system

**snowball sampling:** a non-probability sampling method in which the respondents are selected based on information provided by the initial respondents. This method is used when it is difficult to find suitable respondents.

**social desirability:** the respondents' need to give socially or culturally acceptable responses to the questions posed by the researcher even if they are not true

**societal accountability:** ethical responsibility to professional bodies and the wider community

**Solomon four-group design:** the experimental design that sets up two experimental groups and two control groups, subjecting one experimental group and one control group to both the pre-test and the post-test, and the other experimental group and control group to only the post-test

**source code:** a unique, logical and efficient code that identifies the source of the raw data

**split-half reliability:** the correlation coefficient between one half of the items measuring a concept and the other half

**SPSS (Statistical Package for the Social Sciences):** a specialised statistical package for the analysis of numerical data

**stability of a measure:** the ability of the measure to repeat the same results over time with low vulnerability to changes in the situation

**standard deviation:** a measure of dispersion for parametric data; the square root of the variance

**standard error:** standard deviation of the sample means

**Stapel scale:** a scale that measures both the direction and the intensity of the attributes of a concept

**static panel:** a panel that consists of the same group of people serving as subjects over an extended period of time for a research study

**statistical regression:** the threat to internal validity that results when various groups in the study have been selected on the basis of their extreme (very high or very low) scores on some important variables

**stratified random sampling:** a probability sampling design that first divides the population into meaningful, non-overlapping subsets, and then randomly chooses the subjects from each subset

**structural variables:** factors related to the form and design of the organisation such as the roles and positions, communication channels, control systems, reward systems and span of control

**structured interviews:** interviews conducted by the researcher with a predetermined list of questions to be asked of the interviewee

**structured observational studies:** studies in which the researcher observes and notes down specific activities and behaviour that were clearly delineated as important factors for observation, before the commencement of the study

**subject:** a single member of the sample

**summarising:** where the interviewer restates the major ideas, facts, themes and/or feelings of the interviewer

**synopsis:** a brief summary of the research study

**systematic sampling:** a probability sampling design that involves choosing every $n$th element in the population for the sample

**telephone interview:** the information-gathering method by which the interviewer asks the interviewee over the telephone, rather than face to face, for information needed for the research

**$t$-test:** a statistical test that can be used to test the mean difference in a variable between two groups (for small sample sizes)

**test–retest reliability:** a way of establishing the stability of the measuring instrument by correlating the scores obtained through its administration to the same set of respondents at two different points in time

**testability:** the ability to subject the data collected to appropriate statistical tests in order to substantiate or reject the hypotheses developed for the research study

**testing effects:** the distorting effects on the experimental results (the post-test scores) caused by the prior sensitisation of the respondents to the instrument through the pre-test

**thematic apperception test (TAT):** a projective test that requires the respondent to develop a story around a picture

**theme coding system:** a means of reorganising the raw qualitative data according to conceptual themes recognised by the researcher

**theoretical framework:** a logically developed, described and explained network of associations among variables of interest to the research study

**treatment:** the manipulation of the independent variable in experimental designs so as to determine its effects on a dependent variable of interest to the researcher

**triangulation:** cross-checking the meaning of data. There are at least four methods — researcher to respondent, with other sources, using other data collection methods and using two researchers to analyse the data separately.

**trustworthiness:** a qualitative researcher always tries to observe, report and interpret the complex field experience as accurately and faithfully as possible.

**Type I error:** the error made when the null hypothesis is rejected when it is true

**Type 2 error:** the error made when the null hypothesis is accepted (not rejected) when it is false

**unbalanced rating scale:** an even-numbered scale that has no neutral point

**unbiased questions:** questions posed in accordance with the principles of wording and measurement, and the right questioning technique, so as to elicit the least biased responses

**unit of analysis:** the level of aggregation of the data collected during data analysis

**unobtrusive measures:** measurement of variables through data gathered from sources other than people, such as examining birth and death records or counting the number of empty bottles after a party!

**unrestricted probability sampling:** *see* simple random sampling

**unstructured interviews:** interviews conducted with the primary purpose of identifying some important issues relevant to the problem situation, without prior preparation of a planned or predetermined sequence of questions

**unstructured observational studies:** studies in which the researcher observes and makes notes of almost all activities and behaviour that occur in the situation without predetermining what particular variables will be of specific interest to the study

**validity:** evidence that the instrument, technique or process used to measure a concept does indeed measure the intended concept

**variable:** anything that can take on differing or varying values

**variance:** indicates the dispersion of a variable in the data set, and is obtained by subtracting the mean from each of the observations, squaring the results, summing them and dividing the total by the number of observations (less one)

**verification:** in qualitative research, not accepting anything at face value. A qualitative researcher uses triangulation to check data.

**website:** a computer site accessible on the Internet or intranet, created by individuals and organisations for the purpose of sharing information

**word association:** a projective method of identifying respondents' attitudes and feelings by asking them to associate a specified word with the first thing that comes to their minds

**World Wide Web (the Web):** a mass market means of communication. The Web is a collection of standards and protocols used to access information available on the Internet.

**$z$ test:** a statistical test using the standardised normal distribution, which is a symmetrical, bell-shaped curve with mean zero and standard deviation equal to one

# INDEX

abridged applied business research report (case example)  375–84
abridged basic research report (case example)  371–5
abstract databases  59
accountabilities  21–2
   conflict among  24–5
Accounting Chair Data Set  337
   analysis using Excel  337–46
   Cronbach's alpha  338
   frequency distribution  339
   hypothesis testing  342–6
   measures of central tendency and dispersion  340
   overall interpretation  346
   Pearson correlation  341
accuracy  30, 133–5
acknowledgements  358
Adjusted R square  436
alternate hypothesis  100–2, 415
ambiguous questions  230
ANOVA  328–30, 344–5, 430
   using SPSS  41
*APA Manual*  71
   referencing style  72–3
appendices (research reports)  360
applied research  12, 13
approvals  127
area sampling  261–2, 270
attitudinal factors  53
audience, written reports  353–4
author–date style of referencing  71–3
authorisation letter  356
axial coding  174

background information of the organisation  51–2
bar charts  359
basic research  12, 13–15
behavioural factors  53
Beta coefficients  434–5
bias
   interviews  153
   observational studies  161–2
   qualitative research  136
   questions  230–2
bibliographic databases  58–9
bibliography  59, 71
blank responses, handling  316
body of the report  358
box-and-whisker plot  411–12
budget (for the project)  127
business research  5
   and ethics  21–5
   context  8
   definition  5–6

   evaluation  389–92
   philosophical bases  8–12
   types of  12–15
business research areas  6–7
Business Research Class Questionnaire  226
   responses  403
   variable labels  404
business research methods  12

canonical correlation  442
CAPI (computer-assisted personal interviewing)  151, 152
CAPPA system  240–1
case studies (research method)  112, 164
   internal validity in  298
catalyst for research  37–8, 49–50
categorising data  318
category scale  203–4
CATI (computer-assisted telephone interviewing)  151, 152
causal study  113, 114
chi-square ($\chi^2$) test  331, 342–3, 422–3
   using SPSS  423–4
*Chicago Manual of Style*  71
clarification investigation  113
classification data  232–3
client, researchers responsibility to  23
closed questions  142, 229
cluster analysis  443
cluster sampling  260–1, 269
coding data  316–18
comparative scale  209
completely randomised design  309
complex probability sampling  257–62
comprehensive report offering alternative solutions  353
   case example  369–71
computer-aided survey services  152
computer-assisted interviewing  151–2
   advantages of  53
computer packages, qualitative analysis  176–81
concepts  78–9
   and the conceptual framework  79–81
   definition  33
conceptual framework
   and concepts  79–81
   components  82
   *see also* theoretical framework
confidence  273–4
   in estimation  274–5
   trade-off with precision  275–6
consensus scale  208
consequentialist view  21
constant comparative analysis  172
constant sum rating scale  206–7

construct validity   213–15
constructs, definition   34
consultants
    external   19–20
    internal   18–19
    locating and selecting   16–17
content analysis   171
    conducting   171–5
    using NVivo program   178–81
content level (interviews)   150
content of questions (questionnaires)   228
content validity   213, 238
contextual factors   51
contrived settings   119
convenience sampling   262–3, 270
convergent validity   213, 321
corporate accountability   21
correlation coefficient   321
correlational analysis   214, 321
correlational study   113, 114
correlations   418–21
countries as unit of analysis   121
criterion-related validity   213, 321
critical research   10–11
critical value   415
Cronbach's alpha   324, 338
cross-cultural research   241
    data collection issues   242
    sampling   272
    special issues in instrumentation   241–2
cross-sectional studies   121–2

data analysis   40–1
    qualitative   169–81
    quantitative   319–46
    using Excel   337–46
data categorising   318
data coding   316–18
data collection   40
    comparison of methods   243–6
    cross-cultural research   242
    ethics   165–6
    multimethods   242–4
    overlap with data analysis   169–70
    qualitative methods   134–66
data editing   315–16
data index   173
data mining   54
data representation   359
data warehouses   54
databases   58–9
    for business research   66–8
date entry   318
deception   22–3
deciles   411
decision-making processes and different types of research   388–9
deduction   35–6
demographic questions   232–3, 235–6
deontological view   21

dependent variables   83
descriptive statistics   325–6, 339–40, 402, 405–13
descriptive studies   109–11, 388
    see also simple descriptive report
dichotomous scale   203
directional hypothesis   99, 100
discriminant analysis   442
discriminant validity   213, 321–2
disproportionate stratified random sampling   259–60
divisions as unit of analysis   120
double-barrelled quertions   230
double-blind studies   303
double sampling   262, 270
doughnut charts   359
dyads as unit of analysis   119, 120
dynamic panels   164, 165

editing data   315–16
electronic questionnaires   240–1, 244, 246
element, definition   252
employee perceptions   53
entering data   318
estimation, sample data, precision and confidence   274–5
ethics   64
    business research   21–5
    data collection   165–6
    experimental research   305–6
    researcher   165–6
    respondents   166
evaluating business research   398
    conceptual/overview questions   390
    framework questions   390
    method questions   391
    reader's abstract   392
    results or conclusion questions   391
ex post facto design   303
Excel for data analysis   337–46
executive level (interviews)   150
executive summary   357
experimental designs   118, 285–7
    field experiments   292
    laboratory experiments   287–92
    managerial implications   306–7
    simulation   303–5
    types of   299–303, 309–12
    validation issues   292–9
experimental groups   295
experimental research ethics   305–6
expert systems   334
exploratory study   108–9
external consultants/researchers   17, 19–20
external reliability   291–2
external validity   292
    factors affecting   298–9
    trade-off with internal   293
extraneous variables   287–8

face-to-face interviews   150–1, 243, 245
face validity   212, 238
faces scale   207
facilitator team   156
factor analysis   214, 238, 439–41, 442
factorial design   311–12
factorial validity   321
field experiments   117, 118, 119, 292
    validation comparison with lab
        experiments   292–3
field studies   117, 119
final part of the report   358
fixed sum rating scale   206–7
focus groups   12, 153–4
    conducting   155–9
    group composition   154–5
    logistics   154
    maintenance roles   158
    structured and unstructured   154
    task roles   157
forced choice   208–9
framework development   39
    conceptual framework   79–81, 82
    need for a framework   77–8
    theoretical framework   82–95
fraud   22
frequencies   405–6
frequency distributions   228, 325, 339, 406–7
full-text databases   59
fundamental research   12, 13–15
funnel sequence   143, 232

general appearance of the
    questionnaire   234–7
generalisability   31
goodness of data, testing   320–2
goodness of measures   209–10, 214–15
    reliability   210–12
    validity   212–14
graphic rating scale   207
group composition   154–5
group dynamics   157–9
groups as unit of analysis   119–20

handling questions (oral presentations)   362
history effects   293–4, 297
homogeneity (focus groups)   155
human-as-an-instrument   135
hypothesis, definition   98–9
hypothesis development   98–103
hypothesis testing   111–12, 322, 328–33,
    342–6, 414–18
hypothesis-testing studies   388–9

ideal research design   238–9
if–then statements   99
independent variables   84, 90
    distinction from moderating variables   86–8
    manipulating   288–9
individuals as unit of analysis   119, 120

induction   36–7
industry as unit of analysis   121
indwelling   135
inferential statistics   327–8, 341, 402, 414–41
inkblot tests   163
instrumentation effects   295, 297, 299
inter-item consistency reliability   211
inter-rater reliability   211
internal consistency of measures   211–12
internal consultants/researchers   17, 18–19
internal validity   291, 292
    factors affecting   293–6
    in case studies   298
    threats to   297–8, 301–2
    trade-off with external   293
Internet   5, 56
interpretation (qualitative research)   136
interpretation of findings   41
interpretivist research   9
interquartile range   410
interval scale   196–8, 200
intervening variables   88–9, 90
interview pattern   138–9
    activity no. 2   140
    entrance time investment   139–40
    exit time investment   141
    intimacy   141
interviews   12, 138–53, 243
    advantages/disadvantages   245
    face-to-face   150–1, 243, 245
    level of   150
    listening   142
    non-verbal behaviour   147–8
    paraphrasing   143–4
    probing   144–6
    questioning   142–3
    structured and unstructured   148–50
    summarising   146–7
    telephone   151, 243, 245
    types of   150–3
intranet   55
introduction (research proposal)   124
introductory section (research report)   358
investigation types   113–14
item analysis   210
itemised rating scale   206

judgement sampling   263, 270
justification (of research project)   125

Kendall's rank correlation   420

laboratory experiments   117, 118, 119, 287
    controlling extraneous variables   287–8
    external reliability   291–2
    internal validity   291
    manipulating independent variable   268–9
    selecting and assigning subjects   289–91
    validation comparison with field
        experiments   292–3

language and wording of the
      questionnaire   229
latent content   175
Latin square design   310–11
leading questions   231
length of questions   232
libraries   56
Likert scale   205
line charts   359
listening (interviews)   142
literature survey   39, 56–7
   conducting   58
      extracting relevant information   59
      identifying relevant sources   58–9
   examples   60–1
   reasons for   57–8
   writing up   59–60
loaded questions   231
longitudinal studies   122–3

mail questionnaires   240, 243–4, 245
management action   41, 386–92
management information systems (MIS)   54
management philosophy   52
management research   6
   measures   216–19
manager–researcher relationship   17–18
managerial decision making
   and scientific research   386–9
   using statistical methods   443
managers
   and research   6–7, 15–16
   locating and selecting a researcher or
      consultant   16–17
manifest content   175
MANOVA   442
marketing research   6
   measures   220–3
matching groups   289
   differences from randomisation   290–1
maturation effects   294, 297
mean   408
measurement
   principles (questionnaires)   234
   variables   187–8
measurement scales   194–200
measures   209–10, 214–15
   from management research   216–19
   from marketing research   220–3
   reliability   210–12
   validity   212–14
measures of central tendencies   325–6, 340,
   408–9
measures of dispersions   325–6, 340, 409–13
median   408
mode   408–9
moderating variables   85–6
   distinction from independent
      variables   86–8
moral accountability   21
mortality   296, 298, 300

motivational research   162
multidimensional scaling   208, 443
multiple regression analysis   331–2, 345–6,
   432–3, 437–8
   using SPSS   438–9
multistage cluster sampling   261
multitrait, multimethod matrix of
   correlations   214

nature of information to be collected   50
   broader issues and context   51–4
   is it worth the effort?   53–4
   specific information   50
negatively worded questions   229–30
nominal scale   195, 199
non-contrived settings   117
non-directional hypothesis   99–100
non-parametric correlations   421
non-parametric statistics   402
non-parametric tests   417
nonparticipant-observer   160
non-probability sampling   257, 262–5, 267
non-verbal behaviour   147–8
normal distribution   255, 410, 412
null hypothesis   100–2, 415
numerical scale   205
NVivo program   176–7
   and content analysis   178–81

objectivity   30–1
observational studies   159–60, 244
   advantages/disadvantages   161
   bias in   161–2
   structured and unstructured   160–1
observations   12
   definition   32–3
observer roles   160
open coding   173
open-ended questions   142, 229, 237
operational definition   188–92
   and the concept of learning   193–4
   what it is not   192
oral presentation   360
   deciding on content   360–1
   handling questions   362
   the presentation   361
   the presenter   361
   visual aids   361
ordinal scale   196, 299
organisational records   54–5
outside information gathering   55–6

painting the path (qualitative research)   136–7
paired comparisons   208
panel studies   164–5
paradigms   8
   approach for business   11–12
   comparison   10–11
   critical research   10
   interpretivist research   9
   positivist research   8–9

parallel-form reliability   211, 320
parametric statistics   402
paraphrasing (interviews)   143–4
parsimony   31–2
participant-observer   160
pass time (interviews)   139
pattern of an interview   138–41
Pearson correlation   241, 327–8, 342, 419, 421
percentiles   410
personal information (questionnaires)   232–3, 235–6
   sensitive data   236–7
personally administered questionnaires   239–40, 243, 245
pictorial representation of data   359
pie charts   359
pilot study   238–9
plagiarism   22
population
   definition   252, 254
   normal distribution   255
population frame   252
population parameters   254
positively worded questions   229–30
positivist research   8–9
post-test   295
post-test only with experimental and control groups   300
precision   273
   in estimation   274–5
   trade-off with confidence   275–6
preliminary information gathering   39, 50–6
   nature of information to be collected   50–4
   sources of information   54–6
presentation (oral)   361
presenter (oral presentation)   361
pre-test   295
pre-test and post-test experimental and control group designs   300–1
pre-test and post-test experimental group design   299–300
pre-testing questionnaires   238–9
primary data   51
primary question   142
principles of measurement (questionnaires)   234
principles of wording (questionnaires)   228
   biases in questions   230–2
   classification data   232–3
   content of questions   228
   language and wording of the questionnaire   229
   sequencing of questions   232
   type and form of questions   229–30
probability sampling   257–62, 266
probing (interviews)   144–6
problem definition   39, 61–3
   ethical issues   64
   examples   63
   managerial implications   63–4

process and sequence (qualitative research)   136
process level (interviews)   150
professional accountability   21
projective methods   162–3
proportionate stratified random sampling   259
propositions (hypotheses)   99
pure research   12
purpose of the study   107–13
   and the research method   114–15
purpose of written report   351–3
purposive research   388
purposive sampling   263–5
purposiveness   29

qualitative analysis   169–70
   computer packages   176–81
   content analysis   171–6
   important comments   175–6
   purpose   170
   structured and unstructured methods   170
qualitative research   12, 34–5, 108, 134, 389
   accuracy and replicability   135–7
   assumptions   134–5
   focus groups   153–9
   interviewing   138–53
   methods   137–65
   observational studies   159–62
   sampling   137
   special data sources   162–5
quantitative analysis   314, 319
   expert systems   334
   getting a feel for the data   319–20
   getting data ready for analysis   315–18
   hypothesis testing   322, 328–33
   testing goodness of data   320–2
   Wollongong Enterprises case study   322–34
quantitative research   12, 34, 35, 169
   experimental designs   285–312
   measurement of variables   185–223
   questionnaire design   225–47
   sampling design   251–80
quartiles   411
quasi-experimental designs   299–300
question and answer sessions (oral presentations)   362
questioning (interviews)   142–3
questionnaire design
   concluding the questionnaire   237
   demographic data   235–6
   general appearance   234–7
   guidelines   227–8
   introduction to respondents   234–5
   open-ended questions at end   237
   organising questions   235
   principles of measurement   234
   principles of wording   228–33
   sensitive personal data   236–7

questionnaires  12, 246
   advantages/disadvantages  245–6
   electronic  240–1, 244, 246
   importance of  225–7
   mail  240, 243–4, 245
   personally administered  239–40, 243, 245
   pre-testing  238–9
questions
   biases in  230–2
   sequencing of  232
   type and form (questionnaires)  229–30
quota sampling  264–5, 271
quotations in the text  75

$R$ square  432, 435–6
radar charts  359
randomisation  279–80
   differences from matching  290–1
randomised block design  310
range  409
ranking scales  203, 208–9
rating scales  203–8
ratio scale  198–9, 200
reality (less than ideal) research design  239
recall-dependent questions  230–1
recording (focus groups)  156
references  71, 358
referencing
   author–date style  71–3
   in the business article or report  73–5
referential adequacy  136
reflection on feeling  143–4
regression analysis  432–9
regression ANOVA  435
regression coefficients  434
reliability (of a measure)  210–12, 320–1
   Cronbach's alpha  324, 338
replicability  30, 133–5
report preparation and distribution  41, 127
reporting on research  350
   case examples  363–84
   oral presentation  360–2
   written report  351–60
representation (focus groups)  155
research
   and managerial effectiveness  20
   approaches to  34–7
   what is it  4–5
research design  40, 106–7
   experimental designs  118, 285–312
   ideal (pilot study)  238–9
   less than ideal (pilot study)  239
   managerial implications  127
   measurement and measures  187–201
   purpose of the study  107–13
      and the research method  114–15
   questionnaire design  225–47
   research proposal  123–7
   researcher interference  115–17

   sampling design  251–80
   study setting  117–19
   time horizon  121–3
   type of investigation  113–14
   units of analysis  119–21
research method  114–15
research objectives  39–40, 95
   hypothesis development  98–103
   research proposal  124–5
   research questions  96–8
research process  37–43
   catalyst, preliminary information collection and problem definition  48–64
   experimental designs  285–312
   framework development and research objectives  77–103
   qualitative data analysis and interpretation  169–81
   qualitative data gathering  134–66
   qualitative research design  106–28
   quantitative data analysis and interpretation  314–46
   quantitative research design  186–201
   questionnaire design  225–47
   research reporting  350–84
   sampling design  251–80
research proposal  123–7
research questions  96–8
research report  355
   abridged applied business research report  375–84
   abridged basic research report  371–5
   acknowledgements  358
   appendices  360
   authorisation letter  356
   body of the report  358
   executive summary  357
   final part of the report  358
   introductory section  358
   references  358
   table of contents  356
   title page  356
research reporting  350
   oral presentation  360–2
   written report  351–60
research schedule  126
research subjects  23–4
researcher interference  115–17
researchers
   and ethics  165–6
   external  18–19
   internal  18–19
   locating and selecting  16–17
   responsibility to client or sponsor  23
resources (for the project)  127
respondents, ethical behaviour  166
restricted probability  257
rigour  29
rituals (interviews)  139

sample data, precision and confidence in estimation 274–5
sample size 59, 272
  determining 276–8
  in sampling design 279
  precision and confidence 272–3
sample statistics 254
sample variance 409–10
samples
  definition 253, 254
  representativeness of 255–6
sampling 253–4
  efficiency 279–80
  in cross-cultural research 272
  non-probability 257, 267
  probability 257–62, 266
  qualitative research 137
  reasons for 254
sampling design 251–2, 256, 271–2
  and sample size 279
  choice points 267
  examples 265–71
sampling distribution 412
sampling frame 252–3, 254
scatter diagrams 419, 420
scientific research 28
  and managerial decision making 386–9
  characteristics 28–32
  limitations to in management 32
search engines 71
secondary data 51
  qualitative research 163–4
secondary questions 142
selection bias effects 295–6, 297
selective coding 174
'sell' an idea report 352
  case example 367–9
semantic differential scale 205
semi-structured interviews 148–50
sensitive personal information 236–7
sequencing of questions 143, 232
significance level 415–18
simple descriptive report 351–2
  case example 363–6
simple random sampling 257, 265–8
simple regression 433–6
  using SPSS 436–7
simulation 303–5
single-stage cluster sampling 260–1
size of focus groups 155
size of sample 59, 272–3, 276–9
skewed distribution 412
snowball sampling 263–4, 271
social desirability (questions) 231
societal accountability 21, 22–3
SOLER System 147–8
Solomon four-group design 301
  and threats to internal validity 301–2
source code 171–2

sources of information 54
  Internet 56
  knowledge of the staff 55
  libraries 56
  organisational records 54–5
  response patterns and outside information gathering 55–6
Spearman's rank correlation 420–1
special data sources (qualitative research) 162–5
split-half reliability 211–12, 320
sponsor, researchers responsibility to 23
SPSS
  ANOVA 431–2
  chi-square test 423–4
  multiple regression 438–9
  simple regression 436–7
  $t$-test 426–30
stability of measures 210–11
staff knowledge 55
standard deviation 410–11
standard error of the estimate 436
standard error of the mean 273, 413
Stapel scale 207
statement of hypotheses 99
static panels 164–5
statistical hypothesis testing 111–12, 322, 328–33, 342–6, 414–18
statistical regression 296, 298, 301
statistical test, choosing a 415, 416
statistics *see* descriptive statistics; inferential statistics
strangers versus acquaintances (focus groups) 155
stratified random sampling 258–60, 268
structural factors within the organisation 52
structural variables 52
structured focus groups 154
structured interviews 148
structured observational studies 160
study setting 117–19
subjectivity 136
subjects
  definition 253
  for research 23–4
  selecting and assigning 289–91
summarising (interviews) 146–7
synopsis (research reports) 357
systematic sampling 258, 269

$t$ statistic 435
$t$-test 328, 343–4, 425–6
  using SPSS 426–30
table of contents 356
telephone interviews 151, 243, 245
test–retest reliability 211, 320
testability 29–30
testing effects 295, 297, 299
thematic apperception tests (TAT) 163
theme coding system 172

theoretical framework   91
   components   91–5
   variables   82–90
   *see also* conceptual framework
thinking time (focus groups)   156
Thurstone Equal Appearing Interval scale   208
time horizon   121–3
title page (research report)   356
title (research proposal)   124
trace measures   164
triangulation   136
true experimental designs   300–1
trustworthiness   135
tunnel sequence   143
Type I errors   415, 418
Type II errors   416, 418

unbiased questions   153
units of analysis   119–21
unobtrusive measures   164
unrestricted probability sampling   257
unstructured focus groups   154
unstructured interviews   148
unstructured observational studies   160–1

validity   212–15, 321–2
   external   292, 298–9
   internal   291, 292, 293–8
   lab and field experiments   292–3
values   18
variables   79, 82–3
   dependent   83
   extraneous   287–8
   independent   84, 90, 288–9
   intervening   88–9, 90
   measurement   187–8
   moderating   85–6
variance   409–10
verification   135–6
visual aids   156, 361

websites for business research   69–70
Wollongong Enterprises (case study)   322–4
   Cronbach's alpha reliability measures   324
   frequency distributions   325
   hypothesis testing   328–33
   measures of central tendencies and dispersions   3256
   overall interpretation and recommendations   333–4
   Pearson correlation   327–8
word-association techniques   162–3
written reports   351
   abridged applied business research report   373–84
   abridged basic research report   371–5
   audience   353–4
   characteristics   354–5
   comprehensive report offering alternative solutions   353, 369–71
   purpose of   351–3
   'sell' an idea report   352, 367–9
   simple descriptive report   351–2, 363–6
   structure   355–60

Printed in Australia
08 Mar 2016
446538